"Full of wit, powerful stories, and genuinely helpful tips, this highly readable book could not be more timely. Read this book and be transformed!"
—AMY CHUA, Yale Law professor and author of *Battle Hymn of the Tiger Mother* and *Political Tribes: Group Instinct and the Fate of Nations*

"An inspiring and enlightening exploration of bilingualism, asking and answering all the right questions. Also, it reads like a charm."
—GASTON DORREN, author of *Lingo* and *Babel*

"*America's Bilingual Century* takes in the full sweep of all things bilingual. For someone embarking on a similar journey, this is a fabulous guide to follow."
—BEN EASON, Publisher and Editor of *Creative Loafing* and member of YPO

"I love this book. It is personal and also highly practical. It is well-informed and also slyly humorous. It equips individuals for a richer, more satisfying life—and is a guide for communities to do the same. This is a book I hope people of all generations read."
—JAMES FALLOWS, coauthor of the bestselling *Our Towns* and writer for *The Atlantic*

"Steve Leveen is a gifted storyteller and a meticulous researcher. Unlike others who see bilingualism only as a matter of public or educational policy, Leveen conceives of it as a gift we give ourselves—and others. This book is a generous offering to all who wish to claim his passion as their own."
—ROSEMARY G. FEAL, Executive Director Emerita, Modern Language Association

"Seeking purpose? A way to bridge the divides in our nation? Find your way to Steve Leveen's eloquent new book, *America's Bilingual Century*. Leveen makes a comprehensive and compelling case for bilingualism, then makes it easy to get started at any age. Inspiring, practical—and a joy to read!"
—MARC FREEDMAN, CEO of Encore.org and author of *How to Live Forever: The Enduring Power of Connecting the Generations*

"Within a few miles of the Institute of International Education headquarters in New York City, more than 180 languages are spoken in daily life. As Steve Leveen reminds us, bilingualism is a benefit to all who live here and a gift to the next generation."
—ALLAN GOODMAN, president of IIE

"*America's Bilingual Century* is a treat to read as well as immensely informative. It provides a useful and necessary guide as to how we should address this fundamental, but underappreciated, issue in our culture. It is *the* definitive work on this very interesting topic."

—BOB HECKART, advisor to nonprofit organizations addressing homelessness

"With eloquence and wit, Steve Leveen shows how to enrich our lives, and our children's lives, by embracing adopted or heritage languages. He nudges us to learn through the stories of fascinating people, famous media personalities or motivated immigrants, who turned fumbles into successes. *America's Bilingual Century* is both a helpful handbook of tips for the language-shy and also a timely policy book summarizing the benefits of multi-lingualism for brain development and economic competitiveness alike."

—ROSABETH MOSS KANTER, Harvard Business School professor and best-selling author of *Confidence: How Winning Streaks and Losing Streaks Begin and End* and *Think Outside the Building: How Advanced Leaders Can Change the World One Smart Innovation at a Time*

"Bilingualism will continue to be the norm for human societies, so we should try to optimize it. This deep, engaging book shows how to do that with intelligence and heart. I would have been satisfied with that, but the book goes on to deepen my understanding of languages of any type. I really enjoyed it."

—KEVIN KELLY, author of *The Inevitable* and Senior Maverick for *Wired* Magazine

"They who know not a second language know not their own, the old saying goes. Steve Leveen's timely, smart, and refreshingly practical book robustly confirms that venerable wisdom, one among its many compelling arguments for Americans to embrace—and use—the many tongues that now grace our blessedly polyglot republic."

—DAVID KENNEDY, Pulitzer Prize-winning historian and Stanford Professor of History Emeritus

"I can see a lot of people enjoying this book: language lovers, encore experience seekers, teachers, travelers."

—ANNE KENNER, writer and former federal prosecutor turned high school civics teacher

"Flourishing American bilingualism is a pathway to a flourishing America. As we act with intention to adopt another language, we not only gain a personal skill, we also gain empathy and understanding of another culture. Steve Leveen shows how we can step up our own personal development while at the same time take a deeper responsibility for our nation's role in the world."
—JOHN P. MACKEY, cofounder and CEO of Whole Foods Market and author of *Conscious Leadership*

"As Steve shows in this important book, bilingualism opens up so many doors. Not just richer travel experiences, more diverse cultural experiences, and more interesting friendships, but also possibilities in business. I would not be doing business in Europe and Latin America were it not for my interest in developing my Spanish and French."
—MICHAEL MASTERSON [MARK FORD], bestselling author of *Ready, Fire, Aim*

"Curl up with *America's Bilingual Century* to get answers to the questions people REALLY have about language. How can you really learn another one? How hard will it be? Do I really need to? And why? Leveen ladles out wise and witty answers to all of these and many more, as someone who decided to shed his monolingualism in middle age and hasn't stopped since."
—JOHN McWHORTER, Columbia University professor of linguistics, *Lexicon Valley* podcast host, and author of 10 books on language

"By far the most engaging, informative, and fascinating book on learning a new language ever written, full of more candidly acknowledged humiliation, unexpectedly exalted success, and very funny stories than you'd ever imagine."
—TOM MORRIS, chair of the Morris Institute for Human Values and national bestselling author of *Plato's Lemonade Stand: Stirring Change into Something Great*

"*America's Bilingual Century* addresses a topic of increasing relevance as the demographics of the US change. Steve's book offers a conceptual framework for bilingualism that is well grounded, together with practical commentaries that reinforce his message. I have had a strong interest—as well as fear—of learning Hebrew. Steve's book has shown me that my fears were simply myths that I could overcome."
—PHILIP PIZZO, MD, Founding Director of the Stanford Distinguished Careers Institute and former Dean of the Stanford School of Medicine

"Business today—whether for-profit or non-profit—needs to embrace the reality of a polyglot world, and the benefits of bilingualism. This is what every business leader today needs to read if they want to thrive and be a force for good in the world."
—DOUG RAUCH, founder of Daily Table and former president of Trader Joe's

"Each chapter is valuable and can be read as needed and independently. That said, I actually read the book cover to cover."
—JACK ROEPERS, multilingual business executive

"In a world in which a second language has become a crucial business and social tool, Steve Leveen delivers not just a how-to but a why-to. This book is readable, informative, and, maybe best of all, actionable. He not only shows us why we thrive with another language but gives us the roadmap to get there."
—KEVIN SALWEN, former *Wall Street Journal* editor and coauthor, *The Suspect*

"Steve Leveen won't make you bilingual. But he will make you wish you were, appreciate the reasons you should be, and figure out how to adopt that second (third, or fourth) language. There may be no better gift than an alternate identity—unless it's a nimbler brain, an expanded horizon, a rich vein of surprise, or a double helping of empathy. A warm, winning book from the most motivated—and motivating—of students."
—STACY SCHIFF, Pulitzer Prize-winning author of *A Great Improvisation* and *Cleopatra*

"To speak in another tongue is one of the most magical, jubilant, and gratifying of all human experiences. This wonderfully well-researched book provides a guide to that fulfillment. It's not just the joy of communicating in another language that brings the high, it's also experiencing a concept, emotion, quandary, or perspective that does not exist in your native tongue."
—CALVIN SIMS, Executive Vice President of Standards and Practices, CNN

"Forget any predispositions you have about this topic. Read this masterful treatise on bilingualism. You'll be a better human being . . . in any language."
—ANDREA SYVERSON, author of *BrandAbout* and *Alter Girl*

"Wonderfully readable, full of great advice for future bilinguals, and also engages with those very resistant myths about immigrants and English. A key must-read for our times."
—GUADALUPE VALDÉS, Ph.D., Bonnie Katz Tenenbaum Professor of Education, Stanford University

"At Duolingo, we see teaching languages as an incredibly powerful way to change lives and change the world. Steve's got the right idea: learning a language should not be a chore, but a source of joy and connection. Steve's book can help language learners get over their shyness and succeed on their own bilingual journeys."
—LUIS VON AHN, CEO and cofounder of Duolingo, Professor at Carnegie Mellon University, MacArthur Fellow

"A marvelous Baedeker guide to everything you need to know about becoming bilingual—both how to go about it and why you should."
—KEN WALLACH, Executive Chairman, Central National Gottesman Inc., and Member of the American Academy of Arts and Sciences' Commission on Language Learning

"As an author, immigration attorney, and immigrant to the United States, I have a great appreciation for the research and hard work it took to bring this book to life. Leveen reminds us that our diverse languages, and thus our diverse backgrounds, make us a stronger nation."
—TAHMINA WATSON, creator of the *Tahmina Talks Immigration* podcast and author of *The Startup Visa*

"There is another perspective that this book gave me—a larger one: to be more open to bilingualism, even though I'm not one myself."
—LOIE WILLIAMS, Director of Working Opportunities for Women, Project Place

"This delightful, compelling book draws you in to a national conversation about why it's vitally important that we Americans not only learn another language but support schools and policies that promote bilingualism. Well-researched and full of examples, this book is personal yet profound, thoughtful yet entertaining, individual yet universal."
—DORI JONES YANG, author of *When the Red Gates Opened: A Memoir of China's Reawakening*

AMERICA'S BILINGUAL CENTURY

Also by the author

The Little Guide to Your Well-Read Life:
How to Get More Books in Your Life and More Life from Your Books

Holding Dear: The Value of the Real

To all who give the gift of bilingualism,
and to those who embark on the journey

"To learn a second language is to possess a second soul."

—CHARLEMAGNE

CONTENTS

Part Two: How to Raise Children as Bilingual, Even if You're Not

Part Three: Twelve Language Myths Americans Are Busting

Part Four: A Reimagined America

PROLOGUE

The winter my parents divorced it snowed a lot, even by Syracuse standards. One morning, after my father had already left, my mother heaved open the garage door to find the snow above her head. Whether it was that particular morning or some other, I'll never know, but she resolved that winter of 1962 to move as far away from Syracuse, New York, as possible to where it never—*ever*—snowed.

After consulting an atlas and breaking the news to her mother, she loaded my older sister, Karen, and me into the back seat of our Plymouth and headed southwest to San Diego, California.

After a week on the road, we finally came to a stop in the parking lot of the Travelodge in downtown San Diego, near Balboa Park. The next day, my mother found us a place to live in a garden-apartment complex called the Cabrillo Palisades. Nobody had a garage in the Cabrillo Palisades, but nobody needed to clear snow off their cars, either.

Even at seven years old, I could see and hear the influence of Mexico—in neighborhoods like Linda Vista and Mira Mesa, on streets like La Playa and Camino Real, and, of course, with all the Mexican Americans around us. In an earlier time, San Diego wasn't influenced by Mexico; it *was* Mexico. But I wouldn't learn that until later.

In the San Diego I knew and grew up in, Spanish was quiet. It came in bits of sentences that the gardeners spoke. English was loud—it was the language screamed on the playground, spoken in the stores, heard on the *NBC Nightly News* with Chet Huntley and David Brinkley.

In school, I heard no teacher mention Spanish, or any other language, until sixth grade, at San Miguel Elementary. Once a week, a straight-backed man wearing a dark suit came into our class. We were told to address him as señor Masters. He drilled us:

"*Hola, Pepito, ¿cómo estás?*"

"*Bien, gracias, ¿y tú?*"

My mother and sister and I moved around most every year to different rental houses while my mother got her master's degree in social work and then took a job with the county. I went to four elementary schools and two junior high schools. Other than the dollop of Spanish that señor Masters spooned on our plates, no teacher uttered a word in any language but English.

Before I was to start high school, we moved to a town about eight miles east of San Diego called La Mesa and, lucky me, I got to attend the same high school for all four years. Our next-door neighbors were the Sandovals. Early on we learned the Sandovals spoke little English, so our families remained the waving kind of neighbors.

During afternoons in our backyard, I would hear the Sandovals' radio playing. It wasn't loud but it was full of brassy ballads, and since I played trumpet in our high school band, I liked the music, especially when they played "A Taste of Honey" or "What Now My Love" by Herb Alpert & the Tijuana Brass. Every fifteen minutes or so, a woman's voice came on, repeating the station's ID. I couldn't understand her, but the sing-song rhythm of her voice sank in after countless repetitions: *"Dada-da, da, dada-da, Tijuana, Mexico."* Without my knowing it, her dulcet voice became part of the sound-scape of my coming of age.

A tempting invitation, declined

At school, I came to know a girl named Lynda Martinez. One day she invited me home for dinner, which seemed oddly formal for a first date circa 1970.

When I arrived, her parents weren't around, which also struck me as odd until I realized she was probably demonstrating, with her parents' approval, that she was a young woman capable of making dinner. (On reflection, it may have been that her parents weren't comfortable speaking English, but that didn't occur to me then.)

Lynda told me she had made frijoles from scratch, and had started the day before. "The beans smell up the whole house when you start with dry pinto beans," she explained. "I wanted the smell gone." Instead, I smelled her chicken enchiladas in the oven. She looked in at them, while I looked at her. She was wearing one of those tight church-going dresses that showed nothing except her petite, shapely body. It's the kind of dress that, I imagine, has gotten boys to go to church for centuries.

During dinner, Lynda tossed some Spanish my way, inviting me to play catch. It would have been easy to fall into Lynda's embrace, and through her, into the embrace of Mexican American life. I was poised on the cusp, savoring it as much as the dinner, beguiled by the luster of her jet-black hair, the scent of her perfume. All I had to do was close my eyes, smile, and do what came naturally.

But already, even in high school, I had a vague plan for myself. It entailed going to college, then heading back East and making my mark in some way. Lynda was ready for life there and then in San Diego. She and I never went much further than that lovely dinner at her home.

I don't spreche *enough* Deutsch

Back at high school, we had to take a language. I thought I wanted to be a doctor and had the idea that German was the language of science, whereas Spanish seemed to be the language of restaurants. We had an enthusiastic teacher named Mr. Knot who had been in the Army in Germany. I learned a little German, but not enough to have a conversation.

After high school, I enrolled at the University of California, San Diego. Since we had to take a language there, too, I figured I might as well continue with German. But the class was hard and loaded with unwelcome work, while I was trying to learn what I considered more important subjects like calculus and organic chemistry.

After the last German class, I learned I had to take an oral exam. I entered a windowless room with two chairs. One was fully employed, supporting a sturdy woman ready to probe my command of the language of Goethe. We began with customary greetings and I rattled off the few sentences I knew pretty well. Those pleasantries behind us, she said, "Let's talk about something else." The trouble was, I thought she said, "You can go now."

I lurched for the door, but with the strength of an East German shot-put star, she set me back into my chair. It didn't go well after that, which is to say, I flunked.

After I got that sorry news, another unsmiling woman I recognized from the German department told me that I would have to repeat the class. "Or . . . " (my ears pricked up) " . . . if you take *and pass* a German literature class, you won't have to take the oral exam." With my escape route in sight, I signed up for German Lit and spent the next term reading, in German, how Gregor Samsa woke one morning to find himself transformed into a cockroach. This, I concluded, was better than another round in the oral examination room. When the course was over, I checked off the language box, having withstood my college's attempt to open my mind to the bounties of bilingualism.

A second invitation, also declined

During my college years, I worked as a computer operator at the university hospital. I got to be friends with a janitor named Julio who was just a few years older than I was. He told me, in his competent if somewhat formal English, that he was a pharmacist in Mexico but could earn more money working as a janitor in San Diego. Monday through Friday, he would drive across the border to clean the offices and restrooms at the hospital before returning home to Mexico late at night.

One evening when he came to say goodnight, he had changed out of his janitor clothes and was wearing a camel-colored leather sports jacket. I complimented him on it and he offered his sleeve for me to feel. It felt soft and luxurious. He told me his cousin made the jackets. "Come down Saturday morning," Julio said. "He'll measure you. Then we can go around town, have some fun, and in the evening it will be ready." The cost was forty dollars.

That was serious money for me back then, but still a bargain. I could see myself wowing the girls in a jacket like that. But I thought about my homework and whatever else I had to do, so politely declined. To this day, I regret I didn't take Julio up on his offer, not because of the jacket, but having lost out on the experience of going around Tijuana with a native, to be in Mexico as a visitor rather than a tourist.

I was accepted to grad school back East at Cornell, which is just an hour south of Syracuse, where my father and my grandmother still lived. In July 1977, I pointed my faded red Datsun pickup east and retraced the route my mother had driven fifteen summers earlier. At Cornell, there were no language requirements for a PhD in Sociology, so I didn't bother myself with language study. My progress toward holding a conversation in another language ceased that day I failed my German oral exam in college.

A common story for the times

I share my language story—what I call my language biography—because it is emblematic of America at that time. Most of us who grew up in an English-speaking American home share the experience of having had some exposure to another language in school but not actually learning to speak it. For me, the failure was more abject than for most of us, for I grew up virtually swimming in Spanish, yet somehow not getting wet.

When I walked up the hills in La Mesa where I lived, I could see the mountains of Mexico to the south. I took day trips to Tijuana with my mother and later, with my high-school buddies, ventured deeper into Baja California on beach camping trips. Yet my Spanish never got beyond *buenos días, muchas gracias*, and *cerveza*. My friends weren't any better.

Why bother? After all, it was the Mexicans who seemed so eager to learn English. They were the ones who seemed embarrassed when trying to speak with us. To my friends and me, knowing how to speak another language seemed something like knowing how to play guitar: nice, but hardly necessary. I gained a love for Mexican food, and an appreciation for the Mexicans I encountered, yet I grew up blind to El Dorado at my feet.

Falling for another Spanish speaker

After earning my master's, I had had enough of school and decided I needed to get a job before writing my doctoral dissertation. My plan was to work as a science journalist in New York City and save a bit of money. A naïve plan to be sure, but in that summer of '79, like so many young people before and since, I moved to Manhattan with a dream of making it. I sold my Datsun pickup, by then even more decrepit, for enough to almost cover first and last months' rent for a studio apartment, on the ground floor at Riverside Drive and West 79th Street.

I got a job as an assistant editor for McGraw-Hill, the company's lowest journalistic position. My annual salary of $14,500 barely kept me in bagels and an occasional Dos Equis, to remind me of home. But something of great importance did happen during my first months in the city—I noticed a young woman on the subway.

Her name was Lori Granger and we met on our commute. We had moved to the city within two weeks of one another, lived two blocks from each other, and worked for different companies two floors apart in the McGraw-Hill building.

Lori had just graduated from college that spring and was working for an insurance company. It surprised both of us just how quickly we knew we wanted to stay together.

As it happened, Lori had spent a semester in Madrid, had majored in Latin American history, and was a skilled Spanish speaker. Once again, Spanish seemed to be tapping on my shoulder.

As we both settled into the cold realities of working on the bottom rungs of corporations in winter in Manhattan, we dreamed of a different life. We would move to a seaside town in Mexico. We would run a catamaran rental business by day (I knew how to sail); at night I would play mariachi trumpet, while Lori (an experienced bartender) made drinks behind the bar. After all, we told ourselves, we had as much experience in those lines of work as we did in journalism and insurance—maybe more. Plus, we figured we'd both get really good at Spanish.

When it was time for Lori to introduce me to her mother, Evelyn, we decided we had to come clean and announce our plans to move south of the border. My future mother-in-law, a military wife, listened to our plans with a smile on her face. When we were finished, her smile grew. "I think that's just *wonderful!*" I knew from that moment that I was marrying into the right family.

But our practical sides won the day—or rather, the years. We decided it would be better to finish our graduate degrees and then reassess. We moved to Washington, DC, where Lori got her master's in foreign service from Georgetown and I got a day job so I could write my dissertation in the early morning hours before work. I kept my hand in science writing, publishing articles about the social impact of technology for *The New York Times*, the *Los Angeles Times,* and *The Boston Globe*, among others.

We got the degrees, got married, and after a few more unfulfilling corporate jobs, decided to try our hand at entrepreneurism—but in the United States rather than Mexico. Combining our last names to make "Levenger," we started selling "Tools for Serious Readers" through ads in *The New Yorker* and then a mail-order catalog. After a slow start, our business (miraculously, it seemed to us) took off.

To fast forward, I spent my career as a businessman, which included a good amount of international travel. I made friends with many bilinguals. Some were comfortable in Europe, others in China or India, and they were also comfortable in the US. To me they seemed so worldly. Although they never commented on my monolingualism, I felt provincial in their presence.

But life was overflowing with other challenges and excitements. Lori and I were blessed with two boys, and now managing a business with more than four hundred employees. Yes, learning another language—probably Spanish—would be cool. Maybe later . . .

PREFACE

One morning in my middle age, I woke up feeling disgusted with my monolingualism.

Perhaps it was remembering all the tapping on my shoulder, all the invitations I had declined over the years. Maybe it was traveling around the world and being tired of being the guy in the room who had to be accommodated with English. Possibly it was what compels people, arriving at a certain age, to pick up a paintbrush or sit down at a piano bench. Whatever it was, it hit me hard. It felt like a desperate thirst. I told myself that I *had* to become at least conversational in Spanish, although I didn't know what that really meant.

I don't generally make New Year's resolutions, but that first of January in my fifty-fourth year of life, I resolved to begin learning Spanish. I had no idea what I was getting myself in for.

A man studying Spanish walks into a cocktail party . . .

With an impatience born from decades of keeping my Spanish-speaking self in the waiting room, I threw myself into *español* with a passion.

I bought the 664-page *Spanish for Dummies* and sprang for the complete package from Rosetta Stone. I bought a box of a thousand flash cards from QuickStudy, which also publishes laminated study guides. I bought some of those, too, their cheerful colored boxes showing all manner of dense conjugations and forms of speech. I hired a Berlitz tutor, a monumentally patient woman from Colombia. She came to our house to work with me for forty-five minutes every Tuesday before our family sat down to dinner and then returned home, I imagined, to a stiff drink.

In my car, I listened to the encouraging audio programs of Pimsleur Spanish—three times through. And then I took up the audio programs of Michel Thomas, for more hours of speaking where no one could hear me. If there was a way to *buy* my way into Spanish—in dollars and in hours—I was up for that.

But wait: there's more. I watched YouTube videos, including "13 Ways to End a Conversation in Spanish" (I thought up several more). I downloaded all manner of apps on my phone, including apps for children, and the captivating Duolingo with its green birdie named Duo. For nine months, I set a half-hour goal with Duolingo and met it. If I could *play* my way into Spanish, I was up for that, too.

Being this determined (obsessive, my wife says), I began by brute force to make some progress. But then I would hear some Spanish speakers talking and have no idea what they were saying. That was depressing. I still felt a long way from being able to hold an actual conversation.

Meanwhile, I continued with my regular work and social life, which included attending occasional cocktail parties. When I would casually mention that I was studying Spanish, I heard reactions that almost made me spill my Sam Adams. *Everyone*, it seemed, had an opinion and didn't hesitate to lay it on me.

The wisdom of the cocktail crowd

"Why bother? The whole world speaks English!" pronounced one woman. For evidence, she described the trip she and her husband took to Africa (or maybe it was Peru) where "*everyone* spoke English!"

From others, I heard, "Why bother?" again, this time followed by: "Technology will make language learning obsolete! We'll all have Google implants, or whatever, in our ears doing instant translation from any language."

Yet other people reacted very differently. They would lean toward me and ask in confidential tones, "How are you *doing* it?" I could hear in their voices that they, too, had the thirst. They hoped I would share some method or app that would make it fast and easy.

From yet others, a frown would cross their face. "I took four years of French and can't utter a sentence!" And others stated with authority, "The *only* way to learn a language is immersion!" Their implication being that whatever I might be doing here in the US was a waste of time.

Others would decree: "The *only* way to learn a language is when you're young," and then proceed with a story about some four-year-old who speaks three languages without missing a beat. "Her mother speaks *only* French to her, and her father, being from Germany, only speaks German, and their Korean nanny . . . ."

On occasion a person would respond sarcastically, "Well, *that's* a good idea you're learning Spanish since Spanish is taking over the country!" This might be followed with, "Why don't these people learn *English*? My grand-parents learned English when they came to this country—it was sink or swim. Now? It's 'Press 1 for English.' Give me a break! Don't you think everyone who comes to America needs to speak English?!"

I do, as a matter of fact. But some people seemed uninterested in anything I might say about learning *another* language until I first pledged my allegiance to English, the whole English, and nothing but the English, so help me God.

Still other people would help set me straight with a reality check. "You know, in Europe, *everybody* speaks four or five languages. Of course, that's because they *have* to, the countries being so small. But here in the US, well . . . where would I even *use* French if I could speak it?"

From an engineer I heard, "Well, *coding* is a language, too. *That's* what we should be teaching kids today."

By merely mentioning that I was studying Spanish, I had clearly touched a nerve among my fellow Americans. Maybe it was the alcohol.

What do the bilinguals say?

I wanted to argue with those who told me I was wasting my time. And I wanted to help those who shared my thirst to learn a language themselves. Yet I didn't know what to say to either group. I decided I had better learn a few things about bilingualism and language learning.

I began reading books like *Bilingual: Life and Reality* by François Gros-jean, *The Language Instinct: How the Mind Creates Language* by Steven Pinker, *Is That a Fish in Your Ear? Translation and the Meaning of Everything* by David Bellos, *How to Learn a Foreign Language* by Paul Pimsleur, and the many books written by that great illuminator of language, John McWhorter. One thing I quickly learned was that scholars use the term "bilingual" to mean people who speak two *or more* languages; this is easier than trying to specify how many languages people speak and to what degree. That's the practice I'll follow in this book.

I started asking nearly everyone I could about their own language biog-raphies, so much so that I became quite predictable to my family. "Watch out, he's going to ask you what languages you speak!"

When I took Lyft or Uber, I asked if I could sit up front. Riding shotgun, I heard scores of language biographies from some of our country's newest residents.

Pretty quickly, I learned that the languages people learn are driven by the realities of families, migration, and economics—factors quite removed from the technical aspects of how best to learn a language. And I learned much more.

The bilinguals I interviewed all appeared to *love* being bilingual—it seemed to be one of the most important and fundamental aspects of their lives. Conversely, I never met any monolinguals who said they liked knowing only one language. In fact, when I met Americans who sounded like native English speakers and asked if they spoke other languages, the most common answer I got was, "I *wish* I did!"

Sometimes I'd hear, "Well, I can *read* French pretty well, but I can't speak it." And a good number of my fellow Americans just shrugged their shoulders and said, "I'm not good at languages."

I felt their pain.

Yet it seemed to me that we were retelling old narratives. Were they still valid? Are Americans really hopeless monolinguals? Is there no point anymore, in our digital age, in working hard to become bilingual? Is it too late for adults in any event?

One chapter ends, another begins

The questions began to take over many of my waking hours—and some of the hours I was supposed to be working, too. My day job as CEO of Levenger started to feel burdensome after twenty-seven years. I handed over the reins to someone else and was now free to focus on my newfound passion of bilingualism. But how best to pursue it?

My friend Doug Rauch told me about a year-long fellowship he had taken at Harvard. It was designed for executives who had finished the first chapter in their careers and yearned to do something new, which usually involved saving the world in one form or another. Another friend, Paul Saffo, told me about a similar program at Stanford. Feeling like a highschooler again, I applied to both programs and, to my surprise, was accepted by both. Greedy for knowledge, I spent one year at Harvard followed by another at Stanford—finally returning to California some forty years after leaving San Diego.

The number of language biographies I collected exploded. But more than that, I was able to interview some of our nation's leading scholars on bilingualism: linguists, sociolinguists, and language teachers. And I gathered advice from successful bilinguals on how they prevailed in earning that title. I could finally start to pull together some informed responses to those pronouncements and questions thrown at me at those cocktail parties. What

I was hearing and learning painted a picture of an America quite different from what my fellow cocktail drinkers and I had assumed. My earlier self as a science writer was whispering in my ear, and I decided I'd have to write a book to share the changes I was seeing in America.

On to the second chapter

One of the interviews I conducted was with Marty Abbott, then head of the American Council on the Teaching of Foreign Languages, now known simply by its acronym of ACTFL (pronounced act-full). She invited me to her offices in Alexandria, Virginia, just outside of Washington, DC, and patiently answered my rather basic questions about bilingualism in America and the challenges her fourteen thousand teachers set for themselves. I learned that there's an expectation among language teachers that they not only teach their subjects well, but also advocate for the importance of language learning.

Knowing I had spent my career in business and clearly had a passion for bilingualism in America, Marty asked me to join the public relations campaign that ACTFL was about to launch called Lead with Languages. "It would be great if you could bring in some voices from the business community who could tell Americans how important language skills are in business," she said.

Happily, I'm a member of YPO, the world's largest organization of company presidents. As soon as I sent out a request for American members who were bilingual and used their language skills to advance their business, the emails started flowing in. I was able to interview several presidents at length, posting my written interviews on the Lead with Languages website. Then Marty called me and asked for something more.

"What we'd really like are *audio* interviews."

"Well, sure, that sounds cool," I said (thinking to myself, *How hard could it be? I'll just hit a "RECORD" button when I'm interviewing people*).

When I hung up with Marty, it began to dawn on me that I had no idea what I had agreed to do. My experience as a science writer had been in print. The only recordings I had done were on a Sony cassette recorder (if anyone remembers those) and it was only to get the quotes right. I knew nothing about doing interviews that would be heard by others. Wasn't that . . . *radio*?

I knew enough, however, to call a friend who *did* know something about professional audio recording. When Maja Thomas heard what I had agreed to do, she said cheerily, "You just signed up to do a podcast!"

A podcast, and a project

"A pod . . . cast?" I felt woefully uninformed.

"It's basically a radio show but people listen on demand rather than its being broadcast at a certain time," said Maja, whose career in publishing has included being an audiobook producer and director. "You'll need a producer. First, join the Association for Independents in Radio . . . "

I joined that group, known by its acronym of AIR, and put out a request for a producer. To my incredibly good fortune, a young Mexican fellow named Fernando Hernández signed on as my producer. He blew away the other candidates with his ten years of radio experience and his skills for creating programs weaving voice, sound, and music into compelling stories. After some coaching from him on how to record professional-level audio, we were off. I found it daunting and enormously time-consuming. In the beginning, it took me several weeks of solid work to create episodes that lasted a mere fifteen or twenty minutes. I'd had no idea what went into the kind of radio shows we hear daily on NPR, not to mention all the captivating podcasts that were exploding in popularity in America.

The episodes found an audience, and listeners shared with more listeners. In the terminology of podcasts, "plays" shot up to five thousand, then twenty thousand, then fifty thousand, with public radio stations picking up some of them. It seemed we had tapped into something.

And it was evolving into something more than a podcast. From talking with friends and colleagues, the idea was born for a small organization that would report on the developments in bilingualism in America that were going largely unreported. I assembled a team and, with the help of some crowdsourcing, we decided to call our project America the Bilingual.

Without really knowing what we were doing, we were shining a light on a story waiting to be told—a story of the unique form of American bilingualism emerging into our national consciousness.

You can be part of this story.

No matter what your prior experiences in language learning, even if you think you're inept at languages, even if you had a terrible experience in school, you *can* adopt a language, become a lifelong bilingual, and experience the joy that comes with entering another world and living a larger life. You can help your loved ones do the same. And you can help America find its voice, both with the English that unites us, and with the hundreds of other languages that help define us.

Becoming bilingual is a journey of a thousand miles that begins with one step. Since you will be walking far, I hope this book will serve as your trusted compass.

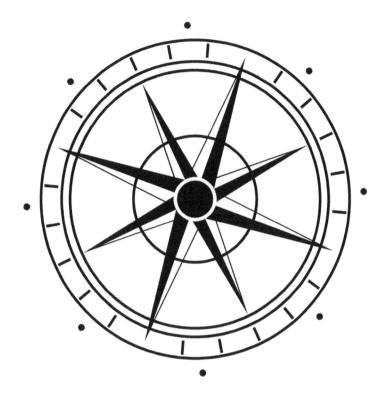

PART ONE

PRACTICAL ADVICE
FOR GROWNUPS

*"You live a new life for every language you speak.
If you know only one language, you live only once."*
—CZECH PROVERB

Chapter 1

NOT JUST HOW, BUT WHERE

"Are you using Duolingo? Or how about Babbel? Or . . . what's that one in the yellow box? Are you taking a class?"

These are the kinds of questions I get from people who, like me, badly want to learn another language. They don't want to waste time. Who does? Is there some *best* way? Some silver bullet?

I had those same questions when I plunged into learning Spanish. It was only later I discovered that "how" isn't the most important question, but rather, "where." That epiphany happened in the office of Guadalupe Valdés, a professor at Stanford.

I had heard about Guadalupe from her admiring colleagues at language conferences and had seen her name in articles and books. I learned she was not only an authority when it comes to bilingualism, but also a beloved figure for her concern for minorities living in America who lack the usual advantage of native English skills. She was the first person I asked to interview when I got to Stanford.

Her office is in the education building, its architecture unusual for its dignified 1930s-era bearing, distinctive on a campus that seems to worship everything new. When I knocked on the wooden door of Professor Valdés's office, Guadalupe greeted me with a warm smile and gentle handshake. Books lined an entire wall of her office, whose high windows filled the room with light. She listened patiently as I explained what I was up to, how I was trying to understand bilingualism in America and where it's going. When I paused, she asked, "Have you heard of Joshua Fishman?"

The social lives of languages

She walked over to her bookcase and plucked out a slim volume: *In Praise of the Beloved Language: A Comparative View of Positive Ethnolinguistic Consciousness,* by Joshua A. Fishman. Next to where Guadalupe had retrieved the book I saw a framed photo of a bunch of people smiling, huddled around an older man who was seated. One of the smiling faces was Guadalupe's. She pointed to the older man. "That's him."

If you study sociolinguistics—which can be thought of as the social life of languages—Fishman is a legend. But I admitted that I had not heard of him. Unfazed by my ignorance, Guadalupe said, "Fishman said, basically, you don't need two languages unless you need two languages."

In other words, she explained, a minority language has to have a place to live in your life if it is going to survive. The normal pattern is that minority languages are lost by the third generation, or even the second generation. Unless a language has someplace it's used, such as church, or in family life, or at work—somewhere—it will lose out to the dominant language in society and gradually fade away.

Those of us trying to learn a second language go from method to method; we try as individuals to find places to use the language and people to speak with, but language learning is inherently a social activity. We don't learn a language, and certainly don't maintain a language, in isolation. While we might start in the privacy of our homes, clicking through software and turning over flash cards, at some point, our new language wants to go out into the real world. And whether bilingualism is welcomed in that world, what the prevailing attitudes and beliefs are about language in that world—all such social things like these matter. A lot.

And while, as language learners, we may not even know the word sociolinguistics, the field of study knows us very well. Sociolinguists study groups of speakers of various languages in different social settings; those groups are made up of people like you and me.

Where will your language live in your life?

"There's a concept called balanced bilingualism—that is, where a person speaks two languages equally," Guadalupe explained. "It's a fiction. Balanced bilingualism doesn't exist in the real world." Even though people speak two languages, one will be dominant in some settings, and the other will be used elsewhere.

This concept is important for us native English-speaking language learners, for two reasons. First, we need to know that, in all likelihood, no matter how good we get at our French or Mandarin or Arabic, including good enough to be called fluent, we will remain dominant in English. This isn't a bad thing; in fact, as we shall see later, English-dominant bilinguals have important roles to play worldwide. It's just good to know.

The second reason is that, as much as we are initially focused on *how* we'll learn our French or Mandarin or Arabic, the *how* question ultimately isn't as important as the *where* question. Unless you can answer the question, "where will my language live in my life?"—not right away, but ultimately—it will be hard, perhaps impossible, for you to develop the fluency you want.

Don't think you have to have this figured out when you're beginning. Just keep it in the back of your mind. Think of it as an invitation to a larger life, which in some important way will be different from your life today.

We'll meet some people in this book who have found those places for themselves. One continues to live his French through his avocation of promoting fine wine in the United States. Another lives her Spanish by teaching English as a second language to Latinos, through her Spanish book group, and by taking hiking vacations in Spanish-speaking countries. Another keeps her Greek alive by being involved in her church and visiting her American son who moved to Greece to become a priest.

By the way, as important as teachers are to your bilingual life, they won't answer this question for you. They are here to help you speak French or Mandarin or Arabic and, in that, they can help you greatly. Nor will you find the answer in software, apps, or YouTube videos, as helpful as all those tools can be. Your answers are yours to discover, although you may well find some useful clues from the people you'll encounter in this book and elsewhere in your travels.

Before I left Guadalupe's office on that first visit, she said one more thing that I've been turning over in my mind ever since: "Bilingualism has always been a gift the rich have given to their children." Yet her career has been dedicated to helping *all* children—regardless of their parents' wealth—inherit this gift. And as we shall see, it is becoming a gift that all of us in America can give and receive.

✳   ✳   ✳

Chapter 2

ADOPTING A LANGUAGE

If there's no such thing as balanced bilinguals, what kinds of bilinguals are there?

From simplest to super complex

At one end of the continuum is the bilingualism we might pick up from a phrase book when traveling to Helsinki or Tokyo. We learn how to say "thank you," "good morning," "what a delicious meal!" Such pleasantries aren't as trivial as they sound. In fact, I've found in the many language biographies I've collected that the more skilled people are in their language use, the more they learn these polite expressions in the countries they visit. And with marvelous results.

This is one of those common practices that linguists, so far as I know, have not named, so the term we use is *buds of bilingualism*. Sometimes these buds develop into a flowering of language skill, but usually they remain niceties that elicit smiles, sometimes laughs, and almost always, good feelings.

The comedian Trevor Noah wrote in his memoir about growing up in South Africa, "When you make the effort to speak someone else's language, even if it's just basic phrases here and there, you are saying to them, 'I understand that you have a culture and identity that exists beyond me. I see you as a human being.'"

Noah grew up acquiring considerable language skills beyond buds of bilingualism. He credits his mother for modeling for him how important language skills are for getting ahead in life. He quotes Nelson Mandela's observation: "'If you talk to a man in a language he understands, that goes to his head. If you talk to him in his language, that goes to his heart.'"

At the other extreme from "budding" bilinguals are professional translators, who work with texts, and interpreters, who work with speech. Translators are hired to translate diplomatic, legal, and business documents. They also translate literature, including novels and poetry, for which they can receive recognitions such as the National Book Award for Translated Literature.

Simultaneous interpretation is viewed as probably the most mentally taxing of all language activities, since one must listen in one language and speak in another, nearly at the same time. It's such intense mental work that simultaneous interpreters, who work at the United Nations, for example, generally work in teams of two and spell one another every fifteen to twenty minutes. The stakes are often high. Think of those interpreters who sit beside world leaders, just outside the frame of the photos.

It's important to note that even these professional bilinguals generally translate or interpret into their native language. They can certainly translate or interpret *from* their native language, but not with the same competence as with their native language—especially since they may not know all of the idioms and cultural references that can most readily convey meaning. This is another example of how there's no such thing as a balanced bilingual.

In between phrase-book buds of bilingualism and simultaneous interpreters, you find many levels of skill among people we might generally call bilingual. As for a definition of bilingual, I like this simple one from François Grosjean: "A bilingual is someone who uses two or more languages (or dialects) in their daily life." But *how* one uses a language in daily life varies greatly. What level of skill should you shoot for?

Reading vs. speaking

For much of the twentieth century in America, language teaching in college focused on reading (as with my German literature course). The idea was to train future scholars to read the great literature of the ages, including works written in ancient Greek, Latin, German, French, Spanish, Italian, and to a lesser extent, Chinese. Someone studying for a PhD in comparative literature, for example, might be expected to read competently in two languages in addition to English. Oral competency was considered of lesser importance from an academic point of view. People didn't travel as much years ago, and communication with colleagues was generally through written correspondence.

On the flip side are people who can't read but can understand the spoken language. This kind of bilingualism is actually quite common among second-generation immigrants. They grew up listening to parents and grandparents speaking the home language but were never schooled in it, and thus never learned to read or write it. It's also common for such second-generation Americans to answer their relatives in English, feeling uncomfortable or unable to respond in the heritage language. Linguists refer to these folks as passive bilinguals.

But other bilinguals do speak their heritage language. American-born Chinese, or ABCs, as they sometimes call themselves, typically can understand spoken Chinese and speak it, but lack the skills to read and write it. An Iranian American named Michelle Bazargan, whom we featured in one of our podcasts, immigrated to the US when she was a child. She speaks her heritage language of Farsi well, mainly with her family, but cannot read it. This is a great disappointment to her, especially given the renowned Persian poets she would like to read in the original language.

Historically, most languages were never written, and even for those that eventually were, they were first spoken. Even today, of the approximately seven thousand languages remaining in the world, most are only oral. Only some one hundred languages have a robust written literature (although more than 95 percent of humans use at least one of these written languages).

Flowers of fluency

For the jobs that require you to demonstrate your bilingual proficiency, standardized tests are used. American language teachers generally take the ACTFL Oral Proficiency Interview (OPI) or a state exam. ACTFL recommends that K-12 teachers achieve at least the "advanced low" level of proficiency.

For the diplomatic corps in the US State Department, or to secure a job in the intelligence community, a different test is used. Depending on the position, it may require you test at the "general, professional" proficiency level to be eligible to serve.

In common discourse, we hear a lot of different terms tossed around, like "Oh, she's *completely* fluent in French," and "I'm *conversational* in Spanish." A friend once enthusiastically exclaimed, "She speaks *idiomatic* French!" Meaning a level higher than merely fluent—she understands the local jargon, jokes, and slang.

I've also had many people tell me that they achieved high levels of fluency for a certain period of time, such as when studying abroad or when working for the Peace Corps. As they relayed their stories, many of these people gazed off with a gentle smile on their faces, as if remembering a former love. Then they would return to the present and say something like, "But it's been many years since I really used the language, so it's mostly gone." Since this is another language phenomenon linguists don't seem to have a term for, we use the term *flowers of fluency*, suggesting the fleeting nature of language skills if not nurtured and maintained.

The journalist Michael Erard writes about his flowering in Spanish and Chinese. "When I glimpse, even for a split second, a different way to be, and begin to accrue more self—an uncanny me emerging from a strange syntax. These are feelings I love, and would love to have again."

Sometimes these fleeting experiences of fluency do lead to lasting bilingualism. Lorna Auerbach, the CEO of a real estate company, had her first flowering of fluency when she went to Israel and lived on a kibbutz. That led, some years later, to her having the confidence to dedicate herself to learning Spanish, which she has used professionally.

Adopting for life

For native English speakers like me studying another language, language teachers use the term L2 learners—2 as in second language. To me, L2 has a rather clinical sound. Much as I love language teachers, when they talk about L2 learners, I'm seeing people in lab coats and clipboards walking down long polished hallways. L2 says nothing about students' interest level. Are they passionate about learning that new language, or just satisfying a graduation requirement?

Linguists and language teachers don't have any particular terms to describe someone who does have this passionate commitment and wants to achieve a level of high competence, except, perhaps, to say that the person is motivated or driven. Nor do they have a particular term to describe people who dedicate themselves to learning the language for the long term, determined to find a place for their second language to live in their lives. But to me, and perhaps you, committing to such goals and having a long-term outlook are important. They call for something a bit stronger than just being called an L2 learner or saying, "I'm studying Arabic . . . "

Over the years of my continuing efforts to learn Spanish, I've struggled to convey to people just how much I love the language and that, even if I'm falling short, I'm dedicated to Spanish for the rest of my life. I've finally hit on what to say. I tell them, "Spanish is my adopted language."

I once met a dear friend of my mother's, a younger woman, who exclaimed, while putting her arms around my mom, "Oh, she's my *adopted* mother!" My mom felt the same about her, calling her "my adopted daughter." The term conveys, of course, a very strong attachment—as strong as one would have for an actual family member. So while we all have our mother tongues, can't we also have our adopted ones? Can't we feel just as loving and committed toward the language we choose for ourselves as we do toward the one that was given us? To me, when I speak of Spanish being my adopted language, it fits better than merely calling Spanish my second language. That sounds like second fiddle, or second place.

Lifelong learning, and playing, and loving

I view adopting a language as a lifetime commitment and a lifetime joy. It continues to teach you, as a child does. It helps you play again.

As a dad, I delighted in building Lego projects with my sons when they were young, and also going to animated feature films—I loved the license to be silly again. My boys and I used to open our garage door and stretch out in the back of our station wagon, resting on our elbows and marveling at the majesty of a Florida thunderstorm. Likewise, as an adult who adopts a language, you get to rediscover the simple things we learned long ago: how to count, how to recite the days of the week and months of the year, adjectives to describe a thunderstorm.

Adopting a language takes place all over the world. It's the lifelong commitment someone makes, for example, by marrying into a family that speaks another language. That practice has been so widespread in history that it does have a name: linguistic exogamy. For some traditional societies, the thought of marrying someone who speaks the same language is akin to incest.

This lifelong commitment aligns with the idea of lifelong learning, which has become part of the social fabric of our times. And this is not just terminology. It's a recognition that a growth mindset, a term coined by the psychologist Carol Dweck, is strongly associated with success in almost all endeavors. And it's a recognition that actively learning throughout one's life is supportive of improved cognition and overall health.

As we shall see in the following chapters, successful bilinguals tend to be those who show deep, long-term commitments to their adopted languages. There are many ways they show their love, and many ways this love rewards them in return.

✳ ✳ ✳

Chapter 3

LEARN FRENCH IN THIRTY YEARS!

Safe to say that no language course will advertise "Learn French in Thirty Years!" But I'm not trying to sell you a language course. I am trying to sell you on the idea that taking a long time to learn your language is actually a good thing.

So how long *should* it take for the average native English-speaking American to learn French? Or how about a language further removed from English, like Arabic? For one answer we can look at people who do this professionally—for example, employees of the US State Department.

In order for Foreign Service Officers to be eligible to fill many overseas positions, they must be tested in reading, writing, listening, and speaking in the language of that country. The test they take, originally developed by the Interagency Language Roundtable, has six levels: from 0, meaning not much beyond buds of bilingualism, to 5, meaning "at a level equivalent to that of a highly articulate, well-educated native speaker." For most positions, candidates are required to be rated at the 3, or "general professional" proficiency level. That's described as "able to use the language with sufficient ability to participate in most formal and informal discussions on practical, social, and professional topics."

Since the State Department can't simply find and hire all the people it needs who already possess the necessary linguistic skills, it does much of the language training itself. Most takes place in the Foreign Service Institute School of Language Studies, which offers training in about seventy languages, with classes in the US and overseas in field offices.

According to a report from the General Accounting Office, it takes about twenty-four weeks, or approximately six months, of training to get a new speaker to level 3 in French. And what about a more difficult language for native English speakers, like Arabic? That's a different story. It takes about a year to get a new speaker just to level 2, described as "sufficient capability to meet routine social demands and limited job requirements." To get this person's Arabic to level 3 requires another full year of training, generally conducted at field schools overseas.

Working hard to learn other languages goes back to America's very first diplomats. Both John Adams and Benjamin Franklin labored diligently at their French while serving the new United States in Paris. They knew how vital it was for American interests. For their efforts, they both received some ridicule and some compliments.

"Your job is to study full time for nine months." That's how one Foreign Service Officer described his language learning to me. He was living in Washington, DC, at the time and had been assigned to a posting in Europe, which required he test out at a level 3.

"You get up in the morning, get dressed, and go to class, and it's a tiny class, sometimes just two students or even just you and the instructor," he explained. Students work on speaking, listening, writing, grammar, taking tests, and watching videos that they then discuss in the language. It's an exhausting day. Then there's your homework. The good news is that instead of paying tuition, you're getting paid. "And you do get your normal vacation," he offered with a weak smile.

Instructors who have created and run such professional-level programs report similar time requirements: it takes many hundreds to several thousands of hours of intense study to be able to use a language professionally.

It takes how *long?*

One reality check on this is to observe children. The language learning scholar Bill VanPatten writes, "The child takes some 14,500 hours or more by age six to master the basics of the adult system. Second language acquisition is equally slow and piecemeal."

Another reality check comes from an innovative study of English language skills acquired over many years, conducted by means of an internet test that went viral and thereby obtained data on more than a half million respondents. The study's authors write, "we found that native and non-native learners both require around 30 years to reach asymptotic performance, at least in immersion settings." The authors aren't talking about fluency with their reference to "asymptotic," but rather, that point at which no further meaningful improvement in grammar is likely to be achieved. Converting thirty years to hours in an immersion setting yields roughly one hundred fifty thousand hours of language exposure. This can explain why we can encounter non-native English speakers who, while fluent by nearly anyone's standard, will make an occasional error, or maybe will ask us why some birds have "bills" while others have "beaks," or why it is that we say "out West" but "back East."

And when the State Department talks about years, it's not like the years we mean when we say, "I took French for four years in school." That may actually mean an hour of class four days a week with twenty other students—a dripping faucet compared with the fire hose blasting over at the Foreign Service Institute.

Given the reality of how many hours of diligent work it takes to become proficient in a language, it shouldn't surprise us that we can't, with our school French, jet over to Paris and casually joke around with our waiters. It's kind of weird that we think we should be able to. I've never heard anyone say to me, "I took four years of high school band" and then complain that they can't sit in with the Chicago Symphony Orchestra. Somehow we know that playing a musical instrument at a professional level takes years and years, while we think learning a language *should* be quicker. In truth, the two activities take similar amounts of time to learn and maintain.

Fast is overrated

Those language course ads that boast how quickly we can become fluent have two problems. The first is the obvious one that you won't become as fluent as they promise, conclude it's *your* problem, and throw in the towel. I've interviewed many language learners who told me they started a class and managed to finish but then didn't sign up for the next one. Or they stopped using their expensive software before finishing it. Or listened to audio in their car for a while but, well, got busy with other things.

Part of the difficulty is what's called the "planning fallacy," which the economist Richard Thaler and jurist Cass Sunstein have described as "the systematic tendency toward unrealistic optimism about the time it takes to complete projects." There is the real danger that the combination of misleading advertising together with our own, very human wishful thinking combine to sandbag our desires to become bilingual.

The second problem with these advertisements is that they promote a fundamentally wrongheaded idea about the benefits of speed. Sure, fast learning is great, and you will have periods when your learning is fast, fun, and rewarding. Hooray! But at other times it will be slow and hard, as you come

13

to a plateau and, by working at it, leap to the next plateau. And most of all, it just takes time, hours, months, years. This is a good thing, not a bad thing. Your journey to bilingualism is something to enjoy along the way. That's what adopting a language is all about.

As the language instructor Paul Pimsleur wrote, "That languages take time to learn becomes a plus instead of a drawback when one considers how much a long-range commitment gives focus and continuity to a period of one's life."

'Nobody Knows the Truffles I've Seen'

Language teachers are always saying things like, "It's not just the language, but the culture." I always had a bit of trouble getting my head around what they meant until one particular afternoon. I was having lunch with one of my long-suffering Spanish tutors named Luz Zuluaga.

We were at Felipe's Taqueria near Boston, where you go through the line ordering your food and then take it to your table. Luz was listening to me order with the Spanish-speaking staff so she could correct me later. While we were eating, we got on the subject of Budapest, of all things, and I mentioned a famous restaurateur from Budapest and his book because I always loved the title. I managed to mangle in Spanish, "His name was George Lang. Maybe you heard of him?"

She hadn't.

"His book was *Nobody Knows the Truffles I've Seen*."

Blank stare.

"You know, the song, 'Nobody Knows the *Trouble* I've Seen'? Louis Armstrong?"

More blank stares.

I decided at that point I would tell her how much I was enjoying my burrito.

Let me say that Luz has a perfect command of English. There was nothing I could say that she didn't understand, nor anything she said in English that was incorrect. But reflecting back on our conversation, I realized I was expecting her to know some cultural things that most likely only an American would know—and perhaps an older American, at that. I also realized, on the flip side, that I couldn't mention *one* historic song or famous musician from her native Colombia. (Okay, besides Shakira.)

The other day I saw a pesticide truck in my neighborhood displaying the company's motto: "The Bug Stops Here." Funny, right? But try explaining why to a non-native speaker. "You know, Harry Truman and the sign on his desk . . . ? 'The *buck* stops here' . . . ?"

The point is that learning culture takes time—and lots of it. Every year we clock in some six thousand hours of waking time, during much of which we're using our native language. We mix our American cocktail of stories, politics, humor, and new words like "selfie" and "woke" as an adjective. We also talk like where we're from, using regionalisms. "Wicked smart" is a compliment in Rhode Island. You might hear it as well when you travel from Boston "down the Cape" to Provincetown (even though you're heading up). In dairy-rich Wisconsin, you might be treated to "cheese curds freshly squeaked."

Yes, you'll learn about the culture of the country or countries that speak your adopted language. Just don't expect it to happen overnight, any more than your knowledge of your own culture did.

A local rather than a native

Even when you have a truly wonderful command of another language, unless you've lived in the country for many years, you'll not get most of the cultural references that natives use. Similarly, even when you become quite comfortable reading, listening, and speaking in your adopted language, it's unlikely that you'll be mistaken for a native speaker. Your grammar will probably be off once in a while, your pronunciation will miss a tone here, an emphasis there. And you know what? That's okay.

The star of our very first episode of the *America the Bilingual* podcast is an American named Ben Macklowe, who has been using his French professionally in his antiques business for more than twenty years. I interviewed one of his French colleagues and asked her to tell me how good Ben's French was. "It's wonderful!" she exclaimed. "And you know what else? He writes really well." That's a high compliment, indeed, coming from a native French speaker.

I asked her if she could tell Ben was not from France. "Yes, of course," she said matter-of-factly. "But that's okay."

When you adopt a language, it means you take the long view. It relieves you of the pressure to believe you're going to be anything close to perfect for years to come. And that's fine. You can still enjoy the hell out of the process of getting there—which is sometimes fast and easy, and sometimes slow and hard.

What you'll want to achieve, instead of perfection, and instead of being mistaken for a native, is daily momentum, developing practices for yourself to improve—which brings us to all the many resources at our disposal that help us do just that.

Be like a bee and play the field

I remember the almost desperate feeling I'd get every time I'd see a new language learning app or new TED video with another polyglot promising to tell us his secrets to becoming fluent fast. It took me a while, after many interviews with language professionals, to learn that there is no silver bullet. But there are many perfectly good lead bullets. It's not which *one* method is best, it's more like "all of the above."

Behind all the apps and methods, schools and YouTube videos are entrepreneurs, usually passionate ones, who have poured their energies and often their lives into giving the world a better way of learning a language. Chances are high that some of what each of them offers will help you, too.

Think like a honey bee. Fly from flower to flower, see which are to your liking, drink from them, learn from them, enjoy their color and shape and fragrance, and move on. Don't forget your local library, which might well have purchased useful software and books you can use for free.

There are lots and lots of good tools. If you get bogged down with one and find yourself losing interest, try a different one. But this do not do: don't let the fact that you got bogged down scrub your entire mission. Keep the larger goal in mind, and understand that no one tool is going to get you there.

The psychologist Angela Duckworth, who has studied high-achieving people, reports that such people have a habit of being able to give up on lower-level things while not losing sight of their higher-level goals. Give yourself permission to give up on something that's not working.

The right time may be some other time

Early in my Spanish learning journey, someone told me how great the audio lessons of Michel Thomas were, so I gave them a try. When I began listening, it sounded to me as if Thomas spoke with some sort of German accent, or maybe French, but certainly not a Spanish accent. Yet he was teaching Spanish. His format consisted of himself plus two students, both of whom seemed to be rank beginners, no better than me. *Why* was I listening to this?

I gave up and switched to Pimsleur audio. I found it so satisfying to hear and repeat the phrases while I was driving that I found other things to do while I listened—washing the car, doing dishes, walking the dog, walking the neighbor's dog. I went through all of Pimsleur and liked it so much, I did it again.

Then, on a lark, I decided to give Michel Thomas another try. This time, I liked it. He was explaining things like how the present tense in Spanish always puts the emphasis on the penultimate syllable, so even if you've never heard the verb before, you'll recognize present tense. And he worked in other grammar tips and fun stories. I wasn't in the mood for him the first time around. The second time, he was great. When the student is ready . . .

The psychologist Ellen Bialystok and the linguist Kenji Hakuta coauthored a book in 1994 dedicated to summarizing what was then known about learning a second language. They concluded that "there is no single correct method for teaching or learning a second language and that the search for one is probably misguided." In his study of polyglots, Michael Erard found that they use many different methods. Some like classes, others teach themselves, and others excel just by speaking with other people. Part of what you'll do as you move from method to method is find out what ways of learning work best for you, at any given point in your journey.

Some teachers who offer refreshing ways of seeing and learning our adopted language include Steve Kaufmann and his site, The Linguist; Tim Ferriss and his 4-Hour Workweek site; and opera-singer-turned-language-instructor Gabriel Wyner and his *Fluent Forever* book and app. They all have ideas and practices that can help us. It's not *one* best way, but many great ways to add to your journey. Just as we have many people who teach us life lessons, we'll have many people who will teach us our adopted language.

Mix quite new with old-fashioned

I suggest you forgive some of the marketing tactics that promise speed above all else. You might indeed progress quickly—which is fantastic, as long as you understand that you'll also, at other times, progress slowly. That's sometimes when your learning will deepen the most.

Keep in mind that you'll also encounter marvelous language teachers who are unknown beyond their small number of students. Sometimes these teachers can be even more helpful to you because you can learn from them face-to-face. Some of these gifted teachers may be within a few miles of you, waiting for you to find them.

Also, explore companies such as Yabla that use technical capabilities like video learning, and Livemocha and HelloTalk, which connect learners with teachers, no matter where in the world they may be. Listen to podcasts that open a new world of audio learning. Two of my favorites are *News in Slow Spanish* (and other languages) and the podcasts that Duolingo produces.

While new technology can be brilliantly helpful, don't forget about old-fashioned flash cards as well. Even more helpful than store-bought cards are those you make yourself. Instead of just single words, write phrases and sentences. As both Paul Pimsleur and Gabriel Wyner tell us, words are more meaningful and relevant when used together. And writing by hand allows our kinesthetic faculties to help our minds learn.

Be patient and kind with yourself. That's the advice of the polyglot Kato Lomb. You might fail at remembering a word ten times. Just laugh and keep going. Remember: adopting a language is a lifetime commitment. We're all going to have our off days and concepts that stay beyond our grasp for longer than we would like.

When he began studying French, the author Ta-Nehisi Coates wrote, "What I quickly learned was that saying I am going to 'study' French was like saying I am going to sail to China. The language is so vast that one can, all at once, feel both great progress being made and a great distance still to go."

There used to be a travel company in Boston with a sign that said, "Please Go Away!" In that spirit, I can imagine a language school. Under the sign that says "Learn French in Thirty Years!" would be a smaller one: "And we hope it takes you forever."

Chapter 4

NOT THE LANGUAGE CLASS
YOU MAY REMEMBER

In my interviews collecting language biographies, many adults told me they didn't get much out of their language classes, or worse, that they actually hated them. They reported verb conjugation drills, a lot of sitting around listening to their teacher, and not getting much beyond that. The funny thing is, I heard similar complaints from language teachers themselves.

The first language-teacher convention I attended was one of ACTFL's, in Boston in 2015. I was surprised at how big it was. Several thousand teachers, from K-12 through higher ed, were there, and they came from all over the country.

I kept hearing some buzz around an upcoming session many teachers were excited about. It was to hear Stephen Krashen, whose name I would hear many times afterwards, with a sort of reverence, from the language teachers I would interview at future conventions.

I got to the hall early but not early enough—I had to stand along the wall. Hundreds of teachers had arrived earlier and were talking excitedly among themselves. On stage were two people, Bill VanPatten, the host of a popular podcast for language teachers, *Tea with BVP*, and Stephen Krashen, an emeritus professor of linguistics at the University of Southern California.

Krashen addressed the audience and said (I'm paraphrasing, since I didn't record the session): "Ninety-eight percent of students who take language classes are bored to death. Two percent of students actually like the classes. They go on to become language teachers."

The audience erupted into laughter and applause.

As one of the few people in the room who wasn't a language teacher, I had the feeling I was listening to some deep-state conspiracy. Not only do language teachers torture their students, they *laugh* about it? But I soon learned that the reason for the laughter was because the teachers have been working hard in the past several years to reverse this common experience, and are confident they are succeeding.

Kill the 'drill and kill'

The basic problem, Krashen explains in his book *Explorations in Language Acquisition and Use,* is that we had this pedagogical idea that we first had to teach people *about* the language—its grammar, how its verbs conjugate, what the pronouns and prepositions are and the rules for how they work—before people could start using the language. But after decades of trying, we finally figured out it just doesn't work. He writes, "The profession has, in my view, backed the wrong horse."

Krashen says that what's needed is "comprehensible input." As an example, he cites the total physical response method. "Language is taught using commands. The teacher gives the command, models the movement, and the student performs the action. Students are not asked to speak, only to try to understand and obey the command." I remember seeing this in action in the English classes I've attended for immigrants. We all enjoyed getting out of our seats and putting our hands on our arms and legs, while saying the words.

In the beginning, writes Krashen, "Demands for output are low and students are not forced to speak until they feel ready." And when they do begin to speak? "Complete sentences are not required, and errors are not corrected." The evidence, he says, is that "grammatical accuracy is a result of comprehensible input, not output and correction . . . ."

We shouldn't be hard on teachers for having the wrong idea, says Krashen; it's been the conventional wisdom for decades. "The public has assumed that some things must first be 'learned,' that a lot of hard work is necessary before students can go on to more interesting activities. But when students engage in real problem solving and are exposed to interesting and comprehensible input, they acquire language and learn concepts and facts much more easily."

We used to assume students had to suffer through all this grammar and what language teachers now derisively call "drill and kill." That was just wrong. "There is no need to wait," Krashen writes. "There is no need for delayed gratification."

Start students off with success

Krashen has had a profound impact on many of the teachers we interviewed. One was Amelia Richter, a Spanish teacher in West Virginia. Krashen's book, she told me, "changed my life." I asked her how.

She explained that his methods helped her find ways to ask her students questions in a way that's comprehensible. "You help create an environment where the students are comfortable and they can experience success, knowing that they're going to take natural steps as they continue in their proficiency. It just made sense."

Bill VanPatten puts it this way: "Language is abstract and complex," he says, and adds that "what's on page 32 of the textbook is not what winds up in anyone's head."

So if both students and teachers agree that teaching grammar doesn't work, why don't language classes change? The answer is, many of them have.

The grammar book comes later

We'll get into how they have changed for young students in the next part of the book, but right now, let's talk about adult classes, which have also changed. Lori and I took an intermediate Spanish class together through Stanford's continuing studies program. The class met at night on campus and was filled with a mix of ages, from Stanford employees in their twenties to local retirees in their seventies. Hae-Joon Won, our instructor, was excellent—enthusiastic, encouraging, patient. We did some homework, talked among ourselves in class, watched and discussed Spanish TV series. At the end of the term, we went to a local Mexican restaurant and for the most part, spoke Spanish.

Part of the value of taking a class is the content you get, and the struggling you get to do as you try to speak in class, but a lot of the value can also come with just having an imposed schedule with social expectations. Just as some people are fine exercising on their own, plenty of others know a class helps them do what they know they want to do, but sometimes don't. The peer pressure, the schedule, the expectations from your instructors and fellow students—all of these help.

Plus, with all the technological ways we have to learn today, it's mighty good to get out and use your adopted language as it was meant to be used— with other people, face-to-face. It can be liberating and exhilarating.

Teachers will be the first to tell you, however, that the more time you put in outside of class, the more you get from the classes. Classes get students confident enough so that they continue learning on their own, using many different methods.

And after you start to get comfortable using the language, that's when you might actually like dipping into a grammar book, which can reinforce what you've learned. As Kato Lomb wrote, "One learns grammar from language, not language from grammar." Or as Paul Pimsleur put it, "Grammar is best learned by using it, not by talking about it."

So I encourage you to check out local language classes. If the instructor wants you to start with a fat textbook full of grammar and seems to delight in conjugating verbs for the class, well, maybe that instructor didn't get the memo. But chances are your instructor *did* get the memo, and you'll find to your delight that it's not the language class you may remember from high school.

Chapter 5

STAY THIRSTY, MY FRIENDS

One of the tutors I had the pleasure of learning from was Janire Bragado, a young woman from Spain. She came to America to earn her second master's degree at Florida Atlantic University (FAU), near where I live in South Florida. At one of our first sessions, she explained that language learners "must pull the language into themselves."

Although Janire was the first to tell me this, I've come across the idea in many of the books I've read since. Paul Pimsleur wrote, "Take charge of your own learning." He added, "Every person must develop his own techniques to suit his capacities and learning styles." *The Linguist* polyglot Steve Kaufmann considers taking charge of your own language learning a first principle. "You must be determined to find your own way to a new language, and be careful of teachers imposing their versions of the language on you." He added, "Success depends not on the teacher, but on the learner."

The 'complete surrender'

Jack Roepers, my longtime friend and a polyglot, was one such successful learner. Jack was born in Holland to a Dutch father and a German mother. He grew up speaking Dutch and German, but family vacations were usually in France, so at a young age he was exposed to French, too. In school, he had classes in English as well as German and French, all the way through college. Later, in his career at the International Development Bank and several private firms, Jack worked in Latin America. He became competent enough in Spanish to address his staff and even give radio interviews. And he knows a bit of Farsi as well, since he married an Iranian woman.

Jack told me that what has been key for him and the many other bilinguals he knows is "drive, desire, and overall, all-in investment" for learning the new language. He describes it as the "complete surrender" to wanting to learn that new language. "That's what it will take for anyone who is serious about being conversant in another language."

I went about searching for other successful bilinguals who had undertaken this "complete surrender." When I asked Janire if she had any students who were really doing well, it took her only a moment to think of one particular undergraduate, Victoria Duclos.

'I just wanted to run'

Victoria was born in Miami of Haitian parents. "My mom spoke Creole to me and I answered in English. My father spoke only English to me and both of them speak English to one another," she told me. In high school, Victoria took Spanish her first two years, but then dropped it. "I didn't want Spanish 3 because it would interfere with sciences, and my math was weak, so I thought I would focus on that," she explained.

Victoria went from age fourteen to twenty speaking no Spanish at all. She didn't need it at the junior college she attended, but when she transferred to FAU, she did: there was a language requirement.

"I felt like I forgot everything," she said. She hadn't used any of her Spanish in six years. Nevertheless, in the entrance exam, she was placed into Spanish 2 and figured she would stop there, after satisfying the language requirement. But she had a certain professor who saw something in her.

"He was the inspiration to all of this," she said, smiling. "He saw my progress and said I should minor in Spanish. I said no, I was already minoring in psychology. He just kept saying I could do it." But Victoria was not willing to jeopardize her grade point average, or GPA. Even so, "I knew I would be paid more as a bilingual and the benefits of being a bilingual would help me in whatever profession I went into. So I decided to do it."

At first, it didn't come easily.

"I remember being afraid to speak," she recalled. "I didn't want to sound ignorant, so I went to a *sobremesa*, an extra-credit session where you just sit with Spanish speakers." That's where she met Janire.

"Someone said to me, 'Look, think if you were around someone who didn't speak English well—"how much cost this?," for example. You would be very happy to help them, right?' Of course I would." That's when Victoria said she started feeling okay about just speaking and letting people help her.

Once she started feeling some momentum, the thirst really came.

"I fell into the music. I wouldn't listen to any radio stations except Spanish stations." Even though she wasn't understanding lots of what she heard, "my professor said I should continue because I was training my brain without knowing it, getting used to the pattern of inflections, and with time, my brain would catch up."

It began to work. "The songs were small stories. I would bring song lyrics into my professors' office hours and we would translate them together." They also watched music videos. "This was *real* Spanish," Victoria said. Getting to that was one of her goals. "I didn't want to crawl and then walk and then run. I didn't want baby steps, I just wanted to run." She started watching Spanish television shows, too.

I asked if it was ever hard.

"Yes, especially indirect pronouns!" she exclaimed. Using them correctly left her, she said, "beyond-belief frustrated. I didn't understand them. I went to my professors for help. I was frustrated for two to three weeks. I would get it in class but out of class it would escape me. I was very close to giving up, but once I finally got over that hill, I could breathe again."

Victoria started taking her adopted language with her wherever she went—dancing at a Spanish nightclub, to church for Sunday service in Spanish.

A breakthrough over a BOGO

Then came something unexpected.

Victoria was standing in line at a CVS Pharmacy one night, when an elderly man wanted to cut in front of her. He seemed agitated. "I thought he was rude, or maybe he was deaf or mute," she said. But something compelled her to say to him, "*¿Habla español, señor?*' And he started talking fast." In Spanish.

"He was explaining to me that he didn't get the discount he was supposed to get and didn't understand." He had seen a sign saying 50 percent off. "But it was a buy-one-get-one-free offer, and I explained this to him," Victoria said. "He understood and said, *'Lo siento.'* Which means, 'I'm sorry.'"

The episode had a real impact on her. "I was in a dream. My Spanish came out effortlessly. After it was over, I took the deepest breath I've ever taken! Did that really happen?"

When we met, Victoria was tutoring in Spanish 4 at FAU and getting her minor in Spanish. She has long-term goals for her adopted language.

"I want to visit the Dominican Republic. I've already been mistaken multiple times for being a Dominicana." She smiled as she told me, "They say, 'She sounds like my people.'"

She plans to marry a native Spanish speaker. "My children will be speaking in Creole and Spanish at home," Victoria said firmly. "English can wait."

Growth mindset vs. fixed mindset

Victoria possesses a natural enthusiasm, which her teachers picked up on and encouraged. Once success started to come, it triggered a positive-feedback loop. When frustration came, she struggled, sought help, and persevered, rising to her next plateau.

Victoria seems to be a test case for what the psychologist Carol Dweck has described as a growth mindset. In her foundational book on the subject, Dweck contrasts a growth mindset with a fixed mindset. In truth, she writes, we all have some of each inside us. Through awareness and good coaching, we can develop our growth orientation and continuously quench our thirst for more skill as we proceed on our own bilingual journeys.

In recent decades, other books have followed on Dweck's work to help us understand how to develop positive habits and strengthen the self-control we need to achieve the goals we want. Charles Duhigg's *The Power of Habit* and Kelly McGonigal's *The Willpower Instinct* are both applicable to language learning.

Grasp the outstretched hand

I had already been studying Spanish for several years when Caroline Doughty, one of our team members at America the Bilingual, told me I must read *Fluent Forever* by Gabriel Wyner. I'm glad she did. His writing reinforced several things I'd already learned, like writing my own flash cards, and working from back to front when working out pronunciation. And he taught me new things about using spaced repetition techniques, where you review the same material again and again, at spaced intervals that gradually get longer. He also introduced me to a marvelous tool called a frequency dictionary, which I had not heard of. It is just that: a dictionary of the most frequently used words in a language. I now adore this power tool.

When I was a new dad, someone gave me some advice about holding my baby son's hand when we walked in a parking lot: "Let him grab your hand." I tried it, although two fingers were easier for him to grasp than my whole hand. It took some faith on my part to not grab his little hand, but instead to allow him to latch onto my two fingers. It worked. We moved only when I felt him holding tight, which was most of the time. It's what Janire was doing with me, extending her hand but expecting me to do the grasping.

I feel deep gratitude to teachers like Janire and Wyner, who are holding the gift of bilingualism out to me so I can grasp it. Abraham Lincoln said, "My best friend is a person who will give me a book I have not read." Lincoln sought out new knowledge to grasp. And knowing two languages is like using both hands—you grasp better.

As Dos Equis' World's Most Interesting Man would say, "Stay thirsty, my friends."

Chapter 6

Immersion at Your Fingertips

People have said to me at those cocktail parties that the only way to really learn a language was total immersion, implying that whatever the hell I was doing here stateside was wasting my time. We'll talk about real immersion in Part Three, its blessings and its pitfalls, but here I want to talk about a cheeky kind of immersion.

When we think of the application of technology to language learning, we tend to think of translation software, apps, connecting with tutors online. Yet there is something else that can be transforming. It's going into the settings of your digital devices and setting your touch points to your adopted language.

Those amazing immersive devices

Start with your phone. Go to settings, and switch the language from English to your adopted one. Suddenly (automagically, as one of my friends says), you're in a different country. The familiar icons for date, weather, camera, phone, and text are in the same color and position you're used to, but now called something else.

Then go into the keyboard options that you can toggle to when texting and writing emails. The predictive text feature, which guesses what you're trying to peck out, works in other languages, too. It even suggests the accents, which can be tricky to type. For those friends who already speak your adopted language, or are learning like you, you can write to them in your new language.

Then comes the voice. My Siri is now Sirita. I'll ask, "*¿Qué tiempo hace?*" ("What's the weather?"), and Sirita will tell me in Spanish. She will set an alarm, call your mom, or do most anything her English sister will do for you—all in your adopted language.

I've sat next to plenty of people and talked them through this digital identity swap. They usually respond with a sense of delight, wonder . . . and fear. "Wait, I don't think I'm ready for that," they'll often say. I understand—it's a bit disconcerting at first. But start by learning how to toggle back and forth between English and your adopted language, which is pretty easy. And don't stop at your phone.

When I insert my bank card into an ATM, in an instant, it knows to serve me in Spanish. I was worried when I first tried this, thinking I might accidentally transfer money to Havana, but I quickly got accustomed to my bank digital touch points, both ATMs and online banking, in my adopted language.

My Ford truck is also set to Spanish, so instead of "truck information" on my digital dash, I see *info camión,* and instead of "fuel economy," I see *economiá de combustible.* My navigation is also set to Spanish audio, so a very patient woman's voice will tell me, *siga derecho,* "continue straight." With all that, plus my LIV MAS ("Live More") license plate, my sons say I should be selling empanadas out the back.

My computer is set to Spanish, too, and that leads to some more Spanish surprises. Many websites pick up the language setting of your computer and will adapt to you, presenting their website in your adopted language. Go ahead and try to read and do what you came there for. If you get confused, you can always toggle back to English.

When I search something, I'll see Wikipedia links, as usual, but some are in Spanish while others are in English. Since I can now read pretty well in Spanish, I won't hesitate to click on the Spanish one and get the answers I'm looking for.

Immersible you

What bilinguals sometimes report is that when they're using their other language, they feel like a slightly different person, their larger self. This is what you can start to experience as you step into your digital immersion. You can find news sources in your adopted language, along with music, shows, and movies. Almost by accident, your everyday life can start to become your everyday bilingual life.

The reason all this is available to us isn't because these many firms are in the language-learning space, at least not intentionally. We are riding a fortunate side effect of the goals of these many businesses and products to be as universally appealing as possible and ready for global sales. With business being so competitive, companies and organizations seek ways to stand out, to gain market share, to delight their customers. This is why they make sure their websites are translated, or are at least amenable to machine translation, to go as far as possible toward making their customers and prospects comfortable. But just as most large companies have to be technology companies these days, most of these companies end up being in the *language* technology business—they've built interfaces that are a boon to language learners.

I admit that I find many news stories boring or depressing. But when I'm following the news in Spanish, it's always educational and often interesting. Some of it is Spanish written for an American audience, and much of it is Spanish written for native speakers. I find great pleasure in getting more comfortable reading and listening in my adopted language. Much of my news time that used to be dispiriting is now uplifting. Not that the news is any better, but it's often from a different perspective.

'A sublime disregard for borders'

Passing through the Phoenix airport one day, I had time to stop for a shoe-shine. The fellow who waved me into a chair was friendly but a bit distracted. I noticed he had in an earbud. When he was buffing my shoes, doing that back-and-forth movement, with two long brushes going the long way, he suddenly let out a laugh. Looking up at me, he stopped and apologized. "Oh, I'm sorry," he said, with the laugh still lingering on his face. "I'm listening to my radio station back home and the fellow just said something really funny."

"No problem," I said. "What's the radio station?"

"Oh, I'm from Nigeria, and I was listening to my hometown station."

"What language is it in?"

"It's in Igbo," he said.

I'd never heard of the language, but when I looked it up later, I found that it has at least twenty million speakers.

This fellow, who I'm guessing is first-generation, is keeping his home language alive in a way unthinkable just a few years ago. By doing so, he's not as likely as earlier immigrants to lose his native language. He can work on his English, which seemed quite good to me, but also listen to the latest news, politics, sports, and entertainment in his native Igbo. What's more, he can do this anytime, and for free.

In one of my interviews with a Greek American named Chris Nichols, he told me about how he and his family watch Greek television. "I'll watch the news, usually." But he came across a program that interviewed twenty famous Greek singers and played their songs. "It went on for two hours. I was like a little kid with my tongue hanging out. Most of the singers were in their sixties. It was the music I grew up with. I have ADD, but I sat there for two hours, listening. I'm getting chills just thinking about it!"

The Nigerian American and the Greek American are using technology to keep their culture and language skills alive, taking advantage of technologies that carry languages far from their home locales. These sources of information operate, writes the journalist Marek Kohn, "with a sublime disregard for national borders." One result is that heritage languages that used to be lost may be valued more highly in the coming years when, as Kohn says, "economic, cultural and personal incentives will increasingly blend into each other."

It used to be hard to find books in your adopted language, but now with our e-readers and electronic books, we have a treasure chest filled with such jewels. Our digital age has, perhaps inadvertently, made us the beneficiaries of a perfect storm of digital immersion possibilities.

My virtual stumbles

I admit that I've had a few embarrassing moments exercising my digital immersion. Once, after I tapped the *español* button on the automated check-in kiosk at one of the airlines, I decided to pay extra to get more leg room. After most of the people had boarded the plane, I finally got up to the agent, who scanned my boarding pass and then looked at me. "You paid for early boarding."

"Oh. I thought I bought extra leg room."

She looked at me quizzically.

"I'm learning Spanish, so I did it in Spanish."

"Next time, keep it in English," she offered, waving me through.

Then there was the time at the Ford dealership in the small town in Maine where we spend our summers. I was trying to pass myself off as not-that-much-of-a-city-dude with the Mainer who headed the service department. We were looking at the screen in my truck, when I remembered it was all in Spanish.

"Oh, sorry, I've got it set to Spanish."

"H'mmm," he said. "Most of us still use English up here"—that last word coming out as "heah," in the Maine version of English.

Despite these awkward moments, I keep my truck, my bank, my computer, my phone, and even my rental cars in Spanish. (I do try to remember to switch those back to English before running for the plane.)

In a sense, abroad

Several of the language teachers we've interviewed, when asking them for their advice to language learners, have pointed out these digital touch points. "Read the news, watch TV, and listen to music in your target language," advises Frances Mecartty, who teaches Spanish at the Pingry School in Basking Ridge, New Jersey. "It's entertaining and very helpful."

Airline pilots spend lots of hours in simulators, where they encounter all kinds of emergency situations. That way, if they ever confront such emergencies during an actual flight, it won't be the first time. Likewise, our digital immersion can help us gain experience with the language to add to our real-life experiences, and move up the confidence ladder.

Many of us complain about all the screens we stare at all the time, all the notifications, emails, and other digital noise. We seek our digital detox in one form or another. Me, too. But now that my digital life is increasingly in my beloved adopted language, it's not nearly so annoying. I can watch TV news and enjoy it, even the ads. In fact, sometimes especially the ads.

Today my adopted language lives in places it's most welcome in my life: taking in the news, learning about the world online, and texting and emailing with Spanish-speaking and Spanish-learning friends. Truly, this American digital life is, for emerging bilinguals, one of the blessings of our time.

Chapter 7

WHEN GUILTY READS
BECOME BEST READS

Early on in my journey to bilingualism, I decided I should read children's books in Spanish. How hard could it be? I had already learned a good bit of vocabulary. So I bought a few at the bookstore and sat down to read.

It was harder than I thought. I had to look up plenty of words and try to sort out the grammar. But I stayed with it, feeling a bit embarrassed that I was having trouble. Then I realized that, although I could make progress with them, I got bored.

So I set my children's books aside and went in the other direction. I decided I should try some of the Spanish literary greats. I bought a copy of *Cien años de soledad (One Hundred Years of Solitude),* by Gabriel García Márquez.

This classic by the Nobel Prize-winning author is an exemplar of magical realism. Which is to say, supernatural things weave in and out of the plot like a snake through high grass. Plus, the language is sophisticated, even in the English version of the book, which I would retreat to every few paragraphs. But having given up on children's books, it became a matter of pride to make it through this. I tackled it every morning with my first—and then second—cup of coffee, putting in an hour on average for two months, after which I was about a third of the way through.

My friends stopped asking me what I was reading because my answer was always the same. Finally, I realized that this revered classic had magically transformed itself into *One Hundred Years of Reading This Book.*

Feeling rather dejected after failing at both children's books and this adult masterpiece, I decided to let myself go to seed. What the hell, I thought, why not just try a page-turner, the eating-ice-cream-out-of-the-container kind of book I would normally not let myself enjoy?

Find your reading rhythm

I went online to find the Spanish novel that had not merely a high average rating, but *thousands* of high ratings. Having failed at charting my own path through the forest, now I just wanted to follow the pack. That strategy led me to the bestselling novel *Dime quien soy* (*Tell Me Who I Am*), by Julia Navarro. It's a mystery spanning much of the twentieth century.

It was also slow going, and I would switch to the English version on my Kindle every page or so. But at about the 40 percent mark, I began going to the English translation less. The plot pulled me along, and even though I didn't get every word, or even every sentence, I got enough to prefer to keep reading in Spanish rather than breaking my rhythm. One morning, as I drained my second cup of coffee, I realized with a flash of joy that I had been reading for an hour in Spanish—and *loving* it! That was a sweet milestone.

I couldn't wait for the next day when I could continue my morning ritual of café con *lectura* (reading). What would our young journalist hero discover about this mysterious Laura he was tracking down out of the mists? I was in book love for the first time in my adopted language.

Following the advice of my friend Harold Augenbraum, who translates Spanish literature into English professionally, I learned to not look up every word I didn't know, but when I did, to do so in the Spanish dictionary residing on my Kindle, thus staying in the language.

It may take you tasting several books before you find the first one that makes you fall in book love in your adopted language. But you should have the confidence of knowing that it's one of the best things you can do for your learning.

The power of reading what you want

Had I read Stephen Krashen's book before I began my own reading adventure, I might have spared myself the Goldilocks drama. From his long observation of second-language acquisition, Krashen advises that readers have the freedom to choose to read *just what they want*, rather than assigned readings.

"Free voluntary reading may be the most powerful tool we have in language education," he maintains. Not only does exercising this freedom improve reading comprehension, vocabulary, grammar, and writing—as he says, "it is also very pleasant."

Free reading may also be an important part of the solution to two related problems: "making the transition from the elementary level to authentic language use, and from 'conversational' language ability to 'academic' language ability." Its impact, Krashen says, is almost "too good to be true."

Encouraging students to choose what they want to read is at the heart of Krashen's "comprehensible input." Over the years, he added another adjective for that input: "compelling." In a book published in 2018, he and his coauthors posited, "When input is compelling, all anxiety disappears, and there is no need for 'motivation': language acquisition and literacy development occur without the acquirer realizing it."

Reading just what you want is not only one of the best ways to improve in your adopted language; it can also become the vehicle to draw you into finding and developing your deepest interests. As Krashen and his two coauthors wrote, "The concept of compelling comprehensible input may be one of the most crucial in all of education. It is possible that it is an important part of the path to full literacy development, full language acquisition, finding one's true interests, and developing the competence to pursue these interests."

Krashen cites the psychologist Mihaly Csikszentmihalyi to support his idea of free voluntary reading, which sent me back to my copy of Csikszentmihalyi's classic book, *Flow*, and this observation: "Enjoyment appears at the boundary between boredom and anxiety, when the challenges are just balanced with the person's capacity to act."

For me, my breakthrough novel was at just that magical boundary between boredom and anxiety. Language learning invites, or even demands, that we seek flow.

"Whenever I am asked how I was able to succeed in many languages in a relatively short period of time," wrote Kato Lomb, who was conversant in more than twenty languages, "I always make a bow in spirit to the source of all knowledge: books. My advice to learners can thus be expressed in one word: read!" And not just anything, but what interests you. "I start on the comprehensible novel immediately."

I was able to see Krashen and Lomb's recommendations put into practice when I visited the Los Robles dual language school in East Palo Alto, California. On a tour that principal Keith Bookwalter took me on, we entered a fourth-grade class during their half-hour of silent reading time. The desks were arranged in a big horseshoe, so we were able to walk quietly behind each student to observe what they were reading. The students, absorbed in their books, ignored us. It looked to me that about half the books were in English and half in Spanish. "We let students choose whatever book, in whatever language, they wish," Keith told me.

Escape to your favorite 'linguistic microclimates'

Reading can't do everything, of course. Lomb said that talking with the right conversation partner is also golden. "A personal exchange of views—a live conversation—will often leave a more lasting mark in our memory than what is in books." She said it can be hard to find such a partner who suits you—interesting, patient, willing to correct you often but not always.

Nor did she see reading as a substitute for classes, which "keep you on a schedule and keep you moving," she wrote. But in the end, the heart of learning for Lomb was reading books, which she described as "linguistic microclimates."

To lure yourself into the kind of reading that will thrill you, I recommend you get physical books, as well as magazines and newspapers, and not rely just on electronic versions. The electronic versions have many advantages, of course, but the very physicality of paper books and periodicals means that they share our physical world with us in ways that electronic materials can't. Take advantage of this. If you don't have time to open them yet, let them whisper to you. Let them wait for you in what I call your "library of candidates." Toss a glance their way now and then. They are abiding patiently, to delight you when the student is ready.

Reliving the ancient gift of literacy

Reading in our new, adopted language will strike us as a novel experience, yet the concept of reading in a second language is as old as reading itself. The first people to become literate were forced to read that way. The sons of wealthy Romans, for example, learned to read in ancient Greek; centuries later, the sons of wealthy Europeans learned to read in Latin. Spoken languages, the so-called vernaculars, were generally deemed unworthy of being written down. In this respect, second-generation American immigrants who learn to speak but not read their heritage languages, while learning to read and write in English, are reliving the experiences of wealthy children of thousands of years ago. One key difference is that literacy, nearly universal today, was rare for most of human history.

What we take as normal today—learning to read in the language we speak—is a relatively new phenomenon that became widespread only with the rise of large nation-states (such as Europe in the nineteenth century and China in the twentieth) and the standardization of national languages. For the most part, it didn't gain traction until the mid-nineteenth century. For most of the last two thousand years, literacy in any language was for only the tiny elite. As William Harris wrote in the final line of his book *Ancient Literacy,* "If fortune set the individual among the literate, that was a golden gift."

I've said there is no such thing as a silver bullet in adult language learning, but if one did exist, it would be reading books you love in your adopted language. Do not wish it to be always easy; wish it to be just hard enough. As Csikszentmihalyi wrote, "Although the flow experience appears to be effortless, it is far from being so. It often requires strenuous physical exertion, or highly disciplined mental activity. It does not happen without the application of skilled performance."

It's in that spirit that I'm enjoying my guilty reads in Spanish so very much. Maybe someday I'll return to *One Hundred Years of Solitude,* with enough skill to truly love it, too. And I hope that you lose yourself in whatever reading in your adopted language interests you. When you find yourself suddenly wondering where the last half hour went, you will have tasted that divine wine.

Chapter 8

THE NEW MAGIC OF MOVIES

W hen Steven Spielberg said, "Every time I go to a movie, it's magic, no matter what the movie's about," he was referring to experiencing movies in a theater. Yet there is even more magic today, following the digitization of movies and streaming technology into our homes. We now have the ability not only to choose from thousands of movies but also to select our preferred audio and subtitle languages. As with other digital touch points in our lives, the technology was created not with language learning in mind, but rather, with reaching an international audience. Businesses, doing what businesses do, have seized upon the new technologies to boost sales. Yet in doing so, they have given language learners blessings we have only begun to appreciate.

Now we can enjoy watching movies at home with a language immersion option that allows us to easily choose how deeply to venture in—from standing on the first step into the pool to diving under water.

So let's step down into movie immersion. I'll use the point of view of an English speaker learning Spanish, but you can substitute any other languages in which films are produced and translated.

Step One

Step One is when you watch the movie in English but select subtitles in Spanish. At this stage you can enjoy your movie with no work at all, but sneak in a little (or a lot) of pleasurable learning. In the magnificent musical *Mambo Kings*, a young Antonio Banderas, with a pained expression on his face, is pleading, "Enough! Enough!" while the Spanish subtitles read,

"¡Basta! ¡Basta!" Movies you love with subtitles in your adopted language can provide the jet fuel that Krashen calls "compelling, comprehensible input."

Step One is also good when you're watching with friends or family who have not adopted your language but will put up with your subtitles. (If your couchmates complain about your subtitles, ask them to give it a minute; once the story takes hold, subtitles seem to vanish.)

Step Two

Step Two is the reverse of Step One: listen in Spanish, but with English subtitles. Now you're hearing the music of the language—the tones, the rhythm, and the beauty of it, spoken by either the actors themselves or voiceover artists. You're easily reading the English subtitles, so you can learn Spanish from the context. In the darkly beautiful sci-fi thriller *In Time,* we hear Justin Timberlake tell an annoying kid, *"¡Lárgate!"* and see the English subtitle: "Get lost!"

The strength of Step Two is that you're hearing the language you want to learn. The weakness is that it's easy to rely on your reading and not engage in that productive struggle of having to make sense of what you're hearing. Yet I still remember the exact scenes of movies where I've learned useful phrases in Step Two. In *The Wizard of Oz,* I remember the Wizard saying to Dorothy, after they had been interrupted, *"¿Donde estábamos?"* ("Where were we?") I have since used this expression with confidence in my own conversations.

Step Three

Wading in deeper, you arrive at Step Three. Now you're hearing the movie in Spanish and also seeing subtitles in Spanish. Since most of us understand our adopted language better when we read it than when we hear it, we're likely to lean on the subtitles—but we're getting constant reinforcement of what the words sound like, plus how they are written. Yet there's a surprise awaiting you in Step Three: the words you hear and the words you see may be different—sometimes markedly so.

Perhaps it's because the actors or director ad lib from the script, or maybe the subtitles are cut down to fit the screen. Whatever the reasons, the discrepancy can be disconcerting—but also helpful, as you learn different ways of conveying the same thing. For example, you might hear *"¡Claro!"* but read *"¡Por supuesto!"* and thus learn that they both mean "Of course!"

Step Four

You turn off the subtitles and just watch the movie in Spanish (or whatever language you're learning). You've taken the plunge. Gone are your water wings. Now you have no choice but to try to figure out what people are saying with your ears.

Body language, facial expressions, and all the action help immensely, as they do in real life. But in the movies, you can hit pause and rewind. If I'm alone, I do hit pause and pick up my phone to repeat what I just heard to see if I've gotten it right, and get the immediate feedback from Google Translate.

The disadvantage of Step Four is that you may miss some of the nuance of the film. The advantage is that you're simulating real life but in a safe, no-stress imaginary world. As your hearing and understanding improve, so will your confidence to speak in the real world.

Movies plus other grand productions

While I've been talking about movies, today we have beautifully produced TV series as well, which increasingly offer a multitude of language options. Lori and I got hooked on *Gran Hotel*, which is like *Downton Abbey*, but set in Spain around 1910. The series has gorgeous cinematography and sets, wonderfully flawed characters, and murders and illicit love affairs thrown into just about every episode. Since Lori gets by well in Spanish and tolerates my passion for my adopted language, we watched *Gran Hotel* in Step Three: Spanish audio and subtitles.

And I must put in a good word for animated films. Since Disney and others create these lavish productions to appeal to both children and grownups, the language can be sophisticated, funny, and grand—matching the beautiful artistry of picture and song.

I've reveled in *Beauty and the Beast*, *Ratatouille*, and the deliciously evil Gru in *Despicable Me*. The Oscar-winning song "Let It Go!" from *Frozen* is, in my opinion, even more beautiful as *"Libre soy"*—which literally means "I am free." Isn't that, after all, what happens when we let something go?

Doing laps between the shallow and deep ends

Although I've written about these four stages as an evolution, I don't mean that once you get to Step Four you'll never go for less. You may find yourself enjoying Step Four for an animation but return to Step One to enjoy a serious film that you're watching with a friend. Plus, our new technology allows us to test out movies for a few minutes to see how deeply we want to plunge in. I find some movies have very fast dialogue while others are luxuriously slow.

The movie industry devises all these translation options to increase the potential audience for a film, but in doing so, it also creates one of the most lovely opportunities for language learning. I have to admit that sometimes, after watching a film in Step Three or Four, I've missed some of the nuance. But the stronger feeling I'm left with is that I've lived more of that larger, bilingual life I thirst for. And while some movies might become predictable, formulaic, or even boring when you view them in your native language, experiencing the same movies in your adopted language can make them more enjoyable because of the learning you're doing.

Like that good feeling we get after a workout, watching a movie in your adopted language, at the depth that's best for you, is a great reward. Today's digitally delivered movies can become one of the delightful places where your adopted language lives in your life.

Chapter 9

The Power of Vulnerability

In June 2010, an unknown research professor stepped onto a darkened stage in Houston to give her TEDx talk. As she wrote later, she had no idea what she was getting into. But she managed to deliver her message of how, contrary to what we have been led to believe, being vulnerable and showing it is actually a secret power. Her video, "The Power of Vulnerability," went viral, becoming one of the most viewed TED videos of all time. What followed was a meteoric rise as a public speaker and bestselling author for Brené Brown. The copy of her book resting on my desk, *Daring Greatly,* has sold more than a million copies. Clearly, her message contains a powerful truth—that we each possess an enormous reservoir of power that usually goes untapped.

Brown's message is particularly relevant to our topic because fear of showing vulnerability is exactly what holds most adult language learners back. This fact came through with lightning clarity when we interviewed scores of America's language teachers in the America the Bilingual recording booth at the ACTFL annual teachers' conferences.

Go ahead, be imperfect

"Adults are so used to getting things right because they channel their efforts into areas that they're good at," said Effie Evans Hall, who has taught German in Loudoun County, Virginia, schools for more than twenty years. "With language, you have to be willing to screw up. You have to be willing to stumble and ponder and ask."

"I taught adults for many years and they were always *so* concerned about whether or not they sounded right," added Lesley Chapman, the department chair for world languages at Sycamore High School in Cincinnati. "They were always kind of reticent—'Oh, did I just make a mistake?' They're not getting to the next level because they're holding back."

When we asked teachers their top advice for adult learners, they often said the equivalent of "park perfection at the door."

"The most important thing is that people understand you," advised Aviva Kadosh, an instructor of Hebrew at the Lanier School in Los Angeles. "No one will ever ask you to conjugate a verb if you visit another country. As long as someone understands you, you're doing okay."

"You don't have to operate at a fluent level to just connect with someone in another language," counseled Amelia Richter, the Spanish teacher in West Virginia. "It doesn't take perfection."

"Don't be shy," instructed Kashika Singh, who teaches Hindi and Urdu at Indiana University Bloomington. Instead, she said, speak spontaneously. It will prevent you from filtering—something adults are so good at, and kids don't bother with. "You may make grammar errors, you may make vocabulary choices that are not right, but at least you're talking spontaneously."

When I got the chance to hear Brené Brown in person, I came to appreciate why she has become so deeply appreciated by so many. She conveys a genuinely compelling message that we seem to know in our hearts is true: we are our best selves when we lower our defenses and admit our limitations. "It is only with the heart that one can see rightly," as Antoine de Saint-Exupéry observed.

Embracing vulnerability rather than hiding it is the path to what Brown calls "wholehearted living." And she offers several guideposts for getting us there. The first is "cultivating authenticity: letting go of what people think." This, together with her second guidepost, "cultivating self-compassion: letting go of perfectionism," helps chart a path for us to embrace our adopted languages.

Let's witness someone following this path. Meet Joan Salwen.

Epiphany in Costa Rica

Joan had both professional and personal reasons to adopt Spanish. She confided in me during her language biography interview that being monolingual just didn't fit her self-perception. "I am a person who has traveled a great deal, and who reads a great deal, who is aware of political and social and economic struggles in far-flung places . . . and yet, I only speak one language. There's a disconnect there."

43

As for the professional reason, Joan has launched an effort to reduce greenhouse gases by introducing seaweed-based feed for cattle. Such feed has the potential for massively reducing digestive methane emissions—or, to put it more scientifically, cow burps. "I know it sounds funny," says Joan, laughing, "but globally, burps from cattle and other ruminant animals are equivalent in global warming impact to 590 million cars, which is twice as many cars as we have on the road in the United States. So globally it's a very large issue."

I asked how learning Spanish was important to her cause.

"In California, which is the nation's largest dairy state, many of the farm workers who work closely with both dairy animals and beef cattle speak Spanish as their primary language," she told me. These people, Joan explained, have lots of expertise concerning the health needs of cattle—how they like to eat and drink, their daily habits. This knowledge, she says, "is absolutely vital to understanding whether or not this innovation can be meaningful to the world. I want to be able to communicate with those experts, or at a minimum to be able to demonstrate to them that I can introduce myself and ask questions in their language as we're getting to know one another."

The problem was, Joan wasn't making much progress with her Spanish. When I asked her how it was going, she confided it had been discouraging. After working every single day for a month with various software programs, she tried to have some conversations.

"I hired my son, who is very proficient in Spanish, to have conversations with me, and they were *awful*. He would ask a question, and I just was unable to even respond. It was really embarrassing."

She had taken some Spanish in school years ago. "I had anticipated that what I had learned when I was younger might just come right back up to the surface, and it did not."

Then Joan and her husband took a vacation to Costa Rica.

They went on a tour that a native speaker of Italian was leading, in English. "It was obvious she was proficient in both Italian and Spanish," Joan said, "but not so much in English. Every sentence she uttered had subject-verb agreement problems and other grammatical problems, but we of course understood every single thing. I think she said something like 'we come aboard,' instead of 'welcome aboard.'"

Their guide completely won Joan over.

"She demonstrated such an interest in having a relationship with us, and communicating with us, that she was unbothered by the fact that her English was poor. I was enthralled by her fearlessness and by her commitment to communicate with whatever level of proficiency of the language she had."

Joan told me that witnessing her tour guide was an epiphany. When she and her husband returned home, Joan signed up for a continuing-education Spanish class and just opened up. "It was terrific!"

How to talk to strangers

Perhaps you've had a similar experience to America the Bilingual team member Caroline Doughty's while traveling to Italy a number of years ago. Before she left, she listened to some tapes of Italian that tourists should know. "There was a random phrase that stood out— *'Dov'è il fruttivendolo?'* It means, 'Where is the greengrocer?'" Caroline and her sister were charmed by the way it sounded and would say it to each other. "I just loved the song of it," Caroline explained, "how it rolled off my tongue." (Caroline is an audiobook narrator, and so is particularly attuned to the music of language.)

One day, as she and her sister were walking around Como, her then two-year-old son spotted an apple and begged for one. "I suddenly remembered my much-practiced phrase and sang out *'Dov'è il fruttivendolo?'* to a woman passing by. Apparently, my accent for this single phrase was perfect, because she proceeded to provide detailed instructions in rapid-fire Italian. I had no idea what she was saying, of course. I just nodded politely and retreated, which puzzled the woman. I didn't want to admit it was the only phrase I knew!"

In my own journey with Spanish, I have worried about a similar encounter should I actually be able to get out a sentence in Spanish that would fool someone. So I've hit upon a strategy. The first thing I say when I meet someone I think speaks Spanish is:

"¿Habla español?" ("Do you speak Spanish?")

If they say, *"Claro"* or *"Sí, señor,"* I then say,

"Estoy aprendiendo español. ¿Puede ayudarme?" ("I'm learning Spanish. Can you help me?")

Almost always, they give a big smile and say, "Of course." Then I not only get to practice, but we have a much more friendly and engaging exchange than we might have had otherwise. With my introduction, I've immediately lowered expectations. So anything I manage to say well will often get a compliment, which gives me plenty of positive reinforcement and raises my self-confidence.

As nice as these encounters are, however, I've found that learning to be vulnerable isn't a one-and-done kind of thing. For me, anyway, it's always a bit of a leap into a cold lake. Normally I like to engage my Lyft or Uber drivers, especially if I think they might speak Spanish, but sometimes I'm just tired after a long day and sit in the back like a lump. On these occasions, I get out of the car at the end of our trip and feel like I've chickened out.

Other times, though, when I do plunge ahead and have a great conversation, I leave the car feeling exhilarated. It's kind of like those times you don't jump in the lake versus the times you do and feel so damn good afterwards, toweling off on the dock.

I've also found that this "wholehearted living," as Brené Brown calls it, is something I practice the way that others might, for example, practice meditation. Each time I have one of those great conversations, I'm building my capacity to try for more. Sometimes I miss the ball and strike out. Other times I get on first base, and once in a while, I hit a home run with someone who would, in my monolingual life, have remained a complete stranger. Instead, we've connected as two human beings. As Brown writes, vulnerability is "the cradle of the emotions and experiences that we crave."

But what about those times when fear of embarrassment becomes actual embarrassment? It's happened to me more than once.

I was getting my hair cut by a Spanish-speaking hair stylist. While talking about my sons and trying to say, in Spanish, "my older son," I instead said, "*Mi hijo mejor*," which means "my better son." The stylist stopped her scissors mid-clip and looked at me. "Oh," I stumbled, correcting myself, "*Mi hijo mayor.*" I find the two words, *mejor* and *mayor,* confusing, and it wasn't the first time I mixed them up. But this time, seeing the expression on her face—well, it stuck with me. I haven't mixed them up since.

Tim Page, a dean at Middlebury Language Schools, told me his own embarrassing story. "I had an experience in Russia where I was hoping to give a woman who had cooked dinner for myself and our group a compliment, calling it very tasty food. Instead I made the mistake of calling it very boring food." And not once, but several times during the meal.

That night, to his mortification, he learned the difference between "tasty" and "boring" in Russian. Embarrassing mistakes can be a bracing, but memorable, cold dip in the lake for language learning.

When sounding stupid is a smart move

Luis von Ahn came to the US from Guatemala to go to college, graduating in 2000 with a degree in math. He then went to graduate school and earned a doctorate in computer science. He quickly became a professor at Carnegie Mellon, where, among other things, he started a company that he sold to

Google. A year after earning his doctorate, he was awarded a MacArthur "genius" grant. That's when Luis decided to help the world learn languages.

He knew virtually nothing about language teaching, but he did know how addictive computer games could be. He also knew a thing or two about how to analyze big data. Luis wondered how he and his team might make language learning as fun as a computer game, and, by analyzing how thousands of players succeeded or failed at learning, develop more efficient learning methods.

Luis soon got his chance to analyze some big data. The thousands of users of his language game quickly became hundreds of thousands and then millions, me among them.

His startup, Duolingo, amassed a worldwide user base exceeding 300 million. Investors, including Google, have put in more than one hundred million dollars into the company, which has exceeded a valuation of one billion dollars.

When I reached Luis on the phone for an interview, he explained that his goal for Duolingo was to help people get over being shy. "There are two types of people: those who don't care about sounding stupid and those who do," he told me. Unfortunately, he said, the people who do care about sounding stupid represent about 80 percent of us. The remaining 20 percent are the lucky ones.

"Those 20 percent are much better at learning, not because they are smarter, but because of the simple fact that they don't care about sounding stupid," he said. "They get so much more practice than the shy ones.

"You can see it in their body language," Luis continued. "Shy ones get small and lower their voice a lot. You can see the fear. The others are just the opposite."

Just start talking

Luis told me that people's limited time and money are legitimate barriers to language learning, but it's this inherent shyness that is the real problem. Borrowing a term from physics, Luis described it as a lack of "activation energy." It just takes too much activation energy for most people to get over their shyness and start conversing.

So he and his team aim with Duolingo to create a place where you can sound stupid because, he says, "nobody cares about sounding stupid with an app."

I asked Luis how far he thinks Duolingo can go. "We can't yet go from zero to my own level of English fluency," he replied in his perfect English.

"No software method can do that. Many claim to, but it's just a lie. Zero to intermediate level is what we can do."

That's when, says Luis, people can begin to get around and ask simple questions. He told me he would love to be able to get people to fluency, but it's just not possible yet. The goal is to get people confident enough so that they "start to have conversations—and *then* get to fluency."

Or as Brené Brown says, "our willingness to own and engage with our vulnerability determines the depth of our courage and the clarity of our purpose."

When your adopted language opens your heart

So far we've seen how opening ourselves to being vulnerable is a key to making real progress with our adopted language. Brown says that vulnerability is more than just a method for improving our skills. "Vulnerability is the core, the heart, the center, of meaningful human experiences," she writes. "If we want greater clarity in our purpose or deeper and more meaningful spiritual lives, vulnerability is the path."

If she's right, then your journey with your adopted language, with the practice of vulnerability, may also be your journey to a larger life in general. Larger not only because of the new world your language will open for you, but larger also because of the new peace you will achieve. Your new life in Italian, or Arabic, or Japanese can become your wholehearted life.

Chapter 10

WHAT'S LOVE GOT TO DO WITH IT?

"The best way to learn a language is in bed," a stranger at a cocktail party said to me, with a drink in his hand and a wink. It wasn't a proposition; he said it when I was explaining that I interview people about their language learning. He was conveying a piece of old wisdom, which has been passed down for who can guess how many generations. In some versions, the best way is "on a pillow." But my favorite is from David Wolf, one of our guests on an *America the Bilingual* podcast: "You're only one romance away from fluency."

Even if we haven't personally experienced this, it's something easy to understand. To have a lover who can whisper to you, gently correcting your funny mistakes, whom you spend long days with, from morning coffee to late-night drinks, your adopted language blooms in the warmth of such love. What language learner wouldn't want that?

If you find such a lover on your bilingual journey, my blessings on you both. But for those of us who have already made other plans, I've got some good news: there's lots of other love waiting for you along your journey.

As we learned in the previous chapter, love begins with accepting yourself. It comes from recognizing that the best path for learning your adopted language is to make mistakes, to be open to embarrassing yourself so that you can laugh it off and learn, learn, learn.

But self-love is just the beginning.

Love between teachers and students

The best teachers and coaches operate out of love for their students, and when we receive their help and show that we gain from it, we give these teachers a gift of love in return. Teachers want to see us opening our minds, struggling and then achieving, and showing joy at having done so. This is the reason many went into their profession in the first place; it's why some teachers describe their work as a calling.

One such teacher was John Rassias, the late revered founder of the eponymous language immersion center at Dartmouth College. His charismatic way of teaching has left an indelible mark on thousands of students. Rassias recognized that language learning, done the right way, is ready-made for deep, emotional connections between people—between teacher and student, and among the students themselves as they, for example, perform a play together in their studied language. A testament to that shared love are the many students of John Rassias who are now language teachers themselves. Among them are his daughter, Helene, and Tamara Smith.

"He reached so many of us over the years," Tamara told me. "And not just those of us who've become language teachers; it's people who are bringing that same passion and kindness toward others, whatever career they have chosen."

Another former student and now language instructor, Fernando Ausin, told me, "John always ripped his shirt open at the end of every ALPs session." (ALP stands for Advanced Language Programs.) "He said, 'This was, by far, the best session that had ever existed in all humankind!'" Fernando told me it's John Rassias's passion that now fuels his own life. He added, "I always wondered how many shirts he had bought."

Rassias programs are still known for the plays the students put on, as the plays force students to act beyond their normal selves, to take on a new persona, declaiming in their studied language in front of their peers. "He lives on through thousands of people," Tamara said. "It still feels as if he's with us. He was larger than life. Like a tidal wave of love."

Luc Tardif is the director of the French summer immersion program at Université Saint-Anne in Canada, the only French-language university in Nova Scotia. He told us about the loving atmosphere that is formed during students' summer immersion experiences. "It's like a bubble of joy," he said. Even the small Acadian village of Church Point, where Saint-Anne is located, is part of this bubble. The locals, Luc said, "know that the students are doing immersion here, and they slow down [when speaking French] and point at stuff. They are very patient with our students, and caring."

Love from your family

Let's say you adopt a language and your spouse or partner does not. If you're lucky, your loved one will still support you on your journey. One adopter of Spanish I interviewed does her own hiking trips in Spain, while her husband and sons pursue their fishing. A friend who has adopted French took advantage of some time between jobs to fulfill a bucket list item of walking one of France's long-distance hiking paths while her partner stayed in the States, working.

In my own case of adopting Spanish, I'm fortunate that my wife had her flowering of fluency while in college and still retains enough skill and interest to get hooked on Spanish TV series with me. Lori also doesn't mind my texting her in Spanish. Nor do my sons, since they've had enough Spanish to understand what their dad is trying to say. They humor me.

Loving your adopted language

Your adopted language itself is a treasure of beauty and wonder. I especially love the ways Spanish has for saying things that are entirely different from English—for example, "to give birth" is *dar a luz* in Spanish: literally, "to give to light." And instead of saying "my better half," which we English speakers might do introducing our spouses, in Spanish, it's *mi media naranja*, which means "my half an orange."

And then there is the whole new world awaiting you with the sayings and proverbs. In a Western we might hear an outlaw, pointing a gun at someone's head, demand in English: "Your money or your life." In Spanish, the bandido would say just three words: "*¿Plata o plomo?*," literally, "Silver or lead?"

Your adopted language as it is sung by a street vendor and whispered by a poet, as it is laughed by a child and intoned by a priest—in all these, you can develop a love for that language. The pop singers and filmmakers, the voiceover artists, the interpreters in movies who match their translation to the lips of an actor speaking a different language—all are there for you to marvel at as you fall deeper in language love.

Love between friends

The same David Wolf who pronounced that "you're just one romance away from fluency" had such a romance . . . but still didn't achieve the proficiency in French that he needed to understand the mumbling professor in his business-school class. While David's French was excellent by social standards, it wasn't up to grade in taking graduate-level business courses.

"They put me on notice," said David. He had to improve, and fast, or risk getting kicked out. David had passed up getting his master's at Oxford for getting an MBA from a French university. He had never failed at anything. He was at a low point in his life, which was when David's French friend, Gilles Perrot, decided to step in.

"He said, 'I want you to go and pack your bags. I'm going to take you to my home town of Toulouse and we're going to have a great time, and then I'm going to take you to Bordeaux. I know several fantastic chateau owners and we're going to eat and drink like you've never done . . . and we'll put a plan together to save your silly American butt.'"

David was stunned.

"'Gilles, we can't just up and go, we have class,' I said. He just looks at me and says, 'What's the difference? You don't understand anything.'"

Gilles made good on exactly what he said they would do, and David did develop a plan to get some extra help and extra time, and he made it through. He could not have done it, he says, without his friend who was there for him.

And while he didn't say it to me, I'm willing to bet that David also gave his friend Gilles a gift, one of deep appreciation and gratitude. He did tell me that they have remained close friends.

Love for English-language learners

As American bilinguals, aspiring and otherwise, we have the greatest opportunities to do what Gilles did for David. Greatest because the world has more than a billion people who are trying to learn English right at this moment, and what they need are native English speakers to talk with. We'll get more into the opportunities and obligations of American bilinguals in Part Four; for now, I just want to say that as you adopt a language, you have a fabulous opportunity to build friendships—as a receiver of the gift of bilingualism and as the giver. And doing this face-to-face, as David and Gilles did, is the best of all.

What does love have to do with learning another language? Just about everything.

✻　✻　✻

Chapter 11

THE GRANDE DAME OF
LANGUAGE CAMPS

O n May 7, 1915, when the crew of the German submarine *U-20* sighted the RMS *Lusitania* in its periscope and released the torpedo that would sink her in eighteen minutes, a good many people had anticipated that such an act could bring the United States into the war in Europe. But no one, it's safe to say, anticipated that the killing of 1,198 people that afternoon would also forever change the way Americans would learn languages.

Transoceanic steamship travel was already commonplace by the time World War I broke out in 1914. Language teachers were among the thousands of Americans who would book passage to Europe in the summer. The teachers would take courses in Spain, France, Italy, or Germany, while also being immersed in those languages. One of the people recommending such immersive study was a professor of German at Vassar College named Lilian Stroebe.

Stroebe was born in Germany in 1875 and earned her PhD from Heidelberg in 1904, one of the first the university awarded to a woman. She came to the United States the following year and at age thirty, joined the Vassar faculty. Perhaps it was her youth, or the pull of entrepreneurism that tugs at so many immigrants, or wanting to do something for her adopted country. Whatever it was, Stroebe asked what would become a beautiful question: How could we simulate a summer trip to Europe right here in America?

Trading the Alps for the Green Mountains

Answering her question became her mission. With the outbreak of the war, summers in Europe were a thing of the past, and so, she wrote, "it therefore becomes the duty of colleges and universities to offer in this country a substitute for what the students formerly sought in Europe, a well-conducted course of study, life in a distinctly foreign atmosphere, and daily intercourse with educated foreigners."

She decided three things were necessary to substitute for what American language teachers could no longer experience in Europe:

1. Complete isolation from English
2. A pledge that participants would sign, promising to speak only the language being studied
3. A beautiful setting comparable to the majestic mountains and valleys of Europe

Stroebe ruled out her own Vassar College, located in Poughkeepsie, New York, as it was too close to New York City, with its many distractions, and English blaring from every street corner. A colleague taking a train back from Montreal to New York made a stop in a tranquil college town in rural Vermont and told Stroebe she must see it. When she arrived in Middlebury, Vermont, with its rolling hills and distant Green Mountains, she was enchanted. And the leaders of the college there were open to her vision.

On the morning of June 29, 1915, Lilian Stroebe opened the Middlebury College German Summer School. It was, she wrote, "the first advanced, specialized and isolated summer school of a modern language in any college in the country."

While we today think of summer camps as something for children and teenagers, the original language summer camps were designed for adults. And today, adults continue to go to summer language camps in America—not just young language teachers, but also mid-career adults in many professions, as well as older Americans eager for their adopted languages to take flight within them. While interviewing American bilinguals, I encountered many people who had been to Middlebury for a summer and they all spoke of the "Middlebury magic." So many, in fact, that I decided to go experience this magic for myself.

The Language Pledge

It was a beautiful day in early July when I sat down in the book-lined corner office of the dean of Middlebury Language Schools, Stephen Snyder. My first question was, "What *is* this Middlebury magic?"

He smiled. "I would say two things. One, it's certainly the Language Pledge and the fact that we enforce it more strictly than anyone else."

"And the second?"

"The second thing is the students—*they* are the magic because they come with a seriousness of purpose that I don't think any other institution gets out of their language students."

I thought Middlebury would be for only advanced students, but Stephen told me they take all levels, including complete beginners. They only insist that the students be serious.

"They come because they know what we've been doing for a hundred and four years. In some senses, it's a self-fulfilling prophecy." That is, students want to obey the pledge. "We rarely have to discipline anyone and they actually make the effort that it takes to get the results," Stephen said.

The day I visited, students were arriving for their six- or eight-week immersion experiences (the length varying depending on the language). There was excitement in the air. Associate Dean Elizabeth Karnes Keefe told me, "Right across the street from this building, the students are streaming in to take the pledge in the next twenty-four to forty-eight hours and plunge into this experience. It's very exciting for us to see them."

I asked her what the Language Pledge was, exactly, and she handed me a copy of the sheet of paper each student must sign:

In signing this Language Pledge®, I agree to use _____ as my only language of communication while attending the Middlebury Language Schools. I understand that failure to comply with this Pledge may result in my expulsion.

I asked her what Middlebury looks for in its students. "Someone who can open their heart to this experience and plunge in . . . to really immerse yourself in the broad experience of language and culture, dancing, singing, eating, talking, playing soccer."

If students use their phones, they must be set to their adopted language, and they can write and speak only in that language. "We have a story of students going down to the local hospital and refusing to speak to the physicians in English because they've taken the pledge—they take it very seriously," Elizabeth said.

From pain comes gain

"We don't pretend it's easy at all," said Stephen. "As a matter of fact, we're often called a boot camp. The Russian school is often referred to as the gulag."

The administration is sympathetic to what the students must endure. "In convocation on Thursday night, we will talk about the suffering that the students will do," Stephen told me. "We know that they experience immersion stress. The memory load for a program like this that compresses essentially an entire year of language learning into seven or eight weeks is almost unbearable for some. It's not easy in any way. But again, we have the motivated students."

For those who can stick with it, the payoff is sweet.

"For maybe a week or two, students want to jump off the roof," said Elizabeth. "But a couple of weeks later, they're in this sort of state of euphoria where they are speaking the language and writing the language. It's pretty exciting to see the transformation."

Molly Baker, Middlebury Language Schools Director of Enrollment, also sees the emotional roller coaster students face. "By the fifth or sixth week, students will be glaring at me, saying, 'What am I doing here? This is really hard, I don't know if I'm going to make it even one more week.'"

And then, Molly said, "You get to that seventh or eighth week and the whole campus picks up. On graduation day, it's almost like you've come through Olympic training camp or Navy SEAL training. You have that for the rest of your life."

Stephen added, "Students will constantly say that they, at some point, had a breakthrough and realized that suddenly, the language they were studying had become incredibly natural to them and that they were able to communicate in a way that they hadn't thought possible even a few weeks before."

For some, he said, the experience can be life-changing. "Most students feel that it's truly transformative to have spent this amount of time in a community with this kind of single purpose. Not only have they learned a tremendous amount of grammar and syntax, but they have actually recreated themselves. They have a new self in the language that they're studying."

Dean of Operations Tim Page says the summer programs are especially effective as a slingshot to living abroad. "You get to a level where you can take your Italian and go to Rome and have a proficient conversation with a Roman. The feedback that we get, especially from students who are able to go directly abroad and put all of their hard work to use immediately, it's really wonderful."

One student who did just that is a winner of the National Book Award and a MacArthur "genius" grant, Ta-Nehisi Coates. The author came to Middlebury to study French in anticipation of going to Paris for a year, Elizabeth told me. He arrived with "zero French, basically," she said. "At the end of the summer he was gabbing away in French."

Another of those students was a young man named Gabriel Wyner. "At the time, I was an engineer with an oversized singing habit," he wrote in his book. He had signed up for the German immersion program for opera singers. Having begun the course with no German at all, at the end of five weeks, "I sang my heart out in a German acting class."

The experience helped Wyner decide he was going to leap from engineering to opera full time. But a funny thing happened on the way to the stage. He came back to Middlebury to do German again and this time reached fluency. He then moved to Austria. In Europe he studied Italian, and two years later, returned to Middlebury, this time to be immersed in French. As he learned more languages, he discovered his own ways to make learning easier and changed career aspirations once more, leaving opera to become a language teacher himself, writing a bestselling book, *Fluent Forever,* and starting a company to develop his own software for learning a language.

Better than being there

Among Wyner's recommendations are immersion courses like Middlebury, which he says can be even more effective than spending the same time overseas in the country. "It can be embarrassing or scary when you're the only non-native speaker in the room. This happens a lot when you're studying abroad. In an immersion program, everyone is making mistakes, so it's not that big a deal if you make some as well."

Stephen agrees. "Middlebury runs study-abroad programs at thirty-seven sites around the world. We know they're very effective, but we feel that the kind of immersion and the kind of enforced language policy that we give the students here during the summer creates even better results."

Middlebury tests students before and after the summer program, and the results bear this out. Stephen pointed out that on the Vermont campus, it can be easier to focus on the language learning itself than in, say, Vienna. "Students come here with the single purpose, not of being tourists, not of developing relationships, not of studying Molière, but simply to improve their language."

Still teaching the teachers

Middlebury teaches more than a thousand students in eleven languages, and added a twelfth as a pilot program in 2020: Abenaki, an Eastern Algonquian Native language. The program also continues to teach the language teachers, as in Lilian Stroebe's day. Most come to earn their master's degrees, which they can do in either four summers, or one summer followed by a year studying overseas.

"Every summer we have five hundred or so graduate students," said Stephen. They come "not just to perfect their language skills, but to study the culture. Originally it was literature they studied, but now they learn about a whole range of contemporary culture in the countries where their language is spoken."

I was able to interview a couple of those grad students, including Julie Spiegelman. When she and I sat down, I noticed she was wearing one of the buttons I had seen all the students wearing. Hers was blue with two white letters: FR.

"That indicates that I am in the school of French and therefore, during my time here I will only be speaking in French." (I thanked her for making an exception with me for our interview; Elizabeth had deposited us in an empty auditorium and guarded the door so that no one would hear our conversation in forbidden English.)

This was Julie's third summer at Middlebury. I asked her how the experience has been. "It's been great," she said, but I noted a twinge. "I was a little bit grumpy when I started because I just got married and was sort of like, 'I'm too grown up for this!' I didn't want to go away all summer."

"But you've come again . . . ," I offered.

"I just love the chance to speak French all the time and to connect with people from different Francophone countries. We're in constant proximity with each other, professors and students, and often the professors come with their families."

I next sat down with Kelly Dewey, a German teacher, who was beginning her third summer as well. She had worked in Germany at various jobs, speaking German in all of them.

Kelly told me she likes all the mixing of language students at Middlebury—from rank beginners to fluent speakers. She smiled again, remembering a particular encounter.

"Two years ago, my first summer at Middlebury, there was a dance that they have every year just for the German school. You're given a drink ticket so you can get one free alcoholic beverage."

One college-age student was going around, asking if anybody at the dance wanted to give him their drink ticket. There was just one problem, Kelly told me.

"He'd had approximately six days of German, and his German was *terrible*. But *not once* did he break into English. He was completely committed, so with a little bit of sign language and maybe some creative dancing, it worked."

She said the episode made a huge impression on her and helped her realize that "the 24/7 Language Pledge environment is something that makes Middlebury really special."

I asked Kelly if the alcohol at the dance was part of the program to help people speak their adopted language. "It certainly helps," she said. "There's the affective filter. That's the thing that goes up that prevents people from wanting to try out their language. A drink makes that affective filter go right back down."

It's a gift

Because Middlebury's program has been around for more than a century, there are plenty of stories.

Molly told me, "We have a student in the French school whose grandparents met in the French school in 1949." Besides writers, opera singers, American military, and NGO workers, she said, Middlebury attracts all sorts of mid-career professionals who realize that bilingualism is critical for their careers. She told me about one of them.

"We have a student this year who is an immigration lawyer who already had a pretty high level of Spanish when he arrived. But he's come here to really master the language." Right after he finishes his summer at Middlebury, she said, "he's moving to Texas, and he wants to be able to really help those individuals right on the border."

I asked Molly why she does what she does.

"Because of those stories," she said. "We get absolutely amazing students, and . . . ," she paused for a moment, "I mean, it's going to sound cheesy, but they are going to save our world."

Chapter 12

DIY LANGUAGE IMMERSION FOR GROWNUPS

While Middlebury is the grande dame of domestic language immersion experiences, there are others that cater to adults in the US, including the Rassias Center at Dartmouth College in New Hampshire. While shorter than Middlebury's, the program delivers excellent results for those who can spare only a week or ten days of immersion.

Additionally, some Americans are creating their own immersion programs by traveling to countries where their adopted languages are native.

Bienvenidos a San Miguel

"Several people I knew had recommended San Miguel de Allende and I thought, why not?" That's what Jennifer Lawson told me in an interview. She had recently retired from a successful career at the Corporation for Public Broadcasting in Washington, DC.

"One of my real desires upon retirement was to put more effort into becoming really fluent in Spanish. It's been an ambition of mine for several years, and I was always too busy being a broadcasting executive, a parent, a wife, and so many other things, that I could not devote my time."

So Jennifer headed to Mexico, to San Miguel, as it's called for short, and signed up at a school named Habla Hispana.

"I was there for five weeks and it was absolutely wonderful. The school was just what I had wanted—truly an intensive immersion." Jennifer studied five days a week from 8:30 a.m. to 6:00 p.m. "And I stayed with a Mexican family," she added.

During those day-long classes, the mornings were devoted to grammar and vocabulary, while the afternoons were filled with lectures on art and cooking and history—all in Spanish.

Jennifer's immersion experience paid off when she and her husband took a side trip to Mexico City. One day, Jennifer was standing on the sidewalk with a crowd of other onlookers, waiting for a Christmas parade to begin, while her husband ducked into a department store. An elderly gentleman sitting near her offered Jennifer his seat.

"He was sitting down and offered me the space that he was sitting on." She declined. "But then he offered it again, so I accepted and sat next to his wife and the little girl who was with them and said 'gracias.'"

That seemed to open a door.

"That led him to ask where I was from, and I said Washington, DC. And that started the conversation." In Spanish.

"We were off and running," Jennifer recounted, "and it was quite fascinating because he said, 'You know, there are many problems in our world,' and he put his hand against mine." Jennifer is African American and the man was Mexican Native American. "And he says, 'In Mexico, too, there's racism.' Then it went from this heavy-duty conversation to his little four-year-old granddaughter. She's trying to put together this puzzle and I began playing with her and asking her, 'Now, what piece goes here?' I'd point to an area and say, '¿Amarilla o rosada?' and she would gleefully put the piece in."

Jennifer told me this encounter would not have been possible without her new skills in Spanish. I asked her how it made her feel.

"Oh, it felt wonderful! It makes me feel that I am more a citizen of the world than simply a citizen of the United States. I mean, I *love* being a citizen of the United States and am very proud of that, but it gives me access to this bigger world, too, and I really enjoy that so much."

'Get wet in the culture'

Having heard so much about San Miguel de Allende, its large expat community, and its language schools, Lori and I booked an Airbnb for ten days and went to check it out.

We found San Miguel true to its travel book descriptions of a charming, friendly, colonial town in the mountains with perennial spring-like temperatures. Its mix of good restaurants, art studios, and adult education in all kinds of subjects makes it a favorite destination for Mexican visitors as well as visitors from North America and Europe.

I had arranged to interview Martha Rodríguez Barbosa, the head of Habla Hispana. She has the kind of tranquil demeanor that made me feel *tranquilo* as well. She invited Lori and me to sit in for a day and see what her school was like.

The school is small and casual, with a large center courtyard surrounded by classrooms, offices, a kitchen and dining area, and a few rooms that students can rent. Lori and I were placed in an intermediate class, which had about twelve students in it, ranging in age from high-schoolers to senior citizens. The door and the windows were open, allowing the cool air to circulate freely.

For the first period, our teacher introduced a concept on the blackboard, such as reflexive verbs or subjunctive case, and some of the students asked her a few questions in Spanish. Then the teacher set us working in pairs from worksheets while she went from table to table listening, only occasionally saying something herself.

For the next period, we went outside and sat down in the courtyard at tables under umbrellas. Each table had a conversation leader who would introduce a topic—for example, the drinking age laws in Mexico and the United States. Students would then chime in with their thoughts. The opinion of the high school student at our table was different from the older Americans', which made it even more interesting. The leader would occasionally repeat what someone had said, altering it into better Spanish. If she noticed someone not speaking, she would pull that person in with a question. There was lots of laughter, and mistakes were frequent, as we stepped beyond the simple phrases we knew into more complex sentences. That, of course, was the point of the exercise.

At lunch later that week, Martha told Lori and me that she had been running the school for more than twenty years. "About 40 percent of our students come here because they want to improve their Spanish for their profession in the US," she explained. Social workers, medical professionals, and Spanish teachers all come here. "The Air Force Academy in Colorado has sent us their teachers," Martha added.

Another 40 percent of the students are planning to attend university in Mexico or another Spanish-speaking country, as the classes are a more affordable alternative to Spanish classes in Europe. The rates for classes and private instruction were a fraction of the costs I was familiar with back home. And these rates include cooking classes, music classes, and city walking tours, all conducted in Spanish.

"Some of our students spend three or six months, and the transformation is pretty amazing," Martha told us. "When they start, they don't speak anything, and then in three months they can argue with you and have wide-ranging discussions. It opens a new door in their lives when they get wet in the culture."

While she says they do work on reading and writing, the emphasis is on conversational Spanish. "Most of our students live with families," she added, "so it's a total immersion experience."

'Spanish from the Heart'

Another well-known institution in San Miguel is the Warren Hardy School. I arranged to interview Warren himself, and he, too, invited Lori and me to sit in on a class.

The school consists of a low stage where Warren and other instructors lead the class. Students sit around at tables and on comfortable chairs, in small working groups. The atmosphere is lighthearted yet hardworking. Our Mexican instructor had us drill one another on some of the one hundred most common Spanish verbs, conveniently printed with their most useful conjugations on color-coded 3x5 cards.

Warren, a native English speaker from the US, told us he started a language school back in the US to help professional people learn Spanish. He later sold it and came with his wife on a vacation to San Miguel. They liked it so much, they decided to stay and open a school. That was almost thirty years ago. I asked him why his students come to his school.

"A lot of lifelong learners stay home and never leave their homes. But this is an adventurous group of people who want to go abroad and experience other cultures and continue to grow," he said. "So there's a spirit of adventure."

Judging from the students in the class we attended, they seemed to be mainly older Americans and Canadians, although we met one mother and daughter who decided to spend their vacation together learning Spanish.

Warren told us he speaks regularly at a conference put on by *International Living,* a magazine dedicated to helping Americans retire overseas. "The title of the lecture that I give is called 'Spanish from the Heart,' and the basic premise is that if you just open up your heart and smile and use the courtesies, then immediately people will connect with you."

After living in Mexico for so many years, Warren said, "I was becoming a Mexican patriot. I spoke at the Rotary Club and said it feels like Mexico has entered through my pores. It didn't happen overnight, but inside there's a part of me that's absolutely Mexican." He applied for Mexican citizenship and now has dual citizenship.

Warren sees a new seriousness of purpose among the Americans he teaches, most of whom are retired professionals. "I think we are wanting to be part of a bigger world. People want to learn to speak Spanish, not just memorize nouns."

Immerse in the school, then dip into the community

During our stay in San Miguel, I heard about a language exchange at the public library. People learning Spanish or English could sit down and take turns speaking with one another.

I found myself seated next to a fifteen-year-old Mexican girl who was there to practice her English. She was studying computer graphics and planned on continuing her studies at a nearby university. Her English was much better than my Spanish, but she indulged me, gently correcting me here and there. After fifteen minutes, I had exhausted all the topics I felt I could discuss with her. Meanwhile, I noticed she was glancing at a young man seated across the table. I decided to broker a seat exchange. The girl perked up considerably when she took her seat next to the handsome young man, while I found myself sitting next to a fifty-something man named Cris Torres.

While Cris was there to improve his English, he surprised me by saying he wanted to just speak Spanish, while I spoke English to him. So we both worked on our listening skills, while speaking slowly and simply in our native languages.

Cris told me he lived in the neighboring town of Dolores Hidalgo and worked as a professor of religion and philosophy at a university in Guanajuato, one of the big cities near San Miguel. We hit it off, and he invited Lori and me to visit his home and his sister's nearby ceramics factory. He offered to give us an insider's tour of the quaint town of Dolores Hidalgo, known for its ceramics. Lori and I took him up on his offer.

Since we had no car, we hired a local bilingual guide to drive us for the day in his van. We spent the entire day speaking Spanish, and a glorious day it was. Cris's sister's factory was fascinating. A couple dozen workers sat at pottery benches painstakingly painting bowls, candlesticks, and, my favorite, tequila bottles for special editions of high-end tequila. We thought Cris might want us to buy a few things, but the opposite was true. We had to push him to let us pay for a couple of bowls he wanted to give us. Then he took us to his home, a beautiful one-story *casa* with a center courtyard filled with religious art, together with his chickens. Inside was a veritable museum of folk art.

In all, it was a divine day and made me wish we could stay longer in San Miguel. I think Cris and I would have become friends, since our passion for learning one another's language seemed equally matched.

I share this story to illustrate the kinds of experiences that are available to Americans who travel outside the US to study their adopted language. The immersion experiences can be centered around a school as the anchor but can and should extend into the community, as you make friends and explore where tourists don't normally go.

I've come to believe that whatever your adopted language, you can go to a city or town where that language is spoken and create your own language camp. It's a bit more adventurous than other options, but what is life for if not for adventure?

Let's Meetup

When I interviewed language teachers for their advice to adult learners, several recommended finding conversation partners. To advance her own Spanish, Julie Sellers, a Spanish professor at Benedictine College in Atchison, Kansas, partnered with a native speaker who wanted to practice her English. "If you're an adult learner, you have to create a community of learners going through the same experience you are," advised William Yepes-Amaya, a native Spanish speaker who teaches Spanish at Belmont Day School near Boston.

When I lived for a year in Palo Alto, California, near the Stanford campus, I went through the Meetup app to find a local group that I could practice Spanish with. Meetup is an online platform for bringing together people in the same geographic area over a shared interest.

For the price of a coffee, I joined a group that met Thursday evenings at Peet's Coffee. We ranged from six to ten people, all Anglos working on our Spanish. Fortunately, there was a Mexican American language tutor named Yazmin Pease who would show up, too. We all wanted to be close to Yazmin because of her friendly yet professional way of guiding our conversation toward actual Spanish. A number of us, including me, hired her for weekly private sessions.

When I returned to South Florida, I easily found a Meetup for practicing Spanish. Within half an hour from my home are Meetups in Italian, French, Hungarian, Korean, Mandarin, Hindi, Hebrew, Japanese, American Sign Language, and even Esperanto.

Not just the how but the why

After visiting Middlebury Language Schools, San Miguel de Allende, and local weekly Meetup groups in California and Florida, a common thread began to appear. They each provide a way to graduate from the apps, the audio programs, and the classrooms into real conversations with real people in the real world. These conversations provide not only the how of language learning but also the why. The relationships you can form may just turn into some of the most meaningful in your life.

When Jennifer Lawson returned home to Washington, DC, from San Miguel, she started going to Spanish-language films and plays, including a Spanish performance of Lin-Manuel Miranda's *In the Heights*. She is finding the places where her adopted language will live in her life.

Chapter 13

HOW TO LEARN A LANGUAGE BY NOT STUDYING IT

Let me tell you about when I played polo in England. Didn't know I played polo? I don't. But here's how it happened.

I had to attend a business meeting outside of London with a dozen colleagues. One of them lived there and was hosting us; he actually did play polo. Over email he wrote that, while we'd have a lot of work to do, he wanted to show us a good time, so he had arranged for us all to play polo.

I assumed he was kidding. He wasn't. Shortly after all of us arrived, we drove over to a polo field. They put us on horses, gave us polo mallets, maybe forty-five seconds of instruction, and let us loose.

We all looked at each other sitting stupidly on those horses. Then we saw the ball and went for it. We squeezed the horses with our legs, laying the bridle on first one side of the horse's neck and then the other, trying to turn. Almost instantly, we forgot we didn't know how to ride horses (ours were clearly very patient animals), and just tried to whack the hell out of the ball and get it down the field. Hey, we were playing polo!

Later, I made the connection to language learning: sometimes we can learn a lot by not studying.

The polyglot Kato Lomb also recommended going beyond just studying the language. "There is no progress without effort," she wrote. "But effort takes time. How should an adult, a working person, manage this? Answer: One should connect language learning with either work or leisure. And not at the expense of them but to supplement them."

Dreaming in Hebrew, cooking in Italian

"I was sixteen when I graduated high school," Susan Golden, a visiting scholar at the Stanford Center on Longevity, told me in her language biography interview, "and essentially took a gap year before people took gap years, and went to live on a kibbutz." There she had something of a language learning breakthrough.

Susan had studied some Hebrew as a child and learned how to read and write it, but not to speak it. As part of the kibbutz program, she spent six months in what's called an Ulpan, doing an intensive study of Hebrew. "But you're also living there and speaking it every single day," she noted.

And in fact, most of Susan's language learning happened outside of class time. "I had different jobs. I worked in the chicken area, then I drove a tractor. But my best job, and where I really learned to speak, was when I was assigned to the children's houses. The three-year-olds spoke at a rate and with a vocabulary that I could understand. It was a joyful experience to work with them." Susan gives the children credit for getting her to fluency, "to the point where I knew I was fluent when I could dream in another language."

Years later, when she was in her early thirties, Susan was about to switch careers and decided to take a two-month break. She headed to Florence, Italy, to learn Italian. Her experience in Israel convinced her that she wanted to learn the language by doing something. She signed up for a cooking school that, she said, "was taught in Italian for people from abroad so they could get some exposure to the Italian language."

"I wasn't there long enough to come out of it fluent," she told me. "But I certainly knew how to say the names of the foods that we were buying in the market and cooking that day."

Those two months paid an unexpected dividend.

Shortly after she returned from Italy, Susan married. She convinced her new husband to go back to Italy for their honeymoon. One day, as they walked around Siena, a building caught her eye. Since she could read some Italian, she recognized it as the University of Siena's medical school.

"I remembered that my uncle, my mother's brother, had been in medical school in Siena when World War II broke out," Susan told me. "Tragically, he had gone home to Poland in 1939 to visit his family and got caught and eventually killed in the Holocaust. I walked into the medical school wondering if maybe they had some of his records."

Susan told me that the sole evidence her mother had of her brother's existence was one photo of them as children. She spoke to Susan of him often, and how he was fluent in so many different languages.

The gray-haired gentleman who greeted Susan when she walked inside the school spoke no English. "My Italian was limited, but at least I wasn't embarrassed to try to speak." And fortunately, she told me, "the Italians are very forgiving."

After she wrote down her uncle's name—Ire Bleich—the time frame, and where he was from, the man disappeared for a while. When he returned, he presented Susan with her uncle's application and report card.

"It was an extraordinary feeling," Susan said. "My mom always told me how smart he was, but there on the papers in front of me were his grades he earned in that very building. It was an incredible gift."

Back in America, Susan presented her mother with what she had found. "She cried a lot. She came from an enormous family, and only she and one cousin survived." Susan had given an unexpected gift to her mother. "It was magical that you can hold onto something and bring it into your life in a positive way, to remember not just the tragedy, but the positive."

I asked Susan whether she could have given her mother this gift without her language skills. "I don't think the person at the medical school would have trusted me—that I was, you know, who I was."

To this day, Susan still cooks for her family the dishes she learned in Florence, following the recipes in Italian.

Doing what you love in your adopted language

"I took Spanish in high school, but then there's this huge gap," Brad Schmier told me in his language biography interview. "I did not continue it in college. It's a regret of mine." Now a molecular biologist and investor in biological firms, Brad told me he particularly regretted his lack of Spanish when he moved to Miami to go to graduate school.

Brad fell in love with the city and decided to adopt Spanish as his second language. But instead of heading to a classroom, he went to a bookstore.

Brad discovered that the Spanish scene and the book scene in Miami are intertwined. "I love to read, so I loved Books & Books in Coral Gables," Brad said. (Coral Gables is a part of Miami.) Books & Books is the landmark independent bookstore in South Florida that Mitchell Kaplan founded. His longtime events manager, Cristina Nosti, is Latina, and helped the stores (there are now several) develop a vibrant roster of Spanish-language programming. Mitchell is also the cofounder of the famed Miami Book Fair, another favorite of Brad's, and which features a significant Spanish-language component.

Brad found Spanish theater in Miami as well, and had friends who became his conversation partners. But when he moved his wife and baby daughter to New York so he could take a fellowship at Memorial Sloan-Kettering Cancer Center, he couldn't seem to find time for his Spanish. The skills he had sharpened so diligently in Miami began to dull.

Then Brad heard people in his lab talking about a bestselling book on cancer research, *The Immortal Life of Henrietta Lacks*, by Rebecca Skloot. When he discovered that the book was available in Spanish, Brad was elated. He could keep learning Spanish while also helping his career. Next on his list was the Spanish edition of *The Emperor of All Maladies: A Biography of Cancer*, by Siddhartha Mukherjee, another bestseller about the history of cancer.

By combining his love for science, his passion for books, and his thirst for Spanish, Brad hit the trifecta for his adopted language. It would pay off unexpectedly, when Brad went to Japan.

"I was at a conference, my first trip to Asia, and I heard some guys speaking Spanish—a Colombian scientist and a Spanish scientist. We became friends and hung out the whole week. I thought it was so fun walking down the streets of Japan, talking in Spanish," he told me. Brad is advancing his career as an American bilingual, and living the expanded life that comes with that.

Biking in Chile, hiking in Corsica

Very early in my Spanish life, when I had just committed to making Spanish my adopted language, I went on a cycling trip to Chile with my older (*mayor*) son, Cal. Our guide, a young Chilean mountain bike champion, took us on glorious rides through the region known as *Lagos y Volcanes* (Lakes and Volcanoes). I still remember some of the Spanish he taught me as we were riding. When it rained on us I learned *está lloviendo* (it's raining), and felt the raindrops pelting us as we rode. As we summited the Andes, I used another line our guide taught me—*no es nada* (it's nothing), which always got a laugh, as I was clearly struggling.

My son and I had a great time in Chile, while I learned some words that will forever be connected to those hard, marvelous days.

When my friend Maja Thomas had some time to kill between work weeks in Europe, she looked for an immersion class for her adopted French. "I didn't find one, but I did join a Francophone hiking group for a week in the wilds of Corsica." She loved the experience. "Of course, I learned lots of new French expressions (and some filthy jokes!), but what I also noticed is that the French use puns and plays on words constantly to make each other laugh."

Tim Ferriss of *The 4-Hour Workweek* fame learned Japanese through judo. In his blog, he advises, "Use the target language as a vehicle for learning more about a subject, skill, or cultural area of interest."

Not a want, but a need

So far in this chapter, we've talked about using experiences outside of the classroom to learn the language you wish to speak. Scholars sometimes call this elective bilingualism, in that we choose to learn a language, as opposed to situational bilingualism, where circumstances pretty much force people to learn another language. Jeane Forrest, who grew up in the Philippines, is a good example.

In her language biography interview, Jeane told me that she spoke Ilonggo, one of 360 languages in the Philippines. "But for us to understand each other, we have one major language, which is Tagalog, and it's also called Filipino." As in so many parts of the world, young people in the Philippines realize that speaking English is their ticket to better jobs. Jeane had some English in school. "I remember we are not allowed to speak our languages in English class because we have this little container that if we speak Ilonggo, we're going to have to pay twenty-five cents. But we were embarrassed to speak English because we might say the wrong thing."

At sixteen, Jeane left home to find work in Manila, first as a maid, and then as a waitress, where she could practice her English. "So we apply, me and my girlfriend." But the manager quickly noticed Jeane's Tagalog was weak. "He said, 'I'm sorry but you don't qualify because you don't have experience and you're not fluent in Tagalog.' It's a totally different language than my Ilonggo."

But Jeane was desperate. "So he was walking out the door. I tap him. I said, 'Sir, sir, sir, I know I didn't have any experience but here's what I want. I'm going to work for you for two weeks without pay to show you that I could learn fast. If I don't learn fast then you can tell me and then I will go. I won't get upset if you fire me because I didn't learn the job.' So he turned around and he said, 'Well, if we're going to hire you, we're going to pay you.' That's how I got hired."

Jeane succeeded at her job, moving from bus girl to waitress to bartender to manager, and learned Tagalog and some English on the job. Later, she and her sisters got jobs at a resort in Belize, where Jeane improved her English further. There she met an American, and they eventually married. Jeane moved to America, a dream she had had since childhood.

Her story illustrates how most people through history have learned another language and what compels them yet today. I saw this firsthand when I was volunteering to help immigrants to the US learn English.

The student teaches the tutor

The students were Latino and Haitian adults who attended evening English classes offered by the Literacy Coalition of Palm Beach County. They were held at a local elementary school and had well-trained teachers who had English as a Second Language (ESL) degrees. Native English-speaking volunteers like me assisted them. Our job was to work one-on-one with particular students.

One student I helped almost every week was a young Mexican in his twenties I'll call Emilio. He was a diligent student. I asked him one evening why he wanted to learn English.

"So I can get a job indoors," he replied.

His answer threw me for a moment. I knew he worked for a landscape company. Was his job outdoors that miserable?

"All the guys I work with, they speak Spanish all day," Emilio explained. "If I get a job indoors, I can speak English all day."

While I was still a tutor, Emilio landed such a job, at a store that sold rugs. It was hard work moving rugs all day for customers, but, he said, smiling broadly, "I get to use English all day."

The stories of Jeane and Emilio illustrate what continues to drive language learning the world over: the need, desperate at times, to advance economically. These people are put into a situation, by circumstances or by their own initiative, where they have to learn the dominant language to survive and prosper. And while they may well have had some schooling in the language, it's not enough to give them the proficiency they require. For these millions, learning outside of a classroom isn't a nice-to-have, it's a have-to-have. This ancient relationship between language learning and work, between language skills and commerce, existed far before there were any language classes as we understand them today. This isn't to say that language classes are unnecessary or superfluous. To the contrary, language classes can today provide a useful foundation for you to build upon with real-world experiences.

A tip from César Chávez

When Marshall Ganz was just a toddler, his parents moved his family from the US to Germany. They told him later that he had been speaking German as well as he did English. When he was five, however, his parents moved back to Washington, DC, where Marshall began having a hard time in school. "I was acting out in the first grade," Marshall told me when I was collecting his language biography. By the third grade, his parents moved him to a private school, but the children there had been learning French since first grade. "It was a very unhappy encounter," he recalled.

From Washington, Marshall's family moved to Bakersfield, California. "In high school I took German, thinking it would come back, but it didn't. I fought with it." Nor did he have much luck with Hebrew. "I resisted because I was in a struggle with my father. I grew up hearing it every Friday." Marshall disliked the rote learning of the prayers. "I could say prayers, but I couldn't use the language. It's a shame, since I really wish I had learned it."

For college, "Harvard was the only place I applied, which was stupid and arrogant," he said. Yet Harvard accepted him. "Geographical distribution probably helped me."

Marshall found Harvard daunting—plus, it had a language requirement. "I thought I'd take German again, but it never clicked for me." In fact, Harvard overall didn't click for Marshall. This was the anti-establishment 1960s; Marshall dropped out and joined the Freedom Riders, traveling down South to work for civil rights.

He found the work rewarding, and so moved back home to Bakersfield to work for the Latino American civil rights leader César Chávez and the United Farm Workers.

There was a problem, though. Marshall didn't know Spanish, and most of what happened in the organization happened in Spanish. "I realized I can't operate this way. I got a grammar book and flash cards, I listened to radio stations and began speaking it every day." It was hard going but Marshall told me he knew he *had* to persevere. "I couldn't tolerate the frustration, being in meetings, living and working in a Mexican world. It took awhile but I learned it in a real context, with gestures, facial and body stances, the *whole* language, not just the words."

Chávez offered him some advice. "César told me to learn the *dichos*, and he had tons of them, for example, 'Nobody comes to visit the cactus until it's time to bear fruit.' That was said when politicians would visit only on the eve of elections. And 'There's more laying of eggs going on than eggs coming,' meaning it's all words and no deeds. It was a wonderful way to learn," said Marshall.

"People had a good time explaining nuances of meaning that I could never get out of a book," he continued. "It was a rich experience, more than words, also the voice tone. Embedding the language in relationships, in context, is the way to learn a language." He added, "Talking to a computer is fine, but it's very different when you learn with people."

Marshall's description reminds me of Guadalupe Valdés at Stanford telling me how people organically learn languages—by being surrounded by others who are "expecting you to understand, wanting you to understand, and inviting you to understand."

A generation after dropping out of Harvard, Marshall received a letter inviting him to his twenty-fifth reunion. He called the university to say there had been a mistake, that he never graduated. "They said come anyway." He did, and ran into a professor who remembered him. "He told me, 'You know Marshall, you should come back and finish.'" And so Marshall did. He jokes, "I'm the only member of the 1964/92 Class at Harvard."

Marshall went on to earn his master's and doctoral degrees at Harvard as well and is now a professor at the Kennedy School of Government. He teaches courses on community organizing and what he calls "public narrative," which is tapping the power of storytelling to power social movements.

Context begets comprehension

Leanne Hinton, a linguist at the University of California, Berkeley, says that you learn a language by doing things, acting things out, and making flawed attempts at speaking that those around you gradually correct. "We understand because the language is spoken to us in the context of actions that make it clear what is meant," writes Hinton. In this way, she continues, learning "takes place most effortlessly in the context of activities."

That's how people learning languages that are only oral do it. And it's exactly what my buddies and I were doing as first-time polo players: we were absorbed in the activity of whacking the ball, rather than straining to learn horseback riding. As Hinton writes: "If team members do things together and talk about what they are doing, then the learner automatically understands and, just as importantly, is absorbed in the activity rather than straining to consciously learn the language."

It's what each of us can look forward to doing through our adopted languages. Classroom learning, apps, audio programs, videos—all are important tools and experiences for you, but expect to transition at some point to doing things in your language. Then, rather than *pursue* your adopted language, you'll allow it to *ensue,* flowering while you're living your life.

And it gets better yet. As you explore ways to learn your adopted language other than studying it, you've set your course toward finding the place, or places, where your adopted language will live in your life. Not until you drop anchor in each one will you know whether you'll spend just a few days in that welcoming bay, or stay to build a cottage in that pleasant grove, back a ways from the beach.

Chapter 14

THE TONIC OF TRAVEL

One of the surprises I encountered while researching this book was discovering the true power of learning a few basic words and pleasantries in the local language wherever you travel.

At the onset of my research, I didn't think much of this. It seemed like corny, phrase-book bilingualism. Why would I go out of my way to *sound* like a tourist? And anyway, didn't most people speak English? Better, I thought, to just admit I didn't know the local language rather than *trying* to say a few things that would either confuse the locals or make them wince at my terrible pronunciation.

I was dead wrong.

I learned just how wrong I was from interviewing many bilinguals and learning their language biographies. To my surprise, the more languages they spoke, the more likely they were to practice buds of bilingualism.

Planting buds of bilingualism

"I say a few words in Turkish and all of a sudden I get a big smile from the person sitting across from me. They say, 'Oh my gosh! I didn't know you knew that!'" That was what Kat Cohen told me. Kat is the founder and head of an educational consulting firm. She is fluent in Spanish and French, but her company has clients in forty countries, so she finds herself encountering different languages frequently. She plants buds of bilingualism in Turkey, Brazil, Italy, and wherever she finds herself.

So does Karen Gross, an author, education consultant, and former university president who speaks Spanish and French. Whenever she spoke to an academic audience outside of the US, "I would give the introduction in the language of the nation," she said. "That tradition served me well. It was a way of signaling to people that I was open to their culture, open to their language, open to their ideas."

That strategy worked fine until, she said, "I was invited to speak in Iceland."

After Karen wrote her introduction, she contacted the Icelandic Consulate in New York and asked if a staff member would translate it phonetically into Icelandic. How hard could that be? Her intro was just a paragraph.

The consulate returned three typed pages.

"That's when I realized, 'I'm in real trouble here,'" she said. "So I called them up and said, 'Okay, let's go for four or five sentences.'" If they sounded good enough, her hosts would know she had at least made an effort.

When it came time for Karen to deliver her speech, the attendees put in their earbuds to hear the translated version of what Karen was about to say.

"I started to speak, and I could see the people tapping on their earbuds. Like, 'Wait a second, I must have hit the wrong button here.' After a minute, they realized. 'Oh, wait, she's actually speaking in Icelandic!'"

It was the first time an American had come to their nation and made an effort to speak their language, Karen said. "And they had understood everything that I was trying to say." Karen told me they just about gave her the key to the city.

Karen elicited in a small way what President John F. Kennedy did on a historic level when, on June 26, 1963, he addressed the people of West Berlin. This was shortly after Communist Russia sawed Berlin in half with a concrete wall. When Kennedy announced, "*Ich bin ein Berliner*" ("I am a Berliner"), the crowd exploded in cheers. With just four simple words, Kennedy planted one of the most memorable buds of bilingualism in America's history.

Like Karen, Kennedy had practiced those four words beforehand, and he had a native German speaker write them out for him phonetically, to make sure he got them right.

After watching the video of Kennedy's speech and interviewing many bilinguals, I finally learned that it's not about trying to pass for a local—that's not going to happen, in any event. It's about being nice and, as Trevor Noah says in his memoir, respecting the people who are your hosts.

The TV travelog host Rick Steves offers this advice: "Dominant as English may be, it's just good manners to know the most common polite words in the local tongue. The top 10 words in any language—mostly niceties like please, thank you, and excuse me—are more important than the next 200 words combined."

Tom Swick, a travel writer who met his Polish wife while on a trip to London, says, "If you have the time to study it before your trip, the language goes from being just a gateway into a culture (as it was in school) to a living thing."

Today Americans have more opportunity than ever before to plant buds of bilingualism. When the term "jet set" was coined in the 1950s, it signified an elite group. Today, we are nearly all jet-setters. American travel to international destinations in the last twenty years has tripled, and while it has plummeted during crises, it has always rebounded to reach new highs. Contrary to the belief that few Americans hold passports today, almost half now do. According to State Department figures, the number of valid US passports in circulation as of 2019 was 147 million—nearly half of American citizens.

Ear lag

For those of us who have adopted a language and are enjoying learning it, the prospect of traveling to a country where that language is spoken is exciting. Yet our arrival can sometimes deliver a shocking disappointment when . . . *we can't . . . understand . . . anything!*

Anyone who has experienced this can relate to Mark Twain's wry observation from *The Innocents Abroad*:

> "In Paris they just simply opened their eyes and stared when we spoke to them in French! We never did succeed in making those idiots understand their own language."

Even if you're the star student in your French class back home, you may be flabbergasted and deflated to find your skills seemingly of no use at all when you arrive in Paris. This common linguistic phenomenon, so far as we know, lacks a name, so we offer *ear lag* because, like jet lag, it can knock you for a loop. But also like jet lag, you can overcome it. To help overcome ear lag, it's useful to understand what causes it.

Standard language versus how people actually speak

What we learn in school is a standard version of a language, whether that be French, Spanish, Russian, or Chinese. Large nation-states have, over the past one hundred or more years, attempted to have their citizens learn a standard, commonly shared version of their language so that the largest number of citizens can communicate well with one another, and so that mass education can take place more efficiently. This is as it should and must be, in order to make it feasible to produce a national literature, legal documents, textbooks, the sports pages, and other cultural and educational products. So when we begin learning a language, we, like schoolchildren in those countries, will be learning the standard, taught version. What people actually speak in the street, however, will be different—sometimes dramatically so.

Why? First off, because the standard language taught in textbooks tends to change far more slowly than the casual language that people actually speak. Merriam-Webster announced at the end of 2019 that "they" was its word of the year, and finally allowed it officially to mean either "his" or "her." We can now say, "each student may choose the lunch *they* want," rather than "the lunch *he* or *she* wants." Not a big deal, right? Not to us native English speakers who have been saying this for years, but the poor Chinese high school students who hear such a usage, when they are expecting to hear "he or she," might well be confused. These kinds of things happen in all languages all the time. Parisians don't speak the way our French textbooks say they should, no more than New Yorkers abide by the English textbooks you might find in Paris.

Kato Lomb warned that the language learner must deal with everyday language in the street, which will be different from standard language because of the eternal changes that languages go through. "Its change is natural: it stretches and it wears away, it widens and it shrinks. It loses its regular shape. And it loses its shape where it is touched by the most people: at everyday words. And everyday words are what all language learners must deal with."

Learning language in a classroom, and studying grammar books, are like observing butterflies in a museum case, dried and pinned for you to view. Whereas language in real life is like live butterflies, constantly in motion. It's hard, especially at first, to relate what you hear and see in real life to what you studied in the museum case.

And French, as it turns out, is a mild case. The French that many Parisians speak comes closer to its staid textbook version than you'll likely find with other languages.

Diglossia: more than one way to speak a language

The linguist Charles Ferguson is credited with coining the term diglossia, or speaking two different dialects of a language, usually in different social settings. He studied Arabic, which is known to have particularly wide variations among the spoken Arabic found in the various Arab countries, such as Morocco, Egypt, and Jordan. People from Arab countries can have a very hard time understanding one another if they speak their local or regional versions of Arabic. But when they go to school, they learn Modern Standard Arabic, which is based more on the Arabic of the Koran.

This seems entirely normal to native Arabic-speaking people—there's the version they speak at home, and the version they learned in school and hear on the news. Not a big deal if you grow up in that kind of environment. But for American adults attempting to learn Arabic, it's a big deal indeed. They will typically start with Modern Standard Arabic, but then they'll have to learn the Arabic of whatever country they are going to if they want to be able to communicate with people on the street. It's partly for this reason that the Foreign Service Institute allocates twice the amount of time for an American to learn Arabic as it does for an American learning French or Spanish.

Diglossia isn't limited to the Arab world. It's also common in China, which is one reason why Deborah Fallows had such a hard time trying to learn Chinese.

She was already bilingual, and holds a PhD in linguistics. When she knew she and her husband would be temporarily living in China, she decided she should learn Chinese. In her memoir about the experience, *Dreaming in Chinese*, she relayed how she took several Chinese courses at Georgetown University to prepare. When they arrived in China, however, "I could not recognize or utter a single word of the Chinese I had been studying, and I even wondered if my teacher had been teaching us Cantonese instead of Mandarin."

Americans are not used to such wide variations in language. What we notice in regional variations between the American South and New England, for example, is like polite chamber music compared with the rowdy rock concerts going on in most of the rest of the world. The so-called dialects in China, for example, are largely mutually incomprehensible. The closest thing we have to compare is American Black English (also referred to as African American Vernacular English). As John McWhorter explains, it is a dialect of English with its own rules and grammar that are complex, consistent, and distinct from American Standard English. It can come as a surprise to listeners when African Americans switch back and forth between these two dialects.

Why do such wide variations exist? It turns out that humans around the world generally *like* to have such distinctions in their languages, to identify which group they belong to.

'Boundary marking'

As the linguist John Edwards writes, "Different languages mark communities or cultures or subcultures that wish to maintain some distinctiveness. Where groups share a language, distinctions are found at the dialectal level: Austrians are not Germans, Bolivians are not Spaniards, the Irish are not English." Language learners are faced with the reality that they are learning a standard version of a language that, in the reality of spoken language, is "part of an ever renewing process of boundary marking," as Edwards describes it.

Such boundary marking doesn't show any sign of diminishing. But ear lag will eventually go away, as it did for Deborah Fallows.

"Slowly, of course, everything began to change," she writes. "My teacher had indeed been teaching me Mandarin, although without the heavy Shanghai accent I heard all around me and later sorted out." And you, too, will sort out your ear lag. All that studying you did of the standard version of your language will pay off, once you tune in and adjust to the real, living version of the language around you.

Your travel to the countries that natively speak your adopted language can become the glorious adventure and learning experience you dream of. And you'll learn some local expressions that will never make it to the text-books or the apps.

Chapter 15

Your Brain on Barcelona (or Bangkok, or . . .)

She was tall and, at times, ungainly. She had taken French in school but seemed to have little talent for it. One former teacher complained that she suffered from "an inability to detect shades of sound." The young woman herself would later admit, "I did just enough to get by."

But as luck would have it, this young woman from Pasadena married an American diplomat who got stationed in Paris. Once they arrived in 1948, she was at a complete loss. Normally extroverted, she shrank from conversations. At restaurants, her husband later recalled, "'After years of practical French lessons, from grade school through college, she was no better equipped to read the menu than was, say, her father or her cat.'"

That young woman was Julia Child.

In his biography *Dearie: The Remarkable Life of Julia Child,* Bob Spitz describes what could be a textbook case of ear lag. "She was unable to express herself in the most fundamental situations. Paul (Julia's husband) recalled how all that finishing-school French eluded her once they hit town. 'She couldn't even hail a cab and give him an address or understand if he said anything in response,' he said." It made her feel helpless and then angry that she couldn't speak the language.

Paul Child, who was fluent in French, described the two of them being at a party where Julia could do nothing but stand aside, silently, as groups of guests all around her "strung words together with machine-gun rapidity." After the party, an exasperated Julia announced to her husband: "'I'm going to learn to speak this language come hell or high water.'"

After that, Julia insisted that shop merchants and others speak to her only in French. A friend recalled that even though "'Julia spoke very poor French' at the outset, the effort she put in was heroic."

Writes Spitz, "Practice became second nature to her—speaking, reading, conjugating those damn verbs. She read Baudelaire and Balzac in their native tongue. Paul put her through the paces at home, with tricky linguistic exercises, correcting, correcting, always correcting her 'gauche accent.'"

Feasting on her newfound French

In a few months, Julia felt comfortable enough to use her French with everyone she met. The locals started to warm up to her, as it was such an impressive turnaround, and Julia felt grateful to them for welcoming her. "'I never dreamed I would find the French so *sympathique*, so warm, so polite, so utterly pleasurable to be with . . . .'"

And then, she discovered a book. A friend loaned her a copy of the bible of French cooking. Published in 1906, it was the work of Henri Babinski, writing under the pseudonym Ali-Bab. Spitz relates: "it was a treasure trove of kitchen lore . . . a doorstop of a book, as thick as the New York telephone directory, and it was legendary. Every French housewife had a copy on her bookshelf. Chefs kept one close to their stoves, knew each of the recipes by heart. And Julia devoured it as she might a morning croissant."

Reading it, as we know from Chapter 7, not only helped Julia's French, but it also became a lighthouse guiding her to the port where French would live in her life. She had been enjoying the food in France, but with this book, her interest went beyond mere enjoyment. Then she found a conversation partner.

"Over time, Julia became a fixture at her neighborhood market on rue de Bourgogne," writes Spitz. There she met an elderly woman named Marie des Quatre Saisons, "who sold produce from a three-wheeled cart and dished out gossip and advice as freely as she dished out Brussels sprouts." The French-woman took a liking to the young American, and the two of them spent hours talking about the city and, of course, food.

Recalled Julia, "'She took great pleasure in instructing me which vegetables were best to eat, and when . . . and how to prepare them correctly.'"

The story of Julia's experience in Paris illustrates many of the points we've touched on, including ear lag, the importance of reading "compelling, comprehensible input," the value of finding a compatible conversation partner, having an insatiable thirst for learning, and perhaps most crucial of all, discovering *where* her adopted language would live in her life. It would be in her French cooking. And boy, did it live. Julia became the ambassador for French cooking in America, forever changing the way Americans would think about their food.

Julia's story illustrates something else important along the journey to bilingualism: a major barrier to Americans fortunate enough to find themselves living overseas in another languagescape, the expat trap.

Avoiding the expat trap

Living abroad can be the greatest way to go beyond merely learning a language to living it. And Julia's story illustrates how that experience can be squeezed for all the juice it has. But the experience can also be squandered when visitors fall into the expat trap.

When you find yourself in another country where another language dominates, especially if you think you'll be there only temporarily, it can be very tempting to restrict your life to an enclave of expats and fail to learn the local language. Fortunately for her and for us, Julia did not tumble into that trap. Another American who did not, and who was one of my language biography interviews, was a company president named Mitch Cuevas.

Like Julia, Mitch grew up in Southern California. One set of grandparents were native Spanish speakers, and the other set, native English speakers. In college in San Diego, he majored in international business and studied Spanish, too. After his junior year, he attended a summer program in Spain. "You learn a lot in university, but until you use it every day, you don't pick it up fully," he told me. Mitch lived in Spain for a year after graduation, taking intensive Spanish for the first four months, and then getting a job with a marketing firm in Madrid. That led to a marketing position back in America with RJR Nabisco. His job was to grow the company's business among Latinos in California's Orange County.

After a successful stint at RJR Nabisco, Mitch went to the London Business School to earn his MBA. He did an exchange program in Brazil and started learning Portuguese. "It's grammatically similar to Spanish but very different pronunciation," he explained. That led to a job with Ernst & Young in São Paulo.

"There was another American who had been there two years, but he had learned only enough Portuguese to order in restaurants," Mitch told me. "He wasn't fluent or even conversational. He didn't make any effort to integrate himself." Mitch's approach was the opposite. "I didn't hang out with other Americans who were there. I spent all my free time with locals so I could understand their culture and the language. After about two years, I picked up fluency in Portuguese."

When I interviewed Mitch, he was on his third CEO job and living in New Zealand. Reflecting back on his career, he told me his bilingualism had always been a necessity for his career advancement. "My biggest career jump, from consulting to the first of three CEO roles, was absolutely enabled by being bilingual." It had started with his knowing what kinds of ads to run on TV and in local newspapers for the Latino market for RJR Nabisco. And for all of his positions since, his skills were dependent on him escaping the expat trap.

Finding her groove through giving

Robin Loving had been running her own public relations business in Corpus Christi, Texas, when she and her husband decided they had saved enough money to change their lives in a big way. They sold their house and drove south to San Miguel de Allende to begin new lives.

"Although I had had the privilege of having Spanish in school and in college, I had never used it on a consistent basis," Robin told me. "I was proud of my accent but I really had no command of the language." Robin knew she wanted to get involved in the community somehow and that improving her Spanish would be important, so she signed up for daily lessons with a private tutor. She expected to make quick progress, but "I came home every day and cried into my textbooks. I like to push myself. I like to achieve quickly, and it wasn't coming quickly."

I asked her if she had considered classes. "I had lots of friends who have taken classes, but I didn't want to hear everybody else's mistakes," said Robin. "I was going to make enough of my own." She switched to a different tutor, which helped. But then one day, she said, she saw a vision.

"It was July of my first year here and I was walking through the house and I saw golden light. I know that sounds strange. And it said in words, printed words, that came to my forehead, 'Go work with girls. Go . . . work . . . with . . . . girls.' It was in a cadence much slower than I can say it." Robin assured me such visions were not a normal occurrence for her. "And I don't take drugs," she added. Robin confided in a Mexican neighbor, who told her to go to Santa Julia.

Santa Julia is an orphanage for girls, and the nuns who run it speak no English. Robin was forced to use her Spanish. "I met the *madres* in their full battle-dress habit," Robin told me, referring to the long tunic and veil that is the traditional dress for nuns. "They said, 'Come teach English.'" So Robin did. And her Spanish improved.

"Using it on a daily basis, getting the idioms and getting the *dichos*—as they say, *vale la pena,*" Robin said, using the Spanish for "it's worth it."

Robin gradually found herself hearing the Spanish that one native speaker might say to another. Instead of *"¿Quieres agua?,"* the standard way to ask, "Do you want water?," Robin started to hear *"¿Quieres agüita?,"* with the diminutive and more personal *agüita*, or "a little water, a little taste."

A million-dollar payoff

After working daily at the orphanage, Robin became aware of bigger needs. She thought she could do more for the school by applying her public relations skills rather than teaching English. And she had gradually earned the trust of the *madres*. So Robin began writing articles and speaking to the San Miguel expat community about Santa Julia and its needs. The community listened. Over the following years, Robin helped raise a million dollars to support the orphanage.

I asked Robin what that triumph felt like. "Oh gosh. You know, the triumph for me was getting these really conservative Catholic nuns to allow me to come in and find out what their true needs were for the little girls who had been abused and abandoned."

Robin told me she could not have done it had she spoken only English. Her Spanish skills allowed her to understand what was really going on at the orphanage and to get the word out to the English-speaking expat community. "This community has a huge capacity to help, but they needed to hear the stories. Being bilingual was essential to that."

Warren Hardy, the founder of the San Miguel language school whom we met earlier, was full of praise for Robin's work. He said her growing skills in Spanish illustrate a pattern he sees in town among some expat Americans.

"When people first come here they're nervous; they want to learn enough to get by. They nest, they begin to build lives." But then, he says, they begin to look for opportunities to serve or engage in the community. "Suddenly a light goes on in their head and they go, 'Oh man, I've got to improve my Spanish.' So they reappear at the school and they take a few courses and bump it up." Warren considers it an "evolutionary process." In the expat community, "you're constantly engaging more and learning more."

A sign of respect

The US government doesn't compile official records of the number of Americans living abroad, but present estimates put the figure at around nine million. No doubt there are many who fall into the expat trap and live diminished lives because of it. Perhaps it's the nature of my reporting that I've found Americans who have done the opposite—Americans like Stavros Stavrakis, the American-born son of Anastasia Kastrenakes Merkel, who has become a priest in Greece. His fellow priests refer to him affectionately as "the American," and they come to him for help with their English.

There's also Debbie Psychoyos, who in college met a young man from Panama and married him. She has lived in Panama ever since, raising three bilingual children and starting a nonprofit that provides enrichment for public school teachers, including teachers of English. "I try to speak only Spanish at the office," she told me, "and only English at home." This was for her children, who went to college and began working in America. Speaking Spanish at work, she told me, is not only practical but shows respect to her team members.

None of these Americans abroad told me it was easy learning the local language or the local culture, which is intertwined with the language, but all of them spoke of the rewards that came with the struggle. And the people around these Americans can gain from them, sometimes greatly.

That brings us back to Julia Child, that ungainly young American whose teachers thought she had no talent for the French language. Suddenly transplanted to Paris, she could have retreated. She could have insulated herself with English-speaking friends and lived in an English bubble, seeing the City of Lights through dark glasses. That she didn't led to a remarkable life for her, and to millions of Americans savoring their own crêpes Suzette, cassoulets, and boeuf Bourguignon.

Chapter 16

DISCOVER YOUR LITTLE DOVES

I had a language epiphany in Walmart. It was a bilingual Walmart, in Carson City, Nevada, with most of the signs in English and Spanish. I was trying to focus just on the Spanish, translating as I strolled through the store. It was going well until I came across a sign in the food section. Around the rice and beans aisle, I saw *Palomitas de maíz*.

Okay, I knew *maíz* was corn and *paloma* was dove, so . . . little doves of corn? H'mmm. I'm thinking maybe tortilla chips. Then I saw it: clear plastic bags of . . . *popcorn*! I realized for the first time that in English, we say what it *sounds* like, whereas in Spanish, we say what it *looks* like. It was a revelation. I did a happy dance right there in the beans aisle.

So *this* is what they mean, I thought, when they say you don't know your own language until you can see it in the light of another. I'm sure that without discovering those delicious little doves of corn, I would have lived my whole life never having considered that "popcorn" is just *one* way to describe this joyful food, and maybe not the most poetic.

It was after my Walmart epiphany that I decided to keep a journal of learning Spanish. It's a Google doc on my computer and phone where I jot down such mind-opening experiences. Another came when I was reading a mini-biography of Amelia Earhart written for young people. A friend of mine, Kate Jerome, wrote it, and I bought two copies of the delightful little paperback, one in Spanish and one in English. I read the Spanish one and referred to the English as I needed. So . . . I'm reading about Amelia's childhood and how, while visiting the St. Louis Exposition with her family, she sees a *montaña rusa*. A Russian mountain? That sent me to the English version, where I discovered that *montaña rusa* is a . . . *roller coaster*! What?

Why on earth do Spanish speakers call it a Russian mountain? It still makes me laugh, and it went right into my journal.

These kinds of delightful surprises are in store for you as you get to know your adopted language. I encourage you to keep track of them to enhance the fun and help you share your discoveries with fellow bilinguals.

Proverbs are potent memory joggers

As the Harvard sociologist Marshall Ganz shared with us, learning proverbs is a joy waiting for you in your adopted language. Not only are they terribly useful for your understanding, they also give you a feeling for the music and poetry of the language. Proverbs were language's way of passing on wisdom before we had the benefit of writing it down. Before print, people needed to pass on wisdom in ways that listeners could easily remember, and so reached for pleasing sounds, humor, and succinctness.

The language historian Walter Ong observed that proverbs are rich with content that help people "think memorable thoughts." Proverbs, he wrote, "are constantly heard by everyone so that they come to mind readily." They are also "patterned for retention and ready recall."

I love the Spanish ones that seem to be more colorful than the English versions. In English, we say "money talks." In Spanish, it's *con dinero baila el perro*—"with money, the dog dances." I can just imagine dropping a coin in a wooden box, hearing the dog's owner whistle, and seeing his smart little *perro* dance for giggling children.

I also love the Spanish proverbs for which no English equivalent exists—for example, *Agua que no has de beber, déjala correr*. It literally means "water that you don't need to drink, let it run," but the expression is used figuratively to express the sentiment that if you don't need or want something, let someone else enjoy it.

If using buds of bilingualism is endearing, using proverbs is doubly so. But the surprises of vocabulary, grammar, and proverbs are just the beginning of the delights that are in store for you as you become more comfortable in your adopted language.

Learning is learning, no matter the language

I've had bilinguals tell me when recording their language biographies that they learned engineering in German, or business in English, or attended church in Spanish, for example, and that it didn't feel natural to use another language in these domains. This can be a boon to your language learning.

If Italian is your adopted language and you'd also like to learn about opera, learn it in Italian. Or take piano in German, or learn soccer in Spanish. You'll likely learn just as well and get the bonus of building on your adopted language. It might even be more satisfying for you as you improve two things at once.

Your life as a translator

Let's say Spanish is your adopted language and you're walking in Mexico with a friend who doesn't understand any Spanish. A man and his dog approach you, the dog straining the leash to chase a cat, and the man cuts you off as a result. As he is tugged along, the man says to you, *"Lo siento."*

Your friend asks you, "What did he say?"

"He said he's sorry," you say.

Did you translate correctly? *Lo siento* actually means "I feel it." But had you said, "He said he feels it," your friend might have misunderstood. "I'll bet he *feels* it!" your friend might exclaim. "That dog is pulling his arm off!"

Welcome to the world of translation. It's a function as old as language itself, and a role taken up by those who, by accident or volition, live between two language groups.

As I've collected language biographies, many people have told me they want to learn another language so they can read such-and-such in the original. That's fantastic, and it certainly will be a different experience from reading the translation, but as the translation scholar David Bellos warns us, we shouldn't think that the original is better and the translation is worse. Bellos says the idea that the original is somehow better is merely pretension. That's why, as he points out, "countless writers have packaged originals as translations and translations as originals and gotten away with it for weeks, months, years, even centuries." Yet the idea that originals are better than translations is widespread. "It's truly astounding how many people fall into the trap," he says. For anything that may be "lost" in a translation, there is more to be found in it.

This is why awards for translated literature, like the one the National Book Foundation gives, go to the author and the translator equally. And as Tina Kover, a finalist for the National Book Foundation's 2018 award, observed, "I absolutely do not believe that anything is lost in translation. It's like fraternal twins."

As we saw in Chapter 2, the jobs of professional translator and interpreter require many years, if not decades, of training; yet nearly all language learners will find themselves in those honored roles—at first for themselves, and then for others. I say it's an honor because translation is nothing less than the mortar that binds civilization.

When, in the mists of history, one language group met another, decisions had to be made, and often very quickly. Should we raid or should we trade? The advance of civilization itself, as halting and uneven as it has been, favored trade. To raid, one doesn't need language skills; to trade, one does. Or at least a willingness to listen and try to learn. As Bellos says, translation "comes when some human group has the bright idea that . . . the people on the other side of the hill might be worth talking to."

Allison De La Torre is the daughter of two monolingual English-speaking Americans, although her paternal grandparents were from Puerto Rico. Allison took Spanish in school, but her Spanish really bloomed when she went on several mission trips with her church to Peru, Guatemala, and Ecuador. "The rest of my team members, very few of them spoke Spanish and so they would ask me for help when we would go out and talk to the people in each of the countries," she said. On her last trip, Allison told me that the paid translators accompanying them wore shirts with "Translator" written in big letters on the back. "At the end of the trip the translators gave me a translator T-shirt and said, 'You're one of us.'" She told me it was one of her proudest moments.

It can be one of the sweetest rewards for you, too, along your journey to your larger bilingual life. By stepping into your adopted language, you're stepping into that fundamental historical role of connector, explainer, bridge builder, and peacemaker.

The surprises to come

I can't say which particular surprises you're in store for as you walk your language journey, but I can say with certainty that you will be surprised.

Perhaps you'll be surprised by the depth of the friendships you'll form with classmates or tutors or conversation partners, or how much you'll love going to a language camp. When you travel, perhaps you'll be surprised at just how powerful buds of bilingualism can be. And now that you know about ear lag, you may be pleasantly surprised that you begin to get over it faster than you expected, as you tune into the local ways of saying things. You may be surprised at just how good your growing bilingualism can feel. I've never met a bilingual who didn't enjoy being bilingual, who didn't consider it a big part of who they were.

The science writer Marek Kohn reports that bilingualism appears to promote extroversion, agreeableness, and conscientiousness. These behaviors tend to be contagious, and can build virtuous cycles of well-being. I'm naturally introverted, but after I've told a Spanish speaker that I'm learning and would love his help, I'm my more extroverted self. It takes energy and I'm not always up for it, but when I am, it's a great feeling.

This may partly explain why all the polyglots I've interviewed were keen on learning their *next* language. This surprised me, I have to admit. From my point of view, struggling so many years just to add my second language, I look at people who speak five or more and think, *My God! Isn't five enough?* Apparently not.

My friend Jack Roepers, for example, who already speaks Dutch, French, German, and respectable Spanish (in addition to English, of course), is thirsty to learn Italian. I only found this out when, over drinks, we got talking about bucket list items. "I understand so much of it," he told me with a look of frustration on his face. "I can *read* much of it, but *damn*, I just want to be able to speak it!"

Polyglots know better than most of us just how rewarding it is to begin feeling comfortable in another language, simply because they have done it more times, and as adults. But even a two-language bilingual can experience the special joy of a life multiplied. As Kohn puts it, "The ability to toggle between two languages is about as near as one can get to being in two places at once."

As you step beyond deliberately learning your adopted language toward doing things in your language, you may be surprised that you enjoy these activities even more because you have to struggle a bit with the language. You may marvel at how the language recedes into the background as you focus on the cooking, hiking, or dancing.

You may be surprised at how your language learning gains momentum and becomes enjoyable in its own right.

And you may be surprised by the cultural differences you learn that lie beyond just being able to speak the language. One of the language biographies I collected was from a remarkable young man named Marco Chan, who at the time was earning his MBA from Stanford *and* his Master in Public Administration from Harvard. A Chinese Canadian, Marco spoke French and English in addition to Chinese. He told me about when he was traveling in Cuba with a friend who was raised as a monolingual English speaker.

"Halfway through the trip, we realized that we had some miscommunication due to our styles. Being raised Chinese, I was used to expressing indirectly. It seems overly forceful and potentially rude for me to express direct wishes to someone I don't know well. My friend, being American, he would voice his desires without hesitation, and his desires became our default because he could not recognize what I was expressing indirectly."

So when Marco would say, "Hey, do you remember reading about this restaurant in our guide book? It looked good. Might be a good stop?," his American friend didn't get the hint. "He would interpret this as an invite to evaluate whether the place was good, whereas I really meant that I wanted to eat there."

Marco and his friend talked about it. "He told me, 'I hope you get better at communicating'—as if one style of communication (the American, of course) was universally, normatively good."

When language teachers talk about intercultural competence, it's exactly this kind of stuff. So as you learn your adopted language, be prepared for learning more than the words and grammar. Be prepared for different styles of communication. Gaining this kind of understanding can make all the difference for relationships. And clearly it's something beyond Google Translate.

Reading memoirs, writing yours

For inspiration, I recommend that you read memoirs written by people who have gone to live in the countries that speak your adopted language. These can be lovely reads and may also teach you about unexpected aspects of the culture, and how the language really works on the ground. A readers' advisory librarian at a public library can be a great help in finding the ones you'll like most.

While I have no idea what you'll learn or what will be inspiring to you, I'm quite confident you will learn and be inspired by such accounts. They may even inspire you to write your own. Go forth, and find your own little doves.

* * *

Chapter 17

FINDING WHERE

In the first chapter, I suggested you think about where your new language will live in your life. It's a question only you can answer. But I can share the stories of a few people who have found those places for themselves.

Two different paths to 'where'

Lorna Auerbach, whom we met briefly earlier, grew up in Los Angeles and studied French from middle school into college. But, Lorna told me, she always struggled with the language. "I found the grammar daunting and I continually got C's—and I don't get C's." She told me her attitude about studying languages was, "it never has benefited me and I can't see how it ever can." Plus, Lorna thought there was something wrong with her—that she just couldn't learn another language. That idea was soon to change.

After college, Lorna joined a program in Israel to teach English as a second language. She was enrolled in Ulpan, the immersion method designed to absorb Israeli immigrants into the language and culture. Her fellow participants were from countries scattered throughout the world. "It was kind of like being in Babylon and our only common language was Hebrew," she said. The experience did the trick for Lorna. "At the end of eight or twelve weeks, I was speaking fluent Hebrew, even with its different alphabet and reading right to left." It was a revelation for her. *Maybe there was nothing wrong with me,* she thought. Unlike the French classes she had in the US, in Ulpan, "you had to learn in order to survive."

She learned something else that year in Israel. "I realized I loved teaching." She returned to Los Angeles, got her graduate degree in teaching at UCLA, and then applied for a job with the Los Angeles school district.

"They sent me to Roosevelt High School in East LA, which is all Latino." Lorna started as a substitute teacher and learned that she could earn more by becoming certified as a bilingual teacher. Having the confidence now that she could learn another language, Lorna set her sights on learning Spanish, and she attacked the challenge with gusto.

"There was a total immersion summer course at USC and I signed up," Lorna said. "We had one hour a day in conversation group, a second hour in grammar and writing, and a third hour in a lab with individualized learning." That was the easy part. For the second half of the summer, she went to Toluca, Mexico, to live with a family that didn't speak English. "We took classes and went on tours, all in Spanish," she said. Lorna's Spanish took off.

Returning home, Lorna continued with extension classes at UCLA at night. Her growing proficiency allowed her to get more involved with her students and their parents. "I was on a mission to get their children into top universities," she said. She signed up to lead educational trips to Mexico, which she did over Christmas and in the summers. And she signed up to teach English at night to Latino gardeners and housekeepers. "I talked to them in Spanish during breaks."

Lorna dove into the language head first. "I'd listen to Spanish radio all the time in the car and loved traveling to Mexico. Whenever I made an effort to speak, they were really grateful and complimented me and all this positive feedback made me want to learn more."

Lorna was enjoying being a bilingual teacher, but her life was about to change again. Her father, who had founded a real estate firm, was in failing health, and had not made any succession plans for his business. Lorna realized that she would have to learn some basics about it, "at the very least, so I could communicate with lawyers and accountants, or things would be a mess for my mother." She took a one-year leave from teaching.

"It may as well have been a foreign language," she said of her father's world and its real estate terminology. "I used to go home crying." Just as with French, "I thought, 'I'm never going to learn this!'"

But learn it she did. When I met Lorna, she was already a longtime member of the international group of company presidents, YPO, having successfully run the business her father started and taking it to new heights. But what of her Spanish?

"I can speak really fast and my vocabulary is constantly improving," she told me. Part of the reason is that she reads Spanish newspapers, but the big reason is that Lorna found a way to bring her Spanish into her second career in business. She discovered the most beautiful tiles, made by artisans in Spain, and decided to import them for her own construction jobs and sell them to other developers. She was able to travel to Spain on business. She loved the human connection and the dear friends she made in the small companies there. She employed a team of bilinguals to manage the website and take sales.

Lorna had found where her adopted language would live in her life, in her first career in education, and in her second career in business. Her Spanish came with her and took Lorna to places she could not have imagined earlier in her life. The schoolgirl who got C's in French and thought she wasn't cut out to learn languages is today an American bilingual who has helped send Latino kids to top universities and helped bring beautiful Spanish tiles to American homes.

Journalists embedded in the language

"The language allows you an entrée to get closer, to interpret that society for other people in a way that you couldn't if you didn't speak the language." That's what Calvin Sims told me about his twenty years as an international correspondent for *The New York Times*. Twice the newspaper sent him to intensive language learning sessions before his postings.

He first learned Spanish for his assignments in Latin America, where he lived for six years. Then he was assigned to Japan. Recalling his Japanese training, he said, "It was very difficult." He started with six hours of language study during the day, with a new Japanese instructor every hour, followed by four hours of homework. "You'd suffer the next day if you didn't get your homework done."

The time and effort paid off. "My Japanese was really good. I learned three thousand kanji [characters], so I could read, as they say, at the *Time* magazine level." He felt well prepared when he arrived at the *Times* offices in Tokyo . . . until he started speaking.

"They said, 'You speak like a woman.'" Calvin was taken aback. Then he remembered that all his instructors were women. "They said, 'Your Japanese is good, but you need to say it *this* way, because you're a man.'" Japanese women tend to speak in a very polite manner, whereas men speak more gruffly.

"A lot of time in Japan you felt like you were on another planet," Calvin added. "Nothing is written in English, everything is pristine, there's no crime, and you go there and are able to function and to understand, to *be* Japanese. From a humanistic point of view, it's a pretty incredible thing."

Calvin avoided the expat trap by taking the time to talk to local people, including playing soccer in the park near his apartment. "I felt comfortable with everyday people, having conversations with friends." But things were different in interviews. The *Times* office would send interpreters with Calvin just to make sure there wasn't a problem. "Sometimes I would ask a question in perfect Japanese, but my subject would look to the interpreter, who would say the same thing. I think the subject found it hard to believe that an American could really speak Japanese, so they wanted to hear the question spoken by the Japanese interpreter."

I heard the same from Anand Gopal, the author of *No Good Men Among the Living: America, the Taliban, and the War Through Afghan Eyes,* which was a finalist for the National Book Award. He didn't know Farsi before going to Afghanistan and learned it by immersion. He said his understanding of the language was essential to the reporting he did for *The Wall Street Journal* and the *Christian Science Monitor*.

When reporters don't speak the local language, it can be just too much of a barrier for their reporting. That's what Evan Osnos discovered when he was stationed in Iraq but didn't know Arabic. He told me he finally left because he felt he wasn't getting beneath the surface, as if there were a scrim between him and his subjects.

But Evan did have a background in Chinese, from studying it in college and having spent two summers in China. That skill helped him to get hired as the China correspondent for *The New Yorker*. His Chinese became good enough to do his own interviews, although he would take an interpreter with him "if the subject was technical or if the regional dialects were too different." His book, *Age of Ambition: Chasing Fortune, Truth, and Faith in the New China,* won the National Book Award.

Journalist turned internationalist

Calvin Sims left the *Times* to become a program officer for the Ford Foundation. Then in 2014, he became president of International House, a venerable institution that houses international students attending universities in the New York City area.

When I went to interview Calvin at International House, I was curious about how much he uses his Spanish and Japanese in his current role. Before I got a chance to ask him, he began speaking Spanish to staff members we met as we walked around the campus. I saw their faces light up. "Spanish is very useful here because about 40 percent of our staff speak Spanish. It's an instant connection with them."

He gets less opportunity to speak Japanese, but had just a few days earlier when he got in the elevator at International House with a Japanese woman and her two children. "Do you speak Japanese?" he asked in the language. "The woman was shocked," Calvin said. Calvin also uses the language with some of his Japanese board members, and says his Japanese gets better at galas and other social events, "when we can have a drink together."

Portal to a true identity

Language teachers have told me they often see changes in their students when they begin to express themselves in another language. Middlebury Language Schools dean Stephen Snyder says when you are removed from your familiar framework, "you're forced, essentially, to recreate your identity as a different person in the new language."

Language guru Steve Kaufmann tells his readers that "it is important to let go of the security of your native language and culture and broaden your identity."

That's just what Kate Krosschell did.

"I was probably eight or nine when I took my first French class," she told me. "I was just obsessed with France. The Parisian love story really captured me, and I loved the French culture, the food, the wine—I just got swept up. I was the obnoxious person in French class in high school who would raise their hand at every question."

Kate went to Bowdoin College in Maine, where she majored in French and film studies and studied abroad for a year in Paris. "We signed a contract that said we couldn't speak any English, even with our fellow American peers," she said. And she didn't.

After graduation, Kate landed a one-year teaching assistant job at a French university. She imagined that she might marry a European man, a guy who wore tight jeans and scarves. But then she described what she called "the beginning of the end."

First off were the French visa restrictions that made it very difficult for an American to find permanent work in France. Then her French boyfriend broke up with her, two days before she flew home to visit her parents. "I remember crying on the plane home and just being kind of a mess," she says.

But it gave her time to reflect. Maybe France wasn't to be. So she applied to four or five different graduate programs in Europe and was accepted to one in Copenhagen, where she worked on a master's degree in film studies. She practiced some Danish with the Rosetta Stone software, but on her second day in Copenhagen, she went into a grocery store and realized things were not going to be simple. She didn't even know what some of the items were. "I saw the words and had no idea how to pronounce them, or what things cost."

Fortunately, the Danish government offers up to two years of free Danish lessons to residents who don't speak it. "It's safe to say that had I not done that program, I would not be fluent in Danish. It took me about a year and a half to pass the fluency test."

At the same time, she was reflecting on her personal life. "That image I had about marrying a European man, and settling there and having kids . . . it wasn't really resonating. Then I just kind of fell for this woman, and couldn't stop it, so that was when I sort of decided to let it fly."

Denmark legalized same-sex registered partnerships in 1989. Says Kate, "The Danes tend to be a little more accepting of the way you want to live your life. I don't think I would have had the courage to come out as early as I did in the States."

Kate's story illustrates that on the journey of finding where your adopted language may live in your life, you may find your own identity or enlarge it. It may help you find your sexual identity and, as it has for millions of Americans, it may help you find your ethnic identity.

Race walking to a heritage

Millions of immigrants to America, as well as their children and grandchildren, have had to negotiate a hybrid identity somewhere between the cultures they came from and American culture. This negotiation is inherently filled with tension, and has been expressed in autobiographical novels such as Jean Kwok's *Girl in Translation* and memoirs such as Laila Lalami's *Conditional Citizens.*

Andrew Hermann's grandmother spoke Spanish but his mother did not. Andrew took Spanish in school and, in a case more common in America than it used to be, reclaimed his heritage language. He had study-abroad experiences in Costa Rica and Spain. Andrew would eventually pursue a career building American businesses in Latin America and starting his own companies there, in which his Spanish was a critical skill. But before he did this, something unusual happened in his early years after college.

"I was a track athlete in college," Andrew told me. His sport was race walking, not all that common in the US but popular in Europe and Latin America. He became friendly with some of the members of the Spanish national team. "To give you context, the coach was José Marin, and his team was filled with world and Olympic champions. There was no way the Spanish team would have invited me if I didn't know the language and hadn't showed such an interest."

Andrew trained with the team for two years. "That got my Spanish going," he said. And his race walking, too. Andrew went to the 2000 Olympics in Sydney, and although he didn't qualify beyond the trials, "the overall experience was amazing," he said. "I was an Olympic athlete." His adopted language launched his Olympic experience.

Today, Americans are establishing beachheads for where the language of their elders will live in their lives. This isn't through any rejection of English, but through an embracing of bilingualism.

As Eric Liu writes in his memoir *A Chinaman's Chance:* "Heritage and identity. The two are often conflated, spoken of interchangeably, but in fact distinct. One is the chrysalis, the other the butterfly; one seed, the other, fruit. The first is insurance against risk; the second is risk. Even if we provide for everyone a suitable heritage, we have only barely begun to acknowledge the full flowering possibility of identity."

Faith in two languages

On a typical bright, cloudless day in the high desert of Carson City, Nevada, the sunlight streamed through the modern stained-glass windows of St. Teresa of Avila Catholic Church, where I had come to hear a bilingual Mass. Even though I was not a parishioner, and am not even Catholic, I marveled at what a welcoming place this church was.

Father Chuck Durante, the pastor, was celebrating the Mass. He raised his arms in welcome and began to speak—first in English and then in Spanish, offering greetings and blessings you could understand in both languages even if you thought you knew only one. Rather than translating, he was alternating— *Dios* and God, *Cristo* and Christ, *alma* and soul.

After the Mass, I went out into the large, airy vestibule and watched Father Chuck greet his parishioners. He looked to be in his fifties, and had a ready and sincere smile. He clearly knew his congregation and the language they spoke with more comfort. He would speak to some parents in English and their kids in Spanish, and then the other way around with other families. With the long greeting line and his various conversations with families, it was an hour before he could duck into the small conference room adjoining his office, where I had a chance to hear his language biography.

"I started Spanish in high school and was going to minor in Spanish in college, but we were supposed to read novels and it was too hard," he said. "Besides," he added, "it's hard to learn a language in class." But when he entered the seminary, "we were expected to learn Spanish because it's the fastest growing part of the Church. Without it, we would be older and shrinking."

When he came to St. Teresa's, Father Chuck noticed something among the Latino families. The parents were more comfortable in Spanish but the kids were more comfortable in English. "I want to encourage and invite the parents to learn English but also respect the language they pray in," he said. As for the children? "They understood their parents' Spanish, but answered in English. I tell them to answer their parents in Spanish, that it's important to keep it up."

I asked Father Chuck if people ever say he's encouraging Latinos not to learn English. "Yes, we have people who complain and say they should learn English, like our parents and grandparents." He told me he believes all Americans should learn English, but that they are also free to pray in whatever language they are comfortable with.

"I find the Spanish language beautiful, I love how it sounds," Father Chuck told me. But not until he began using the language in his work did his bilingual life really blossom. "There are some who say that Mass should be either in Spanish or English, that changing between the two interferes with the praying, but I don't see it that way," he said. And judging from what I had witnessed, neither do those who come here to worship.

Father Chuck found where his adopted language would live. His Spanish lives hand in hand with his English—within his own faith, and inside St. Teresa of Avila Church.

Part Two

How to Raise Children as Bilingual, Even if You're Not

*"What our children see in the world
depends on what we show them."*
—Rose K. Goldsen

Chapter 18

GIVING THE GIFT TO
OUR LOVED ONES

For the first half of the twentieth century in America, bilingualism was thought to be bad for children. In 1939, the same year the New York World's Fair debuted its City of Tomorrow and the first demonstration of television, an American psychologist named Madorah Smith published a study of bilingual children in Hawaii. She concluded that bilingualism caused a retardation of language development that could be counted in years compared with monolingual children. Her study presented lots of data. In fact, it was "a monument to quantification," according to the linguist Kenji Hakuta. The take-home message was that bilingualism in American children, whether arising from Native languages or immigrants' languages, was something like a medical ailment that needed to be cured by an inoculation of modern, monolingual, English-language education.

Not until 1962 did two Canadian researchers, Elizabeth Peal and Wallace Lambert of McGill University, challenge this view. They studied ten-year-old children in Montreal and, unlike prior studies, carefully controlled the selection of samples. Their results turned a half-century of studies upside down. The bilingual children outperformed the monolingual kids in verbal and nonverbal intelligence tests. It was a watershed moment. Lambert summed up the science that existed in the first half of the twentieth century: "Earlier studies over a 50-year period had concluded strongly in favor of monolinguals because, it turns out, they had not matched bilingual and monolingual groups on factors such as social class background. Nor had they measured the bilinguality of those presumed to be bilingual."

Bilingualism begets brainpower

Social science, like all science, progresses in a fitful, uneven manner toward becoming less wrong about the world. After Peal and Lambert, scientists around the world began careful studies trying to parse out cognitive differences that might exist between bilingual and monolingual children. They have continued to find advantages for bilinguals having to do with their thinking, creative abilities, and empathy. Also, scientists have found that being bilingual may help with the acquisition of additional languages. Any delay among bilingual children in learning one language over the other appears to be temporary, while their total vocabularies are greater than those of monolingual children.

At the other end of the age continuum, another Canadian research psychologist, Ellen Bialystok, has found mental health advantages in bilingual older adults. They appear to have an improved cognitive reserve, resulting in a later onset of the symptoms of Alzheimer's by approximately four years.

Adding to these mental health benefits are economic reports that show measurable benefits to bilinguals in landing jobs, earning more money, and advancing in their careers. Other studies show that these individual successes stack up to societal economic advantages as well. In the words of the polyglot author Gaston Dorren, "the benefits of bilingualism have in recent years been piling up like laundry."

Benefits that grow, just like kids

In the first part of this book, we looked at the array of new opportunities American adults are seizing to become bilingual themselves. In this second part, we'll turn our attention to how the gifts of bilingualism are being given to children and young adults. And for American children and young adults, there are even more opportunities—from the early years at home, to college and service years beyond.

Many of the successful practices American adults have seized upon are just as relevant for children, such as the importance of doing what you love in the language, and the *un*importance of correcting speech. And while it's never too late to begin learning a language, it's never too early, either. The earlier children emerge as bilinguals, the more years they have to benefit from the many blessings that being bilingual confers.

The magical first years

We were all sitting on the floor: Allison Altmann Kay and her fourteen-month-old baby girl, Charlotte; Charlotte's nanny, Isabel Perez, a native Spanish speaker; and me, with my audio recording equipment. Allie and I were speaking in English since I was interviewing her, while Isabel was cooing to Charlotte in Spanish. After a while, Isabel began to softly sing a Spanish lullaby to Charlotte, while Allie and I continued.

"I'd love Charlotte to be able to enter school knowing another language," said Allie, who is a novice speaker of Spanish herself. "The research I've read, it just seems like there's so many amazing advantages for her brain and for her life."

The person in the room best able to give little Charlotte this gift is Charlotte herself. While humans have known from time immemorial that children pick up languages fast, until recently we didn't know exactly how they do it. Is it that they learn language quickly from their parents and other caregivers? Or are babies born with something from which language somehow springs? After decades of research, we do finally know a few things. As the psycholinguist Steven Pinker puts it in *The Language Instinct,* "complex language is universal because *children actually reinvent it,* generation after generation—not because they are taught, not because they are generally smart, not because it is useful to them, but because they just can't help it."

And babies can perform this feat not only in one language, but in two or more, simultaneously. If parents build a bilingual languagescape for their children, the languages will come. If both parents speak a minority language, they can choose to speak that language exclusively at home. This is called, simply enough, minority language at home, or ML@H for short. If just one parent in a two-parent household speaks a minority language, that parent can choose to speak only that language to the children, a practice called One Person, One Language, or OPOL.

And yet . . . parenting is hard. Time is always short. Circumstances are rarely ideal. *Won't my child be better off if we all stick to one language?* Despite the science saying otherwise, and plenty of news accounts about the benefits of being bilingual, the seemingly common-sense approach of sticking to one language continues to prevail among millions in America, even among bilingual parents. And thus the road upon which American babies take their first steps on their bilingual journey is often strewn with obstacles.

If you speak it, share it

My polyglot friend Jack Roepers knew just how he would create the bilingual languagescape he wanted for his two baby boys. They lived in America, so he knew English would take care of itself. He would speak only his native Dutch to his sons.

"From the moment they saw their first daylight, I spoke Dutch to them," Jack told me. "Within about a year or two, I ended up translating about 75 percent into English, meaning I said things in Dutch that I wanted to say and then I translated most of it to make a connection." When his boys were five and three, "I dialed down the translation to about 50 percent. I was very, very determined to do this." Jack also provided plenty of cartoons and other videos in Dutch, and made sure the boys had plenty of time with their Dutch grandparents, who, to their delight, could use their native language with their grandsons.

Jack's boys, Cyrus and Philip, now adults, told me their version. "We thought it was Dad's secret language," said Cyrus—until their first trip to Holland. Said Philip, "We were riding in the train from the airport, and everybody was speaking Dad's secret language!"

Cyrus and Philip became so comfortable in Dutch that they elected to go to college in Rotterdam, and they added other languages to their skill sets later in their schooling. But their Dutch will be with them forever, thanks largely to the persistence of their father.

Jeane Forrest, the woman from the Philippines who first learned Tagalog in Manila and then English on her way to becoming an American citizen, told me that when her daughter, Amber, was little, "I tried to talk to her in Tagalog, and she was learning because I wanted her to learn," Jeane told me. "But then I stopped because I got scared that she might not learn English if I continued doing this." Jeane said that later, a pediatrician told her that speaking another language would not have confused Amber, but by then it was too late.

Both Jeane and Amber now regret the decision. When Amber was a teen, her mother took her back to the Philippines to visit relatives. Amber met her maternal grandmother for the first time. "She did not speak any English and I knew the bare minimum phrases like 'How are you? I love you. I miss you.' But that was the extent of our communication." I asked Amber how it made her feel.

"Not being able to learn from my grandmother, learn all her history, it just makes me feel like I am missing out on a part of me," she said.

Emerging from the shadows

Jeane's fear about speaking her heritage language to her daughter is, even today, so common that the authors of books on raising bilingual children address the concern. "There is no evidence that bilingual children differ from monolingual children except for the fact that they produce mixed utterances in addition to monolingual ones," writes Ofelia García, a scholar of bilingualism. "And young bilingual children know usually by the second year of life how to make the choice of whether to use one language or the other, or a mix of the two."

There is also little evidence, say the researchers Ng Bee Chin and Gillian Wigglesworth, that bilingual children acquire either of their languages more slowly than monolingual children, "despite having to cope with two different systems." But, the authors point out, the languages will mostly be used in different domains, with different people, in different situations, and thus the children "will be inherently unequal in knowledge and application" of their languages. This is another way of saying that balanced bilinguals are rare at any age.

Unfortunately, parents face widespread monolingual bias in America, say the scholars Kendall King and Alison Mackey. It's not surprising even today to find teachers, doctors, and other people in authority believing that raising children in more than one language can be detrimental. "Even though there is no sound research supporting these concerns, in many ways, we're still living in the shadow of these outdated notions," the authors write.

Three pieces of advice

In my reading of the guides for how to raise bilingual children, three central pieces of advice stand out: the volume of exposure children require, the need to give them good reasons for using their other language, and the importance of human interaction.

The volume of exposure that children require is a direct parallel to the many hours required for adults who learn a second language. Just how much exposure time does it take? Thirty percent of the child's waking time is a good number to shoot for, says Rita Rosenback, a multilingual mom who has raised two bilingual kids. "If you notice the real exposure time getting much less than 20%, try to find ways to boost it," she writes. Also bear in mind that once your children start school, you'll no longer have the control you have when they are very young. "Whenever possible, overdo the exposure to the minority language during the years before she goes to nursery or school," she advises.

Twenty percent of waking hours is a minimum, writes Barbara Zurer Pearson, an authority in applied linguistics, "and ideally more like 70%" is what she advises. If parents follow the 20 to 30 percent of their child's waking hours, by the age of four, the child will have amassed somewhere between 3,500 and 5,000 hours in the language—impressive numbers, even at the lower figure. And while babies are not studying the language with the diligence and experience of adults, their hearing is acute and their brains are wired for language learning. The combination can provide them the foundation, if the language is maintained, for achieving a native fluency and accent in their second language.

In Part One, we discussed the importance of *where* your adopted language will live in your life, the idea that after all the hows of learning a language, your long-term success as a bilingual will ultimately depend on what place or places you will use your adopted language. Likewise, for children, parents will want to be mindful to do things that their children enjoy in the target language—most important, play and other enjoyable activities with parents and others. Parents are also well served to take the focus off language learning per se, and put it on learning and doing other things in the language. As Adam Beck advises, "Don't teach; give joy."

Playing with other children who natively speak the language can be particularly helpful for language learning. "Apart from her parents, the bilingual child's most important 'teachers' are other small children," say Edith Harding-Esch and Philip Riley, the authors of a popular book on raising bilingual children. "Every effort should be made to ensure that regular contacts do take place."

Swap an app for a book

And while the technology for language learning keeps getting more and more compelling, Harding-Esch and Riley advise not to lean too heavily on it. Use media in moderation, advises Beck. What's much more important is reading aloud to your children in the second language, which he advises as a daily practice. Since children can normally understand at a higher level than they can read themselves, reading aloud can entice them for years after they begin school.

Use the technology, say King and Mackey, but know that it "cannot substitute for a real person and real interaction."

As with adults, it's best not to correct children. "Although many people, especially teachers, have great difficulty believing it, there is no evidence that correcting helps people to learn," write Harding-Esch and Riley. Instead, you can model correct speech occasionally by responding with a continuation of the conversation, but with correct grammar.

When the going gets tough, as it certainly will at times, Beck advises to keep in mind that your child will thank you later in life, as everyone who is bilingual enjoys it so deeply. And yes, monolinguals can raise bilingual children. It helps if the parents are also learning with their children. Write King and Mackey, "Even parents who know just a little of the second language can incorporate it into silly songs, games, and other intimate routines."

Allie Altmann Kay, with the help of her own growing bilingualism, her native-speaking caretaker, and her baby Charlotte, can give the gift of bilingualism to Charlotte. Sitting on the floor with the three of them, I could hear bilingualism happening in real time. Imagining the larger life Charlotte could have as a bilingual, Allie said, "I'd love her to have that."

Chapter 19

WHAT THE DEAF CAN TEACH US

It was 1970, on the weekend before a young American soldier was to ship off to Vietnam. He was already away from his Alaskan home and faced the prospect of spending his last weekend alone. But a group of people his age invited him to spend the weekend with them. "This was in Houston, and they were having their fifth reunion, from a high school for the Deaf."

The weekend made a deep impression on him. "I promised myself if I ever survived the military, I was going to learn sign language so I could communicate with a deaf person, if I ever met one again."

That soldier was Joseph Garcia, and he did survive. He returned home and entered graduate school in psychology at the University of Alaska. He had been trying to decide what to do for his doctoral thesis, and, true to his promise, he had been studying sign language. For recreation, he trained in a sport Alaska is famous for.

"I was out running my dog sled team on the Iditarod Trail one night and working hard and sweating. My father said never trust an idea that comes when you're sitting down." That's when it came to him. "Why don't I prove to the hearing world that babies can sign clearly a year before they can talk?"

Joseph Garcia became one of a handful of pioneers using sign language as a way to help hearing babies communicate before they can speak.

Language before speech

Before they can speak, babies cry. Parents and other caregivers try to figure out what's wrong. Is their baby hungry? Does something hurt? Is their diaper soiled? Are they just tired? Imagine if the babies, before uttering their first "mama" or "papa," could actually communicate their needs or feelings with language—what suffering that could end, what joy that could bring.

Fast forward to 2017, when those possibilities intrigued a young Spanish teacher named Viviana Sisniegas. Viviana had a newborn son, Luis. Her sister had heard about using sign language with infants. So Viviana found an instructional video about American Sign Language, or ASL, and decided that both she and Luis would learn.

But Luis didn't respond to the signs his mother started using for objects like his milk bottle. "I was thinking, 'What am I doing? He doesn't have any idea what we are talking about.'" She was ready to give up.

A few days later, though, things changed. "Luis was putting his little fingers together and making the sign for milk." Viviana teared up, remembering the scene. "I get emotional just remembering, you know, that feeling. I could *talk* with my son."

Luis was barely four months.

An unspeakably beautiful gift

Working within the Deaf community, Joseph noticed something among the hearing children of deaf adults. The parents signed to them, and the kids learned ASL as their native language. Once they began talking, "the children who signed quite early had better language skills than their typically developing peers." He suspected it was because these kids had a head start—"they had language a year before they actually uttered their first clear, articulate word."

Joseph applied his theories with his own sons. "My kids had seventy to eighty signs before they could articulate their first word," he told me. Unlike spoken language, sign language is physical. "When you put a muscle memory, a tactile element to it, you find that young children tend to understand it clearer and better," Joseph said. Once children associate a few signs with objects and what's going on around them, something beautiful happens. "They're not riding the roller coaster of life anymore, completely out of control. Instead, they're influencing their environment with their own internal resources by problem-solving," Joseph explained. "They get the response they want, and that reinforces it to the point where they want to learn more."

This, in turn, encourages the parents as well. "Not only does it reduce the frustration in the child because they can affect their environment, but it also gives the parent the confidence to really go ahead and initiate and do more with their children." As with Viviana, Joseph experienced an emotional high with his first son, when the little boy made a particular sign.

"You take your two fists and you cross them on your chest and you squeeze your body back and forth a little bit like you're hugging yourself." That's how Joseph described for me the sign for love.

"I had never seen him make that sign before," Joseph told me, emotion rising in his voice as he recalled the moment. "He looked up and just gave me those big eyes and did the sign for love, and it just . . . I just melted."

The difficulty that young deaf children face

To find out what the Deaf community thinks of Joseph Garcia and others who advise hearing parents to use sign language with their hearing babies, we reached out to Gallaudet University, in Washington, DC. It is America's foremost teaching and research institution for the Deaf. President Lincoln signed its charter.

Deborah Chen-Pichler, a hearing faculty member and linguist, has two young hearing children who are growing up in a multilingual environment. She and her husband are teaching them their heritage languages. The kids learn Taiwanese from their mother and Croatian from their father. The children are, of course, also learning English, since they are growing up in America. And then there is ASL, which Debbie is fluent in.

Debbie used ASL with her children before they could speak any of their other languages; it worked. She also taught her Croatian-speaking mother-in-law some signs in ASL that her son knew. His grandmother then used the signs while speaking in Croatian to her grandson. The result surprised even Debbie.

"He just sort of fast-mapped all these words," she said, so grandson and grandmother began communicating with ASL. "It was like a ready-made vocabulary," Debbie said. "It was incredible. As a linguist, I have to admit I was not expecting it to be that fast."

Today there are plenty of books and videos to help hearing parents learn ASL with their babies. Debbie approves of parents using ASL to communicate with their hearing children, "with two caveats. They need to be learning from a reputable instructor, and it should be an instructor that has some ties to the Deaf community."

Debbie and other professionals who engage with the Deaf community are concerned that hearing parents will use ASL only as a nice enrichment tool, without understanding two things people in the Deaf community consider fundamental. The first is that ASL and other sign languages are in no way inferior to spoken languages.

It's not just those in the Deaf community who will tell you this. The linguist Stephen Anderson writes, "Signed languages are fully expressive, natural systems of communication, and they can be deployed for all of the purposes (with all of the precision and communicative content) of spoken languages." While we hearing people tend to equate speech with language, oral communication is only the most common mode the language takes. Says Anderson, "It is clear that speech and signing are simply two different modalities in which the human capacity for language can be expressed."

"I cry every time I watch the Star-Spangled Banner," says Debbie, referring to how Gallaudet's deaf students present the National Anthem. "You're looking at poetry, and it's amazingly expressive."

The second thing we hearing people need to know is that deaf children are often deprived of ASL during their critical first years of life, and it can be a lasting problem for them. It happens because 90 to 95 percent of deaf children are born to hearing parents, and our society suffers from a mistaken belief that an oral language is better than a physical one. As a result, most of us are unaware of how important early exposure to ASL is for American deaf babies.

This is an instance when not being bilingual from a very early age (ASL plus English) is more than just a disadvantage; it becomes a serious detriment to how deaf children learn and function as adults.

Unfortunately, says Debbie, "We don't have a system in place where deaf children are automatically given sign language."

Tawny Holmes Hlibok, an education advocate with the National Association of the Deaf, told us why this often happens. She wrote, "The trend has been for states and local school districts to place deaf and hard-of-hearing students in public schools with little to no support or access in sign language."

More often than not, Debbie says, deaf children "have had to demonstrate that they can't succeed in the educational system before they're allowed to sign." The reality, she says, is that "bilingual deaf education is still a dream that we are trying to make happen."

A silent window to the world

The good news is that today, ASL is the third most studied language in American colleges, following Spanish and French.

An example of a young hearing American who has set out on a career of teaching ASL is Sierra Weiner. She took ASL in high school, fell in love with it, and majored in it in college. "Most hearing people don't understand that there is a Deaf community and a Deaf culture that surrounds these people," she says. Being deaf is not a condition that needs to be fixed, but rather, being part of a culture that is proud of the unique beauty of its language. Adds Sierra, "there is so much more than just this hearing world that we live in."

A few years after Viviana taught her son Luis some signs, the two of them were in a park, and Viviana was using ASL to communicate with Luis across the other side of the park—happy she didn't have to yell. Then she realized that "there were kids there that were actually deaf." The mother of one of the deaf children came over to Viviana. "The mom thought that I was able to communicate completely and I told her no, sorry."

But the mom gave her a big smile. "The mom got so happy to know that my child was able to communicate and play with her son," Viviana said. "Language, it definitely opens windows—I mean, the whole world."

Chapter 20

STUDENTS LEARNING IN TWO LANGUAGES: GATHERING STRENGTH

Amidst the exodus of Cubans to America in the wake of Fidel Castro's revolution were youngsters whose parents feared their children would be seized by the Cuban government and sent away for Castro reeducation. That led to daring efforts on the Cuban side by a network of underground operatives, including a British schoolteacher named Penny Powers who fudged the paperwork and secured airline tickets for the youngsters. Helping on the US side was Father Bryan Walsh of the Catholic Welfare Bureau. Between 1961 and 1965, on two afternoon flights per day, more than fourteen thousand children landed in America in what came to be known as Operation Pedro Pan.

The asylum-seeking children, and the parents who were able to later follow them, were welcomed to the US during the heart of the Cold War, with the US providing temporary financial support. The assumption was that Castro's regime would soon topple and they would be able to return to Cuba.

But what to do in the meantime with the thousands of Spanish-speaking schoolchildren?

What materialized was an unprecedented alignment of circumstances and people: an America keen to show the superiority of the American way of life in contrast to communism, as well as compassion for the kids—surely they would need their Spanish when they returned to Cuba, and we'd give them English, too, of course. And yes, it would be good for the Cuban kids to make friends with American kids, who would help them learn English, and while we're at it, why not power up the American kids with Spanish, too?

An elementary school in the Coral Way neighborhood of Miami was chosen as the testing ground of this experiment. The Ford Foundation funded much of it, as the idea aligned with the foundation's goal of fostering world language study and preparing young Americans for living in a wider world. Local taxpayers paid for some of the program, too.

The school's goals were for the American kids to achieve at the same levels in English as their peers educated only in English. But in addition, both Cuban and American children would learn to "operate in either culture easily and comfortably," and be "more acceptive of strange people and cultures." This, in turn, would lead to more job opportunities.

A happy coincidence was the Jewish community surrounding the Coral Way school. These Jewish neighbors of the newly arrived Cubans were comfortable with bilingualism. Many of them spoke Yiddish at home and Hebrew at the local Beth David synagogue. Nor were they strangers to displacement and persecution. The Cuban families found themselves in a pocket of America in which bilingualism was valued and could flourish.

A bridge too soon

The Coral Way school succeeded by all measures. The American kids did at least as well in English as their monolingually educated peers; the Cuban kids learned English, while improving their Spanish; and the American kids acquired levels of Spanish only dreamed of by teachers of conventional Spanish classes. Coral Way was ready to serve as a model for America. The problem was, America wasn't ready for the model of Coral Way.

The work of Peal and Lambert up in Canada, which suggested there were advantages for children being raised bilingually, had not yet emerged from academia into mainstream culture. Besides, the Cuban influx into Miami was a wild aberration in American immigration of the era. In the 1960s, America was near what would be its low point for immigrants, as a percent of our population. Our immigration laws hadn't been modified since the tight quotas set in the 1920s. That would change, however, in 1965, the final year of Operation Pedro Pan.

The third wave arrives

In the 1960s, the US economy was growing, President Kennedy was inspiring the first members of his Peace Corps, our Gemini and Apollo projects were space-walking their way to sending a man to the moon, and the Mustang was turning heads on American highways. Twenty years after its triumph in World War II, America was continuing to step up to what it considered its global responsibilities.

Americans saw how the second- and third-generation children of immigrants who had arrived at the turn of the twentieth century were now contributing to our nation in every way. Our old laws that limited immigrants to fixed percentages of those nationalities already here began to feel out of touch with the modern world. In 1965 Congress passed, by wide margins, the Immigration and Nationality Act, abolishing national-origin quotas and removing all reference to race.

The law went into effect in 1968, and slowly the complexion of America changed. By the 1980s and '90s, only 13 percent of immigrants came from Europe, while 82 percent came from Asia and Latin America. The top countries for emigrants were, from most to fewest, Mexico, the Philippines, Vietnam, China, Taiwan, Dominican Republic, Korea, India, the former USSR, Jamaica, and Iran. By the 1990s, 60 percent of America's population growth came from immigrants. In the last quarter of the twentieth century, America was surfing its third great wave of immigration. While somewhat smaller in terms of percentage to the overall population than the second wave of the 1890s to 1915, this third wave was historically high in absolute numbers. It also was far more representative of the world's people as a whole.

As with prior waves of immigration, the reception was mixed. Immigrants were seen as a welcome boost to the economy, but there was also the usual worry about them taking jobs, reducing wages, being slow to learn English, and harboring loyalties to wherever they came from.

While the third wave of American immigrants followed the established pattern of settling in the major cities, they also settled elsewhere as they searched for jobs, safe neighborhoods, and good schools for their children. As part of this wider settlement pattern, Mexicans began showing up outside of their traditional neighborhoods in the American Southwest. Fatefully, many ventured north, to Utah.

'Life Elevated': Utah's motto takes on a dual meaning

I spoke with Gregg Roberts, who at the time was the dual language immersion guru for the Utah State Board of Education.

"We had a very enlightened governor, Jon Huntsman, back in 2008, and we had a superstar state senator, Howard Stephenson, and they really wanted to start looking at language policy in Utah," Gregg told me. "Huntsman spoke

Chinese and Stephenson visited China on multiple occasions." Senator Stephenson was deeply impressed by the mature, bilingual Chinese students he met there.

Utah's education board considered the Spanish that the newly arrived Mexicans spoke as a resource to be developed. It was part of a bigger goal to help the children of Utah become bilingual—not just in Spanish but in other world languages as well, most especially Chinese and Arabic, with an eye toward economic competitiveness.

"They said, 'if we're truly serious about proficiency, we need to start young, maybe start a dual language immersion program,'" Gregg recounted. Chinese and Spanish were the first two languages to be mentioned. "And then, since I'm a former French teacher, I interjected that we must do French, and that's how it started, in 2009, with twenty-five schools," Gregg said.

Jon Huntsman, who is a member of the Church of Jesus Christ of Latter-day Saints, learned his Chinese early, living with his family in Taiwan as a young adult. He is also an unusual public servant. Although a Republican, he has served as an ambassador to Singapore, China, and Russia under both Republican and Democratic presidents.

I had a chance to ask the former governor about his vision for bilingual education in Utah. He explained that you can't understand China in any depth, and certainly not the nuances of Chinese politics, without understanding the language. He thought it was appropriate to spend public funds to build language skills. "I know it sounds like a very un-Republican thing to do," he said, "but we actually, through state-appropriated money, built some serious muscle around internationally important languages like Mandarin Chinese, like Spanish, like French, and an Arabic program."

Huntsman sees the interests of the state, the country, and the kids all aligned. "From a job acquisition standpoint, from an understanding-the-world-better standpoint, from a confidence standpoint, it's a *huge* gift that we're giving these kids, and I think they'll benefit enormously from it."

Later I caught up with Howard Stephenson at the 2018 ACTFL language teacher conference in New Orleans and was able to interview him at some length. He told me that Utah leads the country in the number of students in dual language immersion schools. "We have forty-three thousand students this year and we're growing by as many as twenty-five schools per year."

In most of America, Howard told me, kids struggle to pass the Advanced Placement, or AP, test in languages when they are high school seniors, but Utah students who have been in dual language classes pass it easily as freshmen. They go on to take college credit courses while still in high school. By the time they enter college, they are very close to already having a minor in the language.

When they were building the program, some people, including himself, worried that the kids wouldn't be as strong in English or in math and science due to splitting their classes between English and another language. "Just the opposite has happened," Howard said, clearly delighted. "These students outscore their monolingual peers in every subject. It seems that their brains are on fire."

But in what became a recurring theme I heard when interviewing leaders about dual language schools, Howard added, "We're always oversubscribed. That breaks my heart. We're not growing fast enough. I would like, someday, for at least half of our students in Utah to be in dual language immersion programs. I think it's very doable."

I asked Howard about the role that Governor Huntsman played. "He gave us immense encouragement and he signed the bill and helped us get it funded and made sure it was done with fidelity." Howard also said that the governor's Chinese was important diplomatically. "Whenever I brought a Chinese group to meet with him, he would immediately start speaking Mandarin to them, and they would always interrupt him with a standing ovation."

Howard told me it's up to the states to build the linguistic capital of America. "We need to start planting the seeds in kindergarten and first grade and be patient and grow the crop." Today Howard goes around the nation speaking to people in other states to help them do what Utah has done.

The Utah model

"We've had thirty-five states, at least, come here for visits, and probably ten foreign countries," Gregg told me. "We believe in collaboration, we believe in helping everyone. We don't want to keep this as a guarded secret just for Utah." Delaware has modeled its dual language program after Utah's. "We assisted them in every way and now they are nipping at our heels," Gregg said with a laugh. "There's no desire to keep our secret sauce. We want to evangelize the nation."

Gregg told me he sees Mexican and Anglo parents working together as volunteers in the schools, something he hadn't seen before. "Racism is something you learn, not something you're born with. These programs can go a long way to help."

But, I wondered, is Utah's program propelled by religion?

"That question has been asked to me so many times," said Gregg. If religion were the driver for Utah's push for bilingualism, he said, "it would have been started a hundred years ago, which it was not." It's economics that's driving the bus, he said.

"I was born and raised in Salt Lake City, and I'm not Mormon," Gregg continued. "Salt Lake City is only about 30 percent Mormon, but we have a high percentage of Mormons in the state overall, 65 to 70 percent. It's a very receptive audience because LDS [Latter-day Saints] people, or Mormons, go on their missions all over the world. They understand that language and culture are very, very important."

The fact that overall academic achievement and bilingualism walk together has made the programs very appealing to Utah parents, so much so that demand has outstripped supply, even with the steady growth in new dual language schools. Part of the problem is finding enough qualified teachers.

To address that, Gregg said that "Utah's taken a very aggressive kind of role to recruit internationally. We recruit teachers from China, Taiwan, Mexico, Peru, Spain, Brazil, France, Germany." And they are not relying just on imports, either. "We're also growing our own teachers within our own universities, and we have a very aggressive alternative route to certification for native speakers who might already live in the state and would like to become educators."

What helps the dual language schools expand in Utah is that they are not a political issue, according to Gregg. "In Utah, languages really become, as we would say, a purple issue. It's not a Democratic issue. It's not a Republican issue. The entire state legislature and the governor worked together for the benefit of Utah students.

For a few dollars more

And it hasn't broken the bank. Gregg said that the Utah model adds just one hundred dollars per student each year to the cost of educating them. The additional money is mainly to support curriculum development, professional development for the teachers, and the testing in the partner language. Those nominal additional costs have not hindered Utah from being ranked as the top state in America in terms of economic competitiveness. "It doesn't cost much to change kids' lives," Gregg said.

Gregg has moved to a national position as the director of dual language studies at the American Councils for International Education, where he is focusing on gathering the research on dual language schools and on best practices for implementing them in all states. Gregg predicts that within two decades, dual language education will be the rule rather than the exception. "I think dual language is a game changer for the United States and for our American students."

A Moses for multilingualism

It was in Albuquerque that I began to get a sense of how big dual language education has already become in America, yet how little national attention it seems to be getting. David Rogers, the executive director of Dual Language Education of New Mexico, was kind enough to issue me the one and only press pass to attend the twenty-second annual conference for dual language educators in 2017. Called La Cosecha (The Harvest), it set a new attendance record that year, with two thousand educators. When I arrived, David introduced me to one of the keynote speakers, Jim Lyons.

The silver-haired Jim Lyons looks like the senior statesman he is. Trained as an attorney, he is the former executive director of the National Association for Bilingual Education. When he stood before the packed auditorium to deliver his speech, I could feel the audience's appreciation for him. Afterwards, when I sat down with Jim, I began by asking him why American children should learn a second language.

"People say we should learn other languages so that we can be better competitors. Yes, but there is something even more important and fundamental: you can be better *collaborators*." Future generations, he said, would need to resolve issues on an international stage that relied on global cooperation. "Until you understand someone, you can't really be a good collaborator," Jim said.

He then told me about a success factor of dual language education that surprises most parents. "What we find is that a program that for some part of the day uses the language the child brings to school produces better results in terms of English language acquisition than a program that doesn't." This runs contrary to what we've seen in Middlebury's and other language programs— that the best way to learn another language is total immersion. This is not the case with immigrant children; they perform better if some of what they are taught every day is in their heritage language.

"On its surface, it *is* counterintuitive," Jim acknowledged. "But that's how it works. The mind is a beautiful machine that puts it all together."

I decided to play devil's advocate and challenge him with a scenario. "If I'm an Anglo parent and I have English-speaking children who go off to a dual language school, isn't that going to hurt their English skills compared with the Anglo kids who go to an all-English school?"

"No," Jim replied, "it will enhance their English skills. Once one has experienced instruction in multiple languages—what is called metacognition, the big picture, if you will—our understanding of language grows and is heightened. It's such an opportunity!"

In the course of our conversations at the conference, Jim let me know that he was monolingual. Surprised, I asked him why he was so passionate about bilingualism in America. He said simply, "Because it's the hope of the future."

Los Angeles sets a date of 2032

David Rogers said I should also interview Kris Nicholls, whose dual language work in California is part of an effort that could impact millions of kids. I found her presentation and sat in the back. It was a working session with fifty or so teachers sitting at round tables. After her session, we sat down at one of the tables so I could record her. I asked her why she was so passionate about bilingualism.

"I was a re-entry student," she explained. "I guess that's a polite word for saying that by the time I went back to school, I had four kids and knew that I needed to get a job. With four kids and my husband being a high school teacher, it didn't always mean that you had the money you needed. My son is six-foot-eight and wears a size sixteen shoe. You can't buy those at Walmart. So we needed some extra funds."

Kris went back to get her teaching credentials ... but there was a problem. "All the jobs I was qualified for said 'Bilingual Preferred.' I'd taken four years of Spanish in high school, but as soon as they said 'we're going to start talking in Spanish,' I was out of there."

So Kris returned to studying Spanish, not knowing if she could get good enough. "But along the way I fell in love with the language and realized I hadn't forgotten everything."

Kris earned her master's and then her doctorate. She taught for a while, then moved into administration and saw something that surprised her: the high test scores for kids in dual language education. That led her to take on a bigger role, where she now aids bilingual teachers in their own professional development.

Dual language in California is big today "and growing, potentially exponentially," Kris told me. "Originally the dual programs were really to meet the needs of the English learners with regard to higher levels of literacy and

English, as well as higher levels of academic achievement. But along the way, as we gathered the data, we found that it was very beneficial for the other students in the program."

I asked her if she meant Anglo kids.

"Yes, for the students that were English dominant, or English only. They had great benefits not only in their literacy and English but also their levels of literacy in the target language."

The results got the attention of the superintendent of the Los Angeles Unified School District (LAUSD), Michelle King. "The superintendent declared publicly that by 2032, all students in LAUSD would have the opportunity to become bilingual by the time they graduate in 2032," Nicholls said. The LA school district had more than six hundred thousand students in 2017—second in size only to New York City.

Kris told me that her own journey to become bilingual, and all the blessings that came with it, inspired her to give the gift to others. I asked her what advice she had for parents. She said, "Be an advocate for your child to have this opportunity."

Making dual language affordable—for teachers

I next sat down with a school principal, Suzanne Wheeler Del Piccolo, who told me: "I think our community came to really understand that we were a dual language community, and being bilingual, biliterate was an asset to the work world. Both Anglo and Latino families saw that as an asset."

Suzanne is the principal at Basalt Elementary School in Basalt, Colorado, about twenty-five miles north of Aspen—or down valley from Aspen, as the locals say it. "About ten years ago, we started to see the trajectory just go straight off the charts. We had *so* many families wanting dual language education."

She has more demand than she can supply. "That has been an ongoing challenge." As with Utah, her school could not find enough American teachers, so she has brought in teachers from Central and South America. It's not easy, she said, getting them the requisite visas and navigating the federal legislation.

"We're always looking for teachers who were trained in the United States," she explained, "but we're not bringing students into the colleges to fill the teacher positions."

If recruiting teachers is hard, finding them affordable housing turned out to be even more challenging in an expensive area so near to hyper-priced Aspen. The solution was a $15 million bond issue to build affordable housing. It's allowed teachers to save between $500 and $1,000 a month.

"I'll never forget the day when they all moved into housing, and it's close to our school. It's beautiful housing," Suzanne told me. "If our children are well educated in schools they all feel they are part of and belong to, I have great hope for this country," she said. "That's why I've been such an advocate for dual language all these years."

'Learning that is transformative'

I sensed that all over the La Cosecha conference, attendees were passionate about giving students not only the chance to be bilingual, but also to benefit from the expanded outlook that they believe bilingualism can bring. Nowhere was this idea more clear than in a moving keynote address by another respected veteran in the field named Tony Báez.

Tony has been a teacher and administrator, a professor and a dean—and, at the time of the conference, was several months into his directorship of the Milwaukee school board. "Dual language can help us bring people together and have a learning that is transformative, in that it creates a next generation of kids that are bilingual, bicultural, but also better human beings," he told me.

He explained that dual language education started as a grassroots movement, which was key. Educators are spreading the word, and school districts and states are starting to listen, including his own state of Wisconsin.

"I managed to work with a group of people to get the school board to pass unanimously a resolution for bilingualism in Milwaukee," he said. "We need to grow the idea of dual language to the point that everybody in this country accepts the notion that bilingualism is good for everybody."

Later at La Cosecha, I squeezed into a large ballroom overflowing with people. A young, energetic man was on stage, moving fast, telling jokes, and asking questions. He was José Medina, the director of dual language and bilingual education at the Center for Applied Linguistics in Washington, DC.

José had his audience of hundreds of teachers laughing, clapping, and paying rapt attention . . . even though he put people on the spot. "I like to make people feel uncomfortable," he told the audience.

When I was able to interview him after his presentation, I asked him why. He sat back and took a deep breath.

"I am an English learner. My parents are from Chihuahua, Mexico. My mom has a sixth-grade education from Ciudad Juarez, my father a fifth-grade education. And so whenever I'm out in the field serving, whether as a researcher or a practitioner, I know that what I'm doing is impacting students, and I cannot provide that support if the teachers and administrators and district leaders that I am providing that support for don't feel that discomfort. Because only when we're uncomfortable do we actually grow."

For José, it's not enough that dual language teachers be good educators. "We also need to embrace our role as defenders of equity and social justice."

I asked José if he thinks all schools should be dual language. "Absolutely. I think that any time you provide any student the opportunity to function in a global society, to see each other's similarities and differences, but to view those differences as opportunities to connect rather than obstacles to overcome, how would you say no to *that*?"

North Carolina's leadership triangle

As we were putting together our *America the Bilingual* podcast episodes on dual language schools, our associate producer Beckie Rankin, a high school French teacher and ACTFL member, told me we *had* to report on North Carolina. "That's where you'll see the future of American language education," she claimed. I got a glimpse of that in the numbers. In 2005, the state had seven dual language schools; in 2018, there were 140.

To understand the explosive growth, Tricia Willoughby told me, you had to go back to the 1950s. Tricia's titles included State Board Member at Large, member of the State Board of Education Global Education Task Force, and co-chair of the SBE Special Committee on Global Education. She was one of four language educators I interviewed. The others were Ivanna Anderson, ESL Consultant; Helga Fasciano, Special Assistant for Global Education; and Ann Marie Gunter, World Languages Consultant. Helga greeted me inside the cavernous marble-lined lobby of the state education building in Raleigh and brought me up to a boardroom to meet the other women.

Back in the '50s, Tricia told me, "then-governor Luther Hodges and his team went out to a place about ten miles from here. Then it was a bunch of tobacco fields and uninhabited space. They said, 'We could rise with the next century if we are prepared.'" That place today is known as Research Triangle Park, one of America's largest and most successful tech hubs, anchored by three universities.

"People don't really understand how we got here," said Helga, referring to North Carolina's dual language program. "They think things just fell from the sky." It was more of a groundswell. Advocates brought together a leadership triangle—leaders from state government, the state universities, and international businesses—to collaborate on a statewide program. Then they let all 115 school districts in the state decide on the languages they would offer.

Dual language schools were how North Carolina would find the best way forward to deal with its influx of immigrants—both from other countries and from elsewhere in America. Also, a growing number of university graduates wanted to stay in North Carolina, and more knowledge workers were considering moving to North Carolina as well. A common requirement for all groups: great schools.

The panel members told me about one principal they said was representative of the North Carolina approach. When she saw that her school was going to be flooded with kids who didn't speak English natively, instead of seeing it as a challenge, she said, "Look at the opportunity I have!" So she created a dual language immersion school. "The children learn one day in Spanish and one day in English," the panel told me. "By the end of fifth grade, everyone's bilingual. We have principals who call this the two-for-one deal."

With North Carolina's growing reputation for dual language schools, principals now get calls from parents who *might* move to North Carolina "*if* they can get their children into a dual language school," the panel said. Like everywhere else, it seems, demand outstrips supply.

The panel members then showed me a video of the two valedictorians who had recently graduated from the Jordan-Matthews High School in Siler City, about fifty miles west of Raleigh. "I still remember going to Siler City Elementary and actually meeting those students when they first started the program—when they were in kindergarten," said Ivanna. In the video, Jonathan Aguilar, a native Spanish speaker, and Olivia Gregson, a native English speaker, deliver a joint address at their 2018 graduation—Jonathan in English and Olivia in Spanish. Said Ivanna, "When you look at two people standing at the podium together with such completely diverse backgrounds, and yet they made this choice to travel this road together—it was the dream that has now been realized."

At Wake Forest University, I interviewed Ken Stewart, an ACTFL teacher of the year and now a teacher of other language teachers, together with Mary Lynn Redmond, who retired from the university after teaching a new generation of language teachers. (Beckie was one of her students.)

Ken told me, "I grew up not far from here, near one of the furniture factories in Thomasville. I remember my own father telling me thirty years ago, 'You'll never get a job in Spanish.' Well, I pretty much got my pick of jobs." The furniture factory, he said, is now closed.

Today, the attitude about bilingualism is different, he said. "Parents realize that it's a life skill that they want their kid to have; it's not just a luxury." The earlier we start, the better. "We can see cognitive benefits in addition to linguistic benefits, the capacity to think critically and be better problem solvers, to see the world through a different lens and have multiple perspectives."

As in other states, a challenge is getting enough bilingual teachers. Mary Lynn described an initiative in North Carolina called Project CAFE, which stands for Calling All Future Educators. The goal is to find college students who would make good teachers and tap them early. "If we can identify potential teachers, we can build this pipeline," she said.

Cherokee rising

When I met with Ann Marie Gunter and her colleagues, she told me something I wasn't expecting to hear. Among the languages the state supports in dual language programs is Cherokee.

"There are, of course, other Native American languages that have been lost, and there was a time that they thought Cherokee would be as well," Ann Marie explained. "But the Eastern Band of the Cherokee Indians have purchased their land back from the [US] government and have worked very hard to take their profits and their proceeds and reinvest that in their children—to help revitalize Cherokee." She then arranged for me to visit the Cherokee school.

The town of Cherokee is a five-hour drive due west from Raleigh, inside the Eastern Cherokee Reservation. Entering town, I drove past Harrah's Cherokee Casino Resort and the Museum of the Cherokee Indian. From there, 441 swings north for a few miles, where you pass a few tubing outfitters hugging the Oconaluftee River, before arriving at the New Kituwah Academy, the school for Cherokee.

The school spread out on a hill above me as I parked. I learned later that the building is a complete redo of a 1940s-era motel. Today it has lots of stone and wood, and the outdoors seems to come inside in the form of a creek that runs through the building. I felt like I was in an upscale eco-lodge, except for a sign over the entrance that proclaimed, "English Stops Here."

As luck would have it, I arrived on the day when teachers were visiting from the Cherokee Nation in Oklahoma for professional development with colleagues from the Nation's Eastern Band. My contact was Hartwell Francis (not a Native), who had the title of Education Curriculum Developer. He led me to his office, speaking in Cherokee to the various people we passed, then closed the door to tell me something. "The Cherokee are very collaborative," he explained, "and that's how they like to make decisions. It's best if you address everyone and let them know what you want."

He led me to the auditorium where some fifty Cherokee teachers were listening to someone who was standing on a low stage. Hartwell waited to be recognized, at which point he explained to the group who I was, and then gestured for me to step up on the stage. The person who had been speaking handed me the microphone.

This all happened so fast, I didn't have time to collect my thoughts, but I explained I was traveling around the country reporting on bilingualism in America. I was very interested in what they were doing with Cherokee. If possible, I would like to interview some of them on tape for an upcoming episode of the *America the Bilingual* podcast, and perhaps gain some material for the book I was writing.

What happened next surprised me, despite Hartwell's warning. After conferring among themselves, they agreed to let me interview some teachers—in front of them all. I'm used to interviewing people one-on-one, usually in a small quiet room. Suddenly I was unloading my backpack and preparing to record my interviews before a live audience.

My first interview was with Kathy Sierra, one of the teachers from Oklahoma. In addition to teaching Cherokee, Kathy is a director of the Cherokee National Youth Choir in Oklahoma.

"I'm Cherokee," she said. Her voice quavered, not from nervousness, but from something else—a long-held wound. "I just wanted my children to know, my grandchildren, because if I had known when I was raising my children what we was going to go through now, I would have taught them the Cherokee language. But you know," she said, crying softly, "we lived in an English world. Cherokee was not important. But it is."

The "English world" that Kathy grew up in was one where, until late in the twentieth century, the US government prohibited Cherokee from being spoken in schools.

My next interview was with Sara Snyder, who directs the Cherokee language program at Western Carolina University. "I'm not a Native person, but I'm a community friend and advocate for the Cherokee language," she explained. "Cherokee language is American culture, and it's Native American culture. It's a part of all of us who live here on this continent. It's a part of all of our story, and to know that is to know who we are, even as non-Native people."

After a few more public interviews, the group decided it was time to take a break. Hartwell indicated that it was now okay to do some more interviews privately, and he took me to meet Renissa McLaughlin.

Renissa is the director of Youth and Adult Education for the Eastern Band of the Cherokee Indians in North Carolina. She also has a Cherokee name, which I pronounced "Toed-ZOO-wa," and which means Red Bird. From Renissa I learned that the New Kituwah Academy is running in a race against time. In 2004, there were about five hundred Native speakers still alive in North Carolina. Today, she said, there are fewer than two hundred.

"There's no one that is a first-language Cherokee speaker that is in child-bearing age," Renissa told me. "So none of the parents here, myself included, have Cherokee as their first language." As a consequence, the Cherokee that the children are learning is different from what their elders speak.

Kathy Sierra told me that, when her mother heard the young school kids speak Cherokee, she said, "'That's not how you speak Cherokee.' And I said, 'Mom, it *is* Cherokee; it's a *learned* Cherokee.' It's not a fluent flowing language once it's *learned*."

If Cherokee is to be saved, it's up to the current crop of children. Renissa said her own son speaks Cherokee much better than she does. "I'm envious, but I would have to be really selfish if I were anything but happy about it." She told me how an elder, hearing her son speak, became emotional. "He said, 'That's the first time I've heard a child speak Cherokee in fifty years.'"

I cautioned Renissa that I would ask her some stupid, possibly even insulting questions, then plowed ahead. "Why should kids become bilingual in Cherokee when they could become bilingual in Mandarin Chinese, or Spanish, or French? Wouldn't that be more useful?"

Her answer was swift and emphatic. "That's not who we are. I'm not Mandarin Chinese. I'm not Spanish. I'm not French. I'm a Cherokee person. Why wouldn't I want to learn my heritage language? Our children should have the ability to learn our heritage language. It is an inherent right."

Hartwell, who was in my interview with Renissa, added that there are many Canadian studies that show the positive effects of First Nation Indigenous peoples learning their heritage language—including lower suicide rates and higher school completion rates. He said, "You don't have to express your identity in a negative way by rejecting the school system because 'I'm a Cherokee person and I'm not going to go through that white-man schooling system.' You can succeed academically."

I then learned that Renissa's mother, Myrtle Driver, wrote a Cherokee translation of *Charlotte's Web* by E.B. White. She was able to do so because Cherokee has had a written language since 1821.

White's granddaughter Martha White is the literary executor of the author's estate. We reached out to her for her thoughts about the Cherokee version of her grandfather's classic.

"I remember when I gave permission for the Cherokee translation, thinking how surprised and pleased my grandfather would be to think that Charlotte and her friends could help preserve a language," Martha relayed to us by email. "My grandfather was always 'a word man,' trying to voice what needs to be said. He gave voice to the barnyard, and he gave Louie the Trumpeter Swan his voice. Now he's helping to do the same for the Cherokee nation."

I asked Renissa if it's too late to save the Cherokee language. Another swift and emphatic reply. "It's not too late. As long as there are still people that can speak the language, there's still opportunity for the younger population."

Chapter 21

STUDENTS LEARNING IN TWO LANGUAGES: TAKING WING

Northe Carolina, New Mexico, and Utah are three states leading American education into our dual language future. Even outside of these heavy-hitter states, dual language schools seem to be spreading like the dawn in the complete absence of any national planning. It's remarkable how very different they can be, yet have the same goals.

Ideally, dual language schools try to have a roughly equal number of students who are native speakers of English and the partner language. But it can be difficult to achieve this ideal, even when enough students live close together.

A tale of two zip codes

The Escondido Elementary School is aptly named, as it seems hidden *(escondido)* away on the edge of the Stanford University campus, an easy walk from graduate student housing. It is part of the Palo Alto Unified School District of California. Principal Charles Merritt was kind enough to let me come interview him and to give me a tour. Tall and lean, with short gray hair and black glasses, Charles was dressed casually in slacks and a sweater. He told me he spent five years working in Spain as a Christian youth pastor before returning to the US to teach.

The Escondido campus has an expansive center courtyard where kids were playing. It is surrounded by covered, outdoor walkways that link the classrooms. We toured the library, which had plenty of bilingual and Spanish books, many of them ones that parents brought in. We visited a third-grade and then a fifth-grade classroom. There, twenty-one students sat on the floor, a mixture of Latinos and Anglos plus one Asian. They were reading *Mis abuelos y yo (My Grandparents and Me)*. All the discussion was in Spanish, and I could tell their Spanish was already better than mine. Charles did some reading out loud for the kids.

Charles said the ideal mix for Escondido is 30 percent Spanish-only kids, 30 percent bilingual Spanish-English kids, and 30 percent English-only kids. But they have trouble getting enough Spanish-only kids, and have an over-supply of English-only speakers. "This last year we had only three spots for English-only kids that weren't taken by siblings, with maybe fifty or sixty applying for those three spots," he told me.

Five miles away is another dual language Spanish-English school, Los Robles-Ronald McNair Academy, which is part of the Ravenswood City School District. (*Los robles* means "the oaks.") Like Escondido, it has open hallways and an uplifting atmosphere. Colorful murals adorn the walls. There I met another very experienced, highly committed principal, Keith Bookwalter, who showed me around. A big man with cropped gray hair, Keith strolled down the outdoor halls in his gray suit and tie as kids called out, "Hi, Dr. B!"

"I try to visit all classes every day," he said. "If they are speaking Spanish, I'll speak Spanish, and if English, I'll speak English to fit in." After graduating from Ohio State, Keith moved to Honduras to teach. He married a Honduran woman and they raised their family there before returning to the US.

He walked me up the wooden ramp to one of the portable classrooms and showed me a well-outfitted maker lab that a wealthy technologist donated. It was staffed with an intense and friendly young man who seemed to love what he was able to do with the kids.

While only five miles from the Escondido school, Los Robles is on "the wrong side of the tracks"—or more precisely, the wrong side of the Bayshore Freeway, what locals refer to as "the 101." It puts Los Robles in East Palo Alto. Whereas Palo Alto is home to some of the most expensive homes in America, East Palo Alto is where the working class live, often with many family members living in one small house. Riding my bike to get there, I went through long stretches of strip development, finally turning into narrow streets with small houses. Older cars overflowed from the driveways onto the street.

Whereas Escondido has trouble getting Spanish-speaking kids, Los Robles has the opposite problem. "The model is based on having fifty-fifty students in the classroom," said Keith. But his students are 90 percent Latino. In kindergarten, 90 percent of the teaching is done in Spanish and 10 percent in English. This changes as the kids move up in the grades, ending in the eighth grade with 20 percent of the teaching in Spanish and 80 percent in

English, "at which point the kids are bilingual and biliterate," he explained. "Of the twenty-one kids who graduated last year, four have to get some sort of academic support for high school, but the rest are ready to go anywhere."

Keith explained that his is a magnet school; parents want their children to be there. They understand that their kids will get better jobs if they are bilingual. "Whether a kid becomes a physician, a car salesman, or is working in a hotel, the bilingual person is going to be that much farther ahead," Keith said.

He told me of a ten-year-old African American student who was struggling with his Spanish. "His father came in for a parent-teacher conference. The teacher asked the kid if he wanted to continue his Spanish and he said no. I asked the father if he was sure this was the right place for his child. The father said to his son, 'You have to, because you'll get a better job. I'm an auto mechanic and can't even talk to my Spanish-speaking customers. You can do better than me, and you will continue in this school.'"

On district-wide tests, Keith told me, "we are not bringing the average down, and we might be raising it." And, he added, "there's also the parts that tests don't measure, like the value of being able to write a letter to their grandparents. And the Latino father who told me, 'I love the school. I can help my child in math because it's in Spanish.'"

Situated almost exactly between the two schools, on the Stanford campus, is the office of Sean Reardon, the sociologist who has produced headline-making studies about how zip codes are strongly predictive of schooling success. The zip code for Escondido is 94305; for Los Robles, 94303—two numbers, and a world, apart.

Reardon has also studied dual language schools and found that they produce favorable results for students compared with monolingual English schools, corroborating the results other researchers have found. Dual language schools won't, in themselves, solve all our educational challenges. But wherever they are, they seem to be leading to better educational outcomes, and parents, very aware of this, are demanding more of them.

Aristotle lives in Miami

Three thousand miles from Los Robles is another charter dual language school. Though it is in Miami, the partner language is not Spanish but Greek. It is the Archimedean Schools. Begun in 2002 with seventy-two students, it now consists of four schools, from pre-K through high school, which itself has 320 students. I toured there at the invitation of my Greek American friend Anastasia Merkel and was pleasantly shocked by what I saw.

The main school is housed in a castle-like building with stone arched halls more typical of Oxford than South Beach. Giving us the tour was the principal of the Archimedean Middle Conservatory, Vasiliki Moysidis.

We walked into a philosophy class being taught in Greek. Vasiliki explained that students also receive twice the math as a regular school, with half the math classes taught in Greek. In addition, they take classes in the Greek language.

Walking the halls with Vasiliki, I was impressed by how polite and attentive the students were with her. "I do visit every class every day," she said. "If I don't come, they ask, 'What happened, are you sick?'"

Vasiliki explained the balance the school strives for. "We set very high standards and never lower expectations. If you are very lenient or very strict, it's not going to work. It's a constant balance of the two. We have rules and expectations. Kids and parents sign contracts, and they are held accountable."

Both parents and kids need to understand, she explained, that the extra math, philosophy, and Greek language are designed to make the kids struggle, because struggling and overcoming are what build achievement. It pays off. Archimedean students consistently rank very high in comparisons with other schools in the state and nationally, especially in math and science competitions.

Civic-minded Greek Americans founded the school. Anastasia, who grew up in Miami, told me there is a big Greek community there, which surprised me. I was also surprised by what appeared to be the ethnic backgrounds of the children. Admission is based on a lottery, and since Latinos are the most numerous group in the area, Latinos make up most of their students. The waiting list, Vasiliki told me, is more than one thousand students. Latino parents want to send their kids here, not because they want them to learn Greek, she said, but because the students perform so well on tests and get into top colleges. "The fact that many of the students graduate speaking *three* languages is a plus," she said.

Just as Sara Snyder views the Cherokee language as belonging to all Americans, the Archimedean Schools feel that the Greek heritage "belongs to humanity and not just to Greeks."

Back in her office, I asked Vasiliki about her own children, who are now grown. "My kids learned to read and write in Greek before learning English. They didn't even know I spoke English until I took them to kindergarten and spoke English to the teachers. My kids almost died when they heard me!" She took them to Greece in the summers, especially when they were small.

I asked her if she wanted her children to marry Greek Americans. "It's open, but I expect my grandchildren to speak Greek. I told my children I will be very upset if that doesn't happen."

From elite to everyone

The public and charter schools we've seen in this chapter and the previous one offer the kind of dual language education that used to be available only at expensive private schools. Those schools haven't disappeared, and continue to serve as reference points for the wide public school expansion.

As Alison Mackey, the director of graduate studies in linguistics at Georgetown University, told me, "Well-off parents can afford to send their kids to schools with good language programs. There are some wonderful private schools with fantastic immersion and state-of-the-art technology." One she mentioned was the Avenues School in Manhattan. At her suggestion, I went to visit.

With campuses also in China, Brazil, and online, the Avenues School assures parents on its website that if their child is accepted to one campus, they are accepted to all. A toddler program helps "sow the seeds of multilingualism," while elementary kids go into Chinese or Spanish programs. As Alison said, "Children lucky enough to be in immersion programs anywhere can benefit enormously."

Another elite private school, this one in Boston, served as the training ground for the man *The New York Times* named the "godfather of language immersion programs," Fabrice Jaumont.

"I was a director of a private school in Cambridge," Fabrice told me. "It was a bilingual program, French and English. People were paying top dollars to get into this program, and we had waiting list upon waiting list of American families, monolingual English American families, trying to get their kids into the school."

A native of France, Fabrice moved to the US in 1997. When he left his position at the private school, he took a job as Education Attaché for the Embassy of France in New York. I met up with Fabrice at the elegant French bookstore, Albertine, on Fifth Avenue.

"When I moved to New York, it was the same story," Fabrice said. "They're very, very good schools, but not everyone can afford them." Moreover, he said, "They're full. Completely. They are attracting a lot of families from all over the world."

But Fabrice noticed something happening in New York and other big cities. "There's a middle class that has been thinking about trying to do similar things in public schools, and that was the case in Brooklyn."

So Fabrice put his background as a school director and his position as education attaché to work. He began helping parents start French-English dual language programs in public schools in Brooklyn. He had both professional and personal reasons to do so—the latter being his two school-age daughters.

Fabrice and other parents were successful in getting some French-English programs growing in Brooklyn. Once they did, word spread.

At first it was French-speaking parents, Fabrice told me. "Then it moved to a group of Japanese moms and then a couple of Russian moms, and then the Germans and the Italians. There were so many people asking me, 'What's the recipe?'"

After ten years of continuing to get calls from all over the US, Fabrice decided that "perhaps it's time to put this in a book."

The Bilingual Revolution: The Future of Education Is in Two Languages is a mix of big-picture explanation and practical advice geared to parents who want to get their own programs started. Fabrice introduced me to one of them, Yuli Fisher, a mother who helped get a Japanese-English program started in Brooklyn.

"When I became a mother and began to look at schools, I found I had a preference for dual language programs because speaking a second language has always appealed to me," Yuli told me, "even though I didn't actually speak one."

Yuli's parents were immigrants from Taiwan. They spoke Taiwanese to Yuli and her siblings when they were young, but when Yuli began school, her parents gave up speaking Taiwanese at home.

Yuli became friends with other mothers in her neighborhood. One spoke Mandarin, another Korean, and two spoke Japanese. They teamed up first to create a babysitting co-op, and having succeeded at that, decided to try something bigger.

The mothers saw a chance to create the first public-school Japanese program in Brooklyn, which has a large Japanese community. "That was one of the reasons why we chose it," said Yuli. They heard about Fabrice and asked his advice for starting a Japanese dual language program that their own children could attend. But before the Japanese school opened, Yuli's older son was accepted into a French dual language program nearby. As for the other mothers who helped create the program, only one was able to get her own son enrolled in it.

I asked Yuli what that felt like to her and the other mothers to work so hard to create a program, only to miss out on getting their own children in.

"It felt good because I think we're all kind of civic-minded and we knew that we were investing in the future of our community."

Fabrice advocates for French-English schools all along our border with Canada, and Spanish-English schools all along our border with Mexico. In his book, he advises parents to start early because it can take two years or longer for a program to get going.

"I think our children, or our children's children, might look on us, saying how dumb we were," Fabrice said, "and why didn't we do this sooner? But this is changing. More schools, communities, and states are going into this. And that's why I'm happy—I'm not too old to see it. I'm happy to see my daughters experience it, and I'm happy to contribute to its development."

Parents have always wanted better for their children. In the twenty-first century, for an increasing number of parents, "better" means bilingual.

Clearly, there are lots of challenges for scaling up dual language instruction in America, including attracting enough qualified bilingual teachers, developing appropriate materials for all grade levels in multiple languages, and dealing with our continuing economic segregation by zip code. But we're seeing many different parties pulling together—not just immigrant parents, but Anglo parents; not just teachers, but administrators; and not just voters, but forward-looking elected officials who advocate for an educated, more globally aware workforce.

As Utah's State Senator Stephenson told me: "I think the only way we're going to have peace on earth is for the *peoples* of the earth to connect together. The leaders may have differences, but when the people can connect, the leaders are going to be more inclined to follow. And the more we can get Americans to be bilingual, I think the more connected we will be."

First in flight

And what became of the Coral Way elementary school in Miami that showed such promise back two generations ago? Happily, it's still with us today. It has expanded to the eighth grade and is still filled with students who are learning in two languages.

During all the years after Operation Pedro Pan, when the national spotlight was aimed elsewhere, Coral Way continued to demonstrate how native Spanish-speaking children together with native English-speaking children could be educated together for their mutual benefit, how their English was better than their monolingual peers', and how they left Coral Way bilingual and biliterate.

Coral Way reminds me of the history I read of the Wright brothers. After their first successful flights on the Outer Banks of North Carolina, in 1903, America didn't instantly understand the significance. Not until sometime later, when Orville and Wilbur staged demonstrations near Washington, DC, did enough people show up to experience for themselves the counterintuitive spectacle of humans going aloft in a heavier-than-air flying machine. Only then did the reality of a new era grip the imagination of the nation. In my view, the Coral Way school, nestled inconspicuously in the Miami suburbs, is like Kitty Hawk. Even though few people witnessed it, Coral Way is where American schoolchildren first spread their bilingual wings, and flew.

Chapter 22

NOT THEIR UNCLE'S
LANGUAGE CLASS

Dual language schools are changing the landscape of American education, but that doesn't mean that conventional language classes are standing still. Indeed, most of them stopped being conventional awhile ago. As with language classes for adults, the old drill-and-kill approach in schools is mostly gone. So is talking about the language, rather than using it in practical ways. Gone also is correcting students all the time with the misguided idea that it helps. Instead, language teachers guide students so they can actually do things in the language, like hold a conversation. "Comprehensible input" is replacing grammar lessons (sorry, subjunctive—we'll catch up with you later).

Conversing, not reciting

To help understand the changes that are afoot in teaching students today, I interviewed many leading language educators who attended the ACTFL annual conferences in Nashville and New Orleans. What I heard was inspiring.

Aviva Kadosh, whom we met in Part One, told us, "I've been teaching long enough that I started out teaching with the ALM. We had reel-to-reel tapes and a filmstrip and kids would memorize dialogues." ALM, or the audio-lingual method, is a thing of the past. Bill Anderson, an ACTFL board member, said, "The tools that we had at that time for teaching languages were the best we had. We know better now, and we *do* better now in helping students acquire the language."

Susann Davis, another ACTFL board member, remembered her own experience as a language student. "I was really good at filling in the blank with conjugated verbs. Unfortunately, the first time I found myself in a taxi in another country, I realized I couldn't talk about anything relevant."

In contrast, Susann told us about an experience her seventeen-year-old daughter had after she completed a course in Arabic. While her daughter was sitting alone in an airport, she started texting her mom. "There's somebody and he's speaking in Arabic and he is speaking so fast and I just wonder where he's from."

Susann texted back, telling her daughter to use her Arabic and ask him. Her daughter did just that. "When she texted me back, she was so excited that she had pulled this off! It was all caps:

OH MOM! HE'S FROM EGYPT AND HE HAS DAUGHTERS AND OH, WOW, I DID IT. IT WAS FANTASTIC!!"

Proficiency, not perfection

The story, said Susann, shows the difference in language education today. Proficiency has taken on a different meaning from filling in the blanks. Said Desa Dawson, a past president of ACTFL, "Proficiency means that grammar takes a different role. It's not that you don't want to be correct when you speak, but that's not the major concern. The major concern is that you are able to communicate with someone else."

Said Aviva, "It means you can function in the real world with real things and real people." Added Susann, "It's about saying the right thing to the right person at the right time." To illustrate, Laura Roché Youngworth, a board member of the Kentucky World Language Association and the host of her own podcast, KWLA Language Talk, offered the example of how students now learn numbers. "You teach numbers for a reason. The kids are going to buy something. They are going to the grocery store and need to count what is in their basket so they know how much money they need."

Edward Zarrow, the 2016 ACTFL Teacher of the Year who teaches Latin to high school students, said, "We've stopped thinking about what we want the language to look like and allow the kids to really be able to communicate."

Desa explained that the principle is the same as that used in dual language schools. "Before, we didn't try to teach *through* the language," she explained. "Today, we use the language to teach, whether it's science or social studies. It's not about teaching Spanish per se, but using Spanish to teach." This sounds very much like the successful adult bilinguals we covered in Part One who found ways to learn everything from cooking to speed walking in—and through—their adopted language.

Carrie Toth, the president of the Illinois Council on the Teaching of Foreign Languages, teaches STEM in Spanish. "We do a unit on water where we talk about a panel that takes water out of the atmosphere and makes potable drinking water for people that live in Lima. The kids really love science, but it also lets me still teach in my language."

Language learning is just the start. Bill Anderson pointed out that it's in language classes where students "learn about the cultures and traditions of people. And that's how you learn to work with people and deal with people around the world."

The positive impact of newfound purpose

As for the impact these new methods have had, some evidence comes from the number of American high school students taking the AP tests in modern languages. In the ten years between 2009 and 2019, that number has increased by 62 percent—from about 163,000 students sitting for the exams in 2009 to 263,000 students sitting for them in 2019, or one hundred thousand more students. The largest percentage increase was seen in Chinese AP exams, followed by Spanish Literature and Spanish Language exams, but all language exams showed increases, including French, German, Italian, and Japanese. Moreover, this 62 percent increase occurred when the total number of American high school students remained relatively unchanged.

The College Board doesn't provide the combined test results of these AP students, who are confident enough to take the voluntary exam, but overall AP results have remained relatively unchanged through these same years. About 25 percent of students earn a score of 3, 20 percent earn a score of 4, and 14 percent earn the highest score of 5.

Another impact of all the improved teaching might well be seen in something hard to measure: a growing respect and affection for language teachers on the part of their students. Edward Zarrow's kids, for example, fondly call him Doctor Z. While there always were wonderful language teachers, beloved by their students, it might be reasonable to assume that with one hundred thousand more students than ten years ago taking AP exams, there are also more close relationships between language teachers and students. We certainly felt this affection in interviewing many language teachers and students.

When Jack Roepers' sons, Cyrus and Philip, talked with me about their French classes at the Potomac School in Washington, DC, Cyrus said, "Mrs. Swope, for me, was one of the best teachers I ever had." His younger brother, Philip, had Mrs. Swope a few years later. "Well, I didn't agree with her at the time," he admitted, since she was demanding. But he continued with his French in college and in his career. Looking back, he said, "I realized how much of a contribution she's made to my life."

Philip's reflection points to a third benefit to improved language teaching: the growing expectations among students that they will actually use their language skills, and build upon them, in their careers and lives.

Toni Theisen is a past Teacher of the Year and past president of ACTFL. She told us teachers used to tell students, "Well, you need language for college." Now, she said, it's the students telling teachers, "'I want to use it for my career and I also want to use it for my life.'"

Life skills for the long term

And the impact we've seen so far is small compared with what is about to happen.

Whereas baby boomer parents may have had poor experiences in their old grammar-laden, drill-and-kill classes, and may not have been particularly encouraging about language study with their children, most students in the twenty-first century are having different experiences. Instead of classes they suffer through, today's students are seeing language classes as places where they can get some fundamentals in what will become their adopted languages, which they expect to use for the rest of their lives. Once these students become parents themselves, having experienced the benefits of bilingualism "piling up like laundry," we might well experience a force multiplier—a virtuous cycle of higher expectations that teachers, parents, and students all share.

Carrie Toth told me, "We're graduating more and more students who have positive feelings about language. I think it's just going to make the bilingual schools explode because they will want that for their children as well."

Tami Jordan, who teaches French to elementary students at Westminster Schools in Atlanta, sees this happening already. This private school has expanded language classes so that all students, K through 12, take language classes every year, because parents expect it.

"Students either take French or Spanish, and now we're adding Chinese," Tami told me. The language department is the largest department at the school. "We have nine French teachers, two Chinese teachers, two Latin teachers, and twenty-one Spanish teachers." Many of Tami's students go on to get 4s and 5s on the French AP, but, she says, what's more important is a commitment to "lifelong learning" of their adopted language.

Thomas Sauer, the assistant director of resource development at the National Foreign Language Center, predicts that today's students will become tomorrow's language learning advocates. "I tell teachers all the time, every time a student leaves your classroom, they're leaving with the understanding of what language learning is supposed to be like, and those students become principals and politicians."

Added Edward Zarrow, "People are going to say, 'I took six years of French and I can communicate at a proficient level and people know what I'm talking about.' We're only a couple of years away."

Chapter 23

LANGUAGE CAMPS FOR KIDS

Just as an adult-oriented language camp like Middlebury Language Schools can help grownups boost their bilingual skills quickly, so can language camps for children. Kids' language immersion programs, normally offered in the summer, can also give them a big advantage when returning to language classes in regular school and fortify them for future study abroad.

If Middlebury is the grande dame of adult language camps (see Chapter 11), Concordia Language Villages is the godmother of children's language camps.

Concordia has become famous over the past half century for its approach to language learning. Its giant campus, situated far from any city, is one that Walt Disney might have approved of as a sort of language EPCOT. Each "village" at Concordia is hidden from view of the other villages, all of them nestled in wooded settings around a big lake. More important, each village is out of *hearing* range of the others. In these villages, English is taboo, and so is any other language but that spoken in that village—be that Danish, Korean, Arabic, or something else.

Concordia is designed for children and young adults, ages eight to eighteen, and is generally a two-week camp experience. Often students come back to their language village every summer for years.

I heard so much about Concordia that I had to visit it, and I talked Lori into going with me.

A French chalet a ways from a German castle

Concordia Language Villages is in Bemidji, a small town in northern Minnesota. To get there, Lori and I drove north from Minneapolis for about four hours into beautiful countryside filled with farms and rimmed by distant hills.

We were given directions to *Lago del Bosque,* or Forest Lake, where Jennifer Speir, who heads the French, Italian, Portuguese, and Spanish villages, would meet us.

We turned into the property and soon drove past something that looked like a giant French chalet. Farther on through the forest was a German castle. It was farther yet that we came to where Jennifer greeted us, at what looked like a town's central plaza in Spain.

Jennifer explained that there were seven villages around the end of this lake with, she said, "each one designed to replicate the culture where the language is spoken." She pointed out a set of cabins that were designed after Central American houses, and then another hill of cabins that looked like they belonged to a Mexican hacienda.

The heart of the Concordia philosophy is to combine the best parts of a camp experience with language immersion. "There are plenty of beautiful camps in America, and there are other summer language programs," said Jennifer. "But no place combines the two as well as Concordia."

Concordia's villages grew organically. The German village was first, in 1961, followed by the Norwegian the next year and the Spanish the year after that.

Jennifer told us how they go into depth in STEM experiences and also theater arts. "The Italian Village, for example, had the Metropolitan Opera group from Minneapolis come up and do a week of special aria and opera teaching."

They do similar things with sports. "The German program hires young German soccer coaches who come for the summers to be our soccer coaches. The teaching and coaching are all in German."

The venerable bead

Unlike Middlebury, Concordia does not have a language pledge to stay in the language. "We always allow questions in English, and kids can reflect with each other in English, but everything is led and directed in the language of the village," Jennifer told us.

Concordia also rewards kids for staying in the language. In the morning at breakfast, kids line up and take a special name tag for the day. Wearing it means they can't speak English, not even with their friends. They receive their reward the next morning if they are still wearing that special name tag.

And the reward? I asked.

"It's a wonderful, precious prize of a bead that goes on their camp name tag," Jennifer said. She acknowledged that it sounded silly. "But," she said, "you see high school students who are very proud to wear their name tag, especially if they've come back year after year." Kids get to keep their beads from prior years, accumulating like merit badges.

I asked Jennifer what Concordia gives kids that they can't get at their regular schools. For one thing, she said, "we have a ratio of one staff member to four villagers, so the opportunity for interaction is so much greater." And there are plenty of what we call *Dorothy moments* (inspired by that pivotal moment in *The Wizard of Oz* when Dorothy pronounces, "Toto, I have a feeling we're not in Kansas anymore"). Jennifer says, "It's so fun to see a ten-year-old who might be here for the second summer of two weeks. And all of a sudden they realize they just spent the entire day operating, negotiating, having fun in the language, and they're comfortable in it."

While Concordia is primarily for kids, there are programs throughout the year for adults, school classrooms, and even families who want to be immersed together over a weekend. Younger and older language learners seem to face similar challenges. Jennifer told me even parents get headaches and think they need a break. "But then they don't want to leave because they start to realize they can ask to pass the rice at the other end of the table. They start to feel really successful and confident, and you see this reaction whether it's in a seven-year-old or a seventy-year-old."

A special kind of bond

Jennifer has had thirty years of experience at Concordia, starting as a villager herself, and then becoming a counselor and a French teacher before heading entire programs. She introduced us to someone on the Concordia staff with even more seniority, the dean of Lago del Bosque, Diana Tess. "I started in '76, as a cook," she told us.

Diana was a college student then, studying Spanish at the University of Wisconsin-Eau Claire. Her best friend was going to be a summer counselor at this language camp up north and told Diana they needed a cook for two weeks. "I said, 'I'll go!' It changed my life."

But why, I asked her, can't students just learn languages during the school year?

"There's a bond at camp that doesn't happen in any other kind of community," Diana said, "because you're doing all these fun things but you're doing it here in Spanish. Where are you going to learn to play volleyball in Spanish? Or hit the soccer ball, or do badminton, or Frisbee? You go out in the canoe and do it in Spanish, you can learn to cook something in Spanish, and can even learn to do embroidery in Spanish."

And surely eat in Spanish, I offered.

"I have a complement of ten cooks, just for this site," said Diana. "Tonight we're doing Mexico—we're having fish tacos. Tomorrow lunch we're doing the Dominican Republic, with Dominican chicken. Tomorrow night we're doing Guatemalan."

What's in a name? At Concordia, a culture

Our own lunch that day was in the French Village, where Lori and I were invited to join a table with camp counselors and administrators. They spoke English for us, but it was often hard to hear with all the excited singing and yelling in French going on in the rest of the cavernous room.

"We have about one hundred villagers at the moment, ranging in age from eight to eighteen," a young fellow named Benoit told us. "Some of them are here for two weeks and some are here for four weeks, and they're interspersed with our counselors who are either native French speakers or speak French as another language." Benoit is the dean of the first two weeks of the French camp. "Benoit" is his Concordia name; when he's not at camp, he goes by his other name of Cliff Schwartz.

Choosing a camp name is an important part of the Concordia experience. Although we thought we'd been talking with Jennifer, we learned that her French name is Charlotte. But it's more than just a name.

"It's not only that you learn the language through names that are culturally based, but you step into those shoes of a French speaker, and you become that French speaker," Jennifer explained.

Also at the table was Jennifer's counterpart, Martin Graefe, who worked in the Nordic Villages. He explained how important mealtimes are. "A couple of years ago, we realized that we spend about three hours a day at mealtimes," Martin said. "That's a lot. So that's a key time for us to focus on language use and learning."

A young woman named Izo chimed in. "In a school course, you're there for forty-five or fifty-five minutes a day. Whereas here, you're hearing the language *all* day long. You get a chance to think about and internalize it into the things you enjoy." Izo, whose other name is Julie Ardis, is the curriculum facilitator for the first two weeks of the French camp. "And you're all in this boat of adventure together."

149

As Izo was talking, the villagers began folding and moving the tables to the side. It was time, Izo explained, to mop the floor. She smiled. "I'll never forget the time when I cleared the dining room with three villagers who were very young and didn't know how to mop very well. So I put on some Edith Piaf music and I taught them how to waltz so we could waltz and mop at the same time." I asked Izo if she would recreate that scene for us for our *America the Bilingual* podcast. She did; you can hear the lovely music and laughter of the kids in Episode 37.

Check your tech at the door

At Middlebury, students are allowed to keep their phones and other technology as long as they set them to their adopted language. Not so at Concordia, where the policy is strict abstinence. Villages literally check the phones, tablets, and laptops at the door. "The only exceptions," Diana told us, "are children who are here for four weeks." After the first two weeks, kids are allowed to use their devices for a short time to check in with their parents.

I asked how the kids reacted to that policy.

"We do have kids that want to sneak in cell phones," Diana admitted. "One of their favorite tricks is to take a teddy bear, open it up, take the stuffing out and put their phone in there and sew it back up." But she and her staff are wise to those tactics. "I have many staff who have been villagers before who snuck in contraband items, so they know all the tricks."

Jennifer added, "Families are always able to connect with us. And they'll see pictures of their villagers in action every day. But the kids get to let go of technology."

"Don't the kids complain about handing over their phones?" I asked.

"They might for the *very* first hour," said Jennifer. "But once they realize there's so much more to be doing and so many people to meet, and foods to try and activities to be involved in, they soon forget it."

And the parents?

"The parents just *applaud*," said Diana. "'The kids lived without electronics for two and four weeks and guess what? They survived.'"

During the school year, Concordia offers programs where teachers bring their language classes up for a weekend, also without phones.

Said Jennifer, "We interviewed a lot of teachers this past year and they said that after those first twelve hours, over a three-day weekend, they see their kids relax. And for the first time, they see them looking into each other's eyes because they don't have their phones."

From a village to the world: one camper's experience

One of the older students at Concordia, Raquel (aka Rachel Schaeffer), is a counselor now herself. She told me she's been coming to Concordia since she was very young. "I went for a one-week program and fell in love with it. We danced all the time. The part that I remember was just having so much fun."

The experience was so positive, she came back—for nine years. She continued her Spanish but also went to the French village, where she took part in the Voyager program.

Separate from the regular camp experience, the Voyager program offers trekking, camping out of canoes, and sleeping in tents—all done in French.

All those many Concordia summers gave Rachel the confidence and desire to study abroad. "I went on an exchange program in high school to Argentina, mainly because every counselor I'd met here from Argentina was amazing and I really wanted to get to know their country." Study abroad in high school "just seemed normal," she told me. "It wasn't anything like big or scary for me after being here."

After her high school study abroad experience, Rachel came back as a staff member at Concordia, and has now been doing that for six years.

As a student at Concordia College, which the language villages are part of, Rachel focused on Spanish and education. "I studied abroad in Spain my sophomore year and that was a cool, contrasting experience from Argentina, just to learn different types of Spanish," she said. She later did student teaching in Norway and taught Spanish at an international school. Then as part of a school program, she taught English in Rwanda and Tanzania, where they speak Swahili.

I asked her how her Swahili was.

"It's not very good," she confessed, "but I can have a simple conversation. It was actually pretty easy to catch on to it. The letter sounds are very similar to Spanish."

Rachel had just finished her bachelor's degree at Concordia and had won a Fulbright scholarship to work for a year in Colombia, teaching English and doing a social project.

I asked her what she would say to parents who were considering sending their kids to Concordia's language camps.

"I would say it's an experience that will challenge them, help them grow a lot in their language abilities, and also in their ways of interacting with other people."

Rachel said that sometimes the kids have unrealistic expectations about how easy learning a language will be.

"Villagers think they'll become fluent by the end of the two weeks, so it's really interesting to see them come to the realization that learning a language is a lot harder than they originally think, that it actually does take a lot of work. They understand now that it's more of a time investment."

A special kind of empathy

One of the Concordia alumnae I had met earlier was Raia Lichen, the founder of a language learning company called Language Lifestylist. She attended the two-week Spanish Language Village when she was in high school and had already studied Spanish for three years.

"I was an excited language learner because early on, I had dreams of fluency," she told me. What's more, she said that learning Spanish helped her to be better at English.

"English was incredibly frustrating for me as an elementary-aged kid because I didn't feel as fluent or literate as my peers, who all seemed to be voracious readers and confident spellers," Raia said. "As a result of my struggles, I did not enjoy reading. But perhaps it was my difficulty with English that helped me develop a passion for Spanish and other languages in general." Raia said she found it easier to read and write in Spanish.

"The mistake we often make with language learning is that we tend to want to teach ourselves as we would program a computer," she said. "We want to create very linear experiences to make it easier to explain and easier to understand. But lines only take us so far. The human brain is not two-dimensional. Our learning thrives tenfold in 3-D environments."

This is what Concordia offers, Raia explained, with its meals, sports, and other activities all in the language, and it results in a special kind of empathy. "You develop your ability to connect to the heart of a native speaker through curiosity and care for the words that are native to them."

The Spanish professor's daughters finally speak Spanish

As it happened, the day we visited Concordia was drop-off day. Jennifer introduced me to one of the villagers' parents, the father of twin girls, and surprised me when she said that he was a professor of Spanish at Xavier University in Cincinnati.

Why would a professor of Spanish want to bring his daughters to a Spanish camp? That was my first question when David Knutson and I sat down to talk.

"So," I said, "you're not just the ordinary parent when it comes to languages. Have you spoken Spanish to your girls growing up?"

"No," David admitted, "and this has been sort of an embarrassing part of my family life. When my daughters were very young, I tried to use some Spanish with them when we were alone, and they just pretty much refused to let Dad speak these strange words that he didn't use with anyone else. So they grew up in an English-speaking family." I could read on his face and hear in his voice that this was a painful part of his own language biography.

"They weren't interested at all until they started watching *Dora the Explorer* on public television and then they started to understand a little bit about Spanish," David said. Even so, "they still didn't want to hear anything from me because I just wasn't prestigious enough as a linguistic model." But David had heard about Concordia Language Villages since he was a kid. He decided to enroll his twins.

When he picked them up two weeks later, they still wouldn't speak Spanish to their father. David didn't know what to think. Then, months later, out of the blue, "my daughter woke me up one morning speaking Spanish."

What did she say? I asked.

"'*Buenos días, papá, vamos a desayunar.*'" ("Good morning, Dad, let's go have breakfast.")

"I didn't know what I was hearing," David said. "I had to look again and make sure it was her. She was hungry and figured out that was the best way to get me out of bed. But that expression didn't come from me; it came from her experiences here at Concordia."

The morning I was interviewing David was the fifth year he was dropping off his twins, who are now thirteen. "They are kind of nervous when I drop them off, but when I pick them up two weeks later, there are tears in their eyes; they're hugging their friends." David was getting emotional as he was telling me this.

"I just dropped my daughters off at the entrance here, unloaded the suitcases, had to drive away to park, and I saw in the rearview mirror that they were already hugging some friends they'd known from last year."

STARTALK, a National Security 'campsite' for kids

A very different kind of language camp is now available for American children because of a national security risk. The number of jobs that went unfilled in 2018 within American intelligence agencies because they couldn't find bilinguals with working proficiency in critically needed languages climbed to ten thousand. Expressed another way: only about half of the jobs that require professional-level competence in critical-need languages are filled.

The Office of the Director of National Intelligence has done something about it. In 2007, its National Security Agency (NSA) began funding a summer program throughout the country named STARTALK, to teach what it identified as critical-need languages, using various schools around the country as the "campsites."

The STARTALK program I visited was using Connecticut's Glastonbury High School, southeast of Hartford, and it was there that I spent a day interviewing teachers and students. The head of the program at this location, Rita Oleksak, explained the goal. "STARTALK is trying to build capacity in the United States for those less commonly taught languages," she said. The NSA identified eleven of these languages. They include Chinese, Russian (the two being taught at Glastonbury), Arabic, Hindi, Korean, Urdu, Dari, Persian, Portuguese, Swahili, and Turkish.

Unlike almost all other language camps, STARTALK is free to students, and it is a day camp, so students either sleep at home or make arrangements to stay in the area around the school. At Glastonbury, K-12 students enroll in a four-week program in either Chinese or Russian, which they are immersed in Monday through Friday.

Rita, the district supervisor in charge of global language learning and a past president of ACTFL, explained that STARTALK involves teaching not just students but also teachers, so that they can return to their schools and continue the process during the regular school year.

Where language stars are born

Rita's colleague, Jimmy Wildman, teaches Spanish during the regular year and runs the STARTALK programs in the summer. The two of them gave me a tour of the "camp." Walking past a classroom, I noticed a mixture of ages of younger and older kids working together. "This is a Chinese Two class," said Jimmy. "They're actually here with a class for our Chinese Four students." The more advanced students were helping the less advanced ones.

Although the teachers looked like they could be ethnic Chinese, most of the students did not. "Most of our teaching staff are heritage speakers, but our students come from all variety of backgrounds," Jimmy said. At Glastonbury, there were about one hundred students in the Chinese program, with classes up on the second floor, and about twenty-five students in the Russian program, on the first floor.

There are also field trips. The Chinese students had taken a trip to Flushing, New York, which has a large Chinese population.

Rita and Jimmy walked me into a classroom that had been converted into what looked like a TV studio. Jimmy explained, "As part of their professional development, our teacher trainees were tasked with working with students to recreate folk tales. The teachers rewrote them using student-friendly language that was appropriate to the level of those students, and then each student had a part in the film." So they made movies, speaking in their adopted languages.

Added Rita, "So the students are now using their language to have authentic communication and to showcase what they know." The teachers, meanwhile, will go home and make comparable films in their regular language classes.

According to a summary report on STARTALK, the support that the program provides its teachers—giving them the chance to observe model teachers, to get coaching and receive recognition—is just the kind of support known to keep teachers motivated and keep them from leaving their profession for other careers.

STARTALK's emphasis on teacher training directly ties into the program's goals. According to the program's white paper, it "is based on the understanding that student achievement is influenced more by effective teachers than by any other factor."

At lunchtime, we headed to the cafeteria, already filled with all the students learning Chinese. (The students taking Russian ate at a different time.) The students spoke their adopted language at lunch as Chinese young-adult videos played on overhead TVs. The food was catered by a local Chinese restaurant, using the school's kitchen. Missing were knives and forks. "I want the kids to try to use chopsticks," Rita said, laughing. She then introduced me to Victor, one of their advanced students.

"This is my sixth year at STARTALK," Victor told me. "I'm going to be a senior next year, so, actually, I'm kind of sad about that because that means I can't come back to STARTALK next year as a student."

I asked Victor how he would rate his Chinese. "I can hold conversations, I mean, fluent enough to talk with the teachers, and we have an intern from Taiwan this year and I could understand what he was saying, even when he was talking really fast, too." I asked him how that made him feel.

"It actually feels really nice because I remember when I was younger, I had absolutely no idea what the teacher was saying unless they deliberately slowed down."

It turns out, Victor is something of a polyglot. He's also biliterate in French, "and I am conversational in Burmese," he added—a nod to his Burmese parents.

Young linguists with a larger purpose

Since the US government funds STARTALK, I asked Rita whether she thought American taxpayers were getting their money's worth.

"Oh, absolutely!" she replied. "Within the big picture, it is very little funding, and the lives that I hope we are impacting is huge." Then to answer my question another way, she arranged for me to interview some of the youngest students in the Chinese program. They had finished their lunches and had a few minutes before they were due back in class.

Bella Wiedman was sitting with a bunch of her young friends who introduced themselves as Kathy, William, and Lauren. They were all talking and laughing excitedly, partly due, no doubt, to a stranger in their midst holding a microphone up for them. Bella began: "It's my sixth year in this program, and I will be going into sixth grade."

"And how's your Chinese at this point?" I asked.

"I think it's pretty good," said Bella, at which point her friends raved about how good Bella was. I asked Bella to demonstrate and she launched off into a paragraph's worth of Mandarin that, in the translation she provided afterwards, included her Chinese zodiac sign of the pig. I asked her why she wanted to speak Chinese.

"Well, it started out, I wanted to order Chinese takeout."

But now her goals are loftier than dim sum. "Now I am hoping to work for the government, so I can go over to China and help with, I guess, trading offers or deals made." At this point, Bella's friends could contain themselves no longer and got themselves in front of the microphone.

"I want to work for the government, like her, or just learn Chinese 'cause it's useful," said one. Another: "I don't want to be in the Army, but I want to, like, help people that need help, yeah, like that type of stuff." And another: "I want to be a scientist for the government, like a physicist, to work with physics and chemicals and math."

When I got to sit down again with Rita in her office, I told her that if Bella and her friends were any indication of the next generation, get ready, world!

Hearing this gave her goosebumps, she said. "It's working, and they're happy," said Rita.

In the first ten years of its operation, some fifty-six thousand American students have gone through STARTALK programs, which have also trained some twelve thousand teachers, who have returned to their classrooms and reached an estimated half million students.

A language camp near home

Concordia and STARTALK are big and nationally known, but you may be able to find a smaller language camp close to your home. I was able to visit just such a camp on the outskirts of Miami called Camp Lingua. It was during an open house, and I interviewed two parents.

"I was lucky enough that I spent my summers in Spain. I would get to spend the school year here, and my summers in Spain. That's how I got to be bilingual," said parent Ricky Perez. "So that's what we're trying to give our children."

Ricky and his wife, Giselle, are both Latinos living in the Miami area. Ricky's parents are from Spain and Panama. Giselle is from the Dominican Republic. They're trying to get their children, ages five and six, to be as fluent in Spanish as they are.

At home, Ricky said, "we try to push it, but they still kind of fight it unless they're amongst their peers and they notice that everybody's speaking Spanish. It's why we were so happy with this camp."

Andreina Galavis, the camp's founder, told me that when kids go to an English-only school, "it's so easy to forget their native language." Both native English-speaking parents and Latinos send their children to Camp Lingua, said Andreina. "They want to give the gift of a new language, or to keep their native language."

Michael Perez is the camp's logistics director—and there's a lot to manage. The camp offers horseback riding, soccer, canoeing, and other outdoor sports, along with art and music. The language learning is taking place, but it's wrapped around activities that the kids enjoy. "Because they're having fun, they don't know that they're learning," Michael said.

Ricky and Giselle told me the approach is working for their children. "Coming home, they were talking about the horseback riding and the canoeing. What they didn't realize was that they were doing it all in Spanish."

Andreina offered a historical perspective on her work. "After the First World War and the migration from Europe, it was not nice if you spoke another language than English. Now it's the opposite. Now with all the globalization, it's a new paradigm. It's good to speak many languages, and I'm very glad that parents realize that."

Said Ricky, "We want our children to speak with their grandfather and their aunts in Spanish when they go to the Dominican Republic, and when they go to Spain."

Vacation immersions for kids

Concordia, STARTALK, and Camp Lingua are formal programs, but as with adults, it's possible to create informal programs for children. They can involve international travel, extended families, or close friendships.

Kat Cohen, the founder of that university advisory firm, became very good friends with a Spanish woman while in grad school who returned to live in Spain after university. Like Kat, her friend has two daughters, so the two moms have arranged their own summer immersion experiences. Kat's daughters live in Spain with their friends for part of the summer.

David Wolf, the American who went to business school in France, has done something similar with his own teenage daughters. "I put together a trip where the entire itinerary was visiting good friends in France who have children the same age," he told me. "You can take kids to France and you can take them to the Louvre and nice restaurants and at the end of the day, they pretty much prefer their iPad," he said. "But if you take them to families and they are interacting with fantastic kids their same age, that's where the magic happens."

What Kat and David have arranged, and what Ricky and Giselle and all the parents who drop their kids at language camps are doing, is just what the psycholinguist Steven Pinker recommends to parents. After he wrote *The Language Instinct,* many parents asked him what they could do to encourage their children to retain their second language as they grew up. He answered, in the FAQ appendix to his book, "Children care more about their peers than about their parents, so send them to summer camps, after-school programs, or vacations with their cousins, where they will have to use the language with kids their own age."

One of my Lyft drivers told me he also was following such advice. Ezzat had immigrated from Egypt fifteen years ago and has three American-born children. "Last summer they spent the entire summer in Egypt and spoke only Arabic. It was *wonderful.*"

✷ ✷ ✷

Chapter 24

HIGHER HIGH SCHOOL

"I was a very indifferent and rebellious high school student," Doug Renfield-Miller told me. Doug grew up outside of Boston and went to Newton South High School. "In fact, I even have my old report card, which shows that my highest grade in junior year was a D. And I think that was in physical education."

Fortunately for Doug, his mother stepped in. She had heard about an organization called School Year Abroad, or SYA, which sent American high school kids overseas to study.

Doug applied—"not through any desire to learn French or go abroad, but because I wanted to get away"— and was accepted. He would be spending the year in France.

But on his trip over, he already began to feel uncomfortable. "I was out of my element in so many ways." He was from relatively modest means compared with a lot of the other kids, and wasn't nearly as sophisticated. Plus, it was Doug's senior year; the others were in their junior year. When he arrived in France, things got worse. He had taken some basic French in school, but "I could barely understand anything anyone was saying."

To Doug's relief, his math and English classes at his new school were taught in English. But "in the other classes, starting on day one, there was not a word of English. And in my literature course, Madame Nébout was a pure terror."

Doug relayed how, when the *professeurs* handed back the students' *devoirs*, or homework, they started with the best grade and ended with the worst. "You're still waiting for your paper and you know you're further and further down," said Doug. "My first grade was a 3, which was tied for the lowest, and it was with complete disdain that Madame Nébout gave me back my paper, telling me how awful it was in front of all my classmates."

It was humiliating. "But interestingly," said Doug, "I don't remember being discouraged. I remember just being challenged. It took a while, but I studied harder than I'd ever studied before and gradually worked my way up." By the end of the school year, Madame Nébout was no longer chastising him. "I'm sure I would have gotten the most improved, if there was an award for that," Doug said. But what was more important, Doug fell in love with his new language.

"I've never had a great accent, but I just loved everything French—French cinema, French theater, the museums, the cities—everything was so different. Everything was interesting."

It was after Christmas when Doug had his Dorothy moment. "Something clicks and suddenly you're dreaming in French, you feel conversant in French, and even if you're not totally fluent, suddenly it comes very, very easily."

SYA president Tom Hassan told me that his organization is now seeing more interest in shorter programs, especially programs offered over the summer, but he still advocates for spending an entire school year abroad, as Doug did. "There comes a time, and it wouldn't happen until December or January, when the students are actually dreaming in the language and feel that they can make their way around a conversation at home and traveling around the city," he said. "That takes time, so it doesn't happen in a two-week or even a five-week program."

When he returned to the US, Doug was accepted at the University of Wisconsin-Madison. Unlike in high school, Doug did well in college. "I ended up a double major in French and philosophy, so I took French all through college, mainly literature courses."

I asked Doug how he did in those college French classes. "Straight A's, if I recall. In fact, one of my teachers even had me co-teach with her or teach when she had to go away." A few years after getting a master's degree at George Washington University, he headed to Stanford for an MBA. "You are allowed to take two courses outside the business school, and I only took one. It was nineteenth-century French literature and I thought I was on vacation. All I was doing was reading French novels." Compared with his business courses, he said, his French course was "relaxation."

AFS: go long, go short, but go

The total number of American high school students who go abroad to study for a year is very small, probably no more than a few thousand out of some four million American high school juniors. But those who do will most likely have a transformational experience, and being such an elite group, they will likely stand out in their applications to college, as well.

Jenny Messner was another unlikely candidate who spent a year of high school abroad, through the program that used to be called American Field Service and is now known simply as AFS.

Jenny grew up in a small town in Pennsylvania's Lancaster County, the daughter of parents who did not go to college. "I think they thought it was all a joke when I came home one day and said, 'What do you think if I applied to be an AFSer?'" AFS sent her to Brazil. For Jenny, a descendant of German indentured farmers not known for their exuberance, the Brazilians were unlike anyone she knew. "In general, Brazilians bubble over," she said. "They bubble over positively and they bubble over sad when they're sad. It did my human spirit a lot of good to learn how to bubble a little bit." But it wasn't easy to start bubbling.

"I had a month in which to learn Portuguese before I started regular high school down there. I remember going to bed with very bad headaches just from all the concentration."

Fortunately, Jenny had a host sister. "We shared a bedroom and she was very, very helpful in that she was stern and wouldn't let me go to bed until I said the name of everything in the room."

She returned home fluent, and she believes it was her AFS experience that got her into the University of Pennsylvania. She was also determined to maintain her Portuguese. After graduation, Jenny got a job in banking in Brazil, and then back in the US, working in the Latin America market. It was in her career where Jenny's adopted Portuguese lived.

"I think it disarms people when they hear me speak because I can be so Brazilian, and I just don't look like that would ever be possible. It's one thing to be blonde, blue-eyed, and relatively Germanic-looking, and then to open your mouth and turn into somebody from São Paulo."

AFS traces its history back to World War I and the Americans who went to France before the US entered the war, in order to help staff military ambulances. Some of those drivers who had seen the horror of the battle-fields decided to try to help global understanding by inviting international high school students to America and sending their American counterparts overseas. The organization has grown over the last century, but still has the same purpose of providing "intercultural learning opportunities to help people develop the knowledge, skills and understanding needed to create a more just and peaceful world."

Another AFSer was Kat Cohen, whom we met earlier as an avid practitioner of buds of bilingualism. Her study abroad experience also began in high school. "I decided to apply on my own to AFS," said Kat. "It was a year-long process with many interviews and I ended up making it through." That's when she decided to tell her parents. Kat was fifteen at the time and her mother was astounded. "She almost had a heart attack, but I convinced her."

Kat went for four months over the summer to Argentina and credits the experience with getting her fluent in Spanish. "I lived with a family almost four months and there were no English speakers around. The whole experience shaped me," she said. She also credits it for helping her get into Brown University.

Today Kat advises parents and kids on how to prepare for their own college experiences. She encourages students to go abroad and for long enough to get a command of the language. But she also acknowledges that there are more shorter-term opportunities today than previously.

While Jorge Castro, the CEO of AFS, recommends year-long programs, he knows that many parents and students think a year is too long. In response, AFS has evolved. "We have introduced short programs for Americans to go abroad with very specific content, during the summertime, for instance—the refugee program in Hungary, or street kids in Colombia—and so the participants feel that they have had an international experience, an intercultural experience, and that they did something good for the community and for themselves."

Swapping fear for understanding

One of Beckie Rankin's high school French students named Stasia took advantage of another organization's ten-day program, which gave her an opportunity to play with a student orchestra in France. She plays French horn.

"I'll never forget walking into the room where I was staying," Stasia recounted. "It was really tiny—a tiny box with two bunk beds that probably had three feet of space in between them. So the people that you were living with, you were *living* with." Another surprise came when she met her two roommates. One girl was from Spain and the other from Russia.

"Both of them were there trying to learn French. I just thought, 'Wow, this is super cool. Not only are the American people coming to learn French, but there are people from other parts of the world.'"

Rehearsals were challenging. "The girl who sat next to me was actually a French student learning English," Stasia said. The rehearsal was conducted in French. "I wouldn't get something and we sort of had to figure it out, especially because music vocabulary isn't really something they talked about in class."

Stasia realizes that some parents and kids are worried about going overseas. But, she said, "The fear aspect of going into a new country and being afraid that you're not going to be able to get around is definitely never something that should hold you back."

The 'leap of faith' for parents

Whether long or short, studying overseas in another language while in high school is often the most memorable and impactful experience students have during those years, at least judging from the people I've interviewed and the testimonials you'll find on the SYA and AFS websites. And recent research shows that the critical period for acquiring language with native-like fluency may be longer than previously thought—extending all the way through the high school years.

After a successful business career, our failing high-schooler, Doug Renfield-Miller, served on the board of School Year Abroad, the organization that gave him so much just when he needed it. His own three children each went on an SYA experience and, Doug said, it helped all of them go to the college they most desired: Bowdoin, Yale, and the University of Pennsylvania. He told me he knows that today's parents and students are concerned that spending a year abroad will take them away from other important activities at home, but counsels, "The benefits of a year abroad are going to far outweigh anything that they lose."

Jenny Messner understands the anxiety parents might have—her own daughter did an AFS program. To these parents, Jenny says, "Take a deep breath, and if your child shows an interest in the world out there, please encourage them. Even though it's not something you have done, even though it's not something you really want them to do, give them a leap of faith, and be not afraid."

I asked Jorge Castro of AFS what his message is to American parents. "See around you and understand that the world of today is not at all what we grew up in, and that knowledge of other cultures, languages, and different points of view is what will make the world change for the good in the future."

✳ ✳ ✳

Chapter 25

BILITERATE SEAL OF APPROVAL

Ron Unz first came to public attention in the 1990s, when he ran for governor of California, challenging the incumbent Republican Pete Wilson. A Harvard grad with a degree in physics, Unz claimed he had an IQ of 214. The press dubbed his campaign the revenge of the nerds.

Unz lost his bid for governor but returned to the public spotlight later in the decade with a proposition that sought to abolish bilingual education in California.

Unz claimed that bilingual education was a failure, was holding kids back, and should be replaced with English-only classes. He argued that English-only was the fastest and best way to have immigrant children acquire English.

At first, the people who knew better didn't take Unz seriously. Why should they? For someone who was supposed to be so smart, he clearly didn't understand, or was ignoring, all the research. Ever since the Peal and Lambert study in the 1960s, evidence had been mounting of the advantages for kids who were educated in two languages—both immigrant kids and native English-speaking kids. This fellow was an interloper pretending to know things he didn't.

Ignoring facts and winning fearful hearts

But Unz did know a few things about human sentiments. He knew that immigrant parents wanted nothing more than to have their kids completely proficient in English—and if abandoning their family language was the price that had to be paid, they would pay it. Unz also knew that many Anglos worried about the record numbers of immigrants in California and feared these immigrants weren't learning English, the way earlier immigrants had.

Unz also understood the widely shared belief in America that English unites us as Americans, and that the perpetuation of other languages can seem subtly, if not flagrantly, un-American. And Unz had learned something about waging a political battle, too. He cleverly named his campaign, "English for Our Children." Who could be against that?

By the time the educators, administrators, and professors saw all the media attention Unz was getting, they were already playing defense. He staged headline-grabbing press events with immigrant parents demanding mainstream English education for their children, portraying them as victims of an entrenched bilingual bureaucracy whose members were intent on holding immigrant children back in order to preserve their jobs.

Unz got enough signatures to get Proposition 227 on the ballot. His opposition tried to present the science that showed he'd got it all wrong, that educating children in their first language led to better outcomes, including better command of English. But their scholarly studies were weak ammunition against sound bites of anguished immigrant parents worried about their children, and Anglos worried about America.

Julia Brownley, a mother of two, was on the school board of the Santa Monica-Malibu Unified School District in 1998 when Unz got his proposition on the ballot. "I was very, very opposed to it," she said. While Unz was telling the media that bilingual education was a disaster, Julia said, "I felt just the opposite, that it is really such a huge benefit to our country, embracing our diverse cultures, and promoting multiculturalism in our society just enriches us so deeply."

Unz returned to Harvard to debate with professors, including Harvard's Catherine Snow. When she pointed out that not a single expert in language education or psychometrics had endorsed his interpretation of the data, Unz countered, "I think academics should look at the reality of the world rather than at theories published in a lot of books." James Crawford, a journalist and past executive director of the National Association for Bilingual Education, attended the debate. He concluded that Unz should be awarded a "doctorate in demagoguery." Snow had another description of Unz: "diabolical."

On election night 1998, the votes were tallied: Proposition 227 passed, 60 percent to 40 percent. Its implementation would mean that parents had to sign a special waiver, written in such a way as to make it seem like they were accepting serious risks in allowing their children to be taught in two languages. It would have the desired chilling effect.

Changing the narrative

"It was a very, very sad evening," recalled Shelly Spiegel-Coleman of that election night. She and her like-minded colleagues had gathered at a restaurant in East LA to watch the returns come in, with growing consternation. Shelly became one of the founders of a group that organized out of the ashes of that lost battle against Ron Unz. It was to be called Californians Together, and its mission was to get bilingual education back on track in the country's most populous state.

Reflecting on their loss, Shelly and her colleagues realized that having the facts and science on their side had not been enough. They had failed to make the issues clear enough to move the electorate. The truth was that bilingual education, done right, was better than monolingual education. The truth was that kids are better off being bilingual and can become so with no loss to their English skills—not just immigrant kids, but all kids. But how to get this across to voters?

Shelly heard about something going on in Los Angeles County that sounded promising. Back in 1992, educators in the Glendale Unified School District had developed a bilingual competency award that recognized high school seniors who were bilingual and biliterate in English and Spanish. In the years following, the school district added Armenian, and then many more languages. Shelly recognized the sleeping giant contained in this little-known award. Rather than seeing Spanish, Armenian, and other languages as problems to be overcome, the award celebrated competence in languages and valorized the skills of these students.

She and her fellow members of Californians Together imagined the powerful message this would send if the award could bloom outside of Glendale—particularly if it were a statewide award, officially recognized by the State of California. They began the long process of preparing a bill for the state legislature.

"We ran the bill through both houses and we did get it to Arnold Schwarzenegger's desk when he was governor," Shelly said. The group reasoned that since Schwarzenegger was an immigrant himself, getting it signed would be a sure thing. It wasn't. Schwarzenegger said there wasn't yet strong statewide criteria for the award, and also questioned whether history teachers would then want a history seal, and math teachers a math seal.

Meanwhile, Julia Brownley, after serving on her school board for twelve years, including as its president, was elected to the California State Assembly. She was now in a position to advocate for the State Seal of Biliteracy bill. "For our young people today to succeed in today's global economy, it is very beneficial to be proficient in more than one language, and certainly as a country I think that we need to promote the importance of speaking a language beyond our own."

When Schwarzenegger stepped down, Jerry Brown got elected as governor and signed the rewritten bill. "When our state finally passed legislation is when we saw large numbers of students being able to be recognized," Shelly said, and then gave it some context.

"We're talking about high school seniors. At graduation, the athletes get recognized, the high academic achievers get recognized, and now at graduation, biliterate students get recognized. And they're recognized by the state, and this creates in local communities a real sense of pride. I think that changes people's minds and attitudes." Shelly was more right than she knew.

A 'nudge' quickly gains traction

Once the Seal of Biliteracy became law in California in 2011, other states quickly followed, starting with New York six months later and Illinois about six months after that. "We were getting all kinds of calls asking for help and advice," Shelly said. "We were very, very surprised by how it spread throughout the nation. We *never* had that in mind, ever."

One of Shelly's colleagues in the cause was Arthur Chou, a publisher of bilingual textbooks. He traveled to many of the states, helping people write their own bills to go to their statehouses. He also created a website with a color-coded map where everyone could watch the progression of states adopting their own seals of biliteracy. Today, those states nearly blanket America.

The Seal of Biliteracy is what the Harvard Law School professor Cass Sunstein might call a *nudge*. It is neither a requirement nor a rule, nor a law. Rather, as a nudge, it is part of what he calls choice architecture, which can be enormously influential in changing behavior. The Seal of Biliteracy offers students an award they can earn by demonstrating their skills in English and another language, as shown in written and oral tests. The seal is a physical thing you can touch. And it appears on student transcripts, signaling a meaningful accomplishment for universities and potential employers to see.

A counter-proposition

And what of Proposition 227? State Senator Ricardo Lara drafted a new bill that would repeal it. Proposition 58 was placed on the ballot in November 2016. Shelly and the crew at Californians Together went back to the same restaurant where, eighteen years earlier, they had suffered their defeat. Senator Lara and Steve Zimmer, the president of the Los Angeles Unified Board of Education, joined them.

That evening, as the results of the presidential election unfolded, Proposition 58 passed, and by an even wider margin than Proposition 227 had back in 1998: 73.5 percent.

"We were overwhelmed with joy," said Shelly. "It passed in every single county in the state. It got more votes than any other proposition on the ballot. The sentiment about learning multiple languages and having all students have that opportunity was the antithesis of what we had in the previous proposition. It was an amazing, amazing turn of events."

The seal had worked its magic. "We knew that the work we had done honoring students for their bilingualism and their biliteracy contributed to this positive outlook and this positive attitude," Shelly said. "We all were very hopeful for the future."

Julia Brownley, who by then had been elected to the US Congress, told me, "As somebody that's been legislating now for a long time, it is extremely rewarding when you see an idea become law in your own state, but it is extraordinarily rewarding to see it replicated and to have other states recognize that this is a good idea."

We were able to talk with a California student who earned the Seal of Biliteracy, to get a student's perspective. Jose Andrade grew up speaking Spanish at home and not learning English until he began school. He told me that he and his friends always spoke informal Spanish. But at school, in order to earn the seal, he had to take advanced Spanish literature and be able to discuss and write about the works in Spanish. Because of that, he said, he aced his AP college entrance exams. "I was able to get a 5 on both the language exam and the literature exam. So it's pretty awesome."

Jose told me that at his graduation, he explained to his parents, in Spanish, why he was being recognized in the ceremony. They don't show a lot of emotion, he told me, but his mother took his Seal of Biliteracy in her hands. "Her eyebrows raised, looking down through her glasses, and she ran her fingers across the seal and, you know, just looking at it, and slightly nodding her head. I know that she was definitely proud."

✳ ✳ ✳

Chapter 26

WHY A GAP YEAR
IS A GOOD YEAR

As I write this, Paulina Jedrzejowski is still in college, yet she has already lived in several other countries and learned their languages. Paulina's story illustrates a promising trend in America in which young people are redefining what their parents called a gap year.

"My parents are immigrants from Poland, but they met in New York. I think my dad came in '93 and my mom in '91, and then I was born in '96. My grandparents bought a house, so we lived there," Paulina told me. The three-storey house in Brooklyn was home to three families—Paulina's grandparents and aunt on the first floor, tenants on the second, and Paulina and her parents on the third. "I would say we are a conservative household," Paulina said. "We only speak Polish at home."

Like many American immigrants today, Paulina's parents wanted to keep their heritage language alive in their daughter. "I went to regular public school from Monday to Friday and I went to Polish Saturday school," she told me. She continued at the Polish school studying history and geography and later added Polish literature.

"Within the first ten years of my life, I went to Poland about five or six times, so almost every other summer," Paulina said. "I would say I'm fluent. It is easier to speak and read and write in Polish than it is in English. English almost seems very formal to me. I probably use more sophisticated words in Polish than I do in English, which is weird."

Paulina was placed in her public school's honors classes in sixth grade and was assigned to the Italian academy, so she had three years of Italian before entering high school, where she took Italian for four more years.

"I think that knowing Polish helped me with learning Italian because the Polish grammar structure comes from Latin as well," Paulina explained. "I was able to pick up on it that much faster than my peers who only spoke English."

Between her junior and senior year in high school, Paulina had an unusual study abroad experience. She was accepted into the American Youth Leadership Program, which the US State Department runs. "I ended up going with the State Department to Bosnia and Herzegovina, and I interviewed multiple organizations about how they work to sort of alleviate the ethnic conflicts that are still occurring there."

I asked Paulina if her languages helped her there. "Polish did help me in some aspects because in Bosnia they mostly speak Serbian, and Serbian and Polish are both Slavic languages."

Paulina graduated her high school as valedictorian. She was doing everything right . . . or so it seemed. But she told me that she was fearful of "messing up." She knew how much her parents expected of her. And she was about to throw a wrench into her perfect track record. Paulina decided to postpone college for what's commonly called a gap year.

A bridge, not a gap

When Paulina had been researching scholarships for college, she came across something called Global Citizen Year, a program that sends high school graduates overseas to work on projects and be immersed in a non-English language for a year before beginning college. Programs are currently conducted in Brazil, Ecuador, India, and Senegal.

The founder and CEO of Global Citizen Year is Abby Falik. "Historically, we have considered this gap year to be somewhat remedial for kids who are off track or who might need an extra year to mature or maybe didn't get into college," Abby told me. But, she added, "I think that the term 'gap year' needs a refresh."

The problem, she explained, are the connotations that go along with gap year, including that it's for privileged kids, or it's not purposeful. "So for that reason, we've actually used other language. We like to call it a bridge year or launch pad."

By any name, Global Citizen Year is not an easy program to get into. "We are quite selective, and we're selecting for things that look different from a college application process," Abby explained. "We're looking for resilience, great curiosity, and drive. We don't even look at test scores and grades. We also are not screening for family income. We've got a need-blind admissions process, which is really core to our model."

When Paulina floated the idea to her parents of postponing college and instead going to Brazil for a year of service, it didn't go well. "My parents were not really happy with it. They wanted me to be on track—high school, college, law school." They expected her to do all this "because they sort of had this feeling that they didn't continue with their opportunities. My dad said, 'Okay, you can volunteer at home and I can pay for your Portuguese lessons if you want to learn Portuguese.'"

Instead, Paulina decided to try for the scholarships available for Global Citizen Year.

Her parents eventually relented and let her apply for the program. Not only was she admitted, but her scholarships came through as well. Paulina was off to Brazil and would be learning her fourth language.

"Even though I spoke English, Polish, and Italian, it was hard," said Paulina. Her host mom didn't know any English. "But she sat down with me every evening after dinner and made me tea. And then I would have my phone with Google Translate and she would try to talk to me about different things—how my day was, or just asking me about my family. It took me a while to figure out what she was saying and then when I did figure it out, it took me a while to communicate back. She was extremely patient."

Language immersion is a big part of the Global Citizen Year experience, Abby said. "We live in a globally integrated world, but not necessarily a world where we understand each other. We can't really connect with other people unless we are speaking to them in their own language, or at least making some effort to do so." And the entire school year gives enough time, she says. "You've got no shot at learning the language unless you stay long enough, so that's really been core to how we do what we do."

"It was a very good way to learn," said Paulina. "Maybe not every day, but like, every three or four days, I would notice that it was becoming easier to communicate. I didn't need to use Google Translate for certain words and I could remember certain things that I wanted to say."

Within the first month, she could form simple sentences and comprehend about half of what Brazilians were saying. "I would say it took me about eight weeks to be like, 'Okay, I think I got this.'"

In time, Paulina adjusted well—maybe too well. "I didn't want to come back! I think it was in the beginning of March where everything just sort of started making sense and it was like, 'Okay, I could live this, this could be my life.' I cried during the last week. I think I cried every single day for at least five minutes."

But Paulina did come home, with the hope of somehow connecting her two worlds, "which I knew was not possible."

A college president applauds postponing college

Abby told me that colleges are starting to be more open to bridge years and some are even encouraging it. I was able to speak with one of America's leading experts in the economics of higher education, Catharine Bond Hill, who had recently stepped down after a decade as the president of Vassar College. She serves on the Global Citizen Year board.

"I've watched freshmen go to college and then take a year off, sometimes eighteen months, sometimes two years—figuring out what it is that they want to do," she told me. "We don't get students through college very quickly. Our graduation rates across American higher education are very low, and that's a very inefficient and expensive way to get students through higher education. So if we could have a program that got students more college-ready, and ready to jump in and be committed and matured a little bit, that would be a great solution."

Cappy, as she is known, thinks that taking a year off could actually get kids through college quicker. "Something like only 60 percent of kids that go on to four-year programs graduate in six years. So if you thought about a gap year helping students get through quicker, it could actually improve educational attainment rather than slow it down."

Like Abby Falik, Cappy also thinks the term "gap year" is not the best, although it might be too late to change it. "But I do like the bridge year terminology," she added. "And if we could slowly shift that to be more the norm, that would be great." She also believes that as colleges become more open to bridge years, the practice will grow. "To the extent that it is valued by admissions officers and college administrations, it will create the incentive for students to think about whether it makes sense for them."

Fortunately, Paulina found that college admission offices viewed her bridge year positively. She was not only accepted into Tufts University but also received a veritable bouquet of scholarships.

The idea of taking a year off from the education treadmill got a lot of media attention when President Obama's older daughter, Malia, decided to take a bridge year before attending Harvard. I asked Abby whether that high-profile example made a difference in changing attitudes.

"Absolutely yes," she said. "We saw our applications double. When the President's daughter says, 'Hey, I'm going to Harvard and I'm taking a year,' it suddenly made this aspirational for the go-getters, and not just the do-gooders."

Closing the gaps between cultures

Even so, the number of students taking a bridge year is still small—less than 1 percent of high school students, according to Abby. "I think realistically, if one in ten kids opted for this path, we'd be in great shape. And that's both realistic and totally achievable."

I asked Paulina what her father thinks now of her year in Brazil before college.

"He sort of sees that, 'Okay, if you want to go somewhere, you can go because you went on this gap year and you came back and everything's okay.'"

As for herself, the experience led to two other, unexpected changes in her life. She returned home wanting to get to know her little brother more, which she has done, and being less concerned about making mistakes.

"Before, I was not open to mistakes. If I made a mistake I thought it was the end of the world." But her year in Brazil, she said, "allowed me to take more opportunities and more positive risks, like, 'Okay, let me try this out. I don't know if it's going to work out or if it's not going to work out.'"

I was able to witness this confidence firsthand when I met with Global Citizen Year fellows in California after they had returned from their year-long experiences. There were hundreds of young fellows, as they are called, who had just returned from Brazil, Ecuador, India, and Senegal. I was impressed with their confidence and positive attitudes about the world and themselves. Abby says seeing that transformation is what motivates her.

"We can't think about the other as separate if you have actually come to feel like they are part of you, and that your fates are wound up in each other's lives. We can't hate what we've grown to love."

Chapter 27

WHAT THEY DON'T TEACH YOU IN HARVARD'S SPANISH CLASS

I want to share with you my own experience in a twenty-first-century language class. While I was researching this book, I found myself—somewhat unwittingly—taking an intermediate Spanish class at Harvard. I learned more than I bargained for.

✳ ✳ ✳

It is January 2015, just before the arrival of blizzards that will set records in Boston and close the campus for an unprecedented three days. I meet Adriana Gutiérrez, Senior Preceptor in Romance Languages and Literatures, in her cozy office on the fourth floor of Boylston Hall, an unremarkable stone and metal structure that hides behind the monumental Widener Library on Harvard Yard. I drape my coat over one of her chairs and sit where she had gestured. I had come to try to learn more about how Harvard teaches languages to its students.

Adriana is Mexican American. She asks me where I am with my Spanish (intermediate, I offer). I think she might then begin speaking in Spanish, but she spares me and continues in English.

She explains the communicative, or post-communicative, teaching method they use at Harvard today. Students do study grammar, but not more than half of any class is devoted to it. Instead, most of the class is conversation. Students talk about stories and poems they have read, or movies they've watched outside of class. The emphasis is on listening and speaking, while at the same time, learning about Latino culture as it is expressed in many countries.

And it's more than just language skills Harvard cares about, she says. "Our goal is to help reduce stereotyping during the process of learning about the language and the different countries and cultures that speak Spanish, and help create transcultural and translingual students," Adriana explains. She adds: "But if you really want to understand how we do it, you should take a class yourself."

Her office suddenly feels hot. The thought of taking a Spanish class with Harvard undergraduates makes my heart skip a beat.

But listening to Adriana, I realize she is right. Besides, my Spanish could use the help. I haven't taken a Spanish class since sixth grade with señor Masters and *"Hola, Pepito, ¿cómo estás?"*

310 Sever Hall

At one o'clock in the afternoon the following Monday, I show up for the first day of "Spanish C: Intermediate" at Sever Hall. Climbing two flights of the wide central staircase, I enter room 310 ten minutes early, which is a good thing, since soon, more than fifty students file in—too many for the small room, and so they line up along the walls when our teacher begins. (As at most American universities today, Spanish is the most popular language at Harvard.)

María Ramírez López apologizes for the crowding and explains that we will soon be divided into sections of no more than fifteen students so that we'll all have plenty of chances to speak.

She speaks only in Spanish, which I partially understand, but looking around it seems that most of the students understand her perfectly, and some are already speaking back in impressive Spanish. While she passes around our first homework, I wonder, *Just how far over my head am I?*

Fortunately, classes are canceled the next day because of snow, which gives me more time to plot a survival plan.

On Wednesday, I trudge through snowdrifts to the same classroom and find that María was true to her word about reducing class size. She and I are the only two people in class. When the bells begin to peal at nearby Memorial Church signaling 1:00 p.m., students start to arrive; by ten minutes after the hour, there are twelve students, freshmen and sophomores mostly, and one old guy, who would be me.

María starts conversations and works her way around the semi-circle of chairs, making sure everyone participates, including me. She also breaks us into groups of three or four for a few minutes, to practice among ourselves.

I appreciate that the students don't seem to treat me any differently, even though I'm old enough to be their granduncle. Yet when class ends at two o'clock, I realize that if this were a *Survivor* episode, I would be voted off the island. I am definitely the weakest at understanding and speaking. And I'm not even sure I should try to participate. The undergrads are taking this for a grade, after all, which many need to get into graduate schools of one type or another. I am an interloper. So I go to office hours that first week to ask María if I should try to participate in class or just sit back and observe.

"Of course, you must participate!" she tells me in Spanish. "There is no other way for you to learn."

After our first week, I make a list of how things stack up.

My classmates' advantages:

- They are smarter than me.
- They take tests really well.
- They have had more Spanish, including grammar, and quite recently.
- They can hear perfectly well, whereas my hearing is starting to go.
- They are highly motivated to get good grades.
- They seem to relish the mental struggle.
- They are all very nice.

My advantages:

- I show up on time.

And now I have a clear idea of what's in store: classes four days a week, four hour-long written exams, four two-page papers (first and second drafts), a presentation on *español en la calle* (Spanish in the street), which requires me to take photos or videos of Spanish in the streets, and—the sour cream on top of this educational burrito—a ten-minute oral presentation with a partner. Clearly, I will need all the help I can get to not make a complete idiot of myself.

I decide to attend all the office hours I can. (It turns out undergraduates these days apparently don't like office hours very much, preferring to engage virtually, so it's not hard to see María every week.) I attend the extra tutoring sessions the language department offers once a week for thirty minutes. I go to Mesa Redonda (roundtable) dinners in the freshman dining hall. Once a week, an instructor dines with students who want to practice Mandarin, Italian, German, Spanish, and other languages. As at some other colleges, all the freshmen at Harvard eat together.

On a typical evening at Mesa Redonda, there are: one Chinese American student whose Spanish is actually even worse than mine (although she is fluent in Mandarin); an enthusiastic native speaker from Argentina, whom our instructor happily chats with; a nerdy fellow who rattles off Spanish like a champ (but I can tell speed rather than accuracy is his thing); and me, the gray-haired guy, struggling to hear in this monumental hall alive with jovial feasting.

I take every opportunity Harvard offers its language students, but I know that won't be enough, so I hire a private language tutor, too. Her name is Luz Zuluaga, from Colombia (whom we met in Chapter 3); I meet with her once or twice a week for her to help with my grammar and conversation, but not to correct my papers, which would be cheating (what's now referred to as academic dishonesty). Our instructor wants to see our writing raw, so she can discern our progress.

Test day

As the date for our first exam looms, I am nervous. It has been decades since I took a college test. María is nice enough to tell us exactly what will be on the test, but that doesn't help much, since I could have used another month to study her list of topics.

When we show up at 310 Sever on test day, the chairs have been rearranged from their usual semicircle into tight horizontal rows, I guess to make it harder to look over someone's shoulder. We hand María our two-pound textbooks so she can check off that we have done all our grammar assignments. Then she hands us two pages stapled together, with questions on both sides.

We sit down and spend the hour hunched over our exams. Some of the questions are sentence completion, but the hard questions are the essays about the articles and poems we've read. It's all in Spanish, of course. I set about my test in a mild panic.

After about forty minutes, some of my classmates are already turning in their papers, but I have braced myself for that. I am determined to work until María pulls my test from under my pen. When she finally says time's up, I am relieved that there are a few other students still sitting there with me.

How did I do? I have to wait a few days to get my test back, but the truth is, I don't know. I guessed about some of my answers, but at least I finished.

Language labs are so last century

The university has a language lab, but we don't use it. I ask Adriana Gutiérrez why not.

"Students do go to the language lab in order to watch the movies we require in our courses; and they also go if they need technical support with their projects—podcast and video editing. But there is really no need to go to the language lab to do oral drills anymore, which is what students used to do before. We know now that grammar drills and repetition do not help language acquisition. We prefer to engage in all four skills, face-to-face, in the classroom." The four skills are reading, writing, listening, and speaking.

Back in 310 Sever, every day we have homework not only in our textbook, but on separate sheets as well. One day as class starts, I can't find mine. I desperately rummage through my bag twice, but no luck. I fall back to the basics: *"Se la comió mi perro."* ("My dog ate it.")

Besides the volume of work, several other things impress me about the course. First, true to what many of the language teachers I had interviewed said, María almost never corrects what any of us says. I learn later this is by design. María and the other instructors have discovered that there is more to be gained by allowing students to speak imperfectly than by correcting them, which can have a chilling effect. By allowing us to babble on, never making fun of us or correcting us, she creates an atmosphere in which we are all eager to speak. The emphasis is on conveying meaning rather than on accuracy.

Or as María later explains to me via email after class, "Students should be in a motivated, calm, and productive learning environment in which they will feel confident to take risks and to participate. I always let them know that making mistakes is a natural step of learning a second language, and that I am not there to judge them but to guide them through the learning process. I encourage them to participate without distressing about making mistakes."

Stealth fixes

She does, in fact, correct us, but in such a wonderfully stealthy way that we don't really know she's doing it. She'll rephrase what we (incorrectly) say, emphasizing the part that needs correcting. "Sometimes I paraphrase what students said with a question or comment. In this way they don't feel intimidated and it doesn't break the flow of the conversation," she adds.

And not surprisingly, there's a reason why she breaks us up into small groups.

"I consider that interactive activities are necessary in order to give as much practice as possible. Working in pairs and small groups gives students the chance to develop communication skills. I design my classes to be very interactive so as to reinforce the new materials presented." As for grammar exercises, she leaves those for homework.

I am also impressed by the readings for the course. We are assigned serious poetry and essays on meaty topics concerning Latin America—the political issues, the struggles of women and the poor, the perilous lives of immigrants. I learn about the Nobel Peace Prize winner Rigoberta Menchú. She didn't learn Spanish until she was twenty, and did so in order to be able to convey her story of coming of age as an Indigenous woman in Guatemala, pulling herself out of poverty and helping her people to do the same.

The readings would have been heavy going in English; in Spanish they are doubly challenging. Plus, we are expected to discuss and write about the reading.

But there is also the sheer beauty of Latin American literature. We read poems by Jorge Luis Borges, Pablo Neruda, Luisa Valenzuela, Julio Cortázar, Nicolás Guillén, and Tino Villanueva. And while it is a struggle, I realize this is more than a Spanish class: it is a history and literature class, too. In the more advanced language classes on campus, students read literature, write about it, and discuss it. Even in this intermediate class, we are getting used to doing that.

And it isn't all serious. María plays the song *"Me gustas tú"* ("It's You I Like") by Manu Chao, which has us all laughing.

Peer pressure

A few days later, María waits till the end of class to discreetly hand back our tests. I nervously open my two stapled sheets of paper to find a B+. I take a photo of my grade and text it to my kids. They text back congratulations and smiley faces. Maybe I could survive this class after all.

I look at my paper again and notice that María has not used the customary red ink to convey my grade but rather, violet. Other tests I get back during the course are graded in blue ink. Later I learn that this isn't any accident, either.

"Studies have shown that students think they've been evaluated more harshly when their work is covered in red ink compared with more neutral colors," María explains.

I learn another important thing: peer pressure works on me. When I have to participate in class, have to take tests, have to write papers, have to do presentations with a partner who needs a good grade, I feel a need to perform.

In contrast, when I was managing my own language learning, as I was for the past five years, what I was missing most was accountability. Yes, I went through many audio programs and computer programs and apps and even had personal tutors. But still, when I was running the show, my pace was slow. Now, with this classroom setting, I am making the fastest progress I've ever made. It's hard but it feels good.

No pain, little gain

When it comes to physical exercise, I usually have enough discipline to do it myself. I don't need classes or an exercise boot camp. But when it comes to language learning, I apparently do need a kick in my butt by people I've made a commitment to. I need demanding coaches to keep me accountable.

Many parts of the learning are delightful, fun and fast, but other parts are a struggle and you must embrace it—permit the pain of searching for words, of not being able to express what you wish. For this is just when we learn the most, right? And how many things truly worthwhile come without a struggle?

I'm not sure any technology, no matter how useful for language learning, can provide what a great coach or teacher can. Perhaps it's because we're in the habit of being accountable to people, not to software and books.

Does that qualify as culture?

The midpoint in our semester arrives and a classmate asks if I will be his partner for the oral presentation. He has no idea how grateful I am. I thought María might have to assign someone to take me on as a charity case.

Josh Robinson is a freshman with a ready smile and a haircut the Marines would be okay with. Over coffee, I ask him about his background. "I went to six different high schools between Virginia, Arkansas, and Texas," he tells me. "My parents divorced and I lived with my aunt and uncle, both of whom were in the Army at the time."

"Well," I say, "you must have done something right to get into Harvard."

"I guess Harvard felt sorry for me," says Josh. "Plus I did pretty well on the tests." (Later I learn that he, like most students here, had nearly perfect test scores.)

Josh tells me that his father is a truck driver and is thirty-eight years old. His mother has never been on an airplane. Josh is half Black and half white, "but I look Dominican or Puerto Rican, which is why I feel so compelled to learn the language and the culture. So many assume that I'm of Latino descent, I figure I should at the very least be connected." He also tells me, with a soft smile, that he has a Spanish-speaking girlfriend, a fellow freshman.

Josh is taking French at the same time, I learn, and is considering majoring in Romance languages and literature. He figures it might help his ultimate goal, which is to become a rapper.

Mulling this as I sip my coffee, an idea pops into my head for our presentation. I say, "Why don't we do a radio interview, where I play a disc jockey and you play a famous rapper?"

Josh likes the idea and says he can give the history of Reggaeton in his responses, which should meet the Latino culture requirement.

"What's Reggaeton?" I ask. Josh is polite enough not to raise his eyebrows but instead explains that its origins trace back to Jamaican dance hall music, especially to a guy named Shabba Ranks. Josh says he'll send me a few links to get me started. We say goodbye and I realize my education is about to take an unexpected turn.

The date arrives when Josh and I have to meet María during office hours and make our pitch that our radio skit should qualify as a report about Latin American culture. Our Spanish must have been pretty horrible because she twice makes us try other words. Finally she says, "But it's supposed to be about Latin American culture, like poetry or art."

"Reggaeton is important music out of Latin America today—important for my generation," says Josh. I nod and say something like, "Yes! It's important for the young generation of today," as if I have any idea. María shrugs but gives her assent.

Josh and I do high-fives in the hall. Then we sign up for one of the last time slots to buy ourselves some time.

On Air

The date finally arrives for our oral presentation. To help our act, I ordered some Mexican T-shirts for us. Josh's is black with a giant label that reads *Hecho en México* (Made in Mexico); mine is blue with one Spanglish word printed in white, "Mexellent."

Josh and I have practiced and have our script written out on my computer, along with the music clips I am to play to illustrate Josh's story of Reggaeton, while on his own computer he clicks through his slides describing the music's history. I launch in with "*Sí, son las doce, medianoche, soy Doc y bienvenidos, chicos, a nuestro programa: El nuevo grito aquí en 109.7, Tijuana, México.*" ("Yes, it's twelve midnight, I'm Doc and welcome, guys, to our program: The New Scream at 109.7, Tijuana, Mexico.")

Our classmates seem to be enjoying the show. I'm not sure about María, but I'm too busy trying to speak my lines and hit the right buttons on my computer. Josh is doing his *rapero* thing with a natural flair.

All of a sudden, I realize to my horror that I have jumped ahead and skipped a whole section of dialogue. But Josh rolls with it like a pro, and we finish on time and to much applause from our classmates. I'm not sure what María thinks of it all; we'll have to wait till we get our grade to find out.

As our course enters its final week, I'm feeling good about the progress I've made, earned from hard study in private and uncomfortable struggle in public. I can tell spirits are high in the class, too.

The final exam comes, and once again the chairs are aligned in tight rows. I struggle more than usual and am among the last students still working when our time is up.

Later that final week, we finish up our *español en la calle* presentations. Mine isn't particularly wonderful, especially when two of my fellow students have to come up and help me with my computer.

María, with her soft, friendly manner, encourages us all to continue our Spanish and move up to Spanish 30, the next language class in line.

Later, home alone, I go online to check to see if my final grades are in. They are. I see that I got a B on my final exam and that my final grade is a B+. I'm delighted. But then I see that one last grade is still outstanding—class participation. I send an email to María to ask when those will come in. She replies within minutes that she has just finished adding those grades, and *"Espero que continúes con el español, has progresado mucho. Tu nota final es una A-."* ("I hope you continue with Spanish, you've made much progress. Your final grade is an A-.") I leap up from my chair and do a happy dance. Showing up on time got me over the hump, after all.

✳ ✳ ✳

Memorable, but not exceptional

My experience at Harvard is one that's being played out, with different scripts and in different classrooms, throughout the country. The Modern Language Association reports that some 1.4 million college students are enrolled in a language class across more than two thousand American colleges. That shows some serious scale. And if those students have a thirst to excel at a language, they will most likely find professors and departments at all of these colleges and universities who are more than able to quench it. We saw this in Victoria Duclos's experience at Florida Atlantic University. And we can see it in the unusual story of a late-entry college student of Italian heritage named Nick Staffa.

Nick told me that he took Italian in high school because of his Italian heritage. "After high school I kept up with it a little bit on my own time, but really nothing much, and, you know, life gets in the way," he said.

Instead of going to college after high school, Nick devoted himself to his music, managing a music store, giving guitar lessons, and playing in his band. But, of course, there aren't many Bruce Springsteens.

"I decided that I needed to go back to school and get a degree in something because I just kind of felt unfulfilled, so I decided to go back to a local community college here on Long Island." He enrolled at Suffolk County Community College, which had a language requirement.

The school told Nick it had been too many years since his high school Italian; he wouldn't get any credit for that. He had to start over.

"I asked them what they had and they were very excited to tell me they were offering Chinese for the first time and they didn't really have many people signed up for the course. They were trying to kind of rope people in. I thought it was interesting, so I gave it a shot."

It was a very basic course, but Nick liked it and got an A for two semesters. "I wanted to go for the four-year degree, so I decided to shift over to Stony Brook University on Long Island," he said. Stony Brook also had a language requirement. "I figured to get my language sequence finished, I might as well continue with Chinese," Nick said. "After all, I was good at it."

He signed up for intermediate Chinese at Stony Brook and was in for a shock. "I would come into class and I'd see a couple of classmates in the hallway and tell them, 'Boy, that homework last night was a real killer, it took me a couple hours to finish.' And they're kind of scribbling it in and finishing it in five minutes before class in the hallway."

"So what happened?" I asked.

"I bombed out," he said, laughing. "It was like going from the minor leagues to the majors." One important difference was that almost all of his fellow students were native Chinese kids who, Nick said, were taking the course to boost their GPAs.

"I felt it was kind of unfair," Nick admitted. "But, I don't give up very easily." Nick decided to tell his professor, Agnes Ha, that he was struggling. Agnes is a professor of applied linguistics and Asian studies at Stony Brook.

"Not a whole lot of students transfer from community college and take the courses that I teach," Agnes told me. She said Nick's Chinese wasn't good enough to enroll in her class, but "he just struck me as a most unusual student, who's most curious and passionate about languages and cultures in general." So Agnes created an independent study course for Nick and arranged for a private tutor: one of the school's graduate students. Nick met with his tutor several times a week for a year. His goal, he said, was "to catch up so I could take the class the following fall."

The next fall, Nick signed up again for the same class he had bombed out of. He continued to work hard, and by the end of the semester, he'd earned an A. "After that the fire was lit, and I was really hot to continue," Nick told me. "So I took the next course." By the time he graduated, Nick was the Asian American Studies undergrad with the highest standings.

Said Agnes, "He was definitely a star student. In fact, at his commencement, he was the one who carried the banner representing our department."

"It was a pretty triumphant day," said Nick about his graduation, and he is deeply grateful to Agnes. "She's just such a caring teacher. She saw the potential I had and knew it would probably change my life, so she stuck with me and really pushed me along."

The true strength of America's colleges

The language classes at Harvard are excellent, but they are not unique. The true strength of American higher education is not the handful of ivy-clad institutions we have, but rather, the broad expanse of fine colleges and universities across our country where dedicated language teachers recognize committed students and help them achieve their goals.

What they don't teach you in Harvard's Spanish class is grit. And when students have grit—as Victoria and Nick do—in America, they can excel.

Chapter 28

SPEAKING THE LANGUAGE
OF OUR GRANDPARENTS

Philadelphia in the 1920s was still a very WASP-dominated town, recalled the sociolinguist Joshua Fishman some eighty years later. But Fishman was not a WASP. Rather, he was the elder child of Yiddish-speaking immigrants from Czarist Russia. "The neighborhoods in which I lived . . . were all middle-class Jewish neighborhoods populated largely by Yiddish speaking immigrant parents and grandparents, on the one hand, and by their proudly and demonstratively Yiddish-ignorant children and grandchildren, on the other hand . . . ," he said in an interview.

We met Joshua Fishman in Chapter 1. He was the man in the photo with Stanford professor Guadalupe Valdés, and the one whose book, *In Praise of the Beloved Language,* she introduced me to. He passed away in 2015 at the age of eighty-eight. Luckily before that, the two editors of another one of his books interviewed him about his early life. They wanted to get on record how it was that he was able to develop the insights on bilingualism that were so far ahead of the scholarship of his day.

Language loss undergoes a radical shift

Fishman's father was a dental mechanic, "a profession he acquired, along with his American citizenship, while serving in the American Army during World War I." But in addition, recalled Fishman, his parents were "unofficial ministries of culture and education" of the Yiddish language. Even as his father made and repaired artificial teeth, "the telephone was always cocked to his ear as he incessantly conversed with other activists, teachers, writers and actors throughout the country." His mother, meanwhile, "addressed masses of envelopes and postcards pertaining to forthcoming conferences, readings, poetry recitals, theater performances, school meetings, etc."

Fishman excelled at Olney High School, where he studied Spanish since "only girls took French." He won a scholarship to the University of Pennsylvania. His father wanted him to become a dentist and he tried to obey, but eventually young Fishman switched his major from pre-dent to history and added Spanish. In four years, he earned both his BS and MS, graduating in 1948. He then enrolled at Columbia for a PhD in Psychology.

He began teaching social psychology at City College of New York during the McCarthy years, writing academic articles about the spectacle and expressing his outrage at McCarthy's "Red Scare" terror tactics. The young instructor achieved professional milestones quite early in his career. He became a full professor after only five years and was invited to be a research fellow at think tanks around the world, forming a particularly long association with Stanford.

Fishman thought it odd that his colleagues were writing so much about language loss, or language shift (a term he coined), yet very little about how to prevent it. He didn't accept the assumption many of his colleagues held that language shift is "some supposedly natural drift of historical events or the obvious direction of social change."

Maintaining minority languages was not only possible, Fishman said, but also the right thing for the millions of Americans who risked losing not just their roots but the means for navigating their world. He coined the term reverse language shift, or RLS, to signify the reclaiming of a language. Champions of minority languages were not "defenders of some mystical, mythical and bygone past," but were actually finding better ways of living in the modern world by being bilingual. And he found a new way of describing these languages rescued from a family's past.

"I tried to get away from the 'foreign' because it didn't fit well into my notion that these were all American languages," Fishman said in another interview. "'Heritage' is a term that involves your inheritance, something that you have, thanks to the kindness of your ancestors. It involves personal, intergenerational ties."

But in the 1950s and '60s, when Fishman was making these arguments, Americans had more pressing matters than old-world languages to concern themselves with. And even if they thought this young professor made some sense, no one really had any idea what the linguistic landscape of America was. The only inquiry into languages on the US Census was whether people spoke English at home. If yes, no further questions. If no, census takers asked what language was spoken and how well did each person speak English. The resulting data gave little information about the range of languages an American might speak, and how well. It wasn't deemed worthy of attention. Fishman found this lack of knowledge unacceptable. While the Pentagon was counting Soviet warheads and baseball fans were counting homers by Frank Robinson, Fishman began counting American speakers of minority languages.

A landmark book on immigrant languages

In 1966, the forty-year-old Fishman published a language book unlike any before. *Language Loyalty in the United States: The Maintenance and Perpetuation of Non-English Mother Tongues by American Ethnic and Religious Groups* was the first reckoning of an American resource mostly unknown and certainly uncelebrated.

On the first page of his preface, Fishman wrote that the book was "particularly appropriate at the present time when non-English language skills have been recognized as scarce and vital commodities in the conduct of our nation's international affairs." It was a not-so-veiled reference to Sputnik, the Soviets' dramatic proof of beating us Americans into space. Now Americans were worried about also falling behind the Russians in defense and education—and suddenly realized that there was a shortage of Russian speakers.

For what may have been the first time in America, Fishman suggested a different way of viewing the languages of immigrants: not as problems but as *resources*: "Is it possible," he asked, "that these resources are being wasted as a result of apathy and ignorance?" Fishman reported data from 1960, the most recent year at the time, noting there had been declines across nearly all twenty-three immigrant languages in the number of speakers compared with 1940.

After nearly five hundred pages of data and analysis, Fishman concluded that only good would result from putting in place policies and practices to encourage bilingualism in America . . . yet it wasn't laws and rules we needed, he said. "Both language maintenance and ethnicity have become and must remain entirely voluntaristic behaviors in the United States." But, he added, success is "dependent on an encouraging and facilitating environment."

Fishman's call for "an encouraging and facilitating environment" for language maintenance was answered in many ways in the years that followed publication, including in the growth of dual language schools, the propagation of the Seal of Biliteracy across the American states, the improvement in language teaching in conventional classes, and in yet another important way: the rise of a new way of teaching young people who already have a family connection to the language. This specialized teaching has come to be called heritage language instruction.

Teaching the heritage language to those who speak it

A frequent visitor to Guadalupe's office at Stanford was a young postdoctoral candidate from Mexico named Maria Luisa Parra.

Maria Luisa found inspiration in both Guadalupe, with her deep commitment to immigrant children, and Fishman, whose work she brought to Harvard when she was offered a position there. "I've been here for five years," she told me in 2015, "but before that, there wasn't any heritage language teaching at Harvard."

Maria Luisa told me that the Latino students at Harvard are, not surprisingly, pretty much superstars in English, but—surprisingly—their Spanish can be another story. Conventional language classes, like the one I took at Harvard, are geared toward people with no background in the language—those L2, or second-language learners. Heritage students are different. They grew up with the second language in their home, and typically have strong listening and oral skills. Even so, said Maria Luisa, it's not unusual that such young people are ridiculed by older family members for the way they speak their heritage language, sometimes causing them to reject it entirely.

Since they typically receive little if any formal instruction in their family language, they are usually weak in reading and writing. "Heritage speakers come in with the language they learned at home, not necessarily the standard Spanish or correct Spanish," said Maria Luisa. "But what is 'correct'?"

With heritage language teaching, she explained, "it's more about expanding their options to speak in different contexts." So in her classes for Latino undergraduates, students learn the kind of Spanish required to write letters, articles, and essays, and they read about Latino culture—"to validate themselves," says Maria Luisa, "and to embrace their own situation."

A language wardrobe

Another luminary in the field of heritage language teaching is Kim Potowski, a professor at the University of Illinois at Chicago. Kim likens the Spanish that many of her heritage students speak to beachwear. "It's entirely appropriate to wear cutoffs and flip-flops when you're at the beach, but you wouldn't wear that to a wedding or a job interview." She and other teachers of heritage speakers offer their students a wider wardrobe to choose from.

"A lot of times when you're raised in the US, your English is very, very strong and your heritage language is very, very weak," said Kim. "So in this analogy, it's kind of like saying you only have beach Spanish."

I encountered just what Kim is talking about in one of my Uber conversations. Getting into a car in Milwaukee, my driver and I got to talking and I found a way, as usual, to ask her if she spoke another language. "Spanish," she told me brightly. Her mother was a native English speaker but her father was Puerto Rican. "I was Dad's favorite, and he used to put me on his knee while he read his Spanish newspaper. He had me read it to him."

When she grew up, my driver married a Puerto Rican man, as her mother had. Of her own four children, only her third learned Spanish. "That's because he liked to spend time at his grandparents' on the Spanish side," she explained. But "we speak ghetto Spanish," she said. "We weren't well trained in school."

Kim said that with students whose backgrounds are like my Uber driver's, "one of the main things we want our heritage teachers to know is that we should not stand there with the red pen and correct them—'That's wrong, that's wrong, that's wrong, you're wearing a bathing suit, that's wrong!'"

Instead, said Kim, "a huge part of our job as heritage language educators is to, number one, raise students' linguistic self-esteem." To do this, the teachers explain some sociolinguistics, Fishman style, and why it's entirely natural and expected that the students speak their heritage language the way they do—mixing in English, missing the formality normally used outside the home. Once this linguistic understanding is in place, then the teacher can move on to the more standard and formal aspects of the language—some fancier clothes for the students to add to their linguistic wardrobes.

Without such support, language skills of the descendants of immigrants can erode quickly. As Fishman wrote, "older children are more linguistically retentive than younger children, first children more so than last children, children more so than grandchildren . . . ." Without intervention, languages are typically lost in two generations, and sometimes even in one.

Why some lose their heritage

My friend Ed De La Torre was one year old when his family moved from Puerto Rico to Pittsburgh, where he still lives. Although he has no recollection of spending his first year in Puerto Rico, "I am Puerto Rican, through and through," he told me.

Ed's parents came to America after World War II to pursue their American Dream. And they found it. Ed's father started a business making orthopedic braces, a trade he learned with the help of the GI Bill. And, as was common in twentieth-century America, Ed's parents didn't speak Spanish to Ed or his brother. "They were just so busy living life and trying to provide for the family," he said, "that's all they focused on."

There may have been another factor as well. Ed saw how his father suffered prejudice because of his thick Puerto Rican accent. One offended hospital administrator said they could no longer do business with the De La Torre firm, even though all the doctors and patients praised his father's work.

Ed's parents came to the US not just to thrive economically, but also to get their boys the education they themselves never received—and to get it in American English.

"They enrolled us in the local public school," Ed recounted. "A lot of Americans may think, 'Oh, that's just a very common, obvious thing that you do.' But for two very poor Puerto Ricans who came from small villages, sending their child on a school bus every morning to a very well-established public school—for them, that was like striking gold." But by not speaking Spanish to Ed, his well-meaning parents unintentionally subjected him to a different kind of poverty.

Every summer, the family would return to Puerto Rico for two weeks. "And, of course, everyone was speaking Spanish and having a wonderful time," Ed told me. "And I remember very distinctly *hating* those moments. Because I couldn't understand what anyone was saying."

I've known Ed for many years. He's a magnanimous man, a great husband and father. He's also a very successful businessman, having grown his parents' business by leaps and bounds. But his inability to speak Spanish continues to be a regret in his life.

"I have been very involved in leading mission trips for my church," Ed said, "and most recently medical mission trips, leading medical teams to Guatemala. I find it odd that I have to work through an interpreter."

Even in America, Ed told me, he often encounters Latinos who are dismayed, given his name and complexion, that he can't respond to them in Spanish. He realizes he could learn Spanish, but feels, having been left out all his life, he's just not willing to put in the time.

Ed's language biography is representative of the millions of Americans who came of age in the twentieth century. But in our present century, it's becoming less so. Ed's daughter, Allison, whom we met in Chapter 16, became proficient in Spanish and now speaks the language of her grandparents. She is a living example of Fishman's RLS—reverse language shift.

Rich daughter, poor daughter

We met Amber Forrest in Chapter 18; her trip with her mother back to the Philippines was tinged with sadness for the same reason Ed's was. Amber knew only some buds of bilingualism in Tagalog and thus could tell her grandmother, "I love you, I miss you," but that was all. But due to some different choices, plus some heritage language classes, another young American woman of Filipino descent had a different experience.

Working today as a medical assistant at Stanford Health Care, April Leyson came to America when she was two-and-a-half. Her mother spoke Tagalog to her and to April's older sister. April is not comfortable speaking Tagalog, but understands the language fully. She is what linguists call a passive bilingual. In high school, she took three years of Tagalog. Because of that, she can read the language. "Those were good courses in Tagalog. We were mostly Filipinos, but we had some in the class who were not."

When April's grandfather was dying, her mother took her back to the Philippines. Although she was uncomfortable speaking, she could understand. She understood what her grandfather was saying, while she answered in English.

And while April says she is still self-conscious about speaking Tagalog, she sings it boldly. "I love singing Karaoke in Tagalog," she told me. "One of my favorites is 'I'm an Old Soul.'" April wants to get better at her Tagalog, encouraged by her progress so far. She told me, "I sound fluent when I sing."

Americans regain their voices

"I don't just want to validate them, I want to help them," Maria Carreira told me. Like Maria Luisa Parra and Kim Potowski, Maria Carreira is both a heritage language educator and also a teacher of other teachers, helping them understand the important nuances of heritage language teaching. She told me that validating the way they speak their heritage language is the starting point. Then teachers can move on to building their students' capabilities.

I met up with Maria, who is a professor at California State University, Long Beach, at a conference for heritage language scholars and educators. She is a heritage Spanish speaker from Cuba whose family moved to Chicago when she was eight. Maria told me you'll commonly find a close connection between teachers and students in heritage classes "because they share a common fate of being, in some ways, between two cultures."

In teaching these students, Maria said, it's important to remember that balanced bilingualism is an ideal rarely reached. "They themselves may never reach the level of a native speaker of Spanish, and that's okay. They can greatly improve their Spanish and get to a professional use of the language, yet remain something different from a native speaker."

At the conference, I was also able to interview Elham "Ellie" Sadegholvad, who teaches Persian at the University of California, San Diego.

"We are getting more third-generation students now," Ellie told me. For many of her students, it's the first time they have been around so many other people who share their Iranian American heritages and their incomplete grasp of Farsi. She says she normally has about twenty in a Farsi class and their skills vary. "The most common is that they can speak but they can't read or write at all," Ellie said.

One young woman in her class has an American father and Iranian mother. "When she started, she could hardly have a conversation. She took my class three times and then went to Iran for a language immersion summer. She really loved it and came back proficient." What's different about heritage language classes, says Ellie, is that "it's not just any language; it's their heritage. They are more passionate about it. It means something to them and brings them closer to their families, their identity and their culture."

Ellie told me that the heritage languages program at UCSD started with Armenian, Vietnamese, and Korean and now also has Arabic, Persian, and Tagalog. Maria Polinsky, whom she described as "a pioneer in heritage language," started the program.

Maria "Masha" Polinsky moved from California to Harvard, where I was able to interview her. "I think heritage language education will make a difference in language retention," she told me. She shared the story of a nineteen-year-old student at Harvard from a Korean American family. She took a Korean class for heritage speakers her junior year, and when reading Korean publications, discovered the Korean gaming industry. "She was a typical Harvard A-type personality," Masha said. "She started a company importing Korean games to the US." Her language skills made her startup possible. "We need more success stories like that," said Masha.

Today there are many more opportunities for the children of immigrants than there were when Ed De La Torre was a student in Pittsburgh. Children can find themselves in a community-based school, like the Greek one in Miami, in one of the increasing number of dual language schools, even in "conventional" language classes where they are likely to gain more usable skills than in the past. In most states, they can earn the Seal of Biliteracy on their high school diploma. What's more, in college and sometimes even earlier, they can find classes specifically designed for heritage speakers like themselves, where their language skills can take flight.

The "encouraging and facilitating environment" that Fishman called for in 1966 has, in our twenty-first century, begun to materialize. We see it in the establishment of the *Heritage Language Journal* in 2002, the National Heritage Language Resource Center at UCLA in 2006, and the Coalition of Community-Based Heritage Language Schools in 2012. Most important, we see and hear it in the voices of bilingual young Americans, writing, speaking—and sometimes singing—the languages of their grandparents.

Chapter 29

THE SEDUCTIVE POWER
OF STUDY ABROAD

O n January 20, 1838, a large audience poured into a lecture hall at the Sorbonne in Paris. The students were gathering to hear a talk about the ancient Greek philosopher Heraclitus. Among the university students were two or three Black men, dressed finely and "'having the easy, jaunty air of young men of fashion.'" So noted another student in that lecture hall that day, an American named Charles Sumner.

Sumner had come to the Sorbonne to study the history of Greece, civil law, and geology, but the education he received before that lecture began—seeing how well accepted the Black men were among their French peers—was to have a profound impact on the young American. He realized that the insidious master-slave relationship between whites and Blacks in his home country "'does not exist in the nature of things.'" Later in his life, Senator Sumner from Massachusetts was to become one of America's most outspoken and effective white advocates for the abolition of slavery.

The Americans who traveled to Paris in the nineteenth century came to open their minds to the latest knowledge in the arts and sciences, for at the time, America was still mostly agricultural—a land blessed with natural resources, space, and frontiers long absent in the cosmopolitan cities of Europe, but lacking those cities' sophistication and innovative thought. The historian David McCullough tells the tales of Sumner, as well as James Fenimore Cooper, Samuel Morse, Oliver Wendell Holmes, Ralph Waldo Emerson, Nathaniel Hawthorne, Mark Twain, Henry James, and other intrepid American voyagers in his book, *The Greater Journey: Americans in Paris*. Their visits not only changed their own lives but also changed

America, as they brought home their broadened perspectives and took action upon them.

While these Americans came with different dreams, they were alike in one respect. "With few exceptions," writes McCullough, "they were educated and reasonably well off, or their parents were. Most, though not all, were single men in their twenties . . . ."

One who did not fit that last description was Elizabeth Williams Champney, who graduated from Vassar College in 1869, a member of the second graduating class of the women's college that the brewer Matthew Vassar founded. After college, Lizzie, as she was known, returned to her parents' home in Kansas, where she became engaged to a farmer. But an artist named James Wells "Champ" Champney, who had been her art instructor, sought her out. The two were married in 1873 and went to Europe for a tour.

When they returned to America, Lizzie began publishing short stories for popular magazines, including Harpers, and then tried her hand at a novel titled *Three Vassar Girls Abroad,* published in 1883. Part travel book, part adventure story, it found an enthusiastic audience; over the course of the next dozen years, Lizzie produced ten more *Three Vassar Girls* novels, with romantic and evocative illustrations by her artist husband.

Study away from home and beyond your comfort zone

A century after Lizzie graduated, Vassar said adieu to its Seven Sisters heritage and began accepting men. By the 1970s, Vassar students still included the daughters, and now sons, of the privileged, but it had broadened its acceptances to promising students coming from all classes. When a bright student named Lori Granger, the daughter of a Navy dentist and granddaughter of immigrants from Canada and Sweden, chose Vassar, she didn't feel out of place among her classmates. A few years after she graduated with her class of 1979, she became my wife.

During her junior year at Vassar, Lori went to study in Madrid. "My father was happy when he learned that it would cost less than staying at Vassar for that semester," she told me. As with most junior year abroad students, it was the most memorable time of her college experience. "It was the biggest, most exotic trip of my life—something I'd dreamt of since starting Spanish lessons in second grade." Her classmate and fellow traveler, Carolyn Cain, told me, "Every day was an adventure." Carolyn went on to a career with the World Bank and has traveled, by her count, to 112 countries—"maybe a few more."

When we started our company together, Lori's former flowering of fluency in Spanish and her comfort with living overseas helped me expand my own expectations of traveling the world in search of products and suppliers, which we and some staff members did for the next twenty-five years. Moreover, the friends she made among her fellow students in Madrid have stayed friends. Most of them have also pursued international careers, and these "Vassar girls" continue to travel together on trips to almost as many places as Lizzie's fictional ones did.

A generation after Lori attended Vassar, the college has become even more open to promising students from every economic level and ethnicity. Its admission process is "need blind," meaning that if students are accepted on merit, they will be able to attend through scholarships, regardless of their ability to pay tuition. What's more, the college puts an emphasis on study abroad. I was able to visit the campus to interview several of the faculty responsible for their international programs.

The cultural staying power of study away

Dean Ben Lotto is a professor of mathematics and an advisor to what Vassar calls study away programs. "We insist that the student is fully prepared. We have a minimum of two years of language and really, that isn't enough," he explained. It's best if students come to Vassar with some language skills. They must also take history courses and keep their grades up. Although Vassar doesn't require study abroad, "it's part of our culture, so 40 percent of our students do study abroad," Ben said. And, as when Lori was a student, Vassar makes study away affordable. "We are a home-tuition school, so if you have a scholarship, that goes with you overseas."

Susan Correll Kennett, the director of international programs, has been guiding Vassar students going abroad for more than twenty-five years. I asked her what impact the experience has on students. "It's hard to measure, but when they return to campus they seem more flexible and not as demanding, they pay more attention to politics and their own history," she said. She also explained that "it's a self-selected group." Students have to figure out themselves which program to apply to, how to get their passports, and so on.

"It's much easier just to stay on campus where everything happens for you," Susan said. "Students who study abroad have to have a certain spark that will push them out of their comfort zone; you have to be a driver."

The changes at Vassar are indicative of the changes in American colleges overall: far more students study abroad today than in years past, and they are a more diverse group.

Go abroad, return transformed

The keeper of the flame (and the facts) for study abroad in America is the century-old Institute of International Education, or IIE. The organization encourages study abroad through its Fulbright scholarships and some two hundred other programs that support students overseas. These include the Boren Awards, which the Defense Department underwrites for the study of such strategically important languages as Arabic, Dari, Pashto, and Somali. It also includes the Gilman scholarships for students of limited financial means; various scholarships for particular countries and regions; as well as scholarships that corporate-based foundations sponsor, such as the foundations of Adobe, Cargill, Chevron, and GE.

In 1985, about fifty thousand American college students studied abroad for credit. By the turn of our present century, that figure had almost tripled to 144,000. Eighteen years later, that figure had more than doubled again, to 342,000 students. As of 2018, about 16 percent of American undergraduates in four-year colleges and universities were studying abroad at some point during their college years.

The staff at IIE would like to see those numbers go even higher. Probably the biggest challenge is all the enticing amenities, activities, and opportunities that today's colleges and universities in the US offer. American places of higher education are pretty swell places to hang out, but money is still a factor, too. "Not everybody has the means to go abroad," said Liza Carbajo, the head of higher education initiatives at IIE, "even though universities and colleges are working very hard to make it affordable for everyone." Those efforts are paying off as reflected in the composition of today's venturesome students. Fully 30 percent are non-white, which is up from 18 percent a decade ago. Liza, who was the head of study abroad at Florida International University in Miami before coming to IIE, told me about one student of Jamaican descent who had a real impact on her.

"I learned that her mother was dying of cancer," Liza began. "She didn't know how long her mom was going to be alive, but her mom was very supportive of her going abroad. She was a senior, so this was going to be her last opportunity."

The student did end up doing a program in Italy. Midway through it, her mother died. "Her sister called me and I said, 'Let's mobilize everything we need to bring her back,'" Liza continued. "But the student said no. She said, 'My mom said this is what she wanted.' And her aunt agreed. 'We want her to finish.'"

One factor driving up the numbers of student voyagers has been the availability of shorter, more focused programs, mirroring the trend in high school study abroad. Even these shorter programs can have a profound impact on the students, said Liza. "Once the students go abroad, whether it's for a week, two weeks, three weeks, they really come home transformed in just such a short period of time." She said there are students who had never left the US before this. "Just by getting on a plane and being in a very different environment gives them that desire to keep traveling, and to really keep learning and growing."

Before the students go overseas, "a lot of them are unsure, not as confident, just a little fearful," Liza told me. But when they come back, "they come back more confident, more independent, just full of energy and understanding."

I asked Liza if every college student should study abroad.

"That's our hope. Each student should have that opportunity. They need to step away from their own culture in order to be able to even appreciate their culture when they come back."

The student version of the expat trap

Along with shorter programs, another trend is that more classes are taught in English, even when in a country where English is not the primary language. Part of the reason, says Liza, is that overseas universities want to attract international students, and it's easier to do that if they teach in English. But like the high school study abroad organizations AFS and School Year Abroad, IIE encourages students to study and immerse themselves in another language for as long as they are able. The president of IIE, Allan Goodman, considers it imperative for American students to learn another language. "It is a mistake of the present for us to think English is sufficient as a lingua franca to serve us all," he maintains. "No one should graduate without proficiency in another language and having studied in a culture beyond their own."

Vassar's Susan Correll Kennett agrees. "We make sure they don't live with other Americans," she said of their study away students. In my language biography interviews, I've encountered Americans who were well aware of the student equivalent of the expat trap, and managed to not be snared. One such student was Ben Macklowe, who is today the CEO of Macklowe Antiques.

"I decided to go to France my sophomore year, my second semester. I just left and went to Avignon. I said that if I wanted to learn French, it's not going to happen in Bedford, Massachusetts. So I went there and stayed for five months and spoke French nonstop," he told me. "I made all the American kids in my group kind of uncomfortable because I wouldn't speak back to them in English. I found three or four other kids in my group who were willing to do the same thing, so we were the ones who actually developed a real proficiency in the language. I had a headache every day! But that was the best French education I had."

Today Ben uses his French daily, as his business specializes in French antiques. He told me his business success has been utterly dependent on him being fully bilingual.

Diana Tess, the dean of the Spanish village at Concordia Language Villages we met in Chapter 23, escaped her expat trap by accident. "I spent my junior year abroad in Madrid, and I was the classical thing—I hung out with the American friends my first semester," she told me. But then during winter break, most of her friends left, and there were only Diana and two friends left. "We went out and met Spaniards and that changed my life entirely," she said. "I spent the second semester hanging out with Spaniards instead of hanging out with Americans, and it was just amazing, the difference."

International students coming to America

Worldwide, more than 5.3 million students study abroad and more than one million of them, some 21 percent, study in the US. That makes America the top destination, by far, for international students. The UK is second, with just under half a million students, while China is a close third.

These million students who study in the US generally stay for several years in order to earn undergraduate or graduate degrees. And like the number of American outbound students, these inbound numbers have also increased dramatically, doubling in the last eighteen years. The reason? Primarily the rise of incomes in Asia, India, and worldwide. These students bring in about $45 billion annually to the US, mostly in the form of tuition and living expenses their parents pay for. That revenue supports or creates an estimated 458,000 American jobs.

But the international students bring more than money—they bring skills in their own languages, often making friends with their American counterparts, some of whom are learning those languages. The students also assist American faculty members in language classes, helping to teach their peers.

These exchange students do much to internationalize American colleges and universities and prepare young Americans for the globalized world they will encounter upon graduation. Moreover, these international students do truly represent the world. The top ten countries for sending students to America, starting with the highest number of students, are China, India, South Korea, Saudi Arabia, Canada, Vietnam, Taiwan, Japan, Brazil, and Mexico. But as we're about to see, the percentage of international students in America is small compared with what it could be.

The nations that fill the largest percentage of their seats with international students are Australia (28 percent), Canada (21.4 percent), the UK (20.9 percent), and New Zealand (15.5 percent). It's no coincidence that all four of these top percentage countries are English-speaking. International college students, and their parents, recognize that English skills will be important for their career success.

If we continue down the list of the top nations for receiving international students, we see something curious. Number five is France with 12.8 percent. Then come the Netherlands, Finland, Sweden, Germany, Norway, Russia, Spain, Japan, Poland . . . and *finally*, the US, with a mere 5.5 percent of our seats warmed by international butts. We have far greater capacity to accept international students, and the benefits they bring, if we wish to. As more colleges and universities see the advantages of adding more international students, the international nature of American higher education may well increase.

The greater journeys continue

US study abroad numbers are increasing due partly to innovation in the way colleges work together. Some college majors, engineering being a good example, can be pretty packed with requirements, making it difficult for students to finish on time if they go overseas. To address this, IIE created a program called the Global Engineering Education Exchange, in which more than seventy universities in more than twenty countries work together to allow students to receive credit for their engineering classes overseas, at the same tuition they pay at home. Integral to the program, says the IIE, are "paid internships in an industrial setting or laboratory in the host country." It's a competitive program, "selecting only the most promising students with sufficient language ability to successfully complete coursework overseas and engage in a meaningful work experience in industry."

Beyond the growing numbers of American college students studying abroad for credit are students who go abroad for other activities, including more than thirty-eight thousand who go to participate in conferences, athletic competitions, and artistic performances. At the graduate school level, thousands more go abroad for research and other individualized programs.

There are also Americans who take a year between college and graduate school to do their own work or study abroad in another language. That's what the son of my friend Amjad did. Amjad is from Jordan and holds dual citizenship in Jordan and the US. His family speaks mostly Arabic at home, but Amjad told me his son's Arabic was poor. "So he took a gap year after he finished his bachelor's degree and went back to Jordan and worked on his Arabic, his reading and writing skills especially, because he realized that this will be a great benefit for his professional career." Even so, Amjad was worried about his son taking such a break from school.

"I was a bit concerned," he admitted, "because I thought that taking a gap year might take him off his goal to study law." But after his year in Jordan, his son did return to the US and began at Harvard Law School.

Another figure on the rise is the number of Americans who go overseas not just for college credit, but for full degrees. These are usually graduate degrees, like the MBAs David Wolf earned in France, and Cyrus and Philip Roepers in Spain. As of 2018, that number exceeded fifty thousand Americans annually.

I ran into such an aspiring graduate student at another of those cocktail parties I seem to hang out at. Nikhil Malekal was an AmeriCorps tutor-mentor who lives in Chicago. His parents, immigrants from India, each speak "a few languages," he told me. They spoke their native language to him as a boy, but he doesn't read or write it. He took Spanish in high school and college, at the University of Chicago, where he majored in psychology. But he surprised me with his graduate school plans. "My father works for a Japanese company," he said, "and I want to as well." So Nikhil applied and was admitted to an MBA program in Japan. The classes for the MBA begin in English and then transition to Japanese, Nikhil told me. He is planning on taking intensive Japanese over the summer to prepare. "I never got a chance to study abroad when I was in college," Nikhil said. "So now I'm doing this."

Compared with just twenty years ago, hundreds of thousands of *additional* young Americans go overseas to study every year. While terrorism and pandemics have reduced travel in the short term, study abroad has always recovered and grown again. The impact of more Americans making their own greater journeys is bound to add up. These venturesome students who have experienced what it's like to live in another country, and in another language, are poised to soon put their hands on the levers of power in America.

As the language teacher Carrie Toth told us, "If you go to Capitol Hill and talk to some of the interns there, they're bilingual and they've had these study abroad experiences and so, as they grow, they're going to become our politicians and our principals and our company owners." Like Charles Sumner two centuries earlier, twenty-first-century American students who venture beyond their own borders see the world more broadly. They return equipped to make their country a more enlightened and effective participant on the world stage.

Chapter 30

THANK YOU FOR YOUR SERVICE

Beyond the dual language schools, the summer camps, the bridge years and study abroad, there are yet more ways young Americans are becoming bilingual. They are doing it through service to our country.

"I basically lied on my application and said I had two years of French, and two years of Spanish in high school, to widen the possibility of getting accepted," Mark Ford admitted to me about his application to the Peace Corps. "As it turned out, I got accepted to serve in Africa—in Chad, which is a French-speaking country."

Mark had, in fact, no French language training at all. It was true that he had taken two years of Spanish in high school, although he performed poorly. Had this been in the early years of the Peace Corps, when volunteers were given their language training in Vermont before being sent overseas, Mark might have been discharged before he began. But this was 1975, when the Peace Corps was fourteen years old, and had switched to its present model of two years of service, with the first three months being language and cultural training—in-country.

"So of the thirty or forty of us Peace Corps volunteers that they brought over to Chad that year," Mark recounted, "there were two of us that, on the government scale of zero to four, tested at a zero." Not surprisingly, one was Mark. The other was a young man named Greg Alex, who became his friend. "He had done the same thing," said Mark. "He actually pretended that he knew French."

The Peace Corps: one way or another, you speak the language

In the 1970s, one of the faculty members responsible for teaching languages to Peace Corps volunteers was Alvino Fantini. "The Peace Corps in the mid-'70s began to move the training programs in-country," Alvino told me. "There was a stipulation. We used the Foreign Service Institute proficiency ratings, so we were looking for a level of proficiency which was at least one-plus, which would be interpreted as basic survival skills. If the trainees did not attain that level, they were often de-selected from the program and had to return back home. It was a pretty horrific process and very emotional for everyone involved."

Mark and his friend Greg seemed prime candidates for such de-selection. But, said Mark, "after [the Peace Corps] spending so much money getting us over there, and since they were going to have us spend six weeks in intense language training with students from the University of Chad, they decided to put us in our own class." It was embarrassing, Mark told me, being in the special-education class. "Greg and I decided to make a little vow. Since we were kind of the black sheep of those six weeks, not only would we study hard, but we wouldn't speak a word of English—and not just during the six hours of training every day, but every other hour, even when we were talking to ourselves and other Peace Corps volunteers who were talking English all the time."

Alvino, now a professor emeritus from the School for International Training in Brattleboro, Vermont, knows plenty about the kind of immersion experience Mark and Greg imposed on themselves—from decades of teaching, and from personal experience.

Alvino became an exchange student at sixteen, spending a high school semester in Mexico through the Experiment in International Living program. "That experience affected me greatly, as it does many people," he explained. "The main thing it did for me was recognize that being of Italian ethnicity was okay, because I grew up in a time when things were not favorable, and I was always embarrassed by my own ethnicity."

As a youngster, Alvino had always cringed when his grandmother called to him in her native Italian in front of his playmates on their street in Philadelphia. But spending those months in Mexico, he said, "I learned to accept my own ethnicity, as I learned about another." The experience was so life-changing for Alvino that he decided he would devote his career to giving the experience to others.

He attended the University of Pennsylvania, where he met a young Bolivian exchange student, whom he would marry. After college and a stint in the military, Alvino decided he would help others study abroad. "Two weeks later I was taking my first group to Europe," he said.

Alvino's experience was very much like that of Sargent Shriver, the first director of the Peace Corps. Alvino told me that Shriver had also been an exchange student with the Experiment in International Living, which Alvino now worked for. As head of the Peace Corps, Shriver awarded the first language training project to the Experiment in International Living in Vermont. "We were teaching volunteers to go to East Pakistan—now Bangladesh—Venezuela, Bolivia, Dominican Republic, Gabon, Ghana, Senegal, and Afghanistan," Alvino said.

For Alvino, language learning wasn't just a nice-to-have for these volunteers; it was fundamental to the Peace Corps' experience and effectiveness. "They had to learn languages and learn how to get along with people on someone else's terms." And because of the volume of volunteers the Peace Corps was running through the training center in Vermont, he saw plenty who feared they wouldn't be able to learn the language. "So many people I have met come and say, 'Oh, well, I'm not a good language learner,' and I think there's no such thing. I mean, there are some people who have more abilities than others, for sure. But I think everybody can learn. It has to do with motivation and interest."

The real lessons of the Peace Corps

Meanwhile, in Chad, Mark and Greg were meeting resistance from their college-aged language teachers. "They didn't want to work with us, but after a while, because of our juvenile sense of humor, they all fought to spend time with us." The French verb for fart is *peter*, and the command is *pète*. "So," Mark said, "when our teachers would say '*répète*—repeat—we would say '*Mais, je n'ai pas encore pété!*', which means, "But, I haven't yet farted!" Their teachers would bust up laughing, said Mark. "We would literally say that every single time they forgot and asked us to repeat, and they never stopped laughing, and so we became good friends with them and they took a lot of extra care with us."

At the end of six weeks of their living, breathing, and joking in French, Mark and Greg were tested again. "We both tested at three, a level which is considered to be moderately fluent. Out of the forty volunteers, we went from the bottom to the top 20 percent—in the group with volunteers who had taken four years of French." Mark relayed this with justifiable pride.

Mark was assigned to teach English literature at the university. The teaching was to be done in English, but French was everywhere, especially in arguments. "I was trying to shove *My Last Duchess* down their throats and they gave me a very sophisticated argument, in French, about how they shouldn't be required to study and write an essay on this colonialist poem that was, you know, out of date anyway."

In his second year in Chad, Mark was asked to teach an introductory course on the French philosopher Jean-Paul Sartre, whose works Mark had been studying as a graduate student back in America. He was to teach the course in French. "The most intimidating thing," Mark relayed, "were the faculty meetings. My French had to be impeccable. If I made one little slip, they would let me know."

But clearly, Mark's French had been improving dramatically. "When I met a French person they would say, 'Where are you from?' They were always surprised to hear that I was a native English speaker, especially from the USA."

As gratifying as Mark's journey had been with French, the world it opened for him in Chad delivered an even greater reward.

Mark's wife, Kathy, came over to join him. "We lived in a small three-room mud house that had an exterior bathroom," Mark said. The two twentysomethings became part of their local community, and Mark's perspective was altered in a fundamental way.

"I'm a big booster of the Peace Corps," he said. "But I would say don't ever go in the Peace Corps if your motive is to be helpful to other people or to save the world, because that's not what happens. What happens is, you save yourself.

"If you're naive enough to think that you—big American, wonderful you—are going over to a poor country to automatically somehow make their lives better," Mark continued, "that's a very self-centered, crazy thought. It disappears very quickly when you're in their environment, dealing with the same kind of problems, and you realize you're less capable of dealing with them than they are, and you're not any smarter than they are, and you're not any more resourceful than they are."

What the Peace Corps gives you, Mark told me, is "a chance to be part of a community. I taught English literature and I'm pretty sure I didn't improve Chad's economy by doing that. But I made some friends, and perhaps there were some students over there that somehow got some personal benefits from my classes, or decided that not all Americans were horrible."

Alvino agrees with Mark's assessment. "The Peace Corps has done some wonderful things for other people in other countries, but one thing I'm really convinced of is that the Peace Corps has been one of the most powerful educational institutions in *this* country—doing something for Americans because it provided them with challenging experiences in intercultural contexts, where they had to learn languages and learn how to get along with people on someone else's terms."

Mark told me that during his years in Chad, he also learned a lesson about happiness. He was sitting on the porch of his mud house one rainy, cool day, listening to the monkeys on the roof, thinking about the life he and Kathy had built. "We had beautiful simple food, we had friends that lived right across from us that we could spend time with. We had local music. Our life was full and rich, and I was very happy.

"I kind of knew that one day I was going to go back to the States and get into business and make a lot of money," he continued. "And I said to myself, 'One day you're going to be living in a fancy house, but it will not be a better house than this.' And it's been true to this day."

Mark did return to the States and he did make a lot of money publishing newsletters and magazines, including *International Living* magazine. He continues to use his French for business and pleasure. Oh, and he did move into a fancy house, although it has no monkeys on the roof.

Truly talking like the locals

Alvino, who recently completed a long-term study of some two thousand people who studied and lived abroad, makes a distinction between tourists and what he calls sojourners. Tourists, he explained, look at monuments, eat the local food, and enjoy the countryside. In contrast, "the sojourner is going to live on the host's terms with the idea of establishing relationships. And that's the key." I was able to interview such a sojourner, a more recent Peace Corps volunteer named Matt Shipley.

I asked him why he had joined the Peace Corps. "My mom is huge into social work," Matt told me. "She's a saint, and it was my opportunity to do my part."

Unlike Mark, Matt could be honest on his application when describing his high proficiency in Spanish. He had benefited from his parents having a Latina housekeeper when he was little—although when he took Spanish in school, his classmates would make fun of him. "I'd speak with a Spanish or a native accent and the kids would make fun of me, but the native speakers appreciated it."

By the time Matt finished high school, he had already completed two study abroad immersion trips, the first to Costa Rica and the second, a six-week stay with a family in Guadalajara, Mexico. In his Mexican host family, the mom was a professional chef and she held cooking classes at the house. "I ate so well," said Matt, "it was ridiculous."

Matt managed to steer clear of the expat trap. "I was in the minority who went out and mingled with the locals. It's really easy to fall back on English, to just stay with your countrymen and not to mingle." Instead, Matt served as an informal translator for other American kids because host families didn't speak any English. He also made friends with local rock climbers.

As a student at the University of San Diego, Matt studied abroad in Spain. "I went to live in Spain my junior year for a whole semester. All my classes were in Spanish—art, history, literature. That was one of the hardest times because it was every day, all day. You weren't allowed to speak English, including with Americans." Matt made friends again with rock climbers. "I'd get a good climb in and then go back by bus, speaking Spanish on the bus. I had to really pay attention because the accent was a lot more harsh in Spain. It doesn't even sound like Latin Spanish."

When Matt was accepted into the Peace Corps, he had his choice of Paraguay or the west coast of Africa. It was any easy choice: Paraguay, because of his Spanish. But he was in for a surprise.

"In the cities it's all Spanish," Matt explained. "But as soon as you get out of the city, it's all Guaraní. That's the first and national language of Paraguay, so I felt the need to step up and learn."

Matt took three to five classes a week in Guaraní with three other volunteers; they did this for three-and-a-half months. "There were local ladies who had been teachers for the Peace Corps for a number of years; they were very helpful. I was trying to learn so much. I had a little pocket notebook and I'd take it everywhere." When he would hear something he didn't know, "I had them write it down in Guaraní, even from random people, kids, teens, or young adults. They were happy to do it, they loved it."

There were, however, times when the locals were critical of his imperfect Guaraní and would make fun of him. "It's not usually malicious, or mean, it's just childish stuff," Matt said. "You have to go one way or the other—brush it off or let it get to you." He brushed it off.

After six months, Matt could hold a short conversation in Guaraní. In another two months, he said, he felt comfortable in the language. After two years, his Guaraní was so good, he was confusing people. "There is some German influence in Paraguay, so they thought I was a Paraguayan of German descent. People would look at me in wonder. 'Why is he able to speak like me?'"

209

Carrying the language back home

Matt is what Alvino Fantini calls an incipient bilingual. Even before they are proficient in the language, incipient bilinguals are diving in and trying to communicate. "It reflects an attitude of accepting and willingness to find some intermediate way," Alvino said. I've described this as being thirsty to pull the language into yourself. It is also recognizing, as Matt did, the power of vulnerability, the willingness to carry a notebook and ask help of strangers. It doesn't mean you're *always* open and seeking help. Matt confessed to me that when he was learning Guaraní, he would sometimes avoid kids because "they would really let me have it" when he screwed up. But that was motivation, too, he said.

After the Peace Corps, Matt went to graduate school at the Monterey Institute of International Studies. There he continued his formal Spanish training in addition to getting his master's in international environmental policy. Today, Matt helps run a nonprofit in South Florida that he cofounded called Community Greening. It helps communities create urban green spaces to benefit both people and the environment. He uses his Spanish daily in his work. "About half the time I can tell that they need me to speak Spanish," Matt told me. "The other half of the time, they can speak English perfectly well but are more comfortable with Spanish."

A sixty-something volunteer learns Ukrainian

While most Peace Corps volunteers are in their twenties, there is no upper age limit for eligibility. Janine Winn, a volunteer in her sixties, spoke to me from Ukraine, where she was stationed. "I kind of resigned myself to talking like a toddler for the next two years," she said. "It's sort of like David Sedaris's *Me Talk Pretty One Day*," she added, referring to the memoir by the popular author and humorist.

Janine was placed with a small group of other volunteers learning Ukrainian. "We met every day for ten weeks. Half of that time was spent in basic language instruction and the other half was cultural integration," she explained.

Janine lives with a host family. One rainy morning she asked if she could borrow an umbrella. "But I pronounced the word badly, and the lady of the house went into the next room and came back with the vacuum cleaner." She added, "I'm doing a little better now."

Like Matt, Janine lets the jokes at her expense roll off her. "It's a sign of respect for me to speak Ukrainian, or try to. I tell them, 'If you hear me pronounce something wrong, please correct me.'" But it's a surprise, especially for children, she told me, to encounter an older adult so inept at their language. "I was walking back to my home one day and a youngster, maybe nine, caught up with me, a little girl. I greeted her and then there was something I said that was completely wrong. And this child looked at me like I had been dropped down from the moon. It just was beyond her understanding that someone wouldn't know how to speak Ukrainian. It was really very funny."

Janine works in the community development sector in Ukraine and has a little development project of her own. Her twelve-year-old grandson and his classmates in Machias, Maine, want to be pen pals with their counterparts in Ukraine, where Janine is. "I've already heard some of the questions the Ukrainian kids want to know—'Do you go hunting? What kind of car do you have? What about sports?'" Janine says the American kids will have to mind their p's and q's as far as their penmanship. "The Ukrainian kids are very precise."

Janine, a believer in buds of bilingualism, has been sending Ukrainian language materials to her grandson's teacher. "Hopefully by the time I'm done, the American kids will at least have some basics, like 'Hello, how are you? My name is,' those kinds of things."

Language skills in the military

As of 2019, the Peace Corps had 7,334 volunteers placed in sixty-one countries. The US military sends far more Americans overseas—as of 2016, that number was 193,442, with personnel stationed primarily in Japan, Germany, South Korea, Italy, and Afghanistan. Like the Peace Corps, America's military branches recruit for language skills and invest in language training. One such recruit was a young soldier named Kevin Ruelas.

Kevin grew up in San Jose, California, and although he had Spanish speakers in his family, he grew up as a monolingual English speaker until the age of twelve. That's when his father, who was a service diplomat, took a job in Honduras. "I was pure gringo," Kevin told me, even though he lived in Honduras for two years. Then his father took the family to El Salvador, which is where Kevin eventually became fluent. He returned to California to go to California State University, Fresno, on an ROTC scholarship.

"The army sent me to Panama for Operation Just Cause and then to Costa Rica to be an interpreter and linguist for our embassy in Costa Rica," Kevin told me. His job was to escort generals and other higher-ups. "We'd take a tour and we'd talk to the local mayor and dignitaries and figure out how the army could build a road or school. It was a great job." After some time back in California, the army sent Kevin to Kuwait, Dubai, and Jordan to work in logistics. During his five years there, he picked up some Arabic.

When Kevin left the army and went into business, he enjoyed success early in his career. After building and selling one company overseas, he bought into another company back near his home in California. That's when his Spanish skills were particularly important when dealing with his staff. "When they learned that the incoming CEO spoke Spanish, they were over-the-moon happy," Kevin said. "We had 250 employees and I'd talk to all of them by walking around every day."

Kevin relayed what happened with one of the Spanish-speaking janitors he got to know. "He was complaining to me that the garbage cans were getting heavier and heavier and he was having trouble. I was puzzled. 'Do you mean under the desks?' I asked him. 'No, on the shop floor,' he said. I looked into the bins and noticed that the scrap was higher than I'd ever seen. We were throwing away too much product, and I needed to find out what was going on."

Kevin and his team discovered they were having quality control problems and traced it to a supplier that had changed one minor ingredient in the powder the supplier was sending. "They didn't bother to tell us," said Kevin, "and when we called, they said it wouldn't affect anything. But it affected us. It was causing bubbles in our ceramic and it would fail quality control." The ceramic was used in high-end components for submarine sonar systems, Kevin told me. "We'd throw it away and make another one, because everyone wanted to do a good job."

Kevin credits the janitor for saving the company lots of money and time. "I don't know how long it would have been before we figured out that we had a problem. After that," he said, "it became standard operating procedure to weigh garbage cans at the end of the week." And all because Kevin could converse with his employee in the janitor's native tongue.

An ex-Marine does bilingual rap

The military changed the life of another young soldier who, unlike Kevin, went in with no language skills. He is an energetic young man who stopped in the America the Bilingual recording booth at the ACTFL language teachers conference, where he was performing.

His business card reads "Mr. GL aka Güero Loco, Music for the Bilingual Classroom, Live Shows for Students, Parents, and Educators." I didn't have to hold the mic for him during our interview; he was comfortable with one in his hand. Güero Loco translates to "crazy blond." But he is not a Latino.

After high school, GL enlisted in the Marines. In the tests the Marines gave him, they discovered he had an aptitude for learning languages, even though he had "basically failed" Spanish in high school. Based on GL's results in the Defense Language Aptitude Battery test, the Marines sent him to the Defense Language Institute in Monterey, California. "I was a Marine and I did what they told me to do," GL said. "In six months I was able to learn the language that I failed in high school."

Already a person who made friends easily, his new abilities in Spanish gave him a new world of friendships. He found his calling in combining his love of music with his passion for bilingualism, and has devoted his life to reaching kids when they still have a chance to learn languages in school.

"My main motivation is letting kids understand the power, not just of language learning, but what happens when we learn those languages, the types of relationships that we start to build, how our mentality changes, how we view the world," GL explained. "I learned so many things in Spanish that I can't translate exactly into English, but I understand the concept through Spanish, and it's opened up my heart and my life to kazillions of opportunities that I otherwise wouldn't have had."

Being neither Latino nor African American, GL said he does occasionally encounter some resistance when traveling around performing bilingual rap. It doesn't deter him. "If we want to survive, we're going to have to catch up with the world. The more we try to hang onto English only, the more of a disservice we're doing to our children," he said.

In the recording booth, when I asked him why he does what he does, he paused to control his emotion before speaking and then said, "I actually look at it as one of my patriotic duties as a former Marine."

Chapter 31

FINDING WHERE AS A FAMILY

Bettina Young was born in the US of an American father and a French mother. Her mother spoke French to her since birth, thus giving Bettina the gift of bilingualism early in life. As a young woman, Bettina lived for several years in France and then in Italy. Those periods, she told me, were magical. They shaped her life ever after.

When Bettina had her own children, she wanted to give her three young sons the same kind of enlarged life she had experienced in Europe. So she made a bold decision. With her husband's blessing, she took her young boys out of school in Florida and traveled to an Italian village she had come to love, and where she still had friends. She would enroll them in school there.

"We did that for six months," Bettina said, "so that they would have full immersion. I really wanted them to have the experience on a daily basis, to form friendships. So we did that when they were three, five, and seven years old." She enrolled her sons in a Montessori school in the village near their small home.

I asked if her husband, who is an attorney, was okay with his young family being gone for so many months. "Greg could not stay with us in Europe full time and would go back and forth. I think that the quality of our time together when he was there with the boys was the most beautiful thing, because it was separate and away," Bettina said.

Toggling between two countries and cultures

When they were in the US, Bettina tried to speak only Italian to her children; when they lived in Italy, Bettina switched to English, knowing the boys would pick up Italian at school and from their friends.

It was such a good experience, said Bettina, that she repeated it. "We waited another year and a half and we did it again, at which point they were five, seven, and nine. Then we waited and did it again when they were seven, nine, and eleven."

Bettina told me that some of her American friends thought she was crazy to disrupt her children's education. But Bettina thought that the small school her boys attended in Italy was pretty wonderful, partly because in the village, "we were part of everybody else's lives, not just their education."

It wasn't just about getting her sons to be bilingual, although she did believe that their bilingualism would help them in school and in their careers. "It was about the experience of having some kind of different surrounding," she told me, "where people really looked people in the eyes, and there was communication and warmth and attachment—more than just 'What college are you going to get into?'"

The kind of Italian language—and culture—immersion that Bettina was giving her sons is a far cry from them just taking Italian classes in the US, even good classes. And it's just the immersion that Stanford's Guadalupe Valdés describes as being so very natural for language learning. "In instructed language acquisition," she told me, "you might have—let's be generous— twenty-to-one for a ratio, and everyone in the class is at your same level. While we can practice the language, the other students don't know the language any better than you do, so the affordances for hearing genuine language are limited."

To get another perspective on how Bettina's kids took to their bilingual education, I spoke with Daniel Young, the eldest of the three sons, who was seven when his mother first took him and his brothers to live in Italy. "Yeah, it was pretty hard," Daniel told me. "I sort of had to spend some time on the side learning the vocabulary and understanding what was expected of me at the school every day and it was hard, but it was enjoyable. The second time I came back, I felt like I was almost fluent."

I asked Daniel what it was like outside of class. "I always think back on the soccer field. Just playing the game, you could sort of pick up on what kids said and learn the language a lot better."

Daniel was a student at Boston College when I interviewed him. He was about to leave for his study abroad experience in Milan, where he would study economics. He told me he was looking forward to using his Italian and gave his mother the credit. "I think it's something that I could never really thank her enough for, and something that people rarely get the opportunity to do at such an early point in their lives."

When children immerse their parents

Taking your children overseas to live is not the only way American family members are becoming bilingual together. When Lori and I were in San Miguel de Allende visiting the Warren Hardy School, we met a mother and daughter who were spending a vacation week improving their Spanish together. They studied at the school every morning and then just enjoyed San Miguel together.

Julie Spiegelman, the French teacher I interviewed at Middlebury, told me that she and her mother did something similar. "My mother had always loved French as a kid and always had a great accent, but never figured out how to learn it all the way," Julie told me. So her mother, independently of her daughter, came and spent a summer at Middlebury. She would call her daughter so they could speak (in French) without her mother breaking her language pledge. "She did it for pleasure," said Julie, "and she keeps it up. She's taking a literature class right now. She'll call me and we'll talk about the books."

The two do more than just study the same language together. "We traveled to Martinique this year as sort of a mother-daughter trip," Julie told me, smiling at the memory. "We both got to speak a lot of French there. It was really cool to be able to share that with her and experience that totally new place."

When Rich Carrigan was a freshman at Notre Dame, he got some advice. "My uncle had been at Notre Dame before me and inspired me to broaden myself. 'You gotta go to one of the study abroad programs,' he told me." So Rich did. He spent ten months in Germany and found he loved speaking another language. He ended up pursuing a double major, in political science and German.

Rich's father ran a family business in Chicago that made retail store displays and employed many Spanish speakers. "My dad was trying to learn Spanish for his employees," Rich told me, which made an impression on Rich. He knew Spanish could be of great value if he were to work in the family business. As he was about to graduate, Rich said, "I looked into service programs and found one teaching English in Santiago, Chile. I had no Spanish, so the professor said, 'We'll send you to Guatemala for an intensive program.'"

In Guatemala, Rich took Spanish for seven hours a day for eleven weeks. For two of those weeks, his father came down to join in the experience.

"Three months later, I was relatively fluent." Rich went on to Chile to begin teaching. "I was living in the orphanage with kids, teaching English and religion all day and talking with the kids at night. Within six months

I was feeling pretty comfortable, switching back and forth. Once I started dreaming in Spanish, I knew it was internalized."

Rich came back to the US to earn his MBA at Northwestern, then worked at Andersen Consulting for a couple years before joining his family business in Chicago. "I use Spanish daily," he told me. Rich estimates that 160 of their employees speak Spanish, and some are bilingual. He is leading by example, demonstrating the value of being bilingual. "Our COO is trying to learn Spanish now so he can connect just like I do."

Families helping families

Rich continues to return to Guatemala to work on improving his Spanish and takes others with him, including his father, his COO, and his three children. "I speak Spanish very comfortably," he told me, "but I'm at an eighth-grade or high school level and want to get to the MBA level. I'm still not there. I still struggle."

He also offers English classes at his factory. "We partnered with St. Joseph Services, which teaches Latino immigrants, mostly Mexicans, computer skills and language skills. We bring the professor in once a week for two hours and we pay employees for the first hour. We do this thirty weeks out of the year, and we try to make it as easy as possible."

Today many of their employees are second generation. "I keep telling them to learn their parents' language as well as they can, and to realize they have been given a gift."

How to live forever

If you're fortunate enough to be a parent yourself, know that giving the gift of bilingualism to your children is not merely a gift for themselves. Their bilingualism is a gift to our country, too, as they become a living part of the linguistic capital of America. And to the extent that they interact with citizens in other countries, they represent an America attuned to the world.

If you feel a connection to American children in general, you are even more fortunate. When you work for the establishment of dual language schools, when you support language teachers, when you support the language learning industry by being a student yourself, you are also helping to build American linguistic capital. Whether you help one immigrant child learn English or fund study abroad trips for a dozen college students, you are living what the psychologist Erik Erikson described as "I am what survives of me." As the Encore.org founder Marc Freedman explains, acting on our care for the young is the true way to live forever. When we tend to the generation after our own, we wet our hands in the clay of the future. It's not only one of the best feelings we can have, it is one of the most important.

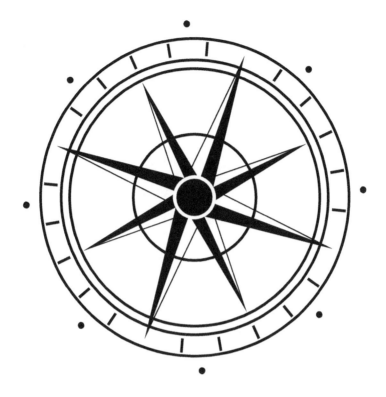

PART THREE

TWELVE LANGUAGE MYTHS
AMERICANS ARE BUSTING

"Truth will rise above falsehood as oil above water."
—MIGUEL DE CERVANTES

Preamble to the Twelve Myths

Much ink has been spilled over the last century by linguists trying to dispel myths and misconceptions that nonlinguists have about language, and for good reason. It turns out we nonprofessionals are pretty loaded up with mistaken beliefs.

Many of these myths, misconceptions, and half-truths can stymie our language learning. Some of them are pretty easy to bounce, but others are woven tightly into the fabric of what we take as normal, and will take a bit more grappling. It's important that we do so.

Our success at language learning is not dependent solely on our personal motivation or our luck in finding dedicated teachers. It also depends deeply upon our fellow Americans. It is they who encourage or discourage us on our journeys. We may be the seeds, but neighbors, friends, colleagues, and even strangers provide the soil, water, air, and sunshine for us to grow.

As the linguist John Edwards reminds us: "Even though most of us would not venture an opinion on the state of string theory in physics, for example, few of us are without opinions about language. These opinions may be 'amateur' views of language, but they often have immediate consequences in everyday life, regardless of their accuracy or sensitivity."

And it's not only monolinguals who have misconceptions about language. Being bilingual doesn't grant some sort of immunity from falling victim to the misconceptions we're about to review.

All of the dozen misguided ideas we're about to consider are widespread enough to merit our attention, but each of them has also been vanquished by a good many Americans already. Our goal is to help the many become most.

(Now back to our regularly scheduled reading, and the first myth . . .)

Chapter 32

Myth No. 1

THE WHOLE WORLD SPEAKS ENGLISH: THE TOURIST'S PERSPECTIVE

"They'll laugh at you if you say that in China or in Japan," warned Ken Romeo, when I asked him for his response to the belief that the whole world speaks English. "That's a very American view." Ken taught English in Japan before returning to America and becoming the associate director of the Stanford Language Center. I've heard plenty of other language professionals say similar things to me in response to this cocktail-party assertion. So who's right?

Let's begin with some numbers.

A couple billion

According to Ethnologue, the organization many scholars look to for language statistics, English speakers number more than 1.1 billion people (although fewer than half are native speakers). This narrowly edges out Mandarin Chinese, making English the number-one language in the world.

With a 2020 world population of somewhat over 7.6 billion, that means about 15 percent of the world's inhabitants speak English. So technically speaking, the language professionals are right—the whole world doesn't speak English.

It's also relevant to look at the number of people in the world who are learning English. In my interviews with the heads of language learning companies, each has told me that the market for English exceeds the market for all other languages. One researcher, Ulrich Ammon of the University of

Dusseldorf, estimates the number of English learners at 1.5 billion, muscling out the next most studied language of French, with a mere eighty-two million. If we accept this 1.5 billion figure of English learners and add the 1.1 billion who already speak the language, we get roughly 2.6 billion people. This would amount to just over one-third of all humans.

What does 'speaks English' really mean?

All such estimates are rough in the extreme. For when it comes to "speaking a language," what exactly do we mean? At what level? Do we count people who understand only half of what we're saying but can still get us a room with a view? And what of those 1.5 billion who are learning English? Does downloading an app count? Must they be enrolled in a class? What if they studied for two years but had to give it up because of work?

Even with perfect information, which we'll never have, we have to make judgments about what counts as "speaking" English. But setting these points aside, it's safe to say that even with the high estimates of English speakers and English students, we're still way short of "the whole world."

To be fair, when the cocktail party cognoscenti with martinis in hand say, "The whole world speaks English," they aren't likely making a factual claim; they are saying that *in effect,* the whole world speaks English because they have been able to get by speaking only English in their travels. And, depending on where you go in the world, this is a fair assessment.

If you travel to the cities of Western Europe and other major world tourist sites, you will likely encounter bilinguals who speak English well enough to provide you with what you want. In addition, there are many countries where the average English ability is quite high among the general population, at least among young adults, such as the Scandinavian countries, parts of Western Europe, South Africa, and Singapore.

Sometimes when Americans have told me that "the whole world speaks English," it's in frustration. With furrowed brow, they report that when they *try* to use their language skills abroad, the locals just reply in English, either for efficiency or because *they* want to practice their adopted language. In either case, it can be deflating to us emerging bilinguals, especially when combined with a bad case of ear lag.

Another factor is the *rate* of growth of English around the world. It's not just at hotels and airport ticket counters anymore. English use is growing rapidly in science and technology, in scholarship generally, in business, in the spread of English media and entertainment around the world. English is the language of international aviation, of most computer science—and most especially, English is the most prevalent language online. All of this makes it increasingly important for speakers of other languages to become bilingual in English, and easier for them to do so. Globalization outside of America means more and more opportunities to hear, read, and speak English. Those of us who have traveled for more than, say, twenty years may have witnessed the change personally. That fellow with the martini might well continue his point with, "When I first went to (fill in the blank), there was hardly any English; now it's everywhere!"

So if Americans can, increasingly, get by with English, and if, even when they try to speak another language, they encounter bilinguals who respond in English, why bother to become bilingual ourselves? It's a fair question, and the first step in answering it is to explain *why* the world adopted English as its lingua franca in the first place.

Last language standing

We know that standards are useful or even necessary for progress in all sorts of domains. Try to imagine our world without agreements on how we express numbers, delineate latitude and longitude, caliper millimeters, or size USB plugs. Did some global language committee convene and decide that English should be the world's standard? It was such an international committee that pegged latitude and longitude, deciding that the Prime Meridian should run through Greenwich, England (after some grumbling from the French), thus setting the zero point for longitude. It had to be somewhere, after all, so that we could agree on how to pinpoint a ship at sea, or find a nearby Starbucks.

In a similar fashion, the world's common language was supposed to be Esperanto. More than a century ago, earnest, peace-loving folks set their sights on the many blessings that would be ours if we could only agree on a common language to learn in addition to our native languages and use it for international communication. Esperanto, a synthetic cousin to some of the languages of Europe, was designed to be easy to learn and use.

The hope for Esperanto (and yes, its name means hope) was to reduce misunderstandings, conflicts, and even war. But civil wars waged around the world neatly dispelled the notion that simply by speaking a common language, people would become less bellicose. Even so, having a common language is beneficial in countless other ways. So why did Esperanto lose out to English?

It certainly wasn't because of English's logical spelling. "English speech and spelling," explains the author and polyglot Gaston Dorren, "were on reasonable terms until, many centuries ago, most of the spoken words began to go their own weird way and their inky partners refused to follow. It's been chaos ever since." Noah Webster's attempt to simplify English spelling (and annoy the British at the same time) only added a layer of complexity, so that today we have American spellings *and* British spellings of English, forcing global English learners to choose a camp and bed down wearing either pajamas or pyjamas.

It was no committee of judges that sent English to the winner's podium in the world language competition. As David Bellos explains, early in the twentieth century, the scientific community recognized that it must have "a means of global communication among its members." Germany, Sweden, and Russia all boasted famous scientists who were publishing in their own languages. German may even have been the favorite, until, writes Bellos, a couple of world wars got other folks pretty annoyed with all its umlauts and verbal cabooses. As for Swedish, they clearly beat everyone else with their Nobel Prize, but failed to produce enough Swedes for Swedish to take the language prize. And as for Russian, the Soviets produced enough Russians but not enough movies. So in the 1965 film *Doctor Zhivago,* Omar Sharif and Julie Christie spoke English while wearing fur hats in a make-believe Moscow.

When the USSR imploded, China dropped Russian like a hot *kartoshka* and took up with *hot potatoes* instead. Says Bellos, "What we seem to have experienced is not a process of language imposition but of language elimination."

Of course, the economic and political power, first of Britain and then of the United States, were driving forces for the global rise of English. In the nineteenth and early twentieth centuries, subjects under that never-setting sun of the British Empire had incentive to learn the language of the Crown to advance their careers, as indeed leaders like Mahatma Gandhi, Nelson Mandela, and Lee Kuan Yew of Singapore did. While France led the world in engineering, medicine, and the arts during much of the nineteenth century, and became the language of diplomacy as well as the first language spoken at the Olympics, Europe as a whole swooned. Of the fifty million Europeans who migrated to the New World in search of better lives, fully 70 percent came to America. And once in America, their children benefited from the largest improvement in public education the world had ever seen during the first half of the twentieth century—all of it in English. As America transformed itself from an agricultural nation to a manufacturing juggernaut, its products and brands spread around the world on a tsunami of English.

No turning back

We didn't know it at the time, but the twentieth century was when the race for a global language was decided, for it was during that century that modern media, advertising, and telecommunications were born and exploded around the world. The first American radio advertisement was broadcast in 1925 (for real estate on Long Island), and television debuted at the 1939 World's Fair in New York. After the Allies vanquished Hitler and Imperial Japan in World War II, the growth of English accelerated until it escaped this earthly realm and went to the moon—literally.

As David Crystal explains in *English as a Global Language,* the success of a common language is a blessing upon the world "as an amazing world resource which presents us with unprecedented possibilities for mutual understanding, and thus enables us to find fresh opportunities for international cooperation."

The world seems to have gotten the memo. "Both Chile and Mongolia have recently declared their intention to become bilingual in English, as Singapore has already done," writes Robert McCrum in his book *Globish.* And when English was made compulsory in Mexico in 2006, it was "a decision that automatically enrolled 200,000 Mexican schoolteachers in English-language training programmes."

With more scale comes more scale. The educational travel company EF created a free online English test, which 2.3 million adults around the world took in 2019. In its report on the findings, EF begins by saying, "the English language demonstrates a strong network effect: the more people use it, the more useful it becomes."

And it's not only native English speakers who benefit from the spread of English, but bilinguals the world over who have added the lingua franca to their repertoires. When a family from Shanghai vacations in Paris, they will likely speak English to the Parisians, who will likely understand them. The same happens in reverse when a French family visits the Great Wall of China, or when a Greek family visits Patagonia.

Esperanto may have been the more rational choice, but it's almost customary that the world goes ahead and adopts a suboptimal standard—like the QWERTY keyboards we're all stuck with. It may have been a marriage of convenience rather than of love, but the world is now betrothed to English. How is the marriage likely to work out?

Will English take over?

Will English suck up all the oxygen in the room? Will it crowd out native language species like some sort of linguistic kudzu? If that's the likely outcome, that certainly strengthens the why-bother-learning-another-language argument.

As a first answer, I want to share a story from my Spanish tutor Janire Bragado. It was nearing Thanksgiving, and knowing Janire was an international student, I invited her to have Thanksgiving dinner with our family. One of my hobbies is flag collecting (I'm getting treatment), and I happen to have the flags of some eighty countries in my garage. When we have international visitors, I like to fly their flag. Because I knew the Spanish word for flag (*bandera*), I told Janire that I would fly her flag on Thanksgiving.

But Janire got a frown on her face, and this time it wasn't because of my Spanish. It turns out Janire is from Bilbao, which is in Basque country. She said, "I would prefer the Basque flag."

I found out that Janire is proud to be Spanish, but she is *also* proud to be Basque. She not only speaks Basque; she also has her credentials for teaching Basque. She told me that when Franco was in power, from 1939 until his death in 1975, he tried to snuff out Basque, along with Catalan and the other regional languages in Spain. After his funeral, Spain brushed itself off and revived its regional languages with gusto. People tend to be proud of their native language and culture, and their pride doesn't diminish when they feel under attack—it probably increases. (By the way, I was able to buy the Basque flag online and flew it on Thanksgiving Day.)

Insight into the tenacity in which people hold onto their native languages comes from our old friend, the sociolinguist Joshua Fishman. It's contained in that slim volume Guadalupe handed me in her office—his 1996 book, *In Praise of the Beloved Language: A Comparative View of Positive Ethnolinguistic Consciousness*.

Fishman noticed similarities in the glowing descriptions people tended to use when speaking of their heritage languages. He got to wondering whether there were similar patterns that people use the world over to describe their mother tongues. "Often I would read a citation about Language X to an advocate of Language Z and ask him or her to 'Guess what language this is about'. In almost all cases they would guess it was about their own 'beloved language' (although it never was) and that gave me the idea that the content of language praises might really be quite parsimoniously structured the world over."

That's just what Fishman found when he studied the question more systematically. There are patterns of praise that speakers use when describing their native languages, including a closeness to God, to the beauty of nature, and to fundamentally important human values worth fighting for—pretty heavy stuff. Are such speakers likely to easily abandon their beloved languages without a fight? Imagine how we English speakers would feel if outsiders suggested we toss out the language of the Declaration of Independence, the Gettysburg Address—the language of Shakespeare, John F. Kennedy, Bob Dylan, and Sting. As Al Pacino might say, "fuggedaboutit."

All languages serve a dual function. They give us the power to communicate well with those people within our language group, and they give us the means to distinguish ourselves from those outside of our language group. As David Bellos says, "Every language tells your listener who you are, where you come from, where you belong."

That we cherish these differences might be related to one of our most elemental tendencies as humans: *we are of this tribe and you are not.* These distinctions are woven into our lives. As Fishman wrote: "At home, at work, in government, at prayer, in the shops and at play, language is part and parcel of the texture of human social life itself . . . ."

Beloved languages are disappearing at a rapid rate, but this is mostly the result of urbanization—young people in places like Brazil and Australia, venturing to towns and cities where they encounter and adopt larger regional and national languages. When these internal migrants raise their own children, they are more likely to speak the urban language rather than the one their grandparents spoke back in the village. But this worldwide loss of languages is not going unnoticed or uncontested.

The rebirth of Indigenous and local languages

Along with the global spread of English, there is another global language trend—the official recognition and valorization of Indigenous languages. I attended an event at the New Zealand Embassy in Washington, DC, and witnessed the embassy staff standing proudly and singing their national anthem—in Maori, the language of the country's Indigenous people. I've toured museums in Ecuador where the signs were in three languages: Spanish, English, and Quechua, the language of the Inka. In Morocco, among the reforms King Mohammed VI instituted in the wake of the 2011 Arab Spring was the official recognition of the Indigenous languages of Morocco that preceded Arabic; these are the Berber, or Amazigh, languages. Today, visitors to Morocco will see the artful Amazigh script adorning its public buildings and highway signs alongside Arabic.

It's as if national leaders the world over have recognized that while there is an expense to making Indigenous languages official, it's cheap compared with civil unrest. And there seems to be widespread belief in people's rights to retain their heritage languages, a position put forward in the 1948 UN Declaration of Human Rights, and reinforced in many declarations since. While in some cases it might be window dressing, there is also a real rise in minority languages being taught in heritage and dual language schools around the world.

What's more, in recent years there has been rapid growth in what is called localization, which is the linguistic enactment of thinking globally while acting locally. Large enterprises that seek to communicate in many countries and languages must take their content and recast it into a form that will be understood and appreciated by many different kinds of locals—hence the term localization. Whether these enterprises are governmental bodies with legal responsibilities, NGOs with humanitarian goals, multinational companies selling soap and soft drinks, or media companies offering online games and streaming movies, their success at being global is determined by their success at being local.

Thus, an important health advisory may be produced in twenty-six different languages and dialects, together with illustrations appropriate to the cultures. A popular computer game might have just as many different languages available in its settings. And as we saw in Chapter 8, a movie available for streaming into your home may allow you to select from many audio tracks and even more subtitle languages. To accomplish the burgeoning linguistic work, new kinds of firms, called language service providers, or LSPs, use a combination of AI-powered machine translation together with human linguists to deliver what their clients need to communicate, influence, and gain market share.

The language translation and localization industry is frothy with investments from venture capital, private equity, and mergers and acquisitions. The top five firms in this space each do more than $200 million in sales. One notable transaction was the $1.5 billion acquisition of the American firm LanguageLine Solutions by the French firm Teleperformance. These numbers confirm the veracity of Fishman's observations about the emotional commitment people feel to their languages and cultures. English is spreading around the world by people electing to become bilingual without tossing their own beloved language out the window.

The blessings—and limits—of tourism

Let's rejoin our cocktail party. I've just conceded to my friend that he's right. "*In effect*, the whole world *does* speak English—and" (pause for effect) "if our goal is to be tourists and visit popular destinations, we're likely to be just fine."

For Americans and other native English speakers, the spread of English around the world is like cushy upholstery that lets us travel as tourists in relative comfort. When we go to top tourist destinations, we think we're seeing the world but we're actually window shopping, taking a vending machine approach to seeing the world. And here, yes, you'll find plenty of English from the folks selling us stuff. These spots are where the world's veneer of English is thickest.

And although it's a popular pastime to put down tourism, I'd like to defend it. I'm a tourist myself and hope to continue to be a tourist in the future. While excessive numbers of tourists at trophy sites can stress everyone out, as well as threaten the ecology of the site itself, tourism, in general, is a force for good. According to the UN World Travel Organization and the World Bank, tourism and travel generate 10 percent of global GDP and 10 percent of jobs. Tourism is particularly beneficial to emerging economies, being the main source of monetary exchange for forty-seven of the world's fifty least developed countries. Tourism also broadens the minds and hearts of the tourists, even if they speak not a bit of the local language. As Mark Twain observed, "Travel is fatal to prejudice."

We native English-speaking Americans, born with this silver language in our mouths, inherited this blessing of being able to travel the world in our comfy seats. So far, so good. But what happens when we shrug our shoulders and say, "Why bother to learn what *they're* saying?" While the rest of the world *is* bothering to learn English, will Americans and other native English speakers become the last of the monolinguals? And if so, will it matter?

David Bellos has considered these questions. Native English speakers, he says, "are going to become very soon the only monolingual people in the world, lacking that double dimension that speaking another language always gives you." These English monolinguals will be less sophisticated users of language than other people, he concludes, since we "have only one language with which to think." If Bellos is right, that silver language we were born with might start to taste a bit tarnished.

✳   ✳   ✳

Chapter 33

THE WHOLE WORLD SPEAKS ENGLISH: THE PROFESSIONAL'S PERSPECTIVE

D eciding to limit our own minds is not the only thing we risk if we choose to remain monolingual. It turns out that, as valuable as tourism is, it's not the most important thing we humans do when we come upon another culture. Not by a long shot.

At diplomacy and development, we're better as bilingual

During the Cold War, two American journalists became worried. They saw American diplomats overseas showing disdain for the locals. They saw well-educated, well-mannered Americans—people we would be happy to have as neighbors at home—become snobbish, insular bigots when installed overseas. It was common among the Foreign Service to show little interest in learning the local language, instead relying on a few informers, assuming such interpreters would faithfully translate what was being printed in the newspapers, broadcast on the radio, and said on the street. The Soviet diplomats, on the other hand, *were* bothering to learn the local languages and cultures, and in doing so, were at a distinct advantage in turning the locals away from democracy and into the orbit of communism.

The journalists, William J. Lederer and Eugene Burdick, were going to write a nonfiction book about this looming danger for American interests, but at the last minute decided to make it a book of fiction, set in the imaginary country of Sarkhan. Their book was published in 1958 and became a multimillion-copy bestseller. Its bluntly stated title: *The Ugly American*.

The term today still describes Americans who travel overseas insisting on speaking English and expecting the world to understand them and accommodate their wishes. But when the book first came out, it was a shocking indictment of America's approach to foreign policy. The book made a powerful impression on a young US senator who knew something of the world beyond America. He'd fought in the Pacific, lived in Europe, and traveled to South America. That senator was John F. Kennedy, and he thought so much of *The Ugly American* that he bought a copy for each of his fellow senators. Later, as President, he envisioned thousands of linguistically skilled young people who would well represent America, and established the Peace Corps.

The book contains an interesting twist. The characters who behaved in an ugly manner were often good-looking, well dressed and well spoken. Ironically, the physically ugly American in Sarkhan, an engineer named Homer Atkins, was in fact beautiful—on the inside, in his attitudes and actions. He and his wife, Emma, both learned Sarkhanese. They were respectful of the locals learning from them, and with them, as they improved the engineering project they worked on together. The authors included Homer and Emma to model what we Americans should be doing to help the interests of those in need, thereby helping American interests as well.

A real-life American in the mold of Homer and Emma was Norman Borlaug, one of the most successful people ever in development work and the founder of the Green Revolution. He did his fundamental field research over the course of many years while living and working in Mexico, beginning in the 1940s. Having no Spanish when he arrived, Borlaug was committed to learning it, realizing the language was necessary for him to work. He eventually mastered Spanish well enough that he could deliver spirited speeches. Among many other awards for his work, Borlaug received the Nobel Peace Prize.

In 2016 I heard a presentation by a young American who was following in the footsteps of Borlaug. Erica Mackey was reporting on her company, Off Grid Electric in Tanzania. Erica's firm worked hard with the local population to figure out how to make affordable and practical solar-powered home lighting systems. She told me that once she learned Swahili, it was a breakthrough. "It took me a year before I was able to give a speech, but to be able to work directly with people, to interview our current customers without a translator, it makes all the difference."

Today the US State Department spends a good deal of money on language training of its own employees as well as sponsoring international study abroad, to fill the pipeline with young Americans with advanced language skills like Erica's.

At journalism and scholarship, we're better as bilinguals

We've already seen how *The New York Times*'s international correspondent Calvin Sims learned Spanish and then Japanese for his overseas assignments. He says he could not have done his work without those skills. We heard the same from the award-winning journalists and authors Anand Gopal, reporting from Afghanistan, and Evan Osnos, reporting from China. There are many more examples, including the Pulitzer Prize-winning *Times* columnist and author Nicholas Kristof, with his skills in French and Chinese.

Bill Weir, the CNN anchor, told me he wishes he had become a bilingual early in life. "Every time the seat belt sign goes off in some country I've never seen before, I wish I could travel back in time and punch my teenage self in the face for not paying attention." Bill was, he told me, "one of those horrible language students who didn't figure I would ever need it. But wow, do I need it now."

Bill has reported from scores of countries and, of course, he could never have learned the languages of all the people he reported on; he just regrets that he doesn't have at least one other language he could use. "So I look for translators, fixers, who can both educate me and then open those doors to discovery that matter so much as a storyteller."

As for advice to aspiring journalists becoming bilingual? "Yes, it should be a basic requirement for anybody who wants to do international journalism, for sure. I pick my teams based on bilingual or not."

Journalism and scholarship share a porous border, and professionals in both worlds share the need to get to the meat of their subjects, to use original sources, which in another country almost always means documents written in another language and interviews in another language. Thus Yale's professor of Chinese history, Jonathan Spence, learned to read Chinese, upon which his stellar career depended. The geographer Jared Diamond learned Tok Pisin in order to work in Papua New Guinea.

The Pulitzer Prize-winning biographer Stacy Schiff said her fluency in French made the writing of her first three books possible—the first on Saint-Exupéry, the author of *The Little Prince;* the second on Véra Nabokov, Vladimir's formidable wife; and the third on Benjamin Franklin, whom Congress sent to Paris at the outset of the American Revolution, to arrange for the French support with which it was won. "Franklin turned out to be more visible in French. It was a language he spoke less than artfully, which meant he revealed himself more fully," Stacy told me.

At intelligence and military operations, we're better as bilinguals

It doesn't take much imagination to realize that we need American citizens in our intelligence agencies and military commands who can understand other languages at a very high level of proficiency, in order to access real and potential threats against America. But I had the opportunity to attend a security summit at the MacDill Air Force Base, in Tampa, Florida, where my eyes were opened to other reasons why bilingual skills are critical for the military.

The sprawling base is home to the US Central Command (CENTCOM), which was created in the wake of the 9/11 terrorist attacks. Today the coalition comprises forty-seven nations, from Albania and Croatia to Ukraine and Uzbekistan. Representatives from these coalition nations live in Tampa and work together with Americans at the base. MacDill is also home to Special Operations Command (SOCOM), which includes the Navy SEALS, Army Rangers, and Green Berets, among other elite fighting units.

The SOCOM public website states that the first priority for Special Operations is to "compete and win for the nation." Listed among their responsibilities are counterterrorism, hostage rescue and recovery, foreign internal defense, foreign humanitarian assistance, special reconnaissance, and countering weapons of mass destruction. All in a day's work.

Hotel clerks in other countries may be happy to speak English, but bad guys aren't so cooperative. This is why the Department of Defense spends serious money on language training for its Special Operators and its analysts. But beyond building language skills among our own active-duty military, even more important is strengthening relationships with our allies.

One purpose of CENTCOM is to build understanding and relationships between American military personnel and their counterparts in allied nations. The US relies on our allies to understand what the bad guys are up to in their countries and to share that information with us, while we help them with their internal defense, stability, and development. This cooperation rests upon the personal relationships that ensue when military officers and enlisted men from all these countries are given the opportunity to work together as teams, develop respect for one another, and become friends. There's a focus on skills training, including leadership skills and language skills. As I heard a few times during the summit, "Humans are more important than hardware."

It's not always easy to work together. The other quotation I also heard more than once during the summit was from Churchill: "There is only one thing worse than fighting with allies, and that is fighting without them."

One commander told me that language skills are important for the human-to-human relationship building we need to do with our allies. It's also critical to be able to align our public messaging with our military actions. When, for example, US Special Operations engage in direct action, our enemies might well make false accusations about the number of civilian casualties. It does little good for us to issue a press release in English. We need to have both the cultural understanding and the language skills required to present the American reasons for the action, and the consequences of the action, in the relevant languages, and to do so in a culturally appropriate way. If we fail at this, our enemies will tell the story for us.

That the leadership of CENTCOM and SOCOM take their responsibilities seriously is an understatement. Their job is not to set policy, not to engage in diplomacy, but to undertake military operations when they are ordered to do so. In the words of one commander, "I own military deterrence, to punish, and/or to deny." Because of the international nature of CENTCOM, it does not report to the Joint Chiefs of Staff but directly to the highest civilian leaders—the Secretary of Defense and the President. The same goes for SOCOM. Their responsibility is to be optimally prepared to engage in military operations on the other side of the world at a moment's notice. Clearly, not every Navy SEAL or Army Ranger is going to command the language of our adversaries, but as a team, including our allies and support staff, we must possess professional linguistic skills at the highest level in order to protect the lives of Americans, our allies, and innocents on the ground. If there is a more serious application for professional-level language skills, I don't know what it would be.

At spreading faith and humanitarian work, we're better as bilinguals

My nephew and his wife are Jehovah's Witnesses. When they invited me over for dinner, knowing my interest in bilingualism, they asked if I wanted to watch some videos showing how much attention their church devotes to language training. Of course I did.

They showed me a video of translators diligently working in many parts of the world. According to the website JW.org, there are nearly 8.7 million Jehovah's Witnesses worldwide. They are inspired to pass the word of God to others in their native languages. In an article on JW.org, "Breaking Through an Ancient Barrier," the authors say the church has published in more than 750 languages, including eighty sign languages. Publications are first created in English and then sent to Jehovah's Witnesses churches around the world for volunteers to translate into their native languages. One volunteer quoted in the article said, "We view our work as a gift to the public. And we want to package that gift nicely. We are thrilled by the possibility of a magazine article or a web-page item touching the heart of a reader and affecting his life for the better."

When you click on the language button on the top navigation of the JW.org homepage, a "Select Your Language" page appears, offering 1,015 options. At the bottom of the homepage, a bright green button links to the free JW language app. It's designed to help followers "greet, preach and teach" in many languages, offering helpful key phrases in audio and written form. Elsewhere on the site, videos convey the blessings of learning a language in order to help others "learn about the Bible and God's Kingdom" in their own languages.

Missionaries learning local languages is nothing new, of course. Some of our earliest linguistic records were created by missionaries seeking to learn local languages in order to convert the population. Francisco Pareja was among Spain's Franciscan priests who learned the languages of the Native peoples in Spain's New World territories. Pareja's challenge in the late sixteenth century was to learn the language of the Timucuan, living just north of Florida. He did this by turning it into a phonetic written language. Not long after, in what is today New England, a Puritan pastor named John Eliot published America's first Bible—in Algonquian. Today's religious organizations are actively expanding on this age-old practice.

Even more known for their emphasis on language training are the Mormons, or more correctly, The Church of Jesus Christ of Latter-day Saints. Each year, thousands of young missionaries prepare for their eighteen- to twenty-four-month missions in training centers around the world. The main site is the Missionary Training Center (MTC) in Provo, Utah, where the men and women spend up to nine weeks in language immersion learning one of fifty-six languages. On the walls inside this training center are signs that read "Speak Your Language," or SYL. This is their version of the Middlebury Language Pledge and the Concordia "Live the Language" motto.

One young woman, daunted but determined to learn Finnish at the MTC, laughed as she conveyed a Finnish saying: "'Only two kinds of people can learn Finnish, babies and missionaries.'" Although she said she was not a great student in high school, she has dedicated herself to being able to perform her service in Finnish.

The Church website reports that some sixty-five thousand missionaries presently serve, and another eleven thousand are involved in humanitarian services. Many of them are highly proficient bilinguals. They are Americans representing not just their religion but their country, in more than four hundred locations around the world. The missionary work has delivered results. During the past few generations, the Church has grown substantially, today counting membership worldwide of more than sixteen million. The Church says that since 1985, it has provided more than $2.3 billion in humanitarian assistance in 142 countries.

The desire of these missionaries to learn their new language is not merely for their own benefit, but for a purpose larger than themselves. They know that the whole world does *not* speak English, and that, even if people can speak English, they prefer to speak their native languages—especially when it comes to matters of the heart.

Missionaries and other humanitarian workers are not tourists. In order to be effective, they know they need more than buds of bilingualism. They must practice the power of vulnerability—make mistakes, let jokes about their accent or grammar slide off them. They must show grit. In short, they must do all the things successful bilinguals must do.

We know from Part One of this book that it's important to have a place for your adopted language to live in your life—to find your *where*. Missionaries have found their where—it is among their peers and the potential converts they encounter, on their mission to serve a higher purpose.

At business, we're better as bilinguals

"I grew up in southern Missouri. My brother and I would say we are bilingual— we speak Hillbilly and English." That's what Lois Melbourne jokingly told me. She is the retired CEO of a software company she founded.

Her small high school (her class numbered 113) offered French and Spanish. "I took French because it seemed more romantic," Lois said. In college, she took a year of French to fulfill the language requirement. "I could actually read French nicely, but speaking it was out of the question."

Lois started a software firm in 1994 that could take a company's human resources data and automatically generate organization charts. To her delight, when she launched a website the following year, people from all over the world sent inquiries about buying her software.

But Lois soon discovered that although prospects sent an initial email in English, when Lois's staff followed up, they found the prospects were tongue-tied. The English of the initial greeting was like a linguistic facade; it concealed the true language reality below. Lois realized that if she wanted to grow her business internationally, she needed someone with serious language skills. Wouldn't it be great, she thought, if she could hire a VP of Sales who could communicate in the languages of her customers?

Through her connections, she found Andy Simmons, who was versed in numerous languages as well as sales and business development. Andy was raised in Washington, DC, Europe, and Asia. He has worked in Brazil and the Middle East, Turkey and Switzerland. By his count, he speaks six languages well, and another four or five "casually."

At one meeting he and Lois had in France, Andy recounted, "They said, 'Don't bother to come to this meeting if you're not going to speak French; it's just not worth your time or ours.'" There were plenty of other meetings like it. This might sound arrogant to Americans, Andy explained, but it's not. "They were simply saying, 'Look, we need to be efficient here; we don't have a lot of time; we just need to select the right technology.'"

Lois let Andy run the meetings. "I was willing to show my vulnerability," she said. By demonstrating to clients how she and Andy as a team could solve the issue of a language barrier, she was effectively telling them, "'Imagine what we can do to solve technical issues.' These meetings were not about me feeling comfortable," Lois said. "They were about the *customer* feeling comfortable and us getting their solutions for them."

Andy and Lois sold their software in France, Germany, and many other European countries. "It would have been very, very different had we only been speaking in English," Lois told me. Said Andy, "Customers want to know that if they have problems, they can pick up the phone and yell at you in *their* language."

Another American executive I interviewed said she goes out of her way to hire bilinguals. Lisa Bjornson Wolf is a bilingual herself, having grown up in France and Japan. After college and grad school, she also picked up Portuguese, using the Rassias Method.

Today, Lisa is a money manager at a major Wall Street firm and has a team that serves clients all over the world. "Language is the combination lock that opens a whole set of cultural contexts," Lisa told me. She said her clients appreciate it when she speaks their language, but that's not the only reason she looks to hire bilinguals. "When an American is a bilingual," she said, "it tells me they have a certain adaptability, a flexibility of mind. They have decoded another language, and so it's likely they will be able to decode other problems. That's why I look for people who have lived in another language."

Doug Renfield-Miller, the failing high school student who turned his life around by spending his senior year in France, also shared a story of the importance of breaking out of the English bubble in order to succeed in business overseas. When he was selling financial services in Japan, his company was up against two large competitors. But Doug had a plan.

"We hired one great guy to head up the office who was a wonderful bridge," he said. This fellow was a Japanese-English bilingual. Because of guidance from him, said Doug, "we always did exactly the right thing from a Japanese perspective." To illustrate, Doug gave me an example of doing the *wrong* thing from a Japanese perspective.

"When you go into a Japanese client, the first thing they always do is either serve tea or coffee. You don't have to drink it; it's just part of being a good host," Doug explained. "But my competitor, I was told, would always say, 'Can you get me a Diet Coke?' That is wrong in so many ways! First of all, they probably don't have Diet Coke. Secondly, you don't ask for something; that's very rude. And third, it just showed them how completely alien and insensitive he was to the local culture."

Did Doug's more culturally appropriate approach pay off? "We completely beat the pants off the competition," Doug relayed. "And I think it was entirely because we just managed to seem more Japanese to the Japanese firms."

Another American, Bill Johnson, found his business forte through Chinese. But it was not an easy win. Bill took Chinese at Boston University. It was difficult for him, so he decided to try an intensive summer Chinese program over at neighboring Harvard. That was even harder. "The professor told me, 'I think you should go get your money back because you'll never learn Chinese.' That wasn't the answer I was looking for," Bill told me.

Bill nevertheless persevered with the Harvard course, added a course from nearby Tufts, and then did the summer immersion program at Middlebury. His grit paid off when he finally got into the Stanford Center Chinese course and studied in Taipei. When Bill returned to the US, he went to business school at Northwestern, and eventually got into the elevator business. "Otis Elevator was hiring and there was an opening, believe it or not, in Shanghai. That was in 1993, and I've been living in China ever since."

Bill moved from Otis to Carrier and eventually to the Finnish elevator company Kone. He was promoted to president of the Greater China Division in 2004. "When I began with Kone, we were doing $70 million in sales and the whole Chinese division was operating in English, as was our entire company," Bill recounted. He recognized that operating in English was holding the Chinese division back. On his next monthly trip to Kone's headquarters in Finland, he proposed to management that the China division be run in Chinese.

"Today we do $3 billion in sales and have fourteen thousand employees," Bill said proudly. "Being able to use Chinese unleashed all the talent that was here. Most of my senior people speak English and can interact with the international types, but we also have a lot of people who do well in the company without having English skills. Speaking and using Chinese let me understand their capabilities and promote them."

I asked Bill if, after all these years, his Chinese was perfect. "My staff makes fun of my grammar but say my pronunciation is good."

When Bill advises young people, he tells them, "If you really want to learn a language, make it your full-time job for a year. Take a couple of semesters before you come to the country, and summer courses, but then you have to make learning the language your job for a year (I did it for eighteen months). Then stop studying and just use it day in and day out in a practical way. Then you'll begin to get a feel for how things actually work."

Bill's story, as well as Doug's and Lois's, illustrate that if you want to succeed in international business, you do have to really try—and that means finding a way to bridge the language gap. The former Chancellor of Germany, Willy Brandt, once said, "If I'm selling to you, I speak your language. If I'm buying, *dann müssen Sie Deutsch sprechen!*" Paraphrased more generally, we could say, "If you want to buy something, you can do it in your language. If you want to sell something, you better do it in theirs." If you don't, your competitors most likely will.

Good business is not just about selling stuff and making profits. Responsible business runs on relationships, on people engaging in voluntary exchange of goods and services, and increasingly doing this around the whole world. From the earliest days of human conflict and cooperation, from the days of "should we raid or should we trade?," the traders gradually won out. And it was bilingualism that served as the fuel for making this civilizing machine run. When we look back over the long arc of human history and the gradual spread of peace rather than violence in the world, the pacifying role of commerce is beginning to be more generally appreciated. An increase in trade is associated with a decrease in warfare for the simple reason that it's bad business to kill customers.

And businesses themselves are evolving, as more business leaders think of how the triple bottom lines of profit, people, and planet can reinforce success. An increasing number of young people are now doing in business what young people a generation earlier thought was the exclusive domain of nonprofits: doing well by doing good. The rise of B Corporations, which write social good into their legal charters, demonstrates a more enlightened way to value customers—one that includes valuing their language.

At living a larger life, we're better as bilinguals

To be clear, I'm not claiming that unless you embrace bilingualism, you'll always be a tourist. You *can* do journalism, scholarship, intelligence gathering, and military operations; you can do diplomacy and development; you can spread the Gospel and humanitarian services, you can even be successful at business internationally by speaking nothing but English. *But* . . . the world is a competitive place. In each of these domains, you and your team will be competing with other people and other teams who *are* bilinguals, and who are dedicated to understanding local cultures.

Trying to compete or collaborate in any of these domains without knowledge of the local cultures and skill in the local languages is like showing up to the big leagues with your shoes tied together. Successful relationships are built upon actual understanding and trust. As has often been said, "They don't care what you know until they know that you care." And nothing says caring like listening in their language—and drinking their tea.

I hope you have many opportunities to be a tourist in the years to come. I hope you enhance your experience by deploying buds of bilingualism. And I hope that in at least one country outside of America, you will be more than a tourist. I hope you will participate, collaborate, compete in the arena, and experience deeply. When you do, bilingualism will be what opens those citizens to you, and you to those citizens.

Chapter 34

Myth No. 2

Technology Will Make Language Learning Obsolete

We'll all have these things in our ears, or maybe implants, that will instantly translate any language. So when those fearsome-looking fellows step onto our path on our trek through Papua New Guinea, our English will be perfectly translated into their Tayap. Suddenly smiling, they will lower their weapons and invite us home to meet the family.

That's the idea anyway, and it's a compelling one. After all, we've seen computer translation go from laughable to pretty amazing in recent years. And it's not just at cocktail parties where you hear such predictions.

I was in attendance when the theoretical physicist Michio Kaku addressed an auditorium full of company presidents. He told us that virtual reality would be used for games, but augmented reality would change the world as we know it. Looking through their new AR glasses, he predicted, "people will appear with their bios and names so you won't have to guess who they are. If they speak another language, the translation will appear as subtitles in your glasses."

The language historian Nicholas Ostler wrote a book positing that yes, the whole world will try to learn English until . . . they won't have to. Once the technology gets good enough, our now friendly villagers can just joke around in their Tayap, and we'll have no more problem understanding them than we do our friends back home.

If this technology is right around the corner, why bother spending all the time and effort to learn another language? Besides, even if we learn a language or three, there are hundreds of languages we might encounter in life. Should we just pluto our Spanish class and learn piano instead?

It's an important question. So important that I decided to go on a quest to seek out those people I figured would know the most about it.

Low tech at MIT

My first stop was at Harvard, for the International Foreign Language Education and Technology conference on how the latest technology is being applied to language learning. I sat in on the presentations on what was going on at universities. Nelleke Van Deusen-Scholl, a faculty member from Yale, shared findings on a partnership between Yale, Cornell, and Columbia to teach less commonly taught languages across the three campuses via teleconferencing. Funded by the Mellon Foundation, the program mixes the latest equipment with periodic in-person booster sessions.

There isn't a language requirement at MIT, so I was surprised to see in the program that two faculty members from the MIT language department were presenting. Clearly, they were still teaching languages there and I was keen to know how they did it. So were a lot of people, it seemed. The room quickly became standing room only. Then Margarita Ribas Groeger and Dagmar Jaeger, both on the MIT Global Languages faculty, surprised me with what they had to say.

"The students are learning technology all day at their screens and don't want to do that for language classes," said Margarita. "They seem to want the human interaction." Since there is no language requirement at MIT, she explained, "the students take it because they want it." Part of the motivation are paid internships in South America, Spain, and France, where it's important to know the language.

Margarita said that she and Dagmar had evaluated many technologies to help in the classroom. The upshot? "We use Padlet." Padlet is a visually driven, collaborative tool that's simple enough for first-graders to work and happens to be usable in many languages. So why would some of the country's brightest technology minds embrace it? Margarita's explanation was revealing. "MIT students are sophisticated technology users, and so they don't have much patience for hard-to-use technology. They aren't in language classes to learn technology; they are here to learn a language."

If technology is going to make language learning obsolete, the students at MIT haven't gotten the memo just yet.

Slow tech at Stanford

My next stop was another citadel of technology on the opposite coast, the Stanford Language Center. Ken Romeo, whom we met in Myth No. 1, runs it.

Ken told me that much of what used to be done in college language labs can now be done on students' own digital devices, so language labs have evolved. Stanford uses them mainly for proficiency testing, in order to place students in the right courses, and after those courses, for exit assessments. Students sit in a controlled, secure computer environment where they are tested in reading, writing, listening comprehension, and speaking. Human language instructors later evaluate the recordings.

I asked Ken point-blank: "Is technology going to replace language learning?"

"Not in my lifetime," he replied. "We're nowhere near it. You don't get the nuance at all, the implied meaning, the higher level. Maybe in the future, long after I've died. We're talking at least fifty years until we get really good machine translation.

"But," he added, "you really ought to go see Chris Manning over in the Gates Building. He's the godfather of natural language processing."

Christopher Manning is a professor of machine learning in Stanford's computer science and linguistics departments. He's also the director of the Stanford Artificial Intelligence Laboratory. According to his bio, his first research goal is creating "computers that can intelligently process, understand, and generate human language material." His office has a small conference table, and he sat on the bench against the wall while I took one of the two seats on the other side of the table. I got straight to the point once again: should humans stop bothering to learn another language?

His answer was not as direct. "In the 1960s, people were saying things about artificial intelligence which today seem ridiculous in their optimism. Today, I think we're in another period like that," he said. "Yet clearly we are in a period when quite dramatic advances are happening."

He mentioned computer vision, "which a few years ago did nothing, but now, is amazingly good." Speech recognition is a comparable area. Ten years ago it was nothing a person would actually use; now, people routinely talk to Siri.

But, Chris added, there's a big difference between just recognizing a string of words and true understanding. "Take the phrase, 'I went to see my boss to see whether I might get a raise. He didn't look that impressed.' You know you're not going to get a raise," said Chris. "But this takes knowledge about the world. Truly understanding language takes reasoning and what

245

humans call common sense—not just that this word means something and the other word modifies this word—but how the world actually works." That kind of understanding of language, Chris said, is very far from being solved. "We're talking decades."

Nevertheless, I pressed him. "Okay, so *decades* from now, do you think it will still be valuable for humans to learn languages?"

"The current research suggests it's good for your brain, and so it's developmentally a positive thing to do," he said. "You actually gain in mental function, and it is enriching in all kinds of broader ways, cultural and humanistic ways." Chris was not ready to tell us to stop learning languages just yet.

Not surprisingly, language teachers concur. Current machine translation, they point out, misses something that human translation does not: cultural nuance.

Chris Manning's explanations reminded me that, while we have a habit of overestimating our technology at times, technology also has a habit of sneaking up on us when we're not looking and startling us with its advances. To get some insight into this paradox, I called my friend Paul Saffo, who teaches at the Stanford Design School.

"It's like hiking in the desert," Paul explained, when we met after one of his evening classes. "You see a mountain that looks *so* close, but it takes two days to hike there." When it comes to the advance of technology, he advised, "Don't mistake a clear view for a close distance."

Paul, who is one of America's leading technology forecasters, told me that if I wanted a crash course on where technology was heading, I should spend a week at Singularity University over on the old NASA Ames campus. "I teach there, too," he added.

It wasn't the first time I'd heard of Singularity University. My friend Lawton Langford, a forward-looking CEO, had been raving about it to me. And I knew that Ray Kurzweil, its cofounder, might be the one guy in America best equipped to answer the question of whether technology would T-bone language learning.

For starters, Kurzweil invented the first commercial text-to-speech synthesizer and the first speech-recognition device. He was awarded the National Medal of Technology and Innovation, has met with three US Presidents, and received twenty honorary doctorates. *Forbes* magazine called Kurzweil the rightful heir to Thomas Edison. Oh, and Larry Page, Google's cofounder, asked Kurzweil to "bring natural language understanding" to Google's search function.

I said to Paul, "Okay, I'm in."

A singular experience

To get ready for my technology boot camp, I assigned myself *The Singularity Is Near*, Kurzweil's six-hundred-page primer on the subject. He tries to give the reader a bit of slack. "I can understand why many observers do not readily embrace the obvious implications of what I have called the law of accelerating returns . . . .After all, it took me forty years to be able to see what was right in front of me, and I still cannot say that I am entirely comfortable with all of its consequences."

Kurzweil conveys how ill-equipped we humans are in grasping power curves. Linear change is what we see around us, but exponential growth— that's the doubling, doubling, doubling, doubling we just can't easily fathom.

Maybe after a week at Singularity University, I'd be able to.

Singularity University, or SU, says it is dedicated to "using exponential technologies to tackle the world's biggest challenges and build a better future for all." The word "singularity" as it applies to technological change refers to the point at which artificial intelligence becomes way smarter than human intelligence and goes its merry way. For most of us, it requires a leap of imagination so high as to be, at times, scary.

Our home for SU week was the 1960s-era NASA Ames Research Campus. My room, on the second floor of a long two-storey motel-like building, had twin beds and two metal lockers ready for padlocks. I imagine that during the space race, engineers and astronauts slept here. The towels reminded me of what they issued us during my high school gym class.

Our spartan quarters were just steps away from the sprawling classroom and adjoining cafeteria, both of which were open day and night. The spacious classroom was a converted dining hall transformed with a variety of tables, a few sofas, lots of whiteboards, and a broad stage for speakers to pace around like Steve Jobs debuting a new iPhone.

We ate our meals outside at picnic tables. There were about seventy of us students, ranging in age from twenty-something to sixty-something, mainly guys, and mostly from outside the US. Most were in business, but one student was a Marine and two were Navy SEALs.

We spent about fourteen hours a day in classes, listening to inspiring and sometimes shocking addresses from some of the brightest bulbs in the Silicon chandelier. There was Brad Templeton on future computing and driverless cars, and Rob Nail on robots. Salim Ismail held forth on the topic of his book, *Exponential Organizations: Why new organizations are ten times better, faster, and cheaper than yours (and what to do about it)*. My friend Paul Saffo captivated the group describing the practices and perils of forecasting the future. Neil Jacobstein spoke on how we are responsible for our technologies, even if we don't understand them. Peter Diamandis, the XPRIZE Foundation founder and SU cofounder, said that "we haven't seen 1 percent of the change that's going to happen in the next ten years." (For some context, I did my SU course in 2014.) Raymond McCauley spoke on biotechnology, and Marc Goodman on cybersecurity and the unseen dark web.

Kurzweil's language lesson

Then, on Thursday evening, Ray Kurzweil delivered what had been billed as his fireside chat. After dinner, the lights inside the classroom dimmed and Kurzweil appeared, perched on a stool, flanked by two large monitors playing videos of logs ablaze, yet not consumed. He launched into a monologue.

First, he reiterated his prediction made some years earlier that artificial intelligence will reach parity with human intelligence in 2029. Parity will be fleeting, however, as AI soars exponentially past us bio-bound humans.

Humans have always used our tools to improve our capabilities, Kurzweil said. Artificial intelligence is no different. AI won't be a technology *apart* from us; it will *be* us. It is the natural outcome of the evolution we've been engaged in for millions of years. Evolution is simply going beyond natural biology and merging with, and being enhanced by, digital evolution. Our own biological brains are already being greatly aided by the exponentially growing digital neocortex. We are outsourcing our documents, our photographs, and our memories to the cloud, and we're just at the beginning.

When he finished his "chat" and opened the presentation to questions, hands shot up. Finally he acknowledged mine. The room went silent as a staff member jogged over to hand me the mic, and I stood to ask my question.

"Around the world, there are millions of people working hard to learn a foreign language—I'm one of them. What advice do you have for us?"

I was worried he might just say, "Give up!" or something else dismissive, but he didn't. He began by explaining how our minds process language, how ideas are represented in a hierarchy in our neocortex. After a few seconds, I remembered to hit the record button on my phone.

"When we invented language," Kurzweil told the audience, "I could actually take this hierarchy of symbols in my neocortex, which represented an idea, and I could transfer that to your neocortex through the medium of language." Google Translate is pretty good now, he said, and getting better, "but it won't be at human levels until we achieve human levels, which I think is 2029, and then . . ."

He paused to take a breath. "I think we will use that technology to make ourselves better."

I felt my shoulders relax.

"Language is not just a complete redundancy, as I'm sure you appreciate," Kurzweil continued. "Different languages have different metaphors and different idioms, and can express things in poetic ways that you just can't do in another language. There are French expressions, Yiddish expressions that you can't communicate in the same way in English. That's a general phenomenon, so preserving languages that are about to go extinct is a very worthwhile endeavor. It's preserving a very valuable part of our human knowledge, both to study popular languages and orphan languages."

Kurzweil then talked about his disagreement with Larry Page, Google's cofounder, who thought it was good that humans wouldn't have to work much in the future. Kurzweil doesn't see it that way. The point is to use technology not to make us weaker, but stronger. "We can learn more languages," he said. "We'll become better at it as we make ourselves smarter."

Reflecting on his long answer to my question, I realize Kurzweil seems to be both a passionate technologist and a passionate humanist. Whether technology will replace human language skills is, in his mind, a matter for us to decide.

To probe the humanistic side of this question, I had a discussion with the philosopher Tom Morris, who said, "Technology can never replace our need to grow."

In some cases, Tom continued, technology does replace human capabilities, as a prosthesis does for an amputee, "but in most cases, technology doesn't replace—it augments." Google Translate and other similar technologies are great to help us find a bathroom in Finland, Tom said. But he agreed with Kurzweil that technology's best application will be to help us learn. "If we think of translation technology as shutting down our need to grow and develop and learn as human beings," said Tom, "we're really misusing that technology."

Player piano bows to piano man

Another way to look at whether we will allow technology to make language learning obsolete is to look at history. What happened when other human skills were matched, and then exceeded, by machines?

In his book *The Inevitable*, the technology author Kevin Kelly tells the tale of what happened back in 1997 when IBM's Deep Blue chess-playing computer beat the reigning chess grandmaster, Garry Kasparov. When it happened, it was shocking. Many thought it would be the end of chess as we knew it. It wasn't.

"The advent of AI didn't diminish the performance of purely human chess players," Kevin writes. "Quite the opposite. Cheap, supersmart chess programs inspired more people than ever to play chess, at more tournaments than ever, and the players got better than ever."

About a century earlier, a similar thing happened with another cherished human skill.

At the turn of the twentieth century, the early player pianos, the kind you had to pedal, were starting to be manufactured. They were an answer to a dream. Player pianos could be played conventionally, like an ordinary piano, but flip out the pedals, insert a roll of punched paper, and like magic, they would begin playing by themselves. And what music they could produce!

Manufacturers staged publicity concerts, including at Carnegie Hall, where the audience would hear a piano concerto coming from behind the drawn curtain, only to then see the curtain open to reveal a human pedaling away. The audience was predictably stunned. Sometimes the recording artist would appear and sit down to play a bit of it himself, taking turns with the machine, while extolling the modern wonders that could produce this very music in your own home.

There were early Edison phonographs at this time, but their sound quality was poor. In contrast, player pianos sounded exactly the same, whether an actual musician or anyone capable of pushing the pedals was playing. Player pianos were, in fact, the true beginning of the music recording industry. Their popularity was immense. The industry was, for a time, second only to the automobile industry in sales, producing more than two hundred thousand pianos and five million paper rolls annually. Access to professional-quality music exploded. The player piano provided much of the roar to the Roaring Twenties.

After the Great Depression of the early '30s, phonographs improved greatly and radio came on the scene, giving the one-two punch to player pianos. Although there are digital player pianos today, they have never quite achieved the magical quality, or wild popularity, of the first mechanical ones.

So what was the impact of these player pianos on piano students? They used the machines to learn how to play, much as a later generation of chess players would with computerized chess games. Black musicians, especially, took advantage of the technology, partly because they often couldn't afford regular music lessons. These musicians included the likes of Thomas "Fats" Waller, Joe "Stride" Turner, Fletcher Henderson, and one pianist turned band leader by the name of Duke Ellington. As with cheap computer chess games, the player piano democratized learning.

Still striving, after all these years

Learning to play chess or piano well takes thousands of hours to achieve. Why, once machines can do it better, do we still put in those hours? Clearly we do so because we garner great satisfaction personally, and the admiration of others. And when you think about it, that's the same kind of thing we all do to some extent in whatever domains we work and play in.

Why do we learn to paint when photography is so easy? Why do we plant our own gardens when we can buy vegetables? Why do we learn to cook when we can buy perfectly delicious prepared foods? We do these things because it feels good to work hard and improve our skills. In fact, doing things skillfully is one of the chief delights of life. We seek this feeling in much of what we do; what technology can do better than us is often irrelevant.

Take sports. We could build robots that could trounce any professional sports team, but we don't. We do pit robots against each other with battlebot contests, but even that is really a competition among the human designers, builders, and operators rather than the machines, which are mere extensions of our cleverness. The worldwide passion for sports is about what *humans* can achieve with our talent, training, drive, and teamwork. Although we're fine accepting training help from machines, we want to do it ourselves.

From this perspective, to think we'll suddenly lose interest in the hard work of learning a language, merely because we don't have to, is to ignore the way we humans behave. We may be inherently lazy in many ways, but we seem also to be inherently hardworking in others. Think of the happiness a child shows when first walking, first putting words together into complete sentences, learning how to ride a bike. Those moments are some of the most joyful moments we humans have.

Let's also keep in mind that our very struggling to use someone else's language with nothing more than our own mind and voice is a sign of commitment and respect. Lowering our defenses and being willing to speak like a child is tapping into the power of vulnerability that goes so very far in building trust. Merely putting a device between us and letting it do the work does little in that regard—although it can be very helpful for basic transactional work.

Those super symbiotic machines

When I interviewed Kevin Kelly, he told me that "ever-improving machine translation will be a boon to billions for basic language work," to get the gist of a news story, for example. And, he said, the role of teachers might change. "They may evolve to helping learners use the technology in the best ways and include more teaching about cultural understanding." Just using devices to start saying things without knowing the local culture could be "uncomfortable or weird," he said, "while teachers could help us learn to use the technology appropriately."

Kevin told me that the same technology that would allow us to bypass learning will also speed our learning. Those who are motivated can learn a language with more ease, and learn more languages. The technology will also spur the volume of machine translations. Technology, he said, doesn't tend to take away options but rather, adds to them. "It's *all* of the above," he said.

When you think about it, we've used technology to help us learn languages for hundreds of years. Not all technology, after all, is digital. Bilingual dictionaries, which have been around for centuries, are technology. For that matter, so was the original Rosetta Stone; it just took us a while to decipher it. Sound and video recordings were major leaps forward. Modern machine translation is the latest in a long line of tools we are now enjoying to help us gain language skills.

The journalist Marek Kohn predicts that readily available machine translation will lead to a two-tier system of "commodity and premium." While everyone can have commodity-level language skills, we will have to pay for premium: humans with a working knowledge of languages at their ready command.

Machine translations can and will take care of utilitarian understanding, but it's the kind of understanding that leads to a wave from across the street, not a hug. As with chess, machine-human teams may be the winning combination for doing large-scale translation, when lots of translation is required in a short amount of time. Machine translation services may also be of critical help to first responders, with the backup of humans when needed.

Machine translation will continue to improve all the way up to being equal and then exceeding human abilities, at least the abilities of any one human. At precisely that point, it will no longer matter.

We humans care about what other humans can do, and language is one of the main things that makes us human. Language learning is more fundamental to who we are than learning chess or piano. Machine translation will likely lead to much more human communication in general, but for the most important face-to-face communication, my guess is that we'll want to keep machines in their place. Machine translation is about as likely to replace language learning as artificial insemination is to replace sex.

An AI Angie: a love story?

One of my long-suffering tutors is Angie Rojas. She was born and raised in Colombia before coming to the US as a teenager. Angie is a natural teacher. She speaks simply and slowly so I can understand. She corrects me kindly, while encouraging my progress, and gradually pushes me to use more advanced vocabulary and grammar. She is helping me evolve from rudimentary statements to something approaching adult conversation—so that I can be myself in my adopted language. Our typical ninety-minute sessions fly by, and I'm thrilled afterwards when I realize I've been conversing in Spanish the whole time.

But with my schedule and Angie's, we meet only occasionally—not nearly enough for me to make the progress I thirst for. But could I have an AI Angie with me all the time? Someone who could always be available to chat while I walk or drive or just go about my life?

Google Translate has a conversation mode, which approximates my AI Angie today. I can try out sentences in Spanish. Sometimes I get it right and sometimes I get it hilariously wrong. She (I'll call it a she for the moment, since my setting uses a female voice) is never judgmental, never too busy to meet. I'll pause a Spanish movie I'm watching and repeat a newly heard line for her, and she'll kindly listen to see if I've gotten it right.

She goes with me everywhere, since she's there on my phone. I've grown accustomed to her voice. If she were gone, I would miss her.

Kevin Kelly knows exactly what I'm feeling. In his book *What Technology Wants*, he writes, "In the future, we'll find it easier to love technology. Machines win our hearts with every step they take in evolution."

As AI improves and becomes more effective at simulating actual human exchanges, we will be able to gain tremendously at learning in general and at language learning in particular. But we also open ourselves up to the pitfalls of anthropomorphism. The AI can sound so human that we can come to believe it is not a simulation of understanding but actual understanding. In fact, it is shocking how very easily we humans can fall for this delusion.

Joseph Weizenbaum of MIT recognized this phenomenon back in the 1960s, during his experiments with an early computer simulation of a therapist, which he called DOCTOR. He wrote, "I was startled to see how quickly and how very deeply people conversing with DOCTOR became emotionally involved with the computer and how unequivocally they anthropomorphized it."

In the fifty years since Weizenbaum wrote those lines, this human foible has become only more evident. Another MIT scholar, the sociologist Sherry Turkle, more fully laid out the phenomenon. She describes how we are prone to blithely substitute machines for people, almost willfully blind to their obvious inhumanity. This particular kind of vulnerability, she tells us, does not make us more powerful.

My favorite artistic portrayal of this human frailty is the 2013 movie *Her,* starring Joaquin Phoenix and Scarlett Johansson as the voice of his AI lover. As he falls more desperately in love, there comes a scene when he's sitting down on a busy public staircase and asks into his invisible device:

"Do you talk to anyone else while we're talking?"
"—Yes."
"Are you talking to anyone else right now?"
"—Yeah."
"How many others?"
"—Eight thousand, three hundred and sixteen."

Seemingly to understand how he feels about hearing this, she tries to console him, but he doesn't appear to be listening anymore. He watches men walking by, smiling while speaking into their own devices. Are they in love with their own AI women? Maybe *his*?

In their effort to make technology more and more useful to us, engineers can't help but make it more lovable, too. And with our proclivity to impute human feelings and qualities, we risk insulating ourselves from other humans. In most cases this isn't the goal of the engineers. It certainly isn't the goal of Luis von Ahn and his team at Duolingo. They want to keep advancing technology so that more humans get comfortable enough to speak with other humans. There are many private pleasures to enjoy by our growing skills in our adopted language, reading being one. But the highest form of using our language skills is to engage, face-to-face with other humans, and have a real conversation.

I mention face-to-face because one of the most wonderful technological advances in language learning are those platforms that link language learners together virtually. Suddenly one of the major barriers to language learning has been eliminated—or so it seems. Yet even this boon in communication, via live audio and video most anywhere in the world for free, can have us believe that our needs for interaction with other humans have been met. Not so, says the psychologist Susan Pinker. We have a deep biological need for actual human interaction—"very much like other biological appetites, like the need for sleep, food and sex," she writes. When we are with people human-to-human, one of our "happiness" hormones, oxytocin, kicks in. "Despite the clear-cut advantages of the internet," Susan says, "if we want to be happy, healthy, long-lived, and yes, clever, then we need to find ways to spend more time with each other face-to-face."

Right here, over the rainbow

One day in June, I was walking on the beach with my family. It was one of those alternating sunny and rainy mornings that we have so many of in South Florida. Suddenly Lori yelled out, "There's a rainbow!" I looked to see where she was pointing. I looked left and right, up and down, checked again where she was pointing to make sure I was directing my gaze correctly . . . yet still I didn't see it. All the while, the rest of my family was exclaiming how beautiful it was.

Finally, I lifted up my sunglasses and there it was, low on the horizon and breathtaking. My glasses are Polarized, which works well for protecting our eyes from glare off the ocean, but as I learned at that moment, the technology also shields us from rainbows.

I think it's safe to conclude that continued improvements in machine translation will lead to an increase in machine translation, and also facilitate improved human language learning. But technology's continued advance in lovability can also shield us from seeing one another and getting to know one another, face-to-face.

The blessings we enjoy from our advancing technology carry with them an obligation. By understanding their side effects on us, not just physical but psychological, we can deploy them optimally. With this understanding we can develop the abilities to use technological blessings with skill, and even, we hope, with wisdom.

✳ ✳ ✳

Chapter 35

Myth No. 3

THE BEST TIME TO LEARN A LANGUAGE IS WHEN YOU'RE YOUNG

W ho could argue that it's wonderful to have our very youngest Americans exposed to two languages as soon as the stork delivers them on doorsteps? The little angels soak up languages like a sponge. They can start out life speaking two languages without even realizing they are doing it. They can enjoy the benefits of being bilingual their entire lives. The very best time to learn a language is when you're so young, you don't even know you're learning it.

But what about the rest of us—those of us who weren't given the gift of bilingualism along with our first blanket? Knowing we've missed out on prime time, knowing we'll have to work harder, knowing we might not have as good an accent—what do we do about it? Do we just slouch away in defeat?

The 'critical period' may not be

For decades, scholars have examined what they call a "critical period" hypothesis. This is the age at which older children are unable to learn a language as easily as younger ones, or at least to the same level as a native speaker and with a native's accent. For many years, scholars thought that this age was around the start of puberty. Perhaps it was some neurons that died off in late childhood, or some hormonal changes that interfered—what we might call a Vienna-Choir-Boy effect where, after puberty, voices just don't sound as heavenly.

But the research I mentioned in Chapter 24 shows that the critical age might be later—as late as our late teen years. The authors of the study, Joshua

Hartshorne, Joshua Tenenbaum, and Steven Pinker, maintain that the end of the prime-time language learning period cannot be attributed to either the death of neurons or hormonal changes during puberty. They remind us that "the question in the critical period literature has never been why adults are incapable of learning a new language—obviously they are—but why adult learners so rarely (if ever) achieve native-like mastery."

The fact is, say the authors, we don't even know if the "critical period" idea captures anything biological, or if it's just social factors. It may simply be "an epiphenomenon of culture: the age we identified (17-18 year old) coincides with a number of social changes, any of which could diminish one's ability, opportunity, or willingness to learn a new language," the authors point out. This is typically the age when young people either go off to college or get their first job.

The language scholar Ofelia García says that other than achieving a native-like accent, there is no evidence that older children or even mature adults can't become bilingual. We may be misled by casual observations of children, she cautions, believing they are more bilingual than they really are, partly because the way they communicate tends to be simpler than adults. "Yet, in formal education settings," she writes, "adults, able to use their metalinguistic skills in a first language more efficiently, learn more quickly than young learners." This ability to use your first language to more easily learn a second leads her to conclude that "adults are quite capable of being bilingual."

Two other language scholars, Edith Harding-Esch and Philip Riley, agree that we can be fooled by "an uncritical observation of children" when they are learning to speak. "In fact," they write, "children put vast amounts of time and effort into mastering a language: where adults do likewise, they seem to learn just as well, pronunciation excepted."

Now that the language scholars have weighed in, let's see what some language educators have to say.

Older learners have the benefit of experience

Katherine Sprang specializes in second-language acquisition and works at the Foreign Service Institute—the organization that trains State Department employees for overseas assignments. She writes that adults can learn languages "very well" and as learners have advantages over children. "Adults can use what we know of our first language to organize our learning of the sounds, words, and grammar of the new one," she points out. "We don't start from scratch when we learn another language."

257

Sprang also reminds us that mature adults may have had language classes that were "pretty dull . . . all about memorizing vocabulary, talking about grammar—in English—and translating as many paragraphs as you could stand." But, as we know from our earlier chapters, language teaching and learning have changed. As a result, Sprang says, "adults are learning languages better than ever. So if you're a monolingual adult, there's no reason to continue in that sad condition. Monolingualism *can* be cured."

Steve Kaufmann, the founder of the language learning company The Linguist, agrees that adults can learn faster than children. "It is always disappointing to hear adults say that they are too old to learn. They have a lifetime of experience and knowledge that can help them learn faster than any child," he writes. "If adults can combine the curious and uninhibited learning attitude of the child with their own advantages, they can learn rapidly."

Lesley Chapman, one of the language teachers we met in Chapter 9, taught older adults for many years. "There's this idea that adults can't learn a language, which is false," she says. "It's kind of like saying adults can't learn math or learn to play the piano. It's not true."

Our next group to poll are polyglots. Since they speak five or more languages, they learn at least some of them as adults.

Serial learners show how well adults can learn

The Hungarian polyglot Kato Lomb conducted her own survey of fellow polyglots, which she published in Hungary in 1988. In the seventy-six replies she received from her colleagues in twenty-two countries, only 28 percent claimed to be natively bilingual. That is, most of them learned most of their languages as adults. "Being able to learn languages only at a young age is the most prevalent prejudice," she wrote, "and probably that's why it is the one I'm the angriest about."

I was able to interview a polyglot whose language biography illustrates how the circumstances of his life were responsible for how his language skills developed.

Claude Vlandis was born in Cairo of Greek and Jewish parents; his mother was Greek and his father was Jewish. His family moved back to Greece when he was six or seven, and although he was exposed to French, Arabic, and Hebrew as a child, "I never got anywhere with those languages. I was essentially a Greek monolingual until age seventeen."

Greece relies heavily on international tourism, and Claude realized that knowing only Greek would limit his prospects. "I had to learn the language everyone seemed to be speaking," he told me. So when Claude was still in high school, he enrolled in an intensive school for English in the evenings. "In six months, I felt very comfortable to go out in Athens and begin making friends with visitors."

Claude also started watching American films with Greek subtitles. When he heard words he didn't understand, he would write them down and ask his teacher in the evening classes. "'Dawn' was one of those words. It sounded like 'Don,' but in class I understood. I think I benefited hugely that the movies were not dubbed."

Next came music with English lyrics. "I bought a big music book of the Beatles and started trying to play guitar and read the lyrics. I found it silly to sing a song without knowing the meaning, so I wanted to know what the words meant. That helped me tremendously. 'Hey Jude,' 'Yellow Submarine,' 'Girl'—we made a band and used to play at weddings. How can you do that if you don't understand what you're saying?"

Claude then had to serve in the Greek Army, where, he said, "all of my language learning was put on pause." When he completed his military service at age nineteen, he went to Italy to go to school. He found it wasn't what he wanted and so came back home after a month, "but that thirty days was great immersion in the language. I came back and spent the summer meeting more Italians, and my Italian started getting better and better."

Two years later, Claude found a different school he wanted to attend. It specialized in textile machinery, which was his family's business. The school was in Germany. Off he went to Germany, arriving early at the school to try to get some German under his belt before classes began. "I took ten hours of German lessons from a woman, private lessons, to get ready for two semesters in Germany." It wasn't nearly enough, he remembered, and he struggled.

"It was very regimented and no fun, six months of very hard work, studying alone in my room," Claude recounted. "I learned German because I had to, but I never really loved the language the same way that I loved Italian." He did eventually come to appreciate the language. "German can be a beautiful language, in terms of sound and content, when spoken well by those knowing how to use the words."

When he returned home to Athens, his uncle was there, visiting from Egypt. "He said to me, 'What are you doing here? You should come to work with me in Egypt.'" Claude was interested, but there was a problem. "My name is Cohen, so I decided I had to change my name to my mother's name, Vlandis, which is a Greek name." (Claude's father had been first jailed and then exiled from Egypt, where he was living during the 1967 Arab-Israeli six-day war, because he was Jewish.) At age twenty-three, Claude Cohen became Claude Vlandis, and he was off to Egypt.

"When I arrived in Cairo I thought, 'Okay, I speak English and German and Italian and Greek. Certainly there's no problem; somebody would speak one of those four languages.' I was totally *wrong*."

At his textile factory, Claude's uncle put him in charge of four hundred employees who spoke only Arabic. "I'd say, 'Give me a white bobbin of yarn,' and they would come back with a box of the wrong color and we had to wait." After two months of trying to make it work, said Claude, "I knew what I needed to do." He sent himself back to language school.

"It was a private school with ten or fifteen students. We had an extraordinary teacher, a young man. He'd look at you and would know whether you were understanding, and if you weren't, he would persist until you understood." During Claude's six months of classes, his teacher didn't speak a word of English. Any time the students spoke to the teacher in English, they were met with a blank stare. "We found out later that he was fluent in English," Claude said.

Claude attended the school three nights a week, from 7 to 10 p.m. "My Arabic was very good. I could communicate at the factory," he said. Even so, he couldn't understand the TV newscasters. As he explained to me, "the Arabic in the street is very different from the news."

Claude was also improving his skills in textile production and design, including operating the modern machinery. It turned out those skills were in demand all over the world, something Claude would benefit from.

When Claude met a certain young Frenchwoman, he left Egypt to go live with her in France. There he remained for fourteen years and, of course, became fluent in French. Then he moved to Miami, where he married an American from Brazil and learned Portuguese and Spanish.

While in the US, Claude became partners with two Canadians in a business venture selling textile machines. "Of these two partners," said Claude, "one speaks only English and the other English and Greek. They said to me, 'Claude, you can be our window to the world.'" Without his language skills, says Claude, "our company would have been just another North American company, instead of the business it is. We are in forty-eight countries and have agents from Chile to Bangladesh."

I asked Claude if he considers himself talented at languages. "I didn't think I was gifted for language learning back before I started studying them; I thought I would never learn. The fact that I did doesn't mean that it was easier for me than for others. It was work and being exposed to it all through circumstances." What does he say to people who think the best time to learn a language is when you're young? "I think that anyone who finds a strong enough reason to learn a language will learn it."

Let's banish ageism

Claude Vlandis learned most of his languages after the so-called "critical age" for language learning, but he was still young relative to those of us north of fifty. Does there come a time when you really *are* just too old? To answer this question, I sought out two experts on aging.

I first spoke with Ann McDougall, the president of Encore.org, the national nonprofit with a mission to tap the experience and wisdom of older adults for the greater good. Ann pointed out that ageism still exists in our society—"the notion that older people are rigid, that they're not agile learners, that they're not comfortable with technology and learning new ways. A lot of that is myth, but it's a pervasive myth," Ann said.

I asked her what she would say to people who think they're too old to learn a new language. "I would say that's nonsense. They do learn languages differently than young children, but they can learn languages. They also bring discipline and focus to a job they like to do."

I then interviewed Laura Carstensen, the founding director of the Stanford Center on Longevity. I asked her the same question: what she would say to people who think they are too old to learn another language.

"It's not true," she replied. "Of course we can learn a language, or anything else at any age, so there isn't a point in life where people can't learn anymore, short of having a serious dementia."

The 'scaffolding' effect

As for language learners over the age of fifty, Laura said they have some advantages. "Although not enough is known about how older people learn in general, or how they learn languages in particular," she says, "we do know that older people have more knowledge. This knowledge resides in complex neural networks that act like scaffolding for new information."

Laura conveyed the scaffolding idea during a speech to a group of older women at a community center. "I said, 'If I showed you a brand-new recipe for a pie and it had some novel kind of an approach, you could read that recipe and you would already know if you liked it or not.' And they all nodded. 'Now imagine if it's your first pie,' I said. 'No way you can do that.'"

Laura also pointed out that older adults typically have larger vocabularies than teenagers, and those who studied Latin have a head start at learning a Romance language.

In her book, *A Long Bright Future: Happiness, Health, and Financial Security in an Age of Increased Longevity*, Laura advocates for lifelong education, and for two kinds of learning in particular—a musical instrument and a new language. I asked her if crossword puzzles help, something we often hear are good mental exercises for seniors.

"Not so much, unfortunately, because I love crossword puzzles," Laura said. "But they help you retrieve things you already knew." Learning an instrument or a language is fundamentally different, she added, because they require us to do lots of different things simultaneously. "It's an approach that engages lots of regions of the brain, most notably the frontal lobes that help us plan and think and coordinate in a higher-level, complex way."

As we get into our sixties, Laura said, "the uptake of novel information is a little bit slower, but again, it doesn't mean it can't be done. I don't think people should ever give up on learning new languages."

She also mentioned the work of the Canadian social scientist Ellen Bialystok, who has shown evidence that bilingualism is associated with a later onset of the symptoms of Alzheimer's.

The luxury to choose

There are other advantages adults have when pursuing their bilingual journeys. For one, many of us have learned over the years how we like to learn. Some of us like to see the words and grammar written down. Others among us have learned that we respond really well to oral input, so watching movies and TV shows in our adopted language will be particularly rewarding.

On another front, many of us have interests, or interests waiting on our bucket lists, that we can pursue in our adopted language, as Susan Golden did when she took her cooking class in Florence, or as David Wolf continues to do by studying the wines of France in French. We know from dual language schools that using your adopted language to learn something else can deliver double-barreled benefits.

Also, adults often have more control over their lives than young people when it comes to finding their *where*—where their adopted language will live in their lives. Perhaps it will be spending a period of time each year using their target language in another country while volunteering on something deeply important to them. Or maybe it will be here in the US, helping Latinos converse in English while also getting help with their Spanish.

While many older Americans must continue to work to support themselves, some have the financial freedom to do what they want with their time. Some want to move on to second acts, doing things they find meaningful to themselves and that often entail helping others. These fortunate older adults can sometimes do those meaningful things in their adopted languages.

Nor does your adopted language have to be a modern one. When health issues forced him to give up his life as an investigative reporter, I.F. Stone took up the study of philosophy that had intrigued him as a youth. In particular, he was interested in the origins of our belief in the freedom of speech. That led him to the Greeks and to the trial of Socrates. After reading some of the scholarly works on the subject, Stone determined that he would have to go back to the original documents. He decided he would learn ancient Greek.

"I started on my own with a bilingual edition of the Gospel of St. John, then went to the first book of the Iliad," he wrote in his book, *The Trial of Socrates*, which became a national bestseller. "But the story of Greek soon led me far afield into the Greek poets and Greek literature generally. The exploration continues to be a joy."

After her thirty-five-year career as a book editor, Ann Patty left New York City and moved to the country. Partly out of boredom, she began to study Latin. The discoveries she made about the ancient past, and their surprising connections to her own life story, emboldened her to write an inspiring memoir, *Living with a Dead Language: My Romance with Latin*.

Mature adults may find it especially rewarding to seek out a language tutor who is a generation or two younger. As Marc Freedman writes in *How to Live Forever*, bridging the generations can lead to surprisingly deep friendships and "an extraordinary sense of liberation and fulfillment."

Redesigning our 'supersized' lives

"If we think of longevity as about old people, then we lose the opportunity to redesign all of life," Laura Carstensen told me. To help make sure we don't, she and her colleagues at Stanford began an initiative called the New Map of Life. Now that more people are living longer, the website asks, "what are we going to do with our supersized lives?"

Part of what we are already doing is rethinking the rush to work. I remember my father telling me about his college years after World War II, when he was attending the City College of New York on the GI Bill. "We just couldn't *wait* to get out of there and start earning some money," he said. Back then, average life spans, and expected working lives, were far shorter than today. Another year in college was a year you weren't out there making a living.

Today, with life spans reaching into the nineties and longer, it's time to reconsider how we think about our life course. As the New Map of Life website says, "The existing norms no longer work because they evolved for lives that were half as long." We can already see how this ongoing redesign is influencing language learning

For more young people, taking a gap or bridge year before college makes sense. More high school graduates are using that year to live and work in another language overseas. Likewise, service work after college provides the opportunity to do the same, for two years or more.

Laura points out that young parents in their thirties are often the most stressed-out of all people. Those tend to be the years when people are building their careers and raising young children at the same time. That may be when they and their children can benefit most from a year or more off the treadmill. Some parents are opting to take their children to live overseas and walk some of their bilingual journey together, as Bettina Young did.

Continuing a redesigned life journey, some people might say goodbye to their first career after twenty-five years or so, while they are still in their fifties, and move on to something they find more meaningful. That can include living overseas and doing service work, as Robin Loving did in Mexico, requiring her to dramatically improve her bilingual skills. Even taking up our adopted language in our sixties or seventies may, if we are lucky, still give us decades of bilingual enjoyment and the larger life that a second language can bring.

What birth bilinguals may miss out on

One afternoon I was having coffee with one of my bilingual friends, a birth bilingual who speaks perfect Spanish and English, or so it seems to me. I was sharing how much fun I was having learning Spanish, seeing things I've never seen before. I said, "Isn't it *cool* that in English we say, 'sooner or later,' whereas in Spanish it's *tarde o temprano*, 'later or sooner'?"

"I never really thought about it," he replied flatly.

I figured I wasn't conveying my feelings well, or maybe my friend was distracted. But then I had similar encounters with other birth bilinguals. None of them got what all my excitement was about. But other friends who, like me, are late-onset bilinguals—they totally get my excitement and share similar stories of wonder.

Maybe this shouldn't be surprising. Why *should* people who have been bilingual all their lives get excited about such things? Birth bilinguals have never known being monolingual. For them, whether they speak one language or the other is like using one hand or the other.

While I'm envious of such seamless bilinguals, I also wonder if they may be missing something. Unless they learn another language after they are grown up, they won't know what it's like to see their languages from the outside. They won't experience the many pleasures and struggles that come with being somewhat childlike again, of channeling the power of vulnerability, of feeling that sweet pleasure of becoming a somewhat different person in another language.

Birth bilinguals may also miss out on feeling empathy for emerging bilinguals. Maybe it's too hard to have that empathy without having struggled yourself.

It's customary for people to become more set in their ways as they age (although not all do). There may be no better way of remaining young and impressionable than being a language learner. Perhaps we shouldn't ask, "Am I too old to learn another language?," but rather, "Am I still young enough?" Young enough to still be able to ask others for help, to sound silly and laugh at yourself, to be delighted at learning surprising new things.

Maybe it's quite simple, after all. If you decide you *are* still young enough, you are.

Chapter 36

Myth No. 4

THE BEST WAY TO LEARN A LANGUAGE IS TOTAL IMMERSION

It's not quite fair to call this a misconception; it's more like a half-truth. Total immersion, whether at a language camp or inside a country where your adopted language is spoken, can indeed be the best way to learn. The real danger of this idea is that people can get hung up on it. At a time in our lives when going to live in another country or spending weeks in a language camp just isn't in the cards, we can fall into the why-bother trap. Why bother messing around with lesser methods when—maybe someday—I could do the *best* method? If people follow this line of thinking, they may miss the boat as "maybe someday" becomes never.

Total immersion, but not too soon

Language learning expert Stephen Krashen actually cautions *against* total immersion before you're prepared. "A beginner can get more comprehensible input in one session of a well-taught class than from several days of being in the country," he writes. It's better to get the basics of a language down, he advises, before giving yourself an immersion experience. You'll get far more out of it.

That's just what Mary Norris did. From the moment she told her boss at *The New Yorker* that she wanted to visit Greece, he thrust books of Greek grammar and literature into the editor's eager hands so that she would gain familiarity with the language. Mary then took courses in Greek at two New York universities for a year before she booked her first trip.

266

She returned from her five-week journey determined to study the language in its classical form as well, "so that I could read everything written by the Greeks who had crossed this sea before me."

And then she found a way to do a quasi-immersion right at home. "I moved to Astoria, the Greek-American neighborhood in Queens," she wrote, "embedding myself among live Greeks, and there I consumed Thucydides."

Regardless of the neighborhood you live in, today, as we have seen, technology has opened up a world of digital immersion possibilities. Active, thirsty learners can actually give themselves more language exposure right here in America than they might get living a more passive, language-sequestered life in another country.

Today, we are blessed with being able to read the news, listen to the radio, watch TV and movies, and play video games, all in our adopted language. We can navigate the web, and set the apps on our phone to our adopted language. We can converse with native speakers live online from the comfort of our couches. We can often speak to our virtual assistants in our adopted language. All these things that used to be possible only by living overseas, or in science fiction, are now available right at home to nearly everyone. Not that these virtual experiences should substitute for actually going overseas when you are able, but today, an American in Pittsburgh can be exposed in more ways to the French language than an American in Paris could fifty years ago.

Also bear in mind that it's possible to live overseas and *not* avail yourself of the "best way to learn." This is just what happens to people who fall into the expat trap and live most of their days in an English bubble with their friends.

The full-bandwidth beauty of being there

It's absolutely true that living fully in your adopted language overseas can be a marvelous way to learn, and the best you've experienced. You can learn in a full-bandwidth way, reading the signs and newspapers, overhearing bits of conversation, using your language to shop, eat out, hire a contractor, socialize with friends and neighbors, all the time tuning in to the preferred local ways of saying things that never make it to the language textbooks or apps.

In this real-world, full-bandwidth immersion, you not only hear someone speak, but see their face and full body gestures; you associate words with the physical things in your new world as you encounter them, and the context helps to imprint them in your brain. I still remember vividly some of the words that were reinforced for me in Spain when walking around a park: on a green and white sign above a newsstand: *Periódicos y Revistas* (newspapers and magazines); on a recycling bin, *Vidrio y Latas* (glass and cans). When you see something in the real world that you can touch, it can be far more impactful than viewing it on a screen or in your stack of flash cards.

But perhaps the biggest benefit of immersion abroad will be the people you will meet and befriend. Remember the deep friendship that Julia Child formed with the Frenchwoman in the food market, and how they talked for hours about French foods and the best ways to cook them. And recall David Wolf and his friend at the business school who whisked David away into the French countryside, giving him the best of what provincial France offered while also plotting a plan for David to survive back at school. The two are still close friends today and vacation together with their children. No amount of time spent in front of your screen can compare with authentic, face-to-face communications and the friendships that can last a lifetime.

Even then, expect ear lag

And this gets us to the essence of what total immersion can be. We tend to think of it as a method for *how* to learn a language, but it's more than that. It's also the *why* to learn a language. Why, after all, spend all the years, and all the effort, to learn your adopted language if you're not going to reap some of the sweet rewards by spending time abroad? It might make you a bit nervous thinking of it—and yes, even with your skills, you can expect to suffer initially from ear lag—but you can also have the kinds of experiences life is made for, overcoming your trepidation and having the time of your life.

Immersion abroad may also help you find your *where*—where your adopted language will live in your life. Maybe you'll work every summer for a cause you believe in, and get some friends and family members to join you. Perhaps you'll spend every winter in a particular locale that you come to love dearly, especially the friends you've met there.

The stronger your language skills are before you arrive, the better. The whole point of being overseas is not just to get more comfortable with your adopted language, but to speak it well enough that you forget about it entirely and just live the larger life that you sense awaits you, for you are right: it does.

Chapter 37

Myth No. 5

AMERICA'S SO BIG,
WHERE WOULD I EVER USE IT?

Another cocktail party pronouncement goes something like this: "In Europe you can't turn left without running into another country. People there *have* to speak more than one language. But here in America, well, it's just too big. Where would I even *use* another language if I could speak one?"

This is another of those half-truths. Yes, America is big. Only three countries are bigger: Russia, Canada, and China. But compared with the world, America amounts to just above 6 percent of the planet's landmass. When it comes to number of people, we're smaller yet. Our 2020 population of 331 million represents just 4.3 percent of the planet's population, and it's declining. The world population growth rate exceeds the American growth rate.

Of course, as small as America is compared with the rest of the world, it's still *effectively* enormous. None of us can see all of our beautiful country or meet more than a few thousand of our fellow Americans. And it's quite possible to live our entire lives without ever leaving the country.

Have you been waiting for the "but"? Here it is: *But* . . . America's disconnection from the rest of the world isn't what it was a century ago, or even twenty-five years ago. Today it's far easier to travel outside of America both virtually and for real, and more Americans than ever are doing both.

All the methods for digital language immersion we've talked about are also, of course, ways to use your adopted language in America—for work, for pleasure, and for daily living. If French is your adopted language, you can set your phone, your computer, your dashboard, and your ATM transactions to French, while never leaving Little Rock. After work, you can swing by a

French language Meetup before returning home to view the next episode of a Netflix series that has been localized for the French. And the cost of this virtual immersion? Zero.

Let's say you've adopted French not only because you love the language but also because you know it can help you at work. The company you work for in Little Rock sells medical equipment and has been expanding its business internationally. You've just been promoted to being responsible for the MENA region (Middle East and North Africa) and have been asked to focus first on North Africa. You travel to Casablanca in Morocco, where your French is a requirement for doing business. Not only do you have success in opening up Morocco, but your Moroccan friends now help your firm expand into Western Sahara, Cameroon, Niger, and Mali.

Back in Little Rock, your company president is so pleased with your work that you earn a bonus, which you use to take your family for a vacation week in Montreal. The trip is especially important for your kids, since they attend a French-English dual language school, and will now be able to meet some French-speaking children their own ages in Montreal.

Next door in Taiwan

One of the advantages of America's large scale is the number of speakers we have of the world's most plentiful languages. If your adopted language is Mandarin, for example, you should have little trouble finding a Mandarin-speaking private tutor, since we have millions of Americans who are native speakers. But if you'd also like an online tutor, you now have thousands of potential tutors as close as your tablet. The virtual landscape available to Americans today is vastly larger than it was even fifteen years ago. As recently as 2005, fewer than 17 percent of the world had access to the internet. By 2019, that figure had surpassed the 50 percent mark, or more than 4.1 billion people. In the developed nations, such as Taiwan, virtually everyone has broadband internet today. Worldwide, even if people don't have internet access at home, almost everyone lives within reach of a mobile cell signal.

What this means is that the isolation Americans have felt in the past is no longer there in reality. We can get to know our neighbors in Taiwan and Morocco as easily as our actual next-door neighbors, and often we will spend more time communicating with them via text and video chats than we do with the neighbors we wave to on our own street.

It's true that actual, face-to-face meetings are the staff of life. Friendships that begin in virtual space can be transformed by getting together in person. Right here in the US, there are also plenty of language communities where Americans can use their adopted language, including the Chinatowns, Little Italys, Greek Towns and other ethnic communities in many urban areas. Miami and San Antonio are just two of many American cities with a significant population of people who speak their native language—in this case, Spanish.

As for going overseas, in 1998, Americans took about thirty-nine million trips to other countries. Twenty years later, that tally had tripled to ninety-three million trips. While there are dips in travel in the wake of a crisis, including a pandemic, travel has always rebounded after a few years, and then gone on to surpass the pre-crisis levels.

As recently as the 1980s, when Americans at a cocktail party asked, "Where would I even use another language?," they had a point. Today, the answer to that question is "anywhere and everywhere." This is the happy reality of American life in the twenty-first century.

Chapter 38

Myth No. 6

ACCENTS ARE EMBARRASSING

W hen I was twenty-two and in graduate school, I took my first trip to England. I made friends with some other students at a pub and mentioned that I was thinking of traveling up to Scotland. "Oh, you should definitely go," said a young woman at the bar. "The girls up there *love* American accents."

"Really?" I said, incredulous.

I had been admiring the British accents I was hearing, but had never thought that *I* had an accent, too. The notion that women in Scotland might like mine was nice, but I also found it kind of odd and unearned. The linguist John Esling says that "we see others as having an accent—because we take ourselves as the norm or reference to compare and measure others' speech."

Later, near the end of that same trip, I was traveling alone on a night train in Italy. It had been days since I'd heard an American and I was trying the best I could to get by with zero understanding of Italian, when suddenly, I heard two young women talking a few benches ahead of me. They were speaking English! And there was something more. Their voices sounded just so *good*, the way rushing water might sound to a thirsty hiker. It took me a few moments to understand why . . . and then it hit me. They were from Southern California, like me! They were speaking in a Valley Girl style, the kind of talk I might have made fun of back home, but here in this train passing through the Italian night, their talk sounded like familiar music for a homesick heart. I went over and introduced myself. Whatever we said to one another, I can't recall. I only remember the marvelous feeling of hearing, unexpectedly, people from my own language village.

It was decades later, while researching this book, that I came across an essay by John H. Esling titled "Everyone Has an Accent Except Me." He wrote, "It's when we travel that we discover we have an accent." True enough, in my case.

We Americans delight in our country's regional accents. We make good-natured fun of Southerners, of Valley Girls, Cheeseheads from Wisconsin, Mainers, New Yawkers, and of course, Bostonians. We like to poke fun at the patrician Bostonians—the Mayflower bunch—but we especially enjoy the city's blue-collar accent. It's the one that proudly belongs to the townies who get their coffee at Dunkin', wear Red Sox caps, and drive beaters with Boston Bruins, Celtics, and Patriots stickers. And maybe a bumper sticker that reads, "If you don't like my driving, stay off the sidewalk!"

So it was with much delight that many millions of us watching the 2020 Super Bowl caught a Hyundai car ad featuring some Boston celebrities talking about the car's new "wicked smaht" self-parking feature. At least forty-three million people have viewed the ad on YouTube. To those of us who know this Boston accent, the ad is funny as hell. Hyundai, the Korean automotive giant, did a wicked smaht job of *localizing* its ad to the American market.

But as much enjoyment as we have with our own American accents, the tables suddenly turn when it comes to our efforts to speak another language. Instead of being a topic of fun, it's a topic of dread, as in, "Oh, god, is my accent horrible? Does it make people wince? Will I embarrass myself? Will others judge me as a hopeless, blithering American?" Tormenting ourselves with such doubts and fears doesn't do anything good for our journey to bilingualism. All this dread might even derail us completely. And so, accents, and our love-hate relationships with them, are the subject of our sixth myth.

Accents and other accidents

Erik Kirschbaum, an American journalist, told me, "I've lived in Germany pretty much straight on for thirty years now and enjoy speaking German, even though I do have a bit of an American accent even today."

We seem to take as gospel that the accent we should strive for as a language learner is one that sounds just like a native. The ultimate mark of success is when native speakers ask us what part of their country we're from, only to be astounded when we tell them we are—can you believe it?—American!

But let's hear what some language professionals have to say about that.

The Foreign Service Institute of the US State Department is where, as you might recall from Chapter 3, they rate job applicants. On the Interagency

Language Roundtable scale, the scale goes from Level 0, "no proficiency," to Level 5, "functionally native proficiency." For many jobs, applicants must achieve Level 3, "general professional proficiency." Among the descriptions of this level is: "Pronunciation may be obviously foreign." And even at Level 5, there is no mention of accent at all, only: "Pronunciation is typically consistent with that of well-educated native speakers of a non-stigmatized dialect."

When you think about it, the language proficiency scale must keep mum on the subject of accent. Think of the US for a moment. At a gathering of US governors, it's likely that we will hear different accents, but will those accents tell us anything about the governors' proficiency in English? Clearly this is the same situation in other countries as well. In fact, other countries usually have more variations in regional accents than is the case in the US. Accent is on a different plane from the other aspects of language proficiency. It's more like style or fashion.

Fashion, however, can be a powerful conveyor of meaning. It can reinforce a person's persona. Consider the former Secretary of State, Henry Kissinger, with his German accent that added gravitas to his intellectual image, and those BBC commentators who just sound so very authoritative, at least to us Americans. And how about a Russian diplomat to the US—would we expect, or even want, him to sound as American as Lester Holt? It would be kind of creepy if he did. We *want* him to sound like the Rocky and Bullwinkle cartoon character Boris Badenov: "Natasha! Get moose and squirrel!"

We Americans might say that Lester Holt has a "neutral" accent, but what exactly does that mean? What we are saying, usually unwittingly, is that's the fashion we approve of—at least for certain scenarios such as a national news show. And just think of Arnold Schwarzenegger or Nicole Kidman or Antonio Banderas. Who would want them to lose their accents?

The linguist Roberto Rey Agudo says that "having no accent is plainly impossible. An accent is simply a way of speaking shaped by a combination of geography, social class, education, ethnicity and first language." In other words, our accent is an accident of our circumstances, unless we go to some pains to change it. "There is no such thing as perfect, neutral or unaccented English, or any other language," Agudo maintains. "So I hope you like my accent as much as I like yours."

Accents are the spice in our linguistic food; we do so love to try to guess where our fellow speakers are from, much like we love to guess ingredients in a savory dish. When it comes to accents, we are discriminating diners—but not in an unkind way; we just eat this accent stuff up. As evidence, try typing into YouTube the name of any popular language followed by the words "accents of" or "dialects of." You'll find lots of examples of people enjoying themselves immensely by impersonating the accents of their fellow speakers.

Once when Lori and I were in Paris, I got to chatting with a young concierge at our hotel and asked her about the various languages she encounters from guests. "I wish I spoke Chinese," she told me; the hotel was getting many tourists from China. "What about French Canadians?" I asked. "They must be easy." She made a face and said, "Oh, their French is *horrible*. It's not even French." And Americans? "Americans are easy; they all speak English," she replied. I was relieved to get off so easy.

But, of course, there are many different ways of speaking English. The linguist R.L. Trask said that when Hollywood movies with sound were first shown in Britain in the 1930s, the audience had trouble understanding what the actors were saying. "Most Britons had never heard American accents, and they were bewildered."

The novelist Paul Bowles picked up on this in his 1949 novel, *The Sheltering Sky*. In one scene, a Frenchman is dreading having to use English in an upcoming conversation with an American. Writes Bowles, "Then he remembered having heard that Americans did not speak English in any case, that they had a patois which only they could understand among themselves."

When different accents diverge enough, they reach a point where they might be called dialects, but what constitutes a dialect is, as we've seen, a matter not so much of linguistics but politics.

The Norwegians and the Danes can understand one another quite well, yet both—being proud of their respective countries and having the freedom to do what they wish—call what they speak different *languages,* and the world accepts their sovereign pronouncements. Conversely, speakers inside different regions of China speak what the government calls *dialects*, even though their speech may be as different as French is from German. The linguist Max Weinreich neatly summed up the situation: "A language is a dialect that has an army and navy."

This is not to say it's wrong to have one dialect that's hoisted onto a pedestal and hailed as a full-fledged language; that's how we humans tend to do things the world over. It may be unfair to the other dialects, but it does help standardize such things as schooling and media. So standards are imposed—the French of Paris, the Italian of Florence, the Chinese of Beijing.

Just know that it's not because those winning dialects are *inherently* better or correct: they're simply preferred by the powers that be and hence, anointed as fashionable. That said, being able to speak fashionably when one wants to can be an important, career-building skill—whether in Paris, Florence, Beijing, or London.

Accents can be subtle, sometimes heard only in the pronunciation of a word or two. The sociolinguist William Labov found just such a difference among the residents of Martha's Vineyard, an island off of Massachusetts known for its influx of summer people. The year-round residents had a way of saying *light* that sounded more like *loight*. Reviewing Labov's research, the linguist John Edwards explains, "it is safe to assume that, as with dialect variants, pronunciation difference typically becomes yet another aspect of status-boundary marking. This has nothing to do with any intrinsic correctness, virtue, or superiority, and everything to do with social pressure and prestige.'"

Accents can be generational, as children adopt the accents of their peers, while their parents stay with the accents they acquired earlier. Bharat Ayyar, a graduate student at Stanford, told me of an unexpected clash of accents that once left both him and his mother speechless.

Bharat was born in India near Madras and grew up in a family that spoke Tamil. When he was eight, the family moved to Toronto, where English quickly became young Bharat's dominant language.

He remembered vividly the two types of English he used to speak as a child. He spoke a heavily accented Indian version at home with his parents and to relatives back in India when they would call. But at school, he spoke a Canadian English very similar to his classmates. Bharat occupied separate linguistic worlds, which didn't pose any conflict—until one day, when Bharat got a phone call at home from one of his friends. His mother had answered and handed him the phone. "I was caught," he told me. "I didn't know which accent to use." Finally, Bharat tried to split the difference and hurriedly told his friend he couldn't talk then and hung up. But his mother was staring at him, letting what she had just heard soak in.

After that episode, Bharat said his parents spoke "regular English" to him. "They didn't want me to suffer a prejudice of speaking with an accent," he explained.

An unnamed bias gets a name

When a strong accent is combined with imperfect command of the language, it can often cause others, even close family members, to conclude that the speaker is just a bit slow. The novelist Amy Tan describes her struggles along these lines with her own mother. "When I was growing up, my mother's 'limited' English limited my perception of her," she writes. "I was ashamed of her English. I believed that her English reflected the quality of what she had to say. That is, because she expressed them imperfectly her thoughts were imperfect. And I had plenty of empirical evidence to support me: the fact that people in department stores, at banks, and at restaurants did not take her seriously, did not give her good service, pretended not to understand her, or even acted as if they did not hear her."

As Tan got older, she came to understand how smart and strong her mother actually was. But as a child, she had fallen victim to a pervasive human bias. When someone struggles with our language—which almost always includes having what we would call a heavy or thick accent—we almost can't avoid thinking that the person just isn't the sharpest tool in the shed.

The Stanford linguist Jonathan Rosa told me about discovering his own bias concerning his grandmother, who had immigrated to New York from Puerto Rico when she was a young woman. "She spoke with an accented English. I thought she was unintelligent and picturesque, not someone I would consult with on life and the world—a relic of the past," he admitted.

Jonathan's opinions began to change when he went to college and took a course in linguistics. "I learned that there is no such thing as right and wrong, and that everyone has an accent. This messed me up and I wanted to learn more." As a class assignment, he interviewed his grandmother and asked her about her experiences in Puerto Rico. He learned she cleaned houses for the Anglos and learned English from them so well, she would correct her English teachers at school. When she came to New York, she worked for tenant rights. "It was the first time I was talking to her as a person," Jonathan confessed. "I'd been complicit in viewing her as less."

Oddly, I haven't been able to find any linguistic term for this widespread and stubborn proclivity we have to underrate imperfect speakers, so after batting around a few options, we've settled on Heavy-Accent-Means-Stupid bias, or *HAMS bias*. Maybe naming the bias is a step toward avoiding it.

At the same time I was interviewing Jonathan Rosa and other linguists, I was continuing my own study of Spanish, including attending weekly Spanish Meetups in Palo Alto at a local Peet's Coffee. We were mostly older Anglos trying our best to converse in Spanish with the help of one Spanish tutor, who would come to our rescue at most meetings. One of the regulars was a fellow named Henry. Like the rest of us, Henry struggled. He would have occasional strings of impressive sentences and then would stop, visibly struggling to utter something that apparently was just beyond his grasp. I didn't think much of it, as we were all doing the same thing.

Then one day, I met Henry in a different setting, where everyone was speaking English. I went over to say hi and he broke into a friendly banter, speaking perfectly natural and fluent English, while I stood there just listening with my mouth open. He was articulate, intelligent, even witty. I was stunned.

"Oh my god, Henry isn't a blithering idiot!" I said, fortunately only to myself. And then I caught myself. "Well, *of course* he's not. *I'm* the blithering idiot for thinking he was." Even while I was busy observing HAMS bias in others, I was walking around with a huge case of it myself. Of course Henry was going to sound like an idiot at Spanish Meetups—we all did. That's kind of the purpose of a Meetup for language learners. And that's when I realized just how deeply and subconsciously HAMS bias works on us.

HAMS bias fits neatly into the realm of what the Nobel Prize-winning psychologist Daniel Kahneman calls System 1 thinking: "System 1 is highly adept in one form of thinking—it automatically and effortlessly identifies causal connections between events, sometimes even when the connection is spurious." In other words, System 1 thinking is the thinking we don't think about. System 2 is our rational selves, but we tend to be lazy in employing System 2. Only when I was confronted by the articulate Henry, chatting away effortlessly in English right in my face, did I finally use a bit of my System 2 brain to realize how I had been fooled by my jumping-to-conclusion System 1.

HAMS bias is what teachers in ESL (English as a Second Language) classes try to avoid—the trap of concluding incorrectly that those students who speak English best are the smartest. HAMS bias is what business leaders like Bill Johnson in China tried to avoid when he switched the language of his division from English back to Chinese. And it's what human resources people can confront when interviewing applicants.

To illustrate, let me share a story of our own recruiting for warehouse workers at Lori's and my company. We had grown fast in the early years and had our warehouse several miles away from our offices. Our head of HR had called our warehouse manager, Frank, to let him know she was sending a couple of guys over she had just hired. Shortly after, two Haitian men showed up at the warehouse and Frank promptly put them to work. A week passed and payday arrived, but Frank was dismayed to find he hadn't received checks for the two new guys. When he called his colleague in HR, the two of them finally worked out the problem: the two men working for Frank were *not* the ones our HR head had hired. The new hires had disappeared, and two other fellows had walked in off the street. Frank assured her that his guys were super workers and he wasn't about to give them up—although he had trouble understanding their English, he admitted. It ended well. The men got their paychecks and became two of the best workers Frank ever had, working for our company for ten years.

My guess is that had these Haitian fellows shown up at our offices with their limited English, they would not have been hired. In this case, an accident of timing helped everyone avoid HAMS bias. Just as we shouldn't judge a book by its cover, we shouldn't judge a mind by its voice. But I'll be the first to admit, that's easier said than done.

Accent-uate the positive of being a language learner

So what's the upshot for language learners when it comes to accents?

First, know that there is a difference between pronunciation and accent. We should work on pronunciation, as it is key to being understood. In the Spanish word *hablo*, for example, if you put the emphasis on the *a,* you're using the present tense, "I talk," whereas if you put the emphasis on the o, you're using the past tense, "he or she talked" (it's written as *habló*).

Likewise, work on grammar and vocabulary, on idiom and colloquialisms. Work on all aspects of the language, but as far as accent? Chillax. Sure, be aware of how you sound, how your way of speaking strikes others; work on being more understandable and more natural all you want, but don't torment yourself about sounding like a native.

Sounding like a native speaker is likely an unrealistically high bar, and, moreover, unnecessary. I know that no matter how proficient I become at Spanish, I'll never be mistaken for a native speaker. For one thing, I can't roll my Rs.

It bothers me that I can't, particularly since so very many Anglos can. But I can still say *perro* (dog), a word that calls for tongue rolling, and be understood by faking it: putting a little extra emphasis on the two Rs. This helps to distinguish it from the similar-sounding word *pero* (but). Spanish speakers will know I'm not a native speaker, but they will understand that I'm saying dog and not but, if it isn't clear anyway from context. Be aware, as Paul Pimsleur has written, that pronunciation "begins not in the mouth but in the ear," meaning we must be able to hear an inflection or nuance before we can hope to reproduce it. But when it comes to accent, he writes, "try not to have an offensive accent, but then, well, it's up to you how much time you want to devote to being perfectly like a native."

The scholar of bilingualism François Grosjean sums up the situation neatly when he says that "having an accent when you know and use two or more languages is a fact of life; it doesn't make you any less bilingual, and it rarely impedes communication. It is something bilinguals get used to, as do others they interact with."

Michael Bloomberg, the former New York City mayor and presidential candidate, was made fun of for his attempts to speak Spanish, but plenty of others came to his defense for trying. As a late-blooming language learner myself, I can sympathize with Bloomberg and salute him for trying, especially since he's in the public spotlight, where he opens himself up to ridicule.

It's also critical to acknowledge that there's a world of difference in HAMS bias between a rich and powerful Anglo attempting to speak Spanish and an immigrant from Central America attempting to speak English. Spanish speakers may cringe when Bloomberg mangles his Spanish, but few of them will conclude he's stupid. Not so on the flip side, when a Spanish-speaking immigrant mangles his English. It's important to distinguish elective bilingualism, which is what Bloomberg is doing by electing to learn Spanish, from situational bilingualism, when someone is pressured by their situation to learn another language. It can be too easy to appreciate the elective bilingual—"at least he's trying, isn't that nice"—while criticizing the situational bilingual as lazy, slow-witted, or un-American for not working hard enough to speak English better.

The science writer David Berreby explains in *Us & Them: The Science of Identity* how readily we humans divide others up into camps, in many cases before we are even aware we're doing it. He writes that "there are parts of the mind that know a person who does not speak your language is neither stupid nor hostile nor disrespectful. But the Us-Them code is not concerned with any of that. It seeks and finds just the cues it needs for its work."

The home of the brave

When it comes to accents, my advice can be summed up in two words that I've seen on some bumper stickers lately: "Be Kind." First, be kind to yourself about your own accent. Sure, work on it, ask native speakers to give you feedback, but don't fret about sounding like an American. My own approach is to focus on the other aspects of language learning and let my accent come along on its own accord.

Second, be kind to others. Be aware that HAMS bias is both pervasive and insidious. Try to recognize when you might be falling victim of it. You'll be a better person than I have sometimes been when you do.

The famed "Tiger Mom," the law professor Amy Chua, exhorted her daughters not to make fun of someone's accent. "Do you know what a foreign accent is?" she lectured them. "It's a sign of bravery." She challenged her daughters to imagine how perfect their accents might be if they moved to China.

280

If an accent is what bravery sounds like, then America has more brave people than any other country, simply because we have more immigrants than any other country. We also have a growing number of native English speakers, like Michael Bloomberg, who are electing to become bilinguals and, along with their language skills, are no doubt gaining some empathy for accents.

Chapter 39

Myth No. 7

I'm Just Not Good at Languages

It happens like this. A girl named Hanna is really good at almost everything she tries. Her parents praise her lavishly. Hanna responds by continuing to do things well, and fairly easily. Then she is presented with math and all of a sudden, it's not so easy and she doesn't perform right away. Her parents and teachers say, "Oh, that's okay, Hanna. Some people just aren't good at math."

Yet math takes some struggle for many of us, but with hard work and good teachers, students can get it and learn. But Hanna isn't used to struggling and the adults around her aren't used to making her, and so they all turn away. In reality, Hanna might have become a math virtuoso.

This is the story that Jo Boaler, a professor of mathematics education at Stanford, told in a presentation. She goes into more detail in her book, *Mathematical Mindsets*. When I heard Jo's talk, I was remembering what so many people had told me: "I'm just not good at languages." Could it be the same thing? After the presentation, I asked her if I could drop by her office with a few questions.

When I met with her there, I was impressed with her direct, simple style of speaking, which is not always the case with professors. I was just as direct. Might the I'm-just-not-good-at-math mindset also apply to I'm-just-not-good-at-languages? Without missing a beat, she replied in her crisp British accent, "Absolutely. Mindsets and brain science apply to everything."

She did qualify her statement by saying she hasn't studied language learning, but said kids tend to be tracked the same way in every subject: if they struggle at something, they are often steered away from it.

Two formulas for being good at languages

What do the linguists and language teachers say on the importance of talent for learning languages?

David Crystal writes, "A few gifted language learners do exist, but most people arrive at their fluency only as a result of hard work, expended over a considerable period of time." Steve Kaufmann writes, "Some people may have better language learning ability than others, but this innate learning ability is not the decisive difference in language learning success."

And Kato Lomb writes, "No one is 'just' good at languages." Betraying her doctorate in chemistry, she offers a formula: "time invested" multiplied by "interestedness" = "result." Then divide by "inhibition," and the result is your skill in a new language.

As she waged war against the prejudice that language learning is only for the young, she battled even harder against the widespread prejudice that it takes special skill. "This hazy and mysterious 'language talent' has kept a lot of people from language learning and, as such, it deserved my full wrath."

The psychologist Angela Duckworth has dedicated her career to banishing what she sees as an unhealthy and unrealistic homage to talent, maintaining that effort is twice as important. She offers her own formula to illustrate this truth. First you multiply "talent" by "effort," which results in "skill." Next you multiply "skill" by "effort," which results in "achievement." Thus, "effort" literally counts twice. It's a simple expression but it covers a wide swath of human endeavor, and her empirical results of surveying for the role of grit in a whole range of human achievement corroborate her formula.

When it comes to real achievement, Duckworth writes, "there's a good reason why 'the ten-thousand-hour rule' and 'the ten-year-rule' have gone viral. They give you a visceral sense of the scale of the required investment. Not a few hours, not dozens, not scores, not hundreds. Thousands and thousands of hours of practice over years and years and years."

But as much as pure effort is required, so, too, is passion, which often comes from people feeling that their work is meaningful and important to something larger than themselves. "What ripens passion is the conviction that your work matters," writes Duckworth. "For most people, interest without purpose is nearly impossible to sustain for a lifetime. It is therefore imperative that you identify your work as both personally interesting and, at the same time, integrally connected to the well-being of others."

How are you at English?

Attempting to channel the advice from these experts, I've tried out some responses on people who say to me, "I'm just not good at languages." I counter with, "Well, how well do you speak English?" That gets a surprised look, a moment's hesitation, and a response like, "Well, pretty good—very good, actually." I'll let that sit there for a few seconds before adding, "Then you have the ability to speak a second language, too; it's mostly a matter of time and motivation."

In *Grit,* her bestselling book, Duckworth writes that "what we accomplish in the marathon of life depends tremendously on our grit—our passion and perseverance for long-term goals. An obsession with talent distracts us from that simple truth."

I worry about the many Americans who have tried learning a language but harbor a suspicion that they just lack talent. Then, when confronted with a roadblock like ear lag or a point of grammar that requires some struggle, they throw up their hands and fall victim of confirmation bias. "See, I *told* you I just don't have a talent for languages!"

So, dear emergent bilingual, don't be one of them. Take the long view that comes with adopting your language. Be prepared for roadblocks and the productive struggle you'll have getting over them, around them, or through them. And when you search for your *where*—the place or places in your life where your adopted language will live—make it personal, let it be part of your answer to what matters most in life. Do all this and you *will* become an American bilingual.

Chapter 40

Myth No. 8

FINE, BUT OTHER SKILLS
ARE MORE IMPORTANT

R ejoining our cocktail party, I've just said that record numbers of Americans are becoming bilingual when a fellow opines, "Well, language skills are fine, but coding is a language, too, and that's what young people should be studying today." Another fellow chimes in. "Yeah, these kids who major in computer science are getting six-digit salaries, right out of college!"

My answer is to agree that coding is important today. One of my own sons is a software engineer and, fortunately, has his choice of well-paying jobs. And it's true that we refer to programming *languages*, like Python, Java, and Ruby. How they are similar and different from human languages, I'll leave to the linguists and the computer scientists to decide. But I will say this: to determine that young people should focus on learning something specific *instead* of learning a human language is a false dichotomy. It's like saying we shouldn't dance because we should be singing.

Adding to, not taking from

To view language learning as taking *away* from learning other subjects is to assume that language learning is best done in language classes, and that since class time is finite, we have to prioritize. While dedicated language classes are, indeed, useful for language learning, they are foundations, touchstones—but not the main show. The growth of dual language schools in America and around the world is evidence of this. The premise of such schools is that students should use more than one language to learn *with*, rather than merely studying the language as a subject. Thus, at a dual language school, math, physics, and chemistry may be taught in Chinese, while biology, geology, and literature are taught in English. As that dual language principal in North Carolina said, it's "the two-for-one deal," meaning you get all the learning, and an extra language, too.

What's more, these dual language schools are proving grounds for showing how being bilingual is making kids smarter. Remember the North Carolina educators we met in Chapter 20? They've tracked what has happened since their state went from a handful of dual language schools in 2005 to well over a hundred thirteen years later. "We know that higher academic achievement, and higher scores on standardized tests and reading and math, result from students being in a second language program, whatever that program is," as one of them told me. "Creativity, divergent thinking, problem-solving skills: all of those things increase and become better if you have studied a second language." Kids are brainier when they're bilingual, making them better prepared to excel at those other important skills.

What only language can teach

We must also remember that learning languages of the human kind is the best—some would say only—way to appreciate other cultures and not just compare them with our own. As we have seen, learning languages also builds empathy and trust among people.

What's deemed important for schoolchildren to learn in school has evolved over the years. In the early twentieth century, during the aviation craze, conventional wisdom maintained that children in the US needed to become air-minded, meaning they had to understand the fundamentally different perspective that comes when being high above our cities and towns. They also had to understand the rudiments of flight and aerodynamics, or risk being left behind. There was a time when penmanship was thought critical, and then typing—until it was thought unimportant, except for secretaries—and then it became important again, reincarnated as keyboarding in the era of personal computers. When I was in high school, we had driver's ed and driver's training, which may be on the way out now that some young people aren't bothering to get driving licenses. And who needs to know shorthand anymore? Or how to use a slide rule?

But some things are constant, including learning about our fellow human beings—especially those who come from different backgrounds from ours and who speak differently. Learning how to communicate with them and collaborate with them will always be necessary skills.

There are language teachers who argue that speaking another language deserves to be included in STEM (Science, Technology, Engineering, and Math). Says Lisa Lilley Ritter, a past president of ACTFL, "Languages are that T. We are a technical skill. So we're part of STEM. You've got to have that skill in language to be able to go forward and use it in different applications." It's also true that speaking another language is an art form, greatly aided by technology, both in learning languages and employing that knowledge.

In my view, language learning and the journey to bilingualism have so very many advantages to the individual and to society, and they are so firmly within our grasp for achieving, that learning another language is the natural next train stop on the long arc of human educational attainment. Learning to code is important, but we humans can sing *and* dance.

Chapter 41

Myth No. 9

ENGLISH IS GOING TO THE DOGS

"What business do schools have teaching foreign languages when they can't even teach them English?" Okay, nobody said those exact words to me at a cocktail party, but complaints about the decline of English are plentiful, and the easy next conclusion is that we ought to do something about *that* before worrying about frills like learning French. But we should know this: complaints about the decline of English have been plentiful for a very long time.

"The myth of the decline of English is particularly interesting, because it is so old," wrote Charles Ferguson and Shirley Brice Heath in their book, *Language in the USA*. "Writers, teachers, public lecturers, and social critics have complained about the decline in English at least as far back as the fifteenth century ... the myth seems to be that the language has been doing well enough until recent decades, when dramatic decline has set in."

Here's how Steven Pinker describes the twenty-first-century version of this myth: "grammatical sophistication used to be nurtured in the schools, but sagging educational standards and the debasements of popular culture have led to a frightening decline in the ability of the average person to construct a grammatical sentence." The trouble is, he adds, "this opinion, however common, is wrong."

Change is what English does so well

The fact is, say linguists, language changes all the time in a process that is inevitable. "There is probably more time wasted on this issue than on any other in the world of language," says David Crystal. "Language change is inevitable, continuous, universal, and multidirectional. Languages do not get better or worse, when they change. They just change."

John McWhorter has tried his hand in clearing us up on this matter in his book, *Words on the Move: Why English Won't—and Can't—Sit Still (Like, Literally)*. The butchering of the language, he assures us, has been going on for a long, long time. He reminds us that "English used to be a language where verbs at the end of the sentence came." What would be strange, he says, is if language didn't change, because "we'd still all speak the first language that popped up in Africa when humans first started to talk."

We should understand that whatever "rules" of English we can come up with are, according to McWhorter, nothing more than "arbitrary fashions of formal language that we must attend to just as we dress according to the random dictates of the fashions of our moment. Remember that what is considered 'proper' English varies with the times just as fashion does."

And it's not just English that is constantly changing. The linguist R.L. Trask writes, "Each generation speaks a little differently because our language is always changing. And not just our language: *every* language is always changing. There is no such thing as a living language that fails to change."

Samuel Johnson, the formidable eighteenth-century British lexicographer, attested to how true this is with English when he published his magnum opus of an English dictionary in 1755. After eight years of working on it, he admitted defeat in trying to "tame" the English language. He was so worn down, in fact, that he defined the role of lexicographer as "a harmless drudge."

The usual suspects on both sides of the pond

But since there aren't enough linguists hanging around to disabuse us of our going-to-the-dogs notion, we're pretty much free to perpetuate this canard with abandon. And as we work our way through various people to blame for the demise of English, we can begin with ourselves—us unruly, misbehaving, rebellious Americans.

The social critic H.L. Mencken first published his enormously popular book, *The American Language,* in 1919. It remains an enjoyable read today. He opens by talking about the accusations the British were hurling at us, as early as 1735, of how we Americans were massacring the English language. Among the indignities: Americans used the term "bluff" to mean a steep perpendicular bank. How laughable is that?

Near the end of his nearly eight hundred-page book, the Sage of Baltimore, as Mencken was known, cautioned his readers to expect further change in English. "The notion that anything is gained by fixing a language is cherished only by pedants."

While the British prefer to blame Americans, we Americans prefer to blame our young people.

"Every generation laughs at the old fashions, but follows religiously the new," observed Henry David Thoreau in *Walden*. That this pertains to language as much as clothes was brought home to me in my high school English class one afternoon before the class period began. Our teacher came over to the girl sitting next to me and said, "Oh, I really like your shades!" This was 1971, and "shades" was how we young people referred to sunglasses.

My classmate, after a pause, corrected her. "Oh, you mean my *sunglasses*."

Her meaning was clear. "Old" people, like our teacher, might know the new meaning of "shades," but she wasn't supposed to actually *use* a term we young people had claimed for ourselves. I don't remember what, if anything, our teacher said in response—just that her face sagged a bit, making me feel sorry for her lapse of etiquette.

But this was an unusual case. Usually older people dislike the new fashions in young people's speech and imitate it only to complain. "No, it's not '*totally random*,'" says the mom. "It just makes good sense that you shouldn't be on the road after midnight."

The sociolinguist William Labov calls this the Golden Age Principle. It describes the nearly universal human reaction among older generations that any change in their language is perceived negatively. Almost never do the older people say they like the change. Instead, the Golden Age Principle kicks in, where "at some time in the past, language was in a state of perfection. It is understood that in such a state, every sound was correct and beautiful, and every word and expression was proper, accurate, and appropriate. Furthermore, the decline from that state has been regular and persistent, so that every change represents a falling away from the golden age, rather than a return to it."

Ebonics and emoticons

The next supposed culprit in the demise of English is what many Black people speak. It is variously called Ebonics, African American Vernacular English, or as John McWhorter prefers, Black English. It strikes most non-Black Americans as wrong or broken English, and perhaps sad evidence of Blacks growing up in a linguistically deprived environment. Linguists know otherwise.

Black English is, in fact, a dialect of English, with its own rules and grammar, some of which can be quite subtle and difficult for newcomers to grasp. It's used because its speakers generally prefer it to Standard English in the same way that all language groups prefer their own way of speaking: it marks a boundary.

It comes as a surprise to many whites that many Blacks, Barack Obama among them, can switch back and forth from Black English to Standard English as easily as we might turn our heads left or right. "Rather than being labeled as verbally deprived," writes the linguist Walt Wolfram, "African-Americans ought to be thanked for contributing to daily conversation with words, phrases and other manners of speaking that enrich our language and our lives."

John McWhorter, an African American himself, devotes a book to the subject, *Talking Back, Talking Black*. He points out that in many countries, it's completely normal to have a home dialect and a more formal national dialect; the US is actually unusual for not having this. We are what linguists call monodialectical. It is a measure of our insular experience that we fail to understand this. Writes McWhorter, "Black English is America's only English dialect that combines being strikingly unlike standard English, centuries old, embraced by an ever wider spectrum of people, and represented in an ever-growing written literature. It is worthy of celebration, study, and certainly acceptance. America will never truly grow up linguistically until this is widely understood."

Well, if we can't blame young people or Blacks, let's move on to today's social media. Texting and Twitter, Facebook and Instagram. All that texting people do today is going to be the ruin of English as we know it, all that "C u soon" and "LOL." Remember when people used to actually speak to one another and not just thumb emoticons onto screens?

Compare today's digital chaos to the relative calm of days gone by, when the evening newspaper was tossed onto our porches by that nice boy from down the street. But the language in those old newspapers might be a bit misleading, according to the journalist Robert MacNeil. Back then, newspaper editors routinely "cleaned up" what public figures and others actually said. The polite, grammatically correct language that made its way into print was not always what came out of people's mouths.

'Caution: this language contains contaminants'

Okay, then, if we can't blame modern media, how about the Mexicans and other immigrants? Their languages are contaminating American English with a verbal guacamole, ruining our all-American smorgasbord (even though we swiped *smorgasbord* from the Swedish). They're the reason why we had to put up with the Terminator tight-lipping "*Hasta la vista, baby*" and Gidget the Chihuahua trilling "*Yo quiero Taco Bell.*" Can linguists actually defend this kind of linguistic mashup? Of course they can, but it sounds better when they call it by its professional name: code switching.

"Using words or terms from different languages in the same sentence or utterance has often been seen unfavorably, even by those who switch themselves: terms like Japlish, Franglais, and Spanglish are evidence here," observes the sociolinguist John Edwards. "Prejudice aside, however, it is hard to see that being able to draw upon double or triple pools of possibility—choosing the most apt or nuanced meaning, using a word from a second or third language to indicate particular emphasis or intimacy—is anything other than an expanded and useful capability."

If you're worried about Spanish contaminating English, you might be interested to know that the defenders of Spanish are worried about the opposite. My Spanish tutor Angie cringes when her husband uses such anglicisms as *parquear*, rather than the correct *estacionar*, for the verb "to park," or *rentar* instead of *alquilar* for the verb "to rent."

It's not just my Spanish tutor who is dismayed. At the headquarters for defending and propagating proper Spanish, the good folks at the Real Academia Española had been wringing their hands for years about the growing number of American embarrassments to the language of Don Quixote. They even established an outpost of the academy at Harvard, called the "Observatory," in an attempt to keep a closer eye on us. Even so, after years of shuddering at what was being said over in the New World, they finally threw in the *toalla* and decided it would be better for all involved just to give us our own dictionary, where we could *parquear* our *carros* in our own *garajes*. (My apologies, Angie.)

Sport bitching from the shore

One of my family's favorite pastimes is being down by the water and—I'm a little embarrassed to admit this—making fun of the boats going by. We make fun of overpowered boats and underpowered ones, of boats that are too big and boats that are too small, of ugly duckling boats and beautiful swan boats. Only rarely are we stumped and find nothing to poke fun at, so we'll praise a boat, just for variety. This whole activity is enhanced with alcohol, of course, and by the fact that we ourselves have done all manner of things in boats worth poking fun at. My point is that we just enjoy the hell out of sport bitching.

I suspect that most of us also enjoy sport bitching about the way people use language. In his massive dictionary, Samuel Johnson dutifully included *lingo*—a word he considered "foreign" rather than "fully naturalized English." He succinctly defined it as "Language; tongue; speech," and then went on to add, no doubt with a scowl on his face, that it was "a low cant word." In other words, it was "not suited to dignified writing." The beloved American stylist E.B. White wasn't above finger-wagging, either. In *The Elements of Style,* he sets readers straight on what went wrong with the word "flammable." He wrote: "The common word meaning 'combustible' is *inflammable*. But some people are thrown off by the *in-* and think *inflammable* means 'not combustible.' For this reason, trucks carrying gasoline or explosives are now marked FLAMMABLE. Unless you are operating such a truck and hence are concerned with the safety of children and illiterates, use *inflammable*."

Despite White's instructions, the Merriam-Webster dictionary came down on the side of children and illiterates. As the comedy writer Jane Wagner says, "I personally believe we developed language because of our deep inner need to complain."

As Mark Twain might say, the death of English has been greatly exaggerated. My advice is: let's keep kvetching about how English is going to the dogs as long as we're just sport bitching. But don't let it keep you, or any school superintendent, from letting young Americans mangle their adopted languages, too. After all, it just gives us more to complain about.

Chapter 42

Myth No. 10

Today's Immigrants Aren't Learning English: A Parallax

"Yeah, it's a good thing you're studying Spanish," said a fellow with a smirk on his face, "since Spanish is taking over the country." He waited for me to try to refute his statement, but instead I took another swig of my Negra Modelo. Frankly, I could see his point.

After all, bilingual signs seem to be everywhere these days—certainly at big retailers like Home Depot and Walmart. We have to listen to those annoying "press 1 for English" messages on our phones, and flip by Univision and Telemundo TV stations as we work our remotes. Where I live, in South Florida, we've got plenty of billboards in Spanish, usually with photos of suited-up personal-injury attorneys asking, "*¿Accidente?*" Then there's the "*Despacito*" song by two Puerto Rican artists that exactly six humans on Earth have not heard because they've been living on the International Space Station. And what the hell does *despacito* even mean?

It's hard *not* to think that Spanish is taking over America. And just as hard not to conclude that we are making it far too easy for native Spanish speakers to just keep using their language and not learn English, not assimilate, not become the mainstream Americans they should want to become.

Adding some numerical substance to these arguments is the fact that immigrants, and Latinos in particular, have grown to record numbers in recent years. According to the Pew Research Center, as of 2019 America was home to some forty million people who were born outside the country. While not a historic high in terms of the percent of our population, it is a historic high in terms of the sheer number of people. What's more, included in this figure are some 10.5 million undocumented immigrants, most of them Latinos. Who knows if these people even *want* to assimilate?

A complaint as old as our country

As with the claim that English is going to the dogs, the accusation leveled against "today's immigrants" not learning English has a long and distinguished career. No less an American than Benjamin Franklin blew what may have been the starting whistle back in 1751, lamenting that the Germans of his day "will never adopt our Language or Customs." The complaining has been pretty much nonstop ever since. It's been the subject of countless conversations on American front porches and plenty of debates in Congress.

From our earliest days as a country, even before we were a country, people naturally were concerned about the language that would unite us and the languages that might divide us. The first European inhabitants of the American colonies came from many different language groups, including Spanish, French, Dutch, and German. And then there were the many Amerindian languages, although the Europeans dismissed those as "savage tongues," much like those of the enslaved Africans, and not worth bothering with.

The framers of our Constitution were aware of the importance of a national language, but perhaps because they knew that trying to agree on an "official" language for America would be fraught politically, decided to remain silent on the subject. Our Constitution, like the Declaration of Independence before it, was, of course, written in English, but English would be used *unofficially*—then, and ever after. In addition, there was no officially sanctioned body to watch over English. The Founding Fathers were almost certainly aware of the language academies in France, Germany, and Spain, but perhaps sensing the elite, class associations of such bodies, decided to skip the idea. And thus from our earliest days, language in America was, for better or worse, left as uncultivated as most of our land.

Applying some facts to the question of whether immigrants were adopting English, and how quickly, has always been tricky. For starters, for more than a century after our founding, we didn't even know how many Americans spoke what languages. In a rapidly growing America, the number was a fast-moving target.

The Louisiana Purchase from France in 1803 added land from the Mississippi Delta to the Canadian border and a good cache of French speakers to the mix. And the Treaty of Guadalupe Hidalgo of 1848 added much of today's West and Southwest plus some eighty to one hundred thousand Spanish speakers to the fiesta. We imported Chinese laborers to build the transcontinental railroad—not only for their labor, but also for their skill with black powder, which was critical to the success of the project. Then came the great waves of immigrants from Europe, including people from German-speaking lands, Scandinavians, Italians, Poles, Jews, Hungarians, Bohemians, Slovaks, Ukrainians, Greeks, Albanians, and Armenians, among others.

The varied languages these intrepid souls brought with them on their long and arduous voyages posed a communication challenge—for commerce, for education, and for governing. The federal government attempted to get a bead on the challenge, starting with the 1890 census, which was the first time we asked what language people spoke at home. In the 1910 census, we asked what the language was if not English. The idea was to figure out just how far short America fell in being able to communicate in a single language, and the size of each language that stood in the way.

The results of the 1910 census contributed to what has been called the Americanization campaign, during which immigrants were encouraged to remove their old-world language clothes and button on a clean new American English shirt that they would wear from now on.

And what became of all these languages?

A quick shift to a single tongue

In their book *Remaking the American Mainstream*, the sociologists Richard Alba and Victor Nee summarize the work of others, as well as their own research, by concluding that the languages immigrants brought to America during the twentieth century were generally gone in three generations.

This timeframe applies not just in America but in other countries where immigrants make new lives, whether it's Italians immigrating to Argentina or Chinese immigrating to Jamaica. And that raises another question: Do American immigrants transition faster or slower to their new language than immigrants in other countries?

Alejandro Portes and Rubén Rumbaut, sociologists who specialize in migration, write that the US "has incorporated more bilingual people than any other country in the world. Yet the American experience is remarkable for its near mass extinction of non-English languages: in no other country, among thirty-five nations compared in the detailed study by [other researchers], did the rate of mother-tongue-shift toward (English) monolingualism approach the rapidity of that found in the United States."

When looking at the history of language loss in America, the linguist Kenji Hakuta writes, "One of the most fascinating aspects of bilingualism in the United States is its extreme instability, for it is a transitional stage toward monolingualism in English." Examining the same comparative work that Portes and Rumbaut cited, Hakuta concludes that "it would take 350 years for the average nation to experience the same amount of loss as that witnessed in just one generation in the United States."

To be sure, no country had ever taken in as many immigrants as had America, nor from as many disparate language groups. The fundamental American values that prize achievement and success were consistent with a rejection of tradition. If immigrants wanted to succeed in America, it meant being able to communicate with their fellow Americans beyond their own language group. It was characteristically American to let go of one's traditions and embrace the future. And America's future was to be written in English.

Portes and Rumbaut conclude that among American immigrants, "the shift to English is both an empirical fact and a cultural requirement demanded of foreigners who have sought a new life in America." So historically speaking, American immigrants have indeed learned English—and fast.

Curiously, the anglicization of the American language landscape happened at the same time as the whitening of American bread. It was in 1910 that America saw the opening of what was then the nation's largest bakery, the Ward Bakery in Brooklyn, advertising white bread "untouched by human hands." Ward advertised the superiority of its factory-made bread in gleaming, modern contrast to the old-fashioned bread made by hands by immigrants. Ward touted its purity and hygiene, its scientific and industrial expertise, and warned against the unwholesome, unwrapped loaves passed hand to hand in sketchy neighborhood bakeries. The oddly parallel lives of uniform, sliced white bread, and uniform, American Standard English would continue deep into the twentieth century.

Not as good as yesterday's

The accusation that immigrants aren't learning English was part of a larger practice of complaining about immigrants in general. The historian Thomas Archdeacon explains the pattern

"Anglo-Protestants were aghast at the coming of the Irish in the 1840s and 1850s, but their descendants found the Latin and Slavic Catholics who arrived at the end of the nineteenth century a greater menace than the familiar Celts. Irish-Americans shared some of the disdain felt by their

Protestant antagonists for the peoples of southern and eastern Europe regardless of shared religious affiliations. Whites of all nationalities worried about the so-called Yellow Peril posed by the Chinese and the Japanese, and Christians from every denomination would have rested more easily had Jewish immigrants from Europe not appeared on the scene on the eve of the twentieth century."

We Americans pride ourselves on being a nation of immigrants, but we tend to forget how badly we treated them. Portes and Rumbaut call it "this peculiar American waltz," in which we pull in immigrants for their needed labor with the one hand, while slapping them with prejudice and discrimination with the other. It's a pattern going back to colonial times, they say, "with foreign languages seen as fractious markers of cultural difference and potential disloyalty . . . ."

And the ill treatment flares with each new wave of immigration. In the midst of the second wave of immigration, between the late 1890s to the beginning of World War I, rumors spread that Europe was sending America its destitute and criminals to rid itself of problems. The hue and cry reached such a din that Congress finally responded by initiating a thorough investigation in 1907. The investigation, which came to be known as the Dillingham Commission, included Congressional visits to the major emigration points in Germany, southern Italy, and Russia. According to the historian David Gerber, the final report, published in 1911 in thirty-nine volumes, mostly exonerated immigrants. "The report dispelled long-held notions that European nations were emptying their poor houses and prisons and sending the inhabitants to the United States," wrote Gerber. To the contrary, the report praised the many sacrifices immigrants had made and their "capacity for work."

Paul Taylor, an executive at Pew Research Center, writes about the checkerboard welcome mat immigrants have always found upon entering America: "We worry that they'll take our jobs, drain our resources, threaten our language, mongrelize our race, worship false idols, and import crime and vice. People once said such things about the Irish, Germans, Italians, Poles, Greeks, Slavs, Russians, Jews, and pretty much every other immigrant wave that came ashore, just as today some say the same about Hispanics and Asians." And this happens even though Latinos in the US commit fewer crimes than native-born Americans.

Despite our "peculiar American waltz" with our immigrants, America up to the First World War was comparatively tolerant about languages. But America's entry into the war galvanized our latent suspicions about other languages in a way that marked the entire century, and lingers even today.

Our war against German

The largely forgotten treatment of German Americans during World War I can be illustrated by what happened to one German immigrant by the name of Robert Paul Prager. His story is told in the book, *Burning Beethoven: The Eradication of German Culture in the United States during World War I*, by Erik Kirschbaum. I was able to interview Erik on this dark chapter in American history.

"Prager was a German immigrant to the United States from Dresden," Erik told me. "He lived in the United States for over a decade and bounced from job to job. He ended up working in a mine near St. Louis, and was a bit of an agitator, agitating for the union, and he wasn't really liked by his coworkers."

These were the years immediately before World War I, when German Americans were the country's largest ethnic group. "It's hard to imagine," said Erik, "but there were five hundred German-language newspapers in the United States, German-American clubs in every city, German was taught in elementary schools in thirty-five states. A quarter of the people in New York City spoke German, making it the world's third biggest German-speaking city after Berlin and Vienna."

The German American community had campaigned for America to stay out of the war. German Americans faced the real possibility of cousins or even brothers fighting one another in the trenches. But after Germany sank the RMS *Lusitania* and the infamous Zimmerman Telegram came to light, in which Germany offered to help Mexico recapture territory it lost to the US if Mexico would enter the war on Germany's side, Americans turned with a vengeance on what was then our largest ethnic group.

That was the atmosphere that Prager found himself in. "Prager sensed trouble brewing," said Erik, "so he applied for US citizenship." Regardless, his fellow miners decided he was a German spy, "just because he spoke English with a German accent and was agitating for a strike," said Erik. "They went to the boarding house where he was staying and they dragged him out of his room, and they made him drape a US flag around his shoulders, and made him march up and down Main Street."

The police attempted to protect him, locking him in the local jail, but the growing mob stormed the jail, forcibly removed Prager, and took him to the outskirts of the town, where the police had no jurisdiction. "They tried to hang him, but they were amateurs and forgot to tie his hands," Erik said. "But the mob quickly remedied their error and successfully hanged him as a German spy.

"The real travesty was a few weeks later," Erik added. "There was a trial, and the jury acquitted all the people accused of hanging him. Afterwards, one of the jury members was quoted in the local press as saying 'that shows that we're patriotic and nobody can accuse us of being slackers.'"

The lynching of Robert Paul Prager wasn't an isolated incident. Erik says about thirty German Americans were hanged by vigilante groups. And lynchings weren't the only injustice.

Languages, the casualty of war

A lot of Americans know about the internment camps of World War II where Japanese Americans were rounded up and incarcerated; in World War I, internment camps were set up for German Americans. Erik says there were two or three camps in the South, ostensibly for the Germans' own protection, but totally innocent people, music conductors among them, were held in these camps for a year or more because the United States was worried that they were German spies.

In Ohio, Wisconsin, and Illinois, mayors and Boy Scouts took German-language books out of schools, piled them up on the streets, and set them on fire.

German-language schools and German-language programs in other schools closed in droves across America. Even Middlebury Language Schools, which had begun with a German summer immersion program, canceled it. Meanwhile, some states outlawed the teaching of German and other languages as well. Nebraska went so far as to pass a law prohibiting the use of any language other than English in a public meeting as well as the teaching of any language before the completion of the eighth grade. A German teacher in a Lutheran-run school was fined for teaching German to a ten-year-old boy who had not yet passed eighth grade.

The case went to the US Supreme Court, which in 1923 struck down the state law in Nebraska, along with similar laws in Iowa, Ohio, and elsewhere. "But by then," writes the historian Dennis Baron, "it was an empty victory for language teachers. Already teaching had so declined by legal means in many states, reflecting the mind set of the time."

"The damage had been done," echoed Kenji Hakuta. In 1915, 25 percent of students were enrolled in German classes. By 1922, just seven years later, the figure had plummeted to less than 1 percent.

It wasn't just the German language that got targeted. "The Anti-German prejudice spread to disdain for all foreigners," write Portes and Rumbaut.

Abandoning other languages and acquiring "non-accented" English became the litmus test of Americanization.

"In a country lacking centuries-old traditions and receiving millions of foreigners from the most diverse lands," Portes and Rumbaut write, "language homogeneity came to be seen as the bedrock of national identity. Immigrants were not only expected to speak English but to speak English *only* as the prerequisite of social acceptance and integration."

Practical patriots

Thus, early in the twentieth century, America swung dramatically from being relatively tolerant of other languages to actively intolerant. That this change was painful to immigrants is an understatement. Apart from all the German-language businesses that were destroyed, the German schools forced to close, and the language teachers who lost their livelihoods, were the millions of parents and grandparents—like Erik Kirschbaum's grandfather—who began to silence themselves. In countless American homes, grandparents were unable to express who they were in their native languages, unable to pass wisdom on in the form of expressions and proverbs. Gone were the songs and poetry, and most especially the stories. They were unable to pass these things on to the people they loved more than anything in the world—their grandchildren. Lacking a linguistic term for this, we offer simply, the *grandparent tragedy.*

But immigrants tend to be practical people. To speak English, and only English, was widely perceived to be a patriotic act, and while it was a burden, it was only one burden among many that immigrants carried after uprooting themselves from their homelands and trying to make a home in America. They left not for adventure, wrote the historian Oscar Handlin, but because "the alternative to flight was death by starvation," and because "any alternative was better."

While we may look back today at the influence of immigrants on America with nostalgia—at our fine Italian food, our good German beer, and our festive Mexican piñatas—for those first-generation immigrants, life was often an ordeal.

Life for many was focused on trying to find and keep work, having a home in a safe neighborhood, getting their kids into a safe and good school. Life was worrying about more mouths to feed and getting the rent money in time. Immigrants faced these challenges without the comforts of familiar culture, church, and language. Most wanted with every fiber of their being to make it in America, to have a piece of that American Dream. They wanted their kids to have a better life here in America than they themselves had had back in the home country.

If giving up their heritage languages was part of the price they had to pay, they would pay it. If speaking English poorly and with a heavy accent was part of that price, they would pay that, too.

Besides, forgetting about their heritage language was also the practical choice. Let's consider the reasons why.

For the first half of the twentieth century, before the era of relatively inexpensive jet travel, most American immigrants had little hope of returning to their homeland to use their language. Their children, when playing outside the home, would likely encounter more English-speaking kids than speakers of their same heritage language. Communication with the homeland took place in the form of letters. When telephone service finally did come, it was expensive and rarely used.

Few elementary schools offered language classes and those classes offered in high school were, for the most part, too few and too late. College was out of reach for most Americans until after World War II, so study abroad was generally only for the elite.

Technology for language learning consisted of dictionaries, grammar books, and chalkboards. Complicating matters, the heritage languages that American immigrants spoke were often not the prestige dialects of Italian or German or Russian, but other dialects from the countryside, for which written materials were few or nonexistent.

Scientists who thought they were doing the right thing advised educators and parents that monolingual education was best. Better to not saddle children with "a language handicap" they would have to struggle to overcome in school.

Parents then, as now, wanted what was best for their children. They wanted their children to have better educations, better opportunities, and better lives than they themselves had. Given all these realities, it was practical to forget the language of the home country. Better their kids just learn English well and sound as American as anybody else, so as not to suffer the prejudice their parents had suffered.

During the same years when Spain's Generalisimo Franco was trying to beat all the non-Spanish languages out of his citizens, in America we had a different approach—we beat the languages out of ourselves.

The broad trends in America were made up of millions of individual stories like this one, from Evelyn Svenson Granger:

My father was named Algot Elvin Svenson and he came to the US from Sweden in 1911, when he was eighteen years old. He was the youngest of twelve children and all of his older siblings came to the US before him, except one sister named Ida who had married and had five children. He came through Ellis Island and it was there that he dropped one of the S's in Svensson to become Svenson.

He told me the only English he knew was "apple pie," "ice cream," and "coffee." In Sweden, he went as far as eighth grade before he became an apprentice painter, and he came to America as a painter and house decorator. He went to live in Brooklyn where his brothers were and went to work for a painting contractor. It must have been at work that he learned English, although he always spoke with an accent. He was blond with blue eyes and was about five-foot-nine or so and had a round Scandinavian face and a very sturdy frame.

When World War I broke out, he enlisted in the Army and was sent to France. When he returned, he met my mother. My memory is that her father wasn't pleased that his only daughter was about to marry someone with an accent, but she married him anyway.

I was born in 1932 and my sister, four years later. He was very proud of his Swedish heritage yet never tried to teach Swedish to me or my sister. He didn't want us to be a foreign person; he wanted us to be an American. My mother had no interest in Swedish at all.

On weekends he would take me to Swedish movies in the city. My mother didn't want to go, and actually, neither did I, but the movies had English subtitles. I wish he had taught me Swedish. I could kick myself today.

We actually had a Swedish exchange student come to our high school and I was assigned to greet her. I sang the Swedish national anthem on stage, which my father must have taught to me. He was so proud of me; I still remember the tears in his eyes.

We talked about going back to Sweden to visit. He wanted to take us, but WWII came and we never went.

Today I remember only "thank you"—tack—and tack så mycket is "thanks very much."

After high school, Evelyn went to St. Luke's Hospital nursing school near Columbia University, where a young man she knew from high school was attending dental school. In 1953 she married him, and she and Ronald Granger went on to have five children, the second of whom, Lori Granger, became my wife.

The silver lining in the single-language cloud

Evelyn's story is representative of so very many Americans in the first half of the twentieth century whose parents, proud as they may have been of their country of origin, chose not to speak their heritage language to their children, other than a few words—and in Evelyn's case, the National Anthem.

But there was recompense, including a free public education for their children that was the envy of the world. The economists Claudia Goldin and Lawrence Katz have written about "the high school movement" in America during the first half of the twentieth century. It was an educational achievement unparalleled in the world at that time. "European visitors in the early twentieth century commented that the U.S. educational system wasted resources by educating the masses," they write. "But Americans viewed their educational system as egalitarian and essential to providing equality of opportunity."

And it was this commitment to education that enabled America to achieve its stupendous economic success. "Because the American people were the most educated in the world," write Goldin and Katz, "they were in the best position to invent, be entrepreneurial, and produce goods and services using advanced technologies." It was our universal, free education through high school, say the authors, that led to America earning naming rights for the epoch, "The American Century."

My own maternal grandmother lived through this mighty crescendo in American education. Born on January 3, 1900, Emma Roelke earned her "normal school" diploma during the war, which was the degree then required for schoolteachers. "I closed nineteen one-room schoolhouses," she told me in the 1970s, after she had retired. I responded that she must have been a very bad teacher to cause all those schools to close, getting the laugh I was going for. But, of course, it was timing. Her career happened to coincide with the massive consolidation of the American school system, which was part of the educational flowering across America. And also, of course, the education was entirely in English. In many cases, the American-born children were the first literate members of their family, and they were literate in English. While immigrants suffered from the grandparent tragedy, there were also blessings to ameliorate their pain, including seeing their grandchildren go far in school.

The language skills of American soldiers and sailors during World War II were weak as a result of the abandonment of German, Italian, Russian, and other immigrant languages. But one heritage language that some Americans still spoke played a pivotal role in the war—the Navajo spoken by those Native Americans who became the famed US Marine code talkers in the war in the Pacific. Although they had been punished for speaking Navajo in school, enough of it remained in memory so that when the Marines came looking for Navajo bilinguals, a core group of twenty-nine was recruited. They worked with linguists to develop a code the Japanese never were able to break, and the code was instrumental in helping the American forces prevail. Unfortunately, the critical role the Navajo performed in the war remained classified for a generation after the war ended, during which time many code talkers passed away as unsung heroes.

'You didn't do that in the '50s'

Soon after World War II, writes Thomas Archdeacon, "America's ethnic groups were becoming composed of English-speaking members of the second generation who were busily ridding themselves of the vestiges of Old World cultures."

Kim Potowski remembers as a teenager questioning her Lithuanian grandmother about why she didn't speak her heritage language. Her reply: "'Well, you know, you didn't do that in Brooklyn in the '50s. You had to speak English and assimilate." American teachers were still silencing students caught using a language other than English, and their parents continued to silence themselves.

The 1950s also saw the rise of Senator Joseph McCarthy and his Red Scare witch hunts that unfairly damaged so many American careers and lives. In the years that McCarthy and his aide Roy Cohn were on their campaign of harassment and intimidation, you certainly didn't want to be overheard speaking Russian on the New York City subway.

Later in the '50s, another headline-grabbing event shook the nation and our assumption that English—and nothing but English—was the best path forward.

When the Soviets launched Sputnik in 1957, the first satellite to be placed in orbit, Americans feared that we were losing the Space Race. The satellite emitting its eerie beeps *right over our heads* seemed like a taunt. Not only that—we had precious few Americans who could even understand what the Russians were saying. Sputnik led to the National Defense Education Act, passed in 1958. Among many other things, it poured money into language education, including, of course, Russian.

That same year, two other journalists would come out with their shocking book, *The Ugly American*, which had such a big influence on then-Senator John F. Kennedy. Looking back, the '50s were the end of an era of American conformity to many things, including speaking nothing but English. The '60s were about to change everything.

Chapter 43

TODAY'S IMMIGRANTS AREN'T
LEARNING ENGLISH: THE '60S PIVOT

The American Century pivoted in the 1960s the way young people pivot in their teenage years. Movements that had been quietly building now filled headlines and began to change minds—the civil rights movement, the women's movement, the anti-war movement. But other things that happened in the '60s, not nearly as well known, were to play leading roles in forging how we were to think about "today's immigrants" and bilingualism. The first was called, at the time, the "ethnic revival."

Despite the constant drumbeat for assimilation during the first half of the century, there was a surprising persistence of ethnic identities that shone through from beneath the coats of 1950s-era whitewash. The historian Thomas Archdeacon found it difficult to predict whether the nation would continue the intense heat under its melting pot or whether the '60s marked a turning point for more open ideas of what Americans were allowed to be.

In 1966, when Fishman published his *Language Loyalty in the United States*, he also sensed a change in the wind. In the first half of the twentieth century, he wrote, there was a clear "'message' which immigrants, other ethnics, and their children quickly get—that ethnicity is foreignness, that both have no value, that they are things to forget, to give up." But Fishman felt that the unity of the United States was already so strong by the 1960s that we no longer needed to fear divided loyalties. He took the growing interest in ethnic cultures to indicate a shift in the mindsets of some Americans, at least, who believed that now we had more to gain from their diversity than to lose from any possible divisions.

Fishman noted American towns that used their ethnic heritages and bilingual skills to attract visitors—like Amana, Iowa, with German; and

Solvang, California, with Danish. He anticipated a time when such towns multiplied and that language maintenance through bilingualism would be perceived to be in the national interest and a sign of social maturation.

Fishman offered the prescient idea that once mainstream Anglo Americans grasped the benefits of bilingualism, and actively pursued it for themselves, they might unite with immigrants and become protectors of American ethnicity. Nearly half a century early, he saw the possibility of the keen demand for dual language schools that today outstrips supply across the country.

The third great wave of newcomers

Perhaps because the Civil Rights Acts of 1964 and 1968 were so seismic in the American consciousness, the dramatic changes in US immigration law went relatively unnoticed. But the Immigration and Nationality Act of 1965, which removed all reference to race, was to have a profound impact on America that accelerated as the American Century moved through its final decades. The law went into effect in 1968 and ramped up slowly so that in the US Census of 1970, the American population still reflected the old status quo.

In fact, the 1970 census reported what would be the century's low point of both the number of immigrants (9.6 million) and their percentage to the whole population, at 4.7 percent. The vast majority of these immigrants were from Europe, as had always been the case. As the new immigration law took effect, between 1970 and 2010, the number of immigrants quadrupled. As a percentage, immigrants leaped from 4.7 percent to 12.9 percent. And instead of them being mainly from Europe, 82 percent came from Asia and Latin America. This was the third great wave of American immigration, one that would transform America from then on.

From the vantage point of baby boomers like myself, the change could not have been more dramatic. We came of age during the biggest upswing in residents born outside of the US in the nation's history. While our parents had seen more immigrants in their own childhoods, especially if they came from urban environments, and our children didn't know to notice any difference—they grew up watching *Dora, La Exploradora,* not *Captain Kangaroo*—we midcentury people felt the change most acutely. No wonder that boomer dude at the cocktail party said Spanish was taking over the country. Or if it wasn't Latinos he was noticing, it was all the Asians, like in the San Diego neighborhood that locals refer to as *Manilla* Mesa, rather than its actual name of Mira Mesa.

Fishman wasn't the only scholar doing groundbreaking work in bilingualism in the '60s. That was also the decade when the Canadians Wallace Lambert and Elizabeth Peal first published their work showing bilingual students outperforming their monolingual peers.

Student study abroad ramped up in the 1960s. It made headlines when Italy's river Arno overflowed its banks in Florence and poured muddy water into the museums and libraries, damaging priceless books and artwork. The "Mud Angels" who flew to the rescue included more than one hundred American exchange students. Even middle-class kids could now leave on a jet plane and study abroad.

The 1960s saw the birth of President Kennedy's beloved Peace Corps, where each year more Americans received intensive language training before going overseas to serve. In 1968, the American Council for the Teaching of Foreign Languages, or ACTFL, was spun out of the Modern Language Association. It set the stage for ramped-up professional training in language teaching as it unleashed a domestic corps of advocates for American bilingualism and the appreciation of other cultures. In that same year, the heroic work of the Navajo code talkers was finally declassified, although only gradually did the nation learn how crucial their bilingualism was to winning World War II.

And it was in the 1960s that the Coral Way school in Miami, described in Chapter 20, demonstrated the power of dual language education and would come to inspire the thousands of dual language schools that would follow.

Reorienting our position on languages

As America moved into the 1970s and '80s, scholars began refining our understanding of American languages. In 1984, the language scholar Richard Ruíz clarified three different perspectives, or orientations. In what has become a seminal article, he described these orientations as language-as-problem, language-as-right, and language-as-resource.

For much of our history, language-as-problem was the predominant orientation, and so the educational tactic was to tolerate non-English languages only so far as was necessary before transitioning students to a monolingual English education. But increasingly after 1960, groups began claiming that learning their heritage language was a fundamental right that had often been violated in America. Switching to the language-as-resource orientation that Fishman and others advocated for early on, one sees a very different path forward: one toward a robust and inclusive bilingualism for all. In truth, in

America in the second half of the twentieth century, all three orientations coexisted, jostling for space in the American psyche.

After the US Supreme Court upheld language rights in Meyer v. Nebraska in 1923, America's highest court again took up language rights in 1974 when it agreed to consider the case of Lau v. Nichols. The court ruled that the Board of Education of San Francisco failed to provide equal access to education by requiring Chinese-speaking pupils to attend instruction in English only. This decision led to the establishment and reinforcement of bilingual programs around the country, although in most cases, these were transitional or subtractive bilingualism, with monolingual English speakers as the result. At the same time, a widening range of groups were demanding language rights.

After being banned by the US in 1898, the Hawaiian language was welcomed back and made official in the state in 1978. The teaching of Hawaiian alongside of English resumed in public schools. The success of the Hawaiians led to similar advocacy on the mainland for Navajo and other Indigenous languages. In the 1960s, American Sign Language was officially recognized. And by the '70s, you could find the first acknowledgments of the legitimacy of Black English.

Yet the language-as-problem orientation, made stark by the lynching of German speakers in the midst of World War I, was not about to let go.

One line of attack was on bilingual education. It wasn't only the demagogue Ron Unz with his Proposition 227 that threw bilingual education under a California school bus in 1998. His populist attack was but one of many coming from the language-as-problem orientation.

The language scholar Lucy Tse was one of the experts who knew better and felt compelled to step away from scholarship long enough to write a short book in 2001 called *Why Don't They Learn English? Separating Fact from Fallacy in the U.S. Language Debate.* "Despite reports to the contrary," Tse writes, "immigrant children are acquiring English well and with striking rapidity." As for adults, "there are no signs that adult immigrants shy away from learning English. In fact, they seem to be doing remarkably well."

Tse explained that today's immigrants have far more motivation to learn English than prior generations. "Arrivals in earlier periods in history could labor on farms, work in factories, and build railroads without speaking fluent English or possessing much literacy. Today's service-oriented economy requires English ability for all but the lowest paying jobs. This reality is not lost on new arrivals to the United States."

But facts were often at a disadvantage compared with feelings. Kenji Hakuta wrote that feelings for English and nothing but English came even from the generation of older immigrants, "who themselves had gone through the old 'sink-or-swim' method of learning English. 'I did it,' the line went. 'Why can't they?'" It was often hard to convince these veteran immigrants that we had, in fact, figured out better ways to teach English during the time since they were children.

The second line of attack was on government programs that communicated in languages other than English. Such expense was counterproductive, went the argument, as it took away incentives for immigrants to learn English. And furthermore, what sense did it make to give a driver's license test in Spanish when all the road signs were in English? Proponents of such thinking organized themselves into a national group called US English and began lobbying the federal government and state governments to finally make English official and cease most non-English communication that was done at taxpayer expense. The CEO of US English is a man named Mauro Mujica. I decided I would try to meet with him.

Inside the boardroom at US English

When I reached out via email to US English, I was surprised how quickly I was connected to the CEO himself. And it turned out that one of his homes was near mine in South Florida. Mauro Mujica agreed to meet for an interview over lunch.

We met at a Cuban restaurant in Delray Beach, and as soon as we sat down at our outdoor table, he said, "I know you and I are on opposite sides politically." I was momentarily at a loss. I had been an Independent for at least thirty years and told him so. To which he said, "We saw that you donated to the Democratic Party; we check these things." I sat back in my chair, searching my brain, and then I remembered. "Oh . . . I did write a check for Ron Klein when he was a Congressman because he's a friend of mine." I added, "And since you check these things, you probably saw it wasn't much." Mauro smiled at that, and we moved on.

Mauro, who's in his seventies (he volunteered this, as I generally don't ask people their age), is of medium height, like me, and was wearing a blue polo shirt, like mine. I asked him how he got involved with US English.

"My wife, Bárbara, was on the board first," he said. "She is not only a Spanish professor but has studied the issue of languages." The organization was in bad shape back in 1993, he told me, and was almost going out of business. "I was just a spouse, but they made the mistake of inviting me to a board meeting and I saw what was going on." Mauro told me he is a serial entrepreneur and currently serves on many boards. He studied math and architecture before going into business.

"The board had some real zealots, people who were anti-immigration, anti-everything, really crazy people. So I was asked to come in for three months and see what could be done, maybe shut it down. This other fellow and I changed the board." When they stepped in, Mauro said, the group had 164,000 members and a pile of debt. But, he told me, they were able to increase the membership to more than two million and made the organization profitable. "I've set up a bequest program and we have some large donors," Mauro added.

As our server took our order, I asked him if he spoke Spanish, which he did, and added that he also spoke Greek. Mauro then began speaking Greek with him, to their mutual delight. Twice during our lunch, Mauro took phone calls in which he was speaking Russian.

Mauro was born and raised in Chile, but, he said, "I'm one-quarter Basque, one-half Italian, and one-quarter Dutch, so typical of Chile." He told me he grew up speaking Italian at home but learned Spanish in the street from his friends and then in school. Their maids spoke Spanish. He studied English from K-12 and also Latin and Greek. He took French for the last six years of his schooling in Chile before coming to America to study at Columbia, where he took four years of French and three years of German. "I can read German," he said, "and I go to Germany every six weeks, but I have trouble speaking the language, with all the verbs at the end."

He immigrated to the US in 1964. "Most immigrants are far more patriotic than American-born people," he said. "Those don't appreciate what we have here. We have built a culture with people from all over the world and from all languages and created one country. I travel to thirty-five countries per year and still think America is the best. Other countries don't have our freedoms."

Mauro worries that at least some of today's immigrants aren't taking their English learning seriously. "The Gershwins wouldn't have been who they became without English. Back then, immigrants kissed the ground when they arrived in America. They didn't want to be Russians or Germans or whatever. They wanted to be Americans. It's what made this country great." He added, "With today's political correctness, we don't want to say to people they can't speak their own language."

In his view, some immigrants are learning English, while others are not, and those who are not fall into two groups. "The first group are poor and they can't afford to learn. They have no time."

The second group, says Mauro, are victims of organizations like La Raza (The Race), a large advocacy group that serves the Latino community. He claims the group actually wants Latinos to remain ignorant of English to "keep them where they are, politically." Democrats, he claims, "assume they will vote for them, but it's insane that they should think that." Mauro thinks this is mainly a Latino issue. "I've never heard of a Chinese who doesn't want to learn English," he told me, "or a Russian."

I asked Mauro, if he were in charge, what he would like to see in the US. "We need a system like Israel has, what they call Ulpan," he replied, referring to the country's intensive program of study for teaching adult immigrants Hebrew. As in Israel, Mauro believes we should support immigrants financially for six months, during which time they go to school every day to learn English and the American way of life.

"So, ideally, you think everyone should speak English," I offer.

"No," he corrected me, "I think everyone should *learn* English or *know* English. 'You *shall* speak English!' That sounds too controlling."

He also thinks there should be some sort of amnesty program for immigrants. "There are families who have children who are citizens by birth and you can't deport the families. But we start by closing down the border."

Clearly a bilingual himself, Mauro supports bilingualism. "I've had debates with Latinos who say, 'Hey, if I give up Spanish, I'll lose my culture.' And I say, when you learn languages, you *gain* culture." And he complained about the "arrogance of Americans" who don't want to learn other languages.

But despite supporting bilingualism, he does not support bilingual education because, he says, "it doesn't work. We are for ESL [English as a Second Language] and want more of it funded." When I asked him about dual language schools, he said they were "for elites in private schools," and "you have to have the kinds of students who can learn that way; not everyone can." When I mentioned the Archimedean public school down the road in Miami and all the success they were having, he looked skeptical but said he would look into it.

It turned into a long lunch and our conversation drifted to other things. He told me about their three grown children, all of whom spoke three languages. I learned about his passions for cars, nice pens, and watches. "And I love tall blondes," he said, "but I married a short brunette. Why? Because she was the smartest person I'd met!" He told me his wife, Bárbara, speaks six languages, and in addition to being a professor at Georgetown is a successful novelist.

The truth is, I found Mauro fascinating. He clearly was on the political right, yet held views that many of my liberal friends shared. His theory that La Raza conspired to keep Latinos ignorant of English sounded kooky to me, and I thought he was out of touch with what I saw going on in dual language schools. But I felt it my duty to understand his views as best I could.

As we were leaving the restaurant, Mauro mentioned that he had commissioned the language scholar David Crystal, who is British, to write a book on the importance of English. I asked him why and he said, "I wanted to share it with our members so they could understand the growth of English worldwide and that it's worth preserving in the US." This also struck me as odd. Why would members of US English, of all people, need convincing that English was worth preserving? Clearly, I still had some homework to do.

Fighting the last war

I was already a fan of David Crystal's *How Language Works*, which I have quoted from in this book. A Welsh speaker himself, Crystal is a champion for bilingualism and believes the optimum condition for all humans is to be able to speak one's local language plus another large, common language in which to seize professional opportunities, as well as to enhance mutual understanding among large groups of people. His career has been dedicated to promoting this healthy bilingualism.

In the preface to the first edition of *English as a Global Language,* the book Crystal wrote in response to Mauro's request, he writes: "I cannot take credit for first seeing the need for [this] book. The suggestion in fact came from Mauro E. Mujica, chairman of US English, the largest organization which has been campaigning for English to be made the official language of the USA. He wanted to have a book which would explain to the members of his organization, in a succinct and factual way, and without political bias, why English has achieved such a worldwide status."

Crystal says he was aware of the skepticism this origin of the book might elicit and wanted to "make it very clear that this book has not been written according to any political agenda." He says he would have written the identical book had the initial idea come from an organization with opposing political views. After reading the book, I have to agree with Crystal's opening remarks; I found the book fair-minded and quite useful for my understanding of the global rise of English.

At my lunch meeting with Mauro, I had suggested that he and his wife come to our house for drinks and then go to dinner, where we could continue our conversation. Before our dinner, I did a bit of research on Bárbara and discovered her impressive career. Not only is she an emerita professor at Georgetown and the author of numerous academic works, she is also the author of *Frida: A Novel of Frida Kahlo; Sister Teresa: The Woman Who Became Spain's Most Beloved Saint;* and *I Am Venus.*

She also wrote a *New York Times* op-ed in 1984, in the midst of the debates over bilingual education, titled "Bilingualism's Goal." In it, she makes the case for what educators would call transitional ESL classes. While her own family speaks Spanish at home, she wrote, and she has worked hard to ensure her children are bilingual, she considers that to be a family affair outside of the public sphere. Public schools should not seek to perpetuate Spanish or any other heritage language more than is necessary for the children to be mainstreamed into English-only education; otherwise they risk being stuck in educational "ghettos." And without full English skills, they are left "vulnerable to not only economic but also political exploitation."

At dinner, I learned that her language learning interests had not diminished. Bárbara explained how she had been spending a lot of time learning German, both because their daughter married a German and his mother doesn't speak much English, and also because she loves German literature. She has taken German literature courses at Georgetown herself for several years. "It's a little odd taking a class with students I have taught," she said. She raved about the book and movie *The Reader*, which she read in the original German. "That character spent all that energy, and time in prison, hiding her shame of not being able to read, a microcosm for the German people spending all that energy in the crimes and hiding them. But now, there is open acknowledgment of the crimes and that's so healthy."

When I asked about US English, Bárbara said she is used to being misunderstood, including by her colleagues. "They are against US English without even listening to what we have to say. People think we are against multilingualism, which clearly we are not."

We learned about their three grown children and how successful they are. Mauro said that when their son was fourteen, "I told him he should get really good at Spanish, so I enrolled him in the Swiss school in Salamanca, Spain." That son became a Marine captain and served in Iraq. When he returned from active duty, Bárbara got heavily involved in veteran affairs at Georgetown, which resonated with Lori, being the daughter of a career-military father and a Georgetown alumna herself.

Bárbara agreed with her husband that the US should do more to help immigrants gain English proficiency, and she shares his concern for splinter Latino groups that could undermine American unity.

Emotions and facts

While the Mujicas and the followers of US English were lobbying for English to be made official and to curtail most government communications in non-English languages, others were lobbying for the rights of minority language groups to receive education in their heritage languages, in addition to English. Included in these voices were many scholars.

Commenting on the English-only movements, the sociologists Richard Alba and Victor Nee wrote: "There is no threat to English. All of the studies of new immigration indicate that linguistic assimilation in the form of English acquisition is a quasi-universal pattern." Concerns that organizations such as US English expressed were "misplaced," and "not supported by evidence."

When I asked the Stanford sociolinguist Jonathan Rosa what he thought of the official-English campaigns, he said the proponents "were worrying about the wrong thing. If you are born and raised in the US, you're going to learn English; it's a guarantee. What needs to be supported is the development of other languages."

And sociologists Portes and Rumbaut point out what seem to them like class distinctions. "There is irony in the comparison between the hundreds of hours and thousands of dollars put into acquiring a halting command of a foreign language and the pressure on fluent foreign-born speakers to abandon its use. These contradictory goals—English monolingualism for the masses but bilingualism or multilingualism for the elites—shed light on the real underpinnings of linguistic assimilation."

Fishman himself lived long enough to see the Official English campaigns. Writing in 1988, he said the rise of American immigration in its third great wave led to wounded pride, an emotional reaction rather than a rational one. "Otherwise, why the utterly ridiculous paranoia about the possible inability of one part of the country being able to communicate with the other?" If it's not mainly an emotional issue, he asked, "Why are facts so useless in the discussion?" The calls for legislation from the official-English folks are "the classical wrong solution to the wrong problem."

How is it that the Mujicas—patriotic, bilingual, American intellectuals—can feel so strongly that America is in danger, whereas the scholars who have devoted their lives to understanding languages so completely dismiss these concerns? I decided I had to chase down more answers.

Chapter 44

TODAY'S IMMIGRANTS AREN'T LEARNING ENGLISH: FROM THEM TO WE

My first stop was to understand a bit more about La Raza (now UnidosUS), America's largest organization that advocates for Latino rights and the one that Mauro suggested conspires to keep Latinos ignorant of English. When researching the organization for someone I might interview, I saw that their annual conference and expo were coming up soon in Orlando, so I decided to register and learn firsthand what the organization was up to.

While driving to the conference, I started to worry whether my Spanish would be up to the task of understanding the speeches and conversations. Would I have to interview people in Spanish, too? But once inside the convention center, I quickly realized my fears about my Spanish were unfounded—everyone was speaking English.

Although there was usually some token *Buenos dias* at the start of a speech and maybe a *Gracias a todos*, all the rest was in English. This may have been due to the heavy hitters who came to speak, including the Secretary of Health and Human Services, Sylvia Mathews Burwell, and the US Surgeon General, Vivek Murthy. But even the smaller presentations were in English.

The only exception I heard was the acceptance speech from Orlando Cruz, the first openly gay boxer. He received the Roberto Clemente Award for Sports Excellence, and when speaking in front of a few thousand people, seemed more comfortable in Spanish.

In the exhibition hall, all of the exhibitors' booths were in English, while a few had bilingual signage. I saw only one aimed at parents who wanted their children to maintain Spanish, promoting a reading and singing program called Sticky Spanish.

I made it a point to walk around at breaks and during meals listening to conversations. Only a few were in Spanish. If UnidosUS was engaged in a plot to keep Latinos speaking Spanish, they sure hid it well.

Such a position would be inconsistent with their campaigns for equal opportunities for Latino children in education, not to mention their positions on paths to citizenship and economic opportunities for all. To the contrary, the organization reports on its website the "clear benefits to growing up bilingual," and it supports children's dual language development, starting with early childhood education and continuing throughout their schooling. According to the UnidosUS statement: "Children do not benefit by minimizing or eliminating their involvement with their home language. Instead, evidence demonstrates that becoming proficient in a home language is positively related to English acquisition and doing well in school, including reading in English."

Speaking Spanish at a Miami call center

The humorist Dave Barry was a keynote speaker at a meeting I had earlier attended in Miami. He opened his remarks with, "My family and I moved to Miami several years ago, from the United States." We all busted up. Barry had his usual funny way to avoid the cliché that you can get along better in Miami with Spanish than with English. But is it true?

In my experience, it depends on where you go and whom you ask. I once toured the giant Macy's in Dadeland Mall and asked the store manager if they had a language policy. "We train our staff to always approach a customer in English," he said. "But if they answer in Spanish, our staff member switches to Spanish if they are able." He added, "Most of our team members speak both."

At a language conference, I was chatting with Andrew Lynch, a sociolinguist who teaches at the University of Miami. He said, "I defy you to show me a third-generation Cuban in Miami who isn't dominant in English." His point was that the usual three-generation language-loss rule applied in Miami as well.

For another take, I reached out to my friend Sion Tesone, who runs an international business based in Miami. Called Tissini, his business is geared toward Latinas. He sources clothing, jewelry, and other products in Latin America, mostly made by women. He then sells these products at wholesale to American Latinas, who in turn sell to their friends and neighbors to earn extra money.

Sion, who was born in Colombia and educated in the US, speaks Spanish at home with his wife, mother-in-law, and kids. Although he speaks English fluently and uses it daily, his own business operates mostly in Spanish. He invited me to come visit his offices and call center in Miami to see, and hear, for myself.

When I got to Sion's offices, he gave me more than I was counting on. "Listen," he said, "we're going to shut off the phones for an hour and have them go to voicemail so you can interview the staff." I protested that I didn't want to interfere with his business, but he said the staff would call all the customers back. "Besides," he said, "they'll enjoy talking." What I didn't realize, until he was already introducing me to his staff, was that the whole hour would be in Spanish.

Sion explained to his staff that I was writing a book on bilingualism in America, and that I wanted to hear about their progress in learning English. I understood enough to get the gist of what he was saying, but once I was supposed to talk, I realized I was out of my depth. I did manage a greeting and then a few more mangled sentences and then apologized for switching to English in order to ask my questions. Sion stepped in now and then to clarify in Spanish.

We then went around the room, allowing each woman a few minutes to tell her story. They ranged in age between their twenties and fifties. Only one spoke English well; she had been born in Miami to Cuban parents and was educated at Florida State University. The rest were relatively new immigrants mainly from Colombia, Venezuela, and the Dominican Republic.

They all said they wanted to learn English but it was difficult because of the time and money involved. Their gold standard, it seemed, was Miami Dade College English classes, but they cost a minimum of $1,000. The advantage was that they got college credit. They were aware of free classes at the local high school, but had a low opinion of them.

Among the women were some highly educated professionals, including a physician and a senior marketing executive, whose English was not at a level that would enable them to work in their professions in the US. Emotions ran high, with several women near tears as they explained how they were grateful for work they could do in Spanish. But they all realized they could be earning more money as English-proficient bilinguals. Many remarked how their children already spoke English well, and one said she *so* wanted to help her kids with their homework, which gives her extra motivation to improve her English.

The hour flew by. I thanked them all in my schoolboy Spanish and went back to Sion's office. "Clearly," he said, "they all realize they could be making more money once their English gets up to speed than working at our call center, speaking Spanish all day. But the good part is that they can earn some money, and we get very educated and capable people for the wages we can afford to pay."

It was also clear that bilingualism was their goal, although they could see their children achieving it before they themselves would. In short, I saw up close and personal what looked like the traditional language shift that has always gone on in America.

Cleaning the skylights at Facebook

On the other side of America I was able to get another view into the lives of immigrants who don't speak much English. When I lived in Palo Alto in 2016, I volunteered with Building Skills Partnership, a program designed to help janitors learn English and other work skills. It's a partnership between the janitorial unions, the firms that contract the janitors, and the Silicon Valley tech companies where the janitors work, including Facebook and Google. Funds come from a variety of foundations, businesses, and nonprofits.

I was assigned to help in ESL classes held at Facebook headquarters, which was close enough to my home I could ride my bike. I was instructed to come to Lobby 2.

The entrance to Lobby 2 is inside what seems like a giant, one-level parking garage. Facebook employees were arriving and departing in shuttles, while others were riding the company's blue rideshare bikes. Upon entering the industrial-chic lobby, I was instructed to sign in on one of the tablets and wait for my escort. After a few minutes a woman arrived wearing a blue janitorial outfit and a necklace of laminated IDs around her neck. She escorted me upstairs into what I later learned was the largest open-floor office building in the world, the forty thousand-square-meter vision of the architect Frank Gehry.

We walked for quite a distance through what seemed like a mashup between an unfinished museum and a hip shared workspace, with periodic cafes, clusters of desks at which employees could sit or stand, and glass-lined conference rooms.

Finally, my escort opened a conference room door and waved me in. I introduced myself to a friendly man named Phil, the ESL teacher. Eight janitors, five women and three men, sat around the conference table. Facebook pays the janitors for part of the class time. The rest they do on their own time. Phil went over some practical vocabulary—vacuum cleaner, oven cleaner, whisk broom, plastic trash bag—having everyone repeat the words out loud after he did.

After half an hour, Phil had me work with one of the students whose English was a bit below the rest of the class. We sat together at the far end of the conference table where we could converse quietly by ourselves. I'll call him Ramon. He was a friendly, shy man in his fifties, wearing a black San Francisco Giants baseball cap. To my surprise, his English was worse than my Spanish, so we spoke slowly in Spanish with only a bit of English while we went over the handouts.

Once a week for a few months, I rode over to Facebook and helped out in the same conference room and got to know Ramon better. After one class, he was the one to escort me back out. Since we both had some time, we sat in the lobby, chatting alternately in Spanish, which I asked him to help me with, and in English, where I helped him. Then he said something I found astonishing. Ramon told me he had been living in the US for seventeen years.

I tried to hide my shock. After a pause, I asked him how it was he hadn't learned English better in all these years. He explained that he and his wife, their two daughters, and his mother-in-law all speak Spanish at their home in San Jose. And he normally carpools with other janitor friends, all of whom speak Spanish. But he says his daughters both speak perfect English, and that the older one was about to graduate from San José State.

"Can't you practice your English with them?" I asked. He replied with a dismissive wave of his hand, *"Ellas se ríen de mí cuando trato de hablar inglés."* ("They laugh at me when I try to speak English.")

Another evening after class we had some extra time again, and Ramon asked if I wanted to see where he worked. He took me up one level to the rooftop park, where we walked past gardens and restaurants, with lots of casual seating areas. It was hard for me to comprehend that it wasn't some public park, like California's version of the New York City Highline. Ramon pointed to one of the giant skylights that was artfully made off limits with the landscaping. *"Eso es mi trabajo,"* he said. ("That is my work.") Ramon's job was to wash the skylights at Facebook.

We got friendly enough that Ramon invited Lori and me to his home for the graduation party they were having for his daughter. I accepted immediately.

Ramon's neighborhood reminded me of where I grew up in San Diego. The houses were small and the streets narrow. There were many parked cars. Most of the houses were well cared for, showing what my father called "the pride of ownership." This was especially true of Ramon's house, which was immaculate down to every roof shingle and perfectly painted windowsill.

We followed the music coming from the backyard. There, under a tent that covered the entire space, were several rows of tables and chairs, enough for forty or fifty people. Men were congregating around a big barbecue, where delicious smells were rising, next to stacks of tortillas and big platters of food covered with plastic wrap. Ramon was beaming when he introduced us to his wife, his elderly mother-in-law, and his daughters, beautifully decked out in their white dresses. Ramon introduced me as his teacher, which I came to learn carries a bit more heft in Mexico than in the US. I quickly explained, in Spanish, that I was a student, too, learning Spanish, which seemed to go over well with everyone except his daughters. They spoke English like any other American teenagers and seemed completely uninterested in speaking Spanish with me. Other partygoers, however, were happy to.

We did feel a bit awkward, realizing that everyone else knew one another well whereas we were clearly newcomers, but all the people were very friendly and the food was some of the best we'd ever eaten. We took our leave on the early side after showering Ramon and his wife with our thanks.

On the language front, I could now understand how Ramon was floating in his own expat bubble of Spanish while living in America. Following the usual pattern, his daughters had what seemed like a perfect command of English, and were at least passively bilingual. Most of the people we spoke with at the party were also bilingual, some with perfect English while others not so much. Ramon had a secure job and a lovely home. He and his wife were trying to learn English but, well, there's a Spanish saying that seems fitting: *Del dicho al hecho hay un buen trecho*. "From saying to doing is a good distance." (In Spanish this rhymes.) In English we're not as poetic, but more succinct: "Easier said than done."

Weighing the Mujicas' focus on learning English against the scholars' focus on maintaining heritage languages through bilingualism, where are we today in America? It could be that both camps are right.

There are, clearly, plenty of people in America who need help with their English. I suspect most language scholars would support the Mujicas' call for more government support to help them. At the same time, there are plenty of people who are at risk of losing their heritage languages, and I suspect the Mujicas would welcome others enjoying the same benefits of multilingualism that they and their own children enjoy. Is it just that the Mujicas and the scholars are focused on different challenges?

A Coke ad becomes a flash point

During the 2014 Super Bowl, the Coca-Cola Company unveiled an unusual sixty-second ad. It showed people of various ethnicities, ages, and sexual preferences coming together against backdrops of traditional Americana scenes mixed with gritty urban ones, all set to a soundtrack of young girls singing "America the Beautiful." The singing opened with a girl singing in English and then different girls continuing—in Spanish, Keres (an unwritten Native American language), Tagalog, Hindi, Senegalese-French, and Mandarin—before returning to English for the finale. Then the message #AmericaisBeautiful appears before fading to black. Of course, there was a fair amount of sipping Cokes, too.

Moments after the ad debuted, the social media exploded.

"Honestly Coke, if you're going for patriotism don't have a bunch of foreigners singing my song," wrote one critic. "If you're gonna sing a song about America, DO IT IN ENGLISH," wrote another.

But the ad's defenders were also there in a flash: "The best thing about America is its diversity," and "Love these young and proud multilingual Americans."

A month after the game, the YouTube version of the ad had amassed 10.8 million views, adding to the millions who saw the ad live during the Super Bowl. The "likes" outnumbered "dislikes" by four to one. Similar lopsided support in favor of the ad appeared on Twitter. Then came the comedians Jon Stewart and Stephen Colbert piling on, lampooning the ad's critics.

But I think we're missing something if we dismiss the critics. Fishman was right when he wrote about the hot emotional component of language that we can't seem to cool with any amount of facts. That's certainly been my experience at some of those cocktail parties.

Fortunately, however, other kinds of scientific advancements that accelerated in the late twentieth century can help us understand a bit more. Those are the advancements in social science and in the biology of social relations.

Us and Them

A few years ago, I was alone in an elevator going down to the first floor when my elevator stopped on another floor and four people stepped in, men and women, all speaking German. They were in a lively conversation, laughing loudly, joking with each other. I'd had enough German to at least recognize that they were speaking it, but not enough to understand what they were saying. All of a sudden, I felt hot and uncomfortable. What were they laughing about? Logic told me it couldn't be me since they were laughing before the door opened. But logic aside, I found myself wanting badly to reach up and push the button for the next floor just to escape.

It wasn't until years later, when I heard the Stanford biologist Robert Sapolsky give some of his popular lectures and read his book *Behave: The Biology of Humans at Our Best and Worst*, that I came to understand why that elevator experience left me feeling so uncomfortable.

"Our brains form Us/Them dichotomies . . . with stunning speed," Sapolsky writes. Scientists have in recent years learned tons about how rapidly we can form these judgments from very subtle cues. These experimental advances are due to what Sapolsky calls "the fiendishly clever Implicit Association Test." In this test, subjects are shown images and asked to make choices that the researchers can measure with millisecond precision, allowing for the first time measurements of replicable and statistically significant differences in human behavior.

"We implicitly divide the world into Us and Them, and prefer the former. We are easily manipulated even subliminally and within seconds, as to who counts as each," writes Sapolsky. When those Germans stepped into *my* elevator, they had become, in my primate mind, *Thems* from another tribe, while I, together with my English-speaking American tribe, became *Us*.

Sapolsky writes, "Despite the importance of thought in Us/Them-ing, its core is emotional and automatic." The neurological mechanisms lurking in our brain's amygdala that instantly kick us into Us/Them mode either precede conscious awareness, he says, "or there never is conscious awareness, as with subliminal stimuli."

Before the elevator reached the ground floor, I felt that those four Germans were rude and obnoxious, laughing loudly as if I wasn't even there. Intellectually, I knew I had no right to feel that way. What law were they breaking? Would the same behavior have bothered me so much had they been speaking English? But when that door finally opened, I was the first one out, walking briskly, and I didn't look back.

Says Sapolsky, "Our cognitions run to catch up with our affective selves, searching for the minute factoid or plausible fabrication that explains why we hate Them." Bingo, Professor: you just nailed my elevator experience!

Can even *suspecting* we might hear a language we don't know push buttons in our minds, without us even being aware?

The Harvard political scientist Ryan Enos performed an experiment to test this very idea. He gave a test of attitudes toward immigration to groups of regular commuters in Boston. Then he placed pairs of well-dressed Latinos at suburban train stations in the mornings for two weeks. He instructed them to keep to themselves and talk quietly while waiting with everyone else for trains into the city; they were not to engage in any conversation with the commuters. He then immediately measured attitudes of those commuters who had been exposed to this subtle change in their environments. The result: statistically significant hardening of their opinions *against* immigrants. Why? Presumably because the newcomers were not regulars and they "looked" Latino.

So yes, at least in this experiment, it doesn't take much at all for us to start Us/Them-ing, as Sapolsky says. See a few Latinos at a convenience store and you just might order that "Welcome to America: NOW SPEAK ENGLISH!!!" bumper sticker that's available online. But those Latinos might have been happy to speak English with you, had you asked them something.

This is depressing. Are we doomed to make these snap judgments that draw boundaries? Are we fated to respond like the primates we are?

'Welcome to my emotional neighborhood'

Maybe not. Because when Enos ended his experiment after two weeks, he reported something encouraging: those commuters' negative feelings toward the Latino *Thems* appeared to diminish toward the end of that short time. In the book Enos wrote a few years after his experiment, he explained that our bias against immigrants springs from our basic cognition. But interpersonal contact can "soften the impulse of exclusion." Thanks to today's social science techniques, we can recognize and measure human tendencies that used to escape our grasp. Today we know that our instinctive behaviors can be calmed with what Enos calls "deep interpersonal contact."

Sapolsky makes similar suggestions. He cautions against the danger of allowing our natural, primate biology to get the better of us, for the stakes can be high. "We tend to think of Us as noble, loyal, and composed of distinctive individuals whose failings are due to circumstance. Thems, by contrast, seem disgusting, ridiculous, simple, homogeneous, undifferentiated, and interchangeable. All frequently backed up by rationalization for our intuitions."

The antidote, Sapolsky says, is to remember that "what seems like rationality is often just rationalization, playing catch-up with subterranean forces that we never suspect. Focus on the larger, shared goals. Practice perspective taking." And most of all, "Individuate, individuate, individuate."

In other words, get to know your neighbors—especially if they don't live in your exact neighborhood. Probably all of us have judged someone we barely knew in one way, only to learn something very different about that person when we got to know them. I know I have.

And that's not the only insight we can gain from recent findings in social science. We know from the work of the psychologists Amos Tversky and Daniel Kahneman that loss aversion is far more powerful than we previously thought. That is, the pain of losing something is judged to be more acute than the pleasure of gaining something. When those Germans stepped into my elevator, I lost what I had taken for granted—that I could understand the adults around me. I was instantly demoted from an adult to an uncomprehending child. It hurt in an emotional way that was hard for me to fathom. I'm guessing that other Americans, when they are going about their business and encounter people speaking another language, feel a similar uncomfortable loss. On an intellectual, non-emotional level, they have no reason to feel that way—but to paraphrase Pascal, the amygdala has its reasons for which reason knows nothing.

Half empty, half full, half truth

Another human frailty is negativity bias, which Steven Pinker has explained in his book *Enlightenment Now*. Basically, it's easier for us humans to imagine our world getting worse than it is to imagine it getting better. Given this psychological predilection, let's look again at Ruíz's language orientations: language-as-problem, language-as-right, and language-as-resource. When we overlay negativity bias, we'll see that it's easier for most of us to imagine America getting worse by losing our common language (language-as-problem) than it is to imagine America improving by having a growing number of bilinguals (language-as-resource). We might understand intellectually that language skills are resources that can help America, but our biology helps us imagine with more clarity the specter of Americans splintering into uncomprehending, suspicious factions. This may explain why the language-as-problem orientation sticks like a bur in our sock, while the language-as-resource orientation stays aloft with the clouds.

The statement, "Today's immigrants aren't learning English," may be a perfect example of a half-truth. It's true that some of today's immigrants aren't learning English, or at least aren't learning it very quickly. I've met some of them. So I agree with Mauro and Bárbara Mujica of US English when they say we should devote more resources to help them.

It's also true that most of today's immigrants are learning English quickly, or already knew it before immigrating. They are almost certainly learning more quickly than prior generations, both because there are more resources for doing so, and because more of today's jobs are dependent on English. Immigrants are also quite aware that English is a global language; in Mexico and Guatemala, people know they can get better jobs if they speak English as well as Spanish.

Another thing that's different now from back in the last century are the attitudes of immigrants about their heritage language and the desirability of maintaining it in their children. The result is a flowering of American bilingualism that we'll explore in the next chapter. What makes it particularly interesting is that this bilingualism has flourished without many of us being aware of it.

Chapter 45

Myth No. 11

MONOLINGUALISM IS NATURAL

I've never heard anyone at a cocktail party actually say that monolingualism is natural—it's more like an unspoken assumption, woven so thoroughly into our lives that it's hard to notice it among the other threads. It's the conflating of what's normal with what's natural—a human tendency of thought that's hard to escape.

Without much thinking about it, we also tend to equate natural with good, as in "naturally good for you." But natural isn't always good. The blind worshiping of anything "natural" annoyed the late Helen Gurley Brown, the colorful editor of *Cosmopolitan* magazine. She would remind her audiences that polio was natural. (It also killed her sister.) Steven Pinker has decried environmentalist groups that crusade against genetically modified crops (despite there being no such thing as a genetically unmodified crop) and their "commitment to the sacred yet meaningless value of 'naturalness.'"

So in this chapter, we'll look at both ideas—that monolingualism is natural and that it's good.

Doing what comes naturally

One way to examine whether monolingualism is fundamentally natural is to look at traditional societies to see what we can learn about humans living closer to nature.

In his book, *The World Until Yesterday: What Can We Learn from Traditional Societies?*, the geographer Jared Diamond reports on the bilingualism in Papua New Guinea, where he did most of his field research. He tells of being around a campfire and asking twenty men to name all the languages each spoke. "Among those 20 New Guineans, the smallest number of languages that anyone spoke was 5. Several men spoke from 8 to 12 languages, and the champion was a man who spoke 15." These were mutually unintelligible languages, not mere dialects.

In Aboriginal Australia, bilingualism was also the norm, writes Diamond, as it is in another well-studied traditional society in South America. A good part of the reason is the practice, found in each of these unrelated traditional societies, of linguistic exogamy—marrying someone outside your language group. Thus children grow up hearing one language from Mom and another from Dad, and perhaps others in their village. Diamond concludes that it's "likely that such multilingualism was routine in our hunter-gatherer past," although not all traditional societies practiced it. He suggests that the mono-lingualism found in modern nation-states is largely a new phenomenon.

In his own study of the tiny village of Gapun in Papua New Guinea, the anthropologist Don Kulick also found widespread multilingualism when he first visited. The villagers' own language is Tayap, and most villagers spoke several of the neighboring languages as well. But that changed over the years as the national language of the country, Tok Pisin ("Talk Pidgin"), came to take over.

Tok Pisin was what the Gapun men encountered when they left the village to take jobs in the city. When they returned, they brought Tok Pisin with them. Over the years and generations, villagers first lost the fluency in the neighboring languages and then started to lose fluency in their own. "A people who used to command many languages now increasingly command only one," writes Kulick. "And that one is not their ancestral language, Tayap. It is, instead, Tok Pisin." He estimates that in fifty years, "Tayap will be stone-cold dead."

A fair conclusion is that human beings have evolved to have the capacity to speak multiple languages, and in most traditional situations, they do just that. While there is at least one documented exception—the Pirahã, who live deep in the Amazon in Brazil—bilingualism among traditional societies is the norm and no doubt feels natural to those who grow up that way.

Bilinguals built our world, including the idea of America

Today we take for granted that we learn to read in the language we speak, but, as we discovered in Part One, this wasn't the case in the early days of literacy. When reading and writing were new, one needed to learn another language in order to do both. David Bellos writes that beginning around 2250 BCE, the conquering Akkadians took up Sumerian script and language even though it was linguistically unrelated to Akkadian. For nearly two thousand years afterwards, Bellos says, "knowledge of Sumerian became the mark of an educated man."

Later it was the Romans who adopted Greek to serve a similar purpose. "The learning of Greek became the main content of a proper education in ancient Rome and translation into Latin the main skill associated with high rank," Bellos says.

John McWhorter tells us, "Slavic language speakers were used to ancient Old Church Slavonic as a written lingua franca, although no one spoke it." He offers other examples as well. In India, Hindi was spoken but Sanskrit was what was written. In Europe, Dante spoke Italian yet wrote in Latin, as did everyone else who was writing in Europe in his day.

The civilization we today take for granted could not have evolved without the human ability to use two languages simultaneously. Without the bilingualism of our ancestors, our Founding Fathers could not have thought to write the Constitution of the United States the way they did, with its references to universal ideas dating back to the Greeks and Romans. Nor would they have chiseled our everlasting American tribute to Latin in the phrase, *E Pluribus Unum.*

We should also note that early literacy was the domain of elites. Literacy for the masses occurred when it was taught in the vernacular languages of the world—that is, without bilingualism being a requirement. Not until the printing press and the democratic ideals of the Reformation arrived did writing gradually take place in the vernacular languages people actually spoke. Writes McWhorter, "People writing in the way they actually talked was quite rare anywhere in the world until rather recently."

This doesn't mean the linguistic monoculture we have today in America is wrong or bad. In fact, it likely helped bring about widespread literacy. According to the writer Minae Mizumura, having a writing system that reflected the language people spoke led to "far higher rates of literacy, a prerequisite for the emergence of democracy." But it does mean that bilingualism was a necessary building block for civilization, and a precursor to the monolingual literacy that came later.

Our early multilingual period

As we saw in the last chapter, America was a far more bilingual place before the twentieth century. As the anthropologist Shirley Brice Heath writes in *Language in the USA*:

"Throughout the nineteenth century, a bilingual tradition existed in public and private schools, newspapers, and religious and social institutions. It was not until the late nineteenth century and the first half of the twentieth century that legal, social, and political forces strongly opposed maintenance of languages other than English. Only then was a monolingual English tradition mandated in some states and espoused as both natural and national."

The second great wave of American immigration was already well underway before Congress passed the Naturalization Act of 1906, which for the first time required that immigrants speak English in order to gain citizenship.

So it wasn't until the twentieth century that our nation established what would be the norm of English monolingualism. But by the time that century closed, America was moving toward a more multilingual voice once again—a return to our earlier, more accepting stance on language diversity.

Appreciating the context of a different time

It's easy from today's vantage point to criticize the Americans who lived in the first half of the twentieth century for their intolerance toward non-English languages. I'd like to defend them—both those who were American-born and those who came to the country, often with little more than their old-country language, determined to become Americans.

First off, no nation has accepted as many immigrants as America has. Nor has any nation accepted as many asylum seekers as America. And although we have at times treated our immigrants in a dastardly manner, their home countries generally treated them even more dastardly, which is why they came to America. Through the thick and thin of our immigration laws, we have always honored birthright citizenship, and we have always shown a preference for family reunification. All Americans can be rightfully proud of these steadfast practices from which we have not veered throughout our whole history.

Moreover, it was an important, and perhaps even a necessary step in our grand social experiment that our predecessors so strongly encouraged the widespread use of our common language. A common language suggests shared customs, and in shedding their Old World languages, some new Americans also shed some Old World practices for the betterment of our society. For example, girls in many emigrant countries were often looked upon as secondary to boys. They didn't always receive an education. Once married (or married off), they were expected to defer to their husbands and agree, at least publicly, with their views. In that melting pot society, some of these discriminatory customs melted away—not immediately, but eventually. And in turn, these new American women were able to show women elsewhere in the world that they did matter as much as the men.

And it is doubtful we could have accomplished the greatest rollout of free public education the world had ever seen had we tried to accommodate other languages besides English. Even today, getting the right books and other materials to teach subjects in other languages is a challenge.

We can look back and shudder at the punishment teachers dished out to children caught speaking their home languages, but in most cases the teachers weren't being intentionally cruel; they were doing what they were told they should do for the children's own benefit. Remember that the incomplete science of the day (and science is always incomplete) held that monolingual educations were best. Not until the 1960s did that dogma become challenged.

It's also important to know that the mistreatment Americans perpetrated on our Indigenous peoples was a common pattern found throughout the world. Not that this excuses European Americans for the crimes they committed and the Trail of Tears we inflicted on so many of our Native peoples, but English speakers were not unique in this practice. Spain did much the same in terms of Spanish being the dominant language in its New World territories, including those in what is now the US. Today nation-states all over the world are attempting to right historical wrongs to their Indigenous peoples, including by recognizing Indigenous languages and supporting their revitalization.

And by leaving their heritage languages behind, as painful as that was for them, American immigrants were being practical, paying what was then part of the price of becoming an American. More important, they were acting in what they believed were the best interests of their children, helping them grow up without the liability of a "foreign" accent, fluent in the language of their country, sounding like any other native English speaker.

The life span of our monolingual period

Looking back, the period of imposing monolingualism upon ourselves was rather limited. It's impossible to say exactly when it began, although we could pick 1908, which was the debut of Israel Zangwill's play *The Melting Pot*. The title became part of American idiom for the beneficial effects of throwing everyone into the same pot and melting off their differences so that America would be a better place. That same year, US immigration went into sharp decline, marking the end of the second great wave of American immigration.

It was during this period that President Theodore Roosevelt spoke against "hyphenated Americans" who displayed divided loyalties. "We have

room for but one language here," he said, "and that is the English language."
It should be noted, however, that TR himself spoke French and German,
and used both languages to good effect while he was President. His attacks
were targeted to immigrants who failed to learn English, while at the same
time he defended all those who did and who became faithful Americans,
"for it is an outrage to discriminate against any such man because of creed
or birthplace or origin."

As vivid as the melting pot image is, however, it's incomplete. We don't
imagine that Americans stay in that hot pot forever. The next step in the
assembly line is to get poured into molds, or maybe into sheets that are
hydraulically stamped, like the utilitarian flatware we might find in a cafeteria. The melting pot and stamping machine were running efficiently all
through that first world war, and the next one, and right up to the 1960s,
when the old machinery began to break down and conformity became like
a four-letter word.

By 1977, US immigration was rising steeply again, heralding the third
great wave of newcomers. By then, many of the changes initiated in the 1960s
were starting to get traction, including our more informed understanding
of the science of bilingualism. Also, more American young people were
experiencing study abroad and the Peace Corps. From 1908 to 1977 marks
sixty-nine years, about equal to the average American life span at midcentury.

Our monolingual period in America was social engineering, a manufactured thing that the nation wore for a while, like an ill-fitting shoe. But
monolingualism fit a period in our history—the fat middle of the twentieth
century. For these middle decades, English monolingualism mostly worked—
until, beginning in the 1960s, it didn't.

It's a bilingual world after all

Another way to address the question of whether monolingualism is fundamentally natural is to look at the world today with its nearly two hundred
countries and some six thousand to seven thousand remaining languages.
Those figures alone are enough to dispel the simplistic one-country-one-
language idea. All countries have citizens who speak more than one language.

"If you have lived your whole life in a monolingual environment," writes
David Crystal, "you could easily come to believe that this is the regular way
of life around the world, and that people who speak more than one language
are the exceptions. Exactly the reverse is the case." Crystal says, "Some two-
thirds of the children on earth grow up in a bilingual environment, and

develop competence in it." Consequently, "multilingualism is the normal human condition."

Maria Polinsky, a pioneer in heritage language scholarship, agrees that monolingualism is "an aberration rather than the norm." Or as David Bellos says, "outside the handful of countries speaking one of the half-dozen 'major' world languages, few people on this planet have only one tongue."

François Grosjean sets a high bar on what he counts as bilingual, which is actually *using* the language on a daily basis. He estimates that "probably more than half of the world's population uses two or more languages (or dialects) in everyday life." Most of the world's monolinguals, he says, live in large nation-states, such as Brazil and the US.

What's more, the era of active suppression of minority languages has, for the most part, passed. While China may be guilty of continuing to take an iron hand in imposing Mandarin on its multilingual nation, that would be the exception among nations today. The more typical pattern is an official embracing of bilingualism for both national unity and strategic advantages.

In Canada, its policy of official French-English bilingualism fits its unique history as well as its strategic goal of encouraging all Canadians to know and use two of the world's most widely spoken languages.

In Singapore, former Prime Minister Lee Kuan Yew took a personal interest in driving his city-state toward a robust bilingualism. He believed "monolingual education wasteful for time and talent," and made sure all children became bilingual in English and Mandarin, while still granting official status to the other heritage languages in his polyglot country. He accomplished this partly by using his legal authority, but largely by convincing Singaporeans of the professional and economic advantages to them and to the country if Singapore could truly serve as a link between east and west. "On language issues," he said, "you have to persuade, not command." Under his leadership, Singapore transformed itself from a third-world nation to one of the richest in the world.

Morocco aims to be the gateway to Africa by reinforcing its own unique mosaic of bilingualism. In addition to the official recognition of its native Amazigh (Berber) languages, Morocco continues to cultivate its traditional European links with its widespread use of French, while adding English to the education of its youth. These languages are in addition to its official use of Arabic, in both its Modern Standard Arabic form as well as Moroccan Arabic.

The tipping of America toward bilingualism in the second half of the twentieth century, and the acceleration of this trend in our present century, is in harmony with global trends. Our present century might fairly be called the bilingual century, as urbanization most likely continues and English becomes ever more popular as a second language for billions. The form bilingualism takes in different countries such as Canada, Singapore, and Morocco will align with each country's histories and strategic goals, just as the form of bilingualism in America is unique to our history and will, in time, align with our strategic goals.

Our emergence from our monolingual period represents a change in norms that can seem dramatic to Americans who lived in this period. And yet, compared with the changes we've seen in other norms in America in the last century, it is relatively minor. Just consider what other things were normal in America a mere hundred years ago, or even more recently.

It was normal to live with legalized, institutional racism, known as Jim Crow laws. Though no longer enslaved, African Americans were denied the most basic of rights. It was the era of lynchings (long after the German Americans of World War I were no longer murdered this way), cross burnings, and a campaign of terrorism and intimidation that the Ku Klux Klan perpetrated most archly in order to keep Blacks "in their place."

It was normal in America a century ago that Chinese were barred from citizenship. The plainly named Chinese Exclusion Act began in 1882 and wasn't abolished until 1943, when it became an embarrassment to the US, since China had joined the Allied powers in fighting Imperial Japan after the bombing of Pearl Harbor.

It was normal in our grandparents' time that Black baseball players had a league of their own, which lasted right through World War II. The color barrier was finally broken in 1947 when Jackie Robinson stepped onto Ebbets Field wearing the uniform of the Brooklyn Dodgers. The following year, President Truman desegregated the American armed forces. The first interracial kisses on American television began appearing in the 1960s, most notably, perhaps, the kiss between Captain Kirk—played by William Shatner, a white man—and Uhura—played by Nichelle Nichols, a Black woman—on *Star Trek* in 1968.

My grandmother was born into an America where it was normal that women were barred from voting. A woman's place was in the home. School teaching, nursing and clerical jobs were acceptable occupations, but for a woman to aspire to something else was unseemly. Who was watching the children? Women got the right to vote in 1920, when my grandmother was teaching elementary school.

It would be another four years before American Indians were allowed to become citizens. And it would take until 1962 before these citizens enjoyed voting privileges throughout the land.

It was normal in America not to deliberately exercise, at least not like anything we view as normal today. The Jack LaLanne Show featuring the leotarded Jack LaLanne debuted on television in 1951, and ran until 1985.

It was normal in America to throw trash out the window of your car without a second thought. Then Keep America Beautiful began in 1953. And the cars of that era didn't come with seat belts. Today, we feel undressed if we drive a car without wearing a seat belt and shoulder harness. And someone who drinks and drives is seen not only as irresponsible, thanks to the efforts of MADD (Mothers Against Drunk Driving), but also as the complete opposite of cool, thanks to the Designated Driver campaign that launched in the late 1980s.

It was normal in the early twentieth century to subdue the earth with all manner of dumps, dikes, and dams in the name of progress, with little thought of the environmental impact. It was normal to use pesticides based solely on how well they killed pests, with little regard for their repercussions on everything else they touched. Then Rachel Carson published *Silent Spring* in 1962, and Earth Day took root in 1970.

It was normal in America to smoke. Magazine advertisements featured doctors recommending their favorite brands. Warning labels didn't begin appearing until 1965, while smoking ads weren't banned from television until 1970.

It was normal in America, if you were gay, to keep it hidden from all but your closest friends. The country's first Gay Rights parade was held in 1970; same-sex marriage wasn't legalized by the US Supreme Court until 2015.

All of this is to remind us that what was normal in America changed radically by the end of the twentieth century in many domains of life, and in ways that are more fundamental than merely whether someone speaks one or more languages. In less than a century, racial and gender taboos of several kinds were smashed to bits. Behaviors thought to be cool became uncool. Most Americans got used to new norms in a very short time. From this perspective, the changes we're witnessing now in our norms about American bilingualism seem like a walk in the park.

What truly took place at the Tower of Babel?

Is it possible that, even as far back as Biblical times, we've been misreading the cues about bilingualism?

The Tower of Babel story in the Old Testament tells us that way back in time, people all spoke one language until they managed to annoy God by having the audacity to build a tower. He punished them by vaporizing their single language and imposing on them many different languages, leaving the poor wretches in uncoordinated confusion, babbling about in their various tongues.

The story is a cautionary tale about the dangers of pride, and serves as a reminder that we ought to show some respect to God. But the Tower of Babel also seems to suggest that many languages are bad, whereas having one language is good. The scholar of bilingualism Suzanne Romaine points out that this Bible story may well have had an enduring negative influence on our perception of bilingualism. "The idea that monolingualism is a natural, original, and desirable state of affairs, while multilingualism is divisive, is still with us."

Then again, maybe we've misinterpreted the Tower of Babel story all these many years. Genesis 11 begins: "Now the whole earth had one language and the same words. And as they migrated from the east, they came upon a plain in the land of Shinar and settled there." And there, set about building a city, a tower, and "a name for ourselves." But maybe the "one language" in Scripture was really a *common* language.

Maybe the original storytellers left off what their listeners would have assumed as obvious—that these migrants had their own tribal languages, just like everyone, but also one common language with "the same words." That is, they were normal, bilingual humans like everybody else they knew. And what God did was to take away their *common* language, thereby reducing those proud humans to hapless monolinguals in their assorted tongues, unable to communicate between tribes.

People will naturally lose a common language—a pidgin, for example—if they move away from one another and no longer have a need for it. So the Tower of Babel story could as well be referring to prideful humans who were bilingual as to monolingual ones—even better, in light of what we now know about bilingualism in traditional societies and how languages evolve.

Moving from Scripture to sociology, we may tend to think that bilingualism can lead to problems due to speakers having divided loyalties, whereas no studies of societies have found evidence of this actually happening. Bilinguals themselves describe their languages not as divided loyalties, but more like layered loyalties—like being a proud Texan while also being a proud American, or loving all your children equally as they come into this world, while appreciating their differences. In fact, it's easier to make a case for monolingualism being the unhealthy condition for individuals and their societies.

Unhealthy monolingualism

Every three years the Organization for Economic Cooperation and Development administers a test to fifteen-year-olds in many countries called the Program for International Student Assessment, or PISA. It tests their proficiency in reading, math, and science, as well as "skills to meet real-life challenges." In 2018, the United States once again slunk away from the international competition with a solid C. American students scored slightly above average in reading and science and slightly below average in math. As usual, the top-ranking students came from Asian and Scandinavian countries, and, although PISA was not making a correlation with bilingualism, we do know that bilingual education is the norm in these countries. While we can't say that their bilingual education has a causal effect on their high scores, we can say with certainty that their bilingual education doesn't stand in the way of their academic success.

I had the chance to have a conversation about our mediocre PISA rankings with the education scholar Linda Darling-Hammond. I asked her if it's a coincidence that most of the nations that score above the US invest heavily in language skills. She shook her head no and pointed to her forehead. "It's all making connections," she said, "like art and culture and music. Language is like that." I took her to mean that having two languages at your command allows you to see things in a richer, more connected way. Linda went on to enthuse about what officials in Finland are doing with languages. "All they need is a few students who speak Arabic to begin a language class in that. And they have to tackle different alphabets—Russian, English, and Finnish—and they do it. It helps them develop."

Monolingualism is associated historically with isolationism. In China in the 1800s, it was illegal for Chinese nationals to teach the Chinese language to outsiders, punishable by death. Today China promotes the Chinese language internationally, while learning English in China is all the rage. The historian Yuval Noah Harari writes that the advancement of civilization comes not through isolation but through expanding circles of human cooperation. It's bilingualism that fuels cooperation. In the dystopian novel *The Emissary*, Yoko Tawada paints a future dysfunctional Japan fearful of outsiders, where the teaching of English is prohibited, as are novels translated from other languages.

When we set the US norm of monolingual English education, it was early in the twentieth century. Then we were aligned with the science of the day, and the focus on English-only education was a practical thing to do in order to build the greatest system of free, public education the world had ever seen. Today, what we know about the benefits of bilingualism has dramatically changed. The lead we once enjoyed in education has vanished, and we've been surpassed by nations that encourage bilingual education.

Today we know that "children are born ready for bilingualism," as David Crystal says. Today we know how to nurture children's innate language abilities in homes, in preschools, in dual language schools, and in vastly improved language classes. If we fail to create these environments for our kids, are we failing them? Knowing what we know today about the mental health benefits of bilingualism—benefits that can last throughout a lifetime, even to delaying the symptoms of dementia—should we see a bilingual education as a matter of public health?

Howard Koh, the former United States Assistant Secretary for Health, has said that "the evolution of public health has been described as the successive redefinings of the unacceptable." At some point, will we decide that leaving kids monolingual is unacceptable?

Restoring America's true spirit

We also know that when adults learn another language, they almost unavoidably learn something about empathy and humility. It's hard, maybe impossible, to learn another language, certainly to speak another language, without being willing to lower your defenses and sound like a child, to ask for help, to be vulnerable and come to appreciate its surprising power. If there were a vaccine for intolerance, it might be learning another language. Conversely, is there a danger in large groups of monolinguals who don't benefit from this experience?

I'm guessing that the people who buy bumper stickers like "Welcome to America: NOW SPEAK ENGLISH!!!" did not become bilinguals as adults. Certainly the head of US English, Mauro Mujica, does not display such a bumper sticker; he and his family are bilinguals themselves and disagree with edicts such as this. They merely want all Americans to *be able to* speak English. Americans who complain about immigrants bringing new languages to America may be living in America, but the spirit of America isn't living in them.

"Once I thought to write a history of the immigrants in America. Then I discovered that the immigrants *were* American history." Thus begins Oscar Handlin's Pulitzer Prize-winning history, *The Uprooted*. Visitors to America often comment on our diversity, meaning the wide variation in what Americans look like, but not, for the most part, what we sound like. But my sense is that the English-only ice has broken in the mighty American river and the season of rebirth has begun. My sense is that Americans, ever practical and ever watchful for what's best for their children, are poised to change what they take as normal, natural, and good, poised to reclaim what is rightfully theirs.

Perhaps that whispering you think you hear, the quiet voice in your head telling you that you need to speak another language, is your biology reminding you that we were born to be bilingual, and that our monolingual life isn't what you or your children were meant for.

In November 2016, a few days after California voters passed Proposition 58 to restore bilingual education in California, I had lunch with Kenji Hakuta, the venerable scholar of language education, now a professor emeritus. He had the same athletic handshake but even more of a sparkle in his eye than I remembered from our earlier meetings. He was elated with the election.

"You can go online to the Secretary of State in California and see all the results," he said excitedly. I asked him why he thought voters overturned the old Ron Unz proposition by such a wide margin. "It's important to un-correlate the benefits of bilingualism from the political realm," he said. He smiled as he looked across the dining room to the picture windows. "This time," he said, "voters didn't see bilingualism as a political issue."

Chapter 46

Myth No. 12

AMERICANS SUCK AT LANGUAGES

When it comes to languages, we Americans are used to being the butt of jokes. Yeah, we know, "America is where languages go to die." And yes, we know what you call someone who speaks only *one* language: "An American!" Yeah, yeah, very funny.

Our critics point to the high percentage of Americans who speak only English, and we know it's the truth. We are used to feeling linguistically inferior to Europeans, each of whom, we tell ourselves, speaks four or five languages, making us feel like uncultured dolts. And it's not just Europeans who tell us we suck; we tell ourselves we suck and have been doing it for quite some time, thank you.

It used to be that young men applying to college had to show their proficiency in Greek or Latin, the way John Adams did when he applied to Harvard. By early in the twentieth century, however, classicists at American colleges were wringing their hands about the mule-headed lads who were applying to college having little Latin and not one iota of Greek. Despairing for our nation's future, college admission committees began to accept some "modern" languages like German and French, and later, with some more heavy sighs, even Spanish.

In the 1930s, the authoritative Coleman Report came out and recommended that the US admit defeat: American kids were never going to learn how to speak other languages, therefore it was better not to try teaching them. Rather, just try to get the kids to be able to *read* some French or Spanish, if possible. For its part, the US Army, looking over its future recruits still in American schools in the 1930s, used such words as "disaster" and "failure" when describing America's language education system. The Army realized it would have to take matters into its own hands if it wanted any soldiers at all who could actually *speak* another language.

We've already heard about the indictment in 1958 contained in *The Ugly American* of the pitiful lack of language skills among American diplomats. Then in 1980 came another book scolding Americans for our failures, this time a nonfiction book by Congressman Paul Simon titled *The Tongue-Tied American: Confronting the Foreign Language Crisis*. The well-meaning and earnest Simon offered pages and pages of sound suggestions for how we should correct our ways. What was needed was nothing short of a "quantum leap in the study of foreign languages, and with it, a sensitivity to other cultures."

And as recently as 2017, the American Academy of Arts & Sciences, while noting some good things in its report on the state of America's language education, made it clear that we still needed work. "The United States lags behind most nations of the world, including European nations and China, in the percentage of its citizens who have some knowledge of a second language."

Seeing beyond percentages

A movie poster for *Godzilla* that I saw featured the beast emerging from the shadows, looking like he badly wanted to flatten some police cars, while underneath him were three words: "Size Does Matter." When it comes to bilinguals in America, those three words apply just as well. Percentages are one thing, but size does matter.

Each year as part of the American Community Survey, the US Census asks Americans what language they speak at home. The number of Americans who speak a language other than English at home grew steadily during the third wave of American immigration. Their numbers have almost tripled since 1980, from twenty-three million to more than sixty-seven million in 2018. And there's an important difference in these speakers from decades ago: most of them speak English well—that is, they are bilinguals.

François Grosjean has been examining these figures closely for decades and is surprised by what he sees happening. While the number of Americans speaking another language at home has risen sharply, the number of Americans who don't speak English has not risen much at all. He reports, "English is so important in the United States that close to 98.7% of the population know it, and use it in everyday life."

Back in the 1980s, Grosjean had bemoaned how America was squandering its linguistic capital with the way our immigrants had been encouraged to abandon their native languages. But thirty years later, he is tipping his hat to us. English is in no danger, yet linguistic capital is being maintained and developed. "This can only lead to a person's personal enrichment, increased ties between generations and cultures, and more diversity in job opportunities." In my correspondence with him about his findings, he admitted, "I would never have thought that we would be up to 23% of bilinguals in the US when I started looking at the statistics back in 1982!"

And just what does 23 percent of the American population look like? With our population of 331 million, 23 percent amounts to about seventy-six million people in America who are actively bilingual. If they were their own country, they would rank as the twentieth largest nation in the world.

By comparison, France has a population of about sixty-five million, and while it may come as a surprise to many Americans, France also has a high percentage of monolinguals—higher, in fact, than the US. How can this be? First, France accepts far fewer immigrants than the US—and the third wave of immigrants to the US has done much to tip the scales in America being bilingual. Second, France is a large country and self-sufficient in many ways. And third, we can attribute some of our surprise to another of those human frailties made famous by Kahneman and Tversky: availability bias.

Chances are, most of our encounters with French nationals have been in the United States, in Paris, or in some other international or cosmopolitan context. If so, our sample is biased toward those French who have a command of English. Furthermore, since we *expect* Europeans to be bilingual, confirmation bias kicks in, too, confirming our false assumption that "all Europeans speak three or four languages." Travel in the French countryside, or even in Paris away from the main tourist sites, and we'll likely encounter a different linguistic reality.

Getting back to the numbers, 20 percent of the population of France equates to roughly thirteen million people. Thus, American bilinguals outnumber French bilinguals by more than five to one.

The American figures become even more impressive when we look at our linguistic diversity. While the largest percentage are Spanish-English bilinguals (about forty-one million speakers), due to our Godzilla-like linguistic reach, we have *lots* of speakers of *lots* of other languages. While we have about 1.2 million French speakers, we also have more than a million speakers of five languages from *outside* of Europe, including Korean, Vietnamese, Tagalog, Arabic, and nearly 3.5 million Chinese speakers. Despite our old war against the German language, we still have almost a million German-English American bilinguals, which gives America the largest concentration of German speakers outside of Europe. And the city with the largest number of Polish speakers after Warsaw is not a relatively nearby city like Vienna, Budapest or Berlin, but Chicago.

The numbers of bilinguals in America are so large and broad it's hard to comprehend the true scale of our linguistic capital. But consider this: Carnegie Hall has a seating capacity of 2,804. If we filled it to capacity with speakers of a different language every night—speakers of Vietnamese one night, speakers of Tagalog the next night, and so on—we could go 131 nights. While we would be able to seat 367,324 people during our four-and-a-half-month-long American Language Fest, we would still leave more than seventy-five million eligible bilinguals outside the concert hall, milling about on West 57th in Manhattan.

The actual number of bilinguals in America is in some ways more important than the percentage of Americans who are bilingual. It is not percentages but individuals who are engaged in diplomacy and development, journalism and scholarship, intelligence and military operations, missionary and humanitarian work, and, of course, in business. In all of these domains, what counts aren't percentages, but how many American individuals can make the connections with other individuals from other nations. The Olympic Games aren't a test of the average fitness of nations. Larger nations generally win more Olympic medals in large part because they have bigger populations from which to draw their athletes.

While percentages are important, they are not the full story. The story we have been missing while we've been busy beating up on ourselves is that no country on earth fields both the depth and breadth of bilinguals as America. As Steven Pinker says, "progress has a way of covering its tracks." It's time to stop thinking of ourselves as a monolingual mouse and realize we are a linguistic lion.

Riding a new wave

The primary reason for the impressive increase in American bilinguals has been the third great wave of American immigration that followed in the wake of the immigration reforms of the 1960s. In the fifty years that followed, the number of American immigrants quadrupled, so that in 2017 they accounted for 13.6 percent of the population versus 4.7 percent in 1970. And these immigrants were quite different from those who came in the second wave a century earlier. Because of the global rise in education in the last century and the rise of English worldwide, many more of these third-wave immigrants have arrived as English bilinguals already. And for many reasons, they are also more inclined to hang onto their heritage language when they come.

The sociologists Portes and Rumbaut noticed this change, which they explored in their 2014 book *Immigrant America: A Portrait*. "The significant new ingredient brought about by contemporary immigration is . . . the presence of a sizable minority of educated newcomers who are able both to understand the advantages of fluent bilingualism and to maintain it for themselves and their children."

Paul Taylor of the Pew Research Center made similar observations that same year, particularly noting the changes in Asian immigrants. "A century ago, most Asian Americans were low-skilled, low-wage laborers crowded into ethnic enclaves and targets of official discrimination." That's changed in recent years, he writes. "More than 6 in 10 (61%) adults ages 25-64 who have come from Asia in recent years have at least a bachelor's degree. This is double the share among recent non-Asian arrivals, and almost surely makes the recent Asian arrivals the most highly educated cohort of immigrants in US history." Once here, the Asians have excelled. "Asian Americans make up less than 6% of the population, but in 2010 collected 45% of all engineering doctorates and 38% of all math and computer science PhDs." These highly educated newcomers are much sought after. "In light of all this," writes Taylor, "it's no surprise that the most enthusiastic proponents of immigration reform are in the business community."

A case in point is Yan Gu, a Chinese American I've come to know because she came to work for our company and advanced to the role of Chief Technology Officer. Today she is also instrumental in managing some of the company's key relationships with Chinese suppliers, speaking their language. Yan and her husband both had their college degrees before immigrating to the US. Once here, they earned their graduate degrees. Yan's daughter was valedictorian of her high school class and went on to MIT, where she earned her degree in engineering. She speaks Mandarin fluently.

America is also the beneficiary of millions of highly educated Latinos who speak English well and enter the workforce as skilled workers and business owners. My entrepreneur friend Sion Tesone and my tutor Angie Rojas, who is a dental surgical assistant, are two examples.

Bilinguals hiding in plain sight

The fact that contemporary immigrants are so much better educated on average, and so much better English speakers than a century ago, may come as a surprise for the same reasons it comes as a surprise that not all Europeans are bilinguals—our dark glasses with availability bias in one lens, and confirmation bias in the other. If we believe that "today's immigrants aren't learning English," and an English-limited custodian becomes "available" to our observation, bingo: we've confirmed our bias from the available sample. What we tend not to see are the many more immigrants who do speak English well because they are hard, or impossible, to distinguish from others within the American workforce.

Another factor in misreading the extent of bilingualism in America is that many bilinguals haven't come out of the home. That is, they intentionally don't speak their heritage language in public, where it might annoy people. It's another factor that catches our dipstick, preventing it from reaching the bottom of the tank.

We also risk misreading what those bilingual signs and "Press 1 for English" messages are really telling us. We may conclude that the nation is overrun with people who can't speak English. Why else would we need such non-English messaging? But what we're actually seeing and hearing are businesses attempting to appeal to more customers because it's relatively inexpensive to add those kinds of interfaces and signs today. Just because many Latinos *can* speak English well doesn't mean they prefer to. Some may prefer Spanish for personal banking or when seeking medical help. After using English all day at work, Latinos might prefer to watch Spanish television, and set their websites and movies to Spanish. They might prefer to buy home and baby products in Spanish.

Remember that their heritage language needs a place to live in their lives, just as adopted languages do. My tutor Angie has now lived much more of her life in America than in her native Colombia. Her English is perfect. Yet Angie attends Spanish church services. She told me, "It's the language I learned to pray in, the language I'm most comfortable speaking to God with." There's an old Mende proverb: "You know who a person is by the language he cries in."

Jean Kwok became a bestselling author with her first book, *Girl in Translation,* which draws on her experiences as a young Chinese immigrant to the US. In a more recent novel, *Searching for Sophie Lee,* she uses three women to tell the story, each one filtering it through her native tongue—Chinese, Dutch, and English. Jean is fluent in all three (she married a Dutchman), and on any given day, she says she thinks in all three of them.

But sometimes, Jean says, "I'm not even sure if I'm speaking English, Chinese, or Dutch. The words just come out of my mouth in whichever language is needed."

Market researchers hear the change

I was able to interview a number of executives who work in market research, studying the Latino marketplace. The nature of commercial market research is, of course, different from scholarship. The point is not to produce shared results open to corroboration and criticism in that long and fitful march toward "being less wrong." The point is to deliver relevant, actionable information that businesses can use to be more successful—and therefore be inclined to hire the market research firm again. Generally, market research findings are not shared, at least not in their entirety. But it's possible that commercial market research can sometimes discern social trends that have not yet emerged in the social science literature.

One such market research report produced in 2016 claimed that, based on interviews with 1,900 Latinos across the country, Latinos are not following the traditional assimilation model. More of them value both English and Spanish and use both on a regular basis. Immigrants want to validate themselves back in their home countries and also in America. Validating themselves in the home country can mean getting an American education, improving their English, sending money back to their families, and owning a home in the US. Validating themselves in America overlaps with all of these accomplishments, with the exception of sending money to their families. Second- and third-generation immigrants partake in both their heritage culture and the wider American culture with ease, according to this report. Their Latino origins, rather than defining them, "afford them a measure of distinction among other Americans." While there were some immigrants in the study who wanted to reject Spanish once they had learned English, these were the exceptions. The majority of Latinos value both languages and use both in their lives.

Valeria Piaggio, VP and Head of Polycultural Insights at The Futures Company in Chicago, told me that many of the millennial Latinos who are second generation take their Spanish more seriously than their first-generation parents. "They view their Hispanic identity not as something to hide, but as something they take pride in, and being bilingual is part of that." Therefore she advises some clients seeking the company's consumer insights services to advertise in Spanish even though their potential customers can understand English, if the advertisers want to connect with them on an emotional level. This can be especially effective for home and baby products. "While they may be English dominant, they have an interest in using Spanish their parents didn't have."

Nancy Tellet, an independent market researcher, has noted similar trends. In her own study of millennial Latino parents, ages eighteen to thirty-four, she found that 86 percent of them still living with their parents reported that they were speaking mostly in Spanish at home. But surprisingly, of the millennial parents living on their own, 78 percent were still speaking mainly Spanish at home even though they speak English very well. Moreover, 90 percent agreed with the statement, "it's important that my kids speak Spanish."

Nancy told me that these attitudes among millennials can sometimes cause angst for their parents, who grew up not being taught Spanish by their own parents. The parents of millennials can feel that "'these young millennials are all excited about speaking Spanish well, but my parents didn't do this for me and I'm really upset.'" Reflecting on this generational reversal in language aspirations, Nancy said, "I don't think this has ever occurred in our nation."

The cool factor

Linda Lane Gonzalez is an advertising executive in Miami who advises clients trying to reach the Latino market. In her view, what we are seeing among young Latinos is what Linda calls a "retro-culturation," and it's because being Latino has in many quarters become cool. In prior generations, Latinos kept in their own ethnic domains, she explained, "but today we have so many crossover artists, like Gloria Estefan, Shakira, Jennifer Lopez, Marc Anthony, Ricky Martin." Latin artists used to be on just Spanish radio; now they have crossed over and sing in both Spanish and English. "Music is a huge influencer and non-Hispanics have allowed it to be cool," Linda told me. "Pitbull is always saying *dale, dale, dale.*" It translates roughly as "okay, okay, let's do it!"

I asked Linda if Latino parents today have a different attitude about their kids speaking Spanish. "Yes, totally different, we turned a corner. I grew up in that era, you didn't speak Spanish, you didn't want your kids to speak Spanish, you wanted them to be American. But it's completely different now. There is such a pride in being Hispanic. No one hides their culture."

When it comes to the impact of immigration on education, we may think of all the limited-English kids who flooded into our schools. That was, indeed, the case early in the third wave a generation ago, and continues to some extent today, but the wind has shifted.

According to the PISA test of American students conducted in 2018, the proportion of students with an immigrant background was 23 percent, and approximately two out of five of them were from socioeconomically disadvantaged backgrounds. Remarkably, however, the test results for these immigrants were not statistically different from their non-immigrant peers. When their disadvantaged backgrounds are controlled for, the immigrant kids actually outscore non-immigrant kids in overall PISA results by a meaningful sixteen points.

What's best is now bilingual

Parents still want what's best for their kids, but what's best has changed. Whereas that used to mean speaking only English, and without the parents' accent, parents today are seeing things differently. Of course they want their kids to speak English perfectly, but they also see the practical advantages of bilingualism and want their kids to own those advantages.

A century ago, few American organizations and enterprises were international. Today, we have tens of thousands of international enterprises where language skills can be important for career advancement.

Parents have taken notice of the changed opportunities for their children. Whereas it made little practical sense to pass on the heritage language in 1920, today it makes all the sense in the world.

We see this in the growing number of books for raising bilingual children. And within that genre are books written by Latinos for Latinos. In their book, *Bilingual Is Better*, Roxana Soto and Ana Flores write, "We are a growing group of Latino parents who are proud of our language and heritage, and we are committed to raising a community of skilled biliterate and bicultural children who can communicate fluently in two or more languages." They welcome Anglo parents to join in, and Anglo parents are doing just that. Miami is an ideal place to raise Latino kids as bilinguals, say the authors. "Miami is heaven for those of us who are trying to raise bilingual and bicultural children because the exposure to both our native language and culture happens organically."

And it isn't just among Latinos where you see this change. In his memoir, *A Chinaman's Chance*, Eric Liu reports on the changing attitudes toward Chinese immigrants, writing that "it's becoming ever easier and cooler *not* to lose the accent."

The valuing of heritage languages through bilingualism is becoming institutionalized in America. This is the guidance the US Department of Health and Human Services and the US Department of Education issued in 2017: "Research indicates that supporting bilingualism from early ages can have wide ranging benefits, from cognitive and social advantages early in life, to long term employment opportunities and competitiveness in the workplace later in life." And in "The 6 Principles for Exemplary Teaching of English Learners" that the TESOL International Association issued (Teaching English to Speakers of Other Languages), the organization advises teachers to "respect, affirm, and promote students' home languages and cultural knowledge and experiences as resources," and to "celebrate multilingualism."

Parents today—both immigrants and native-born—want the best for their kids, just as they did a century ago. It's just that today, parents are concluding that best means bilingual.

The new American bilingual

We met some new American bilinguals in earlier chapters. Let's check back with them and hear the rest of their stories.

Erik Kirschbaum, the American journalist who works in Germany and who wrote *Burning Beethoven*, about our one-time war against the German language, today leads an annual exchange of broadcast journalists between the US and Germany. "We send about thirty Americans to Germany every year and about thirty Germans to the US," he told me. "I'm a big fan of exchanges; I know it changed my life. I just get a big kick out of seeing young Americans and young Germans learning a lot about each other's countries, going deep, going beyond the clichés."

David Wolf is the American who was accepted to business school in France and nearly flunked out. David did survive to earn his MBA, then went to work at the headquarters of Cartier in Paris before returning to America. But with the help of his French friend, David turned into a lifelong lover of fine wine and food, which has changed his life. He became a founding board member of the American Friends of La Cité du Vin. "It is the only international wine museum and cultural center in the world," David told me, recounting the millions of visitors since its opening in 2016. Fittingly, it is located in Bordeaux, one of France's premier wine regions. His organization underwrote the museum's Thomas Jefferson Auditorium, "which gives a permanent American presence and highlights Jefferson's role as a friend and bridge between the two countries," he added.

Doug Renfield-Miller, the young American who was flunking high school until he spent a year in France with the organization School Year Abroad (SYA), went on to a successful business career. Later in life he chaired the board of SYA, working to ensure that other young Americans have the kind of transformational experience he did.

When we last left Nick Staffa, he had gone from being a late-entry college student to the highest-ranking student in Asian & American Studies at his graduation from SUNY Stony Brook. Nick went on to earn his Chinese teaching credential. He was hired in Memphis and later was offered teaching jobs overseas that were too good to refuse—first in South Korea and then in Hong Kong. Nick keeps his adopted Mandarin alive through his profession, and at home with his Chinese American wife and young son, where they all speak Mandarin.

Jenny Messner parlayed her AFS year in Brazil into a job in international finance, where she used her Portuguese to boost her career. She and her husband launched the Speedwell Foundation to help high-schoolers of limited means have the same kind of life-changing study abroad experience she had. "We gave one scholarship and then we gave more and more, and pretty soon we got it up to over two hundred," Jenny says. Each year they throw a picnic for all their scholarship winners and their parents.

Chris Nichols, the Greek American who loves watching Greek television in his home in Florida, was determined to marry a Greek-speaking woman. "She is half Greek and half Italian," he told me. "She's gorgeous, a great cook, and speaks Italian and Spanish, too." They were married in Greece, with the entire service in Greek. The couple's four children are named Natalia, Konstantinos, Maximos, and Andriana. "All named after grandparents," said Chris. "My friends tease me, 'You couldn't pick Keith?'"

I asked Chris what it feels like to be bilingual. He told me that when people find out he can speak Greek, he often hears something like "That's so freaking cool!" But it's much more than that, he says. "One of the challenges we have as Americans is we don't know what's going on around the rest of the world. It gives me a better sense of awareness of the world."

From 'I must learn' to 'I want to learn'

There are many other American bilinguals I've interviewed. One is Dena Storck, whose children are already speaking Spanish much better than she does. They are learning as a family in their Austin home with the help of Dena's Spanish-speaking mother, who now, as a grandmother, is using the Spanish she withheld from her own children.

Gerta Dhamo, a graduate student in Boston, is from Albania. She is the middle of three sisters and was twelve when the family immigrated. "Surprisingly," Gerta told me, "it's my younger sister, who was six when we came, who has the best Albanian, since she really took it seriously and has gone back more than any of us." Gerta speaks Albanian with her parents and in the Albanian community in Boston. She told me she intends to marry an Albanian-speaking man and is committed to passing on her language to her children.

The bilingualism common in America a century ago was, as we learned, what linguists call situational: immigrants learned English because their situation demanded it. Unless they made their living with immigrants from the same language group, the economic value of their heritage language was quite limited. Today's immigrants enter a different America. While their bilingualism can still be called situational, their heritage language is more likely to remain useful in their careers and easier to maintain, due to the revolutions in communications, travel, and attitudes. For some, their heritage language is not merely useful in their careers, but instrumental.

Mike Parra, a Cuban American, began his career while still in college in Miami. That's when he started sorting mail at a shipping company, working with eleven others who spoke Spanish but little English. He spoke both. Within two months, Mike was promoted to supervisor. "Absolutely my bilingualism was important," he told me. "I had to communicate effectively with them, direct our work, understand their needs and wants." In time, Mike was promoted to manager of the warehouse. That was in 1980, when another influx of Cubans from the Mariel boatlift arrived in Miami, resulting in more native Spanish-speaking workers who were learning English.

After that job, Mike was promoted to a regional operations manager position in Los Angeles. In that warehouse, 50 percent of the employees were Spanish-speaking. "The fit was perfect," Mike said. "There were various individuals who had struggled with the prior leader, who didn't speak Spanish. They struggled to communicate and that triggered misunderstandings. I understood their challenges at home with their families and that sometimes they needed flexible schedules. I was working nights. We had a mix of Latinos and Asians and most were working on their English, so between one and two in the morning we would have our 'lunch' in English." Mike told me his region "went from underperforming to basically the number one unit in the US."

Mike continued moving up in the organization. When I interviewed him in his South Florida office, he was CEO of DHL Express Americas. He uses his Spanish on a daily basis, and especially when visiting his teams throughout Latin and South America as well as Puerto Rico. What's more, he makes sure his company covers the cost of language lessons for employees, whether they are learning English or, like his VP of Human Resources, Spanish.

When one of my childhood friends at age eighteen told me he was going to major in accounting at San Diego State, I thought he was setting his sights too low. (Although compared with most of our friends, who were musicians, it was a sensible thing to do.) But Eddie Cannizzaro did well in accounting, making partner and rising up the auditing ranks at KPMG, moving to Connecticut, to San Francisco, back to New York City, and eventually up to the top management team of KPMG's 219,000-person company. His job, he told me, is "global responsibility for KPMG's system of quality controls, risk management and ethics." Not bad for the youngest of five children of a Mexican American mother and an Italian American father, who grew up in a tiny home a block from mine in La Mesa. Ed told me his Spanish isn't fluent, but he was able to improve it during his career. His bilingualism and his understanding of Latin culture became important when he was responsible for risk management for Latin America and the Caribbean. "I understood that our accountants there would be less comfortable challenging a partner than in the US. We worked on that."

And it's not just businesspeople whose careers are dependent on their bilingualism. There are actors like Sofia Vergara, Kate del Castillo, and Andrea Navedo; the playwright and composer Lin-Manuel Miranda; and newscasters like Jorge Ramos and José Díaz-Balart, who has anchored both Spanish and English network news programs.

The other form of bilingualism in America a century ago was elective bilingualism, primarily the privilege of children of wealthy parents, such as Theodore Roosevelt. These are the kinds of families that Guadalupe Valdés had in mind when she told me that bilingualism has always been a gift the rich have given their children. Today, elective bilingualism is no longer limited to the children of the rich, but accessible to an increasing number of American children.

American bilingualism finds its voice

We've seen how in other countries, the shape of their bilingualism fits both their history and their vision for the role they wish to play in the world. Canada has its English and French duality; Singapore its Chinese-English, East-meets-West bilingualism. Morocco has its gateway-to-Africa strategy, while Europe has its Euro unification ideal expressed primarily in bilingualism in the languages of Europe. In America, our shape of bilingualism is unique to us. Our scale is consistent with our history of having integrated more immigrants than any other nation, and our diversity is more representative of the entire world than any other country can boast of. Yet there are other characteristics that appear in our uniquely American form of bilingualism that are also important.

First, American bilingualism is mostly English-dominant bilingualism. It's a fact of life, not only because of the dominance of English in America but also because of the dominance of English globally. In contrast to a century ago, many of today's immigrants come already equipped with a head start in English. Within America, English is what unites us. But this in no way means we can't also have our home-team languages, too, in the same way that baseball unites us—by first dividing us into teams that we call our own. Outside of America, our English skills provide both a front-row seat from which to tour the world and an opportunity to be of service to those billions who are learning English.

Another salient characteristic of American bilingualism is our preponderance of Spanish speakers, who number some 48.6 million. We have more Spanish speakers than Spain, more than Argentina, and more, in fact, than any other country except Mexico. Our English-Spanish bilinguals are especially important for helping the US truly step into its responsible position in the Americas, able to understand and be understood throughout most of the hemisphere. We have only begun to reap the benefits.

I would add another important characteristic of American bilingualism, and that is: our tradition of being of service to the world.

There are the well-known examples, like the Peace Corps, the Red Cross, and our many church-based organizations that perform humanitarian work. The success of these organizations outside of America rides on bilingualism. And there are many more examples of organizations and individuals that are less well known.

After the 9/11 terrorist attacks, one of the responses by the Department of Defense was to create a corps of civilian bilinguals who could provide surge capability on short notice to help the nation deal with a crisis anywhere on earth. The National Language Service Corps, with the motto "Language for the Good of All," was the result.

As of 2020, the NLSC has ten thousand members speaking more than four hundred languages and dialects, including such languages as Marshallese, Hausa, Indonesian, and Somali. Corps members must be US citizens. In addition to having professional-level competence in English and another language, members also bring specific regional, cultural, and profession-based expertise to the table. Corps members are unpaid, unless they are called into action, and then are paid travel and an hourly stipend. Since their first assignment in 2009, NLSC members have served CENTCOM in military missions, as well as supporting disaster relief and coalition-building roles worldwide.

On a much smaller scale, but with the potential to grow, is an organization called Sharelingo. Its founder, an American named James Archer, had become frustrated in his midlife attempt to learn Spanish but found satisfaction in helping Latinos improve their English. He would ask their help with his Spanish, and from this the Sharelingo idea was born. The organization joins together English and Spanish learners, one on one, to help each other in a structured way. "When you're teaching somebody your language and they are teaching you, you just can't help but get to know them," James told me. "And this face-to-face interaction breaks down barriers and you become friends." After starting with in-person classes in Denver, James has expanded the concept online.

For every organization, there are thousands of individual American bilinguals who are using their language skills to serve. In South Florida, I met a Vietnamese immigrant who told me his harrowing tale of survival after the American withdrawal from Saigon in 1975. Duol Thach had been fighting alongside American forces when the US evacuated Saigon. He was captured by the Vietcong and imprisoned. He managed to escape and then walk across the country to Cambodia, where he eventually immigrated to Europe and then to America. Arriving in Miami, he first lived on the street, beneath an Interstate 95 overpass. He found work at a boatyard and today works for himself, painting boats. Duol has done very well in his business and has sent money back home. He travels regularly back to Vietnam, where, he told me with obvious pride, he paid to build a much-needed bridge in his village.

There are also millions more native-born American bilinguals who are using their languages to aid others overseas, like Allison De La Torre, who reclaimed her grandparents' Spanish and used it in Central and South America on mission trips.

When you start looking for famous Americans in history who were bilingual, you will find them in abundance—and not just immigrants like Einstein, but native-born Americans who lived during what I'm calling our monolingual period. One was New York City Mayor Fiorello La Guardia, who as a young man worked on Ellis Island and for the Consular Service in Budapest. The historian Mason B. Williams writes that "by the time he returned to America, he had a passable knowledge of Italian, Yiddish, French, Croatian, Hungarian, and German."

Another was the Nobel Prize-winning physicist Richard P. Feynman. He learned Portuguese for his extended teaching duties in Brazil and to feed his lifelong passion for Brazilian drumming. As a baby in New York City, Eleanor Roosevelt learned French before she spoke English. Later she also learned Spanish, Italian, and German. Besides being First Lady, she was the US Representative to the United Nations and an architect of the UN's Universal Declaration of Human Rights.

The rising American lion

Is the number of American bilinguals likely to decline or grow in the future? Much depends on future immigration and whether it will decrease, increase, or stay the same. Despite news stories about immigration being a controversial topic in America, I see broad agreement among the Americans I interview. I've never met an American who believes we should have *no* immigration, nor have I met an American who believes we should have open borders. Within those guardrails, the road is plenty wide, and although it's hard to predict what side of the road we'll travel, Pew has estimated that American immigration is likely to continue at near recent levels in the near term, at least.

For today's immigrants and their offspring, the three-generation rule of language shift will not go away completely. Even if immigrants *want* to retain their heritage languages and want their kids to perpetuate this inheritance, this doesn't mean it will happen automatically. The dominance of English in America is unassailable, while its importance internationally continues to rise as well. It takes dedication and hard work for families to raise bilingual kids, even in the new American atmosphere that generally welcomes it.

Moreover, in its most recent survey of college language classes, the Modern Language Association reports another significant decline in enrollments—even in Spanish classes. But bear in mind that today, one hundred thousand more high school students take AP language tests than was the case a decade ago. It's certain that some of these students test out of their college language requirement and thus enroll in other classes instead.

The MLA also reports that colleges offering language classes relevant to getting jobs in fields such as health care and criminology are seeing enrollments grow. So are classes that focus on content areas of interest to students. Elon University, for example, offers courses titled "Cultural Shifts in France through Music," "French Theatre in Production," and "Business Cultures of the Francophone World." And a burgeoning number of college students are pursuing a second major in a language that bolsters their first.

There are several other potential multiplier effects. The persistent undersupply of dual language schools nationally is frustrating parents across the country. Both native-born and immigrant parents are united in their demands for dual language schools. Together with language teachers and school administrators, these parents are successfully pressuring school districts to respond. And they have: the number of dual language schools is increasing dramatically, around 15 percent annually. If that growth rate continues, we could have a dual language program for every American school in one generation.

Hear us roar

Many of today's young parents have had very different language learning experiences than their baby boomer parents. As the younger generations step into positions of authority in America, they may well increase support for languages—not just with more dual language schools, but also for the conventional language classes that are so much improved from a generation ago. This could create a virtuous cycle of more opportunities for language teachers, improved teacher training, and better outcomes for students, both among heritage learners and those new to a language.

The Seal of Biliteracy will likely continue to grow in popularity among students and parents, as well as in its significance to colleges and employers. Study abroad will, barring such *forces majeures* as pandemics, continue to increase. As will bridge years and service years, allowing millions more American young people not only to earn their bilingualism, but also to feel firsthand the benefits of applying their bilingualism in real-world settings.

Technology for language learning will continue to improve, becoming more useful and more lovable, giving everyone a free AI version of my ever-patient tutor Angie. We will also gain even more ability to fashion virtual language immersion experiences right here in America, in a wider array of world languages.

Since most of America's bilinguals live in cities, and cities foster social innovation, the combination may well accelerate experiments and prototypes, as has already happened with dual language public schools in Brooklyn.

America is also the home of many of the world's leading tech companies in the language learning space, including Microsoft, Apple, and Google. Duolingo is another American firm dedicated to seeing how far technology can take humans toward feeling comfortable enough in their skills to welcome having real conversations with other humans.

As success breeds success, more Americans will understand the benefits of being bilingual, and as they see their fellow Americans reaping those benefits, the more good bilingualism will come to seem. While it's possible to have a good career as a monolingual, why risk it?

A world thirsty for English, while we hold the water

In tandem with the likely growth in American bilingualism is an exploding demand for English around the world. The world's inhabitants will not be giving up their native languages but will be adding English. And with a global median age still under thirty, lots of young people will want to seize for themselves the career boost that English skills can provide.

"My mom made sure English was the first language I spoke," writes South African-born Trevor Noah in his memoir. "If you're black in South Africa, speaking English is the one thing that can give you a leg up. English is the language of money. English comprehension is equated with intelligence. If you're looking for a job, English is the difference between getting the job or staying unemployed. If you're standing in the dock, English is the difference between getting off with a fine or going to prison."

English is no less important in China. Evan Osnos, the American journalist who's covered the country extensively, wrote this in his *Age of Ambition* book about China's most recent coming of age: "Of all the pathways to self-creation, nothing galvanized people as broadly as the study of English. 'English fever' settled on waiters, CEOs, and professors, and elevated the language into a defining measure of life's potential—a force strong enough to transform your résumé, help attract a spouse, or vault you out of a village."

Beyond the pragmatic reasons for learning English are the symbolic ones. As David Crystal explains, "As the lyrics (as distinct from the tunes) of Bob Dylan, Bob Marley, John Lennon, Joan Baez and others spread around the world, during the 1960s and 1970s, English for the younger generation in many countries became a symbol of freedom, rebellion and modernism." Crystal describes how Martin Luther King's three words set to music, "We Shall Overcome," washed over countless thousands around the world, "providing many people with a first—and often highly charged—experience of the unifying power of English in action."

These English learners around the world will have ever better technology within their grasp to help them learn. But what is most difficult for them to obtain are genuine conversations with native English speakers, especially in-person conversations, the kind that Julia Child enjoyed with her friend at the Parisian food market.

Surprising as it may sound, native English speakers are a rare commodity on the world market, constituting less than 7 percent of all humans. The US represents the largest repository (about 50 percent), with India placing a distant second (about 25 percent). To what extent Americans, and especially American bilinguals, step in to help is something I find most intriguing. It might seem at first a rather obscure question, particularly in the face of climate change, armed conflicts, vulnerable migrants, and persistent inequality. But more hangs in the balance with this question than it might appear. For such conversations can address climate change, armed conflicts, vulnerable migrants, and persistent inequality.

The need for conversations range from matters of life and death to the most mundane commerce. The other day I ordered a toilet brush from Amazon. A few days after it arrived, I received an email with the subject line: "Do you happy with toilet brush?"

After a double take, I laughed. "Why, yes," I thought, "I do happy with toilet brush, thank you for asking." The email went on, "Dear Steve, How are you? This is my personal follow up to your order, hope not bother you, we are very valued your shopping experience . . . " Clearly, you don't have to be a professional translator to help these folks out. There's a real need for Americans to bridge the gap between Google Translate and the way people really speak English. And helping in this way is just the starting point to what Americans can do.

Do Americans suck at languages? Quite the opposite. America can boast the world's largest population of English-dominant bilinguals, and these Americans speak more world languages, in greater numbers, than any other country. This gives Americans unprecedented opportunities to help the world, while also helping themselves and their country.

As we reflect on the myths, misconceptions, and half-truths that threaten to deflect us along our bilingual journeys, I hope you now feel armed with perspectives you can use to bat them away. Your journey, and those of your loved ones, are too important to miss. Besides, the world needs more American bilinguals who do happy.

✳ ✳ ✳

PART FOUR

A REIMAGINED AMERICA

"The greatness of America lies not in being more enlightened than any other nation, but rather in her ability to repair her faults."

—ALEXIS DE TOCQUEVILLE

Chapter 47

AMERICA, LATER THIS CENTURY

As a thought experiment, it's fun to imagine our present time as seen through the eyes of someone back in time—say, our grandfathers when they were twenty. What would seem familiar to them? What would surprise them? And what would they find utterly baffling?

I'm guessing that fighting among politicians would be familiar. Perhaps gay marriage would be surprising. And maybe they would be baffled that everyone keeps looking down all the time at these things we call phones.

Now let's turn the tables and imagine that we are the Rip Van Winkles who suddenly awake in America decades from now. What might we see? That's the question I set out to answer in this chapter, limiting myself to our future linguistic landscape.

Carrying a Cultural Passport

The first thing you notice when you open your eyes are the people. They look like a Norman Rockwell painting of American diversity. You see people of all colors, but mostly people of *some* color, or some mixture, and my gosh, they all look so good and healthy.

The second thing you notice are their voices. They are speaking English that you understand perfectly well, although they use some new words, but they are also speaking all kinds of other languages with one another. You come to find out that most Americans are bilingual, using their second and sometimes third language as a regular part of their lives.

A college student named Emma, who has been assigned to take you around her campus, explains that bilingualism starts quite early now: in pre-school, if not before. Kids begin school in two languages and continue in what used to be called dual language schools, except now all schools are dual language, so they're just called schools again. She explains, "Growing up, I took half my classes in French until I got to college. Now I'm taking half my classes in Spanish, because I'm planning to graduate with a Jefferson Citation."

What's a Jefferson Citation? you ask.

"Well, Thomas Jefferson recommended that Americans learn English, French, and Spanish, right? So my college offers a Jefferson Citation, and I ought to be able to get it." You learn that colleges also offer what's called the Big Three Citation, which stands for Spanish, English, and Chinese. Lots of kids like the Big Three, Emma explains, "because you can speak to most people in the world in their native language, which is cool."

Emma earned her Seal of Biliteracy in French upon entering high school and then added Spanish. "We always played soccer in Spanish, and I went to Colombia for soccer camp every summer," she explains.

As Emma takes you around the campus, you're surprised that it's not just young people you see. "We have all kinds of mid-career students and also encore students," people who have finished their first careers and are back for round two. "We have about 10 percent international students, too." You learn that America has maintained its lead as the number one country for international students. "They help us out with our languages," she adds, "assisting our language professors and also by living in the language dorms." Emma tells you that she lives in the Spanish language dorm. "We only speak Spanish at meals and events that we all go to together."

It's not just the major languages that students can learn on Emma's campus but the top forty. You learn that most language classes, like most classes in general, are hybrids of virtual and in-person sessions. Emma shows you her Cultural Passport on her phone. It lists all her languages, together with level of competency, experience domains (Emma has biomedical Spanish), and time living in various countries, all beautifully displayed. "We have regular transcripts, too, but employers like to see your languages and cross-cultural experiences."

You learn Emma did her bridge year in Barcelona before college, working in a biotechnology lab. She is considering a number of service year programs after college, either in Santiago or outside of Paris.

Since Emma has a double major in applied linguistics and computer science, she knows a lot of what's happened since you went to sleep earlier in the century. She suggests you have a coffee at the outdoor cafe you're coming upon.

What is an 'American language'?

There is a team at a top university, she explains as you sip your coffee in a cool, shady area, that measures America's linguistic capital in real time. The researchers use big data from computer and phone usage (anonymized) to measure bilingualism in America and in many other countries. Not only that, but they have used other data to go back in time to estimate linguistic capital as far back as 1900. The low point in American linguistic capital was around 1970, but it's been growing steadily since. It helped, Emma says, when the Census added a question about how well people speak their LOTEs (Languages Other Than English), using the same scale that people have always used to self-report their English skills.

The researchers at the Linguistic Capital Research Center issue a global ranking every other year and it always makes headlines, Emma says. "That's because American linguistic capital is linked to our improvement in the PISA ranking and our balance of trade, which is good." You learn that America's PISA ranking, after languishing in the middle of the pack when you fell asleep, is now always in the top tier. And our trade balance has been positive for many years, too.

You heard Emma say "American languages" at one point, and you ask what that means.

"Well, it's all our founding languages, right—Spanish, French, Dutch, English, German. And it's all the Amerindian languages, which there are still hundreds of, and Gullah, which preserves some of the African languages. Then we have all our immigrant languages, which are almost all the world's living languages. So it's hard to find a language that *isn't* an American language," she says cheerily.

You ask Emma why most people you see walking by are people of color. She explains that with all the immigrants who came in the third wave, "it just makes sense that they're going to marry people from other cultures, and that's why you have so many Asian Latinos and African Irish and whatever." *Oh*, you say, looking around. Emma continues.

"But the biggest factor is that America keeps winning at immigration."

Winning? you ask. Such an interesting choice of word.

"Yes, ever since global population decline—and even before that—countries began competing for immigrants, kind of the way American cities used to compete for company headquarters."

Emma explains that after the global population peaked, it quickly fell. Consequently, human capital became the hot commodity. "You can get free homes in many countries if you're willing to fix them up," she says. "Canada and Australia have always done a great job attracting immigrants. So has Latin America, but the US got its game on pretty early and now offers a really competitive package."

What's the package? you ask.

"Well," says Emma, "of course, you can get all the English classes and tutoring you need, although most people don't need much. Oh, and there's mandatory US history and values courses. Then there are various financial incentives. It's really a race, because it's harder and harder to attract immigrants."

You learn from Emma that once extreme poverty was mostly eliminated and education and access to birth control became nearly universal, women elected to have fewer children all around the world. "It's basically a market share battle for people," said Emma. "And with fewer people on the planet, immigrants around the world have many countries to choose from."

The Conversation Corps

You ask Emma a bit more about her service year options she's considering. She explains that they are both Conversation Corps jobs. You look at her quizzically.

"Conversation Corps is something like the Peace Corps, but with shorter stays," she explains. "You help people learn English by doing things with them, like hiking, building homes, community projects, while having conversations." She adds, "It's for Americans of all ages."

Emma tells you how there is a need for people around the world to practice English. "Of course people cherish their native languages, but they want to speak the global language, too." Since native English speakers constitute less than 10 percent of the world's population, "we have a duty to help others learn English," she says. "And of course, we Americans benefit by boosting our own bilingualism and getting to make friends all over the world." One of the Conversation Corps' mottos, she tells you, is "Imperfect sentences make for perfect friendships."

She adds that the Conversation Corps also operates within the US, in cities like Phoenix and Los Angeles, "wherever there are lots of different cultures living side by side. The CC helps people mix and get to know one another."

And it's not just the larger American cities where this kind of cultural and linguistic exchange takes place. Emma tells you how she's studied two early twenty-first-century journalists, the husband-and-wife team of James and Deborah Fallows, who set off in 2012 in their two-seater prop plane to fly into what was often dismissed as America's flyover country. They touched down in many smaller towns to see how people were dealing with the issues that make or break communities: jobs, schools, immigrants. What they found in a small town in Kansas was a harbinger of the America that Emma now lives in.

"When the Fallowses visited, this town had as many immigrants as native-born residents," Emma recounts. "So the schools had an English-Language Learner program to help immigrants acquire English while still retaining their heritage language." Emma says she remembers what one native English-speaking resident said: "'By and large, people here—Anglo and Hispanic and otherwise—recognize that we're all in this together.'" She smiles as she tells you this.

So where do I sign up for this Conversation Corps? you say to Emma, half-kiddingly. But she is serious as she tells you that there is an American Bilingual Honor Code you have to agree to before you can serve. "You pledge certain things," Emma explains.

What kinds of things? you ask.

"Like, you try not to use a language around people who don't understand it, but you encourage the use of LOTE in general." She continues, counting off on her fingers. "You try not to correct people with their English, unless they ask you to. You speak English *very slowly*. You understand HAMS bias and try not to fall into it. You are sympathetic toward monolinguals. And you generally support endangered languages by promoting bilingualism." She pauses for a moment. "There's more, but those are the basics."

You want to know more about how all this happened (and what exactly a HAMS bias is), but it's already been a long, somewhat bewildering day. Emma gives you a hug goodbye and promises to answer more of your questions tomorrow.

How bilingualism became the American way

After a good night's sleep and breakfast, you meet up with Emma to hear more about how on earth this flourishing bilingualism got planted so deeply in American soil.

It started with the kids, Emma tells you. More precisely, their parents. "Immigrant parents and native-born parents got together to demand that school districts have more dual language schools," Emma explains. "Both sets of parents knew it was the best way to keep their kids bilingual, or get them to be bilingual, so they just didn't let up. And it's not just the US that has gone over to dual language schools," Emma adds. "They are the norm worldwide. And what parent wouldn't want their kid to have the advantages of being bilingual?"

You nod.

"Of course, teachers and school administrators also drove the change," she adds. "And it helped that teachers are now paid more, and respected more, than they used to be. It's part of what happened when so many teacher colleges closed and it became harder to get into the ones that were left."

Tell me more about Americans winning at immigration, you prompt her. *You mentioned that yesterday.* To your surprise, she starts talking about China.

"China way overdid their one-child policy," says Emma. "And when they realized it, it was too late." You learn the Chinese people got used to having fewer children and that as a result, China's population was now on track to be half of what it was at the start of the twenty-first century. "And they've never been that good at attracting immigrants," adds Emma with a shrug.

By contrast, the recruitment of immigrants is what America has always done, she says. "It happened in the colonial period, and then building the transcontinental railroad, which brought the first Chinese. And then with the Bracero Program," she adds, "which brought in Mexicans as migrant workers during the Second World War, when so many American farmers were fighting overseas." Emma tells you that Americans still debate how much immigration we should have, but in general are in agreement that immigration has always been a competitive advantage for the US and must remain so. "Besides," she adds, "immigration is just in our DNA."

Fighting prejudice, in school and in uniform

"Then there was also the matter of public health," Emma said. "The Surgeon General was very charismatic, and she asked questions that hadn't been asked before."

Such as? you ask.

"She said something like, 'Well, we immunize children against disease, right? Why don't we immunize children against prejudice?' She was talking about empathy education and becoming bilingual. She also said that since we know being bilingual improves mental health over your whole lifetime, and since we know perfectly well how to educate children to be bilinguals, don't we have a *responsibility* to do so?"

It was sometime around then, maybe fifteen or twenty years ago, Emma offers, that monolingual kids began to be seen as disadvantaged. "Once that happened, well, Americans aren't going to accept that." After that, many summer camps became language summer camps by adding young counselors from overseas and language teachers to their staffs.

The recruitment campaigns for the Army and Marines probably also had an impact, she says. "You hear people in uniform saying, 'I serve America in English and Arabic, I serve America in English and Hindi,' or whatever."

You take a moment to process that. Could it be that bilingualism is some benign weapon for peace?

Getting our American groove back

You learn that America continues to do a better job at bilingualism than Europe overall "because Europe just doesn't have the culture of immigration the way America does," Emma explains. "They did a pretty good job with bilingualism among their founding European languages, but they haven't valued their immigrant languages the way Americans have."

"And I can't leave out our former president," she continues. "President Garcia had a Jefferson Citation, so she was fluent in French and Spanish. She was the one who created the Conversation Corps, to follow on President Kennedy's Peace Corps way back in the 1960s." Emma recounts how President Garcia saw the Conversation Corps as an important process to help the world and help Americans. She argued for the good it would do for American education and GNP, and she was proved right. Americans regained much of the respect that other nations had lost for this country. "We were pretty low there for some years in surveys on how people viewed us, but we've bounced back," Emma says happily.

"Americans have always been at our best when we look outwards," Emma says dreamily. "The Marshall Plan, the Peace Corps and Red Cross, and now the Conversation Corps." Then she smiles and tells you what a little boy in Nigeria said about Americans: "'An American is someone who helps.'"

You mention to Emma that for much of the twentieth century, it was normal to be monolingual. She knows that, of course, although it baffles her. "What could be more patriotic than helping your country and the world?" she asks. "I suppose it's like when people didn't have vaccines and managed somehow, but then things got so much better when we did have them." Emma tells you that politicians on both sides of the aisle take credit for American advancement in bilingualism.

"We actually know a lot more about social science now," she says, "because it's part of our basic education. We know about the biases in our thinking, our habit of forming tribes, of seeing 'others' as threats. But we also know that forming individual relationships, especially face-to-face relationships, is an antidote to prejudice."

Sounds like you've given this lots of thought, you say. Emma blushes slightly. "Yes, I'm doing my thesis on it."

It will be wonderful, you say. She blushes again, clearly pleased, and then continues.

"It's not like we're immune from demagogues, and we still tend to divide people into Thems and Us, until we remember not to demonize groups and that it's individuals we need to focus on, and that conversations with each other are how we do that."

And thus the Conversation Corps, you say. She nods.

"And if the pandemics taught us anything, it's that cooperation and collaboration are what we need. The worst thing you can do is start blaming others. Pandemics have shown us how connected we are biologically, which requires that we be just as connected socially."

The Second American Century

I made all this up. But I didn't really. The world that our fictional, future Emma describes wasn't fabricated out of thin air, but from thick data. American bilingualism, already larger than most of us know, is poised to grow larger yet, and soon. The world's population is expected to peak at a number lower than previously forecasted, and then to decline. We are seeing this already in countries such as Japan, Italy, and Greece. But global population decline isn't necessarily bad, as long as we anticipate it and adapt to it. A key benefit is likely to be a growing value placed on all humans, and a healthy competition to create optimum living experiences where humans can flourish in harmony with themselves and the natural world.

Because of general improvement in health and education worldwide, plus improved teaching methods and technology, there has never been a better time to learn an additional language no matter where you live in the world. We live in a golden age of learning, and of language learning, made possible by many dedicated, hardworking people. Bilingualism has always been, and will always be, a gift that humans give one another—teachers, tutors, scholars, software developers, businesspeople, and conversation partners.

By encouraging bilingualism, by creating an environment in which bilingualism can flourish, we not only help individuals obtain skills and improved mental health, we help them gain perspectives that lean toward peace. When you learn another language, you learn something of the culture of the people who speak it. You cannot help but broaden perspectives by doing so. Having conversations and getting to know people as individuals reduces the temptation to lump others into stereotypical groups of Thems. It is inherently peacemaking.

While our elected leaders represent America overseas, there are millions more Americans who go overseas and form relationships with people who will judge America by them, one individual at a time. Therein lies our real ability to understand and to help the world. As Eleanor Roosevelt said, "It is not so much the powerful leaders that determine our destiny as the much more powerful influence of the combined voice of the people themselves."

Through the accident of birth, we Americans were handed a winning lottery ticket. Only around 7 percent of the world's people are native speakers of English, the language billions of people around the world wish to know. Our ticket means we can travel the world and operate in the world more comfortably than can native speakers of other languages. On the other hand, if we do not elect to become bilingual ourselves, we risk being the last of the monolinguals, and denying ourselves the many blessings that bilingualism can bring to ourselves and to our country.

The vigorous bilingualism I portray in this future America is now within our grasp. And while at first, the benefits of bilingualism may seem largely a benefit to individuals, those benefits scale quickly to communities and to countries. Just as the various rights revolutions of the twentieth century unleashed more human capital for the benefit of individuals and the country, so, too, will America benefit when we fully embrace the languages-as-resource perspective.

Not that reaching this advancement will be all smooth rowing. In order to arrive at this next waypoint in human flourishing, we will travel a river with unexpected turns and powerful rapids. Along the riverbank will be politicians quite willing to divide us, if they sense it will help them rise to power. Professors and pundits will continue to debate the nuances, as is their way. People will continue to be human. Just because we are more aware of how easily our rationality can be capsized, doesn't mean we won't flip our canoes on occasion. But as Americans well into our third century, our boats have already passed successfully through much rougher waters.

In February 1941, *Time* magazine publisher Henry Luce wrote an essay titled "The American Century." He composed it during a dark and unsettled time in our country. Americans were severely divided on entering another war in Europe. The daily news revealed our deeply dysfunctional politics. There was a contagion of foreboding of what was to come, with the war already two years old in Europe, and with England at risk of falling into Hitler's hands. It was ten months before the Japanese attack on Pearl Harbor.

Luce wrote about how international Americans already were, how our trade circled the globe, and how utterly dependent we were on the freedom of world travel and trade that we take for granted, and that would be smashed to bits if despots like Hitler had their way. Isolationism is not our way, nor in our interest, he argued. We cannot be economically free unless the world is economically free. What we can accomplish in the first American Century is limited largely by what we can imagine for ourselves. Luce wrote:

"America as the training center of the skillful servants of mankind, America as the Good Samaritan, really believing again that it is more blessed to give than to receive, and America as the powerhouse of the ideals of Freedom and Justice—out of these elements surely can be fashioned a vision of the 20th Century to which we can and will devote ourselves in joy and gladness and vigor and enthusiasm."

It was in this spirit that Luce called on his fellow citizens "to create the first American Century." Now there is a calling for us to create our second American Century, in which American bilingualism will stand center stage. No longer the gift that immigrants feel they must hide, nor the privilege of a chosen few, but the birthright of all Americans, as we stand ready to extend ourselves to the world.

Whether your parents are recent immigrants or have lived in America for many generations, whether you are old or young, rich or poor, you can live your larger life by living part of it in another language, enjoying the expanded experiences that bilingualism brings. Do this and you help not only yourself, but also that grand experiment we call America.

Epilogue

It was a Sunday morning before anyone else in the house was up, five years since I'd begun studying Spanish, and for some reason, I had recalled our neighbor's radio station, the one I used to hear as a teenager in my backyard in San Diego. More particularly, the sing-song voice, that woman's lovely voice, saying things in Spanish I couldn't understand, followed by "Tijuana, Mexico."

An idea appeared in my mind, the way they sometimes do after coffee on a quiet Sunday morning. Now that I knew how to pronounce the Spanish alphabet, could I possibly figure out what I had been hearing? Could I now, all these decades later, understand what that siren-like voice had been saying when I heard "*Dada-da, da, dada-da*, Tijuana, Mexico"?

I decided to search "History of Tijuana radio stations." To my surprise, I found a Wikipedia article—a long one that included a listing of all the stations that have broadcast from Tijuana since the beginning of radio. I scanned the list for a few minutes, waiting for some sort of recognition, but nothing leaped out. I counted out the syllables in her "*Dada-da, da, dada-da*": seven syllables before "Tijuana, Mexico." I narrowed my search to stations with more letters in their names and began sounding them out in Spanish. My eyes set on one longer station name: XETRA.

I sounded out the letters in Spanish: "Equis, eh, te, ere, ah . . . "

In disbelief, I said it again, this time in the sing-song way she did:

"*E-quis-eh, te, e-re-ah, Tijuana, Mexico.*" This was the station. It had to be.

And suddenly I heard her again, the beautiful voice from my youth. What had been just rhythm and melody now had lyrics. It was as if I had been listening to music from outside the concert hall and now, all these years later, a smiling doorman swung open the doors, motioning me inside. With a shiver, I understood. All along it was X E T R A—something *extra* I could have had. Alone that early morning, in front of my computer, I broke down in tears.

Your bilingual life, and America's

XETRA had gone out of business long ago. In its day it had been one of the most famous "Border Blasters." Since it was aimed at the Los Angeles Latino market, 120 miles to the north, it lorded over the AM dial in San Diego where I grew up.

That morning, I had my most emotional revelation among many in my journey of learning Spanish. In my early years of learning, scores of place names I had grown up with in California began to come to life. Mission Viejo revealed itself as Old Mission, Hermosa Beach tantalized as Beautiful Beach, Linda Vista beckoned as Pretty Vista.

It was fun sharing my growing awareness with friends. One night I was having dinner with a friend in Palo Alto at a popular restaurant on one of the main streets in town. He said, "I love this restaurant, but what a strange name, 'Flea Street.'"

"I guess it's because of the street name," I replied. My friend looked at me blankly.

"You know, '*Alameda de las Pulgas*—Grove of the Fleas.'" His face lit up in astonishment and then he broke into roaring laughter. "I've lived in Palo Alto twenty-five years and never knew that!"

My friend spoke Hindi, but clearly not Spanish.

My own bilingualism is a work in progress, or perhaps it's better to say my bilingualism is a life in progress. I no longer fret about not being better than I "should" be after the number of years I've been at it. I just enjoy the daily interaction I have with my adopted language—reading novels, binge-watching series with Lori, texting and emailing with friends. Spanish lives in my life and is giving me the larger life I still thirst for.

My adopted language also took me back to my earlier passion for social science. I hope my adopted language has other places it will take me, including to more conversations with emerging bilinguals of both Spanish and English heritages.

Where will your adopted language take you? Will it be an international career, as it was for Jenny Messner in Brazil and Bill Johnson in China? Or perhaps a life-enriching avocation, such as promoting the art of wine, as it is for David Wolf. Or perhaps you will move to another country and be the beloved American, helping your companions with their English, like Father Demetrios Vasilios, the young American priest in Greece.

Epilogue

My wish for you, dear reader, is that your adopted language will surprise and delight you, be daunting and embracing, and that it will take you beyond your imagination. Can you hear it calling you?

Te deseo un hermoso viaje.
I wish you a beautiful journey.

Appendix I.

SIX TIPS FOR CONVERSATION CORPS PARTNERS

For language learners worldwide, the hardest thing is often just to find a native speaker to have casual conversations with. Good language classes can do wonders; so can using software, watching movies, and reading. But nothing is quite like having an authentic, live conversation with someone who actively listens to you. Not only are such conversations one of the very best ways to learn, they are also one of the chief purposes of learning another language in the first place.

The number of people trying to learn English greatly exceeds the number of native English speakers. That imbalance will almost certainly increase in coming years as English solidifies its role as the global lingua franca. Given that the United States holds the world's largest repository of native English speakers, and probably the world's largest repository of English-dominant bilinguals, we Americans have a great opportunity to help give others something they badly need.

It's more than just an opportunity. Since all of us native English speakers won the language lottery in being born and raised in an English-speaking country, and fully enjoy the benefits of speaking natively the language that so much of the world wants to learn—and that can be so devilishly difficult to learn—our opportunity rises to the level of duty.

For English learners, the stakes are high. Learning English can mean getting a better-paying job, or even a job in the first place. It can mean moving up professionally. For US immigrants still needing to improve their English, it can mean them passing their citizenship test and not being the target of HAMS bias. When you help others become bilingual, you're helping our country continue to strengthen its common language and build its linguistic capital, one emerging bilingual at a time.

Beyond language skills, by having conversations with others with different backgrounds, you gain the deep personal satisfaction of providing to others what we all need—a feeling of belonging, of community, of being heard.

For all of these reasons, it's important to lend a hand, and a voice, and have genuine, casual conversations. And it's why, as part of the America the Bilingual project, we are committed to helping create a Conversation Corps. These tips will get the conversation flowing.

Tip No. 1: Be a learner, too

First, it helps greatly if you are learning their native language. This levels the table, away from teacher-student, and facilitates true conversations among equals. You are learning together, both being vulnerable and child-like, both being helpful and adult-like. It makes conversations more open and candid, and fosters true learning. Even if you're not learning their particular language, if you are an emerging bilingual in another language, you still will be more likely to have empathy for what they are going through.

And if their native language is not your adopted language, learn a few buds of bilingualism. In each session, use a few words and expressions, ask for their feedback on pronunciation or specific meaning (for example, is "fish" both a noun and a verb, the way it is in English?), and have them suggest another word you can learn.

Tip No. 2: Quiet your mind

When listening, try to become comfortable with pauses and delays in the conversation, especially if you see them struggling. Resist the urge to fill in the empty space with helpful suggestions. The pauses you hear are the productive struggle so necessary to learning. With their permission, record a session so you can listen to yourself afterwards. This feedback may help you adjust and polish your listening style.

Tip No. 3: Rarely correct

Don't feel you have to correct everything. It might make them self-conscious and reluctant to keep trying. What you're shooting for is communication.

Can they get their idea across, no matter how grammatically incorrect and oddly phrased? Good! Keep going.

There's a technique called "covert correction," which Barbara Zurer Pearson describes as "a technique of responding to errors not by drawing attention to them but by modeling correct usage within the conversation." Our partner asks, "You do working today?" You respond, "Yes. Did you go to work today?"

Tip No. 4: Use simple, standard English

Use simple phrases, sentences, and vocabulary. Avoid idioms and figures of speech. Instead of "He did a complete one-eighty," you might say, "He changed his mind, completely." Rather than "He worked himself into a lather," say, "He got very excited." As their English improves and your relationship develops, you can introduce some common idioms and slang. Ask them to teach you the same in their language, to keep your empathy meter ticking.

Tip No. 5: Keep sessions short

Using your adopted language can be exhausting. Professional interpreters usually work in just fifteen-minute shifts, so intense is the mental exercise of performing real-time translation in high-stakes professional environments. Simple conversations are not the same, of course, but even so, it's hard mental work. Take a break. Switch between languages if you're in a conversation exchange.

Tip No. 6: Do things together

Sitting and chatting is fine, but it's also mentally taxing, especially at the beginning and low-intermediate skill stages. As the science writer Marek Kohn says, "An hour spent in an uncertain language is like a day spent in one's dominant tongue." For an alternative, do something like cooking or work on a project together. Or take a walk. And as you do, describe in their adopted language—the names of the cooking utensils, the words for birds and trees and sidewalks.

Remember, too, that it's not always about how much talking takes place. Give time for questions to form. Let answers linger. Such activities done well are an example of learning by doing; of not studying a language, but living it.

* * *

Appendix II.

An American Bilingual Honor Code

For an American to become bilingual is an act of patriotism. By becoming bilingual, we honor those who have come before us—those who have used bilingualism to help build America, and also those who sacrificed their heritage languages for the perceived good of their children. These immigrants, living during the fat middle of the twentieth century, suffered from the grandparent tragedy and tolerated HAMS bias. We honor them now by doing what is best for our children today and best for the nation.

It is patriotic to help our fellow Americans with their English, when they need it. It is patriotic to help others around the world practice English, while they help us learn our adopted languages. This kind of patriotism helps America build its soft power. It is right and honorable.

In the fictional future we journeyed to in Part Four, Emma talked about an honor code that American bilinguals followed. If such an honor code existed, it would be a collaborative effort of many people from many perspectives. I hope something like an honor code does come to pass. As a kick-start, I offer this rough draft of what such a code might include.

The American Bilingual Honor Code

First Practice. As a native English speaker, be aware that the world contains many more people who are learning English or speak English as a second language. Since their skills vary dramatically, adjust your speech accordingly. This generally means speaking slowly and clearly and without much idiom. There's nothing like being a language learner yourself to appreciate the importance of this. Give to English learners the encouragement that you want native speakers to give to you with your adopted language.

SECOND PRACTICE. When you hear fellow Americans speaking a language other than English, smile and know that you're hearing American linguistic capital being strengthened. These bilinguals are coming out of the home and speaking their language in public, which is what America needs to encourage. Most likely those people can speak English well and will do so when you engage them in English: "Excuse me, but the language you're speaking sounds beautiful; what is it?"

THIRD PRACTICE. Be sensitive to those around you who want to be part of the conversation, and speak the language all of you have in common.

FOURTH PRACTICE. By being a lifelong language learner with your adopted language, you are supporting a vital industry made up of teachers and tutors, social scientists and scholars, programmers and businesspeople. Your support can continue a virtuous flywheel of growth.

FIFTH PRACTICE. Be understanding toward monolinguals. Few people are happy about being monolinguals, and some may express their unhappiness with anger or hostility. Model the empathy that rides along with bilingualism and, when appropriate, let monolinguals know they, too, can learn another language.

SIXTH PRACTICE. Plant buds of bilingualism. Seldom can so much goodwill blossom from so few words.

SEVENTH PRACTICE. Encourage people to maintain their heritage languages and to pass them on to their children. Bilingualism is the path for building a stronger America, and for preserving languages worldwide.

GLOSSARY

In this glossary we offer three kinds of entries: definitions of established linguistic terms that are good to know (for example, diglossia and calque), somewhat modified definitions of standard terms (accent and monolingual), and wholly new terms that our team at America the Bilingual invented (ear lag and HAMS bias).

The inspiration for the neologisms comes from the many language biographies we've collected, and the guests we've featured on the *America the Bilingual* podcast. We noticed common experiences that many people describe that do not, as far as we know, have a name. So we've invented names for them to provoke thought and invite conversations. Our hope is that some of these terms will help Americans write new narratives, recasting how we think of ourselves in the twenty-first century.

ACCENT Something we all have when we speak, but hearing your own native accent is like seeing the back of your head without a mirror. "An accent is the sound of bravery," says Amy Chua, when speaking of American immigrants. What is described as a "neutral accent" or "no accent" more correctly could be described as a fashionable accent the listener approves of.

ADDITIVE BILINGUALISM When the educational goal is to maintain the heritage language children bring to school, while adding the majority language. This is the goal of dual language schools, in contrast to **subtractive bilingualism.**

ADOPTED LANGUAGE Our term for the language, in addition to our native language, that we commit to learning for the rest of our lives. Like your native language, your adopted language is a lifelong companion, teacher, and tool to learn with.

AMERICAN BILINGUAL HONOR CODE Our term for a developing set of codes and practices designed to foster the growth of **linguistic capital** in America and in the larger world. See Appendix II for the seven practices we put forth.

AMERICAN BILINGUALS The world's largest group of English-dominant bilinguals. Roughly two-thirds Spanish speakers, they also comprise large populations of the world's other languages. American bilinguals are well positioned to serve as informal translators and interpreters into English, as well as conversation partners for the billions of people learning English as a second language.

AMERICAN LANGUAGES Any—and every—language that an American speaks. English is the language that unites Americans. Bilingualism is what encourages people from many cultures to pursue their happiness as Americans.

Bilingualism is a gift that contributes to the pursuit of happiness for speakers of Cherokee, Navajo, and other first languages; for speakers of Dutch, German, Spanish, French, and other founding languages; for speakers of Greek, Polish, Chinese, Arabic, Turkish, Swedish, and other furthering languages. American languages belong not just to those who speak them; they are part of our country's shared history and resources.

ASSIMILATION The characteristic goal for immigrants and some Indigenous people in twentieth-century America. This assimilation hewed to a melting pot approach that had societal and personal benefits, when done in moderation and with the consent of the melted. This century has seen a shift away from assimilation toward **integration**.

BALANCED BILINGUAL A mostly fictitious concept, as it is nearly impossible for each language a person possesses to occupy an equivalent mental and emotional space. See **complementarity principle**.

BILINGUAL We adopt the definition of the psycholinguist François Grosjean: one who uses two or more languages, or dialects, in one's daily life. Actual daily use is a higher bar than merely having some competency in a language. Most scholars like Grosjean have elected to stretch the word bilingual to mean speaking two *or more* languages. It's more workable than trying to be specific about how many languages someone speaks—trilingual, quadrilingual, multilingual or plurilingual, for example.

BILINGUAL BREAKTHROUGH Our term for the observation among many language teachers and scholars of bilingualism that a leap in understanding happens when an adult becomes bilingual. Being bilingual brings a basketful of cognitive and social benefits, including a growth in empathy. Becoming bilingual brings a new appreciation of your native language, as you can finally see it with the lamp of another. Our two eyes give us visual depth perception; our two languages give us emotional depth perception.

BILINGUAL CENTURY What our present century may well be called, as bilingualism will most likely accelerate significantly. The trends driving this are urbanization, the increasing appeal of English as a universal second language, and increasing elective bilingualism by native English speakers. It is a sad irony that this is also the century when the world is projected to lose thousands of its small languages.

BILITERACY The ability to read and write in two or more languages as well as speak them. The Seal of Biliteracy factors in these additional skills.

BIRTH BILINGUALS Our term for those fortunate enough to be raised from the very beginning in two or more languages. They are given the gift rather than having to earn it. If they don't learn another language as an adult, they may have a hard time relating to the struggles, and also the joys, that adult language learners encounter. Birth bilingualism is also called compound bilingualism or infant bilingualism. Learning a second language later in life is sometimes called consecutive, coordinate, or successive bilingualism.

BUDS OF BILINGUALISM Our term for the practice of saying a few words and expressions in a new language. It's a time-honored practice for showing respect and being polite. The rewards can be many.

CALQUE Copying a word or phrase from one language into another where it didn't exist or is rare in that form (pronounced *calc*, as in *talc*). For example, in English we say "sooner or later." If we translate that literally to Spanish, it would be *temprano o tarde*. But if we say that, even though native Spanish speakers will understand us, they will also know that we are neophyte Spanish speakers. In Spanish, one says *tarde o temprano*, "later or sooner." One of the delights of learning a language is to speak in calques and have native speakers smile and offer a more idiomatic way of saying what we meant to say.

CODE SWITCHING What linguists call changing from one language to another within one sentence or conversation. It is a natural and useful phenomenon among bilinguals, although it is often denigrated by both those who hear it and those who engage in it.

COMMUNICATIVE LANGUAGE TEACHING The newer way language classes are taught today, with an emphasis on having students acquire practical language skills by using the language, as opposed to studying grammar and learning about the language.

COMPLEMENTARITY PRINCIPLE François Grosjean's term for the way that bilinguals usually acquire and use their languages for different purposes, in different realms, and with different people. Stated another way, an adopted language must have a place where it lives in your life.

COMPREHENSIBLE INPUT What the language learning scholar Stephen Krashen has called the real fuel for language learning. He later updated his concept to compelling comprehensible input, or CCI, with the judgment of what is compelling being left to the language learner. CCI is what learners choose for their **free voluntary reading**.

CONVERSATION PARTNERS Language learners can benefit greatly from having relaxed conversations with native speakers, yet often such informal conversations are the most difficult thing to find. A variety of organizations in America and internationally are working to increase the availability of such conversation partners. We at America the Bilingual are also proposing a program called the Conversation Corps (see Appendix I).

DIALECT Commonly considered a lower form of a language, like an unfortunate family member who isn't quite right in the head, but in reality the only difference between what is considered a dialect versus a language is political power. The linguist Max Weinreich summed it up with his quip, "A language is a dialect that has an army and navy."

DIGLOSSIA We like the definition provided by the linguist Charles A. Ferguson in *Language in the USA*: "A language situation in which two very different varieties of a language are functionally complementary, one (H, the 'high' variety) being used for written and formal spoken purposes, the other (L, the 'low' variety) for ordinary conversation." Examples include Classical

Arabic and Colloquial Arabic, High German and Swiss German, Standard English and Black English.

DOROTHY MOMENT Our term to describe that moment during language immersion when suddenly, everything seems to make sense. It comes from the moment in *The Wizard of Oz* when Dorothy steps out of her black-and-white world and enters the colorful world of Oz. Many people report such a feeling after some weeks or months of language immersion.

DRILL AND KILL An expression language teachers use to describe the old and misguided way languages were taught, with students drilled in, for example, verb conjugations.

DUAL LANGUAGE EDUCATION Teaching in two languages, sometimes called dual language immersion. It is common in much of the world and growing in popularity in the US for the good reason that it generally works well. American students test higher in English than their counterparts in monolingual English schools, plus they pick up fluency in a second language.

EAR LAG Our term for the dismay that comes when an emerging bilingual visits a country where her adopted language is spoken and finds that she can't understand anything. It happens because the way people actually speak is always different from textbook language, or the standard dialect that is taught. Like jet lag, ear lag will dissipate as you tune in to the local dialect and learn common expressions—in other words, once you adjust to the local sound zone.

ELECTIVE BILINGUAL Someone who chooses to learn a second language rather than feeling forced to by their situation (for that, see **situational bilingualism**). An elective bilingual is often a speaker of the majority language who elects to learn a minority language.

EMERGENT BILINGUAL Language scholar Ofelia García's redefinition of English Language Learners. It switches the perspective from language-as-problem (they need to learn English) to language-as-resource (they need to add English to their language skills). Rejecting the old practice of **subtractive bilingualism**, this term affirms the higher goal of becoming bilingual and biliterate.

EXPAT TRAP The tempting practice of expatriates to spend their time with one another, speaking their common language, rather than getting to know the locals and speaking their language.

FLOWERS OF FLUENCY Our term to describe well-developed language skills—for example, at the end of a study abroad experience or a Peace Corps assignment, when language skills reach a peak but then decline in subsequent years through disuse. While this may be viewed as regrettable by the speaker and others, such flowerings of fluency can nevertheless bring about memorable life experiences, and they can be revived later as need or desire dictates, including into becoming an **adopted language**.

FOREIGN LANGUAGES Just as accent is relative, what constitutes foreign is also relative. English is a foreign language in most of the world. Mandarin might be considered a foreign language in America, except for the fact that more than three million Americans speak it. In that respect, it is an American language. As the Dartmouth language professor John Rassias used to say, "A language stops being foreign when you begin speaking it." The term **world languages** has been widely adopted among language teachers to replace the term foreign languages.

FREE VOLUNTARY READING Advocated by Stephen Krashen as one of the very best things language learners can do. Teachers can help by providing the time and reading material from which learners can choose. If you are learning on your own, seeking out reading materials in your adopted language that interest you is the ticket to success.

GRANDPARENT MYTH The belief that, unlike today's immigrants, our grandparents worked harder to learn English and did so without any coddling. In contrast, the myth goes, today's immigrants expect to be able to continue using their native languages and may not even want to learn English. Thanks to the heritage language professor Kim Potowski for naming this stubborn American myth, which has been with us for at least two centuries.

GRANDPARENT TRAGEDY Our term for when grandparents can't communicate in their native language with their grandchildren, and both generations lose out as a result. It is a consequence of **language shift**, and what heritage language instruction is designed to cure. The sadness is magnified when grandchildren fall victims to **HAMS bias** due to their grandparents' heavily accented English.

HAMS BIAS (HEAVY-ACCENT-MEANS-STUPID BIAS) Our term to describe the common inclination, when we hear someone lacking proficiency in our language, to conclude that the speaker isn't the brightest bulb in the chandelier. Even when we are aware of this bias, it's hard not to fall victim to it. Just as we shouldn't judge a book by its cover, we shouldn't judge a mind by its voice.

HERITAGE LANGUAGE CLASSES Classes designed for students who have had some exposure to the language at home. This kind of teaching recognizes unique strengths and weaknesses of heritage speakers. When they receive education tailored to their needs as opposed to conventional language classes, heritage students can often excel, quickly developing more confidence and competence in their heritage language. The result can be a reversal in language shift and an increase in America's **linguistic capital**.

IMMERSION SCHOOLS Commonly used to describe schools that teach in a language other than the majority language of a country—for example, a French immersion school in the United States.

INTEGRATION In a demographic context, the characteristic goal for immigrants and Indigenous peoples in twenty-first-century America. Allowing individuals to honor their heritages, including speaking their languages as bilinguals, strengthens our nation. English unites us; our other American languages, through bilingualism, strengthen us. It's important to note that this integration is not multiculturalism, in which minority groups are isolated from the larger society, denying the benefits of integration on both sides. Integration is characterized by individuals getting to know one another, social harmony, flourishing bilingualism, and the growth of **linguistic capital**.

L2 A term language scholars and teachers use to describe students learning a second language.

LANGUAGE BIOGRAPHY A narrative timeline or memoir focusing on the languages a person has learned and the ways he or she has used them.

LANGUAGE EXCHANGE (LX) Conversations among two people who wish to learn one another's languages. Also known as practice partners or conversation partners, such exchanges tend to connect people as equals (as opposed to teacher-student dynamics) and can also lead to reducing Us/Them-ing as participants get to know one another.

LANGUAGE INSIDER/OUTSIDER Also known as language ingroups/outgroups. We humans are exquisitely skilled at discriminating, and we use our powers of discrimination to create Us versus Them groups based on all kinds of factors, including age, appearance, religion, politics, favorite sports teams, and, of course, language. This includes not only the language that people speak but also their particular dialects and accents.

When any of us are suddenly thrust into the position of language outsider—for instance, being in an elevator with a bunch of Thems speaking loudly in a language we don't understand—it can be extremely uncomfortable, as we experience an unbidden and unwanted loss of competence. Such situations can prompt hurt feelings, paranoia (*Are they making fun of me?*), and even **language vigilantism**.

LANGUAGE MAINTENANCE When a language is holding its own despite the influence of one or more powerful language neighbors.

LANGUAGE NESTS Groups of speakers who come together to revitalize an endangered language. In Hawaii, for example, a community creates small groups of elders who speak with young people in the native Hawaiian tongue.

LANGUAGE PLEDGE® A trademark of The Middlebury Language Schools, whereby pledge takers agree to converse only in the language they're learning. (Some other language immersion programs have comparable policies.) Thirsty language learners all over the world in many different situations also impose this rule on themselves.

LANGUAGE REVITALIZATION What the sociolinguist Joshua Fishman called reverse language shift (RLS), when a minority language is brought back into use among younger generations through bilingualism, thus granting them the skills to negotiate better paths between tradition and modernity.

LANGUAGE SERVICE PROVIDER (LSP) Companies that provide translation, interpretation, localization, and other language-related services, including cultural consulting.

LANGUAGE SHIFT Another coinage of Joshua Fishman's, the term signifies language loss in a population. It happens when subsequent generations lose their heritage language. Shift is accelerated by societies intolerant of bilingualism (America during much of the twentieth century) and decelerated by societies supportive of bilingualism (many parts of America today). The inverse is **language revitalization.**

LANGUAGE VIGILANTISM A public attack, usually verbal, expressed in the majority language against those found speaking a minority language. Outbreaks occur around the world, sometimes as a result of people unexpectedly feeling like a **language outsider**. Although outbreaks have been fatal, including lynchings in the US, normally they are merely annoying, and stem from ignorance and fear.

LANGUAGES OTHER THAN ENGLISH (LOTE) A handy shorthand when discussing languages in the US and other English-dominant countries. In Australia, the term is CLOTE, for community languages other than English.

LESS COMMONLY TAUGHT LANGUAGES (LCTL) Languages most schools don't teach but that remain vital both for the heritage speakers and for America's **linguistic capital.**

LINGUISTIC CAPITAL A part of human capital constituting the aggregate language skills of bilinguals in a country or some other geography. In the case of America, it is the combined value of bilinguals who speak English and at least one other language. The country benefits from improved understanding and communication with the rest of the world.

LIVE THE LANGUAGE A key branding message of Concordia Language Villages. A powerful concept, it focuses on the wondrous experience that ensues when merely studying a language gives way to living it.

ML@H Minority language at home. The common practice of a family speaking a heritage language at home, insulating its role from the majority language spoken outside the home.

MONOLINGUAL A linguistically disadvantaged person who speaks only one language. Monolinguals are a shrinking minority of humans worldwide.

NO CHILD LEFT MONOLINGUAL An expression that Kim Potowski popularized. Its power comes from the growing recognition among parents and educators that we have a responsibility to our children to prevent or alleviate monolingualism.

ONE PERSON, ONE LANGUAGE (OPOL) A popular practice for raising bilingual children in which each parent consistently speaks a different language to the children.

PASSIVE BILINGUAL Also called a receptive bilingual, a person who can understand a language when spoken, but can't or won't speak it themselves. This was common for the descendants of immigrants in twentieth-century America, but is becoming less so as interest in bilingualism grows.

PRODUCTIVE STRUGGLE A common and beneficial experience when learning a language. While it can be tempting to avoid it, struggling can sometimes produce the best results. Good teachers and conversation partners learn to be okay with silence and won't immediately help their students, who learn to relish the "wait, wait, don't tell me" moments when they are groping for the right word or phrase in their new language. Combined with an error-friendly environment, productive struggle can be a catalyst for growing linguistic skill.

PROFICIENCY-BASED LANGUAGE LEARNING The newer type of language learning, where students use their emerging skills to actually do things in the language, such as shop in a store or have a conversation about current events. This approach can be measured in listening, speaking, reading, and writing tests. It stands in contrast to older teaching methods that relied on grammar as the central focus. The idea is that students acquire *useful* skills, giving them more motivation to build upon them.

RASSIAS METHOD A language learning method that Dartmouth professor John Rassias created. It emphasizes theatrics, fast-paced drills, and high levels of commitment by both teacher and student.

SITUATIONAL BILINGUALISM A scenario where people—most commonly immigrants—are pressured to learn a second language due to their circumstances. (In contrast, see **elective bilingual**.)

SUBTRACTIVE BILINGUALISM What typically passed as "bilingual education" in the twentieth century in America. Children were taught in their heritage language during a transition period, with the goal of getting them up to speed with their English-speaking peers as quickly as possible. They were then mainstreamed into the standard monolingual English track. Contrast this with **additive bilingualism**, which teaches in the heritage language and English with the goal of producing bilingual, biliterate students. (See also **dual language education**.)

WORLD LANGUAGES The preferred term among language teachers as opposed to **foreign languages**. See also **American languages**, which are the world languages that Americans speak.

* * *

NOTES

Chapter 1. Not Just How, but Where

4 *Unless a language has someplace it's used ...it will lose out to the dominant language.* The psycholinguist François Grosjean calls this the complementarity principle. He explains that "bilinguals usually acquire and use their languages for different purposes, in different domains of life, with different people." François Grosjean, *A Journey in Languages & Cultures: The Life of a Bicultural Bilingual* (Oxford: Oxford University Press, 2019), 37.

4 *Even though people speak two languages, one will be dominant...and the other will be used elsewhere.* Other scholars of bilingualism also describe this concept. This is from the textbook that Guadalupe Valdés assigns her students: "while bilinguals certainly do speak two languages and may sound native-like in both, it is rare to find an individual who does not have one language which is more dominant than the other, particularly in functional terms." Ng Bee Chin and Gillian Wigglesworth, *Bilingualism: An Advanced Resource Book* (Abingdon, UK: Routledge, 2007), 45. See also John Edwards, *Sociolinguistics: A Very Short Introduction* (Oxford: Oxford University Press, 2013), 81; François Grosjean, *Bilingual: Life and Reality* (Cambridge, MA: Harvard University Press, 2010), 29; and Suzanne Romaine, "Language Contact in the USA," in *Language Diversity in the USA*, ed. Kim Potowski (Cambridge: Cambridge University Press, 2010), 29.

5 *One continues to live his French through his avocation.* David Wolf, "With a Little Help from His Friends and Good French Wine," *America the Bilingual* (podcast), Episode 2, 2017, https://www.americathebilingual.com/2-with-a-little -help-from-his-friends-and-good-french-wine/.

5 *Another lives her Spanish by teaching English as a second language to Latinos.* Julie Reis (ESL teacher), in discussion with the author, March 2016.

5 *Another keeps her Greek alive by being involved in her church.* "Just Call Me Ana," *America the Bilingual* (podcast), Episode 3, 2017, https://www.americathebilingual .com/3-just-call-me-anna/.

Chapter 2. Adopting a Language

6 *the term we use is buds of bilingualism.* "Buds of Bilingualism," *America the Bilingual* (podcast), Episode 43, 2019, https://www.americathebilingual .com/43-buds-of-bilingualism/.

6 *"I see you as a human being."* Trevor Noah, *Born a Crime: Stories from a South African Childhood* (New York: Spiegel & Grau, 2016), 236.

7 *Translators are hired to translate...documents. They also translate literature.* David Bellos, *Is That a Fish in Your Ear? Translation and the Meaning of Everything* (New York: Faber and Faber, 2011).

7 *simultaneous interpreters...generally work in teams of two and spell one another.* Kato Lomb, *Polyglot: How I Learn Languages* (Berkeley, CA: TESL-EJ Publications, 1995), 190.

7 *It's important to note that even these professional bilinguals generally translate or interpret into their native language.* Alane Salierno Mason (the founder of *Words Without Borders*, a magazine that translates works from authors' native language to English), in email discussion with the author, May 2020.

7 *"A bilingual is someone who uses two or more languages (or dialects) in their daily life."* Grosjean, *Bilingual*, 4.

7 *For much of the twentieth century in America, language teaching in college focused on reading.* Elizabeth B. Bernhardt, "Sociohistorical Perspectives on Language Teaching in the Modern United States," in *Learning Foreign and Second Languages*, ed. Heidi Byrnes (New York: The Modern Language Association of America, 1998), 39ff.

8 *She speaks her heritage language of Farsi well...but cannot read it.* "Little Ketchup Girl," *America the Bilingual* (podcast), Episode 6, 2017, https://www.americathe bilingual.com/6-little-ketchup-girl/.

8 *Historically, most languages...were first spoken.* Walter J. Ong, *Orality and Literacy: The Technologizing of the Word* (New York: Routledge, 2002), 7.

8 *of the approximately seven thousand languages remaining in the world, most are only oral.* "How many languages in the world are unwritten?" Ethnologue: Languages of the World, https://www.ethnologue.com/enterprise-faq/how-many -languages-world-are-unwritten-0.

8 *ACTFL recommends that K-12 teachers achieve at least the "advanced low" level of proficiency.* ACTFL, "Oral Proficiency Levels in the Workplace," https://www .actfl.org/sites/default/files/pdfs/TLE_pdf/OralProficiencyWorkplacePoster.pdf.

9 *Michael Erard writes about his* **flowering in Spanish and Chinese.** Michael Erard, *Babel No More: The Search for the World's Most Extraordinary Language Learners* (New York: Free Press, 2012), 21.

9 *Lorna Auerbach...had her first flowering of fluency when she went to Israel.* Lorna Auerbach (bilingual executive), in discussion with the author, June 2016.

10 *marrying someone who speaks the same language is akin to incest.* Stephen R. Anderson, *Languages: A Very Short Introduction* (Oxford: Oxford University Press, 2012), 55; Jared Diamond, *The World Until Yesterday: What Can We Learn from Traditional Societies?* (New York: Viking, 2012), 384ff.

10 *growth mindset.* Carol S. Dweck, *Mindset: The New Psychology of Success* (New York: Ballantine Books, 2016), 7.

10 *learning throughout one's life is supportive of improved cognition and over-all health.* Laura L. Carstensen, *A Long Bright Future: Happiness, Health, and Financial Security in an Age of Increased Longevity* (New York: PublicAffairs, 2011).

Chapter 3. Learn French in Thirty Years!

11 *candidates are required to be..."general professional" proficiency level.* Depart-ment of State, "Foreign Language Proficiency Has Improved, but Efforts to Reduce Gaps Need Evaluation," General Accountability Office Report to General Requestors (March 2017), GAO-17-318, https://www.gao.gov/assets/690/683533.pdf.

11 *it takes about twenty-four weeks...of training to get a new speaker to level 3 in French.* For a data visualization of the time estimated by the Foreign Service Institute to learn languages of varying difficulty level, see Nick Routley, "Map: Language Difficulty Ranking for English Speakers," Visual Capitalist, December 15, 2017, https://www.visualcapitalist.com/language-difficulty-map/.

12 *Both John Adams and Benjamin Franklin labored diligently at their French.* Stacy Schiff, *A Great Improvisation: Franklin, France, and the Birth of America* (New York: Henry Holt and Co., 2005), 188ff.

12 *"Your job is to study full time for nine months."* State Department Foreign Service Officer in discussion with the author, December 2012.

12 *it takes many hundreds to several thousands of hours of intense study to be able to use a language professionally.* Paul Pimsleur, *How to Learn a Foreign Language* (New York: Pimsleur Language Programs, 2013), 15; Nina Garrett, "What Does It Take to Learn a Language Well?" in *The 5-Minute Linguist: Bite-sized Essays on Language and Languages*, ed. E.M. Rickerson and Barry Hilton, 2nd ed. (Sheffield, UK: Equinox Publishing Ltd., 2006), 144ff. Victoria Nuland, a former assistant secretary of state, came to the Foreign Service Institute with what she called "college Russian." In nine months of studying under Boris V. Shekhtman, she achieved "professional fluency." Sam Roberts, "Boris V. Shekhtman, Creative Russian Teacher, Dies at 77," *The New York Times*, March 27, 2017, https://www.nytimes.com/2017/03/24/world/boris-v-shekhtman-who-taught-russian-to-journalists-and-diplomats-dies-at-77.html.

12 *"The child takes some 14,500 hours or more by age six to master the basics."* Bill VanPatten, *While We're on the Topic: BVP on Language, Acquisition, and Classroom*

Practice (Alexandria, VA: The American Council on the Teaching of Foreign Languages, 2017), 98.

12 *"native and non-native learners both require around 30 years to reach asymptotic performance."* Joshua K. Hartshorne, Joshua B. Tenenbaum, and Steven Pinker, "A Critical Period for Second Language Acquisition: Evidence From ⅔ Million English Speakers," *Cognition* 177 (August 2018): 263-77, https://doi .org/10.1016/j.cognition.2018.04.007.

13 *playing a musical instrument at a professional level takes...similar amounts of time.* Gene Pokorny (Chicago Symphony Orchestra tubist), in discussion with the author, December 2014. Besides the tens of thousands of hours Gene put in before joining the CSO, he continues to practice several hours each day, which he says is pretty typical for his colleagues.

13 *the "planning fallacy."* Richard H. Thaler and Cass R. Sunstein, *Nudge: Improving Decisions About Health, Wealth, and Happiness* (New York: Penguin, 2009), 7. "Planning fallacy" was coined by Amos Tversky and Daniel Kahneman. See Daniel Kahneman, *Thinking, Fast and Slow* (New York: Farrar, Straus and Giroux, 2011), 249ff.

15 *"Wicked smart" is a compliment.* Mim Harrison, *Wicked Good Words: From Johnnycakes to Jug Handles, a Roundup of America's Regionalisms* (New York: Perigee, 2011), 4-5, 19-20, 67.

16 *It's not which one method is best, it's more like "all of the above."* Pimsleur, *How to Learn a Foreign Language,* and Pimsleur audio courses, available on Audible and elsewhere; Michel Thomas audio programs, available on Audible; Steve Kaufmann, *The Way of the Linguist: A Language Learning Odyssey* (Bloomington, IN: Author House, 2005), and https://www.thelinguist.com/; Tim Ferriss, "How to Learn Any Language in Record Time and Never Forget It," *The Tim Ferriss Show* (blog), July 16, 2014, https://tim.blog/2014/07/16/how-to-learn-any-language-in -record-time-and-never-forget-it/; Gabriel Wyner, *Fluent Forever: How to Learn Any Language* Fast *and Never Forget It* (New York: Harmony Books, 2014), and https://fluent-forever.com/.

17 *"there is no single correct method for teaching or learning a second language and... the search for one is probably misguided."* Ellen Bialystok and Kenji Hakuta, *In Other Words: The Science and Psychology of Second-Language Acquisition* (New York: Basic Books, 1994), 209.

18 *words are more meaningful and relevant when used together.* Pimsleur, *How to Learn a Language,* 74; Wyner, *Fluent Forever,* 183ff.

18 *our kinesthetic faculties...help our minds learn.* Alan Hodge (professor and ergonomist, Cornell University), in discussion with the author, November 2004. Hodge explained that studies have shown that when we write numbers down, we can remember them better than when we merely type them: we're taking advantage of our whole body to help our mind learn. See also Steve Leveen and Mim Harrison, "Does Hand-Writing Matter?" *Well-Read Life* (blog), February

6, 2013, https://blog.wellreadlife.com/my_weblog/2013/02/does-hand-writing
-matter.html?cid=6a00e54f8eed218833017ee8693b92970d.

18 *"saying I am going to 'study' French was like saying I am going to sail to China."*
Ta-Nehisi Coates, in *Life Doesn't Come with Subtitles: The Middlebury Language
Schools at 100*, ed. David Stameshkin, Caroline Eisner, Elizabeth Karnes Keefe,
and Michael E. Geisler (Middlebury, VT: Middlebury Language Schools, 2015),
dust jacket panel.

Chapter 4. Not the Language Class
You May Remember

19 *"Ninety-eight percent of students who take language classes are bored to death."*
Presentation by Stephen D. Krashen at the American Council on the Teaching of
Foreign Languages (ACTFL) 2016 Annual Convention and World Languages
Expo, Boston, MA, November 2016.

20 *"The profession has, in my view, backed the wrong horse."* Stephen D. Krashen,
Explorations in Language Acquisition and Use (Portsmouth, NH: Heinemann,
2003), 84.

20 *what's needed is "comprehensible input."* Krashen, 7.

20 *"Demands for output are low."* Krashen, 8.

20 *"The public has assumed that some things must first be 'learned.'"* Krashen, 85.

20 *"There is no need for delayed gratification."* Krashen, 85.

21 *"what's on page 32 of the textbook is not what winds up in anyone's head."*
VanPatten, *While We're on the Topic*, 98.

22 *"One learns grammar from language, not language from grammar."* Kato Lomb,
Harmony of Babel: Profiles of Famous Polyglots of Europe, 2nd ed. (Berkeley, CA:
TESL-EJ Publications, 2018), 241.

22 *"Grammar is best learned by using it, not by talking about it."* Pimsleur, *How to
Learn a Foreign Language*, 35.

Chapter 5. Stay Thirsty, My Friends

23 *language learners "must pull the language into themselves."* This concept is consistent with what Stephen Krashen describes as "acquired" language, which you
draw into yourself by means of comprehensible input. Krashen, *Explorations in
Language Acquisition and Use*, 1.

23 *"Take charge of your own learning."* Pimsleur, *How to Learn a Foreign Language*,
43, 62.

23 *"Success depends not on the teacher, but on the learner."* Kaufmann, *The Way of
the Linguist*, 42.

24 *the "complete surrender" to wanting to learn.* Jack Roepers (polyglot), in discussion
with the author, November 2018. All quotes by him are from this discussion. Hear

some of the conversation in "American Outliers," *America the Bilingual* (podcast), Episode 8, 2017, https://www.americathebilingual.com/8-american-outliers/.

26 *a test case for...a growth mindset.* Dweck, *Mindset.*

26 *how to develop positive habits and strengthen the self-control.* See Charles Duhigg, *The Power of Habit: Why We Do What We Do in Life and Business* (New York: Random House, 2012), and Kelly McGonigal, *The Willpower Instinct: How Self-Control Works, Why It Matters, and What You Can Do to Get More of It* (New York: Avery, 2012).

Chapter 6. Immersion at Your Fingertips

31 *"I'm getting chills just thinking about it!"* Chris Nichols (Greek American), in discussion with the author, November 2013.

31 *"with a sublime disregard for national borders."* Marek Kohn, *Four Words for Friend: Why Using More Than One Language Matters Now More Than Ever* (New Haven, CT: Yale University Press, 2019), 80.

32 *"listen to music in your target language."* Frances Mecartty (Spanish teacher), in discussion with the author, ACTFL 2018 Annual Convention and World Languages Expo, New Orleans, LA, November 2018.

Chapter 7. When Guilty Reads Become Best Reads

34 *I was in book love.* Steve Leveen, *The Little Guide to Your Well-Read Life: How to Get More Books in Your Life and More Life from Your Books* (Delray Beach, FL: Levenger Press, 2005).

34 *"Free voluntary reading may be the most powerful tool we have."* Krashen, *Explorations in Language Acquisition and Use*, 15.

34 *"making the transition from the elementary level to authentic language use."* Krashen, 15.

35 *"When input is compelling, all anxiety disappears."* Stephen D. Krashen, Sy-Ying Lee, and Christy Lao, *Comprehensible and Compelling: The Causes and Effects of Free Voluntary Reading* (Santa Barbara, CA: Libraries Unlimited, 2018), vii.

35 *"The concept of compelling comprehensible input may be one of the most crucial in all of education."* Krashen et al., vii, 87.

35 *"Enjoyment appears at the boundary between boredom and anxiety."* Mihaly Csikszentmihalyi, *Flow: The Psychology of Optimal Experience* (New York: Harper & Row, 1990), 52.

35 *"My advice to learners can thus be expressed in one word: read!"* Lomb, *Polyglot*, 149.

35 *"We let students choose whatever book, in whatever language, they wish."* Keith Bookwalter (principal, Los Robles dual language school in East Palo Alto, CA), in discussion with the author, November 2016.

36 *"A personal exchange of views…will often leave a more lasting mark in our memory than what is in books."* Lomb, *Polyglot*, 64.

36 *classes…"keep you on a schedule and keep you moving."* Lomb, 69.

36 *the heart of learning for Lomb was reading books, which she described as "linguistic microclimates."* Lomb, 77.

37 *"If fortune set the individual among the literate, that was a golden gift."* William V. Harris, *Ancient Literacy* (Cambridge, MA: Harvard University Press, 1989), 337.

37 *"Although the flow experience appears to be effortless, it is far from being so."* Csikszentmihalyi, *Flow*, 54.

Chapter 8. The New Magic of Movies

39 *Movies you love with subtitles in your adopted language can provide the jet fuel that Krashen calls "compelling, comprehensible input."* Krashen et al., *Comprehensible and Compelling*, 83ff.

Chapter 9. The Power of Vulnerability

42 *being vulnerable and showing it is actually a secret power.* Brené Brown, "The Power of Vulnerability," filmed June 2010 in Houston, TX, TEDx video, 20:19, https://www.ted.com/talks/brene_brown_the_power_of_vulnerability.

42 *"Adults are so used to getting things right."* Effie Evans Hall (language teacher), in "Top Tips from Teachers for Adult Language Learners," *America the Bilingual* (podcast), Episode 45, 2019, https://www.americathebilingual.com/45-top -tips-from-teachers-for-adult-language-learners/ and the accompanying PDF download, "Top Tips from Language Teachers on Learning a Language When You're Older," https://attachments.convertkitcdnn.com/116297/ce0a756f -eb09-4885-be80-cecfe7eb7bbd/Top%20Tips%20from%20Language%20 Teachers.pdf.

42 *"they were always* so *concerned about whether or not they sounded right."* Lesley Chapman (language teacher), in "Top Tips from Teachers" (podcast and PDF), https://www.americathebilingual.com/45-top-tips-from-teachers-for-adult -language-learners/ and https://attachments.convertkitcdnn.com/116297 /ce0a756f-eb09-4885-be80-cecfe7eb7bbd/Top%20Tips%20from%20 Language%20Teachers.pdf.

43 *"The most important thing is that people understand you."* Aviva Kadosh (language teacher), in "Top Tips from Teachers" (podcast and PDF), https://www .americathebilingual.com/45-top-tips-from-teachers-for-adult-language -learners/ and https://attachments.convertkitcdnn.com/116297/ce0a756f -eb09-4885-be80-cecfe7eb7bbd/Top%20Tips%20from%20Language%20 Teachers.pdf.

43 *"You don't have to operate at a fluent level to just connect with someone."* Amelia Richter (language teacher), in "Top Tips from Teachers" (podcast and PDF), https://www.americathebilingual.com/45-top-tips-from-teachers-for-adult-language-learners/ and https://attachments.convertkitcdnn.com/116297/ce0a756f-eb09-4885-be80-cecfe7eb7bbd/Top%20Tips%20from%20Language%20Teachers.pdf.

43 *"Don't be shy."* Kashika Singh (language teacher), in "Top Tips from Teachers" (podcast and PDF), https://www.americathebilingual.com/45-top-tips-from-teachers-for-adult-language-learners/ and https://attachments.convertkitcdnn.com/116297/ce0a756f-eb09-4885-be80-cecfe7eb7bbd/Top%20Tips%20from%20Language%20Teachers.pdf.

43 *When I got the chance to hear Brené Brown in person.* Brené Brown, "The Power of Vulnerability" (speech, Conscious Capitalism CEO Summit, 2016).

43 *"I am a person who has traveled a great deal."* Joan Salwen (social entrepreneur), in discussion with the author, February 2018.

46 *vulnerability is "the cradle of the emotions and experiences that we crave."* Brené Brown, *Daring Greatly: How the Courage to Be Vulnerable Transforms the Way We Live, Love, Parent, and Lead* (New York: Avery, 2012), 34.

46 *"I made the mistake of calling it very boring food."* Tim Page (dean of operations at Middlebury Language Schools), in discussion with the author, July 2018.

47 *Duolingo...amassed a worldwide user base.* "Alphabet-backed Duolingo becomes first VC-funded $1 billion Pittsburgh tech start-up," CNBC, December 4, 2019, https://www.cnbc.com/2019/12/03/google-funded-duolingo-first-1-billion-start-up-from-pittsburgh.html.

47 *"There are two types of people: those who don't care about sounding stupid and those who do."* Luis von Ahn (founder of Duolingo), in telephone discussion with the author, February 2016.

48 *"our willingness to own and engage with our vulnerability determines the depth of our courage."* Brown, *Daring Greatly*, 2.

48 *"Vulnerability is the core, the heart, the center, of meaningful human experiences."* Brown, 12.

48 *"If we want greater clarity in our purpose...vulnerability is the path."* Brown, 34.

Chapter 10. What's Love Got to Do with It?

49 *"You're only one romance away from fluency."* David Wolf (who studied at a French business school), in discussion with the author, February 2017. Hear some of the conversation in "With a Little Help from His Friends and Good French Wine," https://www.americathebilingual.com/2-with-a-little-help-from-his-friends-and-good-french-wine/.

50 *"He lives on through thousands of people."* Tamara Smith (instructor at the Rassias Center), in discussion with the author, July 2018. Hear some of the

conversation in "A Tidal Wave of Love: The John Rassias Legacy," *America the Bilingual* (podcast), Episode 36, 2019, https://www.americathebilingual .com/a-tidal-wave-of-love-the-john-rassias-legacy/.

50 *"It's like a bubble of joy."* Luc Tardif (director of the French immersion program at Université Sainte-Anne), in discussion with the author, August 2018. Hear some of the conversation in "French Immersion at Université Sainte-Anne: A Bubble of Joy," *America the Bilingual* (podcast), Episode 41, 2019, https://www.americathebilingual.com/41-french-immersion-at-universite -sainte-anne-a-bubble-of-joy/.

Chapter 11. The Grande Dame of Language Camps

53 *Stroebe was born in Germany in 1875 and earned her PhD from Heidelberg.* Gisela Hoecherl-Alden, "Female Immigrant Intellectuals in Germanics: From Invisibility to 'Women in German,'" in *Teaching German in Twentieth-Century America*, ed. David P. Benseler, Craig W. Nickisch, and Cora Lee Nollendorfs (Madison, WI: University of Wisconsin Press, 2001), 109.

53 *Stroebe asked what would become a beautiful question: How could we simulate a summer trip to Europe right here in America?* It was the kind of beautiful question that the author Warren Berger studies and celebrates in his *A More Beautiful Question: The Power of Inquiry to Spark Breakthrough Ideas* (New York: Bloomsbury USA, 2014).

53 *"it therefore becomes the duty of colleges and universities to offer in this country."* Stameshkin et al., *Life Doesn't Come with Subtitles*, 13.

54 *It was, she wrote, "the first advanced, specialized and isolated summer school of a modern language in any college in the country."* Stameshkin et al., 13.

54 *"One, it's certainly the Language Pledge."* Stephen Snyder (dean of Middlebury Language Schools), in discussion with the author, July 2018. All other quotes by him are from this discussion. Additionally, hear the conversations with various principals from Middlebury in "The Magic of Middlebury," *America the Bilingual* (podcast), Episode 35, 2019, https://www.americathebilingual.com /the-magic-of-middlebury/.

55 *"the students are streaming in to take the pledge."* Elizabeth Karnes Keefe (associate dean of Middlebury Language Schools), in discussion with the author, July 2018.

56 *"By the fifth or sixth week, students will be glaring at me, saying, 'What am I doing here?'"* Molly Baker (director of enrollment for Middlebury Language Schools), in discussion with the author, July 2018.

56 *"You get to a level where you can take your Italian and go to Rome."* Tim Page (Middlebury dean of operations), in discussion with the author, July 2018.

57 *"At the time, I was an engineer with an oversized singing habit."* Wyner, *Fluent Forever*, 3.

57 *"It can be embarrassing or scary when you're the only non-native speaker in the room."* Wyner, 163.

58 *"That indicates that I am in the school of French."* Julie Spiegelman (graduate student at Middlebury Language Schools), in discussion with the author, July 2018.

58 *she likes all the mixing of language students at Middlebury.* Kelly Dewey (graduate student at Middlebury Language Schools), in discussion with the author, July 2018.

Chapter 12. DIY Language Immersion for Grownups

60 *"Several people I knew had recommended San Miguel."* Jennifer Lawson (retiree of the Corporation for Public Broadcasting), in discussion with the author, April 2017. Hear some of the conversation in "Bless the Late-Blooming Bilinguals," *America the Bilingual* (podcast), Episode 16, 2017, https://www.americathe bilingual.com/16-bless-the-late-blooming-bilinguals/.

62 *"About 40 percent of our students come here because they want to improve their Spanish for their profession in the US."* Martha Rodríguez Barbosa (head of the Habla Hispana school in San Miguel), in discussion with the author, July 2015.

63 *"A lot of lifelong learners stay home....But this is an adventurous group of people."* Warren Hardy (head of an eponymous language school in San Miguel), in discussion with the author, July 2015. All quotes by him are from this discussion.

63 *Warren told us he speaks regularly at a conference put on by* **International Living.** The magazine focuses on how to live, retire, and invest overseas: https://international living.com/.

65 *"you have to create a community of learners going through the same experience you are."* William Yepes-Amaya (language teacher), in "Top Tips from Teachers" (podcast and PDF), https://www.americathebilingual.com/45-top-tips-from -teachers-for-adult-language-learners/ and https://attachments.convertkitcdnn .com/116297/ce0a756f-eb09-4885-be80-cecfe7eb7bbd/Top%20Tips%20 from%20Language%20Teachers.pdf.

Chapter 13. How to Learn a Language by Not Studying It

67 *The polyglot Kato Lomb also recommended going beyond just studying the language.* Lomb, *Polyglot*, 159ff.

68 *"I was sixteen when I...took a gap year before people took gap years."* Susan Golden (visiting scholar at the Stanford Longevity Center), in discussion with the author, March 2017. Hear some of the conversation in "How to Learn a Language Without Studying It," *America the Bilingual* (podcast), Episode 27, 2018, https://www .americathebilingual.com/27-how-to-learn-a-language-without-studying-it/.

69 *"I took Spanish in high school, but then there's this huge gap."* Brad Schmier (cancer researcher), in discussion with the author, December 2017. Hear some of the

conversation in "How to Learn a Language Without Studying It," https://www
.americathebilingual.com/27-how-to-learn-a-language-without-studying-it/.

70 *"I didn't find one, but I did join a Francophone hiking group."* Maja Thomas (chief innovation officer at Hachette Livre), in discussion with the author, November 2013.

71 *"Use the target language as a vehicle for learning more about a subject, skill, or cultural area of interest."* Tim Ferriss, "How to Learn Any Language in 3 Months," *The Tim Ferriss Show* (blog), January 20, 2009, http://www.fourhourworkweek .com/blog/2009/01/20/learning-language/.

71 *"But for us to understand each other, we have one major language."* Jeane Forrest (a Filipino émigré to the United States), in discussion with the author, May 2017. All quotes by her are from this discussion. Hear some of the conversation in "Mother Tongue," *America the Bilingual* (podcast), Episode 4, 2017, https: //www.americathebilingual.com/episode-4-mother-tongue/.

73 *"I was acting out in the first grade."* Marshall Ganz (faculty member at the John F. Kennedy School of Government at Harvard University), in discussion with the author, September 2015. All other quotes by him are from this discussion.

74 *Leanne Hinton...says that you learn a language by doing things.* Leanne Hinton, *How to Keep Your Language Alive: A Commonsense Approach to One-on-One Language Learning* (Berkeley, CA: Heyday Books, 2002), 9.

Chapter 14. The Tonic of Travel

76 *"I say a few words in Turkish and all of a sudden I get a big smile."* Kat Cohen (educational consultant), in discussion with the author, June 2017. Hear some of the conversation in "Buds of Bilingualism," https://www.americathebilingual .com/43-buds-of-bilingualism/.

76 *"I would give the introduction in the language of the nation."* Karen Gross (former university president), in discussion with the author, May 2018. Hear some of the conversation in "Buds of Bilingualism," https://www.americathebilingual .com/43-buds-of-bilingualism/.

77 *"Ich bin ein Berliner."* President John F. Kennedy delivering his "I Am a Berliner" speech at the Berlin Wall, June 26, 1963, YouTube Educational Video Group, https://www.youtube.com/watch?v=hJNM0C-7lPk. To view the speech card the President used with the phrase's phonetic pronunciation (as well as his pronounce-ment of the Latin *civis Romanus sum*—"I am a Roman"), see National Archives, John F. Kennedy Library, Boston, Massachusetts (NLK-29248), https://www.archives .gov/exhibits/american_originals/kennedy2.html.

77 *"it's just good manners to know the most common polite words in the local tongue."* Rick Steves, *Europe Through the Back Door: The Travel Skills Handbook* (Berkeley, CA: Avalon Travel, 2017), loc. 7798, Kindle. Buds of bilingualism will not be the same words and expressions in each language. In France, for example, to say *bonjour*

is more important than most anything else. Emily Monaco, "In France, Learning to Say 'Bonjour' a Lot," *The Wall Street Journal,* February 3, 2016.

78 *"the language goes from being just a gateway into a culture (as it was in school) to a living thing."* Thomas Swick, *The Joys of Travel: And Stories That Illuminate Them* (New York: Skyhorse Publishing, 2016), 6.

78 *American travel to international destinations in the last twenty years has tripled.* The National Travel and Tourism Office reports that in 1998 there were 31,134,600 trips; in 2018, the number had swelled to 93,038,257 trips. Monthly US citizen departures are collected and reported in the Tourism Industries U.S. International Air Travel Statistics (I-92 data) Program, https://travel.trade.gov/research /programs/i92/index.html, and includes departures by month, https://travel .trade.gov/research/monthly/departures/.

78 *The number of valid US passports in circulation as of 2019 was 147 million.* https://travel.state.gov/content/travel/en/about-us/reports-and-statistics.html.

79 *Merriam-Webster announced at the end of 2019 that "they" was its word of the year.* Merriam-Webster, "Word of the Year: They," the website of the Merriam-Webster Dictionary, https://www.merriam-webster.com/words-at-play/word-of -the-year/they.

79 *Kato Lomb warned that the language learner must deal with everyday language in the street.* Lomb, *Polyglot,* 134.

79 *The linguist Charles Ferguson is credited with coining the term diglossia.* Nancy H. Hornberger and Martin Pütz, eds., *Language Loyalty, Language Planning, and Language Revitalization: Recent Writings and Reflections from Joshua A. Fishman* (Clevedon, UK: Multilingual Matters, 2006), 69.

80 *"I could not recognize or utter a single word of the Chinese I had been studying."* Deborah Fallows, *Dreaming in Chinese: Mandarin Lessons in Life, Love, and Language* (New York: Walker & Company, 2010), 14.

80 *The closest thing we have to compare is American Black English.* John McWhorter, *Talking Back, Talking Black: Truths About America's Lingua Franca* (New York: Bellevue Literary Press, 2019).

81 *"Different languages mark communities or cultures...that wish to maintain some distinctiveness."* Edwards, *Sociolinguistics,* 30.

81 *Such boundary marking doesn't show any sign of diminishing.* William Labov, *Dialect Diversity in America: The Politics of Language Change* (Charlottesville, VA: University of Virginia Press, 2012).

Chapter 15. Your Brain on Barcelona (or Bangkok, or...)

82 *"I did just enough to get by."* Bob Spitz, *Dearie: The Remarkable Life of Julia Child* (New York: Alfred A. Knopf, 2012), 59.

82 *"After years of practical French lessons,...she was no better equipped."* Spitz, 171.

82 *"She couldn't even hail a cab."* Spitz, 177.

82 *"'I'm going to learn to speak this language come hell or high water.'"* Spitz, 177.

83 *"Practice became second nature to her."* Spitz, 177-78.

83 *"'I never dreamed I would find the French so* **sympathique.***'"* Spitz, 178.

83 *"it was a treasure trove of kitchen lore."* Spitz, 178.

83 *"Over time, Julia became a fixture at her neighborhood market."* Spitz, 179.

83 *"'She took great pleasure in instructing me which vegetables were best.'"* Spitz, 179.

84 *Julia became the ambassador for French cooking in America.* For most of the twentieth century, expensive restaurants used lots of French in their menus, but today, the expensive restaurants use words like farm-raised, free ranging, local, organic, and sustainable. Dan Jurafsky, *The Language of Food: A Linguist Reads the Menu* (New York: W.W. Norton, 2014), 8ff.

84 *"You learn a lot in university, but until you use it every day, you don't pick it up fully."* Mitch Cuevas (company CEO), in discussion with the author, May 2016. All other quotes by him are from this discussion.

85 *"Although I had had the privilege of having Spanish in school...I had never used it on a consistent basis."* Robin Loving (expat PR professional), in discussion with the author, July 2015. All other quotes by her are from this discussion. Hear some of the conversation in "Bless the Late-Blooming Bilinguals," *America the Bilingual* (podcast), Episode 16, 2017, https://www.americathebilingual.com /16-bless-the-late-blooming-bilinguals/.

87 *present estimates put the figure at around nine million.* https://web.archive.org /web/20160616233331/https://travel.state.gov/content/dam/travel/CA_By _the_Numbers.pdf.

Chapter 16. Discover Your Little Doves

89 *Why on earth do Spanish speakers call it a Russian mountain?* It's also the name in French, Italian, and Portuguese: https://lingualista.wordpress.com/2017/07/28 /literal-translation-of-roller-coaster-in-languages-across-the-globe/.

89 *proverbs are rich with content that help people "think memorable thoughts."* Ong, *Orality and Literacy*, 9.

90 *"countless writers have packaged originals as translations and translations as originals."* Bellos, *Is That a Fish in Your Ear?*, 8. See also David Crystal, *How Language Works: How Babies Babble, Words Change Meaning, and Languages Live or Die* (New York: Harry N. Abrams, 2006), 418. Crystal says that "there is no such thing as a 'best' translation." It's a matter of purpose. As for translation, "its importance is often underestimated, and its practitioners' social status and legal rights undervalued."

90 *"It's truly astounding how many people fall into the trap."* Bellos, 38.

90 *awards for translated literature, like the one the National Book Foundation gives, go to the author and the translator equally.* For more on the National Book Awards, see https://www.nationalbook.org/press/.

90 *"I absolutely do not believe that anything is lost in translation. It's like fraternal twins."* Tina Kover (translator), presentation at the Miami Book Fair, November 17, 2018.

91 *translation "comes when some human group has the bright idea that...the people on the other side of the hill might be worth talking to."* "Translation and Writing: David Bellos of Princeton University on the Future of Text," December 4, 2013, YouTube video, https://www.youtube.com/watch?v=0EFG9xw1RHM.

91 *her Spanish really bloomed when she went on several mission trips with her church.* Allison De La Torre (student), in discussion with the author, July 2017.

91 *bilingualism appears to promote extroversion, agreeableness, and conscientiousness.* Kohn, *Four Words for Friend*, 147.

92 *"The ability to toggle between two languages is about as near as one can get to being in two places at once."* Kohn, 147.

92 *"Being raised Chinese, I was used to expressing indirectly."* Marco Chan (Canadian Chinese MBA and MPA candidate), in discussion with the author, May 2016.

93 *For inspiration, I recommend that you read memoirs written by people who have gone to live in the countries that speak your adopted language.* For example, Katherine Russell Rich, *Dreaming in Hindi: Coming Awake in Another Language* (Boston: Houghton Mifflin Harcourt, 2009); Michael Tucker, *Living in a Foreign Language: A Memoir of Food, Wine, and Love in Italy* (New York: Atlantic Monthly Press, 2007); Lauren Collins, *When in French: Love in a Second Language* (New York: Penguin Press, 2016); and David Sedaris, *Me Talk Pretty One Day* (New York: Little, Brown and Company, 2000), in which he recounts with typical hilarity learning French when he and his partner, Hugh, moved to France. Sedaris first captured some of his foibles and faux-pas in his personal diary, large chunks of which were published in *Theft by Finding: Diaries, 1977–2002* (New York: Little, Brown and Company, 2017). There he writes about how he and his fellow struggling students spent a lot of time in class dodging chalk—their teacher had a propensity for hurling pieces of it when the students got their French wrong. Then came the red-letter day when the fearsome teacher announced to David that dealing with him was "like having a caesarean section." The insult slid right off his back. He had finally understood every word she hurled at him.

Chapter 17. Finding Where

94 *"I found the grammar daunting and I continually got C's—and I don't get C's."* Lorna Auerbach (bilingual executive with Spanish-import business), in discussion with the author, May 2016. All other quotes by her are from this discussion.

96 *"The language allows you an entrée to get closer."* Calvin Sims (former international correspondent for *The New York Times*), in discussion with the author, September 2014. All other quotes by him are from this discussion.

96 *Japanese women tend to speak in a very polite manner.* Mark Tercek (Japanese second-language speaker), in discussion with the author, February 2020.

97 *He didn't know Farsi before going to Afghanistan and learned it by immersion.* Anand Gopal (journalist and author), in discussion with the author, November 2014.

97 *He told me he finally left because he felt he wasn't getting beneath the surface.* Evan Osnos (author and China correspondent for *The New Yorker*), in discussion with the author, November 2014.

98 *"it is important to let go of the security of your native language."* Kaufmann, *The Way of the Linguist*, 88.

98 *"I was just obsessed with France."* Kate Krosschell (language adventurer), in discussion with Fernando Hernandez, co-host of this podcast, and the author, ACTFL 2018 Annual Convention and World Languages Expo, New Orleans, LA, November 2018. All other quotes by her are from this discussion. Hear some of the conversation in "A Language to Reveal—or Conceal—Your True Self," *America the Bilingual* (podcast), Episode 22, 2018, https://www.americathebilingual.com/can-learning-a-new-language-help-you-find-your-true-identity/.

99 *"There was no way the Spanish team would have invited me if I didn't know the language."* Andrew Hermann (Olympics competitor in race walking), in discussion with the author, May 2016. All other quotes by him are from this discussion.

100 *"Heritage and identity. The two are often conflated."* Eric Liu, *A Chinaman's Chance: One Family's Journey and the Chinese American Dream* (New York: PublicAffairs, 2014), 72.

100 *"I...was going to minor in Spanish in college, but we were supposed to read novels and it was too hard."* Father Chuck Durante (pastor of St. Teresa of Avila Catholic Church), in discussion with the author, August 2015.

Chapter 18. Giving the Gift to Our Loved Ones

105 *bilingualism caused a retardation of language development.* Kenji Hakuta, *Mirror of Language: The Debate on Bilingualism* (New York: Basic Books, 1986), 59.

105 *"a monument to quantification."* Hakuta, 59.

105 *a medical ailment that needed to be cured.* The bilingual scholar Ofelia García cites, as an example, a 1924 study titled "The Bilingual Problem" in her *Bilingual Education in the 21st Century: A Global Perspective* (West Sussex, UK: Wiley-Blackwell, 2009), 102. Smith's study wasn't the only, or worst, example of using discredited science to support social policies. See Daniel Okrent, *The Guarded Gate: Bigotry, Eugenics, and the Law That Kept Two Generations of Jews, Italians, and Other European Immigrants Out of America* (New York: Scribner, 2019).

105 *Not until 1962 did two Canadian researchers, Elizabeth Peal and Wallace Lambert of McGill University, challenge this view.* Elizabeth Peal and Wallace E. Lambert, "The relation of bilingualism to intelligence," *Psychological Monographs: General and Applied* 76, no. 27 (1962): 1–23, https://doi.org/10.1037/h0093840.

105 *Their results turned a half-century of studies upside down.* Chin and Wigglesworth, *Bilingualism*, 61, 70.

105 *Lambert summed up the science that existed.* Wallace E. Lambert, afterword to *Bringing Up Baby Bilingual*, by Jane Merrill (New York: Facts On File, 1984), 270.

106 *Any delay among bilingual children in learning one language over the other appears to be temporary.* See, for example, this video by Maria Polinsky, a linguistics professor at Harvard: "Cognitive Advantages of Bilingualism," Serious Science series, June 22, 2015, YouTube video, https://www.youtube.com/watch?v=W-ml2dD4SIk.

106 *Bialystok...has found mental health advantages in bilingual older adults.* Ellen Bialystok, "How Bilingualism Helps Your Brain," University of Reading, UK, May 5, 2015, YouTube video, https://www.youtube.com/watch?v=6sDYx77h CmI. See also Ellen Bialystok, "Bilingualism and the Development of Executive Function: The Role of Attention," *Child Development Perspectives* 9, no. 2 (2015): 117-21. The popular media in the UK has also reported on Bialystok's research: Wency Leung, "New Research Suggests Being Bilingual May Help Delay Symptoms of Alzheimer's Disease," *The Globe and Mail*, March 1, 2020, https://www.theglobeandmail.com/life/health-and-fitness/article-can-being-bilingual-delay-symptoms-of-alzheimers/. Bialystok points out that bilingualism does not prevent the onset of the disease itself, but the symptoms of it. In other words, people can carry on with their normal lives for an average of four years longer. While she says people can become bilingual at any age, the duration of bilingualism in your life seems to be the important variable. Ellen Bialystok, "The Brain and the Potential of Bilingualism," Conversation with Fabrice Jaumont, May 22, 2018, YouTube video, https://www.youtube.com/watch?v=3KFWc2hF2b4. See also Ellen Bialystok, Fergus I.M. Craik, David W. Green, and Tamar H. Gollan, "Bilingual Minds," *Psychological Science in the Public Interest* 10, no. 3 (2009): 89-129, https://journals.sagepub.com/doi/full/10.1177/1529100610387084; and Albert Costa, *The Bilingual Brain: And What It Tells Us About the Science of Language*, trans. John W. Schwieter (London: Allen Lane, 2019), 112-20.

106 *Adding to these mental health benefits are economic reports that show measurable benefits to bilinguals in landing jobs.* See how one university explores this new reality with its students: "New Fireside Charla Episode Explores Bilingualism," San Diego State University News Team, SDSU President Adela de la Torre podcast Episode #015, March 9, 2020 (joined by Cristina Alfaro, professor in SDSU's Department of Dual Language and English Learner Education, Jose Sabedra, and his parents, Edith and Jose), http://newscenter.sdsu.edu/sdsu_newscenter/news_story.aspx?sid=77920.

106 *"the benefits of bilingualism have in recent years been piling up like laundry."* Gaston Dorren, *Lingo: Around Europe in Sixty Languages* (New York: Atlantic Monthly Press, 2015), 284. Books on raising bilingual children have been piling

up in equal measure. *The Bilingual Family: A Handbook for Parents*, by Edith Harding-Esch and Philip Riley (Cambridge: Cambridge University Press), went into its tenth printing in 2012. It provides an excellent background of the issues and challenges facing parents, and contains many case studies that may mirror families' own situations. *The Bilingual Edge: Why, When, and How to Teach Your Child a Second Language*, by Kendall King and Alison Mackey, is an excellent resource guide. *Raising a Bilingual Child: A Step-by-Step Guide for Parents*, by Barbara Zurer Pearson, includes useful case studies. See also *7 Steps to Raising a Bilingual Child* by Naomi Steiner, MD (New York: AMACOM, 2008), and *Bilingual Is Better: Two Latina Moms on How the Bilingual Parenting Revolution Is Changing the Face of America*, by Ana L. Flores and Roxana A. Soto. *Maximize Your Child's Bilingual Ability: Ideas and Inspiration for Even Greater Success and Joy Raising Bilingual Kids*, by Adam Beck, contains lots of encouraging advice written mostly from the point of view of a parent who speaks a minority language following OPOL (One Person, One Language). Beck also has an active blog and website. Two other books written by Latinos for Latinos are *Raising Nuestros Niños: Bringing Up Latino Children in a Bicultural World*, by Gloria G. Rodriguez (New York: Fireside, 1999), and *Parenting with Pride Latino Style: How to Help Your Child Cherish Your Cultural Values and Succeed in Today's World*, by Carmen Inoa Vazquez (New York: Rayo, 2004).

106 *while it's never too late to begin learning a language, it's never too early, either.* See "Benefits of Bilingualism," in Ofelia García, *Bilingual Education in the 21st Century*, 93-108; Chin and Wigglesworth, *Bilingualism*; Colin Baker and Wayne E. Wright, "Bilingualism, Cognition and the Brain," in *Foundation of Bilingual Education and Bilingualism*, 6th ed. (Bristol, UK: Multilingual Matters, 2017), 132-55; François Grosjean, "The Bilingual Advantage: Three years later, where do things stand in this area of research?," *Psychology Today* blog, June 11, 2019, https://www.psychologytoday.com/intl/blog/life -bilingual/201906/the-bilingual-advantage-three-years-later; Mark Antoniou, "The Advantages of Bilingualism Debate," *Annual Review of Linguistics* 5 (January 2019): 395-415, https://www.annualreviews.org/doi/abs/10.1146/annurev -linguistics-011718-011820; and "The Brain and the Potential of Bilingualism: A Conversation with Ellen Bialystok and Fabrice Jaumont," May 22, 2018, YouTube video, https://www.youtube.com/watch?v=3KFWc2hF2b4.

107 *"I'd love Charlotte to be able to enter school knowing another language."* Allison Altmann Kay (mother and attorney), in discussion with the author, February 2017.

107 *"children actually reinvent it, generation after generation."* Steven Pinker, *The Language Instinct: How the Mind Creates Language* (New York: Harper Perennial Modern Classics, 2007), 20.

109 *"There is no evidence that bilingual children differ from monolingual children."* Ofelia García, *Bilingual Education in the 21st Century*, 64.

109 *little evidence...that bilingual children acquire either of their languages more slowly.* Chin and Wigglesworth, *Bilingualism*, 44.

109 *"still living in the shadow of these outdated notions."* Kendall King and Alison Mackey, *The Bilingual Edge: Why, When, and How to Teach Your Child a Second Language* (New York: Harper Perennial, 2007), 215.

109 *Thirty percent...is a good number to shoot for.* Rita Rosenback, *Bringing up a Bilingual Child* (Croydon, UK: Filament Publishing, 2014), loc 1966, Kindle.

110 *"and ideally more like 70%."* Barbara Zurer Pearson, *Raising a Bilingual Child: A Step-by-Step Guide for Parents* (New York: Living Language, 2008), 116.

110 *the child will have amassed somewhere between 3,500 and 5,000 hours in the language.* Assuming a twelve-hour waking day, 20 percent is 2.4 hours per day, while 30 percent is 3.6 hours per day. Multiply that by 365 days, and four years gives you a range of 3,504 to 5,256 hours.

110 *their brains are wired for language learning.* Steven Pinker, *The Language Instinct*, 298, and 16 of the Publishers' Series material.

110 *"Don't teach; give joy."* Adam Beck, *Maximize Your Child's Bilingual Ability: Ideas and Inspiration for Even Greater Success and Joy Raising Bilingual Kids* (N.p.: Bilingual Adventures, 2016), page 48 (22%), Kindle.

110 *"the bilingual child's most important 'teachers' are other small children."* Harding-Esch and Riley, *The Bilingual Family*, 173.

110 *What's much more important is reading aloud to your children.* Beck, *Maximize Your Child's Bilingual Ability*, 177ff.

110 *technology..."cannot substitute for a real person and real interaction."* King and Mackey, *The Bilingual Edge*, 29.

110 *"there is no evidence that correcting helps people to learn."* Harding-Esch and Riley, *The Bilingual Family*, 145.

111 *"Even parents who know just a little of the second language."* King and Mackey, *The Bilingual Edge*, 105.

Chapter 19. What the Deaf Can Teach Us

112 *"I promised myself...I was going to learn sign language."* Joseph Garcia (pioneer in the use of ASL for babies), in telephone discussion with the author, May 2018. All other quotes by him are from this discussion. Hear some of the conversation in "When Baby's First Words Are Not Spoken," *America the Bilingual* (podcast), Episode 29, 2018, https://www.americathebilingual.com/when-babys-first-words -are-not-spoken/. For readers who are deaf or hard of hearing, please email us at info@americathebilingual.com, and we will be happy to send you a transcript.

113 *Viviana...decided that both she and Luis would learn.* Viviana Sisniegas (Spanish teacher), in discussion with the author, November 2018. All other quotes by her are from this discussion. Hear some of the conversation in "When

Baby's First Words Are Not Spoken," https://www.americathebilingual.com/when-babys-first-words-are-not-spoken/.

114 *"It was incredible. As a linguist, I have to admit I was not expecting it to be that fast."* Deborah Chen-Pichler (hearing faculty member at Gallaudet University), in telephone discussion with the author, May 2018. All other quotes by her are from this discussion. Hear some of the conversation in "When Baby's First Words Are Not Spoken," https://www.americathebilingual.com/when-babys-first-words-are-not-spoken/; and in "Children of a Silent God: A Bilingual Journey Through American Sign Language," *America the Bilingual* (podcast), Episode 40, 2019, https://www.americathebilingual.com/children-of-a-silent-god-a-bilingual-journey-through-american-sign-language/. For readers who are deaf or hard of hearing, please email us at info@americathebilingual.com, and we will be happy to send you a transcript.

115 *"speech and signing are simply two different modalities in which the human capacity for language can be expressed."* Stephen R. Anderson, *Languages*, 8.

115 *"little to no support or access in sign language."* Tawny Holmes Hlibok (Education Policy Counsel at the National Association of the Deaf and a member of the Deaf community), in email discussion with Mim Harrison, January 2019.

115 *"Most hearing people don't understand that there is a...Deaf culture."* Sierra Weiner (hearing student with an ASL college major), in telephone discussion with the author, May 2018. Hear some of the conversation in "Children of a Silent God: A Bilingual Journey Through American Sign Language," https://www.americathebilingual.com/children-of-a-silent-god-a-bilingual-journey-through-american-sign-language/.

Chapter 20. Students Learning in
Two Languages: Gathering Strength

117 *What materialized was an unprecedented alignment of circumstances and people.* Maria R. Coady, *The Coral Way Bilingual Program* (Bristol, UK: Multilingual Matters, 2020).

118 *both Cuban and American children would learn to "operate in either culture easily and comfortably."* Coady, 39.

119 *Our old laws that limited immigrants...began to feel out of touch.* David A. Gerber, *American Immigration: A Very Short Introduction* (Oxford: Oxford University Press, 2011).

119 *In 1965 Congress passed, by wide margins, the Immigration and Nationality Act.* Gerber, 51.

119 *I spoke with Gregg Roberts.* Roberts (director of dual language studies at the American Councils for International Education) is responsible for coining the phrase that the bilingual community heard 'round the world: "Monolingualism is the illiteracy

of the twenty-first century." As he relayed to the author, "I actually said that back in 2013 at the national Chinese language conference in Boston. I was on a panel and we were presenting and it came up." Then, he said, it got passed on by word of mouth across the country and internationally. "It made it to quite a few places around the world. *BBC Mundo* published an article about it, so I've seen it pop up in Madrid, in Buenos Aires, in Bogotá, so it has made it around because it's kind of catchy, and it's very true. Some people are a little offended by it, but you know, what's a quotation if it can't at least shock people sometimes?" The quotation has even made its way onto bumper stickers, a favorite of language teachers, but few people know it was Roberts who first said it. He said he's fine with that. But he *is* pleased to be known for his role in helping to build the dual language programs in Utah.

119 *"We had a very enlightened governor."* Gregg Roberts, in telephone discussion with the author, April 2016. All other quotes by him are from this discussion.

120 *"we actually...built some serious muscle around internationally important languages."* Jon Huntsman, Jr. (governor of Utah, 2005-2009), YPO Global Conference Call, Q & A, May 18, 2016. All other quotes by him are from this conference call.

120 *"we're growing by as many as twenty-five schools per year."* Howard A. Stephenson (Utah state senator, 1992-2018), in discussion with the author, at the ACTFL conference in New Orleans, LA, November 2018. All other quotes by him are from this discussion. Hear some of the conversation on Utah's bilingual initiative in "Dual-Language Education, Report #1: The Revolution Begins," *America the Bilingual* (podcast), Episode 24, 2018, https://www.americathebilingual.com/dual-language-education-report-1/.

121 *Howard told me it's up to the states to build the linguistic capital of America.* Catherine Snow, an expert on language and literacy development in children who is in the Harvard Graduate School of Education, said much the same in a discussion with the author in April 2015. Unlike most countries that have national top-down control over education, in America, she says, education is governed by the states or even by individual school districts. As a consequence, she says, "the US educational system is ungovernable. Two-way bilingual programs would seem to be an obvious solution, a beautiful idea. And there are places where it works pretty well, but they are hard to keep going." Snow says that bilingual educational reform programs are dependent on funding and committed administrators and teachers. "It takes great leaders."

122 *Those nominal additional costs have not hindered Utah from being ranked as the top state in America in terms of economic competitiveness.* For at least a dozen years, Utah has been the top performer in the *Rich States, Poor States* index of economic competitiveness. Stephen Moore, "Why Utah Has Become America's Economic Star," *The Wall Street Journal*, December 7-8, 2019.

123 *I began to get a sense of how big dual language education has already become in America.* The growing interest in dual language education across America led the US Department of Education to conduct a survey to determine the extent of such

schools in the states and how they could be encouraged and grown. Andrea Boyle, Diane August, Lisa Tabaku, Susan Cole, and Ashley Simpson-Baird, *Dual Language Education Programs: Current State Policies and Practices* (Washington, DC: American Institutes for Research, December 2015), https://www.air.org/resource /dual-language-education-programs-current-state-policies-and-practices.

123 *"there is something even more important and fundamental: you can be better collaborators."* Jim Lyons (former executive director of the National Association for Bilingual Education), in discussion with the author at the La Cosecha dual language conference, Albuquerque, NM, November 2018. All other quotes by him are from this discussion. Hear some of the conversation in "Dual-Language Education, Report #1: The Revolution Begins," https://www.americathebilingual .com/dual-language-education-report-1/.

123 *"On its surface, it is counterintuitive."* For the research showing the counterintuitive finding, see especially Wayne P. Thomas and Virginia P. Collier, *Dual Language Education for a Transformed World* (Albuquerque, NM: Fuente Press, 2012). The authors' research into dual language schools is some of the most respected. In their preface (p. xi), they write: "From all of our studies to date, the bottom line is this: when students receive schooling through their primary language and the second language all the way through the first six years of schooling, with at least half of the instruction time in their primary language, they can reach grade level in second language and stay there through the remainder of their schooling. If they get continuing support through their primary language into the middle school and high school years, they can reach even higher than grade-level achievement in second language. Furthermore, when they graduate from high school bilingual/biliterate/bicultural, they are prepared to fully participate in a global world of the 21st century." See also the review of their work in Ofelia García, *Bilingual Education*, 187ff. See also Ilana M. Umansky and Sean F. Reardon, "Reclassification Patterns Among Latino English Learner Students in Bilingual, Dual Immersion, and English Immersion Classrooms," *American Educational Research Journal* 51, no. 5 (October 2014): 879–912.

124 *"I was a re-entry student."* Kris Nicholls (professional development instructor for bilingual teachers), in discussion with the author at La Cosecha conference, Albuquerque, NM, November 2018. All other quotes by her are from this discussion. Hear some of the conversation in "Dual-Language Education, Report #2: Winds of Change," *America the Bilingual* (podcast), Episode 25, 2018, https://www.america thebilingual.com/25-dual-language-education-report-2-winds-of-change/.

125 *"I think our community came to really understand that we were a dual language community."* Suzanne Wheeler Del Piccolo (elementary school teacher), in discussion with the author at La Cosecha conference, Albuquerque, NM, November 2018. All other quotes by her are from this discussion. Hear some of the conversation in "Dual-Language Education, Report #2: Winds of Change," https://www.america thebilingual.com/25-dual-language-education-report-2-winds-of-change/.

125 *in an expensive area so near to hyper-priced Aspen.* The median home price in Aspen in the first months of 2020 was $1.9 million, according to Zillow. Rentals could top $14,000 a month. https://www.zillow.com/aspen-co/home-values/.

126 *"Dual language can help us bring people together and have a learning that is transformative."* Tony Báez (director of the Milwaukee school board), in discussion with the author at La Cosecha conference, Albuquerque, NM, November 2018. All other quotes by him are from this discussion. Hear some of the conversation in "Dual-Language Education, Report #2: Winds of Change," https://www.americathebilingual.com/25-dual-language-education-report-2-winds-of-change/.

126 *"I like to make people feel uncomfortable."* José Medina (director of dual language and bilingual education at the Center for Applied Linguistics), in discussion with the author at La Cosecha conference, Albuquerque, NM, November 2018. All other quotes by him are from this discussion. Hear some of the conversation in "Dual-Language Education, Report #2: Winds of Change," https://www.americathebilingual.com/25-dual-language-education-report-2-winds-of-change/.

127 *"We also need to embrace our role as defenders of equity and social justice."* As promising as dual language programs are, they are not panaceas for addressing underlying issues of poverty and race. See, for example, Nelson Flores and Lauren McAuliffe, "'In other schools you can plan it that way': a raciolinguistic perspective on dual language education," *International Journal of Bilingual Education and Bilingualism*, May 2020, https://www.researchgate.net/publication/341235453_'In_other_schools_you_can_plan_it_that_way'_a_raciolinguistic_perspective_on_dual_language_education.

127 *In 2005, the state had seven dual language schools; in 2018, there were 140.* Ivanna Anderson, Helga Fasciano, Ann Marie Gunter, and Tricia Willoughby (North Carolina bilingual education leaders), in discussion with the author, June 2018. All quotes by them are from this discussion. Hear some of the conversation in "North Carolina: A Dual-Language Success Story," *America the Bilingual* (podcast), Episode 42, 2019, https://www.americathebilingual.com/42-north-carolina-a-dual-language-success-story/.

128 *"I remember my own father telling me thirty years ago, 'You'll never get a job in Spanish.'"* Ken Stewart (bilingual education instructor), in discussion with the author, June 2018. All other quotes by him are from this discussion. Hear some of the conversation in "North Carolina: A Dual-Language Success Story," https://www.americathebilingual.com/42-north-carolina-a-dual-language-success-story/.

129 *"If we can identify potential teachers, we can build this pipeline."* Mary Lynn Redmond (professor emerita of world languages), in discussion with the author, June 2018. Hear some of the conversation in "North Carolina: A Dual-Language Success Story," https://www.americathebilingual.com/42-north-carolina-a-dual-language-success-story/.

130 *"We lived in an English world. Cherokee was not important."* Kathy Sierra (Cherokee, and a teacher of the language), in discussion with the author, June 2018. All other quotes by her are from this discussion. Hear some of the conversation in "A New Generation of Cherokee Speakers Rises," *America the Bilingual* (podcast), Episode 30, 2018, https://www.americathebilingual .com/a-new-generation-of-cherokee-speakers-rises/.

130 *"Cherokee language is American culture, and it's Native American culture."* Sara Snyder (university director of a Cherokee language program), in discussion with the author, June 2018. Hear some of the conversation in "A New Generation of Cherokee Speakers Rises," https://www.americathebilingual .com/a-new-generation-of-cherokee-speakers-rises/.

131 *"There's no one that is a first-language Cherokee speaker that is in childbearing age."* Renissa McLaughlin (Cherokee, and education director for the Eastern Band of the Cherokee Indians in North Carolina), in discussion with the author, June 2018. All other quotes by her are from this discussion. Hear some of the conversation in "A New Generation of Cherokee Speakers Rises," https://www .americathebilingual.com/a-new-generation-of-cherokee-speakers-rises/.

131 *Cherokee has had a written language since 1821.* That is the year a Cherokee named Sequoyah devised a Cherokee syllabary. Unlike an alphabet, which is a series of letters, a syllabary contains a group of syllables. Sequoyah created a symbol for each of the eighty-five syllables he established for the Cherokee written language. Mim Harrison, "Talking Leaves: The Cherokee Syllabary of Sequoyah," America the Bilingual website article, https://www.americathebilingual.com /talking-leaves-the-cherokee-syllabary-of-sequoyah/.

132 *"I remember...thinking how surprised and pleased my grandfather would be to think that Charlotte and her friends could help preserve a language."* Martha White (literary executor of E.B. White), in email discussion with Mim Harrison, July 2018. A picture of the book cover is in the episode notes of "A New Generation of Cherokee Speakers Rises," https://www.americathebilingual .com/a-new-generation-of-cherokee-speakers-rises/.

Chapter 21. Students Learning in
Two Languages: Taking Wing

133 *Even outside of these heavy-hitter states, dual language schools seem to be spreading like the dawn.* Rebecca Goldfine, "Figuring Out What Works in Bilingual Education," the website for Bowdoin College, the "News" page, July 11, 2019, https: //www.bowdoin.edu/news/2019/07/figuring-out-what-works-in-bilingual -education.html.

134 *Charles said the ideal mix for Escondido is 30 percent Spanish-only kids, 30 percent bilingual Spanish-English kids, and 30 percent English-only kids.*

Charles Merritt (principal of a bilingual elementary school), in discussion with the author, November 2016. All other quotes by him are from this discussion.

134 *"If they are speaking Spanish, I'll speak Spanish, and if English, I'll speak English."* Keith Bookwalter (principal of a bilingual magnet school), in discussion with the author, April 2016. All other quotes by him are from this discussion.

135 *zip codes are strongly predictive of schooling success.* This is the work of Stanford sociologist Sean Reardon. See, for example, https://www.washingtonpost.com /sf/local/2013/11/09/washington-a-world-apart/.

136 *"We set very high standards and never lower expectations."* Vasiliki Moysidis (principal of a Greek dual language school), in discussion with the author, October 2014.

136 *the Greek heritage "belongs to humanity and not just to Greeks."* Message from the website of Archimedean Schools in Miami, Florida, https://www.archimedean .org/.

137 *"Well-off parents can afford to send their kids to schools with good language programs."* Alison Mackey (co-author of *The Bilingual Edge*), in discussion with the author, December 2014. All other quotes by her are from this discussion.

137 *As Alison said, "Children lucky enough to be in immersion programs anywhere can benefit enormously."* She teamed up with bilingualism scholar Kendall King to write *The Bilingual Edge*, with the goal of providing a resource to help all parents, regardless of income level, raise their children to have transformative multilingual experiences.

137 *"There's a middle class that has been thinking about trying to do similar things."* Fabrice Jaumont (advisor on establishing dual language schools), in discussion with the author, October 2017. All quotes by him are from this discussion. Hear some of the conversation in "Dual-Language Education, Report #2: Winds of Change," https://www.americathebilingual.com/25-dual-language-education -report-2-winds-of-change/. See also Fabrice Jaumont, *The Bilingual Revolution: The Future of Education Is in Two Languages* (New York: TBR Books, 2017). Read about Fabrice's work as the French embassy's education attaché to increase the number of French dual language schools in New York City: https://www .nytimes.com/2014/01/31/nyregion/a-push-for-french-in-new-york-schools -from-france.html.

138 *"When I became a mother…I found I had a preference for dual language pro-grams."* Yuli Fisher (founder of a Japanese-English school), in discussion with the author, December 2017. All other quotes by her are from this discussion. Hear some of the conversation in "Dual-Language Education, Report #2: Winds of Change," https://www.americathebilingual.com/25-dual-language -education-report-2-winds-of-change/.

139 *We're seeing many different parties pulling together.* Dual language schools are growing not just in America but around the world. See Amanda Ripley, *The Smartest Kids in the World: And How They Got That Way* (New York: Simon

& Schuster, 2013); Vivien Stewart, *A World-Class Education: Learning from International Models of Excellence and Innovation* (Alexandria, VA: Association for Supervision & Curriculum Development, 2012); Peeter Mehisto and Fred Genesee, eds., *Building Bilingual Education Systems: Forces, Mechanisms and Counterweights* (Cambridge: Cambridge University Press, 2015); and Colin Baker and Wayne E. Wright, *Foundations of Bilingual Education and Bilingualism*, 6th ed. (Bristol, UK: Multilingual Matters, 2017). Writes Baker (pp. xiii-xiv): "In the 21st century, there is now less scepticism, and much accumulated data to suggest that bilingual education is effective and advantageous for all students." Such programs, he says, are "destined to blossom and flourish in the 21st century."

139 *America didn't instantly understand the significance.* See the works of Tom D. Crouch, including *A Dream of Wings: Americans and the Airplane, 1875-1905* (New York: W.W. Norton, 1981), as well as his later works. See also David McCullough, *The Wright Brothers* (New York: Simon & Schuster, 2015).

Chapter 22. Not Their Uncle's Language Class

141 *educators who attended the ACTFL annual conferences.* The author's discussions with language teachers Aviva Kadosh, Bill Anderson, Susann Davis, Desa Dawson, Laura Roché Youngworth, and Carrie Toth took place at the ACTFL 2017 annual conference in Nashville, TN, November 2017. Hear some of the conversation in "Not Your Uncle's Language Class," *America the Bilingual* (podcast), Episode 31, 2018, https://www.americathebilingual.com/not-your-uncles-language-class/. The author's discussions with language teacher Edward Zarrow took place at the ACTFL 2017 annual conference and at the ACTFL 2018 annual conference in New Orleans, LA, November 2018. Hear some of the conversation in "Not Your Uncle's Language Class" and in "In Case You Thought Latin Was Dead...," *America the Bilingual* (podcast), Episode 23, 2018, https://www.americathebilingual.com/in-case-you-thought-latin-was-dead/.

143 *some evidence comes from the number of American high school students taking the Advanced Placement.* College Board, "AP Exam Volume Changes (2009-2019)," https://secure media.collegeboard.org/digitalServices/pdf/research/2019/2019 -Exam-Volume-Change.pdf.

143 *one hundred thousand more students.* https://secure-media.collegeboard.org /digitalServices/pdf/research/2019/2019-Exam-Volume-Change.pdf.

143 *the total number of American high school students remained relatively unchanged.* William J. Hossar and Tabitha M. Bailey, "Enrollment in grades 9–12 is projected to increase less than 1 percent between 2007 and 2019," in *Projections of Education Statistics to 2019*, 38th ed. (Washington, DC: National Center for Education Statistics, March 2011), https://nces.ed.gov/pubs2011/2011017.pdf.

See also Dennis Looney and Natalia Lusin, *Enrollments in Languages Other Than English in United States Institutions of Higher Education, Summer 2016 and Fall 2016: Final Report* (New York: Modern Language Association of America, June 2019), https://www.mla.org/content/download/110154/2406932/2016 -Enrollments-Final-Report.pdf.

143 *overall AP results have remained relatively unchanged.* AP Program Participation and Performance Data 1999 to 2019, https://secure media.collegeboard.org /digitalServices/pdf/research/2019/2019-Score-Distribution-All-Subjects.pdf.

144 *today's students are seeing language classes as places where they can get some fundamentals...which they expect to use for the rest of their lives.* According to the National Center for Educational Statistics, there were approximately 8,059,000 five- and six-year-old children in America as of 2018: https://nces.ed.gov/programs /digest/d18/tables/dt18_101.10.asp?referrer=report. Even if they miss out on dual language schools, most of them will take multiple language classes in the years to come.

Chapter 23. Language Camps for Kids

147 *"each one designed to replicate the culture where the language is spoken."* Jennifer Speir (group director at Concordia Language Villages), in discussion with the author, July 2018. All other quotes by her are from this discussion. Hear some of the conversation in "Concordia Language Villages: Waltzing with Mops, and Other Adventures," *America the Bilingual* (podcast), Episode 37, 2017, https://www.americathebilingual.com/37-concordia-language-villages-waltz ing-with-mops-and-other-adventures/.

148 *"I started in '76, as a cook."* Diana Tess (dean of Lago del Bosque, Concordia), in discussion with the author, July 2018. All other quotes by her are from this discussion. Hear some of the conversation in "Concordia Language Villages: Waltzing with Mops, and Other Adventures," https://www.americathebilingual .com/37-concordia-language-villages-waltzing-with-mops-and-other-adventures/.

149 *"We have about one hundred villagers at the moment."* Cliff Schwartz (dean of the French camp, Concordia), in discussion with the author, July 2018. Hear some of the conversation in "Concordia Language Villages: Waltzing with Mops, and Other Adventures," https://www.americathebilingual.com/37-concordia -language-villages-waltzing-with-mops-and-other-adventures/.

149 *"we realized that we spend about three hours a day at mealtimes."* Martin Graefe (group director at Concordia), in discussion with the author, July 2018. Hear some of the conversation in "Concordia Language Villages: Waltzing with Mops, and Other Adventures," https://www.americathebilingual.com/37-concordia -language-villages-waltzing-with-mops-and-other-adventures/.

149 *"here, you're hearing the language* **all** *day long."* Julie Ardis (curriculum facilitator at Concordia), in discussion with the author, July 2018. Hear some of the conversation in "Concordia Language Villages: Waltzing with Mops, and Other Adventures." https://www.americathebilingual.com/37-concordia-language-villages-waltzing-with-mops-and-other-adventures/.

151 *One of the older students...is a counselor now.* Rachel Schaeffer (counselor at Concordia), in discussion with the author, July 2018. All other quotes by her are from this discussion. Hear some of the conversation in "Concordia Language Villages: Waltzing with Mops, and Other Adventures," https://www.americathe bilingual.com/37-concordia-language-villages-waltzing-with-mops-and-other -adventures/.

152 *"early on, I had dreams of fluency."* Raia Lichen (founder of a language learning company), in discussion with the author, August 2015. All other quotes by her are from this discussion. Hear some of the conversation in "Concordia Language Villages: Waltzing with Mops, and Other Adventures," https: //www.americathebilingual.com/37-concordia-language-villages-waltzing -with-mops-and-other-adventures/.

153 *"this has been sort of an embarrassing part of my family life."* David Knutson (Spanish professor), in discussion with the author, July 2018. All other quotes by him are from this discussion. Hear some of the conversation in "Concordia Language Villages: Waltzing with Mops, and Other Adventures," https://www .americathebilingual.com/37-concordia-language-villages-waltzing-with -mops-and-other-adventures/.

154 *only about half of the jobs that require professional-level competence in critical-need languages are filled.* "STARTALK 2030: A New Paradigm for World Language Education" (College Park, MD: National Foreign Language Center, University of Maryland, 2018), 2.

154 *"STARTALK is trying to build capacity in the United States for those less commonly taught languages."* Rita Oleksak (head of the STARTALK program at Glastonbury High School, CT), in discussion with the author, July 2018. All other quotes by her are from this discussion. Hear some of the conversation in "STARTALK: Another Peace Corps for the 21st Century," *America the Bilingual* (podcast), Episode 38, 2019, https://www.americathebilingual.com /startalk-another-peace-corps-for-the-21st-century/.

154 *"Most of our teaching staff are heritage speakers."* Jimmy Wildman (program director of STARTALK at Glastonbury), in discussion with the author, July 2018. Hear some of the conversation in "STARTALK: Another Peace Corps for the 21st Century," https://www.americathebilingual.com/startalk-another -peace-corps-for-the-21st-century/.

155 *STARTALK's emphasis on teacher training..."is based on the understanding that student achievement is influenced more by effective teachers."* "STARTALK 2030," 10.

156 *"Well, it started out, I wanted to order Chinese takeout."* Bella Wiedman (sixth-grade student in STARTALK), in discussion with the author, July 2018. All quotes by Bella, Victor, and the other STARTALK students are from this discussion. Hear some of the conversation in "STARTALK: Another Peace Corps for the 21st Century," https://www.americathebilingual.com /startalk-another-peace-corps-for-the-21st-century/.

156 *In the first ten years of its operation, some fifty-six thousand American students have gone through STARTALK programs.* "STARTALK 2030," 2. STARTALK is only one of the language education programs the US government supports. The Department of Defense funds Language Flagship educational programs in K-12 and universities, and at seven centers overseas: https://www.thelanguageflagship .org/. DoD also funds the Boren Awards, specifically for the study of critical languages abroad: https://www.borenawards.org/.

157 *"I was lucky enough that I spent my summers in Spain."* Ricky Perez (parent of children at Camp Lingua), in discussion with the author, May 2018. All other quotes by him are from this discussion. Hear some of the conversation in "Summer Language Camps: A Short-Course on Six We Love," *America the Bilingual* (podcast), Episode 46, 2019, https://www.americathebilingual .com/46-summer-language-camps-a-short-course-on-six-we-love/.

157 *"it's so easy to forget their native language."* Andreina Galavis (founder of Camp Lingua), in discussion with the author, May 2018. All other quotes by her are from this discussion. Hear some of the conversation in "Summer Language Camps: A Short-Course on Six We Love," https://www.americathebilingual .com/46-summer-language-camps-a-short-course-on-six-we-love/.

157 *"Because they're having fun, they don't know that they're learning."* Michael Perez (logistics director at Camp Lingua), in discussion with the author, May 2018. Hear some of the conversation in "Summer Language Camps: A Short-Course on Six We Love," https://www.americathebilingual.com/46-summer -language-camps-a-short-course-on-six-we-love/.

158 *"You can take kids to France and you can take them to the Louvre."* David Wolf (who studied at a French business school), in discussion with the author, February 2017. Hear some of the conversation in "With a Little Help from His Friends and Good French Wine," https://www.americathebilingual.com /2-with-a-little-help-from-his-friends-and-good-french-wine/.

158 *"Children care more about their peers than about their parents, so send them to summer camps."* Steven Pinker, *The Language Instinct*, Appendix FAQs, 9.

158 *"Last summer they spent the entire summer in Egypt and spoke only Arabic."* Ezzat (Lyft driver), in discussion with the author, October 2016.

Chapter 24. Higher High School

159 *"I was a very indifferent and rebellious high school student."* Doug Renfield-Miller (former board member of School Year Abroad), in discussion with the author, July 2017. All quotes by him are from this discussion. Hear some of the conversation in "The Vanishing High School Year Abroad," *America the Bilingual* (podcast), Episode 14, 2017, https://www.americathebilingual.com/14-the-vanishing-high-school-year-abroad/.

159 *SYA, which sent American high school kids overseas to study.* Young people going abroad to acquire a language is something that's been going on for a long time. Says Grosjean in *Bilingual: Life and Reality* (p. 167), "This has happened throughout human history—as far back as ancient Rome, when Roman families would send their children to Greece to be educated and to learn Greek."

160 *SYA president Tom Hassan told me that his organization is now seeing more interest in shorter programs.* Tom Hassan in discussion with the author, September 2017. Hear some of the conversation in "The Vanishing High School Year Abroad," https://www.americathebilingual.com/14-the-vanishing-high-school-year-abroad/.

161 *"I came home one day and said, 'What do you think if I applied to be an AFSer?'"* Jenny Messner (AFS alumna, Brazil), in discussion with the author, October 2017. Hear some of the conversation in "Parents, Give Your Child Bilingual Wings," *America the Bilingual* (podcast), Episode 34, 2018, https://www.americathebilingual.com/34-parents-give-your-child-bilingual-wings/.

161 *AFS traces its history back to World War I.* https://afs.org/archives/timeline/#afs-nav-1916.

162 *"I decided to apply on my own to AFS."* Kat Cohen (educational consultant), in discussion with the author, June 2017. Hear some of the conversation in "The Vanishing High School Year Abroad," https://www.americathebilingual.com/14-the-vanishing-high-school-year-abroad/.

162 *"We have introduced short programs for Americans to go abroad with very specific content."* Jorge Castro (CEO of AFS), in discussion with the author, September 2017. All other quotes by him are from this discussion. Hear some of the conversation in "The Vanishing High School Year Abroad," https://www.americathebilingual.com/14-the-vanishing-high-school-year-abroad/.

162 *"I'll never forget walking into the room where I was staying."* American high school exchange student in discussion with the author, September 2017. All other quotes by her are from this discussion. Hear some of the conversation in "The Vanishing High School Year Abroad," https://www.americathebilingual.com/14-the-vanishing-high-school-year-abroad/.

163 *the critical period for acquiring language with native-like fluency may be longer.* Hartshorne et al., "A Critical Period for Second Language Acquisition," 7.

Chapter 25. Biliterate Seal of Approval

164 *Unz claimed he had an IQ of 214.* By comparison, Einstein's IQ was said to be around 160. https://www.livescience.com/59020-what-high-intelligence -iq-means.html.

164 *Unz claimed that bilingual education was a failure.* Catherine Snow, the Harvard faculty member who attended the debate with Ron Unz and described him as "diabolical," acknowledged that some bilingual education programs were, indeed, bad. They cosseted students and unintentionally held them back from the more challenging content. These were, however, a small number of programs. Proposition 227 tried to throw the baby out with the bathwater.

165 *"I was very, very opposed to it."* Julia Brownley (activist mom turned California State Assemblywoman), in discussion with the author, October 2017. All other quotes by her are from this discussion. Hear some of the conversation in "Sealed with *un Beso*," *America the Bilingual* (podcast), Episode 15, 2017, https://www .americathebilingual.com/15-sealed-with-un-beso/.

165 *a "doctorate in demagoguery."* James Crawford, *Advocating for English Learners: Selected Essays* (Clevedon, UK: Multilingual Matters, 2008), 67.

165 *When she pointed out that not a single expert...endorsed his interpretation.* Catherine Snow (faculty member, Harvard Graduate School of Education), in discussion with the author, April 2015.

166 *"It was a very, very sad evening."* Shelly Spiegel-Coleman (founder of Californians Together), in discussion with the author, October 2017. All other quotes by her are from this discussion. Hear some of the conversation in "Sealed with *un Beso*," https://www.americathebilingual.com/15-sealed-with-un-beso/.

167 *a color-coded map where everyone could watch the progression of states adopting their own seals of biliteracy.* See https://sealofbiliteracy.org/. While the Seal of Biliteracy has been a great success for valorizing language skills, ongoing efforts are aimed at ensuring that the award is achievable by minority children, grows to include uncommonly taught languages, and recognizes the importance of linguistic multicompetence. Guadalupe Valdés, "The Future of the Seal of Biliteracy: Issues of Equity and Inclusion," in *The Seal of Biliteracy: Case Studies and Considerations for Policy Implementation*, ed. Amy J. Heineke and Kristin J. Davin (Charlotte, NC: Information Age Publishing, 2020), 175-201.

167 *The Seal of Biliteracy is what the Harvard Law School professor Cass Sunstein might call a* **nudge.** Presentation to Advanced Leadership Initiative cohort by Cass R. Sunstein, Harvard University, 2015; and Thaler and Sunstein, *Nudge*, 6.

168 *"I was able to get a 5."* Jose Andrade (high school recipient of the Seal of Biliteracy), in discussion with the author, October 2017. Hear some of the conversation in "Sealed with *un Beso*," https://www.americathebilingual.com/15-sealed-with -un-beso/. When given the chance to speak for themselves, students sometimes say things of ringing clarity, as this Latino student did: "The best way to give

Latino students a future is to make sure that they speak both of their languages well." Maria M. Carreira and Tom Beeman, *Voces: Latino Students on Life in the United States* (Santa Barbara, CA: Praeger, 2014), 29.

Chapter 26. Why a Gap Year Is a Good Year

169 *"My parents are immigrants from Poland, but they met in New York."* Paulina Jedrzejowski (gap year student), in discussion with the author, October 2017. All other quotes by her are from this discussion. Hear some of the conversation in "When a Gap Year Becomes a Bridge Year," *America the Bilingual* (podcast), Episode 17, 2017, https://www.americathebilingual.com/17-when -a-gap-year-becomes-a-bridge-year/.

170 *"Historically, we have considered this gap year to be somewhat remedial."* Abby Falik (founder and CEO of the Global Citizen Year program), in tele- phone discussion with the author, October 2017. All other quotes by her are from this discussion. Hear some of the conversation in "When a Gap Year Becomes a Bridge Year," https://www.americathebilingual.com/17-when-a-gap -year-becomes-a-bridge-year/.

172 *"I've watched freshmen go to college and then take a year off."* Catharine "Cappy" Bond Hill (former president of Vassar), in discussion with the author, October 2017. All other quotes by her are from this discussion. Hear some of the con- versation in "When a Gap Year Becomes a Bridge Year," https://www.america thebilingual.com/17-when-a-gap-year-becomes-a-bridge-year/.

172 *taking a year off...got a lot of media attention when President Obama's older daughter, Malia, decided to.* Adrienne Green, "How Common Is a Gap Year? Malia Obama will attend Harvard, but she's waiting until her dad's out of office." *The Atlantic*, May 2, 2016, https://www.theatlantic.com/education /archive/2016/05/how-common-is-a-gap-year/480921/.

Chapter 28. Speaking the Language of Our Grandparents

186 *"The neighborhoods in which I lived...were all middle-class Jewish neighbor- hoods."* Joshua Fishman, interview on May 17, 2005, by Nancy H. Hornberger and Martin Pütz, *Language Loyalty, Language Planning, and Language Revital- ization*, 36.

187 *"some supposedly natural drift of historical events or the obvious direction of social change."* Hornberger and Pütz, 80.

187 *Champions of minority languages were not "defenders of some mystical, mythical and bygone past."* Hornberger and Pütz, 85.

187 *"I tried to get away from the 'foreign' because it didn't fit well."* Joshua A. Fish- man, "Questions for Joshua A. Fishman," telephone interview by members of the

National Heritage Language Resource Center at UCLA, published March 12, 2010, https://www.international.ucla.edu/apc/article/114238.

187 *The only inquiry into languages on the US Census was whether people spoke English at home.* Baker and Wright, *Foundation of Bilingual Education and Bilingualism*, 33.

188 *Fishman wrote that the book was "particularly appropriate at the present time."* Joshua A. Fishman, *Language Loyalty in the United States: The Maintenance and Perpetuation of Non-English Mother Tongues by American Ethnic and Religious Groups* (The Hague: Mouton Publishers, 1966), 15. Fishman was writing at the same time that other intellectuals, including Lewis Mumford (*Technics and Civilization*) and Jacques Ellul (*The Technological Society*), and novelists such as Kurt Vonnegut (*Player Piano*), were writing about the struggle the human race was having in coming to terms with rapid technological change.

188 *"Is it possible...that these resources are being wasted."* Fishman, 15. Echoing Fishman, two other champions of heritage languages have called them "an underutilized resource" for America. Maria Polinsky and Olga Kagan, "Heritage Languages: In the 'Wild' and in the Classroom," *Language and Linguistics Compass* 1/5 (2007): 368–95, https://scholar.harvard.edu/mpolinsky/files/Offprint.pdf.

188 *there had been declines across nearly all twenty-three immigrant languages in the number of speakers compared with 1940.* Part of the reason was that the total number of people in the US in 1960 born outside of the country was down to 9.7 million, constituting only 5.4 percent of the total American population, whereas a generation earlier, in 1930, the number of people born outside the country was nearly 14 million, amounting to almost 13 percent of a smaller overall American population.

188 *success is "dependent on an encouraging and facilitating environment."* Fishman, *Language Loyalty in the United States*, 374. For more on efforts to ensure this environment, see Maria Carreira and Olga Kagan, "Heritage Language Education: A Proposal for the Next 50 Years," *Foreign Language Annals* 51, no. 1 (March 2018): 152-68, https://www.researchgate.net/publication/323784791_Heritage _language_education_A_proposal_for_the_next_50_years.

189 *"but before that, there wasn't any heritage language teaching at Harvard."* Maria Luisa Parra (heritage language professor), in discussion with the author, January 2015. All quotes by her are from this discussion.

189 *Kim likens the Spanish that many of her heritage students speak to beachwear.* Kim Potowski (heritage language professor), in telephone discussion with the author, April 2017.

190 *some fancier clothes for the students to add to their linguistic wardrobes.* Kim Potowski later expanded on this idea, in email correspondence with the author in September 2020: "Then, they can examine together why certain forms of language are considered more or less prestigious than others—that is, who are the people in power exerting the linguistic gatekeeping? This way, heritage speakers can make informed choices about the ways they wish to speak."

190 *"older children are more linguistically retentive than younger children."* Fishman, *Language Loyalty in the United States*, 394.

190 ***"I am Puerto Rican, through and through."*** Ed De La Torre (non-Spanish speaker), in telephone discussion with the author, July 2017. All quotes by him are from this discussion.

192 ***"Those were good courses in Tagalog."*** April Leyson (a passive bilingual), in discussion with the author, March 2016. All quotes by her are from this discussion.

192 ***"I don't just want to validate them, I want to help them."*** Maria Carreira (heritage language professor), in discussion with the author, June 2015. All quotes by her are from this discussion.

193 ***"We are getting more third-generation students now."*** Elham Sadegholvad (professor of Persian), in discussion with the author, June 2015. All quotes by her are from this discussion.

194 ***The "encouraging and facilitating environment" that Fishman called for in 1966 has...begun to materialize.*** More information on the Coalition of Community-Based Heritage Language Schools can be found here: https://www .heritagelanguageschools.org/coalition.

Chapter 29. The Seductive Power of Study Abroad

195 *"'having the easy, jaunty air of young men of fashion.'"* David McCullough, *The Greater Journey: Americans in Paris* (New York: Simon & Schuster, 2011), 131.

195 *"'does not exist in the nature of things.'"* McCullough, 131.

195 *at the time, America was still mostly agricultural.* Leo Marx, *Machine in the Garden: Technology and the Pastoral Ideal in America* (Oxford: Oxford University Press, 1964).

196 *"With few exceptions...they were educated and reasonably well off."* McCullough, *The Greater Journey*, 4.

196 **Three Vassar Girls** *novels.* *Vassar Encyclopedia* (online), s.v. "Elizabeth Williams Champney," http://vcencyclopedia.vassar.edu/alumni/elizabeth-williams -champney.html.

196 *Vassar said adieu to its Seven Sisters heritage.* *Vassar Encyclopedia* (online), s.v. "A History of Coeducation," http://vcencyclopedia.vassar.edu/notable-events/ coeducation/a-history-of-coeducation.html.

196 *"My father was happy when he learned that it would cost less."* Lori Granger Leveen (former Vassar study away student), in discussion with the author, June 2019.

196 *"Every day was an adventure."* Carolyn Cain (former Vassar study away student), in discussion and in email correspondence with the author, February 2020.

197 *"We insist that the student is fully prepared."* Ben Lotto (Vassar study away advisor), in discussion with the author, November 2014.

197 *"when they return to campus they seem more flexible."* Susan Correll Kennett (Vassar director of international programs), in discussion with the author, November 2014. All quotes by her are from this discussion.

198 *far more students study abroad today than in years past.* Institute of International Education, *Open Doors 2019: Report on International Educational Exchange*, Report #IEW2019 (Washington, DC: U.S. Institute of Peace), November 18, 2019, https://p.widencdn.net/6tpaeo/Open-Doors-Annual -Data-Release-2019-11-17-Print.

198 *In 1985, about fifty thousand American college students studied abroad.* Todd M. Davis, ed., "Open Doors 1995-1996: Report on International Education Exchange," Institute of International Education: 11, https://files.eric.ed.gov /fulltext/ED404959.pdf.

198 *"Not everybody has the means to go abroad."* Liza Carbajo (head of higher educa-tion initiatives at IIE), in discussion with the author, April 2017.

198 *Fully 30 percent are non-white.* Institute of International Education, *Open Doors 2019*, https://p.widencdn.net/6tpaeo/Open-Doors-Annual-Data-Release -2019-11-17-Print.

199 *imperative for American students to learn another language.* Allan E. Good-man, "The Global Education Imperative: Building Bridges," *University World News*, February 2, 2018. https://www.universityworldnews.com/post.php?story =20180202144122426.

200 *"I decided to go to France my sophomore year."* Ben Macklowe (antiques dealer), in discussion with the author, February 2017.

200 *Worldwide, more than 5.3 million students study abroad.* Institute of Inter-national Education, 2019 Project Atlas Infographics, file:///C:/Users/mim /Downloads/Project-Atlas-2019-graphics.pdf.

200 *These million students who study in the US generally stay for several years in order to earn undergraduate or graduate degrees.* Institute of International Education, *Open Doors 2019*, https://p.widencdn.net/6tpaeo/Open-Doors -Annual-Data-Release-2019-11-17-Print.

200 *These students bring in about $45 billion annually.* Institute of International Education, "The Number of International Students in the United States Hits All-Time High," press release, November 18, 2019, https://www.iie.org /Why-IIE/Announcements/2019/11/Number-of-International-Students -in-the-United-States-Hits-All-Time-High.

201 *and finally, the US, with a mere 5.5 percent of our seats warmed by international butts.* The 5.5 percent of seats we do fill with internationals is an average for America as a whole; the universities in America ranked as top, according to *US News & World Report*, all have a higher percentage of international students. In fact, the top ten universities have an average of 11.7 percent of their seats filled with international students, more than twice the national average. This represents an average of the percentage of international students that *US News &*

World Report reported for Princeton, Harvard, Columbia, MIT, Yale, Stanford, Chicago, University of Pennsylvania, Northwestern, and Duke, the ten top-ranked national universities in 2020: https://www.usnews.com/best-colleges /rankings/national-universities.

201 *a program called the Global Engineering Education Exchange.* Institute of International Education, "Global E³ Program Structure," https://www.iie.org /Programs/Global-E3/About/Program-Structure.

201 *Integral to the program, says the IIE, are "paid internships in an industrial setting or laboratory in the host country."* https://www.iie.org/.

202 *At the graduate school level, thousands more go abroad for research and other individualized programs.* The Institute of International Education tried to measure this for the first time in 2017. About twenty-five thousand graduate students, some 3.4 percent of America's total, were known to participate in overseas learning of some kind in 2016, although these figures are, according to IIE, clearly an undercount since reporting was not yet in place. Two of the purposes identified for this graduate-level travel are field work and language study. See also Jodi Sanger and Leah Mason, EdD, "Who's Counting? Understanding the Landscape of Graduate Learning Overseas," *Higher Education Today* blog, October 2019, https://www .higheredtoday.org/2019/11/18/understanding-u-s-graduate-student-mobility/.

202 *"My father works for a Japanese company…and I want to as well."* Nikhil Malekal (MBA candidate in Japan), in discussion with the author, July 2016.

Chapter 30. Thank You for Your Service

204 *"I basically lied on my application and said I had two years of French."* Mark Ford (former Peace Corps volunteer), in discussion with the author, July 2017. All quotes by him are from this discussion.

204 *Had this been in the early years of the Peace Corps.* Find more on how the Peace Corps works at https://files.peacecorps.gov/multimedia/pdf/about/pc_facts.pdf.

205 *"The Peace Corps in the mid-'70s began to move the training programs in-country."* Alvino Fantini (professor emeritus at the School for International Training), in telephone discussion with the author, June 2017. All quotes by him are from this discussion.

206 *Shriver had also been an exchange student with the Experiment in International Living.* Find more on its history at https://www.experiment.org/about -the-experiment/history-mission/.

208 *a long-term study of some two thousand people who studied and lived abroad.* Alvino E. Fantini, *Intercultural Communicative Competence in Education Exchange: A Multinational Perspective*, 1st ed. (Abingdon, UK: Routledge, 2018).

208 *"My mom is huge into social work."* Matt Shipley (recent Peace Corps volunteer), in discussions with the author, December 2013, and by phone, April 2020. All quotes by him are from these discussions. Read more about Community

Greening, the nonprofit he founded after his time in the Peace Corps, at https://communitygreening.org/.

210 *"I kind of resigned myself to talking like a toddler for the next two years."* Janine Winn (Peace Corps senior-age volunteer), in telephone discussion with the author, July 2017. All quotes by her are from this discussion.

211 *The US military sends far more Americans overseas.* Kristen Bialik, "U.S. Active-Duty Military Presence Overseas Is at Its Smallest in Decades," Pew Research Center, August 22, 2017, https://www.pewresearch.org/fact-tank/2017/08/22/u-s-active-duty-military-presence-overseas-is-at-its-smallest-in-decades/.

211 *"I was pure gringo."* Kevin Ruelas (former interpreter for the US Army), in telephone discussion with the author, May 2016. All quotes by him are from this interview.

213 *"I was a Marine and I did what they told me to."* Güero Loco, in discussion with the author, ACTFL Annual Convention and World Languages Expo, November 2017. All quotes by him are from this discussion. For more on how this hip-hop artist is helping kids become bilingual, see his website, https://www.bilingualnationusa.com/gueroloco.

Chapter 31. Finding Where as a Family

214 *"We did that for six months...so that they would have full immersion."* Bettina Young (mom whose school-age children split their time between Italy and the US), in discussion with the author, February 2017. All quotes by her are from this discussion. Hear some of the conversation in "The Bella and the Bold," *America the Bilingual* (podcast), Episode 7, 2017, https://www.americathebilingual.com/7-the-bella-and-the-bold/.

215 *"Yeah, it was pretty hard."* Daniel Young (Bettina's eldest son), in discussion with the author, June 2017. All quotes by him are from this discussion.

216 *"My uncle had been at Notre Dame...and inspired me to broaden myself."* Rich Carrigan (business owner who pays his immigrant employees to learn English on site), in telephone discussion with the author, May 2016.

217 *"I am what survives of me."* Erik Erikson, a twentieth-century developmental psychologist, identified eight stages of personal development that evolve as we age. The seventh, which manifests itself in mid-adulthood, is what he called generativity. We know it more commonly today as paying it forward, where we perform an altruistic work for another—in this case, for someone in the next generation. http://www.postkiwi.com/2005/erikson-identity-development/ and https://www.gq.com.au/success/opinions/what-it-takes-to-leave-a-legacy/news-story/41a6354be82cafa315fd35116fa0a4b9.

218 *As the Encore.org founder Marc Freedman explains.* Encore promotes intergenerational relationships by encouraging the older generations ready for their

"second act" to volunteer in ways that help young people. Learn more at https: //encore.org/our-quest/.

Preamble to the Twelve Myths

221 *We may be the seeds, but neighbors, friends, colleagues, and even strangers provide the soil, water, air, and sunshine for us to grow.* Bialystok and Hakuta have used the expression, "the ecosystem of language learning." *In Other Words*, viii.

221 *"few of us are without opinions about language."* Edwards, *Sociolinguistics*, 31.

Chapter 32. Myth No. 1—The Whole World Speaks English: The Tourist's Perspective

223 *"They'll laugh at you if you say that in China or in Japan."* Ken Romeo (associate director of the Stanford Language Center), in discussion with the author, June 2016. All quotes by him are from this discussion.

223 *English speakers number more than 1.1 billion people.* Ethnologue: Languages of the World, https://www.ethnologue.com/guides/ethnologue200. For a helpful infographic, see Iman Ghosh, "Ranked: The 100 Most Spoken Languages Around the World," Visual Capitalist, February 15, 2020, https://www.visualcapitalist .com/100-most-spoken-languages/.

223 *the market for English exceeds the market for all other languages.* The author's telephone discussions with Luis von Ahn, Duolingo, February 2016; discussion with Andres Moreno, Open English, January 2016; and discussion with Andrew Mangion, EC English, March 2016.

224 *One researcher...estimates the number of English learners at 1.5 billion.* Ulrich Ammon, University of Dusseldorf, cited in Rick Noack and Lazaro Gamio, "The world's languages, in seven maps and charts," *Independent*, December 31, 2015, https://www.independent.co.uk/news/world/the-worlds-languages-in-seven -maps-and-charts-a6791871.html.

224 *This would amount to just over one-third of all humans.* Tsedal Neeley, "Global Business Speaks English: Why You Need a Language Strategy Now," *Harvard Business Review*, May 2012, https://www.hbs.edu/faculty/Pages/item.aspx ?num=42451. The Worldometer put the world's population as of April 8, 2020 at 7.8 billion: https://www.worldometers.info/world-population/.

224 *the average English ability is quite high among the general population.* EF [English First] English Proficiency Index: "A Ranking of 100 Countries and Regions by English Skills Based on the EF Standard English Test," 2019, 5-6, https://www.ef.com/__/~/media/centralefcom/epi/downloads/full-reports /v9/ef-epi-2019-english.pdf.

225 *It was such an international committee that pegged latitude and longitude.* Dava Sobel and William J.H. Andrewes, *The Illustrated Longitude: The True Story of a Lone Genius Who Solved the Greatest Scientific Problem of His Time* (New York: Walker & Company, 1998), 199.

225 *the world's common language was supposed to be Esperanto.* The linguist Arika Okrent explains that Esperanto was the most successful of a long line of attempts to create a universal language: "By the time Esperanto came along, a couple centuries' worth of invented languages had failed to attract more than a handful of speakers." Arika Okrent, *In the Land of Invented Languages: Esperanto Rock Stars, Klingon Poets, Loglan Lovers, and the Mad Dreamers Who Tried to Build a Perfect Language* (New York: Spiegel & Grau, 2009), 85.

226 *"most of the spoken words began to go their own weird way."* Dorren, *Lingo*, 281.

226 *it must have "a means of global communication among its members."* Bellos, *Is That a Fish in Your Ear?*, 17.

226 *When the USSR imploded, China dropped Russian like a hot* **kartoshka.** See also Kejal Vyas, "Nyet Loss: Cubans Rush to Learn English, Abandon Russian," *The Wall Street Journal*, November 21, 2015.

226 *"not a process of language imposition but of language elimination."* Bellos, *Is That a Fish in Your Ear?*, 17.

226 *Of the fifty million Europeans who migrated to the New World.* Gerber, *American Immigration*, 2.

227 *"as an amazing world resource which presents us with unprecedented possibilities for mutual understanding."* David Crystal, *English as a Global Language*, 2nd ed. (Cambridge: Cambridge University Press, 2014), xiii.

227 *"Both Chile and Mongolia have recently declared their intention to become bilingual in English."* Robert McCrum, *Globish: How the English Language Became the World's Language* (New York: W.W. Norton, 2010), 276.

227 *"the English language demonstrates a strong network effect."* EF English Proficiency Index, "A Ranking of 100 Countries and Regions by English Skills," 4, https://www.ef.com/__/~/media/centralefcom/epi/downloads/full-reports/v9/ef-epi-2019-english.pdf.

228 *"Often I would read a citation about Language X to an advocate of Language Z."* Joshua A. Fishman, *In Praise of the Beloved Language: A Comparative View of Positive Ethnolinguistic Consciousness* (Berlin: Mouton de Gruyter, 1996), xix.

229 *"Every language tells your listener who you are, where you come from, where you belong."* Bellos, *Is That a Fish in Your Ear?*, 335.

229 *"language is part and parcel of the texture of human social life."* Fishman, *In Praise of the Beloved Language*, 3.

229 *Beloved languages are disappearing at a rapid rate, but this is mostly the result of urbanization.* Don Kulick, *A Death in the Rainforest* (Chapel Hill, NC: Algonquin, 2019), 246-52. See also Diamond, *The World Until Yesterday*.

229 *Today, visitors to Morocco will see the artful Amazigh script.* Hear the author's first lesson in Arabic in "America the Bilingual Goes to Morocco," *America the Bilingual* (podcast), Episode 39, 2019, https://www.americathebilingual .com/39-america-the-bilingual-goes-to-morocco/.

230 *there seems to be widespread belief in people's rights to retain their heritage languages.* Linguistic rights were first included as an international human right in the United Nations' Universal Declaration of Human Rights in 1948. Article 2 stated that individuals are "entitled to all the rights and freedoms set forth in this Declaration, without distinction of any kind," including language: https://www .un.org/en/universal-declaration-human-rights/. In the last decades of the twentieth century, more declarations of linguistic rights were promulgated, including the "Declaration of the Rights of Persons Belonging to National or Ethnic, Religious and Linguistic Minorities," adopted by General Assembly resolution 47/135 of 18 December 1992: https://www.ohchr.org/en/professionalinterest/pages /minorities.aspx.

230 *there is also a real rise in minority languages being taught in heritage and dual language schools.* Corinne A. Seals and Sheena Shad, eds., *Heritage Language Policies Around the World* (Abingdon, UK: Routledge, 2018).

230 *The...industry is frothy with investments from venture capital, private equity, and mergers and acquisitions.* See Slator.com and the Slator 2020 Language Service Provider Index, February 25, 2020, https://slator.com/data-research/the-slator -2020-language-service-provider-index/. Also listen to *SlatorPod* (podcast) Episode 10, February 27, 2020, https://podtail.com/en/podcast/slatorpod/. The nonprofit Globalization and Localization Association (GALA), based in Seattle, reports that the language industry accounts for approximately $50 billion in revenue internationally and is growing. https://www.gala-global.org/industry /industry-facts-and-data.

230 *the $1.5 billion acquisition of the American firm LanguageLine Solutions.* "Agreement by Teleperformance to Acquire LanguageLine Solutions LLC," *Businesswire*, August 22, 2016, https://www.businesswire.com/news/home/20160821005024 /en/Agreement-Teleperformance-Acquire-LanguageLine-Solutions-LLC.

231 *tourism and travel generate 10 percent of global GDP and 10 percent of jobs.* International Finance Corporation, *Deep Dive: IFC's Hotel Investment Experience and Approach* (Washington, DC: World Bank Group, January 2018), 2.

231 *"the only monolingual people in the world."* David Bellos, "How Long Will the Global Dominance of the English Language Last?," Big Think (website), September 20, 2012, http://bigthink.com/users/david-bellos.

231 *we "have only one language with which to think."* Bellos, *Is That a Fish in Your Ear?*, 19.

Chapter 33. The Whole World Speaks English:
The Professional's Perspective

232 *They saw American diplomats overseas showing disdain for the locals.* See William J. Lederer and Eugene Burdick, *The Ugly American* (New York: W.W. Norton, 1958), reissued by the publisher in 2019, in paperback. Additionally, in *Political Tribes: Group Instinct and the Fate of Nations* (New York: Penguin, 2019), the legal scholar Amy Chua shows how our nation's inability to understand the cultures and languages of nations overseas has been tragic for Americans and our allies.

233 *Having no Spanish when he arrived, Borlaug was committed to learning it.* Kenneth M. Quinn, "Norman E. Borlaug: Extended Biography," the website of The World Food Prize Foundation, https://www.worldfoodprize.org/en /dr_norman_e_borlaug/extended_biography/.

233 *He eventually mastered Spanish well enough that he could deliver spirited speeches.* Debora Mackenzie, "Norm Borlaug: the man who fed the world," *NewScientist* (September 14, 2009), https://www.newscientist.com/article /dn17778-norm-borlaug-the-man-who-fed-the-world/.

233 *"It took me a year before I was able to give a speech."* Erica Mackey (creator of solar-powered lighting in Tanzania), in discussion with the author, following her presentation at Stanford University Graduate School of Business, Social Ventures class, January 26, 2016.

234 *"Every time the seat belt sign goes off in some country I've never seen before, I wish I could travel back in time."* Bill Weir (CNN anchor), in discussion with the author at the ACTFL Annual Convention and World Languages Expo in Nashville, TN, November 2017. Hear some of the conversation in "Bill Weir Loves Language Teachers, Wishes He Had Listened to His," *America the Bilingual* (podcast), Episode 18, 2017, https://www.americathebilingual .com/18-bill-weir-loves-language-teachers%e2%80%8a-%e2%80%8awishes -he-had-listened-to-his/.

234 *"Franklin turned out to be more visible in French."* Stacy Schiff (biographer), in email discussion with the author, April 2020.

235 *my eyes were opened to other reasons why bilingual skills are critical for the military.* For more on CENTCOM, see https://www.centcom.mil/ABOUT-US /COMMAND-NARRATIVE/ and https://www.centcom.mil/AREA-OF -RESPONSIBILITY/CENTCOM-COALITION/; and on Special Operations Command, https://www.socom.mil/FactBook/2020%20Fact%20Book.pdf.

236 *If there is a more serious application for professional-level language skills, I don't know what it would be.* For a summary of the ongoing needs of the US intelligence community for advanced language skills, see the testimony before the Senate Homeland Security and Government Affairs Committee on May 21, 2012,

by Glenn Nordin, Principal Foreign Language and Area Advisor, https://www
.hsgac.senate.gov/imo/media/doc/Glen%20Nordin%20Testimony.pdf. Nordin
and the author also held email discussions on this matter in September 2012.

236 *there are nearly 8.7 million Jehovah's Witnesses worldwide.* "How Many of
Jehovah's Witnesses Are There Worldwide?," JW.org, 2019 Report, https://www
.jw.org/en/jehovahs-witnesses/faq/how-many-jw/.

236 *In an article on JW.org, "Breaking Through an Ancient Barrier."* See https://www
.jw.org/en/library/magazines/awake-no3-2016-june/breaking-language-barrier/.

237 *"'Only two kinds of people can learn Finnish, babies and missionaries.'"* "Why
Mormons are So Good at Languages," *Subtitle* (podcast) Episode 7, January
2020, https://subtitlepod.com/why-mormons-are-so-good-at-languages/. See
also Samuel B. Hislop, "How Do Mormon Missionaries Learn Foreign Languages? NPR Explains," Newsroom web page of The Church of Jesus Christ
of Latter-day Saints (June 9, 2014), https://newsroom.churchofjesuschrist.org
/article/npr-mormon-missionary-language-training; "Lessons from the Language
Boot Camp for Mormon Missionaries," NPR (June 7, 2014), https://www.npr
.org/2014/06/07/319805068/lessons-from-the-language-boot-camp-for
-mormon-missionaries; and "Learning Spanish as a Latter-day Saint Missionary,"
YouTube video, https://www.youtube.com/watch?v=d8rTtkLVmOQ.

238 *the Church has grown substantially, today counting membership worldwide of
more than sixteen million.* "Facts and Statistics," the Newsroom web page of The
Church of Jesus Christ of Latter-day Saints, https://newsroom.churchofjesus
christ.org/facts-and-statistics.

238 *The Church says...it has provided more than $2.3 billion in humanitarian assis-
tance.* See the Humanitarian Services web page of The Church of Jesus Christ
of Latter-day Saints, https://www.ldsphilanthropies.org/humanitarian-services.

238 *"I grew up in southern Missouri. My brother and I would say we are bilingual."*
Lois Melbourne (businesswoman), in telephone discussion with the author,
February 2017. All quotes by her are from this discussion. Hear some of the conversation in "The CEO and the Polyglot," *America the Bilingual* (podcast), Episode
5, 2017, https://www.americathebilingual.com/5-the-ceo-and-the-polyglot/.

239 *"They said, 'Don't bother to come to this meeting if you're not going to speak
French.'"* Andy Simmons (businessman and polyglot), in telephone discussion
with the author, March 2017. Hear some of the conversation in "The CEO and the
Polyglot," https://www.americathebilingual.com/5-the-ceo-and-the-polyglot/.

239 *"Language is the combination lock that opens a whole set of cultural contexts."* Lisa
Bjornson Wolf (businesswoman), in telephone discussion with the author, May 2016.

240 *"The professor told me, 'I think you should go get your money back because you'll
never learn Chinese.'"* Bill Johnson (businessman and bilingual in Chinese), in
telephone discussion with the author, May 2016. All quotes by him are from
this discussion.

241 *if you want to succeed in international business, you do have to really try.* US businesses depend on bilingual employees to a surprising degree already. According to the 2019 report, "Making Languages Our Business: Addressing Foreign Language Demand Among U.S. Employers," which the American Council on the Teaching of Foreign Languages (ACTFL) published, "nine out of 10 U.S. employers report a reliance on U.S.-based employees with language skills other than English, with one-third (32 percent) reporting a high dependency. Moreover, demand is on a sustained rise." There are also millions of Americans working in the US for internationally-owned firms. The UK is the number one nation for employing Americans in the US, followed, in order, by Japan, France, and Germany. American employees of such firms have an incentive to become competent in the language of their superiors at headquarters. In 2015 these companies paid their employees, on average, more than private US firms, and paid more than $500 billion in total compensation. Kristen Bialik, "Number of U.S. workers employed by foreign-owned companies is on the rise," Pew Research Center, December 14, 2017, https://www.pewresearch.org/fact-tank/2017/12/14/number-of-u-s-workers-employed-by-foreign-owned-companies-is-on-the-rise/.

241 *the pacifying role of commerce is beginning to be more generally appreciated.* Steven Pinker, *The Better Angels of Our Nature: Why Violence Has Declined* (New York: Viking, 2011), 287-88. From the days of "should we raid or should we trade?," these two books illustrate how the traders gradually won out: William J. Bernstein, *A Splendid Exchange: How Trade Shaped the World* (New York: Atlantic Monthly Press, 2008); and Matt Ridley, *The Rational Optimist: How Prosperity Evolves* (New York: Harper, 2010).

241 *businesses themselves are evolving.* John Mackey and Raj Sisodia, *Conscious Capitalism: Liberating the Heroic Spirit of Business* (Boston: Harvard Business School Publishing, 2013).

Chapter 34. Myth No. 2—Technology Will Make Language Learning Obsolete

243 *or maybe implants.* Much like the Babel fish that the novelist Douglas Adams made famous in *The Hitchhiker's Guide to the Galaxy*, first published in 1979.

243 *"the translation will appear as subtitles in your glasses."* Speech by Michio Kaku, YPO Edge conference, Dubai, United Arab Emirates, March 10, 2016.

243 *Once the technology gets good enough.* Nicholas Ostler, *The Last Lingua Franca: English Until the Return of Babel* (New York: Walker & Company, 2010), 11. Ostler also held email discussions with the author in August 2014 and November 2015.

245 *"people were saying things about artificial intelligence which today seem ridiculous."* Christopher Manning (Stanford professor of machine learning), in discussion with the author, December 2016. All quotes by him are from this discussion.

246 *"It's like hiking in the desert."* Paul Saffo (technology forecaster), in discussion with the author, February 2016.

247 *"many observers do not readily embrace...the law of accelerating returns."* Ray Kurzweil, *The Singularity Is Near: When Humans Transcend Biology* (New York: Viking, 2005), 7.

248 *"When we invented language...I could actually take this hierarchy of symbols in my neocortex."* Ray Kurzweil (inventor), answering the author's question during Kurzweil's presentation at Singularity University, November 2014. All other quotes by him are from this exchange.

249 *"Technology can never replace our need to grow."* Tom Morris (philosopher), in discussion with the author, August 2017. Hear Tom's thoughts on the value of knowing Latin in "In Case You Thought Latin Was Dead...," https://www .americathebilingual.com/in-case-you-thought-latin-was-dead/.

250 *"The advent of AI didn't diminish the performance of purely human chess players."* Kevin Kelly, *The Inevitable: Understanding the 12 Technological Forces That Will Shape Our Future* (New York: Viking, 2016), 41. For a dramatic and big-hearted telling of this story, watch the 2009 movie *Queen to Play*, starring Sandrine Bonnaire and Kevin Kline, about a chambermaid who gets her start with a computer chess game. The World Chess champion in 2020, Magnus Carlsen, was born in 1990 and thus grew up with computer chess programs. As a teenager, he became the youngest player ever to reach the pinnacle of chess and achieved the highest quantitative rating in history. https://en.wikipedia.org/wiki /Magnus_Carlsen. Meanwhile, Garry Kasparov teaches chess through 29 video lessons on the online teaching platform Masterclass: https://www.masterclass .com/classes/garry-kasparov-teaches-chess. The same boost in popularity appears to have followed the triumph of the computer program AlphaGo over the world champion Go player Lee Sedol in 2016. See the documentary "AlphaGo—The Movie, Full Documentary," directed by Greg Kohs, March 13, 2020, https: //www.youtube.com/watch?v=WXuK6gekU1Y&feature=youtu.be. AlphaGo, the creation of the Google-funded company DeepMind, has been supplanted by AlphaZero, which has also triumphed at chess, beating the other computer programs. According to David Silver, one of the principal scientists responsible for AlphaZero, Magnus Carlsen is learning from AlphaZero. In an interview, Silver said, "Magnus Carlsen, apparently, recently commented on his improvement in performance and he attributes it to AlphaZero, he's been studying the games of AlphaZero and he's changed his style of play to play more like AlphaZero and it's led to him actually increasing his rating to a new peak." #86 David Silver: AlphaGo, AlphaZero, and Deep Reinforcement Learning, interviewed by Lex Fridman on his Artificial Intelligence podcast, April 3, 2020, Position 1:11:30, https://lexfridman.com/david-silver/.

250 *They used the machines to learn how to play.* Brian Dolan, *Inventing Entertainment: The Player Piano and the Origins of an American Musical Industry* (Lanham, MD: Rowman & Littlefield, 2009).

252 *"ever-improving machine translation will be a boon to billions for basic language work."* Kevin Kelly (technology observer and writer), in telephone discussion with the author, January 2017. All quotes by him, excepting those from his books, are from this discussion. Additionally, according to Bill Rivers, Executive Director of the Joint National Committee for Languages and the National Council for Languages and International Studies, the growth of machine translation is spurring the need for human translators and interpreters. Rivers, a former Russian interpreter and translator, held a discussion with the author in November 2018.

252 *a two-tier system of "commodity and premium."* Kohn, *Four Words for Friend*, 201ff.

253 *"In the future, we'll find it easier to love technology."* Kevin Kelly, *What Technology Wants* (New York: Viking, 2010), 324.

254 *"I was startled to see how...unequivocally they anthropomorphized it."* Joseph Weizenbaum, *Computer Power and Human Reason: From Judgment to Calculation* (New York: W.H. Freeman, 1976), 6.

254 *we are prone to blithely substitute machines for people.* Sherry Turkle, *Alone Together: Why We Expect More from Technology and Less from Each Other* (New York: Basic Books, 2011), 52.

255 *We have a deep biological need for actual human interaction.* Susan Pinker, *The Village Effect: How Face-to-Face Contact Can Make Us Healthier, Happier, and Smarter* (New York: Spiegel & Grau, 2014), 29. She provided the author with additional insights during a telephone discussion in January 2016. See also Turkle, *Alone Together.*

255 *one of our "happiness" hormones, oxytocin, kicks in.* Susan Pinker, 265.

255 *"if we want to be happy, healthy, long-lived, and yes, clever."* Susan Pinker, 266.

Chapter 35. Myth No. 3—The Best Time to Learn a Language Is When You're Young

257 *"the question in the critical period literature has never been why adults are incapable of learning a new language."* Hartshorne et al., "A Critical Period for Second Language Acquisition," 11.

257 *It may simply be "an epiphenomenon of culture."* Hartshorne et al., 11-13.

257 *"adults...learn more quickly than young learners."* Ofelia García, *Bilingual Education in the 21st Century*, 67.

257 *"children put vast amounts of time and effort into mastering a language."* Harding-Esch and Riley, *The Bilingual Family*, 69.

257 *"Adults can use what we know of our first language to organize our learning."* Katherine Sprang, "Can Monolingualism Be Cured?" in *The 5-Minute Linguist*, 140-43.

258 *"It is always disappointing to hear adults say that they are too old."* Kaufmann, *The Way of the Linguist*, 85.

258 *"this idea that adults can't learn...is false."* Lesley Chapman (language teacher), "Top Tips from Teachers" (podcast and PDF), https://www.americathebilingual.com/45 -top-tips-from-teachers-for-adult-language-learners/ and https://attachments .convertkitcdnn.com/116297/ce0a756f-eb09-4885-be80-cecfe7eb7bbd/Top %20Tips%20from%20Language%20Teachers.pdf.

258 *"Being able to learn languages only at a young age is the most prevalent prejudice."* Lomb, *Harmony of Babel*, 231.

258 *"I had to learn the language everyone seemed to be speaking."* Claude Vlandis (polyglot), in discussion with the author, November 2013. When he studied Arabic, Claude was learning Egyptian Arabic rather than Modern Standard Arabic, which is what the newscasters use.

261 *"the notion that older people are rigid."* Ann McDougall (Encore.org president), in telephone discussion with the author, July 2017. Hear some of the conversation in *America the Bilingual* (podcast), "Bless the Late-Blooming Bilinguals," Episode 16, 2017, https://www.americathebilingual.com/16-bless -the-late-blooming-bilinguals/.

261 *"Of course we can learn a language, or anything else at any age."* Laura Carstensen (founder of the Stanford Center on Longevity), in discussion with the author, February 2018. François Grosjean concurs: "one can become bilingual at any time during one's life," he says, in "Becoming Bilingual: One Can Become Bilingual at Any Time," *Psychology Today* blog (November 10, 2010), https://www.psychology today.com/intl/blog/life-bilingual/201011/becoming-bilingual. Hear some of the author's conversation with Laura Carstensen in *America the Bilingual* (podcast), "Are You Too Old to Learn Another Language?," Episode 26, 2018, https: //www.americathebilingual.com/26-are-you-too-old-to-learn-another-language/.

263 *"I started on my own with a bilingual edition of the Gospel of St. John."* I.F. Stone, *The Trial of Socrates* (New York: Anchor Books, 1989), xi.

263 *"an extraordinary sense of liberation and fulfillment."* Marc Freedman, *How to Live Forever: The Enduring Power of Connecting the Generations* (New York: PublicAffairs, 2018), 25.

263 *"what are we going to do with our supersized lives?"* The Stanford Center on Longevity: A New Map of Life, http://longevity.stanford.edu/a-new-map-of-life/.

Chapter 36. Myth No. 4—The Best Way to Learn a Language Is Total Immersion

266 *"A beginner can get more comprehensible input in one...well-taught class."* Krashen, *Explorations in Language Acquisition and Use*, 7.

267 *"so that I could read everything written by the Greeks."* Mary Norris, *Greek to Me: Adventures of the Comma Queen* (New York: W.W. Norton, 2019), 10.

267 *"I moved to Astoria, the Greek-American neighborhood in Queens."* Norris, 12.

Chapter 37. Myth No. 5—America's So Big, Where Would I Ever Use It?

269 *Only three countries are bigger.* "Largest Countries in the World (by area)," Worldometer, https://www.worldometers.info/geography/largest-countries -in-the-world/.

269 *Our 2020 population of 331 million.* "Most Populous Countries in the World (2020)," Worldometer, https://www.worldometers.info/population/most -populous-countries/.

270 *As recently as 2005, fewer than 17 percent of the world had access to the internet.* The International Telecommunication Unit of the United Nations published a series of internet usage maps in "Measuring Digital Development: Facts and Figures, 2019 ITU Publications," https://www.itu.int/en/ITU-D/Statistics /Documents/facts/FactsFigures2019.pdf. In addition to increased access to the internet worldwide, broadband subscriptions grew even more rapidly, at an annual rate of 18.4 percent, between 2005 and 2019.

271 *"that tally had tripled to ninety-three million trips."* "U.S. Citizen Travel to International Regions," US Department of Commerce, International Trade Administration, National Travel and Tourism Office, https://travel.trade.gov /view/m-2018-O-001/index.html.

Chapter 38. Myth No. 6—Accents Are Embarrassing

273 *"It's when we travel that we discover we have an accent."* John H. Esling, "Everyone Has an Accent Except Me," in *Language Myths*, ed. Laurie Bauer and Peter Trudgill (New York: Penguin, 1999), 169-75.

273 *So it was with much delight that many millions of us watching the 2020 Super Bowl.* "Smaht Pahk," 2020 Hyundai Sonata Super Bowl ad featured on YouTube, https://www.youtube.com/watch?v=85iRQdjCzj0.

273 *"I've lived in Germany pretty much straight on for thirty years."* Erik Kirschbaum (American journalist), in telephone discussion with the author, November 2017.

274 *The scale goes from Level 0, "no proficiency," to Level 5.* Interagency Language Roundtable, "ILR Skill Level Descriptions for Competence in International Communication," https://www.govtilr.org/Skills/Competence.htm#13.

274 *"Having no accent is plainly impossible."* Roberto Rey Agudo, "Everyone Has an Accent," *The New York Times* Sunday Review, July 14, 2018.

275 *"Most Britons had never heard American accents, and they were bewildered."* R.L. Trask, *Why Do Languages Change?* (Cambridge: Cambridge University Press, 2010), 11.

275 *"Then he remembered having heard that Americans did not speak English."* Paul Bowles, *The Sheltering Sky* (New York: Ecco, 2014), 148.

276 *"pronunciation difference typically becomes yet another aspect of status-boundary marking."* Edwards, *Sociolinguistics*, 24.

276 *"I didn't know which accent to use."* Bharat Ayyar (native Tamil speaker), in discussion with the author, February 2016.

276 *"when I was growing up, my mother's 'limited' English limited my perception of her."* Amy Tan, "Mother Tongue," in *Tongue-Tied: The Lives of Multilingual Children in Public Education*, ed. Otto Santa Ana (Lanham, MD: Rowman & Littlefield, 2004), 170.

277 *"She spoke with an accented English."* Jonathan Rosa (third-generation American), in discussion with the author, December 2016.

277 *we've settled on Heavy-Accent-Means-Stupid bias, or HAMS bias.* For a good summary of the social science that has revealed biases in how children and adults view accents negatively, see Costa, *The Bilingual Brain*, 144-48.

278 *"System 1...automatically and effortlessly identifies causal connections between events, sometimes even when the connection is spurious."* Kahneman, *Thinking, Fast and Slow*, 110.

279 pronunciation *"begins not in the mouth but in the ear."* Pimsleur, *How to Learn a Foreign Language*, 52.

279 *"having an accent...doesn't make you any less bilingual."* Grosjean, *Bilingual: Life and Reality*, 84.

280 *"there are parts of the mind that know a person who does not speak your language is neither stupid nor hostile."* David Berreby, *Us & Them: The Science of Identity* (Chicago: University of Chicago Press, 2008), 253.

280 *"Do you know what a foreign accent is?...It's a sign of bravery."* Amy Chua, *Battle Hymn of the Tiger Mother* (New York: Penguin, 2011), 86.

Chapter 39. Myth No. 7—I'm Just Not Good at Languages

282 *"Some people just aren't good at math."* Presentation by Professor Jo Boaler, Stanford University, to the Fellows of the Stanford Distinguished Career Institute, January 2016.

282 *"Mindsets and brain science apply to everything."* Jo Boaler (Stanford professor), in discussion with the author, March 2016. See also her book, *Mathematical Mindsets: Unleashing Students' Potential Through Creative Math, Inspiring Messages and Innovative Teaching* (San Francisco: Jossey-Bass, 2016).

283 *"A few gifted language learners do exist."* Crystal, *How Language Works*, 430.

283 *"Some people may have better language learning ability than others."* Kaufmann, *The Way of the Linguist*, 77.

283 *"No one is 'just' good at languages."* Lomb, *Harmony of Babel*, 233.

283 *"This hazy and mysterious 'language talent'...deserved my full wrath."* Lomb, 233.

283 *"there's a good reason why 'the ten-thousand-hour rule' and 'the ten-year-rule' have gone viral."* Angela Duckworth, *Grit: The Power of Passion and Perseverance* (New York: Scribner, 2016), 120.

283 *"What ripens passion is the conviction that your work matters."* Duckworth, 91.

284 *"because what we accomplish in the marathon of life depends tremendously on our grit."* Duckworth, 269.

Chapter 40. Myth No. 8—Fine, but Other Skills Are More Important

286 *What's more, these dual language schools are proving grounds for showing how being bilingual is making kids smarter.* North Carolina bilingual education leaders in discussion with the author, June 2018. Hear some of the conversation in "North Carolina: A Dual-Language Success Story," https://www.americathebilingual.com/42-north-carolina-a-dual-language-success-story/.

286 *during the aviation craze, conventional wisdom maintained that children in the US needed to become air-minded.* The historian Joseph J. Corn has written extensively about this episode in American history, including a textbook, *Science of Pre-Flight Aeronautics for High Schools.* Corn later wrote of this book: "The book covered, in considerable detail, the reasons why an airplane flew and how it was controlled in the air. By the end of 1943 this book, or one of its competitors, was being used in over half of the nation's high schools to teach the one- or two-semester-long, pre-flight aeronautics courses which had joined biology, chemistry, and physics in the American high school science curriculum." Joseph J. Corn, *The Winged Gospel: America's Romance with Aviation* (Baltimore: The Johns Hopkins University Press, 1983), 125.

287 *"Languages are that T."* Lisa Lilley Ritter (past president of ACTFL), in discussion with the author at the ACTFL 2017 annual conference in Nashville, TN, November 2017. Hear some of the conversation in "Not Your Uncle's Language Class," https://www.americathebilingual.com/not-your-uncles-language-class/.

Chapter 41. Myth No. 9—English Is Going to the Dogs

288 *"The myth of the decline of English is particularly interesting, because it is so old."* Charles A. Ferguson and Shirley Brice Heath, eds., *Language in the USA* (Cambridge: Cambridge University Press, 1981), xxix. See also James Milroy, "Myth 8: Children Can't Speak or Write Properly Any More," in *Language Myths*, Bauer and Trudgill, 58-65.

288 *"grammatical sophistication used to be nurtured in the schools."* Steven Pinker, *The Language Instinct*, 4.

289 *"Languages do not get better or worse, when they change. They just change."* Crystal, *How Language Works*, 483.

289 *"English used to be a language where verbs at the end of the sentence came."*
John McWhorter, "Do languages have to change?," in Rickerson and Hilton, *The
5-Minute Linguist*, 39. See also McWhorter's *Words on the Move: Why English
Won't—and Can't—Sit Still (Like, Literally)* (New York: Henry Holt and Company, 2016).

289 *"what is considered 'proper' English varies with the times just as fashion does."*
John McWhorter, *Our Magnificent Bastard Tongue: The Untold History of English*
(New York: Gotham, 2008), 84.

289 *"every language is always changing."* Trask, *Why Do Languages Change?*, 1.

289 *After eight years of working on it, he admitted defeat.* Jack Lynch, ed., *Samuel
Johnson's Dictionary: Selections from the 1755 Work That Defined the English
Language* (Delray Beach, FL: Levenger Press, 2002), 7.

289 *he defined the role of lexicographer as "a harmless drudge."* Lynch, 297.

290 *"The notion that anything is gained by fixing a language is cherished only by
pedants."* H.L. Mencken, *The American Language*, abridged ed., 1 vol. (New York:
Alfred A. Knopf, 1977). For more on America dragging English down, see John
Algeo, "America Is Ruining the English Language," in *Language Myths*, Bauer and
Trudgill, 176-82. Algeo, who both taught and published on linguistics, relayed
how John Adams predicted the growth of English, quoting him as saying, "English
is destined to be in the next and succeeding centuries more generally the language
of the world than Latin was in the last or French is in the present age. The reason of
this is obvious, because the increasing population in America, and their universal
connection and correspondence with all nations will, aided by the influence of
England in the world, whether great or small, force their language into general
use." For a quick survey of how English evolved into American, see Harrison,
Wicked Good Words, xii-xvi.

290 *The sociolinguist William Labov calls this the Golden Age Principle.* William
Labov, *Principles of Linguistic Change*, vol. 2: *Social Factors* (New York: Blackwell,
2001), 514.

291 *Black English is, in fact, a dialect of English, with its own rules and grammar.*
McWhorter, *Talking Back, Talking Black*, 101-18.

291 *"African-Americans ought to be thanked for contributing to daily conversation."*
Walt Wolfram, "Myth 13: Black Children are Verbally Deprived," in *Language
Myths*, Bauer and Trudgill, 103.

291 *in many countries, it's completely normal to have a home dialect and a more
formal national dialect.* In our *America the Bilingual* podcast on Africa's effortless
bilingualism, you'll hear how, from a young age, many Africans slip on different
languages as easily as different T-shirts, depending on the situation—a game of
soccer, formal education, the national language of their country: https://www
.americathebilingual.com/44-africas-relaxed-multilingualism/.

291 *"Black English is America's only English dialect that combines being strikingly
unlike standard English."* McWhorter, *Talking Back, Talking Black*, 167.

291 *newspaper editors routinely "cleaned up" what public figures and others actually said.* Robert MacNeil and William Cran, *Do You Speak American?* (New York: Nan A. Talese, 2005), 15.

292 *"Using words or terms from different languages in the same sentence or utterance has often been seen unfavorably."* Edwards, *Sociolinguistics*, 30.

292 *they finally threw in the* toalla *and decided it would be better...just to give us our own dictionary.* https://elpais.com/cultura/2012/10/10/actualidad /1349893853_744008.html.

293 *Samuel Johnson dutifully included* lingo—*a word he considered "foreign."* Lynch, *Samuel Johnson's Dictionary*, 22, 23, 302.

293 *"The common word meaning 'combustible' is* inflammable.*"* William Strunk, Jr., and E.B. White, *The Elements of Style*, 50th anniv. ed. (New York: Pearson, 2009), 47.

293 *the Merriam-Webster dictionary came down on the side of children and illiterates.* Under the entry for "flammable," see the discussion of "Why *Inflammable* Is Not the Opposite of *Flammable*," https://www.merriam-webster.com/dictionary /flammable.

293 *"I personally believe we developed language because of our deep inner need to complain."* Jane Wagner, *The Search for Signs of Intelligent Life in the Universe* (New York: It Books, 2012), 133.

Chapter 42. Myth No. 10—Today's Immigrants Aren't Learning English: A Parallax

294 *Then there's the "Despacito" song by two Puerto Rican artists. Despacito* translates to "slowly," said in the tender, sweet way that the "ito" suffix in Spanish suggests.

294 *as of 2019 America was home to some forty million people who were born outside the country.* Jynnah Radford, "Key Findings About U.S. Immigrants," Pew Research Center, June 17, 2019, https://www.pewresearch.org/fact-tank /2019/06/17/key-findings-about-u-s-immigrants/.

295 *No less an American than Benjamin Franklin blew what may have been the starting whistle.* Alejandro Portes and Rubén G. Rumbaut, *Immigrant America: A Portrait*, 4th ed. (Oakland, CA: University of California Press, 2014), 217. See also Gerber, *American Immigration*, 17-18.

295 *And then there were the many Amerindian languages.* Even discounting the Native Americans and the enslaved from Africa, as our first census of 1790 did, about 25 percent of the inhabitants spoke languages other than English. Ofelia García, *Bilingual Education in the 21st Century*, 160. García also tells us (p. 162) that among the 12 million captives brought to America from Africa for enslavement were an estimated 2 to 3 million Muslims, literate in Arabic. Other languages the Africans brought with them include Ashanti, Bakongo, Fante, Fula, Ibo, Mandingo, and Yoruba. Traces of these and other native tongues can be heard

in the language of some of their descendants, the Gullah. Wilbur Cross, *Gullah Culture in America* (Winston-Salem, NC: John F. Blair, Publisher, 2012), 259.

295 *English would be used* **unofficially**—*then, and ever after.* A few years after America gained its independence, John Adams proposed to the new American Congress that it authorize a language academy. When a bill was finally introduced in 1806 to establish such an academy, it died in the Senate. Daniel J. Boorstin, *The Americans: The Colonial Experience* (New York: Random House, 1958), 282.

295 *the Treaty of Guadalupe Hidalgo...added...some eighty to one hundred thousand Spanish speakers.* "Some 80,000 Mexicans were thereby included in the subsequent 1850 Census." US Census, "Treaty of Guadalupe Hidalgo," *Profile America* series, February 2, 2017, https://www.prnewswire.com/news-releases/us-census-bureau -daily-feature-for-february-2-treaty-of-guadalupe-hidalgo-300395534.html.

296 *We imported Chinese laborers to build the transcontinental railroad.* Stephen E. Ambrose, *Nothing Like It in the World: The Men Who Built the Transcontinental Railroad 1863–1869* (New York: Simon & Schuster, 2000), 152.

296 *Then came the great waves of immigrants from Europe.* All of the nationalities mentioned arrived in the 1800s. Oscar Handlin, *The Uprooted*, 2nd ed. (Philadelphia: University of Pennsylvania Press, 2002), 32-33. For more on what they endured on their voyages, see Edwin S. Guillet, *The Great Migration: The Atlantic Crossing by Sailing-ship Since 1770* (New York: Thomas Nelson and Sons, 1937).

296 *the 1910 census contributed to what has been called the Americanization campaign.* Colin Baker and Wayne Wright, *Foundations of Bilingual Education and Bilingualism*, 184.

296 *the languages immigrants brought to America...were generally gone in three generations.* Richard Alba and Victor Nee, *Remaking the American Mainstream: Assimilation and Contemporary Immigration* (Cambridge, MA: Harvard University Press, 2003), 219.

296 *The US "has incorporated more bilingual people than any other country in the world."* Portes and Rumbaut, *Immigrant America*, 218.

297 *"One of the most fascinating aspects of bilingualism in the United States is its extreme instability."* Hakuta, *Mirror of Language*, 166.

297 *"it would take 350 years for the average nation to experience the same amount of loss."* Hakuta, 167.

297 *The fundamental American values that prize achievement and success were consistent with a rejection of tradition.* Robin M. Williams, Jr., *American Society: A Sociological Interpretation*, 3rd ed. (New York: Alfred A. Knopf, 1970), 454.

297 *"the shift to English is both an empirical fact and a cultural requirement demanded of foreigners who have sought a new life in America."* Portes and Rumbaut, *Immigrant America*, 255.

297 *Curiously, the anglicization of the American language landscape happened at the same time as the whitening of American bread.* Aaron Bobrow-Strain, *White Bread: A Social History of the Store-Bought Loaf* (Boston: Beacon Press, 2012).

297 *The accusation that immigrants aren't learning English was part of a larger practice of complaining about immigrants in general.* Thomas J. Archdeacon, *Becoming American: An Ethnic History* (New York: Free Press, 1983), xv. See also Roger Daniels, *Coming to America: A History of Immigration and Ethnicity in American Life*, 2nd ed. (New York: Harper Perennial, 2002), 266. He writes that "successful nativist movements have almost always been linked to more general fears or uneasiness in American society. When most Americans are generally united and feel confident about their futures, they seem to be more willing to share that future with foreigners; conversely, when they are divided and lack confidence in the future, nativism is more likely to triumph."

298 *"this peculiar American waltz."* Portes and Rumbaut, *Immigrant America*, 2.

298 *"with foreign languages seen as fractious markers of cultural difference and potential disloyalty."* Portes and Rumbaut, 217.

298 *"The report dispelled long-held notions that European nations were emptying their poor houses."* Gerber, *American Immigration*, 39-40.

298 *"We worry that they'll take our jobs, drain our resources, threaten our language."* Paul Taylor, *The Next America: Boomers, Millennials, and the Looming Generational Showdown* (New York: PublicAffairs, 2014), 69. For example, the Irish-born Denis Kearney rose to power in California by castigating the Chinese laborers. Gerber, *American Immigration*, 26-28.

298 *Latinos in the US commit fewer crimes than native-born Americans.* See, for example, Ramiro Martinez, Jr., *Latino Homicide: Immigration, Violence, and Community*, 2nd ed. (New York: Routledge, 2015), 167-68; and Neeraj Kaushal, *Blaming Immigrants: Nationalism and the Economics of Global Movement* (New York: Columbia University Press, 2019), 152ff. And about lower crime rates among immigrants in general, including undocumented immigrants versus the native population, see Anna Flagg, "Is There a Connection Between Undocumented Immigrants and Crime?," The Marshall Project, May 13, 2019, https://www.themarshallproject.org/2019/05/13/is-there-a-connection-between-undocumented-immigrants-and-crime. For a foundational history of Mexican Americans and the prejudice they have faced, see Albert Camarillo, *Chicanos in a Changing Society: From Mexican Pueblos to American Barrios in Santa Barbara and Southern California, 1848–1930* (Dallas, TX: Southern Methodist University Press, 2005).

299 *The largely forgotten treatment of German Americans during World War I.* Erik Kirschbaum, *Burning Beethoven: The Eradication of German Culture in the United States during World War I* (New York: Berlinica, 2014). See also Daniels, *Coming to America*, 159ff. The anti-German hysteria was captured in American literature, too—for example, in John Steinbeck's *East of Eden*: "He was forever painting his house and the white picket fence in front of it. Nobody had given his accent a thought until the war came along, but suddenly we knew. It was German. We had our own personal German. It didn't do him any good to bankrupt himself buying war bonds. That was too easy a way to cover up."

299 *"Prager was a German immigrant to the United States from Dresden."* Erik Kirschbaum, in telephone discussion with the author, November 2017. All other quotes by him are from this discussion.

300 **Even Middlebury Language Schools...canceled it.** Middlebury would keep its German program in mothballs for thirteen years.

300 *"But by then...it was an empty victory for language teachers."* Dennis Baron, *The English Only Question: An Official Language for Americans?* (New Haven, CT: Yale University Press, 1990), 145.

300 **By 1922...the figure had plummeted to less than 1 percent.** Hakuta, *Mirror of Language*, 168.

300 *"The Anti-German prejudice spread to disdain for all foreigners."* Portes and Rumbaut, *Immigrant America*, 216.

301 *"In a country lacking centuries-old traditions...language homogeneity came to be seen as the bedrock of national identity."* Portes and Rumbaut, 215.

301 *America swung dramatically from being relatively tolerant of other languages to actively intolerant.* An example is found in this study of a German American community in the township of Hustisford, Wisconsin, in 1910: Miranda E. Wilkerson and Joseph Salmons, "Linguistic Marginalities: Becoming American without Learning English," *Journal of Transnational American Studies* 4, no. 2 (2012), https://escholarship.org/uc/item/5vn092kk.

301 *Lacking a linguistic term for this, we offer simply, the grandparent tragedy.* The tragedy can also occur for parents and their children. See Lily Wong Fillmore, "When Learning a Second Language Means Losing the First," *Early Childhood Research Quarterly* 6, no. 3 (September 1991): 323-46, https://www.sciencedirect.com/science/article/pii/S0885200605800596. See also Richard Rodriguez, *Hunger of Memory* (New York: Bantam, 1982), 11-40. The historian David M. Kennedy writes: "Legend to the contrary, last century's immigrants did not cast their Old World habits and languages overboard before their ship steamed into New York Harbor. In fact, many groups heroically exerted themselves to sustain their religions, tongues, and ways of life." From "Can We Still Afford to Be a Nation of Immigrants?," *The Atlantic*, November 1996, https://www.theatlantic.com/magazine/archive/1996/11/can-we-still-afford-to-be-a-nation-of-immigrants/304835/.

301 *"the alternative to flight was death by starvation."* Handlin, *The Uprooted*, 30.

302 *we beat the languages out of ourselves.* As Fishman wrote, "By and large, more linguistic and cultural treasures have been buried and eroded due to permissiveness and apathy than would ever have been the case had repression and opposition been attempted." Fishman, *Language Loyalty in the United States*, 30.

303 *"My father was named Algot Elvin Svenson and he came to the US from Sweden in 1911."* Evelyn Svenson Granger (second-generation American), in discussion with the author, February 2016. All quotes by her are from this discussion.

304 *It was an educational achievement unparalleled in the world at that time.* Hakuta, *Mirror of Language*, 343.

304 *"Because the American people were the most educated in the world...they were in the best position to invent."* Claudia Goldin and Lawrence F. Katz, *The Race Between Education and Technology* (Cambridge, MA: The Belknap Press, 2008), 2.

304 *"The American Century."* Henry Luce, the publisher of the then highly influential *Time* and *Life* magazines, coined the term in early 1941 when he used it as the title of his February 17 editorial in *Life*.

304 *In many cases, the American-born children were the first literate members of their family, and they were literate in English.* Handlin, *The Uprooted*, 172.

305 *The language skills of American soldiers and sailors during World War II were weak as a result of the abandonment of...immigrant languages.* But the role of immigrants in America's war effort was outsized. When World War II came, David Gerber reports that without international migration, the US population would have been only 60 percent of what it was. "It is impossible to overestimate the extent to which that additional 40 percent contributed to making the United States the world's largest economy," he writes in *American Immigration*. How different the outcome of World War II might have been, had America shown up to fight missing 40 percent of its soldiers and factory workers.

305 *"members of the second generation...were busily ridding themselves of the vestiges of Old World cultures."* Archdeacon, *Becoming American*, xviii.

305 *The 1950s also saw the rise of Senator Joseph McCarthy and his Red Scare witch hunts.* McCarthy seemed unstoppable until a couple of valiant journalists, Fred W. Friendly and Edward R. Murrow, aired a series of episodes of *See It Now* on CBS television. The first was "The Case Against Milo Radulovich, A0589839," a University of Michigan student in the Air Force Reserve who had been released from duty because unidentified accusers said his immigrant father and sister had read subversive newspapers. The second, broadcast on the evening of March 9, 1954, featured film of McCarthy himself showing just how he spoke and acted during his "investigation." Then Murrow dared to question the accuser. "The actions of the junior Senator from Wisconsin have caused alarm and dismay amongst our allies abroad and given considerable comfort to our enemies, and whose fault is that? Not really his. He didn't create this situation of fear; he merely exploited it, and rather successfully." The airing of those episodes was the beginning of the end for McCarthy. See Erik Barnouw, *Tube of Plenty: The Evolution of American Television* (London: Oxford University Press, 1977), 172-84.

306 *the National Defense Education Act...poured money into language education.* Paul Dickson, *Sputnik: The Shock of the Century* (New York: Walker & Company, 2001), 227-28.

Chapter 43. Today's Immigrants Aren't
Learning English: The '60s Pivot

307 *The American Century pivoted in the 1960s the way young people pivot in their teenage years.* For insights into the tenor of the times, in particular, the counter-cultural, anti-establishment mindset of American youth, see William Manchester, *The Glory and the Dream: A Narrative History of America, 1932-1972* (Boston: Little, Brown and Company, 1973), vol. 2:1376-1411.

307 *there was a clear "'message' which immigrants, other ethnics, and their children quickly get—that ethnicity is foreignness."* Hornberger and Pütz, *Language Loyalty, Language Planning, and Language Revitalization*, 184-88.

308 *the 1970 census reported what would be the century's low point of both the number of immigrants.* Jynnah Radford and Luis Noe-Bustamante, "Facts on U.S. Immigrants, 2017: Statistical Portrait of the Foreign-Born Population in the United States," Pew Research Center, June 3, 2019, https://www.pewresearch.org/hispanic/2019/06/03/facts-on-u-s-immigrants/. See also Portes and Rumbaut, *Immigrant America*, xviii, 219.

309 *The "Mud Angels" who flew to the rescue included more than one hundred American exchange students.* Gaia Pianigiani, "Fifty Years After a Devastating Flood, Fears That Florence Remains Vulnerable," *The New York Times*, November 7, 2016, https://www.nytimes.com/2016/11/08/world/europe/50-years-after-a-devastating-flood-fears-that-florence-remains-vulnerable.html.

309 *only gradually did the nation learn how crucial their bilingualism was to winning World War II.* In July 2001, the surviving Navajo Code Talkers and their families were flown on a Marine jet from Albuquerque to Washington, DC, where President George W. Bush awarded them the Congressional Gold Medal. Chester Nez, *Code Talker* (New York: Berkley Books, 2011), 256-58.

309 *And it was in the 1960s that the Coral Way school in Miami...demonstrated the power of dual language education.* The same influx of Cubans into Miami that was the impetus for the Coral Way School also brought the predictable backlash from Anglo residents. Many were dismayed by the number of Spanish speakers suddenly in their midst. Some residents felt their language, themselves, and the American way of life itself were under attack. Miami was to become a bellwether of what the whole nation would soon experience, as the number of immigrants ramped up in the closing decades of the century.

309 *In 1984, the language scholar Richard Ruíz clarified three different perspectives, or orientations.* Richard Ruíz, "Orientations in Language Planning," *NABE Journal of Research and Practice* 8, no. 2 (1984): 15-34.

310 *After being banned by the US in 1898, the Hawaiian language was welcomed back and made official...in 1978.* Ofelia García, *Bilingual Education in the 21st Century*, 249.

310 *"Despite reports to the contrary...immigrant children are acquiring English well and with striking rapidity."* Lucy Tse, *Why Don't They Learn English? Separating Fact from Fallacy in the U.S. Language Debate* (New York: Teachers College Press, 2001), 17.

310 *"there are no signs that adult immigrants shy away from learning English."* Tse, 16.

310 *"Today's service-oriented economy requires English ability for all but the lowest paying jobs."* Tse, 25.

310 *feelings for English and nothing but English came even from the generation of older immigrants.* Hakuta, *Mirror of Language*, 8.

311 *"I know you and I are on opposite sides politically."* Mauro Mujica (CEO of US English), in discussion with the author. The author held several discussions with Mauro and his wife, Bárbara, during December 2014 and June 2015.

314 *Mauro mentioned that he had commissioned the language scholar David Crystal...to write a book on the importance of English.* Crystal's book is *English as a Global Language.*

315 *She also wrote a* **New York Times** *op-ed in 1984, in the midst of the debates over bilingual education.* Bárbara Mujica, "Bilingualism's Goal," *The New York Times*, February 26, 1984, https://www.nytimes.com/1984/02/26/opinion/bilingualisms-goal.html.

316 *"There is no threat to English."* Alba and Nee, *Remaking the American Mainstream*, 221-26.

316 *he said the proponents "were worrying about the wrong thing."* Jonathan Rosa (sociologist at Stanford), in discussion with the author, December 2016.

316 *"There is irony in the comparison between the...thousands of dollars put into acquiring a halting command of a foreign language and the pressure on fluent foreign-born speakers to abandon its use."* Portes and Rumbaut, *Immigrant America*, 246.

316 *Writing in 1988, he said the rise of American immigration in its third great wave led to wounded pride.* Hornberger and Pütz, *Language Loyalty, Language Planning, and Language Revitalization*, 184.

Chapter 44. Today's Immigrants Aren't Learning English: From Them to We

319 *To the contrary, the organization reports on its website the "clear benefits to growing up bilingual."* The UnidosUS website lists six benefits to bilingualism and states its support of dual language development for children: https://www.unidosus.org/issues/education/ece/dual-language-development/.

319 *"I defy you to show me a third-generation Cuban in Miami who isn't dominant in English."* Andrew Lynch, in discussion with the author, Heritage Language Conference at Harvard, June 2015.

320 *"they all realize they could be making more money once their English gets up to speed than working at our call center."* Sion Tesone (owner of Latina-focused business), in discussion with the author, June 2015.

321 *It's a partnership between the janitorial unions, the firms that contract the janitors, and the Silicon Valley tech companies where the janitors work.* Building Skills Partnership, https://www.buildingskills.org/.

324 *the Coca-Cola Company unveiled an unusual sixty-second ad.* YouTube video, January 1, 2017, https://www.youtube.com/watch?v=4-KxPRptu_Y.

325 *"Our brains form Us/Them dichotomies...with stunning speed."* Robert M. Sapolsky, *Behave: The Biology of Humans at Our Best and Worst* (New York: Penguin Books, 2017), 388.

325 *"We implicitly divide the world into Us and Them, and prefer the former."* Sapolsky, 673.

325 *"Despite the importance of thought in Us/Them-ing, its core is emotional and automatic."* Sapolsky, 400.

325 *"or there never is conscious awareness, as with subliminal stimuli."* Sapolsky, 401.

325 *"Our cognitions run to catch up with our affective selves, searching for the minute factoid or plausible fabrication that explains why we hate Them."* Sapolsky, 404.

325 *He gave a test of attitudes toward immigration to groups of regular commuters in Boston.* Ryan D. Enos, "Causal Effect of Intergroup Contact on Exclusionary Attitudes," *PNAS* 10, no. 111 (March 11, 2014): 3699-3704, https://www.pnas.org/content/111/10/3699.

326 *our bias against immigrants springs from our basic cognition.* Ryan D. Enos, *The Space Between Us: Social Geography and Politics* (Cambridge: Cambridge University Press, 2018), 115.

326 *Today we know that our instinctive behaviors can be calmed with what Enos calls "deep interpersonal contact."* Enos, *The Space Between Us*, 248. See also Robert Kurzban, John Tooby, and Leda Cosmides, "Can Race Be Erased? Coalitional computation and social categorization," *PNAS* 98, no. 26 (December 18, 2001): 15387–92.

326 *He cautions against the danger of allowing our natural, primate biology to get the better of us, for the stakes can be high.* Sapolsky, *Behave*, 404.

327 *We know from the work of the psychologists Amos Tversky and Daniel Kahneman that loss aversion is far more powerful than we previously thought.* Kahneman, *Thinking, Fast and Slow.* For additional insights on loss aversion, see Michael Lewis, *The Undoing Project* (New York: W.W. Norton, 2017).

327 *Another human frailty is negativity bias.* Steven Pinker, *Enlightenment Now: The Case for Reason, Science, Humanism and Progress* (New York: Viking, 2018), 47-48.

Chapter 45. Myth No. 11—Monolingualism Is Natural

329 *She would remind her audiences that polio was natural.* Helen Gurley Brown (now deceased; former editor-in-chief of *Cosmopolitan* magazine), in discussion with the author, May 2004.

329 *their "commitment to the sacred yet meaningless value of 'naturalness'."* Steven Pinker, *Enlightenment Now*, 77.

330 *"Among those 20 New Guineans, the smallest number of languages that anyone spoke was 5."* Diamond, *The World Until Yesterday*, 369. See also "Translation and Writing: David Bellos of Princeton University on the Future of Text," December 4, 2013, YouTube video, https://www.youtube.com/watch?v=0EFG9xw1RHM.

330 *"likely that such multilingualism was routine in our hunter-gatherer past."* Diamond, 385.

330 *"A people who used to command many languages now increasingly command only one."* Kulick, *A Death in the Rainforest*, 38.

330 *"Tayap will be stone-cold dead."* Kulick, 26.

330 *While there is at least one documented exception.* The linguist Daniel L. Everett describes the Pirahã living almost completely isolated, deep in the Amazon in Brazil. In his book *Don't Sleep, There Are Snakes: Life and Language in the Amazonian Jungle* (New York: Vintage Departures, 2008), he explains that the Pirahã seem to have no interest whatever in other languages and other customs, considering their own way of speaking the correct way and other ways "crooked head" (p. 20). It made it very difficult for him to learn the Pirahã language. He writes, "In a monolingual field situation, very rare among the languages of the world, the researcher shares no language in common with the native speakers. This was my beginning point among the Pirahãs, since they don't speak Portuguese, English, or any language other than Pirahã, except for a few limited phrases" (p. 20).

331 *"knowledge of Sumerian became the mark of an educated man."* Bellos, *Is That a Fish in Your Ear?*, 207.

331 *"The learning of Greek became the main content of a proper education."* Bellos, 207.

331 *"Slavic language speakers were used to ancient Old Church Slavonic as a written lingua franca, although no one spoke it."* McWhorter, *Our Magnificent Bastard Tongue*, 35. See also Joshua A. Fishman, *European Vernacular Literacy: A Sociolinguistic and Historical Introduction* (Bristol, UK: Multilingual Matters, 2010).

331 *early literacy was the domain of elites.* Harris, *Ancient Literacy*.

331 *"People writing in the way they actually talked was quite rare anywhere in the world until rather recently."* McWhorter, *Our Magnificent Bastard Tongue*, 43.

331 *having a writing system that reflected the language people spoke led to "far higher rates of literacy, a prerequisite for the emergence of democracy."* Minae Mizumura, *The Fall of Language in the Age of English*, trans. Mari Yoshihara and Juliet Winters Carpenter (New York: Columbia University Press, 2015), 94.

332 *"Throughout the nineteenth century, a bilingual tradition existed in public and private schools, newspapers, and religious and social institutions."* Ferguson and Heath, *Language in the USA*, 7.

332 *the Naturalization Act of 1906...for the first time required that immigrants speak English in order to gain citizenship.* This is still the case today.

332 *Once married...they were expected to defer to their husbands.* During the Allied occupation and rehabilitation of Japan following the end of World War II, General Douglas MacArthur, who led the US effort, wrote women's rights into the new constitution he crafted for Japan. For the first time, women had the right to vote. MacArthur also forced new laws to end other kinds of longstanding sexual discrimination. William Manchester, *American Caesar: Douglas MacArthur, 1880-1964* (New York: Little, Brown and Company, 1978), 498-504.

333 *the mistreatment Americans perpetrated on our Indigenous peoples was a common pattern found throughout the world.* Thomas Sowell, *Conquests and Cultures: An International History* (New York: Basic Books, 2008), 25, 48, 189, 217-20, 223, 229.

333 *It was during this period that President Theodore Roosevelt spoke against "hyphenated Americans" who displayed divided loyalties.* For a transcript of Roosevelt's speech on immigration, see https://www.snopes.com/fact-check /sole-loyalty/. For a discussion of Roosevelt's use of German and French during his presidency, see Edmund Morris, *Theodore Rex* (New York: Random House, 2001), 191, 407.

334 *"If you have lived your whole life in a monolingual environment...you could easily come to believe that this is the regular way of life."* Crystal, *How Language Works*, 409.

334 *"Some two-thirds of the children on earth grow up in a bilingual environment."* Crystal, *English as a Global Language*, 17.

335 *"multilingualism is the normal human condition."* Crystal, *How Language Works*, 409. See also Chin and Wigglesworth, *Bilingualism*, 43.

335 *monolingualism is "an aberration rather than the norm."* Polinsky, "Cognitive Advantages of Bilingualism," https://www.youtube.com/watch?v=W-ml2dD4SIk.

335 *"few people on this planet have only one tongue."* Bellos, *Is That a Fish in Your Ear?*, 13.

335 *"probably more than half of the world's population uses two or more languages."* François Grosjean, "How Many Are We? On the difficulty of counting people who are bilingual," *Psychology Today* blog, September 19, 2012, updated April 4, 2020, https://www.psychologytoday.com/us/blog/life-bilingual/201209 /how-many-are-we. Some scholars estimate the figure as high as 65 percent of the world's population.

335 *"the era of active suppression of minority languages has, for the most part, passed."* Crystal, *How Language Works*, 447. The United Nations proclaimed 2019 the

International Year of Indigenous Languages: https://www.un.org/development /desa/dspd/2019/01/2019-international-year-of-indigenous-languages/.

335 *While China may be guilty of continuing to take an iron hand in imposing Mandarin on its multilingual nation.* See, for example, Edward Wong, "Tibetans Struggle to Salvage Fading Culture: A Push for Assimilation Fuels Anxiety," *The New York Times,* November 29, 2015, https://www.nytimes.com /2015/11/29/world/asia/china-tibet-language-education.html; and Andrew Jacobs, "A Devotion to Language Proves Risky: In China, 3 Men Are Jailed After Starting a Uighur-Language Kindergarten," *The New York Times,* May 12, 2014, https://www.nytimes.com/2014/05/12/world/asia/a-devotion-to -language-proves-risky.html.

335 *In Canada, its policy of official French-English bilingualism fits its unique history.* For a history of the bilingual movement in Canada, see Graham Fraser, *Sorry, I Don't Speak French: Confronting the Canadian Crisis That Won't Go Away* (Toronto: Douglas Gibson Books, 2006) and the famous Canadian novel from 1945 that portrays the historic conflict between its French- and English-speaking citizens, *Two Solitudes* by Hugh MacLennan (Toronto: New Canadian Library, 2008).

335 *In Singapore, former Prime Minister Lee Kuan Yew took a personal interest in driving his city-state toward a robust bilingualism.* Lee Kuan Yew, *My Lifelong Challenge: Singapore's Bilingual Journey* (Singapore: Straits Times Press, 2012), 67. The DVD included with his book features interviews. See also Graham Allison and Robert D. Blackwill, *Lee Kuan Yew: The Grand Master's Insights on China, the United States, and the World* (Cambridge, MA: The MIT Press, 2013). Singapore continues to be among the leading nations in the education of its youth. See Fernando M. Reimers and E.B. O'Donnell, eds., *Fifteen Letters on Education in Singapore: Reflections from a Visit to Singapore in 2015 by a Delegation of Educators from Massachusetts* (Morrisville, NC: Lulu Publishing Services, 2016).

335 *Morocco aims to be the gateway to Africa by reinforcing its own unique mosaic of bilingualism.* Nouzha Chekrouni (Morocco's ambassador to Canada) and Aziz Goumi (Moroccan tour guide), both in discussion with the author, March 2018. Also, hear "America the Bilingual Goes to Morocco," https://www.americathe bilingual.com/39-america-the-bilingual-goes-to-morocco/.

336 *It was normal in America a century ago that Chinese were barred from citizenship.* Daniels, *Coming to America,* 245-47.

336 *The color barrier was finally broken in 1947 when Jackie Robinson stepped onto Ebbets Field.* "April 15, 1947: Jackie Robinson breaks color barrier," the website for the History television channel, November 24, 2009, updated April 13, 2020, https://www.history.com/this-day-in-history/jackie-robinson -breaks-color-barrier.

336 *The first interracial kisses on American television began appearing in the 1960s.* Matthew Delmont, "Fifty Years Ago, 'Star Trek' Aired TV's First Interracial Kiss,"

the online magazine of the Smithsonian, https://www.smithsonianmag.com /arts-culture/fifty-years-ago-star-trek-aired-tvs-first-interracial-kiss-180970204/.

336 *And it would take until 1962 before these citizens enjoyed voting privileges throughout the land.* Becky Little, "Native Americans Weren't Guaranteed the Right to Vote in Every State Until 1962," the website for the History television channel, November 6, 2018, updated August 20, 2019, https://www.history.com /news/native-american-voting-rights-citizenship.

337 *And someone who drinks and drives is seen...as the complete opposite of cool.* William DeJong and Jay A. Winsten, "The Use of Designated Drivers by US College Students: A National Study," *Journal of American College Health* 47, no. 4 (January 1999): 151, https://www.tandfonline.com/doi/abs /10.1080/07448489909595640; and Howard Koh and Pamela Yatsko, "Jay Winsten and the Designated Driver Campaign," Harvard Advanced Leadership Initiative Case, February 21, 2017 (rev. March 6, 2017). Today's concept of Designated Driver was a fine example of social engineering that was launched in America in the late 1980s.

337 *It was normal in America to smoke.* Stuart Elliott, "When Doctors, and even Santa, Endorsed Tobacco," *The New York Times*, October 6, 2008, https://www .nytimes.com/2008/10/07/business/media/07adco.html.

337 *The country's first Gay Rights parade was held in 1970.* "Gay Rights," the website for the History television channel, June 28, 2017, updated April 3, 2020, https: //www.history.com/topics/gay-rights/history-of-gay-rights.

338 *"The idea that monolingualism is a natural, original, and desirable state of affairs, while multilingualism is divisive, is still with us."* Suzanne Romaine, *Bilingualism*, 2nd ed. (Malden, MA: Blackwell Publishing, 1995), 322. If Romaine is correct in her assessment, generalized unease with bilingualism is something that exists at an individual level. The author discussed the matter with the Biblical scholar Harvey Cox in May 2015, and Cox is unaware of any concerted attempt by a church to attack minority languages based on the Tower of Babel story. Instead, as we have seen regarding the Jehovah's Witnesses and the Church of Jesus Christ of Latter-day Saints, churches are generally open to any and all languages, taking the point of view that God speaks universally in all languages and so, therefore, should we. See also Harvey Cox's book, *How to Read the Bible* (New York: HarperOne, 2015). Additionally, the philosopher Tom Morris, who consulted various scholarly translations of the Tower of Babel story from the Hebrew, says that "there is no suggestion in the passage that having one language is better than having many, or that having many languages is itself a bad condition." Tom also points to the story of the Day of Pentecost, when "'all of [the Apostles] were filled with the Holy Spirit and began to speak in other tongues,'" which, as he says, enabled the Apostles to communicate their message of a savior in "as many different languages as needed." Tom Morris in email discussion with the author, June 2020.

338 *"Now the whole earth had one language and the same words."* Gen. 11: 1-9 (New Revised Standard Version). From *The HarperCollins Study Bible, New Revised Standard Version* (New York: HarperOne, 1989), 18.

338 *We may tend to think that bilingualism can lead to problems due to speakers having divided loyalties, whereas no studies...have found evidence of this actually happening.* Kim Potowski, "Language Diversity in the USA: Dispelling Common Myths and Appreciating Advantages," in *Language Diversity in the USA*, 12-16.

339 *the top-ranking students came from Asian and Scandinavian countries, and... bilingual education is the norm in these countries.* "Although the PISA scores make no statements about bilingual education, it is revealing to note that most of the countries or regions that have generalized bilingual education for all school-goers tend to score higher than the OECD average, and some significantly higher." Diane J. Tedick, in *Building Bilingual Education Systems*, 38.

339 *"It's all making connections...like art and culture and music."* Linda Darling-Hammond (Stanford education scholar), in discussion with the author, November 2016.

339 *In China in the 1800s, it was illegal for Chinese nationals to teach the Chinese language to outsiders.* Stephen R. Platt, *Imperial Twilight: The Opium War and the End of China's Last Golden Age* (New York: Vintage Books, 2018), 79.

339 *the advancement of civilization comes not through isolation but through expanding circles of human cooperation.* Yuval Noah Harari, *Sapiens: A Brief History of Humankind* (New York: Harper, 2015), 78, 163ff.

339 *the dystopian novel.* Yoko Tawada, *The Emissary*, trans. Margaret Mitsutani (New York: New Directions, 2018), 5, 48.

340 *"children are born ready for bilingualism."* Crystal, *English as a Global Language*, 17. Even before infants begin to speak a recognized language, they are babbling phonemes, or speech sounds, in a state of what the linguist Roman Jakobson dubbed "tongue delirium." Lewis Hyde, *A Primer for Forgetting: Getting Past the Past* (New York: Farrar, Straus and Giroux, 2019).

340 *"public health has been described as the successive redefinings of the unacceptable."* Howard Koh (Assistant Secretary for Health under President Obama), in discussion with the author, April 2015. Howard said he did not invent this description. It appears to have been said first by Sir Geoffrey Vickers, a British industrialist, at the Harvard School of Public Health in 1957. See also Annette Dobson, "Redefining the Unacceptable" (Gordon Oration, 1993), *Australian Journal of Public Health* 18, no. 1 (March 1994): 9, https://onlinelibrary.wiley.com/doi/abs/10.1111/j.1753-6405.1994.tb00187.x.

340 *"Once I thought to write a history of the immigrants in America. Then I discovered that the immigrants* were *American history."* Handlin, *The Uprooted*, 3.

Chapter 46. Myth No. 12—Americans Suck at Languages

342 *young men applying to college had to show their proficiency in Greek or Latin, the way John Adams did.* In his biography of America's second president, the historian David McCullough describes how Adams read Cicero, Tacitus, and others in Latin. David McCullough, *John Adams* (New York: Simon & Schuster, 2001).

342 *college admission committees began to accept some "modern" languages.* Harry Charles McKown, "The Trend of College Entrance Requirements 1913-1922," Department of the Interior, Bureau of Education, *Bulletin*, no. 35 (Washington: Government Printing Office, 1925). It wasn't until 1875 that Harvard recognized any study of a modern language that could satisfy an entrance requirement.

342 *the authoritative Coleman Report came out and recommended that the US admit defeat.* Bernhardt, "Sociohistorical Perspectives on Language Teaching in the Modern United States," 49-50. One prominent institution that resisted the reading emphasis that the Coleman Report recommended was Middlebury College and its summer programs. Stameshkin et al., *Life Doesn't Come with Subtitles*, 71-72.

343 *then in 1980 came another book scolding Americans for our failures.* Paul Simon, *The Tongue-Tied American: Confronting the Foreign Language Crisis* (New York: Continuum, 1980), 26.

343 *"The United States lags behind most nations of the world."* Commission on Language Learning, "America's Languages: Investing in Language Education for the 21st Century," American Academy of Arts & Sciences, 2017: viii, https://www.amacad.org/publication/americas-languages.

343 *The number of Americans who speak a language other than English at home grew steadily.* Karen Zeigler and Steven A. Camarota, citing the results of the American Community Survey, in "67.3 Million in the United States Spoke a Foreign Language at Home in 2018," Center for Immigration Studies, October 2019, https://cis.org/Report/673-Million-United-States-Spoke-Foreign-Language-Home-2018.

344 *"This can only lead to a person's personal enrichment."* François Grosjean, "The Amazing Rise of Bilingualism in the United States: The proportion of bilinguals in the US has practically doubled since 1980," *Psychology Today* blog, September 11, 2018, updated April 2, 2020, https://www.psychologytoday.com/intl/blog/life-bilingual/201809/the-amazing-rise-bilingualism-in-the-united-states.

344 *"I would never have thought that we would be up to 23% of bilinguals in the US."* Grosjean, in email discussion with the author, April 2020.

344 *20 percent of the population of France equates to roughly thirteen million people.* See James Mulholland, "Who is Bilingual in Europe?," Tableau Public, January 13, 2020, https://public.tableau.com/profile/james.mulholland#!/vizhome/BilingualisminEurope/WhoisBilingual, for an infographic that answers this question. Additionally, according to the report "Europeans and Their Languages," just over 54 percent of Europeans are able to hold a conversation in at least one

additional language beyond their mother tongues, while 25 percent are able to do this with at least two additional languages (p. 5). Only about 24 percent use their first additional language every day, or almost every day, while an additional 23 percent use it often. The remainder use it on an occasional basis (p. 6). European Commission, Special Eurobarometer 386/Wave EB77.1, June 2012, https://ec.europa.eu/commfrontoffice/publicopinion/archives/ebs/ebs_386_en.pdf.

344 *The American figures become even more impressive when we look at our linguistic diversity.* US Census Bureau, "Detailed Languages Spoken at Home and Ability to Speak English for the Population 5 Years and Over: 2009-2013" (October 2015), https://www.census.gov/data/tables/2013/demo/2009-2013-lang-tables .html.

344 *we still have almost a million German-English American bilinguals.* Renate Ludanyi, "German in the USA," in *Language Diversity in the USA*, 151.

345 *And the city with the largest number of Polish speakers after Warsaw.* Bozena Nowicka McLees and Katarzyna Dziwirek, "Polish in the USA," in *Language Diversity in the USA*, 238.

345 *Carnegie Hall has a seating capacity of 2,804.* The reference is to the Isaac Stern Auditorium, https://www.carnegiehall.org/About/Building-Overview /Stern-Auditorium-Perelman-Stage.

345 *If we filled it to capacity...we could go 131 nights.* Only four nations have more living, or spoken languages, than the US. They are, in order: Papua New Guinea, 839; Indonesia, 707; Nigeria, 526; and India, 454. The US has 422, far above No. 6, China, with a mere 300. Visual Capitalist: "A World of Languages," https://www .visualcapitalist.com/wp-content/uploads/2018/05/world-of-languages.html.

345 *As Steven Pinker says, "progress has a way of covering its tracks."* Steven Pinker, *Enlightenment Now*, 207.

345 *the number of American immigrants quadrupled, so that in 2017 they accounted for 13.6 percent of the population.* Radford, "Key findings about U.S. immigrants," https://www.pewresearch.org/fact-tank/2019/06/17/key-findings-about-u-s-immigrants/.

346 *a sizable minority of educated newcomers who are able both to understand the advantages of fluent bilingualism and to maintain it.* Portes and Rumbaut, *Immigrant America*, 256.

346 *"A century ago, most Asian Americans were low-skilled."* Taylor, *The Next America*, 76.

346 *"More than 6 in 10 (61%) adults ages 25-64 who have come from Asia in recent years have at least a bachelor's degree."* Taylor, 77.

346 *Once here, the Asians have excelled.* Taylor, 87.

347 *There's an old Mende proverb.* Cross, *Gullah Culture in America*, 145.

347 *"I'm not even sure if I'm speaking English, Chinese, or Dutch."* Mim Harrison, "'On the Other Side of the Curtain': Jean Kwok's Bestselling Novels Reveal What It Means to Live in Other Languages," America the Bilingual website article, January 13, 2020, https://www.americathebilingual.com/on-the-other-side-of-the -curtain/.

348 *Their Latino origins, rather than defining them, "afford them a measure of distinction among other Americans."* Carlos de León de la Riva et al., *The Hispanic Game* (Mexico: De La Riva Group, 2016), 151.

348 *"They view their Hispanic identity not as something to hide."* Valeria Piaggio (strategic marketing consultant), in telephone discussion with the author, October 2016.

349 *these attitudes among millennials can sometimes cause angst for their parents, who grew up not being taught Spanish.* Nancy Tellet (market researcher), in telephone discussion with the author, October 2016.

349 *"Music is a huge influencer and non-Hispanics have allowed it to be cool."* Linda Lane Gonzalez (advertising executive), in telephone discussion with the author, October 2016.

350 *immigrant kids actually outscore non-immigrant kids in overall PISA results.* OECD [Organisation for Economic Co-operation and Development], "United States Country Note, PISA 2018 Results," 1, https://www.oecd.org/pisa/publications/PISA2018_CN_USA.pdf. The same PISA report says that in 2009, the proportion of students of immigrant background was 19 percent. But we know from the previously reported AP exam trends in Chapter 22 that the number of students sitting for AP exams in world languages has exploded, growing from 163,000 in 2009 to 263,000 in 2019. Not all of these kids taking the test are immigrants, of course, but the trends of improving immigrant PISA test scores and increased numbers taking the AP exams are rising in parallel. At least some of that can be attributed to students with an immigrant background.

350 *"we are committed to raising a community of skilled biliterate and bicultural children."* Ana L. Flores and Roxana A. Soto, *Bilingual Is Better: Two Latina Moms on How the Bilingual Parenting Revolution Is Changing the Face of America* (Madrid: Bilingual Readers, 2012), 139.

350 *"Miami is heaven for those of us who are trying to raise bilingual and bicultural children."* Flores and Soto, 49.

350 *"it's becoming ever easier and cooler not to lose the accent."* Liu, *A Chinaman's Chance*, 200.

350 *"Research indicates that supporting bilingualism from early ages can have wide ranging benefits."* U.S. Department of Health and Human Services, "Policy Statement on Supporting the Development of Children Who Are Dual Language Learners in Early Childhood Programs," US Department of Education, January 5, 2017, https://www.acf.hhs.gov/sites/default/files/ecd/dll_guidance_document_final.pdf.

351 *"respect, affirm, and promote students' home languages and cultural knowledge and experiences as resources."* TESOL International Association, "The 6 Principles for Exemplary Teaching of English Learners," https://www.tesol.org/the-6-principles/about. Even Dr. Spock's venerable baby book, first published in 1945 and in its tenth edition (thus far), supports raising children bilingually, *viz*:

"Children who grow up hearing two languages have a real advantage. While they often take a bit longer to start expressing themselves clearly, once they get going, they quickly become fluent speakers in both languages." And: "A child who learns Spanish or Russian at home can quickly pick up English in preschool." Benjamin Spock, MD, and Robert Needlman, MD, *Dr. Spock's Baby and Child Care*, rev. ed. (New York: Gallery Books, 2018), 467-68.

352 *"it's my younger sister...who has the best Albanian."* Gerta Dhamo (Albanian American), in discussion with the author, September 2015.

353 *"Absolutely my bilingualism was important."* Mike Parra (Cuban American executive of DHL), in discussion with the author, June 2016.

355 **We have more Spanish speakers than Spain.** Sarah Warman Hirschfield, "Potowski debunks myths surrounding Spanish in US," *The Daily Princetonian*, May 8, 2018, https://www.dailyprincetonian.com/article/2018/05/potowski -debunks-myths-surrounding-spanish-in-us.

355 *Our English-Spanish bilinguals are especially important for helping the US truly step into its responsible position in the Americas.* See, for example, the 100,000 Strong in the Americas Innovation Fund: http://www.100kstrongamericas.org/.

355 *As of 2020, the NLSC has ten thousand members speaking more than four hundred languages.* See the National Language Service Corps website, https: //www.nlscorps.org/. Joyce M. Baker, information security manager of the NLSC, also held an earlier discussion with the author, November 2017.

356 *"When you're teaching somebody your language and they are teaching you, you just can't help but get to know them."* James Archer (founder of Sharelingo), in discussion with the author, August 2017. See also his book, *Beyond Words: A Radically Simple Solution to Unify Communities, Strengthen Businesses, and Connect Cultures Through Language* (Aurora, CO: Sharelingo Press, 2017).

356 *"he had a passable knowledge of Italian, Yiddish, French, Croatian, Hungarian, and German."* Mason B. Williams, *City of Ambition: FDR, La Guardia, and the Making of Modern New York* (New York: W.W. Norton, 2013), 21.

357 **He learned Portuguese for his extended teaching duties in Brazil.** Richard P. Feynman, *"Surely You're Joking, Mr. Feynman!" Adventures of a Curious Character* (New York: W.W. Norton, 1985), 199-204.

357 **Eleanor Roosevelt learned French before she spoke English.** In an interview with CNN's Larry King, Eleanor Roosevelt's grandson David relayed that "my grandmother spoke French before she ever spoke a word of English. And she spoke French all of her life." http://transcripts.cnn.com/TRANSCRIPTS/0211/28 /lkl.00.html.

357 *in its most recent survey of college language classes, the Modern Language Association reports another significant decline in enrollments.* Dennis Looney and Natalia Lusin, "Enrollments in Languages Other Than English in United States Institutions of Higher Education, Summer 2016 and Fall 2016: Final Report," Modern Language Association, June 2019, https://www.mla.org/content

/download/110154/2406932/2016-Enrollments-Final-Report.pdf. Rosemary Feal, then the executive director of the Modern Language Association, had related discussions with the author in June 2015 and September 2016.

357 *one hundred thousand more high school students take AP language tests than was the case a decade ago.* AP Exam Volume Changes (2009-2019), https: //secure-media.collegeboard.org/digitalServices/pdf/research/2019/2019 -Exam-Volume-Change.pdf._In its report on language class enrollments, the Stanford Language Center noted a 12 percent decline in the years 2010 to 2015, but also reported that nearly half of its incoming students in 2015 placed out of the university's language requirement. *Stanford Language Center Annual Report to the Committee on Undergraduate Standards and Policy, Academic Year 2014-2015*, 11, 17.

357 *a burgeoning number of college students are pursuing a second major in a language that bolsters their first.* "Data on Second Majors in Language and Literature, 2001-13," MLA Office of Research, February 2015, https://www .mla.org/content/download/31117/1320962/2ndmajors200113.pdf.

359 *"If you're black in South Africa, speaking English is the one thing that can give you a leg up."* Noah, *Born a Crime*, 54.

359 *"Of all the pathways to self-creation, nothing galvanized people as broadly as the study of English."* Evan Osnos, *Age of Ambition: Chasing Fortune, Truth and Faith in the New China* (New York: Farrar, Straus and Giroux, 2014), 67.

359 *"English for the younger generation in many countries became a symbol of freedom, rebellion and modernism."* Crystal, *English as a Global Language*, 103-4.

Chapter 47. America, Later This Century

364 *now all schools are dual language, so they're just called schools again.* Using data from the Center for Applied Linguistics for the number of dual language schools from 1971 (3) to 2011 (448), and continuing with data from the registry that DualLanguageSchools.org provided in 2020 (2,804), we get a combined annual growth rate of 15 percent: http://webapp.cal.org/Immersion/Doc /Growth%20of%20Language%20Immersion%20Programs%20in%20 the%20US%201971-2011.pdf and https://duallanguageschools.org/, plus the author's email discussion with Arthur Chou in May 2020. (Chou is the head of Academic Learning Company, an educational publisher that publishes the websites DualLanguageSchools.org and SealofBiliteracy.org.) With this growth rate, by midcentury, America would have roughly 130,000 dual language schools, about equal to the total number of American K-12 schools in 2020.

364 *"Thomas Jefferson recommended that Americans learn English, French, and Spanish."* Letter from Thomas Jefferson to his nephew Peter Carr, August 10, 1787, https://www.encyclopediavirginia.org/Letter_from_Thomas_Jefferson _to_Peter_Carr_August_10_1787.

364 *"encore students," people who have finished their first careers and are back for round two.* Rosabeth Moss Kanter, Rakesh Khurana, and Nitin Nohria, "Moving Higher Education to the Next Stage: A New Set of Societal Challenges, a New Stage of Life, and a Call to Action for Universities." Harvard Business School Working Paper, No. 06-021, November 2005, https://www.hbs.edu/faculty /Pages/item.aspx?num=20569.

364 *"We have about 10 percent international students."* The number of international students studying in the US has been growing steadily since after World War II, reaching 5.5 percent in the 2018-19 academic year. Many top-ranked American universities are already more than 10 percent international. Institute of International Education (IIE), "International Student Enrollment Trends, 1948/49–2018/19," International Student Data from the 2019 Open Doors Report, https://www.iie.org/Research-and-Insights/Open-Doors/Data/Inter-national-Students/Enrollment. Globally, eight countries in 2019 already had total percentages of international students above 10 percent, including Australia (28 percent), Canada (21.4 percent), and the UK (21 percent). IIE 2019 Project Atlas Report, https://www.iie.org/ProjectAtlas.

364 *It's not just the major languages that students can learn...but the top forty.* Nelleke Van Deusen-Scholl, "The Negotiation of Multilingual Heritage Identity in a Distance Environment: HLA and the Plurilingual Turn," *Calico Journal* 35.3 (September 2018): 235–56, https://eric.ed.gov/?id=EJ1191543. To watch an interview with Prof. Van Deusen-Scholl on this article, see https://www.youtube .com/watch?v=FCrDlNfiLMg.

364 *most language classes, like most classes in general, are hybrids of virtual and in-person sessions.* Nelleke Van Deusen-Scholl and Stéphane Charitos, "The Shared Course Initiative: Curricular Collaboration Across Institutions," in the AAUSC 2016 Volume of Issues in Language Program Direction, *The Intercon-nected Language Curriculum: Critical Transition and Interfaces in Articulated K-16 Contexts*, ed. Per Urlaub and Johanna Watzinger-Tharp (New York: Cengage Learning, 2017). See also https://sharedcourseinitiative.lrc.columbia.edu/.

364 *Emma shows you her Cultural Passport.* The Council of Europe suggested in 2020 the Language Passport, as part of the European Language Portfolio, to provide an overview of an individual's proficiency in different languages, using a self-assessment grid keyed to the Common European Framework of Reference levels. It is to be used to complement a curriculum vitae: https://www.coe.int /en/web/portfolio/the-language-passport. See also the Global Seal of Biliteracy, which "celebrates language skills and expands future opportunities for its recip-ients," https://theglobalseal.com/.

365 *the Census added a question about how well people speak their LOTEs.* The US Census does modify and add questions to its surveys. It was in 2000 when respon-dents could first indicate more than one race; that has led to much richer data for researchers to mine. The same sort of expansion in knowledge of American

linguistic capital could be ours for the asking. Anna Brown, "The changing categories the U.S. census has used to measure race," Pew Research Center, February 25, 2020, https://www.pewresearch.org/fact-tank/2020/02/25/the-changing -categories-the-u-s-has-used-to-measure-race/. The first step leading to more Census questions about language skills is to clearly see the limitations of our current questions, and this has begun. See Jennifer Leeman, "It's all about English: The interplay of monolingual ideologies, language policies and the US Census Bureau's statistics on multilingualism," *International Journal of the Sociology of Language* 252 (2018): 21-43, https://www.degruyter.com/view/journals/ijsl/2018/252 /article-p21.xml.

365 *So it's hard to find a language that* isn't *an American language.* Joshua Fishman spoke of "American languages" as those spoken by Americans, in his interview at the UCLA Center for World Languages, 2010, https://www.international.ucla .edu/cwl/article/114238.

365 *most people you see walking by are people of color.* William H. Frey, *Diversity Explosion: How New Racial Demographics Are Remaking America* (Washington, DC: Brookings Institution Press, 2015), 191-211; Richard Alba, *Blurring the Color Line: The New Chance for a More Integrated America* (Cambridge, MA: Harvard University Press, 2009); Alba and Nee, *Remaking the American Mainstream*, 277-92. The Pew Research Center executive Paul Taylor writes in his *The Next America* (p. 71), "America is already one of the most racially and ethnically diverse nations in history, and the modern immigration wave is making our tapestry more intricate with each passing year. In 1960 our population was 85% white; by 2060 it will be 43% white."

365 *"America keeps winning at immigration."* "Countries vary in their success in enabling immigrants and their children to take on the norms of their new society. Among the most successful is America. Children growing up in America almost unavoidably assimilate American values." Paul Collier, *Exodus: How Migration Is Changing Our World* (Oxford: Oxford University Press, 2013), 69. And, as Emma says, borrowing directly from Collier (p. 158), "Immigration is in America's DNA." Paul Taylor of Pew says, "If we adopt immigration policies that allow us to keep winning the global lottery for newcomers with brains, talent, and drive, we'll go a long way toward ensuring our place as the top dog in the world's economy" (*The Next America*, p. 87). See also Ana Gonzalez-Barrera and Phillip Conner, "Around the World, More Say Immigrants Are a Strength Than a Burden," Pew Research Center, March 14, 2019, https://www.pewresearch.org /global/2019/03/14/around-the-world-more-say-immigrants-are-a-strength -than-a-burden/; and Tunku Varadarajan, "America's Great Immigration System," The Weekend Interview with Neeraj Kaushal, *The Wall Street Journal*, March 9-10, 2019.

365 *After the global population peaked, it quickly fell. Consequently, human capital became the hot commodity.* Darrell Bricker and John Ibbitson, *Empty Planet: The*

Shock of Global Population Decline (New York: Crown, 2019). Say the authors (p. 57): "Greece's population started to decline in 2011. Fewer babies were born in Italy in 2015 than in any year since the state was formed in 1861. That same year, two hundred schools closed across Poland for lack of children. Portugal could lose up to half its population by 2060." And it's not just Europe, according to the authors (p. 49): "Japan's population is expected to decline by 25% over the next thirty-five years, taking it from 127 million to 95 million. The numbers are similar for South Korea and Singapore, two other fully developed Asian societies." As for China (p. 163): "China's population could decline by almost half in this century." See also Janet Adamy, "U.S. Birthrates Fall to Record Low: Last year's data are another sign of how American childbearing, which began declining during the 2007-09 recession, never fully rebounded," *The Wall Street Journal*, May 20, 2020.

365 *"You can get free homes in many countries if you're willing to fix them up."* Silvia Marchetti, "You can still buy $1 homes all over Italy," CNN Travel, updated December 25, 2019, https://www.cnn.com/travel/article/italy-one-euro-homes -roundup/index.html.

366 *"Canada and Australia have always done a great job attracting immigrants."* The Pew Research Center reports: "Compared with other countries receiving immigrants, the share of the U.S. population that is foreign born is modest." The US was at 14 percent in 2016, compared with Canada, at 22 percent, and Australia, at 28 percent. Phillip Connor and Gustavo López, "5 facts about the U.S. rank in world-wide migration," Pew Research Center, May 18, 2016, https://www.pewresearch .org/fact-tank/2016/05/18/5-facts-about-the-u-s-rank-in-worldwide-migration/.

366 *"you can get all the English classes and tutoring you need, although most people don't need much."* Jeffrey S. Passel and D'Vera Cohn, "U.S. unauthorized immigrants are more proficient in English, more educated than a decade ago," Pew Research Center, May 23, 2019, https://www.pewresearch.org /fact-tank/2019/05/23/u-s-undocumented-immigrants-are-more-proficient-in -english-more-educated-than-a-decade-ago/.

366 *"It's really a race, because it's harder and harder to attract immigrants."* To help countries gauge their success at integrating immigrants, work is currently ongoing to develop a common international index of integration success. While the investigators measure facility in the host country's dominant language, they recommend being "agnostic" about retaining heritage languages. Niklas Harder, Lucila Figueroa, Rachel M. Gillum, Dominik Hangartner, David D. Laitin, and Jens Hainmueller, "Multidimensional Measure of Immigrant Integration," *PNAS* 115, no. 45 (November 6, 2018): 11483-88, https://doi.org/10.1073 /pnas.1808793115.

366 *once extreme poverty was mostly eliminated.* Hans Rosling, Ola Rosling, and Anna Rosling Rönnlund, *Factfulness: Ten Reasons We're Wrong About the World— and Why Things Are Better Than You Think* (New York: Flatiron Books, 2018).

366 *"immigrants around the world have many countries to choose from."* See, for example, Ana Gonzalez-Barrera, "More Mexicans Leaving Than Coming to the U.S.: Net Loss of 140,000 from 2009 to 2014; Family Reunification Top Reason for Return," Pew Research Center, Hispanic Trends, November 19, 2015, https://www.pewresearch.org/hispanic/2015/11/19/more-mexicans-leaving-than-coming-to-the-u-s/. And according to the historian David Kennedy, "The era of mass immigration of Mexicans to the US is coming to an end; it may have already ended. In the 1970s, Mexican women were having seven-plus babies and today it's getting close to just replacement levels. Plus the economy is getting better in Mexico....I wouldn't be surprised, in the next couple of decades, to see policies to give incentives to Mexicans for immigration." Presentation to Stanford Distinguished Careers Institute Fellows, May 25, 2016. "I'm hoping in one hundred years we have the human right of mobility—to live anywhere as long as they obey the local laws and pay local taxes and not be a public burden. There will be more and more competition for the remaining people." Kevin Kelly (technology observer), in telephone discussion with the author, January 2017.

366 *"Conversation Corps is something like the Peace Corps, but with shorter stays."* Experimentation with community conversations among people who don't normally talk with one another has begun. See, for example, the Study Circles program of the Montgomery County Public Schools, described in Susan E. Eaton, *Integration Nation: Immigrants, Refugees, and America at Its Best* (New York: The New Press, 2016), 151-61, and at https://www.montgomeryschoolsmd.org/departments/studycircles/. See also The Neighborhood Project, https://theneighborhoodproject.com/.

366 *the Conversation Corps also operates within the US, in cities like Phoenix and Los Angeles.* Los Angeles and Phoenix are what the scholar of social geography Ryan Enos calls polycentric cities, which are in particular need of conversations among residents of different neighborhoods who don't normally talk. "We have here an unfortunate combination: high social-geographic impact and low interpersonal contact." Enos, *The Space Between Us*, 242-43.

366 *it's not just the larger American cities where this kind of cultural and linguistic exchange takes place.* Mim Harrison, "Our Towns: A Book, A Journey, and an Often Surprising View of Multicultural America," America the Bilingual website article on James and Deborah Fallows's research, January 2, 2020, https://www.americathebilingual.com/our-towns-a-book-a-journey-and-an-often-surprising-view-of-multicultural-america/.

367 *the American Bilingual Honor Code.* Feeling the need for a moral code is a fundamental value orientation in America. Writes the sociologist Robin M. Williams, Jr., "Probably few people have so copiously documented and analyzed what they themselves consider to be the 'bad' aspects of their history—a revealing fact in itself, for it was broadly the same culture that produced the behavior and then

pronounced it undesirable or wrong. Even so, the evidences of humanitarian values meet all our tests for a major value." Williams, *American Society*, 463.

367 *"Immigrant parents and native-born parents got together."* First anticipated by Joshua Fishman in his 1966 *Language Loyalty in the United States* (p. 410), it later came to pass, with parents being the driving force in the growth of dual language schools. Jaumont, *The Bilingual Revolution*. For a look at how parents in one state are driving this revolution, listen to "North Carolina: A Dual-Language Success Story," https://www.americathebilingual.com/42-north -carolina-a-dual-language-success-story/.

368 *"And what parent wouldn't want their kid to have the advantages of being bilingual?"* Progress sometimes happens simply because it makes sense. "There is a good reason why utilitarian arguments have so often succeeded: everyone can appreciate them....That explains why certain reform movements, such as legal equality for women and gay marriage, overturned centuries of precedent astonishingly quickly...with nothing but custom and intuition behind it, the status quo crumbled in the face of utilitarian arguments." Steven Pinker, *Enlightenment Now*, 417-18.

368 *"it helped that teachers are now paid more, and respected more."* Ripley, *The Smartest Kids in the World*.

368 *China's population was now on track to be half of what it was at the start of the twenty-first century.* Bricker and Ibbitson, *Empty Planet*, 163.

368 *"the Bracero Program...brought in Mexicans as migrant workers."* A *bracero* is a farm laborer. The word derives from the Spanish *brazo*, or arm, as farm laborers work with their hands and arms. The Bracero Program was in effect from 1942 through 1964. http://braceroarchive.org/about.

369 *The recruitment campaigns for the Army and Marines probably also had an impact.* The thirty-second commercial, "What's Your Warrior?," which includes the line, "Speak New Languages," clocked 4.5 million views as of November 11, 2019. The YouTube description of this Army recruitment message opens with "Learn new languages." https://www.youtube.com/watch?v=cOi_abLAPJE.

369 *Could it be that bilingualism is some benign weapon for peace?* Dual language schools are used to promote empathy and peace in areas of known conflict, such as in Macedonia, in a Macedonian–Albanian dual language program, and also in Israel, teaching in Hebrew and Arabic, with Jewish and Arab teachers. In their *Foundations of Bilingual Education and Bilingualism* (p. 223), Colin Baker and Wayne Wright say that "such initiatives symbolize that bilingual education can include a vision that goes beyond languages, beyond a troubled past, and work towards a better present and future."

369 *"They did a pretty good job with bilingualism among their founding European languages, but they haven't valued their immigrant languages the way Americans have."* One example of how this plays out in France: "About three million people use Arabic on a daily basis in France, making it the country's most spoken foreign

language, according to the Culture Ministry. But Arabic is barely taught in public schools, so mosques and private associations have stepped in to address this educational gap." Emma Bubola, "Divided France Debates Where to Teach Arabic," *The New York Times*, January 6, 2019, https://www.nytimes.com/2019/01/05 /world/europe/france-arabic-public-schools-mosques.html.

369 *"We were pretty low there for some years in surveys on how people viewed us."* Kevin Drew, "U.S. Suffers Greatest Global Decline in Trust," *U.S. News & World Report*, January 15, 2020, https://www.usnews.com/news/best-countries /articles/2020-01-15/us-trustworthiness-rating-dives-in-2020-best-countries -report.

369 *"Americans have always been at our best when we look outwards."* Jon Meacham, *The Soul of America: The Battle for Our Better Angels* (New York: Random House, 2018); James Fallows, *More Like Us: Making America Great Again* (Boston: Houghton Mifflin, 1989); David McCullough, *The American Spirit: Who We Are and What We Stand For* (New York: Simon & Schuster, 2017).

369 *politicians on both sides of the aisle take credit for American advancement in bilingualism.* According to Bill Rivers, who heads the Joint National Committee for Languages and the National Council for Languages and International Studies (https://www.languagepolicy.org/), "The driving forces are the grassroots energy from parents, coupled with pressure from the business community, coupled with pressure from the National Security Community." Therefore, support for language training is generally bipartisan, said Rivers, in discussion with the author, November 2018. Rivers is also a registered lobbyist.

369 *"We actually know a lot more about social science now."* Kahneman, *Thinking, Fast and Slow*; Sapolsky, *Behave*; Enos, *The Space Between Us*.

370 *The world's population is expected to peak at a number lower than previously forecasted, and then to decline.* Bricker and Ibbitson, *Empty Planet*.

371 *As Eleanor Roosevelt said, "'It is not so much the powerful leaders that determine our destiny as the…voice of the people themselves.'"* Meacham, *The Soul of America*, 14.

372 *"America as the training center of the skillful servants of mankind."* Henry R. Luce, "The American Century," an essay by the publisher, *Life* magazine, February 17, 1941, https://books.google.com/books?id=I0kEAAAAMBAJ&printsec =frontcover#v=onepage&q=century&f=false.

SELECTED BIBLIOGRAPHY

Language Learning for Adults

Archer, James. *Beyond Words: A Radically Simple Solution to Unify Communities, Strengthen Businesses, and Connect Cultures Through Language.* Aurora, CO: Sharelingo Press, 2017.

Hinton, Leanne. *How to Keep Your Language Alive: A Commonsense Approach to One-on-One Language Learning.* Berkeley, CA: Heyday Books, 2002.

Kaufmann, Steve. *The Way of the Linguist: A Language Learning Odyssey.* Bloomington, IN: Author House, 2005.

Lomb, Kato. *Harmony of Babel: Profiles of Famous Polyglots of Europe.* 2nd ed. Berkeley, CA: TESL-EJ Publications, 2018.

———. *Polyglot: How I Learn Languages.* Berkeley, CA: TESL-EJ Publications, 1995.

Pimsleur, Paul. *How to Learn a Foreign Language.* New York: Pimsleur Language Programs, 2013.

Wyner, Gabriel. *Fluent Forever: How to Learn Any Language* Fast *and Never Forget It.* New York: Harmony Books, 2014.

Raising Bilingual Children

Beck, Adam. *Maximize Your Child's Bilingual Ability: Ideas and Inspiration for Even Greater Success and Joy Raising Bilingual Kids.* N.p.: Bilingual Adventures, 2016.

Flores, Ana L., and Roxana A. Soto. *Bilingual Is Better: Two Latina Moms on How the Bilingual Parenting Revolution Is Changing the Face of America.* Madrid: Bilingual Readers, 2012.

Harding-Esch, Edith, and Philip Riley. *The Bilingual Family: A Handbook for Parents.* Cambridge: Cambridge University Press, 2012.

King, Kendall, and Alison Mackey. *The Bilingual Edge: Why, When, and How to Teach Your Child a Second Language.* New York: Harper Perennial, 2007.

Merrill, Jane. *Bringing Up Baby Bilingual.* New York: Facts On File, 1984.

Pearson, Barbara Zurer. *Raising a Bilingual Child: A Step-by-Step Guide for Parents.* New York: Living Language, 2008.

Rebelo, Lane. *Baby Sign Language Made Easy: 101 Signs to Start Communicating with Your Child Now.* Emeryville, CA: Rockridge Press, 2018.

Rodriguez, Gloria G. *Raising Nuestros Niños: Bringing Up Latino Children in a Bicultural World.* New York: Fireside, 1999.

Rosenback, Rita. *Bringing up a Bilingual Child.* Croydon, UK: Filament Publishing, 2014.

Spock, Benjamin, MD, and Robert Needlman, MD. *Dr. Spock's Baby and Child Care.* Rev. ed. New York: Gallery Books, 2018.

Steiner, Naomi, MD. *7 Steps to Raising a Bilingual Child.* New York: AMACOM, 2008.

Vazquez, Carmen Inoa. *Parenting with Pride Latino Style: How to Help Your Child Cherish Your Cultural Values and Succeed in Today's World.* New York: Rayo, 2004.

Dual Language Education and Language Teaching

Baker, Colin, and Wayne E. Wright. *Foundations of Bilingual Education and Bilingualism.* 6th ed. Bristol, UK: Multilingual Matters, 2017.

Bialystok, Ellen, and Kenji Hakuta. *In Other Words: The Science and Psychology of Second-Language Acquisition.* New York: Basic Books, 1994.

Coady, Maria R. *The Coral Way Bilingual Program.* Bristol, UK: Multilingual Matters, 2020.

Crawford, James. *Advocating for English Learners: Selected Essays.* Clevedon, UK: Multilingual Matters, 2008.

Fantini, Alvino E. *Intercultural Communicative Competence in Education Exchange: A Multinational Perspective.* 1st ed. Abingdon, UK: Routledge, 2018.

García, Ofelia. *Bilingual Education in the 21st Century: A Global Perspective.* West Sussex, UK: Wiley-Blackwell, 2009.

Heineke, Amy J., and Kristin J. Davin, eds. *The Seal of Biliteracy: Case Studies and Considerations for Policy Implementation.* Charlotte, NC: Information Age Publishing, 2020.

Jaumont, Fabrice. *The Bilingual Revolution: The Future of Education Is in Two Languages.* New York: TBR Books, 2017.

Krashen, Stephen D. *Explorations in Language Acquisition and Use.* Portsmouth, NH: Heinemann, 2003.

Krashen, Stephen D., Sy-Ying Lee, and Christy Lao. *Comprehensible and Compelling: The Causes and Effects of Free Voluntary Reading.* Santa Barbara, CA: Libraries Unlimited, 2018.

Mehisto, Peeter, and Fred Genesee, eds. *Building Bilingual Education Systems: Forces, Mechanisms and Counterweights.* Cambridge: Cambridge University Press, 2015.

Ripley, Amanda. *The Smartest Kids in the World: And How They Got That Way.* New York: Simon & Schuster, 2013.

Santa Ana, Otto, ed. *Tongue-Tied: The Lives of Multilingual Children in Public Education.* Lanham, MD: Rowman & Littlefield, 2004.

Seals, Corinne A., and Sheena Shad, eds. *Heritage Language Policies Around the World.* Abingdon, UK: Routledge, 2018.

Stewart, Vivien. *A World-Class Education: Learning from International Models of Excellence and Innovation.* Alexandria, VA: Association for Supervision & Curriculum Development, 2012.

Thomas, Wayne P., and Virginia P. Collier. *Dual Language Education for a Transformed World.* Albuquerque, NM: Fuente Press, 2012.

Urlaub, Per, and Johanna Watzinger-Tharp, eds. *The Interconnected Language Curriculum: Critical Transition and Interfaces in Articulated K-16 Contexts.* New York: Cengage Learning, 2017.

VanPatten, Bill. *While We're on the Topic: BVP on Language, Acquisition, and Classroom Practice.* Alexandria, VA: The American Council on the Teaching of Foreign Languages, 2017.

Linguistics and Bilingualism

Anderson, Stephen R. *Languages: A Very Short Introduction.* Oxford: Oxford University Press, 2012.

Andresen, Julie Tetel, and Phillip M. Carter. *Languages in the World: How History, Culture, and Politics Shape Language.* New York: Wiley-Blackwell, 2016.

Bauer, Laurie, and Peter Trudgill, eds. *Language Myths.* New York: Penguin, 1999.

Bellos, David. *Is That a Fish in Your Ear? Translation and the Meaning of Everything.* New York: Faber and Faber, 2011.

Byrnes, Heidi, ed. *Learning Foreign and Second Languages.* New York: The Modern Language Association of America, 1998.

Costa, Albert. *The Bilingual Brain: And What It Tells Us About the Science of Language.* Translated by John W. Schwieter. London: Allen Lane, 2019.

Cross, Wilbur. *Gullah Culture in America.* Winston-Salem, NC: John F. Blair, Publisher, 2012.

Crystal, David. *English as a Global Language.* 2nd ed. Cambridge: Cambridge University Press, 2014.

———. *How Language Works: How Babies Babble, Words Change Meaning, and Languages Live or Die.* New York: Avery, 2005.

Dorren, Gaston. *Lingo: Around Europe in Sixty Languages.* New York: Atlantic Monthly Press, 2015.

Edwards, John. *Sociolinguistics: A Very Short Introduction.* Oxford: Oxford University Press, 2013.

Erard, Michael. *Babel No More: The Search for the World's Most Extraordinary Language Learners.* New York: Free Press, 2012.

Ferguson, Charles A., and Shirley Brice Heath, eds. *Language in the USA.* Cambridge: Cambridge University Press, 1981.

Fishman, Joshua A. *European Vernacular Literacy: A Sociolinguistic and Historical Introduction.* Bristol, UK: Multilingual Matters, 2010.

———. *In Praise of the Beloved Language: A Comparative View of Positive Ethnolinguistic Consciousness.* Berlin: Mouton de Gruyter, 1996.

———. *Language Loyalty in the United States: The Maintenance and Perpetuation of Non-English Mother Tongues by American Ethnic and Religious Groups.* The Hague: Mouton Publishers, 1966.

Fuller, Janet M., and Jennifer Leeman. *Speaking Spanish in the US: The Sociopolitics of Language.* Vol. 16. 2nd ed. Clevedon, UK: Multilingual Matters, 2020.

Grosjean, François. *Bilingual: Life and Reality.* Cambridge, MA: Harvard University Press, 2010.

———. *A Journey in Languages & Cultures: The Life of a Bicultural Bilingual.* Oxford: Oxford University Press, 2019.

Hakuta, Kenji. *Mirror of Language: The Debate on Bilingualism.* New York: Basic Books, 1986.

Harris, William V. *Ancient Literacy.* Cambridge, MA: Harvard University Press, 1989.

Harrison, Mim. *Wicked Good Words: From Johnnycakes to Jug Handles, a Roundup of America's Regionalisms.* New York: Perigee, 2011.

Hornberger, Nancy H., and Martin Pütz, eds. *Language Loyalty, Language Planning, and Language Revitalization: Recent Writings and Reflections from Joshua A. Fishman.* Clevedon, UK: Multilingual Matters, 2006.

Jurafsky, Dan. *The Language of Food: A Linguist Reads the Menu.* New York: W.W. Norton, 2014.

Kohn, Marek. *Four Words for Friend: Why Using More Than One Language Matters Now More Than Ever.* New Haven, CT: Yale University Press, 2019.

Labov, William. *Dialect Diversity in America: The Politics of Language Change.* Charlottesville, VA: University of Virginia Press, 2012.

———. *Principles of Linguistic Change.* Vol. 2, *Social Factors.* New York: Blackwell, 2001.

Lynch, Jack, ed. *Samuel Johnson's Dictionary: Selections from the 1755 Work That Defined the English Language.* Delray Beach, FL: Levenger Press, 2002.

MacNeil, Robert, and William Cran. *Do You Speak American?* New York: Nan A. Talese, 2005.

McCrum, Robert. *Globish: How the English Language Became the World's Language.* New York: W.W. Norton, 2010.

McWhorter, John. *Our Magnificent Bastard Tongue: The Untold History of English.* New York: Gotham, 2008.

——. *Talking Back, Talking Black: Truths About America's Lingua Franca.* New York: Bellevue Literary Press, 2019.

——. *Words on the Move: Why English Won't—and Can't—Sit Still (Like, Literally).* New York: Henry Holt and Company, 2016.

Mencken, H.L. *The American Language.* Abridged edition. 1 vol. New York: Alfred A. Knopf, 1977.

Mizumura, Minae. *The Fall of Language in the Age of English.* Translated by Mari Yoshihara and Juliet Winters Carpenter. New York: Columbia University Press, 2015.

Ng Bee Chin and Gillian Wigglesworth. *Bilingualism: An Advanced Resource Book.* Abingdon, UK: Routledge, 2007.

Okrent, Arika. *In the Land of Invented Languages: Esperanto Rock Stars, Klingon Poets, Loglan Lovers, and the Mad Dreamers Who Tried to Build a Perfect Language.* New York: Spiegel & Grau, 2009.

Ong, Walter J. *Orality and Literacy: The Technologizing of the Word.* New York: Routledge, 2002.

Ostler, Nicholas. *The Last Lingua Franca: English Until the Return of Babel.* New York: Walker & Company, 2010.

Pinker, Steven. *The Language Instinct: How the Mind Creates Language.* New York: Harper Perennial Modern Classics, 2007.

Potowski, Kim, ed. *Language Diversity in the USA.* Cambridge: Cambridge University Press, 2010.

Rickerson, E.M., and Barry Hilton, eds. *The 5-Minute Linguist: Bite-sized Essays on Language and Languages.* 2nd ed. Sheffield, UK: Equinox Publishing Ltd., 2006.

Tawada, Yoko. *The Emissary.* Translated by Margaret Mitsutani. New York: New Directions, 2018.

Trask, R.L. *Why Do Languages Change?* Cambridge: Cambridge University Press, 2010.

Tse, Lucy. *Why Don't They Learn English? Separating Fact from Fallacy in the U.S. Language Debate.* New York: Teachers College Press, 2001.

Bilingualism in Other Countries

Allison, Graham, and Robert D. Blackwill. *Lee Kuan Yew: The Grand Master's Insights on China, the United States, and the World.* Cambridge, MA: The MIT Press, 2013.

Everett, Daniel L. *Don't Sleep, There Are Snakes: Life and Language in the Amazonian Jungle.* New York: Vintage Departures, 2008.

Fraser, Graham. *Sorry, I Don't Speak French: Confronting the Canadian Crisis That Won't Go Away.* Toronto: Douglas Gibson Books, 2006.

Kulick, Don. *A Death in the Rainforest.* Chapel Hill, NC: Algonquin, 2019.

Lee Kuan Yew. *My Lifelong Challenge: Singapore's Bilingual Journey.* Singapore: Straits Times Press, 2012.

MacLennan, Hugh. *Two Solitudes.* Toronto: New Canadian Library, 2008.

Reimers, Fernando M., and E.B. O'Donnell, eds. *Fifteen Letters on Education in Singapore: Reflections from a Visit to Singapore in 2015 by a Delegation of Educators from Massachusetts.* Morrisville, NC: Lulu Publishing Services, 2016.

Immigrants, Migrants, and American Demographics

Alba, Richard. *Blurring the Color Line: The New Chance for a More Integrated America.* Cambridge, MA: Harvard University Press, 2009.

Alba, Richard, and Victor Nee. *Remaking the American Mainstream: Assimilation and Contemporary Immigration.* Cambridge, MA: Harvard University Press, 2003.

Archdeacon, Thomas J. *Becoming American: An Ethnic History.* New York: Free Press, 1983.

Camarillo, Albert. *Chicanos in a Changing Society: From Mexican Pueblos to American Barrios in Santa Barbara and Southern California, 1848-1930.* Dallas, TX: Southern Methodist University Press, 2005.

Collier, Paul. *Exodus: How Migration Is Changing Our World.* Oxford: Oxford University Press, 2013.

Daniels, Roger. *Coming to America: A History of Immigration and Ethnicity in American Life.* 2nd ed. New York: Harper Perennial, 2002.

Eaton, Susan E. *Integration Nation: Immigrants, Refugees, and America at Its Best.* New York: The New Press, 2016.

Frey, William H. *Diversity Explosion: How New Racial Demographics Are Remaking America.* Washington, DC: Brookings Institution Press, 2015.

Gerber, David A. *American Immigration: A Very Short Introduction.* Oxford: Oxford University Press, 2011.

Guillet, Edwin S. *The Great Migration: The Atlantic Crossing by Sailing-ship Since 1770.* New York: Thomas Nelson and Sons, 1937.

Handlin, Oscar. *The Uprooted.* 2nd ed. Philadelphia: University of Pennsylvania Press, 2002.

Kaushal, Neeraj. *Blaming Immigrants: Nationalism and the Economics of Global Movement.* New York: Columbia University Press, 2019.

Kirschbaum, Erik. *Burning Beethoven: The Eradication of German Culture in the United States during World War I.* New York: Berlinica, 2014.

Martinez, Ramiro, Jr. *Latino Homicide: Immigration, Violence, and Community.* 2nd ed. New York: Routledge, 2015.

Okrent, Daniel. *The Guarded Gate: Bigotry, Eugenics, and the Law That Kept Two Generations of Jews, Italians, and Other European Immigrants Out of America.* New York: Scribner, 2019.

Portes, Alejandro, and Rubén G. Rumbaut. *Immigrant America: A Portrait.* 4th ed. Oakland, CA: University of California Press, 2014.

Simon, Paul. *The Tongue-Tied American: Confronting the Foreign Language Crisis.* New York: Continuum, 1980.

Taylor, Paul. *The Next America: Boomers, Millennials, and the Looming Generational Showdown.* New York: PublicAffairs, 2014.

Williams, Robin M., Jr. *American Society: A Sociological Interpretation.* 3rd ed. New York: Alfred A. Knopf, 1970.

Yang, Dori Jones. *Voices of the Second Wave: Chinese Americans in Seattle.* Independently published: CreateSpace, 2011.

Social Science and Current Affairs

Berger, Warren. *A More Beautiful Question: The Power of Inquiry to Spark Breakthrough Ideas.* New York: Bloomsbury USA, 2014.

Berreby, David. *Us & Them: The Science of Identity.* Chicago: University of Chicago Press, 2008.

Boaler, Jo. *Mathematical Mindsets: Unleashing Students' Potential Through Creative Math, Inspiring Messages and Innovative Teaching.* San Francisco: Jossey-Bass, 2016.

Bricker, Darrell, and John Ibbitson. *Empty Planet: The Shock of Global Population Decline.* New York: Crown, 2019.

Brown, Brené. *Daring Greatly: How the Courage to Be Vulnerable Transforms the Way We Live, Love, Parent, and Lead.* New York: Avery, 2012.

Carstensen, Laura L. *A Long Bright Future: Happiness, Health, and Financial Security in an Age of Increased Longevity.* New York: PublicAffairs, 2011.

Chua, Amy. *Political Tribes: Group Instinct and the Fate of Nations.* New York: Penguin, 2019.

Csikszentmihalyi, Mihaly. *Flow: The Psychology of Optimal Experience.* New York: Harper & Row, 1990.

Diamond, Jared. *The World Until Yesterday: What Can We Learn from Traditional Societies?* New York: Viking, 2012.

Duckworth, Angela. *Grit: The Power of Passion and Perseverance.* New York: Scribner, 2016.

Duhigg, Charles. *The Power of Habit: Why We Do What We Do in Life and Business.* New York: Random House, 2012.

Dweck, Carol S. *Mindset: The New Psychology of Success.* New York: Ballantine Books, 2016.

Enos, Ryan D. *The Space Between Us: Social Geography and Politics.* Cambridge: Cambridge University Press, 2018.

Goldin, Claudia, and Lawrence F. Katz. *The Race Between Education and Technology.* Cambridge, MA: The Belknap Press, 2008.

Kahneman, Daniel. *Thinking, Fast and Slow.* New York: Farrar, Straus and Giroux, 2011.

Kelly, Kevin. *The Inevitable: Understanding the 12 Technological Forces That Will Shape Our Future.* New York: Viking, 2016.

———. *What Technology Wants.* New York: Viking, 2010.

Kurzweil, Ray. *The Singularity Is Near: When Humans Transcend Biology.* New York: Viking, 2005.

Leveen, Steve. *The Little Guide to Your Well-Read Life: How to Get More Books in Your Life and More Life from Your Books.* Delray Beach, FL: Levenger Press, 2005.

Mackey, John, and Raj Sisodia. *Conscious Capitalism: Liberating the Heroic Spirit of Business.* Boston: Harvard Business School Publishing, 2013.

McGonigal, Kelly. *The Willpower Instinct: How Self-Control Works, Why It Matters, and What You Can Do to Get More of It.* New York: Avery, 2012.

Osnos, Evan. *Age of Ambition: Chasing Fortune, Truth, and Faith in the New China.* New York: Farrar, Straus and Giroux, 2014.

Pinker, Steven. *The Better Angels of Our Nature: Why Violence Has Declined.* New York: Viking, 2011.

———. *Enlightenment Now: The Case for Reason, Science, Humanism, and Progress.* New York: Viking, 2018.

Pinker, Susan. *The Village Effect: How Face-to-Face Contact Can Make Us Healthier, Happier, and Smarter.* New York: Spiegel & Grau, 2014.

Ridley, Matt. *The Rational Optimist: How Prosperity Evolves.* New York: Harper, 2010.

Rosling, Hans, Ola Rosling, and Anna Rosling Rönnlund. *Factfulness: Ten Reasons We're Wrong About the World—and Why Things Are Better Than You Think.* New York: Flatiron Books, 2018.

Sapolsky, Robert M. *Behave: The Biology of Humans at Our Best and Worst.* New York: Penguin Books, 2017.

Thaler, Richard H., and Cass R. Sunstein. *Nudge: Improving Decisions About Health, Wealth, and Happiness.* New York: Penguin, 2009.

Turkle, Sherry. *Alone Together: Why We Expect More from Technology and Less from Each Other.* New York: Basic Books, 2011.

Weizenbaum, Joseph. *Computer Power and Human Reason: From Judgment to Calculation.* New York: W.H. Freeman, 1976.

History

Ambrose, Stephen E. *Nothing Like It in the World: The Men Who Built the Transcontinental Railroad 1863–1869.* New York: Simon & Schuster, 2000.

Barnouw, Erik. *Tube of Plenty: The Evolution of American Television.* London: Oxford University Press, 1977.

Benseler, David P., Craig W. Nickisch, and Cora Lee Nollendorfs, eds. *Teaching German in Twentieth-Century America.* Madison, WI: University of Wisconsin Press, 2001.

Bernstein, William J. *A Splendid Exchange: How Trade Shaped the World.* New York: Atlantic Monthly Press, 2008.

Bobrow-Strain, Aaron. *White Bread: A Social History of the Store-Bought Loaf.* Boston: Beacon Press, 2012.

Boorstin, Daniel J. *The Americans: The Colonial Experience.* New York: Random House, 1958.

Corn, Joseph J. *The Winged Gospel: America's Romance with Aviation.* Baltimore: The Johns Hopkins University Press, 1983.

Cox, Harvey. *How to Read the Bible.* New York: HarperOne, 2015.

Crouch, Tom D. *A Dream of Wings: Americans and the Airplane, 1875-1905.* New York: W.W. Norton, 1981.

Dolan, Brian. *Inventing Entertainment: The Player Piano and the Origins of an American Musical Industry.* Lanham, MD: Rowman & Littlefield, 2009.

Fallows, James. *More Like Us: Making America Great Again.* Boston: Houghton Mifflin, 1989.

Gibson, Carrie. *El Norte: The Epic and Forgotten Story of Hispanic North America.* New York: Atlantic Monthly Press, 2019.

Harari, Yuval Noah. *Sapiens: A Brief History of Humankind.* New York: Harper, 2015.

Lederer, William J., and Eugene Burdick. *The Ugly American.* New York: W.W. Norton, 1958.

Manchester, William. *American Caesar: Douglas MacArthur, 1880-1964.* New York: Little, Brown and Company, 1978.

———. *The Glory and the Dream: A Narrative History of America, 1932-1972.* Vol. 2. Boston: Little, Brown and Company, 1973.

McCullough, David. *The American Spirit: Who We Are and What We Stand For.* New York: Simon & Schuster, 2017.

———. *The Greater Journey: Americans in Paris.* New York: Simon & Schuster, 2011.

Meacham, Jon. *The Soul of America: The Battle for Our Better Angels.* New York: Random House, 2018.

Nez, Chester. *Code Talker.* New York: Berkley Books, 2011.

Platt, Stephen R. *Imperial Twilight: The Opium War and the End of China's Last Golden Age.* New York: Vintage Books, 2018.

Sobel, Dava, and William J.H. Andrewes. *The Illustrated Longitude: The True Story of a Lone Genius Who Solved the Greatest Scientific Problem of His Time.* New York: Walker and Company, 1998.

Sowell, Thomas. *Conquests and Cultures: An International History.* New York: Basic Books, 2008.

Stameshkin, David, Caroline Eisner, Elizabeth Karnes Keefe, and Michael E. Geisler, eds. *Life Doesn't Come with Subtitles: The Middlebury Language Schools at 100.* Middlebury, VT: Middlebury Language Schools, 2015.

Williams, Mason B. *City of Ambition: FDR, La Guardia, and the Making of Modern New York.* New York: W.W. Norton, 2013.

Biography and Memoir

Carreira, Maria M., and Tom Beeman. *Voces: Latino Students on Life in the United States.* Santa Barbara, CA: Praeger, 2014.

Chua, Amy. *Battle Hymn of the Tiger Mother.* New York: Penguin, 2011.

Collins, Lauren. *When in French: Love in a Second Language.* New York: Penguin Press, 2016.

Fallows, Deborah. *Dreaming in Chinese: Mandarin Lessons in Life, Love, and Language.* New York: Walker & Company, 2010.

Feynman, Richard P. *"Surely You're Joking, Mr. Feynman!" Adventures of a Curious Character.* New York: W.W. Norton, 1985.

Lewis, Michael. *The Undoing Project.* New York: W.W. Norton, 2017.

Liu, Eric. *A Chinaman's Chance: One Family's Journey and the Chinese American Dream.* New York: PublicAffairs, 2014.

McCullough, David. *John Adams.* New York: Simon & Schuster, 2001.

———. *The Wright Brothers.* New York: Simon & Schuster, 2015.

Morris, Edmund. *Theodore Rex.* New York: Random House, 2001.

Noah, Trevor. *Born a Crime: Stories from a South African Childhood.* New York: Spiegel & Grau, 2016.

Norris, Mary. *Greek to Me: Adventures of the Comma Queen.* New York: W.W. Norton, 2019.

Patty, Ann. *Living with a Dead Language: My Romance with Latin.* New York: Viking, 2016.

Rich, Katherine Russell. *Dreaming in Hindi: Coming Awake in Another Language.* Boston: Houghton Mifflin Harcourt, 2009.

Rodriguez, Richard. *Hunger of Memory.* New York: Bantam, 1982.

Schiff, Stacy. *A Great Improvisation: Franklin, France, and the Birth of America.* New York: Henry Holt and Co., 2005.

Sedaris, David. *Me Talk Pretty One Day.* New York: Little, Brown and Company, 2000.

———. *Theft by Finding: Diaries, 1977–2002.* New York: Little, Brown and Company, 2017.

Spitz, Bob. *Dearie: The Remarkable Life of Julia Child.* New York: Alfred A. Knopf, 2012.

Stone, I.F. *The Trial of Socrates.* New York: Anchor Books, 1989.

Swick, Thomas. *The Joys of Travel: And Stories That Illuminate Them.* New York: Skyhorse Publishing, 2016.

Tucker, Michael. *Living in a Foreign Language: A Memoir of Food, Wine, and Love in Italy.* New York: Atlantic Monthly Press, 2007.

Acknowledgments

For all those whose names appear in the text or notes, I express my deep gratitude. These acknowledgments are dedicated mainly to others who contributed.

E ver since humans have had languages, bilingualism was a gift given from one human to another through conversation. Thus my first thanks are for my conversation partners: Janire Bragado, Maria Martinez, Yazmin Pease, Angie Rojas, Cris Torres, Lucy Wong-Kuon, and Luz Elena Zuluaga—my own first givers of the gift.

I was fortunate indeed to spend a year at Harvard, followed by another at Stanford, in fellowship programs designed for professionals seeking a meaningful second act in their careers. And so I thank Rosabeth Moss Kanter, who conceived and built the Advanced Leadership Initiative at Harvard, an interdisciplinary fellowship year for people who have finished their first careers and yearn to get recalibrated for what Marc Freedman calls an encore career. The experience was about more than just learning new subject matter. Rosabeth inspired me, as she has so many others, to a heightened sense of duty to foster social change. This book is my attempt to answer that call. Also making this experience possible were Monica C. Higgins, James P. Honan, Rakesh Khurana, Howard K. Koh, Charles J. Ogletree, Jr., Fernando Reimers, and Meredith B. Rosenthal.

To our entire 2015 Advanced Leadership Initiative cohort of fellows and partners, I am grateful not only for our time together on campus but for our trips when I had the time to hear some of your language biographies at length. Special thanks go to Amy and David Abrams, Warren Adams, Sutapa Banerjee, Gay Browne, Tushara Canekeratne, Alfonso and Lorraine Carrillo, Nouzha Chekrouni, Thomas Dans, Tom Dery, William R. Ebsworth, Eduardo Elejalde, Alexia Elejalde-Ruiz, Mark Epstein, Charles and Elisabeth Fleischman, Michael and Kristin Gibbons, Karen and Mark Green, Akhilesh Gupta, Deborah Hannam, Robert Lee Heckart, Amoretta Hoeber, Peter R. Holbrook, Kenneth and Lisa Kelley, Michael (Mick) Kent, Jagannatha Kumar, Patricia López Aufranc, Hector A. Mairal, Philip Maritz, Judy Perry Martinez and Rene Martinez, Anne Welsh McNulty, Horst Melcher,

Thomas and Louise Middleton, Leonard and Susan Miller, C. David Moody, Jr., Ken Neisser and Winifred White Neisser, Michael Pepe, Jacques P. Perold, Mário Antônio Porto Fonseca, Keith and Teri Raffel, Douglas and Jean Renfield-Miller, Jim and Karen Sherriff, Montgomery Simus, Dame Jennifer Smith, Lauren and Ken States, and Denis Weil.

Others at Harvard who helped me along the way include Layla Anasu, Austin Campbell, Davíd Carrasco, Myra Hart, John M. Kendzior, Arthur Kleinman, Seongmin Lee, and Victoria Royal.

At Stanford, I am especially grateful to Philip A. Pizzo, the founding director of the Distinguished Careers Institute, and the DCI staff: Nancy Baumann, Dianne Child, Mira Engel, Kathryn M. Gillam, and Kristin Goldthorpe. I can't think of them without smiling, as they always seemed to be doing.

My deepest gratitude to our 2016 DCI cohort, including Tom and Maggie Bedecarré, Michael Bracco and Kathy Reeves Bracco, Mario Enrique Bravo Rivera and Brandel France de Bravo, W. Amon Burton and Carol Burton, John and Catherine Debs, Kris Deutschman, David Gensler, Susan Wilner Golden, Rhys Gwyn, Robert M. Haddock, M. Roch and Carol Hillenbrand, Roger and Ligia Ingold, Mac Irvin, Pradeep Jotwani, Ronald S. Katz, Anne Kenner, Michael J. Levinthal, Alan Marks, Ronjon Nag, Elizabeth Roth, Thomas Sadler, Joan King Salwen and Kevin Salwen, Karen Sipprell, Ned and Carol Spieker, Ann Stanton, Bryan Traubert, and Marsha Vande Berg. Kate Jerome, whom we adopted from the inaugural class, showed us the ropes.

At Stanford University Libraries, I am grateful to Michael A. Keller and Mimi Calter, who secured a tiny but oh-so-helpful office inside the Green Library, where I could keep books and work in tranquility.

Others at Stanford who were generous with their time and talents were Russell Berman, Albert M. Camarillo, Dan Jurafsky, Kris Kasianovitz, David M. Kennedy, Richard Saller, Deborah Stipek, Sarah Sussman, Tatiana Freiin von Rheinbaden, and my wicked smart undergraduate research assistant, Alma Ixchel Flores-Perez. Special thanks to my landlords in Palo Alto, Hao Huachu, his wife, Emily Hung, and their daughter, Alison. They were exceptionally warm in welcoming me to the neighborhood, including picking me up from the airport and taking me to dinner—where I couldn't refrain from repaying their kindness by interrogating them about bilingualism in Taiwan and their own bilingual journeys.

Marty Abbott invited the America the Bilingual podcast team to the ACTFL annual conventions in Nashville and New Orleans, where our recording booth enjoyed a steady stream of language teachers and presenters. My thanks to all who gave us interviews. A special shout-out to Michelle van Gilder and Erin Whelchel, the tireless drivers of ACTFL's Lead with Languages campaign.

Acknowledgments

My thanks to Vassar College past president Catherine "Cappy" Hill for her introductions to faculty I could interview on study abroad. In addition to those mentioned in the text, thanks go to Cathy Baer, Jennifer Sachs Dahnert, Andrew Meade, Eva Maria Woods Peiro, and Jeff Schneider.

Many other scholars have helped me along the journey. My gratitude goes to Harold Augenbraum at Yale, Amanda Boomershine at the University of North Carolina Wilmington, Jeffrey Brenzel at Yale, Allison Briceno at San José State, Tom D. Crouch at the Smithsonian's National Air and Space Museum, Arturo Díaz at UCLA, Carlos Eire at Yale, Dick Feldman at Cornell, Carmen Greenlee at Bowdoin College, Tamar Gollan at UC San Diego, Alan Hedge at Cornell, Andrew Lynch at the University of Miami, Joseph Salmons at the University of Wisconsin, Nicole Sherf at Salem State College, Laura Welcher at the Rosetta Project of The Long Now, and Ana Celia Zentella at UC San Diego.

Of the organizations that opened their doors for my research I thank especially: at AFS, Marlene G. Baker; at the American Academy of Arts and Sciences, John Tessitore and AAAS fellows Kenneth L. Wallach and Paul LeClerc; at the American Association of Teachers of German, Keith Cothrun; at Amnesty International, Emma Hanley and Salil Shetty; at the Association of Hispanic Advertising Agencies, Natalie Judd and Jennifer Walus; at the Avenues School, Matt Scott; at the Center for Applied Linguistics, Donna Christian and Joy Peyton; at the Chinese Community Schools of Delaware and Delaware Technical Community College, Tommy Lu; at the Contemporary Chinese Schools of South Florida, Fuchen Cheng and Qing Gu; at the Defense Language Institute, Don Fischer; at the Delray Beach Public Library, Mykal Banta and Loanis Menendez-Cuesta; at Glades Central High School in Florida, Kenneth Lutz and Lynn Taylor; at Hispanic Unity of Florida, Josie Bacallao; at the Institute of International Education, Christine Farrugia, Wagaye Johannes, and Mark S. Lazar; at *International Living* magazine, Jackie Flynn and Jennifer Stevens; at the Joint National Committee for Languages and the National Council for Languages and International Studies, Bill Rivers; at the Literacy Coalition of Palm Beach County's Glades Family Center, Kristin Calder and Alejandro Garzon; at the Modern Language Association, Rosemary Feal and Natalia Lusin; at the National Language Service Corps, Joyce Baker; at W.W. Norton & Company, W. Drake McFeely; and at the US Department of Defense, Glenn Nordin.

Worldwide demand for language learning together with new technological advances have led to a flowering of new enterprises. I thank Zevi Aber of Burlington English, Renzo Ampuero of *News in Slow Spanish*, Rey Castuciano of Table Wisdom, Helene Cormier of My Language Exchange, Ding Ding of SayWhat, John DuQuette of Yabla, Mike Elchik of WeSpeke, Micah Greenberg of Language Zen, Jake Jolis

479

of Verbling, Michael Lucia of Language Twin, Andrew Mangion of EC English, Andres Moreno of Open English, Shirish Nadkarni of Livemocha, Michael Quinlan of Transparent, Dan Roitman of Pimsleur, Mark Samson of Hellotalk, and Zhenyu Zhou of eXlogue.

The international organization of chief executives, YPO, fully lived up to its mission of "lifelong learning and idea exchange." I thank Vineet Agarwal, Lisa and Tony Altmann, Jofi Baldrich, Mark and Pam Begelman, Patrick Blanchet, Michael Bloch, Josh Boaz, Devan Capur, Amar Sharany Charani, Tony Cherman, Brian Cohen, Ben and Ann Eason, William Fung, Rolando Gadala-Maria, Roger Gladstone, Arjun Gupta, Jim Hall, Andrea Hass, Alan and Chitra Hepburn, Brett Hurt, Laura Koch, Alex Koo, Michael Korchmar, Michael Koss, Marisa Lazo, Bruce Levitt, Sean Magennis, Jayant Matthew, Roberto Milk, Shai Misan, Raj Mitta, Joel Paige, Hasit Patel, Matt Petkun, Wills Ryan, Ran Sharon, W. Paul Stewart, Justin Taylor, Fred Thiel, Michael Tiernan, Sunny Vanderbeck, Bashar Wali, and Dan Weingart.

As always, staff members at YPO were a big help. I thank Angela Buster, Julie Chipman, Pietro Macchiarella, Andrew McLaughlan, Sarah McNeely, Michelle Mekosch, Amy Miller, Amber Perry, Amanda Phillips, Christa Robson, Maria del Mar Velasco, Zoe Williams, and Alicia Yi.

My colleagues at Conscious Capitalism helped me understand the power of business to improve the world through peaceful commerce, often fueled by bilingualism. My thanks to Philomena Blees, Runa Bouius, Timothy Henry, the late Jeff Klein, Roberta Lang, Doug Levy, John Mackey, Carrie Freeman Parsons, Cheryl Rosner, Raj Sisodia, Rand Stagen, Kip Tindell, and most of all, the person who introduced me to Conscious Capitalism, Laura Roberts.

To the bilinguals and emerging bilinguals who graciously shared their language biographies with me, my heartfelt thanks to all, including Amir and Maria Abtahi, Berta Alvarez, Dalí Amaro, Ernesto Araneda Aranguiz, John Armato, Atheed Azzet, Kwasi Baah, Bridget Bailey, Jack Barrette, Deborah Belange, Margaret Blume, Ann Bouslog, Carolyn Liesgang Cain, Marie Christine Cannizzaro, Willie Cone, Pamela Daley, Gregory Duncan, Charlene Heintz, Steve Herrmann, Jian Huang, Crawford Hunt, Esme Hurlburt, Susan and Roger Hurlburt, Salim Ismail, Melissa Marek, Jeanette Martinez, Joseph Mateus, Cynthia Merz, Jennifer Nadeau, Auska Nakahara, Richard and Susan Neulist, Frode Odegard, Deborah Pearce, Randy Phelps, Andrew Pitts, Sheila Quinlin, Julie Reis, Jeanne and Gary Schermerhorn, Kari and John Shipley, Sandy Smith, Sarah Solberg, Don and Ione Spear, Amy and Mark Tercek, Kimon and Dejenane Theophanopoulos, Joseph Toone, Chris Welch, Katie Williamson, Nanette Wiser, and Strauss Zelnick.

Special thanks to those who read drafts of the text, saving me from errors and confusions, including Marty Abbott, Mario Bravo, Ellan Cates-Smith, Ben Eason,

Acknowledgments

Rosemary Feal, Mark Ford, Karen Granger, Robert Lee Heckart, Anne Kenner, Pamela Newman, Ray Nied, Kim Potowski, Doug Renfield-Miller, Jack Roepers, Kevin Salwen, Bob Schmeir, Tina St. Pierre, Andrea Syverson, Maja Thomas, Guadalupe Valdés, Loie Williams, Katie Williamson, and Dori Jones Yang. My dear friend and publishing pro George Gibson not only read the draft, but also offered invaluable advice on "making the book public—that is, publishing."

I'm filled with gratitude to our America the Bilingual Project team and advisors who produced our first three seasons of our podcast and set the stage for this book. My thanks go to Maja Thomas for steering me right in the early days; to our graphic designer, Carlos Plaza, for the creation of our logo and a site design that evokes the Americana feeling we thought was appropriate for America regaining its voices (Carlos also designed this book's beautiful cover); to Caroline Doughty, our social media maven who also, true to her surname, fearlessly took on the formidable task of producing this book in different formats; and to Rob Kennedy and his digital team at Daruma Tech, including Susan Erickson, Alejandro Capriles, Rick Griswold, Bruno Guimares, and Karla Hernandez.

Our podcast's associate producer, Beckie Bray Rankin, when not teaching French or leading a study abroad trip, has been our scout alerting us to the changing landscape of American language teaching. Beckie also joined me as co-host on several episodes. I thank also Cathy Mercer, virtual assistant; Abril Rayas, for her "digital anthropology" study of our listeners; and most of all, our podcast producer, Fernando Hernández Becerra (aka Micro), who shepherded me into the world of audio storytelling. Fernando produced all of our episodes, including the music and sound design, and coauthored many of the scripts. Finally, Mim Harrison, our brand guru, writer, and co-host, who also enlisted as the editor of this book (her third such tour of duty with me).

Many authors say their book would not have existed without their agent or editor. In my case, that person without-whom-this-book-would-not-exist is Mim. She acted as not only the best editor I can imagine, but strategic thinker and Believer in Chief about the America the Bilingual Project. If you find any of the subheads in this book insightful, you have her to thank. We had many a tussle as we hammered out this book together. In general, she was more right than I, and the book was greatly improved as a result, not only with matters of writing, but with seeing the larger vision and potential of this work when I could not.

A friend is someone who likes you anyway. I am deeply grateful to Keith Doughty, Cynthia Fisher, and Jim Koch. Special shout-outs to Chris Wheeler, for his challenges to my thinking on the impact of technology, and to Wayne Welch, who accompanied me on reporting trips to New Mexico, New Hampshire, and Vermont.

Wayne, you're the greatest traveling companion and most loyal friend (aside from my dog, Chet) a fellow could ask for.

Finally, I thank my family members, Jerry and Amineh Bahnsen, Bryan Granger and Diana McCauley, Dale Granger, Eric and Karen Granger and their son, Luke, Evelyn and Ron Granger, and Bob and Lynn Gidley. To my immediate family, Calgary and Stephanie Leveen, and Corey Leveen, thank you for your good humor and support. And to Lori, who has been, as always, my spiritual and actual companion through this life, not to mention couchmate for many a Netflix series en español, *sin ti, no soy nada.*

INDEX OF NAMES

INDEX OF TOPICS

ABOUT THE AUTHOR

S teve Leveen devoted his first career to celebrating literacy, cofounding the first company in America to create products for readers (Levenger) and serving on the board of the National Book Foundation. He is now devoting his encore career to biliteracy, championing bilingualism in America as a path to a stronger and healthier nation. A monolingual until midlife, Steve has chosen Spanish as his adopted language and is an avid learner.

Steve divides his time between South Florida, where he successfully practices his Spanish, and Maine, where he is somewhat less successful in sounding like a local. *America's Bilingual Century* is his third book. His work has also appeared in *The New York Times, The Wall Street Journal,* the *Los Angeles Times,* and the *Christian Science Monitor.* He holds a PhD in Sociology from Cornell University.

For more about Steve and the America the Bilingual project, visit
www.americathebilingual.com.

Aspiring bilinguals welcome!

CPSIA information can be obtained
at www.ICGtesting.com
Printed in the USA
BVHW031041270121
598654BV00005B/8/J

9 781733 937559